Readings *on* Argumentation

Readings *on* Argumentation

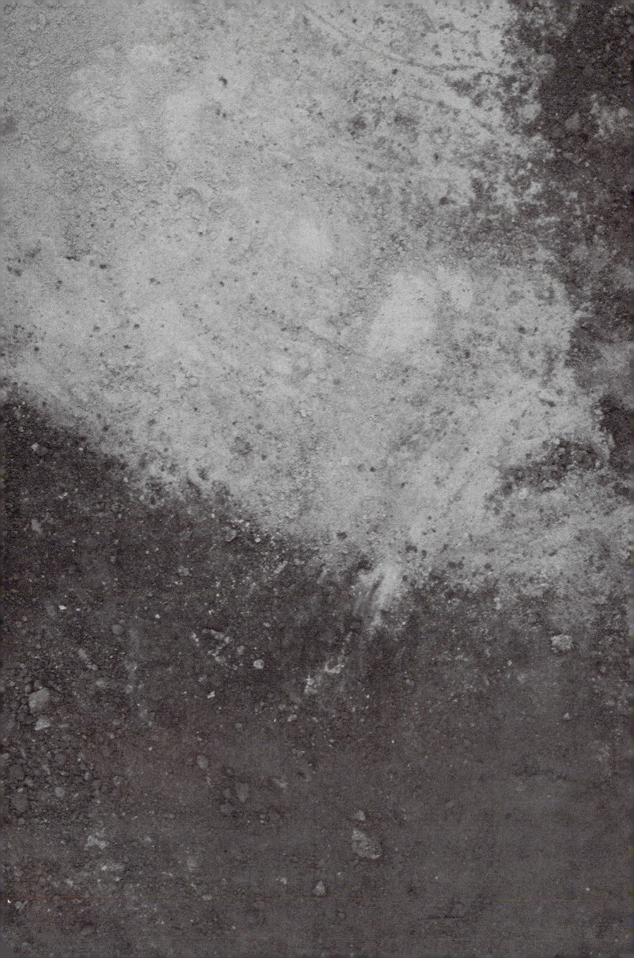

Readings *on* Argumentation

edited by

Angela J. Aguayo
Eastern Illinois University

Timothy R. Steffensmeier
Kansas State University

Strata Publishing, Inc.
State College, Pennsylvania

9 8 7 6 5 4 3 2 1

Readings on Argumentation

Published by:
Strata Publishing, Inc.
P.O. Box 1303
State College, PA 16804
telephone: 1-814-234-8545
fax: 1-814-238-7222
web site: http://www.stratapub.com

Text and cover design by WhiteOak Creative.
Cover image and background image on pages i, iv, 5, 7, 69, 101, 141, 143, 191, 249, 251, and 329: Robin Cracknell/Stockbyte/Getty Images.
Printed and bound in the United States by Malloy Incorporated.

Credits and acknowledgments appear on pages vii–viii and on this page by reference.

Library of Congress Cataloging-in-Publication Data

Readings on argumentation / edited by Angela J. Aguayo, Timothy R. Steffensmeier.
    p. cm.
  Includes bibliographical references and index.
  ISBN-13: 978-1-891136-20-7 (pbk. : alk. paper)
  ISBN-10: 1-891136-20-8 (pbk. : alk. paper)
  1. Reasoning. 2. Logic. 3. Critical thinking.   I. Aguayo, Angela J., date.
 II. Steffensmeier, Timothy R., date.
  BC177.R343155 2008
  168--dc22
                                        2008004309

ISBN (10) 1-891136-20-8
ISBN (13) 978-1-891136-20-7

Credits and Acknowledgments

Wayne Brockriede, "Where is Argument?" *Journal of the American Forensic Association* 9 (Spring 1975): 179–182. Used by permission of the American Forensic Association.

Argumentation, 17, 2003, 387–403, "The Development of the Pragma-dialectical Approach to Argumentation," Frans H. van Eemeren and Peter Houtlosser, © 2003 *Kluwer Academic Publishers*. With kind permission from Springer Science and Business Media.

Ralph H. Johnson and J. Anthony Blair, "Informal Logic: An Overview." *Informal Logic* 20, 2 (2000): pp. 93–107. Used by permission of *Informal Logic*.

David A. Frank, "Argumentation Studies in the Wake of *The New Rhetoric*." *Argumentation and Advocacy* 40 (Spring 2004): 267–283. Used by permission of the American Forensic Association.

David Zarefsky, "Persistent Questions in the Theory of Argument Fields." *Journal of the American Forensic Association* 18 (1982): 191–203. Used by permission of the American Forensic Association.

Daniel J. O'Keefe, "Two Concepts of Argument." *The Journal of the American Forensic Association* 13 (1977): 121–128. Used by permission of the American Forensic Association.

From *Philosophy and Rhetoric*, "On Defining Argument" by Robert C. Rowland, vol. 20, no. 3, pp. 140–159. Copyright © 1987 by The Pennsylvania State University. Reprinted by permission of Penn State Press.

Argumentation, 16, 2002, 299–309, "A Concept Divided: Ralph Johnson's Definition of Argument," Christopher W. Tindale, © 2002 *Kluwer Academic Publishers*. With kind permission from Springer Science and Business Media.

Wayne Brockriede and Douglas Ehninger, "Toulmin on Argument: An Interpretation and Application." *Quarterly Journal of Speech* 46 (1960): 44–53. Used by permission of the National Communication Association.

Barbara Warnick and Susan L. Kline, "*The New Rhetoric*'s Argument Schemes: A Rhetorical View of Practical Reasoning." *Argumentation and Advocacy* 29 (Summer 1992): 1–15. Used by permission of the American Forensic Association.

Argumentation, 15, 2001, 365–379, "Walton's Argumentation Schemes for Presumptive Reasoning: A Critique and Development," J. Anthony Blair, © 2001 *Kluwer Academic Publishers*. With kind permission from Springer Science and Business Media.

Douglas Ehninger, "Validity as Moral Obligation." Copyright 1968 from *Southern Speech Journal* by Southern States Communication Association. Reproduced by permission of Southern States Communication Association, http://ssca.net

Thomas B. Farrell, "Validity and Rationality: The Rhetorical Constituents of Argumentative Form." *Journal of the American Forensic Association* 13 (Winter 1977): 142–149. Used by permission of the American Forensic Association.

From *Philosophy and Rhetoric*, "Universality in Rhetoric: Perelman's Universal Audience" by James Crosswhite, vol. 22, no. 3, pp. 157–173. Copyright © 1989 by The Pennsylvania State University. Reprinted by permission of Penn State Press.

Douglas N. Walton, "Bias, Critical Doubt, and Fallacies." *Argumentation and Advocacy* 28 (Summer 1991): 1–22. Used by permission of the American Forensic Association.

Argumentation, 16, 2002, 179–196, "How to Distinguish Good and Bad Arguments: Dialogico-Rhetorical Normativity," Wouter H. Slob, © 2002 *Kluwer Academic Publishers*. With kind permission from Springer Science and Business Media.

Deborah Orr, "Just the Facts Ma'am: Informal Logic, Gender and Pedagogy." *Informal Logic* 11 (Winter 1989): 1–10. Used by permission of Deborah Orr.

Argumentation, 13, 1999, 297–315, "Justifying *My* Position in *Your* Terms: Cross-Cultural Argumentation in a Globalized World," Yameng Liu, © 1999 *Kluwer Academic Publishers*. With kind permission from Springer Science and Business Media.

Argumentation, 13, 1999, 183–201, "Argument Quality and Cultural Difference," Harvey Siegel, © 1999 *Kluwer Academic Publishers.* With kind permission from Springer Science and Business Media.

G. Thomas Goodnight, "The Personal, Technical, and Public Spheres of Argument: A Speculative Inquiry into the Art of Public Deliberation." *Journal of the American Forensic Association* 18 (Spring 1982): 214–227. Used by permission of the American Forensic Association.

Charles Arthur Willard, "The Creation of Publics: Notes on Goodnight's Historical Relativity." *Argumentation and Advocacy* 26 (Fall 1989): 45–59. Used by permission of the American Forensic Association.

Robert Asen, "Toward a Normative Conception of Difference in Public Deliberation." *Argumentation and Advocacy* 35 (Winter 1999): 115–129. Used by permission of the American Forensic Association.

Erik W. Doxtader, "The Entwinement of Argument and Rhetoric: A Dialectical Reading of Habermas' Theory of Communicative Action." *Argumentation and Advocacy* 28 (Fall 1991): 51–63. Used by permission of the American Forensic Association.

Argumentation, 13, 1999, 139–160, "Regulating Disagreement, Constituting Participants: A Critique of Proceduralist Theories of Democracy," Darrin Hicks and Lenore Langsdorf, © 1999 *Kluwer Academic Publishers.* With kind permission from Springer Science and Business Media.

Ronald Walter Greene, "Social Argumentation and the Aporias of State Formation: The Palestinian Declaration of Independence." *Argumentation and Advocacy* 29 (Winter 1993), 124–136. Used by permission of the American Forensic Association.

David S. Birdsell and Leo Groarke, "Toward a Theory of Visual Argument." *Argumentation and Advocacy* 33 (Summer 1996): 1–10. Used by permission of the American Forensic Association.

Catherine H. Palczewski, "The Male Madonna and the Feminine Uncle Sam: Visual Argument, Icons, and Ideographs in 1909 Anti–Woman Suffrage Postcards." *Quarterly Journal of Speech,* 91 (November 2005): 365–394. Used by permission of the National Communication Association.

Kevin Michael DeLuca, "Unruly Arguments: The Body Rhetoric of Earth First!, Act Up, and Queer Nation." *Argumentation and Advocacy,* 36 (Summer 1999): 9–21. Used by permission of the American Forensic Association.

Argumentation, 12, 1998, 147–166, "The Space of Argumentation: Urban Design, Civic Discourse, and the Dream of the Good City," David Fleming, © 1998 *Kluwer Academic Publishers.* With kind permission from Springer Science and Business Media.

Argumentation, 15, 2001, 381–395, "The Search for Grounds in Legal Argumentation: A Rhetorical Analysis of *Texas v. Johnson,*" S. J. Balter, © 2001 *Kluwer Academic Publishers.* With kind permission from Springer Science and Business Media.

Contents

....

PART I
The Realm *of* Argumentation
5

Chapter 7   Places and Uses   329

Preface

As teachers and students of argumentation, we wanted a book that would present the scholarship of the study in a framework that would help our own students understand the central issues, concerns, and current directions. We wanted the book to reflect the diversity of scholarship, the interdisciplinary expansion of argumentation studies over the last several decades, and the increasing attention to the intersection of argumentation and democracy. Through conversations with many other people in our field, we discovered that they, too, wanted such a book for their own courses.

This book is intended for use in courses that explore the conceptual and theoretical dimensions of argumentation. Courses that focus on public deliberation, public sphere theory, and deliberative democracy may also find this book pertinent. The essays included in the book reflect and exemplify significant theoretical work by scholars of rhetoric, speech communication, informal logic, and philosophy. These essays explore argument in various contexts and spheres, with a particular focus on argumentation as a fruitful means for people to negotiate differences. Our aim, in selecting and organizing these works, was to represent significant trends in argumentation studies, illuminating both the traditions and current directions of this increasingly diverse study.

Our goal in this book is to draw attention to major themes and questions in the scholarship on argumentation, to show traditional approaches and recent developments, and to provide a foundation that would guide future study. The essays in this book reflect the *rhetorical, dialectical,* and *informal logical* perspectives that have permeated the published research in recent decades, as well as the groundbreaking perspectives from Chaïm Perelman, Stephen Toulmin, and Jürgen Habermas. As our world becomes more integrated with new media, as the speed of information exchange increases, and as visual arguments become more saturated in public culture, the essays in this book show how our theoretical understanding of argumentation should and will be challenged.

We faced the usual challenges of editing an anthology. A selection of thirty essays cannot encompass every significant thread, every noteworthy scholar of argumentation studies. To address the sheer volume of material, which appears in numerous books, multiple journals, and detailed conference proceedings, we began by constructing an intellectual map of argumentation studies that shaped our selection criteria. We chose, for a variety of reasons, to focus on scholarly essays published in peer-reviewed journals. We selected some essays because they introduced key ideas and scholars to the study, others because they show the evolution of a dynamic body of scholarship and highlight the increasingly diverse realm, definitions, and uses of argumentation. Some innovative works also address new forms and places for the study of argument. In some cases, our particular choices reflected our sense of what would be accessible to students. We also tried to select essays that, collectively, would provide instructors and students with the flexibility to explore the interdisciplinary scholarship in ways that meet their own needs and goals.

Many excellent essays that, for various reasons, we did not reproduce in full are listed in the selected bibliography at the end of the book. This list, organized topically, is intended to provide additional resources and guidance for students and instructors who wish to investigate specific aspects and topics in more depth.

ORGANIZATION OF THE BOOK

We have organized the book around three overarching themes. Part I addresses the primary question: *what is the realm of argumentation?* The essays in this section deal with the diverse frameworks and rich historical lineage of argumentation studies. They also establish definitions and schemes for arguments. Part II addresses the question: *how do we judge and evaluate arguments?* It explores theoretical models that guide conceptions of judgment, including validity, normativity, fallacies, and difference. The essays here connect prevailing uses of judgment in argument evaluation and construction with critiques of those practices. Part III explores the question: *where are the spheres and uses of argument?* This section addresses the connections among public spheres, democracy, and contemporary argumentation in practice. It also reflects emerging scholarship on visual argument. This three-part organization is intended to provide students and instructors with a broad view of argumentation studies. By addressing these three central questions, we also hoped to provide a heuristic for students' own future scholarship.

The chapters within these three major sections address specific themes and issues. Each chapter follows a progression of ideas and intellectual exchange among authors, in order to help students identify core concepts, theoretical tensions, and conceptual concerns.

Part I: The Realm of Argumentation provides a framework for the study of argumentation. Chapter 1, "Perspectives," includes key essays that represent three divergent approaches to argumentation: *rhetorical, dialectical,* and *informal logical* perspectives. It also introduces important thinkers and approaches to argumentation studies. Chapter 2, "Definitions," outlines the robust debate among scholars regarding definitional boundaries of argumentation studies. The scholarly exchange involves what is at stake with particular conceptions of argument and highlights various conceptual concerns. Chapter 3, "Structures and Schemes," introduces students to the building blocks of argument, how they are structured, and on what grounds.

Part II: Judging and Evaluating Arguments explores the evolving conversation about judgment as a significant dimension of understanding arguments. Chapter 4, "Validity," discusses the manner in which the soundness of an argument is characterized and assessed. Many of the articles respond to formal logicians' traditional conceptualizations of validity. Chapter 5, "Normativity," is concerned with standards for assessing argument quality: how theorists and critics analyze arguments and on what grounds. This chapter also reflects on intercultural and feminist critiques of argument normativity and the degree to which culturally specific and socially constructed arguments are bound by context.

Part III: Spheres and Uses of Argument explores the implied connection between argumentation and essential practices of democracy that is at the core of argumentation study. In addition, it addresses how argumentation is employed in particular social contexts. Chapter 6, "Public Sphere and Democracy," focuses on the democratic potential of argument in public deliberation. Influenced by Jürgen Habermas's work, these articles discuss public argument, the problem of difference in the public sphere, and contingent conditions of democratic deliberation. Chapter 7, "Places and Uses," investigates the practice of argument in various contexts and forms. Many of the essays in Part III expand traditional conceptual boundaries by addressing how various places and spaces enable, challenge, and maintain the process of argument.

The Selected Bibliography provides a list of additional works to guide students in their further reading. We organized this list around broad themes and lines of inquiry that we thought would be of interest to students of argumentation. Because of the dynamic nature of journal articles, however, it is impossible to exhaust an essay's contribution under one theme or subject heading. The organization of the book is intended to reflect the diverse approaches to argumentation studies as well as the common questions that drive the breadth and depth of the scholarship. The range of articles reflects the history, theoretical assumptions, perspectives, and critical approaches that continue to shape the broader study. Our framework also emphasizes the rhetorical approach to the study. There are many ways to organize such a complicated and dynamic body of work, however, and teachers may choose to organize the readings differently, according to the goals of their own courses.

As editors, we worked diligently to replicate the original publication of each essay accurately. We corrected a few minor typographical errors. We inserted "[*sic*]" in a few places where the original phrasing was unconventional, to indicate the accuracy of the transcription. (Unitalicized appearances of "[sic]" are in the original publication.) Footnotes were converted to endnotes for consistency throughout the text.

ACKNOWLEDGMENTS

This book would not be possible without the insightful words, innovative ideas, and hearty exchange among argumentation scholars during the last forty years. Their research and passion for the study and practice of argumentation motivated this project and paved a sturdy road for the interdisciplinary and international study of argumentation.

This book began with a simple curiosity that grew into a thirst to know more about where argumentation studies have been and where they are going. We quickly learned that beyond the need to map the trajectory of argument studies, there was a sincere need to compile the key lines of inquiry in order to pass this scholarly legacy on to future students of argumentation. In the early stages of this project, Richard Cherwitz at the University of Texas was incredibly supportive and a valuable advisor to the ambitious task before us. Benefiting from his guidance and decades of teaching argumentation, we were able to develop a concept for this reader that could function as a pedagogical and scholarly contribution. We also thank Charles E. Morris III at Boston College for helping us navigate the process of publishing this project. Chuck is a generous and brilliant scholar who is kind enough to provide us with some very helpful advice and introduced us to a wonderful publisher.

The diligent attention to details required to complete a reader like this would not be possible without the hard work of some very extraordinary editorial assistants. Dana Wyant at Eastern Illinois University and Joshua Hersch at Kansas State University provided important support with scanning and editing the selected articles. We thank our home institutions, Eastern Illinois University and Kansas State University, for providing the space and resources to make completing this project possible.

Throughout the development of this book many reviewers provided important and valuable feedback on the selected readings and structure of the book. We thank those who provided insightful advice and encouragement with this project: Robert Asen, University of Wisconsin–Madison; Don R. Brownlee, California State University, Northridge; Beth Brunk-Chavez, University of Texas at El Paso; Locke Carter, Texas Tech University; William Keith, University of Wisconsin–Milwaukee; Peter Marston, California State University, Northridge; Kelly M. McDonald, Arizona State University; Brian R. McGee, College of Charleston; Jerry Miller, Ohio University; Matthew J. Sobnosky, Hofstra University; Robert Trapp, Willamette University; Danielle Wiese, Grand Valley State University; and Kelly M. Young, Wayne State University.

We also thank those journal editors, publishers, and association directors who assisted us in gaining permission to reprint the essays in this book. These people include: Frans van Eemeren, *Argumentation;* Ralph Johnson, *Informal Logic;* Katie Novak, *Philosophy and Rhetoric;* Randall Lake, *Argumentation and Advocacy;* J. Emmett Winn, Southern States Communication Association; and Roger Smitter, National Communication Association.

Working with Strata Publishing, Inc., has been an incredibly valuable experience for us, as scholars and people. Our publisher, Kathleen Domenig, has been an invaluable resource in every phase of producing this book. Her focused energy, patience, and attention guided this project from start to finish. We feel quite lucky that our paths crossed with an extremely thoughtful and professional publisher. We also thank Brian Henry for his assistance with the many particulars that go into producing a book.

We also give thanks to our friends and family who provided the necessary emotional and sometimes editorial support for this project. Certainly, this book would not be possible without the love and support of our partners, Daniel Elgin and Tina Steffensmeier. We also thank our colleagues at the University of Texas, who contributed to a community of excellence that cultivated this book idea. There were also countless others who made this work possible with their encouragement, insights and kind words: among them, Barry Brummett, University of Texas; Dana Cloud, University of Texas; Rosa Eberly, Pennsylvania State University; and Ronald Greene, University of Minnesota.

Early in our education, several gifted teachers imparted upon us the potential and necessity for argumentation to mediate a complicated world. Their passion and dedication for public speech and argument cultivated our fondness for the practice and study of this work. We dedicate this book to Matthew Taylor at Fullerton College, Liana B. Koeppel at Cypress College, and Patricia Koch-Johns at Lincoln High School.

Introduction

Why study argument? One reason is that argumentation is a method of inquiry. Through argument people explain and understand the world, discover ideas or generate new ones. In social settings, we often argue informally and generate theories about important issues of the day. These discussions can help us create new ideas on issues such as religion, sexuality, racism, economics, and law.

A second reason is that argument is a means of negotiating cultural differences. In the classroom, for example, we commonly bridge our differences by engaging in the process of argumentation; we give words to our experiences and find points in which our experiences and values intersect with those of our fellow students, despite differences in our backgrounds and cultures. In a world increasingly connected by communication technologies, where diverse cultural practices influence almost every place and every idea, argument serves as a means for people to locate common ground.

A third reason argument is worthy of study is that it is intrinsically connected to democracy. Argumentation studies have flourished alongside democratic ideals since ancient Greek times. In an ideal democracy, citizens are civically engaged in public deliberation about their common concerns. People advance rational arguments to solve problems and sustain democratic governance. For example, in local communities, groups come together to address shared problems such as water pollution, crime, or substandard housing. Solving these problems requires citizens who come from disparate backgrounds to work together for a common interest, to negotiate differences and settle disputes using argument.

These three functions of argumentation—producing knowledge, enabling cross-cultural exchanges, and nourishing democracy—are woven through our society, offering the hope of civility, of solving problems and reaching agreement through peaceful means.

Argument serves similar functions among individuals in their personal lives. You deploy and consume arguments daily at work, in your home, and with loved ones. Whether you are voicing objections about unfavorable work policies, looking for ways to reduce monthly expenses, or quarreling over who should wash the dishes, you are creating and evaluating arguments. You may also watch arguments unfold on television or read political blogs, prompting you to inquire about larger public controversies. In these cases, the consumption of arguments shapes your thoughts and relationships with others.

Admittedly, some individuals are inclined to engage in argumentation more frequently than others. Some activities call for a constant stream of argument, others less so. Yet, one clear fact remains: the practice of argumentation is inescapable on a societal and individual level.

Still, healthy argument practices and theories are not a given. The art of deliberation, as communication scholar Thomas Goodnight contends, is subject to atrophy.[1] In many contemporary political messages, letters to the editor, and college classroom discussions, the practice of argument falls markedly short of democratic ideals. In place of argument aimed at sound, collective decision-making, monologues and shouting matches occur where erroneous claims are plentiful and good reasons are scarce.

Argumentation is a dynamic organism. People must cultivate and nourish its practice in order to use it productively. In building theory, developing sound arguments, or evaluating the arguments of others, the study of argument helps to foster healthy argument in our personal lives and in the society at large. By bringing together an array of prominent essays that offer diverse contemporary argumentation theories, this book aspires to play a role in sustaining the study and practice of argumentation, with a particular emphasis on the relationship between argumentation and democracy.

While some evidence substantiates Goodnight's fears that the practice of argument has atrophied, the essays in this reader illustrate that the study of argumentation is gaining momentum globally. This scholarship offers hope that argumentation can serve as a counterforce to oppressive regimes and institutions, especially in political climates in which people are disengaged or feel incapable of participating in civic affairs.

The scholarship on argumentation is vast, producing a significant body of work that addresses theoretical and practical functions of argumentation from many perspectives. The essays in this book explore argumentation in a social context. That is, the authors view argument as emerging from particular social conditions and carried out through human interaction.

This collection of essays reflects the vibrant development of argumentation studies over the past half century. Because argumentation is neither the domain of any one discipline nor exclusive to one method of study, the scholarship evolves from many academic departments, including Communication, Rhetoric, Philosophy, and English. The cross disciplinary and methodologically diverse study of argumentation has produced a rich offering of ways to define, evaluate, and produce arguments. From the wide breadth and scope of the scholarship, this book brings together major thinkers, foundational articles, and new directions for the international study of argumentation.

This diverse, fruitful scholarship produces few agreed-upon assumptions, but dominant lines of inquiry and shared questions for study do emerge from it. The authors of these essays generally agree that the use of argument in human interaction is fertile ground for study. Collectively, they demonstrate the value and utility of argumentation studies by addressing the question: how do people produce, analyze, and evaluate arguments?

The seven chapters in the book are organized in three parts. Part I provides diverse perspectives and insights into the lineage of argumentation studies. The essays in these chapters present major perspectives from three areas of argument inquiry—rhetoric, pragma-dialectics, and informal logic—and from two influential argumentation theorists—Chaïm Perelman and Stephen Toulmin. These perspectives provide various theoretical vantage points to establish the realm of argumentation—the scope and reach of argumentation in society. This section also includes discussions of the basic building blocks of argumentation, including definitions and structures of argument, that are foundational to understanding the range of possibility in argumentation studies. An interdisciplinary framework is offered in this section for you to begin developing an intellectual map of argumentation studies.

Part II addresses how to judge arguments. The essays introduce theoretical models that guide conceptions of judgment in argumentation theory, including ways for theorists and evaluators of argument to determine what makes a logically sound argument (validity) and what leads to errors in reasoning (fallacy). The essays also introduce the concept of normativity in argumentation—socially constructed norms of what ought (and ought not) to be involved in a good argument. They explore argumentation in a diverse global environment, specifically focusing on differences in the ways people conceive of and practice argumentation.

Part III explores the places where argument is practiced and how it is used. In particular, the essays in this section focus on the intersection between argumentation, democracy, and public spheres—the public spaces where people come together to interact. Many of the essays draw from philosopher Jürgen Habermas's writing on public sphere theory. The ways in which argument functions to engage citizens in civic life is a primary area of concern. This section also includes scholarship on emerging fields of social argument, which emphasizes the role context plays in argument development and evaluation. The essays here also reflect new avenues of research, such as visual argument, that expand argumentation studies.

Collectively, the thirty essays in this book provide foundational material for understanding the interdisciplinary study of argumentation. By focusing on the realm of argumentation, on the judgment and evaluation of arguments, and on spheres and uses of argument, the book shows the common concerns, issues, and questions of a large, diverse, and interdisciplinary body of research. Our hope is that this collection of essays will help you understand the paths scholars have taken to create innovative and thought-provoking ways to enhance the study of argument as well as its practice in a diverse, democratic society.

NOTES

[1] G. Thomas Goodnight, "The Personal, Technical, and Public Spheres of Argument: A Speculative Inquiry into the Art of Public Deliberation," *Journal of the American Forensic Association* 18 (Spring 1982): 214–227. Reproduced in this volume.

PART I

The Realm
of Argumentation

Chapter 1

Perspectives

The study of argumentation spans two millennia, stretches across the globe, and dwells in numerous academic departments. It is an academic domain occupied by a host of characters, including rhetoricians, informal logicians, philosophers, and social scientists, each with particular ways of seeing and using argumentation. The rich and diverse traditions of argumentation theory are impressive; yet, the expanse leaves the realm of argumentation a contested territory. Conceptions about the definition, function, and aim of argumentation vary radically among camps of scholars.

The essays in this chapter introduce five major theoretical perspectives on argumentation. The first three articles represent predominant scholarly camps in the study of argumentation: rhetoric, pragma-dialectics, and informal logic. One distinction among these camps is in how they examine the behavior of arguers. Rhetorical approaches are primarily concerned with the *process* of argumentation, pragma-dialectics with *procedures,* and informal logic with the *products* of argumentation.[1] The fourth essay focuses on the scholarship of Chaïm Perelman, one of the most influential argumentation theorists and the co-author (with Lucie Olbrechts-Tyteca) of the groundbreaking book *The New Rhetoric.* The final article addresses an overarching issue found throughout the essays in this book—the context in which arguments are created and used.

Wayne Brockriede's essay "Where is Argument?" (1975) represents a rhetorical approach to argument. This approach focuses on the process arguers employ to reason with audiences. According to Brockriede, an argument is not a thing or an object; rather, it is "a perspective that people take." Situating the study of argument in its practice, Brockriede defines argumentation as a dynamic process that changes as arguments develop. His essay centers on where arguments can be found and on characteristics of human behavior that overlap with argumentation practices. Brockriede ties the essay together with the overarching assertion that arguments deal with the problematic: people call on argument when they encounter an issue that is both uncertain and significant.

Frans H. van Eemeren and Peter Houtlosser's 2003 essay, "The Development of the Pragma-Dialectical Approach to Argumentation," provides a detailed chronology of the scholarship that shaped pragma-dialectics as a comprehensive theory of argumentation. The pragma-dialectical perspective, which van Eemeren and colleagues at the University of Amsterdam originated, focuses on procedure; that is, on establishing rules of critical discussion that ultimately enable arguers to resolve "differences of opinion." The authors also explore a rhetorical dimension of pragma-dialectics, "strategic maneuvering"—arguers' attempts to influence discussion in favor of their own best interests. This essay outlines the primary tenets of pragma-dialectics and offers a guide to contemporary research projects that advance the pragma-dialectical approach.

Ralph H. Johnson and J. Anthony Blair's 2000 essay, "Informal Logic: An Overview," offers a thorough and concise summary of informal logic as well as a distinction between informal and formal logic. Informal logic typically focuses on the argument itself, the product created through reason. While formal logic operates on an abstract symbolic level (as in geometric proofs), informal logic is concerned with natural languages (peoples' everyday argument use). By studying everyday human language use, informal logicians evaluate how people reason in their own lives. Blair and Johnson define informal logic by addressing misconceptions about the perspective, discuss topical areas of recent research, indicate directions for future scholarship, and provide a list of informal logic resources.

In "Argumentation Studies in the Wake of *The New Rhetoric*" (2004), David A. Frank assesses Chaïm Perelman and Lucie Olbrechts-Tyteca's book, *The New Rhetoric: A Treatise on Argumentation,* which Frank contends is "the most important system of argumentation developed in the twentieth century." His essay emphasizes *The New Rhetoric*'s perspective that because human beings are unique and particular, argumentation theory should take a pluralistic view of human nature. In other words, argumentation is as diverse as the people who use it. Seen from this perspective, argumentation is not governed by a sole logic aimed at producing uniform agreement; rather, argumentative exchange produces "an appreciation of the irreducible plurality of human values." Frank outlines significant developments in *The New Rhetoric,* including the alignment of rhetoric and dialectic—a move that connects rhetoric's focus on audience with dialectic's focus on reason. The article concludes with a rebuttal of pragma-dialectical theorists' reading of *The New Rhetoric.*

David Zarefsky's "Persistent Questions in the Theory of Argument Fields" (1982) focuses on the contexts in which arguments exist and on the implications for those contextual frameworks. Zarefsky employs the term "field" to indicate places where argument standards, such as the grounds for sound evidence or valid reasoning, develop. The purpose of the "field" construct is to explore the ways in which context-specific arguments are constructed, understood, and evaluated. For example, the fields of science and law evaluate arguments differently. Exploring how these fields invent and deploy arguments is intellectually and practically helpful, especially if people in these fields are to converse with each other. Building on rhetorical scholarship and on Stephen Toulmin's discussion of argument fields, Zarefsky's essay represents argument as contextually bound and constrained by the culture in which it exists.

The five essays in this chapter collectively demonstrate the significance of understanding shared and divergent assumptions that shape perspectives of argumentation. To borrow from the rhetorical tradition, as Brockriede does, creates a view of argumentation that is based on audience. Van Eemeren and Houtlosser's pragma-dialectical approach begins from very different points and focuses on resolving differences of opinion through critical discussions. The informal logic perspective moves beyond the abstract deductive method of formal logic to evaluate natural language arguments. *The New Rhetoric* too breaks from formal logic; Perelman and Olbrechts-Tyteca turn to rhetoric to construct a pluralistic notion of reason, one that acknowledges multiple forms of reasoning. Zarefsky's essay complements the previous essays by explicitly focusing on the role of context in argumentation. In these essays, we can begin to see why and how scholars approach argumentation from so many different perspectives.

NOTES

1 Joseph Wenzel develops this distinction in "Jürgen Habermas and the Dialectical Perspective on Argumentation," *Journal of the American Forensic Association* 16 (Fall 1979): 83–94.

Where is Argument?

WAYNE BROCKRIEDE

Before looking for the clues that may lead to the discovery of where "argument" is, perhaps I should state some of my biases so you may be less surprised if I don't go instantly to where you presume I could find the culprit without difficulty. My principal bias is a humanistic point of view that denies an interest in logical systems, in messages, in reasoning, in evidence, or in propositions—*unless these things involve human activity rather directly.* One of the most famous cliches during the past fifteen years in the study of communication, originated by I know not whom but popularized by David K. Berlo, is that meanings are not in words but in people.[1] Arguments are not in statements but in people. Hence, a first clue on the whereabouts of argument: people will find arguments in the vicinity of people.

Second, argument is not a "thing" to be looked for but a concept people use, a perspective they take. Human activity does not usefully constitute an argument until some person perceives what is happening as an argument. Although defining the term on this basis is not as neat as speaking of necessary and sufficient conditions, seeing argument as a human activity encourages persons to take into account the conceptual choices of the relevant people. Hence, a second clue: only people can find and label and use an argument.

Third, because arguments are in people and are what people see them to be, the idea of argument is an open concept. Seeing it as an open concept is consistent with the ideas that arguers are people, that people change, and that the filtering concepts people use when they make perceptions also change. Hence, a third clue: the location of argument may change, and so may the road map.

Fourth, because argument is a human process, a way of seeing, an open concept, it is potentially everywhere. During the past four years some undergraduate students at the University of Colorado have found argument lurking in some strange places. We asked them specifically to look for it beyond the traditional habitats of the law courts (where textbook writers tend to find their doctrine) or the legislative assemblies (where teachers typically want students to imagine presenting their arguments). We asked them to look in such relatively exotic places as the aesthetic experience, the interpersonal transaction, and the construction of scientific theory or the reporting of research studies. I've read some interesting papers by students who have applied an argumentative perspective to a novel by Camus, to a symphony by Bernstein, to marriage and divorce, to Zen Buddhism, and to Thomas S. Kuhn's *Structure of Scientific Revolutions*.[2] Throughout the reading of the arguments of such papers, I have been able to maintain my bias that "argument" has not been stretched out of shape, that it constitutes a frame of reference that can be related potentially to any kind of human endeavor (although, obviously, the idea of argument is not the only perspective that can be applied to a novel or a symphony). And until someone disabuses me of this eccentricity, I'm stuck with this fourth clue: the perspective of argument may pop up unexpectedly and usefully in a person's head at any time.

Fifth, but even though I appear to have constructed the idea of argument out of elasticity, I do not wish to argue that all communication is usefully called an argument. At this moment I see six characteristics that may help a person decide whether argument is a useful perspective to take in studying a communicative act. These characteristics, taken as six ways of looking at the same gestalt, define argument as *a process whereby people reason their way from one set of problematic ideas to the choice of another.*

The six characteristics of my construct of argument imply three primary dimensions. First, argument falls squarely into the realm of the problematic. What people argue about are nontrivial enough to pose a problem, but they are not likely easily to resolve the problem and so the issue remains somewhat problematic for a significant period of time. Second, each of the six characteristics of argument is a function of the variable logic of more or less and not a function of the categorical logic of yes or no. That is, each characteristic, and the construct as a whole, lies within the midrange of the more-or-less continuum. If an argument is not problematic enough or if any characteristic is too minimal—no argument. Too much of a problematic character or too much of any of the characteristics—no argument. Third, as my preliminary biases imply, argument is based on the perceptions and choices of people.[3]

Characteristic One. —an inferential leap from existing beliefs to the adoption of a new belief or to the reinforcement of an old one. One way to explain what I mean by an inferential leap is to contrast an argument of the sort I am talking about with a syllogism, the most famous member of the analytic family. Because its conclusion is entailed by the premises, no inferential leap is needed: nothing is stated in the conclusion of a syllogism that is not stated in the premises. As long as people stay within the closed system of a syllogism, nothing is problematic. To question a definition or a premise, people must leave that closed system by leaping inferentially into problematic uncertainty, and by doing so they may then make the kind of argument I am delineating in this paper. To function as an argument an inferential leap occupies the midrange of the more-or-less continuum. A person has little to argue about if the conclusion does not extend beyond the materials of an argument or extends only slightly; but one may be unable to make a convincing argument if the leap is too large, perhaps perceived as suicidal.

Characteristic Two. —a perceived rationale to support that leap. An arguer must perceive some rationale that establishes that the claim leaped to is worthy at least of being entertained. The weakest acceptable rationale may justify saying that the claim leaped to deserves entertainment "for the sake of argument." A stronger rationale may justify a person's taking a claim seriously—with the hope that after further thought it may be accepted. A still stronger rationale may convince someone to accept a claim tentatively until a better alternative comes along. If a rationale is too slender to justify a leap, the result is a quibble rather than an argument; but a rationale so strong a conclusion is entailed removes the activity from the realm of the problematic and hence from the world of argument. If the perceived rationale occupies either polar region, it fails to justify the label of argument because the claim either appears ridiculous (not worth arguing about) or too risky to entertain.

Characteristic Three. —a choice among two or more competing claims. When people quibble or play the analytic game, they do not make arguments because they cannot see a situation as yielding more than one legitimate claim. The right to choose is a human characteristic, but people are not free to choose without constraints. They are limited by what they know, what they believe, what they value. They are limited by how they relate to other people and to situations. They are limited by cause and by chance. But within such constraints people who argue have some choice but not too much. If they have too little choice, if a belief is entailed by formal logic or required by their status as true believers, they need not argue; but if they have too much choice, if they have to deal with choice overload, then argument may not be very productive.

Characteristic Four. —a regulation of uncertainty. Because arguers make inferential leaps that take claims beyond a rationale on which they are based, because they choose from among disputed options, they cannot reach certainty. If certainty existed, people need not engage in what I am defining as argument. When uncertainty is high, a need for argument is also high, especially if people are uncertain about something important to them. Usually arguers want to reduce uncertainty, but sometimes they may need to employ a strategy of confrontation to increase uncertainty enough to get the attention of others. Only then may such people be receptive to arguments designed to reduce uncertainty. If people have too little uncertainty to regulate, then they have no problems to solve and argument is not needed. But if the regulation of uncertainty is too difficult, if people have too much trouble reducing or escalating the degree of uncertainty, then they may be unable or unwilling to argue.

Characteristic Five. —a willingness to risk confrontation of a claim with peers. In his evolutionary theory of knowing, Donald K. Darnell argues that scientists and other kinds of people gain knowledge by taking an imaginative leap from an accumulated and consolidated body of information on a subject and then by undergoing the risk of confronting self and others with the claim that results, a risk that may lead to the disconfirmation or modification of the claim.[4] Arguers cannot regulate uncertainty very much until their claim meets these tests of confrontation. A person confronting self has no public risk (unless someone overhears one self arguing aloud with another self), but the private risk is that an important claim or an important part of a self may have to be discarded. When two persons engage in mutual confrontation so they can share a rational choice, they share the risks of what that confrontation may do to change their ideas, their selves, and their relationship with one another. If the leap is too little, the rationale too minimal, the choice too slender, the problem of uncertainty-reduction too miniscule, then the potential risk of disconfirmation after confrontation probably is not enough to justify calling the behavior argument. But if these characteristics are too overwhelming, the risk may be too great and a person may be unwilling to subject an idea through argument to confrontation and almost certain disconfirmation.

Characteristic Six. —a frame of reference shared optimally. The emergence of this characteristic is consistent with the idea that argument is an open concept. Until the spring of 1974 I knew of only five characteristics of argument, those I have just discussed. Then while working on a doctoral dissertation, one of my advisees, Karen Rasmussen, wrote a chapter on argument that added this sixth characteristic. She argued that arguers must share to an optimal degree elements of one another's world views or frames of reference.[5] This idea squares with a position Peter A. Schouls took in contending that professional philosophers (and, one may presume, others as well) cannot argue with one another very effectively if their presuppositions share too little or are virtually irreconcilable; but argument is pointless if two persons share too much.[6] It also squares with Kenneth Burke's doctrine of identification, which implies that polar extremes are empty categories—that the uniqueness of individuals makes for at least some divisiveness (which occasionally makes argument necessary), but on the other hand individuals are consubstantial in sharing at least a few properties (which occasionally makes argument possible).[7]

So this is my argument about where argument may be discovered: among people, by people, in changing forms, potentially everywhere, but especially where six characteristics are joined. I have contended that argument deals with the problematic and ignores the trivial or the certain, that it depends on the perceptions and choices of people who will decide whether viewing an activity as an argument is appropriate, and that it lies in the midrange of the more-or-less continuum of a variable logic and not a categorical logic.

I argue that what I have done in writing this essay is an illustration of my construct of argument. I have made some inferential leaps. I have presented what I perceive to be a rationale for supporting those leaps. I have made some choices. I may have succeeded in regulating some uncertainties. I have presumed throughout that our frames of reference overlap at some points but not at too many. I now invite your confrontation.

NOTES

[1] *The Process of Communication* (New York: Holt, Rinehart and Winston, 1960), pp. 174–175.
[2] 2nd ed. enlarged (Chicago: University of Chicago Press, 1970).
[3] An earlier exposition of five of these characteristics of argument, as applied to rhetorical criticism, appeared in my "Rhetorical Criticism as Argument," *QJS*, L (April 1974), 165–174. A more detailed discussion of the construct will appear as Chapter VII, "Argument," in Donald K. Darnell and Wayne Brockriede, *Persons Communicating* (forthcoming).
[4] Chapter III, "An Evolutionary Theory of Knowing," in Darnell and Brockriede.
[5] "Implications of Argumentation for Aesthetic Experience: A Transactional Perspective" (unpublished Ph.D. dissertation, University of Colorado, 1974), Chapter III.
[6] "Communication, Argumentation, and Presupposition in Philosophy," *Philosophy & Rhetoric*, II (Fall 1969), 183–199.
[7] *A Rhetoric of Motives* (1950; rpt. Berkeley: University of California Press, 1969), pp. 20–23.

The Development of the Pragma-Dialectical Approach to Argumentation[1]

FRANS H. VAN EEMEREN AND PETER HOUTLOSSER

1. THE DEVELOPMENT OF PRAGMA-DIALECTICS

The pragma-dialectical perspective on argumentation combines a dialectical view of argumentative reasonableness with a pragmatic view of the moves made in argumentative discourse. The dialectical conception of argumentative reasonableness is inspired by critical rationalist and other analytic philosophers, such as Karl Popper, Hans Albert, and Arne Naess, and by formal dialectical logicians, such as Charles Hamblin, Paul Lorenzen *cum suis*, Else M. Barth and Erik C. W. Krabbe. It is manifested in the pragma-dialectical ideal model of a 'critical discussion'. In this model argumentative discourse is conceived as aimed at resolving a difference of opinion by putting the acceptability of the 'standpoints' at issue to the test by applying criteria that are both problem-valid as well as intersubjectively valid.[2] The pragmatic conception of the argumentative moves as speech acts in a discursive exchange is firmly rooted in John L. Austin and John R. Searle's philosophy of verbal communication, Paul H. Grice's theory of conversational rationality, and other studies of verbal communication by discourse and conversation analysts. This conception is manifested in the definition of the moves made in the various stages of the resolution process as 'speech acts' such as presenting a standpoint, casting doubt on a standpoint, advancing arguments in favour of a standpoint, and concluding what the result of a discussion is.[3]

Together, Frans H. van Eemeren and Rob Grootendorst founded the pragma-dialectical theory or argumentation. In the 1970s and early 1980s, they first gave shape to their meta-theoretical starting-points of (1) functionalisation, (2) externalisation, (3) socialisation, and (4) dialectification. First, argumentation was, in their view, not to be studied as a structure of logical derivations, psychological attitudes or epistemic beliefs, but as a complex of linguistic (and sometimes also non-linguistic) acts with a specific communicative function in a discursive context. Second, rather than speculating on people's internal motives or dispositions for assuming a certain argumentative position, they advocated a focus on the public commitments that arguers undertake in their performance of argumentative speech acts and on the consequences of these commitments for the argumentative process. Third, they emphasized that argumentative speech acts are not performed in a social vacuum, but between two or more parties who are having a disagreement and interact with each other in an attempt to resolve this disagreement. Fourth, to transcend a merely descriptive stance in studying argumentation, they insisted on explicating the critical standards to which reasonable arguers appeal and to which they hold each other accountable when engaging in a regulated process of resolving a difference on the merits.

Van Eemeren and Grootendorst presented the basics of their pragma-dialectical theory of argumentation for the first time in English in *Speech Acts in Argumentative Discussions* (1984). As stands to reason, this fundamental book is strongly philosophical and theoretical. When viewed analytically, a critical discussion consists, according to van Eemeren and Grootendorst, of four different stages. There is a confrontation stage in which a difference of opinion manifests itself. There is also an opening stage, in which the procedural and material points of departure for a critical discussion about the standpoints at issue are established. In the argumentation stage the standpoints are challenged and defended. And the critical discussion closes with a concluding stage, in which the results of the discussion are determined. In order to comply with the dialectical standards of reasonableness, in all four stages the speech acts performed in the discourse have to be in agreement with the rules for critical discussion that van Eemeren and Grootendorst formulated. These rules range from the prohibition to prevent each other from advancing a particular position in the confrontation stage of the discussion to the prohibition to generalize the result of the discussion in the concluding stage. Any move made in the discourse that does not comply with the rules can be seen as an obstruction to achieving the critical aim of the discussion and may therefore (and in this particular sense) be considered fallacious.

This approach to the fallacies was intended as an alternative to the standard treatment of the fallacies so severely criticized by Hamblin in the early 1970s and was fleshed out by van Eemeren and Grootendorst in *Argumentation, Communication, and Fallacies* (1992). Instead of viewing the fallacies in the pre-Hamblin fashion as arguments that seem valid but are not valid, they defined the fallacies as discussion moves that violate in a particular way a particular rule for critical discussion that applies to a particular stage of the discussion. They thus replaced the single norm of logical validity by a collection of different norms that argumentative discourse has to comply with and that are expressed in the rules for critical discussion. In this way, many of the traditional fallacies can be characterized more clearly and consistently, while 'new' fallacies that went earlier unnoticed are now detected.

To make clear how the fallacies can be pinned down in argumentative practice, van Eemeren and Grootendorst first had to explain in what way argumentative discourse could be fruitfully analysed. In this endeavour, they make use of concepts such as unexpressed premise, argumentation structure and argument scheme. In *Argumentation, Communication, and Fallacies* each of these concepts is defined from a pragma-dialectical perspective. In dealing with the identification of unexpressed premises, van Eemeren and Grootendorst propose to differentiate first between a 'minimal logical' and an 'optimal pragmatic' analysis, the former amounting to a reconstruction of the 'associated conditional' motivated by the logical requirement of valid reasoning and the latter to a contextual specification or generalization of that conditional motivated by the Gricean requirement of being informative. The subordinate, coordinate and multiple structures into which a complex constellation of arguments may evolve are defined in terms of different responses to the critical questions the arguer anticipates or answers in the process of supporting a standpoint before a critical judge. These critical questions are in turn conceived as pertaining to the argument scheme on which an argument can be based, i.e., the relation of support between an individual argument and a standpoint of either a causal or a symptomatic or an analogical nature.

The main focus of *Argumentation, Communication, and Fallacies* is theoretical, but its content is to some extent also analytical and practical. The analytical component of pragma-dialectics is further developed in *Reconstructing Argumentative Discourse* (1993), written by van Eemeren and Grootendorst, Jackson and Jacobs. This study in 'normative pragmatics' combines van Eemeren and Grootendorst's ideas about the normative and dialectical dimension of argumentative discourse as viewed from the perspective of a critical discussion with the descriptive and empirically oriented approach developed by Jackson and Jacobs over the years in a series of articles dealing with argumentation in conversations (1980; Jacobs and Jackson, 1981, 1982, 1983). *Reconstructing Argumentative Discourse* sets forth the theoretical characteristics of the type of analysis that is carried out when a specimen of argumentative discourse is pragma-dialectically reconstructed as an instance of critical discussion by comparing critical normativity in various ways with 'naïve' and other kinds of normativity favoured in argumentative practice. It also develops the analytic tools that are to be applied in this endeavour, i.e., the transformations of deletion, addition, permutation, and substitution by means of which elements in the discourse that are not directly relevant for the aim of dispute resolution, such as remarks that are unrelated to the ongoing discussion, are eliminated; elements that are needed but lacking in the discourse, such as implicit and indirect premises and 'virtual standpoints', are included; a resolution-oriented order is imposed on the discourse to replace its sequential order where this is called for; and uniformity is secured in the verbal description of the moves that fulfill the same critical function.

From the outset, the four authors of *Reconstructing Argumentative Discourse* already shared some important starting points, most notably regarding the use of Searlean and Gricean insight in the analysis of argumentative discourse. Nevertheless the combination of views opened new venues for a further integration.

Reconstructing Argumentative Discourse demonstrates, among other things, that certain pieces of real-life argumentative discourse that, at first sight, seem strikingly unreasonable may be, at second sight, reasonable. Or that they can at least be viewed as reasonable when it is taken into account that certain 'higher order' conditions for critical discussion were unfulfilled during the exchange. As Jacobs (1982) has shown, a case in point is the witnessing and heckling by preachers and bystanders on an American campus site. More evidence is adduced from letters to the editor and, more particularly, from conversations during third-party dispute mediation. Their joint publication of a later date provides further confirmation of the usefulness of integrating a normative and a descriptive approach in the analysis of argumentative discourse (van Eemeren et al., 1997).

The last monograph van Eemeren and Grootendorst have published together is *A Systematic Theory of Argumentation* (2003). The book offers an overview of the main insights concerning the study of argumentation van Eemeren and Grootendorst developed during their collaboration of almost thirty years. The five components of the pragma-dialectical research program are explained, from philosophical and theoretical research to empirical, analytical and practical research. It is emphasized that practical improvement of argumentative procedures and skills—the alpha and omega of argumentation studies—can only be realised if first a philosophically motivated conception of reasonableness is explicated and given shape in a theoretical model of reasonable argumentation, systematic empirical insight is gained in the particularities of argumentative reality, and analytic tools are developed that can be applied in carrying out a methodical reconstruction of argumentative discourse that bridges the gap between the theory and practice.

2. RECONCILING DIALECTICAL AND RHETORICAL INSIGHT

Some five years ago, the present authors instigated a new development: the inclusion of insight from classical and modern rhetoric in the pragma-dialectical theory, more particularly in its method of analysis and evaluation. As it is generally perceived, in classical Greek argumentation theory, the difference between dialectic and rhetoric amounted initially to no more than a division of labour. In later years, however, these disciplines have gradually grown apart. In classical Roman argumentation theory, rhetoric was dominant, absorbing certain insights from dialectic and remaining very influential for ages. In late medieval times dialectic gained the upper hand and took over some crucial parts of rhetoric, such as dealing with the aspects of order in an oration (*dispositio*). These changes have been carefully documented and examined, albeit seldom from the perspective of argumentation theory.

According to Toulmin's *Return to Reason* (2001), the division between dialectic and rhetoric became 'ideological' after the Scientific Revolution in the seventeenth Century, and resulted in the existence of two mutually isolated paradigms, which were regarded incompatible. Rhetoric has become a field of study for scholars in the humanities interested in communication, discourse analysis and literature. With the further formalization of logic in the nineteenth Century dialectic, which was adopted by representatives of the exact sciences and viewed as a part of logic, almost disappeared from sight. Since the second half of the twentieth Century, the study of argumentation has witnessed a remarkable revival of both rhetorical and dialectical perspectives on argumentation. Regrettably, however, and in spite of a tendency to diminish the differences, there is still a yawning gap in the conceptual approaches and mutual understanding between those who favour a dialectical approach and the protagonists of a rhetorical approach. In fact, until recently, rhetoricians largely ignored the results of dialectical theorizing, and the same applies the other way around.[4]

In order to remedy the undesirable separation between dialectic and rhetoric, we have made an attempt to develop a conceptual and theoretical basis for systematically conjoining rhetorical and dialectical lines of analysis, showing that dialectical and rhetorical views on argumentative discourse are not incompatible, as is often claimed, but can even be complementary (van Eemeren and Houtlosser, 1998, 1999, 2000a, 2000b, 2002).[5] The combination of rhetorical and dialectical analysis we propose amounts to a systematic integration of rhetorical considerations in a dialectical theoretical framework. Given that it is in argumentative discourse, whether it takes place orally or in writing, generally not the arguers' sole aim to conduct the discussion in a way that is considered reasonable, but also to win the discussion in the sense of having their point accepted, we view the arguers' rhetorical attempts to have things their way as being incorporated in their efforts to realize their dialectical aspiration of resolving the difference of opinion in accordance with the proper standards for a critical discussion. We take it that, in practice, in every stage of the resolution process, irrespective of whether it is the confrontation stage, the opening stage, the argumentation stage or the concluding stage, the parties may, while being out for the optimal rhetorical result at that stage in the discussion, be presumed to hold also to the dialectical objective of the discussion stage concerned, so that the dialectical aim of each of the four stages of the resolution process may be taken to have its rhetorical analogue. To reconcile the simultaneous pursuit of these two different aims, which at times may seem to go against each other, the arguers can make use of what we have termed *strategic manoeuvring*. This strategic manoeuvring is directed at diminishing the potential tension between pursuing at the same time a dialectical as well as a rhetorical aim.

Strategic manoeuvring may take place at several levels of an argumentative move. The basic aspects of strategic manoeuvring are, in our view, making an expedient selection from the topical potential available at a certain discussion stage, adapting one's contribution optimally to the specific expectations and demands of the audience, and using the most effective presentational devices. When the choices that are made at the various levels go together in a concerted succession of moves, this amounts to conducting a full-fledged argumentative strategy. What the best way of strategic manoeuvring is, will in the last resort always depend on the limits set by the dialectical situation and the audience that is to be persuaded in the context concerned.

A good example of a mode of strategic manoeuvring that clearly exhibits all the three levels we distinguish can be found in the argumentative use of the figure that rhetoricians call *conciliatio* (van Eemeren and Houtlosser, 1999). The figure of conciliatio involves using an argument that is at a certain point put forward by the opponent in order to support the standpoint of the proponent. As we see it, in terms of strategic manoeuvring conciliatio consists in making a selection from the available argumentative potential which is expedient to the arguer (the argument is readily available) and at the same time optimally adapted to the other party's point of departure (the argument has already been accepted). On top of that, if the conciliatio is used as a strategic manoeuvre, a presentational device will be used, such as asking a rhetorical question, which is effective in making clear that the argument is indeed already considered part of the opponent's commitments. Because the opponent's adherence is then secured in advance, this mode of strategic manoeuvring can be rhetorically strong whereas it is also pre-eminently dialectical because the argumentation proceeds *ex concessis*.

In our opinion, a pragma-dialectical analysis can benefit in at least three ways from using this conception of strategic manoeuvring in reconstructing argumentative discourse. By getting a clearer view of the rhetorical aspects of the discourse, a better and more comprehensive grasp is gained of what may rightly be called argumentative reality. By achieving a more thorough and subtle understanding of the rationale behind the specific instantiations of the various discussion moves made in the argumentative discourse, the analysis becomes more profound. Last but not least, by combining the two achievements just mentioned, the analysis can also be more clearly justified.

3. DIALECTICAL BOUNDARIES OF RHETORICAL OPTIONS IN STRATEGIC MANOEUVRING

In the strategic manoeuvring that takes place in argumentative discourse to maintain the balance between dialectical and rhetorical objectives, the pursuit of these two different aims can well go together. Nevertheless there may certainly be tensions and even incompatibilities. This predicament explains the occurrence of certain *derailments* of strategic manoeuvring in a lot of real-life specimen of argumentative discourse. These derailments are to a large extent similar to the wrong moves in argumentative discourse that are traditionally known as fallacies.[6] How to distinguish between sound and fallacious argumentative discourse is one of the central problems in the study of argumentation. In our view, this problem can neither be solved completely from a purely dialectical and logical perspective nor from a purely rhetorical and pragmatic perspective.

To solve the problem, a clear demarcation is needed between argumentative moves that are to be considered as reasonable and argumentative moves that are not. In pragma-dialectics, this demarcation is achieved by giving shape to the critical ideal of reasonableness in a well-defined set of functional norms for conducting argumentative discourse aimed at resolving a disagreement concerning the tenability of a standpoint. An argumentative move is considered sound if it is in agreement with the rules applying to a specific stage of a critical discussion and it is considered fallacious if it violates any of these rules and hinders the resolution of a dispute. The problem of distinguishing between sound argumentation and fallacious argumentation thus coincides with the problem of determining whether or not a pragma-dialectical rule for critical discussion has been violated. However, in order to be able to determine systematically for all stages of the resolution process whether or not certain argumentative moves are fallacious, clear criteria are required for deciding when exactly a discussion move violates a particular rule applying to the discussion stage concerned. Establishing these criteria meets with considerable problems. We believe that our conception of strategic manoeuvring can be of help in identifying such criteria.

In our conception, strategic maneuvering is aimed at alleviating the potential tension in argumentative discourse between the extremes of arguing perfectly reasonably and just having things one's own way. Although this view implies that both aims are considered as represented in all the moves made in argumentative discourse, we have already observed that they will not always automatically be in perfect balance. On the one hand, the persuasive interests may be neglected, e.g., for fear of being (perceived as) unreasonable; on the other hand, the commitment to the critical ideal may be neglected due to assiduity to win the other party over to one's own side. Neglect of persuasiveness may result in bad strategy—or even in a blunder, as Walton and Krabbe (1995) choose to call it. Such moves will harm the arguer but not the adversary, and are therefore not 'condemnable' as being fallacious. However, if a party allows its commitment to a reasonable exchange of argumentative moves to become overruled by the aim of persuading the other party, the strategic maneuvering may 'derail' and is then condemnable for being fallacious, because the other party has become the victim of the strategic manoeuvring. In the view of strategic manoeuvring that we have developed, all derailments of strategic manoeuvring are fallacious and, in principle, fallacies can be viewed as derailments of strategic manoeuvring.

The approach of the fallacies as derailments of strategic manoeuvring can be of help in developing criteria for identifying fallacious argumentative moves. In our view, each type of strategic manoeuvring has, in a manner of speaking, its own "continuum" of sound and fallacious acting. Although fallacy judgments are in the end always contextual judgments of specific instances of situated argumentative acting, this does not mean that no clear criteria can be established in advance to determine whether a particular way of strategic manoeuvring goes astray. Particular 'types' or 'categories' of strategic manoeuvring can be identified, and for each of these types specific conditions can be determined that need to be fulfilled if the manoeuvring is to remain sound. Certain manifestations of strategic manoeuvring can then be recognized as legitimate while other manifestations can be pinned down as fallacious because the relevant conditions have not been met.[7]

In our view, derailments of strategic manoeuvring can occur only by virtue of the existence of sound strategic manoeuvring. Because in practice there is a continuum between sound and fallacious strategic manoeuvring and the demarcation line between the two is not always clear in advance, our account also explains why certain fallacies may not always be immediately manifest or apparent to others. In everyday argumentative discourse, arguers will usually expect each other to uphold a certain commitment to reasonableness and to live up to that commitment, despite their aim to have their own position accepted. Thus, an assumption of reasonableness is conferred on every discussion move (see also Jackson, 1995). This assumption is operative even when a particular way of manoeuvring violates a certain discussion rule and is therefore fallacious. Echoing Aristotle's definition of a fallacy as cited by Hamblin (1970, p. 12), we may say that the manoeuvring then still 'seems' to obey the rules of critical discussion, although in fact it does not.[8] If a deliberate rule violation is at stake, the party that is guilty will even be forced to emphasize that the commitment to reasonableness still stands. If it had been clear that the commitment to reasonableness had been withdrawn, the persuasive effect of the move would be lost immediately. If the violation is unintentional because the move is simply a mistake, it is still a fallacy in the pragma-dialectical sense: although the move concerned may seem rhetorically strong as well as dialectically acceptable to the offender, it is in fact not reasonable. Such unintended infringements are, of course, not irreversible: once the other party points out that an offence against reasonableness has been committed, it can be repaired instantly.

The criteria for determining fallacious manoeuvring can be more fully and systematically developed if we can rely on a well-motivated classification of the diverse modes of strategic manoeuvring and a specification of their soundness conditions. Such a well-motivated classification of modes of strategic manoeuvring is to be based on a methodical specification of the critical and persuasive aims that the parties involved in a dispute may be supposed to attempt to achieve at the various stages of an argumentative exchange. In our view, the pragma-dialectical model of a critical discussion provides a good starting point for identifying these aims. Although the model specifies only the critical objectives of the parties in the four stages of resolving a difference of opinion, each of these dialectical objectives has, as we have argued before, its rhetorical complement. This means that both parties can exploit all the room that is left in attempting to realize each of the critical objectives to their own persuasive intent and arrive at making the move that furthers their own case optimally. In the confrontation stage of a critical discussion, for instance, the dialectical objective of the parties is to come to a clear definition of the issue(s) on which the parties differ and the positions they assume. All parties involved can attempt to shape the issues and the positions they assume with respect to these issues in the way they think they can handle best. Of course, such stage-related 'local' aims are to be further specified in order to achieve a more precise idea of the modes of strategic manoeuvring that are pertinent to, and put to good use in, the confrontation stage. For now, these observations should suffice to show that the strategic manoeuvring by the parties at this particular stage will be aimed at maintaining the balance between an accurate definition of the difference of opinion and an interpretation of the dispute that is advantageous to one of the parties involved. In this way, we have at any rate identified in an exemplary way one general mode of strategic manoeuvring. This makes it possible to examine the soundness conditions applying to this mode of strategic manoeuvring more precisely and to identify the criteria that have to be taken into account in deciding whether or not the strategic manoeuvring has got derailed and a particular fallacy has been committed.

To illustrate how the identification of such demarcation criteria may proceed, we take again the specific case of strategic manoeuvring by means of conciliatio that aims at securing in the argumentation stage that the argument is rhetorically strong and complies at the same time with the dialectical requirement of advancing only arguments whose content is in the opening stage agreed upon by both parties in the discussion. In the conciliatio case, the danger of derailment stems from the fact that the other party, although he may safely be assumed to agree with the propositional content of the argument, may not just like that be assumed to agree with the way in which this propositional content is used to argue for a standpoint that is precisely the opposite of his own standpoint. We think that this discrepancy can be illuminated by making use of the pragma-dialectical analysis of the speech act of advancing argumentation. According to this analysis, an argument can only count as a felicitous attempt to convince the other party if both parties do not only accept the propositional content of the argument but also view the proposition concerned as a potential justification of the standpoint at issue. Typically, in a conciliatio the propositional content of the argument that is used is indeed accepted by the other party. Its justificatory potential for the standpoint at issue, however, is not—at least not automatically. This pragmatic speech act analysis makes it possible to derive a condition that can be of help in evaluating actual instances of conciliatio. Such manifestations of conciliatio can be considered sound if the protagonist may be supposed to be capable of supporting the view that the argument he has taken over from the other party has an unquestioning and overriding justificatory potential with regard to his, i.e., the protagonist's, standpoint and the other party may decide whether this is indeed the case. The use of conciliatio is a derailment of strategic manoeuvring if it is simply presupposed that the argument taken over from the other party has an unquestioning justificatory potential for the standpoint at issue and there is no room left for questioning this presupposition.[6] If a conciliatio derails in this way, the fallacy of 'begging the question' has been committed: the protagonist relies on a starting point that is not yet accepted by the other party.

Two examples of conciliatio may suffice to illustrate how the condition we have explained can be of help in determining whether a derailment of strategic manoeuvring has taken place—and the fallacy of begging the question has been committed. The first example is part of an 'advertorial' in which one of Shell's defences of its involvement in Nigeria consists of justifying its not pulling out of Nigeria's Liquefied Natural Gas project by pointing out that not Shell would suffer if Shell pulled out but the Nigerian people and the environment:

> If we do so now, the project will collapse. [. . .] A cancellation would certainly hurt the thousands of Nigerians who will be working on the project, and the tens of thousands more benefiting in the local economy. The environment, too, would suffer, with the plant expected to cut greatly the need for gas flaring in the oil industry.

Shell chooses its arguments for not pulling out of the project from two of its opponents' professed concerns: their concern for the people of Nigeria and their concern for the environment. Shell's opponents may, in view of their political preferences, be assumed to be in favour of a prospering native population and a non-polluted environment. At the propositional level, Shell can therefore be sure of acceptance. But how does the oil company proceed to ensure the opponents' acceptance of the justificatory potential of the two arguments for its standpoint that it should not pull out of the project? Shell does so by claiming that there is a causal relation between its pulling out of the project and a deterioration of the human and environmental circumstances, thus lending direct support to the view that the justificatory power of the opponents' arguments for Shell's standpoint is unquestionable. Although the addition of 'certainly' suggests that the harmful effects are obvious, Shell does not really deter the reader from questioning the supposed causal link, so that no actual derailment of strategic manoeuvring with conciliatio can be said to have taken place, and there is no sufficient reason to accuse Shell of making a move that amounts to question begging.

The second example of conciliatio we would like to discuss stems from John LeCarré's novel *A Perfect Spy*. The main character in the book is a boy who is raised by everyone but his father, a real, albeit amiable, charlatan. Now and again the father comes to visit the boy. Each time when the father gets ready to leave again the boy starts to cry. The father wants him not to start crying and tries to achieve this by saying:

> Do you love your old man? Well then . . .

This is a more complex manifestation of conciliatio than the previous one, because the proposition that is to be taken over first needs to be attributed to the boy. This happens by means of a rhetorical question. A further difference with the Shell case is that the father suggests that adherence to the proposition forces the boy to accept his standpoint. By adding 'well then . . .' the father implies that, given that the boy loves his old man, he should stop crying. Because the father does not add any further support for this implication and his wording suggests that this is all there is to be said, we can only conclude that this manifestation of strategic manoeuvring by means of conciliatio has got derailed.

These analyses show how a fundamental problem in the study of argumentation, i.e., distinguishing between sound and fallacious moves in argumentative discourse, can be clarified by viewing fallacies as derailments of strategic manoeuvring. By gaining a deeper and more realistic insight in the strategic design of the discourse, a more mature sense can be achieved of the whys and wherefores of the various non-fallacious and fallacious moves that occur in certain circumstances in ordinary argumentative practice. Our approach to the demarcation problem differs considerably from how it is dealt with by other argumentation theorists, such as Biro and Siegel (1992) and Johnson (2000), who give precedence to absolute epistemological considerations. It also differs from Willard's (1995) and Leff's (2000) approaches, who rely on empirical—and relativistic—social considerations. Instead, in our approach normative and descriptive insights are systematically integrated and we treat fallacies as modes of strategic manoeuvring that violate, in spite of the maintenance of a general commitment to dialectical reasonableness, a certain rule for critical discussion because the conditional constraints pertaining to a specific type of strategic manoeuvring have been ignored and rhetorical interests have gained the upper hand over dialectical interests.

4. SOME CURRENT PROJECTS
IN PRAGMA-DIALECTICAL RESEARCH

Currently, we continue first of all our ambitious research project *Rhetorical and dialectical analysis* in which we examine the relations between rhetoric and dialectic and the ways in which insight from these disciplines can be of help in developing a comprehensive method for analysing and evaluating argumentative discourse. We already described how, in this endeavour, we incorporate rhetorical insight in means of persuasion in a dialectical framework for resolving differences of opinion in a reasonable way. The integrated method for critical analysis thus developed we use exemplarily in reconstructing a historically important case of argumentative discourse: William of Orange's *Apologie* [Apologia] (1581). The *Apologie* is a long pamphlet that justifies William the Silent's actions in the Dutch Revolt against the Spanish rulers that started in 1568. The justification is a response to King Philip of Spain's *Ban Edict* in which William was outlawed. It involves an intricate display of strategic manoeuvring between dialectical commitments and rhetorical objectives (van Eemeren and Houtlosser, 2003).

Besides *Rhetorical and dialectical analysis*, in the pragma-dialectical research programme, which has in the 1990s become much more international,[9] there are several other (clusters of) research projects in the process of being carried out. Although the efforts have always been directed at covering all five components of the research programme, initially the main emphasis was, as we have explained, primarily on the philosophical and theoretical components. Later on the analytical component has been given more substance and recently the empirical and practical components have also been studied intensively. Presently pragma-dialectical research generally concentrates on the problems involved in bridging the gap between abstract philosophy and theory of argumentation and the empirical, analytical and practical study of argumentative discourse.[10] A concerted effort is being made to determine how the theoretical conceptual tools of pragma-dialectics can be methodically adjusted for systematic and viable employment in dealing with the varied and often unruly features of argumentative practice.[11] This means that the research projects that are currently carried out usually relate to several components of the research programme at the same time. Let us close our overview by mentioning some prominent themes that can be distinguished.

First, there is an extensive research project, *Conceptions of reasonableness,* aimed at testing the conventional validity of the pragma-dialectical rules that is based on their intersubjective acceptability. In this project, experimental empirical investigations are undertaken to determine systematically the extent to which the rules for critical discussion agree with the norms applied (or rather favoured) by ordinary arguers when evaluating argumentative discourse. For this purpose, ordinary language users are requested to assess the reasonableness or acceptability of fragments of argumentative discourse that contain fallacious (and non-fallacious) discussion moves. On the basis of the results of persuasion research carried out in social psychology it is assumed that a number of factors will affect their judgements: the type of discourse involved, the degree to which the standpoints at issue are loaded, the evaluator's perception of the speaker or writer, the type of discussion move at stake, its verbal presentation, et cetera. All these factors are taken as variables in the tests. The results of these empirical investigations are also relevant to the teaching of students about fallacies. They provide an empirical basis for developing more pedagogically adequate textbooks in which appropriate attention is paid to each of the specific argumentation rules, elaborating more intensively on the rationale for rules that are intuitively not immediately clear and acceptable than on those that are. In a more general sense, the results of these investigations provide insight into ordinary language users' rationality or reasonableness conceptions, the consistency of these conceptions, and eventually, as the case may be, in the social, cultural and other differences between them.

Second, there is an elaborate project, *Characteristics of argumentative discourse,* which deals with the pragmatic features of argumentative discourse. In this project it is being investigated which tools certain characteristics of argumentative discourse may provide for its analysis. The project focuses in the first place on those explicit and implicit elements in the text or context that are relevant to making a pragma-dialectical reconstruction of the discourse that results in an adequate analytic overview. Starting from the assumption that all speech acts performed in an argumentative discourse can be reconstructed as part of an attempt at resolving a difference of opinion, the project concentrates on the various types of verbal moves that can play a constructive role in the consecutive stages of a critical discussion. In this endeavour, insight from speech act theory, discourse analysis, conversation analysis and other branches of pragma-linguistics are used to make a systematic inventory of the means that are used in argumentative practice to indicate the communicative and interactional functions of certain moves. In our broad conception of indicators of argumentative moves or, for short, 'argumentative indicators', they are words, expressions or other signs that can serve as clues for identifying argumentative moves and relations between such moves that are relevant to resolving a difference of opinion. The project aims not only at making a systematic inventory of potential verbal indicators and classifying them in terms of argumentative moves, but also at identifying the conditions that have to be fulfilled for a certain expression to serve as a specific indicator. The scope of the project is not restricted to relational indicators of argumentation and standpoints in the 'narrow' or 'broad' sense, such as "therefore" and "that is why" respectively, but extends to indicators of other crucial elements of argumentative discourse, such as antagonism, concessions, rebuttals, counter-arguments, and relations between arguments.[12]

Third, we would like to mention a cluster of projects, referred to as *Institutional argumentation,* which is aimed at developing instruments for analysing and evaluating argumentative discourse in institutional settings. The project concentrates primarily on the reconstruction of argumentation in legal discourse and political discussions. The central questions are which argumentative procedures and techniques are in juridical and political settings used for resolving differences of opinion and which insights are crucial to an adequate analysis and evaluation of juridical and political argumentative discourse. In investigating argumentative discourse in a legal context, the assumption is that to a great extent the legal process can be viewed as critical discussion. Starting from this assumption, the research focuses on the reconstruction of juridical discussions, taking into account the specific characteristics of legal discourse and the specific characteristics of legal rationality. The aim is to develop a comprehensive theoretical framework in which ideas concerning the analysis and evaluation of legal argumentation taken from argumentation theory and from legal theory are integrated. To this end, it must be established how, in which stages and according to which rules legal discussions are conducted and which general and specific legal criteria of rationality are applied. It must also be established how various forms of complex argumentation occurring in the justification of legal decisions can be reconstructed. Further, it must be established how argument schemes that are frequently used to justify legal decisions, such as those of analogy, *a contrario* and pragmatic argumentation, can be analysed and evaluated in a rational way. Last but not least, it must be established which combinations of rhetorical and dialectical techniques are used to convince a legal audience of the acceptability of legal standpoints. Discussions in political settings are studied along similar lines and in a similar way. Hence the focus is on the function of the procedures and rules in the resolution of political disputes. Among the main questions are whether a political context requires additional rules, whether it requires a specific formulation of the general rules and whether it is necessary and justified to acknowledge certain restrictions to the applicability of the general rules for critical discussion. More specific questions are, for example, how the various argument schemes are used in a political context, in what way pragmatic arguments need to be analysed and evaluated in such a context and which dialectical and rhetorical techniques certain politicians use to convince their audience.

NOTES

[1] As one might expect, this paper is based on a list of earlier publications: they will be mentioned only when this seems helpful. Other versions of (parts of) this paper will be published elsewhere.

[2] The notions of problem-validity and intersubjective validity, which are based on insight developed by Crawshay-Williams, are introduced by Barth and Krabbe (1982). Problem validity refers to an assessment of the suitability of certain theoretical tools to fulfill the purpose for which they are designed, intersubjective validity to their acceptance by the company of people that is supposed to apply them. In van Eemeren and Grootendorst (1988a, 1988b, 1992) an account is given of the problem-validity of the pragma-dialectical norms; the intersubjective validity of these norms is being investigated empirically in a series of experimental tests, e.g., van Eemeren et al. (2000). See also section 4 of this paper.

[3] In this short description of the development of pragma-dialectics we do not discuss publications that were in the first place intended as a general service to the discipline, such as *Fundamentals of Argumentation Theory* (van Eemeren et al., 1996), *Argumentation: Analysis, Evaluation, Presentation* (van Eemeren et al., 2002) and *Crucial Concepts in Argumentation Theory* (van Eemeren, Ed., 2001).

[4] The collection of essays published in *Dialectic and Rhetoric* (van Eemeren and Houtlosser, Ed., 2002) may be regarded as efforts to stimulate a rapprochement between dialectic and rhetoric. They not only illustrate some of the major problems one is confronted with when trying to achieve such a rapprochement, but also the various angles from which, and ways in which, it can be aimed for.

[5] Viewed from our current perspective, pragma-dialectics as it was initially developed by van Eemeren and Grootendorst (1984, 1992, 2003) can be regarded as an attempt to create a dialectical approach to argumentation that keeps an open eye for the rhetorical aspects of argumentative reality by studying argumentative discourse from a pragmatic perspective.

[6] Before Hamblin published his well-known study *Fallacies* (1970), the 'logical' conception prevailed of a fallacy as an argument that seems valid but is in fact not valid. For the various pre-Hamblin and post-Hamblin theoretical approaches to the fallacies, see van Eemeren (2001).

[7] In some clear-cut cases a certain mode of strategic manoeuvring can be immediately recognized as manifestly violating a discussion rule applying to the specific discussion stage concerned, but this is usually not the case.

[8] This characterization can thus be of help in explaining the deceptive character of the fallacies.

[9] *Studies in Pragma-Dialectics* still gives an overview of the state of the art in pragma-dialectics by means of a collection of essays by the Amsterdam group (van Eemeren and Grootendorst, Eds., 1994). Its successor, *Advances in Pragma-Dialectics* consists of essays written by an international group of scholars (van Eemeren, Ed., 2002).

[10] See van Eemeren (Ed., 2002).

[11] Several scholars, such as Jackson, Aakhus and Groarke, have also made proposals to widen the scope, or 'inclusiveness', of pragma-dialectics in various respects. See van Eemeren (Ed., 2002, ch. 7, 8, and 9).

[12] Since the model for critical discussion specifies the moves that can play a constructive role in the various stages of the resolution process, it constitutes an appropriate theoretical framework for classifying the indicators of argumentative language use. For each stage, the investigation will identify which expressions are available in ordinary language for indicating the moves pertinent to the resolution process in the stage concerned and it will be specified which kind of information is conveyed by the use of a particular indicator, and under which conditions the analysis of the use of a certain expression as an indicator of a specific discussion move is justified.

REFERENCES

Barth, E. M. and E. C. W. Krabbe: 1982, *From Axiom to Dialogue: A Philosophical Study of Logics and Argumentation.* Walter de Gruyter, Berlin/New York.

Biro, J. and H. Siegel: 1992, 'Normativity, Argumentation and an Epistemic Theory of Fallacies', in F. H. van Eemeren, R. Grootendorst, J. A. Blair and C. A. Willard (eds.), *Argumentation Illuminated,* Sic Sat, 1, Amsterdam, 85–103.

Eemeren, F. H. van (ed.): 2001, *Crucial Concepts in Argumentation Theory,* Amsterdam University Press, Amsterdam.

Eemeren, F. H. van (ed.): 2001, *Advances in Pragma-Dialectics,* Sic Sat/Vale Press, Amsterdam/ Newport News, VA.

Eemeren, F. H. van and R. Grootendorst: 1984, *Speech Arts in Argumentative Discussions: A Theoretical Model for the Analysis of Discussions Directed towards Solving Conflicts of Opinion.* Foris/Mouton de Gruyter, Dordrecht/Berlin.

Eemeren, F. H. van and R. Grootendorst: 1988a, 'Rationale for a Pragma-dialectical Perspective', *Argumentation* 2, 271–291.

Eemeren, F. H. van and R. Grootendorst: 1988a, 'Rules for Argumentation in Dialogues', *Argumentation* 2, 499–510.

Eemeren, F. H. van and R. Grootendorst: 1992, *Argumentation, Communication, and Fallacies: A Pragma-Dialectical Perspective,* Lawrence Erlbaum, Hillsdale, NJ.

Eemeren, F. H. van and R. Grootendorst: 2003, *A Systematic Theory of Argumentation. The Pragma-Dialectical Approach,* Cambridge University Press, Cambridge.

Eemeren, F. H. van and R. Grootendorst (eds.): 1994, *Studies in Pragma-Dialectics,* Sic Sat, 4, Amsterdam.

Eemeren, F. H. van, R. Grootendorst, S. Jackson and S. Jacobs: 1993, *Reconstructing Argumentative Discourse*, The University of Alabama Press, Tuscaloosa/London.

Eemeren, F. H. van, R. Grootendorst, S. Jackson and S. Jacobs: 1997, 'Argumentation', in T. A. van Dijk (ed.), *Discourse as Structure and Process. Discourse Studies: A Multidisciplinary Introduction, Volume I*, Sage, London, 208–229.

Eemeren, F. H. van, R. Grootendorst, A. F. Snoeck Henkemans, J. A. Blair, R. H. Johnson, E. C. W. Krabbe, Chr. Plantin, D. N. Walton, C. A. Willard, J. Woods and D. Zarefsky: 1996, *Fundamentals of Argumentation Theory: A Handbook of Historical Backgrounds and Contemporary Developments*, Lawrence Erlbaum, Mahwah, NJ.

Eemeren, F. H. van, R. Grootendorst and A. F. Snoeck Henkemans: 2002, *Argumentation: Analysis, Evaluation, Presentation*. Lawrence Erlbaum, Mahwah, NJ.

Eemeren, F. H. van and P. Houtlosser: 1998, 'Rhetorical Rationales for Dialectical Moves: Justifying Pragma-dialectical Reconstructions', in J. F. Klumpp (ed.), *Argument in a Time of Change: Definitions, Frameworks, and Critiques*. Proceedings of the Tenth NCA/AFA Conference on Argumentation. Alta, Utah, August 1997, National Communication Association, Annandale, VA, 51–56.

Eemeren, F. H. van and P. Houtlosser: 1999, 'Strategic Manoeuvring in Argumentative Discourse', *Discourse Studies* 1, 479–497.

Eemeren, F. H. van and P. Houtlosser: 2000a, 'Rhetorical Analysis within a Pragma-dialectical Framework', *Argumentation* 14, 293–305.

Eemeren, F. H. van and P. Houtlosser: 2000b, 'Managing Disagreement: Rhetorical Analysis within a Dialectical Framework', *Argumentation and Advocacy* 37, 150–157.

Eemeren, F. H. van and P. Houtlosser: 2002, 'Strategic Maneuvering: Maintaining a Delicate Balance', in F. H. van Eemeren and P. Houtlosser (eds.). *Dialectic and Rhetoric: The Warp and Woof of Argumentation Analysis*, Kluwer Academic Publishers, Dordrecht, 131–159.

Eemeren, F. H. van and P. Houtlosser: 2003, 'The Rhetoric of William the Silent's Apologie: A Dialectical Perspective', in L. Komlósi, P. Houtlosser and M. Leezenberg (eds.), *Communication and Culture. Argumentative, Cognitive and Linguistic Perspectives*, Sic Sat, Amsterdam. Also published in: T. Suzuki, Y. Yano and T. Kato (eds.), *Proceedings of the 1st Tokyo Conference on Argumentation*, Japan Debate Association, Tokyo, 37–40.

Eemeren, F. H. van and P. Houtlosser (eds.): 2002, *Dialectic and Rhetoric: The Warp and Woof of Argumentation Analysis*, Kluwer Academic Publishers, Dordrecht.

Eemeren, F. H. van, B. Meuffels and M. Verburg: 2000, 'The (Un)reasonableness of the *Argumentum Ad Hominem*', *Language and Social Psychology* 19, 416–435.

Hamblin, C. L.: 1970. *Fallacies*. Methuen, London. Reprinted at Vale Press, Newport News.

Jackson, S.: 1995. 'Fallacies and Heuristics', in F. H. van Eemeren, R. Grootendorst, J. A. Blair and C. A. Willard (eds.), *Analysis and Evaluation*. Proceedings of the Third ISSA Conference on Argumentation (University of Amsterdam, June 21–24, 1994). Volume II, Sic Sat, Amsterdam, 257–269.

Jackson, S. and S. Jacobs: 1980, 'Of Conversational Argument: Pragmatic Bases for the Enthymeme', *Quarterly Journal of Speech* 66, 251–265.

Jacobs, S.: 1982, *The Rhetoric of Witnessing and Heckling: A Case Study in Ethnorhetoric*. Ph.D. dissertation. University of Illinois at Urbana-Champaign.

Jacobs, S. and S. Jackson: 1981. 'Argument as a Natural Category: The Routine Grounds for Arguing in Natural Conversation', *Western Journal of Speech Communication* 45, 118–132.

Jacobs, S. and S. Jackson: 1982, 'Conversational Argument: A Discourse Analytic Approach', in J. R. Cox and C. A. Willard (eds.), *Advances in Argumentation Theory and Research*, Southern Illinois University Press, Carbondale, IL, 205–237.

Jacobs, S. and S. Jackson: 1983, 'Strategy and Structure in Conversational Influence Attempts', *Communication Monographs* 50, 285–304.

Johnson, R.: 2000, *Manifest Rationality. A Pragmatic Theory of Argument*. Lawrence Erlbaum, Mahwah, NJ.

Leff, M.: 2000. 'Rhetoric and Dialectic in the Twenty-first Century', *Argumentation* 14, 241–254.

Toulmin, S. E.: 2001, *Return to Reason*, Harvard University Press, Cambridge, Mass.

Walton, D. N. and E. C. W. Krabbe: 1995. *Commitment in Dialogue: Basic Concepts of Interpersonal Reasoning*, State University of New York Press, Albany, NY.

Willard, Ch. A.: 1995, *Liberal Alarms and Rhetorical Excursions. A New Rhetoric for Modern Democracy*, University of Chicago Press, Chicago.

....

Informal Logic: An Overview

RALPH H. JOHNSON AND J. ANTHONY BLAIR

INTRODUCTION

The issues we address in this paper are contained in the question that were put to the symposium on informal logic and philosophy at the World Congress of Philosophy at Boston in August 1998:

- What is the philosophical significance of informal logic?
- What are its applications/implications for other areas of philosophy?

In this overview we are not going to attempt to answer these questions in detail, though our views will become evident at the end of our agenda, which is as follows.

We begin with a brief statement about the nature of informal logic, what it is and what it is not. We then outline the problems and the issues informal logic addresses, followed by a brief account of the recent developments in the field, the resources available, and, finally, our view about its implications for philosophy. (We have added references to some of the work appearing since the World Congress.)

1. INFORMAL LOGIC: WHAT IT IS

A. Towards a definition. Many have noted the strong Canadian presence in research in the field of informal logic. Perhaps coincidentally, both Canadians and informal logicians seem to be involved in an ongoing questioning about their identity. What is Canadian, as distinct from American, or British, French, and so on? Informal logicians find themselves asking: What is informal logic, as distinct from formal deductive logic, epistemology and critical thinking? Walton and Brinton (1997) say, in a recent anthology about the history of informal logic, that:

> Informal logic has yet to come together as a clearly defined discipline, one organized around some well-defined and agreed upon systematic techniques that have a definite structure and can be decisively applied by users. (9)

This observation is significant, if irksome. For although there remain misconceptions about what informal logic is about, its leading practitioners (among whom we include Walton, Govier, and ourselves) more or less agree that its mandate is the study of norms of arguments (as contrasted with those of inference or implication). We propose once again (see Johnson and Blair 1987, 148) the following as a way to construe informal logic that fits with what both Govier (1987) and Walton (1989) have said:

> Informal logic designates that branch of logic whose task is to develop non-formal$_2$ standards, criteria, procedures for the analysis, interpretation, evaluation, critique and construction of argumentation in everyday discourse.

"Non-formal$_2$" is borrowed from the Barth-Krabbe (1982) distinction of three different senses of 'form.' This logic is *non*-formal in the following respects. It does not rely on the chief analytic tool of formal deductive logic, the notion of logical form. Nor does it rely on the main evaluative function of formal deductive logic, validity. But that does not mean this logic is non-formal in the sense that it abandons reference to standards, criteria or procedures.

One problem with this definition, however, is that it limits informal logic to everyday discourse, a restriction that now seems to us both unnecessary and counterfactual. Historically informal logic's realm of interest has been what might be called natural-language argument, which has two sub-domains: (a) everyday discourse (discussions of public affairs, such as newspaper editorials) and (b) what Weinstein (1990) called "stylized" discourse, namely, the domain-specific styles of arguments, inference tickets and epistemologies of the special disciplines, such as the different sciences. The crucial divide is not between everyday and stylized discourses, but between artificial and natural languages. The latter is the focal point for informal logic (as distinct from formal deductive logic's focus on artificial languages and logistic systems), whatever the discourse.

B. Some misconceptions and competing conceptions of informal logic. We are going to run through an inventory of other responses to the question: "Just what is informal logic?" some of which anyone at all familiar with the research of the past 25 years will recognize as plainly wrong, and some of which are views of knowledgeable colleagues with which we disagree. We begin with what some consider a *locus classicus*—Ryle's (1954) statement, in which he uses the label 'informal logic' to refer to the implications of substantive concepts (such as *time* and *pleasure*), whose logic is "informal," as opposed to the logic of concepts such as conjunction and disjunction, whose logic is "formal." For Ryle, "informal logic" appears to be synonymous with "philosophical analysis." That is a much broader understanding than will be found in most of the work of informal logic's leading practitioners.

A second misconception of informal logic is that it is simply and exclusively the study of the informal fallacies (Carney and Sheer 1964, Kahane 1971). The study of informal fallacies does constitute a part, but only one part, of informal logic's subject matter.

A third misconception of informal logic is that it is formal logic without the formality. This idea is illustrated by the way that Copi produced his textbook, *Informal Logic* (1986), which consists simply of excerpts from his *Introduction to Logic* (1986) textbook, omitting the chapters covering formal logic. This view is wrong because, on the one hand, where formalism$_2$ illuminates, informal logic employs it (see Woods and Walton, 1982); and on the other hand, the principal focus of informal logic is where formalism in that sense does not illuminate.

A point of disagreement within the field is the view that informal logic has the task of mediating between formal logic and reasoning in natural language. Such a view can be found in Goldman (1986) and Woods (1995). In our view, where deductive implications occur in natural language argumentation, they can be formalized (sometimes with profit, sometimes not). Implications that are not entailments, and other aspects of argument analysis and evaluation, are not amenable to such formal treatment.

A second view with which we disagree (which finds favour with such authors as McPeck (1981), Siegel (1988), and Weinstein (1994) is that informal logic is applied epistemology in the sense that it is the application of epistemological findings to the evaluation of arguments. We might agree, but only if epistemology were stretched to include logic, dialectics and rhetoric.

Finally, we disagree with Fisher and Scriven (1997), who hold that informal logic is "the discipline which studies the practice of critical thinking and provides its intellectual spine" (76). Given our view that informal logic's defining subject-matter is arguments and argumentation, and that critical thinking, in Fisher and

Scriven's view, is "skilled and active interpretation and evaluation of observations and communications, information and argumentation" (21), we would assign to informal logic a narrower scope than they do.

2. RECENT RESEARCH

In this section we look at some of the most recent areas of research in the field of informal logic.

1. The history of informal logic. One important development is the emergence of work on the history of informal logic. It has sometime been said that very little happened in informal logic between the time of Aristotle and the publication in 1970–71 of Hamblin's *Fallacies* (1970) and Kahane's *Logic and Contemporary Rhetoric* (1971). But Hansen and Pinto's anthology *Fallacies, Classical and Contemporary Readings* (1995) includes several studies of historical treatments of informal fallacies. And Walton and Brinton's *Historical Foundations of Informal Logic* (1997), with chapters on Isaac Watts, Whately, Bentham, Mill and Kant, shows how much applicable work did occur in the interstitial two millennia or so.

2. Argument as dialogue. A second area of research has been the modeling of arguments as dialogues of different kinds, carried out by Walton (1996) and Walton and Krabbe (1995). Their work might be seen as an elaboration of the pragma-dialectical theory, with which it has close ties. It also informs their theory of fallacy. More recently, some limitations of the dialogue model have been suggested (Tindale 1996, Blair 1998).

3. Extending the concept of argument. Various scholars have been suggesting that the concept of argument be revised in other directions. Gilbert contends that argument is not exclusively verbal, but also emotional, visceral and "kisceral"(1997). Groarke (1996), Birdsell and Groarke (1996) and Blair (1996) include visual communications such as works of art as arguments. Most recently, Tindale (1999) argues for considering the rhetorical perspective as basic.

4. Reason and argument. At two levels, the relation of reason and argument has been explored in recent literature. At the micro level, reasoning and argument have been distinguished and related (Pinto 1995, Blair 1999). At the macro level, the connection between argument and rationality has been explored—both the place of argument in rationality, and the constraints of rationality on argument (see Walton 1990, Finocchiaro 1992, Johnson 1996,).

5. New theory of inference. When someone adduces grounds in support of a claim, they may believe that the grounds deductively imply the claim, or they may believe that the grounds supply strong inductive support for the claim. Traditionally, these have been thought to be the only two possibilities for rational support for a claim. Citing Wellman and Wisdom, Govier (1987) has long contended that grounds may support a claim in other ways. Wellman (1971) used the term 'conduction' to parallel deduction and induction. Rescher (1976) used the term 'plausible reasoning' in a similar connection. More recently, Scriven (1987), using the term 'probative reasoning,' and Walton (1996b), using the term 'presumptive reasoning,'

have argued for such a third kind of evidentiary support. These authors are pointing in the direction of a new theory of inference.

6. Argument schemes. In the last several years the idea has emerged in the research of various scholars that argumentation schemes may hold the key to important problems in the theory of argument. Kienpointner (1992) has identified over 80 argument schemes, and classified them in an organizing typology. Walton (1996b) finds in argument schemes patterns of presumptive reasoning, and sees many fallacies as misused or abused argument schemes.

7. Structures and diagrams. A certain amount of attention in the literature has been devoted to the structure of arguments within argumentation, and to attendant models of argument diagramming. Freeman (1991) provided a Toulmin-inspired model crossed with a dialectical conception of argument, Snoeck Henkemans (1992) offered an analysis grounded in the pragma-dialectical approach, Walton (1996a) developed his own pragmatic, dialogue-based analysis.

8. Fallacy theory. The study of fallacy is closely associated with informal logic. Several important developments have taken place since Woods and Walton's (1989) classic series of papers on individual fallacies appeared in the 1970s and early 1980s. First, there is the fine recent collection of articles and research edited by Hansen and Pinto noted above: *Fallacies: Classical and Contemporary Readings* (1995). Second, Walton has proposed a kind of classification or hierarchy on mistakes (1995). Third, there has been a shift in the direction of seeing a fallacy as a certain kind of procedural or strategic mistake (Walton & Krabbe 1995, van Eemeren & Grootendorst 1992, Hintikka 1987). Fourth, we should mention Walton's continuing research on the fallacies. For the past decade, Walton has been producing a series of book length studies of the individual fallacies: to date he has published monographs on begging the question (1991), appeal to emotion (1992a), slippery slope (1992b), the argument from ignorance (1994), *ad hominem* 1998). In addition, besides numerous articles on individual fallacies, he has two monographs on fallacy theory and fallacies in general (1987, 1995).

9. Premise adequacy. In distinction from the modern tradition of barring questions about the doxastic, epistemic or dialectical adequacy of premises of argument from logic, informal logic's focus on argument evaluation has led its practitioners to consider the criteria of premise adequacy. There is quite widespread interest in the relevant-sufficient-acceptable triad first proposed by Johnson and Blair (1977). Among the authors who have embraced that doctrine (sometimes with slightly different terminology) are: Govier (1985) (who changes "sufficient" to "adequate"), Damer (1987), Freeman (1988), Little, Groarke and Tindale (1989), Barry (1992) and Seech (1992). Johnson and Blair (1994), Pinto and Blair (1993), and Freeman (1992) have argued for some norm of acceptability of premises, a modification of van Eemeren and Grootendorst's model (1984). More recently Blair (1995) has taken a relativistic position, while Johnson (1998) has insisted on truth as one criterion of premise adequacy. There have been numerous informal logic papers on relevance in the past decade (see, for examples, the papers by Tindale, Woods, Blair, Freeman, and Hitchcock in the special 1990 issue of *Argumentation* on relevance). Sufficiency has received less attention (but see Blair 1991).

10. Developments in the theory of argument criticism. Walton (1995) argues that argument criticisms are not all of a piece, some are more serious than others; and that we must differentiate, for example, between weak execution and misuse or abuse. He also presents a possible typology of fallacy, distinguishing between a paralogism and sophism. In (1996) Johnson argues for a distinction between the evaluation of an argument and criticisms of an argument, and argues that we need to develop principles of argument criticism, among them: the principle of vulnerability, the principle of discrimination and the principle of logical neutrality. The latter have both been incorporated into Johnson and Blair's *Logical Self-Defense* (1994) but further discussion is needed as to how these are best formulated, how best justified, and whether there are other principles.

11. Investigation of argument's social role. In developing a theory of argument criticism, Johnson (1996) has been led to examine the role of argument as a social practice and to generate norms for the social obligations of arguers in both using the practice appropriately and in maintaining it in a healthy state. Govier (1987) and Walton (1990) also draw attention to the role of argument in the life of the society.

12. Impact of feminist theory. Feminist critical examination of the metaphors employed in the practice and the theory of argument have led to their revaluation (see Ayim 1988). The general concern raised about the privileging of the rational and the marginalization of the emotional have led to a debate among informal logicians about extending the conception of argumentation and about limiting the social role of argumentation (see Orr 1989, 1995, Nye 1990, Govier 1993, Menssen 1993, Gilbert 1994). Both Gilbert (1997) and Tindale (1999) devote sympathetic chapters to the influence of feminist insights on theory of argument.

13. Return to rhetoric. It is the burden of Tindale's *Acts of Argument* (1999) that a rhetorical perspective is both essential and fundamental for argument theory. Gilbert's *Coalescent Argument* also urges a turn toward a rhetorical perspective.

14. Argumentation as pragmatic. Walton has for some time been developing a pragmatic theory of argument (see, for example. *Argument Structure: A Pragmatic Theory,* 1995), and Johnson's recent book *Manifest Rationality: A Pragmatic Theory of Argument* (2000), presents a theory of argument that, while differing in many respects from Walton's, is similarly pragmatic.

3. PROBLEMS AND QUESTIONS FOR FUTURE RESEARCH

The recent theoretical developments just listed represent an ongoing research program for informal logic. To that extent, "problems and questions for future research" are constituted by the problems and questions stimulating current ongoing research. Still, a classification of the issues can be useful. In our view there are four areas of "problematic" around which research in informal logic theory can be organized, all of which are clearly interrelated.

1. The theory of argument. How are argument and argumentation to be understood? Some, such as the proponents of the pragma-dialectic theory of the Amsterdam school (van Eemeren and Grootendorst 1984), hold that a general unified theory of argumentation is necessary to underwrite anything but *ad hoc*

research in argumentation. Others believe useful work can be done on specific problems without working out a global theory of argumentation. The pragma-dialectical theory is one of the most comprehensive theories developed to date although aspects of it have come under criticism (Blair and Johnson 1993, Woods 1994, Tindale 1996). If modifications are needed, what are they? Is some form of pragma-dialectical theory the correct global theory of argumentation? If not, what is the alternative?

What logical types of argument are there? The old distinction between inductive and deductive arguments has been criticised as not being exhaustive (see "conduc-tive," "probative," "presumptive" under item 5, above).

Several of the items of recent and ongoing research listed above fit comfort-ably within the "theory of argument" rubric: historical studies (item 1), relating dialogue to the dialectical nature of argument (item 2), stretching the concept argument (item 3), relating reason and argument (item 4), developing a new theory of inference (item 5), studying argument schemes (item 6) and working out the theoretical implications of certain insights of feminist theory (item 12).

2. The analysis of arguments. What is the correct way to analyze particular argu-ments? How is "correct" here to be parsed? It seems evident the question should be answered in terms of the purposes of such analysis, so these need to be identi-fied. In the background are theories about the possible types of argument (which brings us back to the theory of argument); a corollary is a theory of how arguments may be diagrammed (see item 7, above). Should rhetorical (and other possibilities) as well as logical elements be kept track of, and if so, how is that best done? The rhetoric/logic distinction remains problematic still, so the problem of argument analysis raises it again.

Taking a broader perspective, however, identifies arguments as a type of dis-course. Hence, theories of discourse analysis have a bearing on argument analysis. We here enter the cognate fields of pragmatics.

Clearly one's general theory of argument will be pertinent to issues of the analysis of arguments. If arguments are conceived as essentially dialogues between individuals, that will call for a different kind of analysis than if they are understood as addresses to general audiences. If arguments are to be identified as belonging to different schematic types, that too will affect how they are analyzed. So item 2 (argument as dialogue), item 3 (extending the concept of dialogue), item 5 (new theory of inference) as well as item 7 (structures and diagrams) all fit under the rubric of argument analysis.

3. The theory of evaluation. Here the initial motivating question is: What distin-guishes a "good" argument from a "bad" one? The reply will be: it depends on the perspective. The standard story is that an argument can be logically good, rhetori-cally good, or indeed good from a number of other possible perspectives. However, are these norms independent of one another? Some (e.g., Tindale 1992, 1996, 1999, Gilbert 1995) claim the need for a theory of evaluation that integrates different perspectives. Here too the issues of argument types and their related norms apply. Once argumentation is understood as a social, functional enterprise, pragmatics, social epistemology and communication theory in general (Willard 1983, 1989) would seem to have a bearing on its evaluation. Research into theories of fallacy, and into individual fallacies (item 8 above) and the close analysis of criteria of good argument (item 9 above) belong here as well.

4. The theory of criticism. We have long held out for a distinction between evaluation (identifying the criteria of good and bad) and criticism (the act of criticism, including the application of the criteria of good and bad argument, but also the public act of critique). The act of argument criticism presupposes a normative theory of the function of such criticism. Such a theory in turn presupposes a normative theory of the roles of argumentation. If argument is properly used to accomplish a set of aims, then the public critique of arguments will be related to their contribution to achieving those aims (see Walton 1990). Here is where we would situate item 10 (developments in the theory of argument criticism), item 11 (investigation of argument's social role) and item 12 (impact of feminist theory).

4. INFORMAL LOGIC: RESOURCES

1. Journals. The journal *Informal Logic* has been the journal of record in the field since 1983, but articles on topics in or related to informal logic also appear regularly in *Argumentation* (founded 1986), *Philosophy and Rhetoric, Argumentation and Advocacy* (the journal of the American Forensic Association), and *Inquiry: Critical Thinking Across the Disciplines* (founded in 1988). Articles on informal logic topics have also appeared in a wide range of general philosophical journals including, but not at all restricted to, *Synthese, Logique et Analyse* and *American Philosophical Quarterly.*

2. Academic programs. To our knowledge, there are no undergraduate or graduate programs devoted to informal logic. Virtually every college and university in the United States and Canada has an introductory-level course that teaches some informal logic (usually as part of either a "critical thinking" or "reasoning" orientation, or an introduction to logic course). We know of only a handful of upper-level undergraduate courses, and another handful of courses at the M.A. and Ph.D. levels, mostly in Canada.

3. Conferences. The original conferences on informal logic were held at the University of Windsor (Windsor, Ontario) in 1978, 1983 and 1989. Conferences in both informal logic and critical thinking have been held at Sonoma State University (Rohnert Park, California) yearly since May, 1981 and at Christopher Newport University (Newport News, Virginia) each year from 1984 to 1988. Oakton Community College hosted five conferences on critical think[ing] from 1988 to 1992 (Des Plains, Illinois), and a conference was held at George Mason University (Fairfax, Virginia) in 1995. The Association for Informal Logic and Critical Thinking has, since its inception in 1983, organized sessions on informal logic in conjunction with the Eastern, Central and Pacific meetings of the American Philosophical Association, and at some of the meetings of the Canadian Philosophical Association. Papers on informal logic have been on the program of the International Society for the Study of Argumentation conferences of 1986, 1990, 1994 and 1998 (University of Amsterdam, The Netherlands). Finally, the Ontario Society for the Study of Argumentation has held conferences devoted largely to informal logic in 1995, 1997 and 1999 (Brock University, Ontario).

4. Challenges. In our view, the field of informal logic faces two major, and related, practical challenges. It needs to find the support and resources to mount graduate

level instruction, so that more young scholars become aware of its problematic and its literature, and make informal logic one area of concentration in their research programs. And it needs to penetrate the philosophical establishment, so that its theoretical findings become known and better reflected in undergraduate instruction.

5. IMPLICATIONS FOR PHILOSOPHY

What implications does informal logic have for philosophy, and indeed for the broader world we inhabit?

1. The end of deductivism. Philosophical reasoning and argument need informal logical analysis. It is a theoretical prejudice, not a fact, that the only respectable philosophical reasoning and argumentation employ deductive inferences. Ryle recognizes this when he says:

> Whether a given philosophical argument is valid or fallacious is, in general, itself a debatable question. Simple inspection cannot decide. More often it is a question of whether the argument has much, little or no force. (1954, 112)

Perhaps the most important contribution of informal logic is that it helps to complete the revolution begun by the pragmatists who took issue with the classical (Platonic/Cartesian) theory of knowledge. Their work can be seen as an attempt to reconceptualize knowledge according to the model of the empirical sciences. Work in informal logic can be seen as an attempt to reconceptualize argumentation and free it from its historical attachment to what Toulmin and Perelman called the geometrical or mathematical model. This means, among other things, the end of deductivism—the idea that all implications are either deductive or defective; the end of the notion that argument should be conceived as proof; and the end of the class divisions between types of beliefs—elite beliefs being either necessary truths or truths that follow necessarily from premises known to be true, while second best are beliefs warranted by some probability calculus and all the rest are untouchable, not warranting acceptance by a reasonable person.

2. The demise of the view that logic is the theory of reasoning. By identifying reasoning with implication and taking the view that logic is essentially deductive logic, it was possible to believe that logic is in fact identical with the theory of reasoning. But once we adopt a broader view of logic and reasoning, it becomes clear that there is more involved in the construction of a theory of reasoning than formal deductive logic can provide (Finocchiaro 1984, Johnson 1996). If we are right, philosophical education needs to change its standard story about argument, reasoning, and logic.

Another implication of the work in informal logic has been to make it clear that logic is still developing. It does not carry this responsibility alone; other developments also attest to it, such as fuzzy logic (Zadeh 1975) and dynamic logic (van Benthem 1995). Yet, as mentioned, the vast body of philosophical education remains untouched by the findings of informal logic. As a consequence, serious mis-education continues.

3. The re-evaluation of formalism. Another result of informal logic has been to challenge the strong attachment to formalism and all that goes with it: algorithms,

proof procedures, model theories, etc. Thus, it is not just the deductive bias inherent in traditional logic that informal logic has helped reveal; it is also the preference for formalism. This is what Toulmin is referring to when he says:

> From the mid 17th century, Modern Philosophers regarded the formal issues a[s] central—not least, because they would be discussed in general, "decontextual" terms. So, logic became equated with *formal* logic. (1992, 4)

Here it is crucial to emphasize the point made earlier, that there are different senses of the term, 'formal' (see Barth & Krabbe 1982, Johnson and Blair 1990). This realization opens the door to seeing that informal logic is not therefore a contraction or oxymoron, as some have alleged. We want to emphasize that informal logic is in no way incompatible with procedures, the application of criteria, or rigour. It is a question of *which* criteria, and here informal logic is informal because it rejects the logicist view that logical form (*à la* Russell) holds the key to understanding the structure of all arguments; and also the view that validity is an appropriate standard to demand of all arguments.

Another way of making this point is to say that informal logic is allied with the movement to make logic more empirical, less *a prioristic* (Barth 1992, Toulmin 1958, Weinstein 1990).

6. BROADER PRACTICAL IMPLICATIONS

Finally, it can be argued that the practice of argumentation has fallen on hard times in this culture. Serious observers have noted a decrease in literacy skills in the culture, the level of public debate seems at an all-time low, and public rhetoric is dominated by the confessional mode of television "talk-shows." Where in all this is the practice of argumentation to be cherished and nurtured, if not in the Academy? The teaching of high standards of argument interpretation, evaluation and critique that have practical application is the goal of the pedagogical side of informal logic.

Outside the Academy, in what some would call the "life-world," we have witnessed the withering away of the old world order. The post WWII coalitions existing under the threat of military force and power are now everywhere giving way to new alignments based on common interest and rational persuasion. The Balkan states, the mid-East, and parts of Africa, and the India-Pakistan subcontinent, are noteworthy exceptions. The human community must understand that the only force that we can expect to make use of is "the force of the better argument." Yet, paradoxically, it seems that just when there has never been a greater need for argumentation in the life-world, never has it been in greater danger as a cultural practice in the very societies premised on its healthy operation, the democratic societies. More than ever, we the philosophical community, and particularly those committed to the study of everyday argumentation, have something to contribute in educating the world.

Through its commitment to the development of better theories of argumentation, then, informal logic has an important service to render not merely to the theory of reasoning and to the academy, but also to the life-world.

REFERENCES

Ayim, M. (1988) Violence and domination as metaphors in academic discourse. In T. Govier (ed.), *Selected issues in logic and communication*, 184–195. Belmont, CA: Wadsworth.

Barry, V. and Rudinow, J. (1992). *Invitation to critical thinking*. 2nd ed. New York.

Barth, E. M. (1985). A new field: empirical logic/bioprograms, logemes and logics as institutions. *Synthese* 63: 376–388.

Barth, E. M. and Krabbe, E. C. W. (1982). *From axiom to dialogue. A philosophical study of logics and argumentation.* Berlin/New York: Walter de Gruyter.

Benthem, J. van. (1995). *Logic and argumentation.* In F. H. van Eemeren, R. Grootendorst, J. A. Blair and C. A. Willard (eds.), *Proceedings of the third international conference on argumentation.* Vol. 1, 18–35. Amsterdam: SicSat.

Birdsell, D. S. and Groarke, L. (1996). Toward a theory of visual argument. *Argumentation and Advocacy,* 33.1, 110.

Blair, J. A. (1991). What is the right amount of support for a conclusion? In F. H. van Eemeren, R. Grootendorst, J. A. Blair and C. A. Willard (eds.), *Proceedings of the second international conference on argumentation,* Vol. 1A, 330–337. Amsterdam: SicSat.

Blair, J. A. (1995). Premise adequacy. In F. H. van Eemeren, R. Grootendorst, J. A. Blair and C. A. Willard (eds.), *Perspectives and approaches, Proceedings of the third ISSA conference on argumentation,* Vol. II, 191–202. Amsterdam: SicSat.

Blair, J. A. (1996). The possibility and actuality of visual arguments. *Argumentation and Advocacy,* 33.1, 23–39.

Blair, J. A. (1992). Premissary relevance. *Argumentation* 6.2, 203–217.

Blair, J. A. (1999). Walton's argument schemes for presumptive reasoning: A critique and development. In F. H. van Eemeren, R. Grootendorst, J. A. Blair and C. A. Willard (eds.), *Proceedings of the fourth International Society for the Study of Argumentation conference.* Amsterdam: SicSat.

Blair, J. A. and Johnson, R. H. (1987). The current state of informal logic and critical thinking. *Informal Logic* 9, 147–151.

Blair, J. A. and Johnson, R. H. (1993). Dissent in fallacy land, Part I: Problems with van Eemeren and Grootendorst. In R. E. McKerrow (ed.), Argument and the Postmodern Challenge, Proceedings of the Eighth SCA/AFA Conference on Argumentation. Annandale, VA: Speech Communication Association.

Carney, J. D. and Sheer, R. K. (1964). *Fundamentals of logic.* New York: Macmillan.

Copi, I. (1986). *Introduction to logic.* 7th ed. New York: Macmillan.

Copi, I. (1986). *Informal logic.* New York: Macmillan.

Damer, T. E. (1987). *Attacking faulty reasoning.* 2nd ed. Belmont, CA: Wadsworth.

Eemeren, F. H. van and Grootendorst, R. (1984). *Speech acts in argumentative discussions.* Dordrecht/Providence: Foris Publications.

Eemeren, F. H. van and Grootendorst, R. (1992). *Argumentation, communication and fallacies: A pragma-dialectical perspective.* Hillsdale, NJ: Lawrence Erlbaum Associates.

Finocchiaro, M. (1984). Informal logic and the theory of reasoning. *Informal Logic* 6(2), 3–8.

Finocchiaro, M. (1989). Methodological problems in empirical logic. *Communication and Cognition* 22, 313–335.

Fisher, A. and Scriven, M. (1997). *Critical thinking: Its definition and assessment.* Point Reyes, CA: Edgepress.

Freeman, J. B. (1988). *Thinking logically: Basic concepts for reasoning.* Englewood Cliffs, NJ: Prentice-Hall.

Freeman, J. B. (1991). *Dialectics and the macrostructure of argument: A theory of argument structure.* Amsterdam: Mouton de Gruyter. Waveland Press.

Freeman, J. B. (1992). Relevance, Warrants, Backing, Inductive Support. *Argumentation* 6.2, 219–235.

Freeman, J. B. (1995). Premise acceptability, deontology, internalism, justification. *Informal Logic* 17.2, 270–278.

Gilbert, M. A. (1994). Feminism, argumentation and coalescence. *Informal Logic* 16.2, 95–113.

Gilbert, M. A. (1997). *Coalescent argumentation.* Mahwah, NJ: Lawrence Erlbaum Associates.

Goldman, A. (1986). *Epistemology and cognition.* Cambridge: MIT Press.

Govier, T. (1987). *Problems in argument analysis and evaluation.* Dordrecht: Foris Publications.

Govier, T. (1993). When logic meets politics: Testimony, distrust and rhetorical disadvantage. *Informal Logic* 15.2, 93–104.

Groarke, L. (1996). Logic, art and argument. *Informal Logic* 18.2&3 (to appear).

Hamblin, C. L. (1970). *Fallacies.* London: Methuen.

Hansen, H. V. (1990). An informal logic bibliography. *Informal Logic* 12, 155–184.

Hansen, H. V. and Pinto, R. C. (Eds.). (1995). *Fallacies: Classical and contemporary readings.* University Park, PA: The Pennsylvania State University Press.

Hintikka, J. (1987). The fallacy of fallacies. *Argumentation* 1, 211–238.

Hitchcock, D. (1992). Relevance. *Argumentation* 6.2, 251–270.

Johnson, R. H. (1996). *The rise of informal logic.* Newport News, VA: Vale Press.

Johnson, R. H. (2000). *Manifest rationality: A pragmatic theory of argument.* Mahwah, NJ: Lawrence Erlbaum Associates.

Johnson, R. H. and Blair, J. A. (1977). *Logical self-defense.* 3rd ed., 1993. Toronto: McGraw-Hill Ryerson. U.S. ed., 1994. New York: McGraw-Hill.

Johnson, R. H. and Blair, J. A. (1991.) Contexts of informal reasoning: Commentary. In J. Voss, D. Perkins, and J. W. Segal, (eds.), *Informal Reasoning and Education,* Ch. 7, 131–150. Hillsdale, NJ: Lawrence Erlbaum Associates.

Kahane, H. (1971). *Logic and contemporary rhetoric.* Belmont, CA: Wadsworth.

Kienpointner, M. (1992). *Alltagslogik: struktur und funktion von argumentations-mustern.* Stuttgart-Bad Cannstatt: frommann-holzboog.

Little, J. F., Groarke, L. A. and Tindale, C.W. (1989). *Good reasoning matters.* Toronto: McLelland and Stewart.

McPeck, J. (1981). *Critical thinking and education.* New York: St. Martin's Press.

Menssen, S. (1993). Do women and men use different logics?: A reply to Carol Gilligan and Deborah Orr. *Informal Logic* 15.2, 123–138.

Nye, A. (1990). *Words of power.* New York: Routledge.

Orr, D. (1989). Just the facts Ma'am: Informal logic, gender and pedagogy. *Informal Logic* 11.1, 1–10.

Orr, D. (1995). On logic and moral voice. *Informal Logic* 17.3, 347–363.

Pinto, R. C. and Blair, J. A. (1993). *Reasoning, A practical guide.* Englewood Cliffs, NJ: Prentice-Hall.

Pinto, R. C. (1995). The relation of argument to inference. In F. H. van Eemeren, R. Grootendorst, J. A. Blair and C. A. Willard (eds.), *Perspectives and approaches, Proceedings of the third ISSA conference on argumentation,* Vol. 1, 271–286. Amsterdam: SicSat.

Rescher, N. (1976). *Plausible reasoning: An introduction to the theory and practice of plausible inference.* Assen: Van Gorcum.

Rescher, N. (1977). *Dialectics: A Controversy-oriented approach to the theory of knowledge.* Albany: State University of New York.

Ryle, G. (1954). *Dilemmas.* Cambridge: Cambridge University Press.

Scriven, M. (1987). Probative logic: Review and preview. In F. H. van Eemeren, R. Grootendorst, J. A. Blair and C. A. Willard (eds.), *Argumentation across the lines of discipline,* 7–32. Dordrecht/Providence: Foris Publications.

Seech, Z. (1992). *Logic in everyday life: Practical reasoning skills.* 2nd ed. Belmont, CA: Wadsworth.

Siegel, H. (1988). *Educating reason: Rationality, critical thinking and education.* New York: Routledge.

Snoeck Henkemans, A. F. (1992). *Analysing complex argumentation.* Amsterdam, SicSat.

Tindale, C. W. (1992). Audiences, relevance and cognitive environments. *Argumentation* 6.2, 177–188.

Tindale, C. W. (1996). Fallacies in transition: An assessment of the pragma-dialectical perspective. *Informal Logic* 18.1, 17–33.

Tindale, C. W. (1999) *Acts of arguing: A rhetorical model of argument.* Albany: State University of New York Press.

Toulmin, S. E. (1958). *The uses of argument.* Cambridge: Cambridge University Press.

Toulmin, S. E. (1992). Logic, rhetoric & reason: redressing the balance. In F. H. van Eemeren, R. Grootendorst, J. A. Blair and C. A. Willard (eds.), *Argumentation illuminated,* 3–11. Amsterdam: SicSat.

Walton, D. (1987). *Informal fallacies: Towards a theory of argument criticisms.* Amsterdam: John Benjamins.

Walton, D. (1989). *Informal logic: A handbook for critical argumentation.* Cambridge: Cambridge University Press.

Walton, D. (1991). *Begging the question.* Westport, CT: Greenwood.

Walton, D. (1992a). *The place of emotion in argument.* University Park, PA: The Pennsylvania State University Press.

Walton, D. (1992b). *Slippery slope arguments.* Oxford: Oxford University Press.

Walton, D. (1994). *Arguments from ignorance.* University Park, PA: The Pennsylvania State University Press.

Walton, D. (1995a). *A pragmatic theory of fallacy.* Tuscaloosa and London: The University of Alabama Press.

Walton, D. (1996a). *Argument structure: A pragmatic theory.* Toronto: University of Toronto Press.

Walton, D. (1996b). *Argumentation schemes for presumptive reasoning.* Mahwah, NJ: Lawrence Erlbaum Associates.

Walton, D. (1998). *Ad hominem arguments.* Tuscaloosa, Alabama: University of Alabama Press.

Walton, D. and Brinton, A. (Eds.). (1997). *Historical foundations of informal logic.* Aldershot: Ashgate.

Weinstein, M. (1990). Towards a research agenda for informal logic and critical thinking. *Informal Logic* 12, 121–143.

Weinstein, M. (1994). Informal logic and applied epistemology. In R. H. Johnson and J. A. Blair (eds.), *New essays in informal logic,* 140–161. Windsor: Informal Logic.

Wellman, C. (1971). *Challenge and response, justification in ethics.* Carbondale and Edwardsville, IL: Southern Illinois University Press. London and Amsterdam: Feffer & Simons, Inc.

Willard, C. A. (1983). *Argumentation and the social grounds of knowledge.* Tuscaloosa: The University of Alabama Press.

Willard, C. A. (1989). *A theory of argumentation.* Tuscaloosa: The University of Alabama Press.

Woods, J. (1992). Apocalyptic relevance. *Argumentation* 6.2, 189–202.

Woods, J. (1994). Is the theoretical unity of the fallacies possible? *Informal Logic* 16.2, 77–85.

Woods, J. (1995). Fearful symmetry. In H. V. Hansen and R. C. Pinto (eds.), *Fallacies: Classical and contemporary readings.* University Park, PA: The Pennsylvania State University Press.

Woods, J. and Walton, D. (1982). *Argument, the logic of the fallacies.* Toronto: McGraw-Hill Ryerson.

Woods, J. and Walton, D. (1989). *Fallacies: Selected papers, 1972–1982.* Dordrecht/Providence: Foris Publications.

Zadeh, Lotfi. (1975). Fuzzy logic and approximate reasoning. *Synthese,* 30: 407–428.

Argumentation Studies in the Wake of *The New Rhetoric*

DAVID A. FRANK

Those who resisted the Nazi tyranny, Jonathan Glover observes in his *Humanity: A Moral History of the Twentieth Century,* tended to come from homes in which children were encouraged to reason through argument (382). Children raised by parents who used physical means of gaining compliance or an authoritarian style of childrearing were much less likely to rescue Jews. Glover cites research conducted by the Oliners, who carefully document why some chose the moral path during World War II. Glover and the Oliners conclude that habits of reasoning, expressed through argument and questioning, elicit concern for the other and recognition of values beyond one's own. Chaïm Perelman and Lucie Olbrechts-Tyteca detected this connection between argumentation and moral action.

Seeking a philosophical balm for the wounds of post-war Europe, Perelman and Olbrechts-Tyteca re-discovered rhetoric and argumentation, seeing that they could foster the "contact of minds" necessary for the reconstruction of civil society. This is an odd phrase, but it reflects their aspiration that reasoning rather than violence should be the primary means of dealing with disagreement. Between 1947 and 1984, Perelman, alone and in collaboration with Olbrechts-Tyteca, translated this aspiration into the New Rhetoric Project (NRP), which was expressed in a number of books, articles, and conference papers. The most complete expression of the project was published in 1958 as *Traité de l'argumentation: la nouvelle rhétorique* (known in French speaking countries as *Traité*), which was translated into English in 1970 as *The New Rhetoric: A Treatise on Argumentation* (known in English speaking countries as *The New Rhetoric*). Perelman set the agenda for the collaboration, as his solitary writings on a host of subjects before his collaboration with Olbrechts-Tyteca identified the key issues and problems addressed in the NRP. Olbrechts-Tyteca played a major role in the development of the examples and middle range theory (Warnick, 1998; Olbrechts-Tyteca, 1963).

In this article, I consider the influence of the NRP on studies of twentieth-century argument in our field, and its relevance in the new millennium. My rehearsal of the argument in the NRP is not meant to duplicate the fine surveys of Perelman's work in Foss, Foss, and Trapp; Conley; and other anthologies and overviews of rhetoric. Rather, my purpose is epideictic in the Perelmanian sense in that I hope to strengthen a commitment to the study of argument as a humane art with philosophical and pragmatic expressions. I seek to recall the larger purpose Perelman and Olbrechts-Tyteca envisioned for argumentation and to trace the influence of the NRP on argument studies in the United States. In so doing, I will call attention to some key books and scholarship that draw from the NRP to develop insights on argument. In the conclusion, I suggest the NRP is the most important system of argument produced in the twentieth century and can serve as an ecumenical site for the development of argumentation theory.

My purpose may seem benign, but it directly confronts two movements in the field. The first is the continued fragmentation of the field into a set of case studies with little shared sense of purpose, which David Zarefsky has rightly lamented as a failure of disciplinary coherence. Another movement, pragma-dialectics, originating in the Netherlands, begins with a misreading of the NRP to launch a system of argument with quite different goals than those set forth by Perelman. The pragmadialecticians seek uniform standards for all argument and see conflict resolution as the objective of argumentation. I believe the NRP's system navigates between fragmentation and enforced uniformity, and remains the most ethical and powerful framework available to scholars of argument. The NRP is a blueprint for civil society, with a strength and coherence lacking in other systems. To better understand the tension among these movements, it is necessary to resituate the NRP and its influence on argumentation studies in the United States.

THE NEW RHETORIC PROJECT IN CONTEXT

Before and during War II [*sic*], totalitarians seized reason and designed ideologies to contain it in what Hannah Arendt in her *Origins of Totalitarianism* termed the "cold logic" of the syllogism (468–472). Ideological reasoning is distinguished by its adherence to a premise, which governs a chain of logic that does not acknowledge experience. Such reasoning embraces apodictic logic and is expressed in a hyper-rationality that values nothing outside itself. Scholars have identified the role of a ruthless expression of ideological rationality in many of the twentieth century genocides. A disembodied rationality, devoid of humanity, is no guarantee of humane behavior.

Arendt in her *Eichmann in Jerusalem* described the advent of ideological thinking and the peculiarly modern form of evil she saw on display in the trial of

Adolph Eichmann, the Nazi in charge of the final solution. Eichmann, according to Arendt, was trapped by the assumptions and language of ideology, thereby blocking recognition of experience. She saw Eichmann as a uniquely modern expression of monstrosity because he did not seem to command the capacity to think outside of realm of ideology. Rereading *Eichmann* as a scholar of argumentation, I find it striking that no one confronted or argued with Eichmann, making his flight to ideology comfortable. The internal dialogue that makes up authentic thinking, so essential in Arendt's vision of moral action, requires argument. Arendt, Perelman, and a number of other postwar philosophers understood the need to consider the role played by reason in totalitarian movements that captured Eichmann and his colleagues. Some conflated reason with totalitarian thought, and abandoned rationality; others rallied and sought an expanded sense of reason and a new rationalism.

After the liberation of Belgium in September 1944, Perelman joined those who sought a reconstituted sense of reason. Until that point, he was a logical positivist, holding that reason was limited to formal logic and to the *vita contemplativa* (See Frank and Bolduc, From *Vita Contemplativa to Vita Activa*). While leading the Jewish underground during the War, he finished a book titled *On Justice*. He concluded in *On Justice* that values could not "be subject to any rational criterion" and that they are "utterly arbitrary and logically indeterminate . . . " (*The Idea of Justice and the Problem of Argument* 56–57). Perelman was "deeply dissatisfied" with his conclusion that there was no reasonable basis for value judgments (*The New Rhetoric and the Humanities* 8). He resisted the limitations of logical positivism and saw that the other dominant alternative, existentialism, did not give the grounds for justice or judgment (see Frank and Bolduc, "Chaïm Perelman's First Philosophies").

As he worked through his dissatisfaction, he decided to use the method adopted by Gottlob Frege, the subject of Perelman's dissertation, to study value reasoning. Frege analyzed particular instances of mathematical reasoning to build general principles of logic. Similarly, Perelman set out to examine examples and illustrations of arguments to determine how humans reasoned about values. In 1947, Lucie Olbrechts-Tyteca joined him in his search and after a ten-year exploration, the collaborators published their *Traité de l'argumentation: la nouvelle rhétorique*. The NRP was a major force in the "rhetorical turn" of the 1950s. Gerard Hauser notes:

> By mid-century, philosophers such as Richard McKeon and Chaïm Perelman were turning to rhetoric as a mode of thought and analysis that could address basic questions of knowledge and action in an age lacking a dominant set of shared assumptions. During the last third of the century these important but relatively isolated initial statements exploded into a flurry of intellectual work aimed at theorizing rhetoric in new terms. (1)

This "flurry of intellectual work" was, in part, a result of philosopher Henry W. Johnstone's encounter with Perelman when he visited Belgium in the 1950s. There, Johnstone became familiar with Perelman's work, understood Perelman's agenda, agreed that argument justified philosophical inquiry, and brought the NRP to the attention of American philosophers. Although Johnstone disagreed with Perelman on several issues, there is little question that Perelman's work helped to justify the philosophical study of argumentation in the United States.

Perelman brought the NRP to the United States and Pennsylvania State University when he was invited by Johnstone and Robert T. Oliver to serve as a visiting professor in 1962. During this visit, he discovered the field of speech communication. As Oliver observes in his history of Perelman's visit, Perelman did not know about the American field of rhetoric and speech, nor did American scholars of speech know much about Perelman. The mutual ignorance is explained by the fact that Perelman's view of rhetoric stemmed from his frustration with logical positivism, his reading of Paulhan and Latini, and his rediscovery of the Greco-Roman rhetorical tradition. The speech field in 1962 was, according to Oliver, aligned with social psychology, and U.S. rhetoricians were concerned with historical studies of great speakers (578–580). Oliver reports that William James and John Dewey were the philosophers most often cited by American scholars of speech, cultivating a pragmatism primarily concerned with effects of rhetorical practices (578–580). Oliver and American speech scholars saw in Perelman's work a philosophical justification for the study of speech, one endorsed by a celebrated continental philosopher.

After his 1962 visit, Perelman recognized he had strong allies in the field of speech communication. Perelman wrote Emily Schossberger, his editor at the University of Notre Dame, that he wanted to title the English translation *The New Rhetoric: A Treatise on Argumentation* rather than a literal translation of the French title, *A Treatise on Argumentation: The New Rhetoric* in order to attract potential readers in the American speech communication discipline (Perelman to Schossberger). His visit also inspired the study of argument as a subject of philosophical inquiry. In the abstract of their 1965 book, *Philosophy, Rhetoric and Argumentation,* Johnstone and his colleague Maurice Natanson informed their readers the book was "intended as evidence that a new field of philosophy has appeared—a field in which the concepts of rhetoric and argumentation, including the rhetoric and argumentation of the philosopher himself, are subjected to philosophical scrutiny" (v). The founding of the journal *Philosophy and Rhetoric* was another result of Johnstone's encounter with Perelman.

Reflecting the tie between Perelman and the field of speech, Carroll Arnold wrote the introduction to Perelman's *Realm of Rhetoric*. Recognizing the importance of the NRP in argumentation studies in the United States, this journal dedicated a special issue, edited by Ray Dearin, to the work of Perelman and Olbrechts-Tyteca. A survey of scholarly articles published in *Argumentation and Advocacy* in the last 13 years reveals that a number of argument scholars draw on the NRP for insights on the practice of argumentation. Some of our most promising scholars, such as Theodore Prosise and Brian McGee, have deployed the NRP in their articles and understand Perelman's larger ambition to situate argument as an expression of philosophical reason. Unfortunately, they are the exceptions. Scholars of argument, as David Zarefsky notes, have lost track of what binds the field together. Reflecting the fragmentation in the field, scholars often pluck a concept or notion out of the NRP for the purpose of illuminating a particular case study, neglecting the larger purpose of Perelman and Olbrechts-Tyteca's efforts. The pragma-dialecticians are not interested in the intent of the NRP because of its purported "bias against logic" (van Eemeren and Grootendorst, *Argumentation, Communication, and Fallacies* 3–4). When placed in context, the texts of the NRP display a coherent vision of argument as an expression of reason.

I hope, in what follows, to highlight for argument scholars the key notions in the NRP that have lost focus, been misread, or are underappreciated. In particular, I wish to revisit their rescue of reason and persuasion, novel interpretation of the relationship between dialectic and rhetoric, and their illuminating take on audience, epideictic, loci, and the techniques of argument.

ARGUMENT IN NEW RHETORIC PROJECT

Perelman recognized the defining characteristic of totalitarian thought: the absolute commitment to the "cold logic" of deductive reasoning. Having resisted the "myth of the twentieth century," the Nazi belief in racial superiority, Perelman identified pluralism as the necessary bulwark against another outbreak of totalitarianism. To erect this bulwark, he contested Descartes' notion that if two people disagree, one must be wrong. Disagreement, in Perelman's view, was a sign of societal health as long as argument and a "contact of minds" rather than violence and irrationality were responses (Perelman, *New Rhetoric and the Humanities* 112–113).

The only absolute metaphysic Perelman defended was that all metaphysical principles were subject to revision and that humans deserved liberty and freedom of choice. (See Perelman, *Participation aux Deuxiemes Entretiens de Zurich*). Parties in a disagreement might all hold partial truths and uniform agreement was not the primary goal of the rhetorical encounter. Indeed, the NRP endorsed dissent and fostered pluralism, doing so by nesting different and incompatible values within a larger realm of rhetoric.

In this realm, deduction does not rule and many different logics flourish. Accordingly, in the NRP truth is in process, dissent revealing the irreducible plurality of values, and argument serving as a form of reason designed to allow for judgment. Two key values recur in the NRP and undergird the moral basis of argument: *rapprochement* and *einfuehlung*. The first word, from the French, calls for a realignment of forces out of conflict into harmony; the second, from the German, means empathy. Placing the work of Perelman and Olbrechts-Tyteca in context, these two values capture the intent of the NRP to humanize reason by bringing it into alignment with the lived reality of human beings. Perelman sought a rapprochement between reason and rhetoric, and broadened the domain of reason to include sentiment and values. He also integrated Classical Greek thought with Jewish patterns of reason, an important gesture of reconciliation in the post war setting (Frank, "Dialectical Rapprochement in the New Rhetoric"). Argumentative exchange, in this vision, was not intended to produce uniform agreement but an appreciation of the irreducible plurality of human values. Those who make reasonable arguments put themselves "in the place of others" and understand that humans are moved by sentiment and will (*The New Rhetoric and The Humanities* 118). The realm of rhetoric calls for a broad and robust sense of reason, one that includes empathy and sentiment. To put these values into play, Perelman and Olbrechts-Tyteca saw that they needed to develop a new definition of reason constituting a "break" with the Enlightenment definition of reason, which featured formal rationalism and apodictic logic (*The New Rhetoric* 1).

In response to the compulsion of apodictic logic, embodied and misused as it was in totalitarian thought, Perelman and Olbrechts-Tyteca gave a philosophical grounding to persuasion. Perelman and Olbrechts-Tyteca highlighted the importance of choice and liberty in human affairs. Demonstrative reason, they noted, does not provide choice. Apodictic logic forms a chain of premises and conclusions that cannot be challenged (Perelman and Olbrechts-Tyteca, *The New Rhetoric* 2–4). In comparison, argumentation gives audiences the choice of adherence. The notion of adherence is at the philosophical and spiritual heart of NRP. The audience has the liberty to accept or reject the reasoning offered by an advocate: "the use of argumentation implies that one has renounced using force alone, that value is attached to gaining the adherence of one's interlocutor by means of reasoned persuasion, and that one is not regarding him as an object, but appealing to his free judgment" (Perelman and Olbrechts-Tyteca *The New Rhetoric* 55). Persuasion becomes an important philosophical value, not merely a technique.

Perelman and Olbrechts-Tyteca attended the notions of persuasion and adherence with a rhetorically inflected sense of reason. They developed one of the first systems of non-formal logic in the post-war period. Their system of argumentative logic moved beyond deduction, and did not yield to systems demanding allegiance to a first premise, other than those acknowledging the need for continual revision. The logic in the NRP functioned paratactically (the linking of ideas in a non-hierarchical constellation), avoiding the hypotatic impulse (one which demands subordination) embedded in totalitarian logic (Perelman and Olbrechts-Tyteca, *The New Rhetoric* 158). Paratactical argument does allow for judgment, though such judgments are open to revision and challenge.

The NRP took a different tack on the relationship between rhetoric and dialectic. Olbrechts-Tyteca noted in her 1963 retrospective that those interested in argument did not connect it to rhetoric (Rencontre avec La Rhétorique). Olbrechts-Tyteca cites Toulmin's 1950 *The Place of Ethics in Reason* as a primary illustration of a work on argument that both denigrates rhetoric and ignores the role played by audience in argumentation. In contrast to Toulmin, Perelman and Olbrechts-Tyteca sought a rapprochement between dialectic (reason) and rhetoric (the art of adapting arguments to audiences). Perelman and Olbrechts-Tyteca aspired to bring them into alignment, and refused to completely conflate the two, seeing both a "tie" and a "distance" between them. This "tie and distance" Perelman and Olbrechts-Tyteca establish between dialectic and rhetoric produces an inherent equivocation frustrating to those who seek essential and clear definitions.

Formal logic provides definitional clarity, Perelman argued, because it is isolated from the world of experience, and is limited to the realm of abstraction and the *vita contemplativa*. The intent of the NRP was to inflect logic with rhetoric, thereby displaying the expressions of reason used by humans in the *vita activa* (Frank and Bolduc, "*From Vita Contemplativa to Vita Activa*"). The quality of logic is ultimately dependent on the judgment of the audience. There are, of course, stronger and weaker expressions of logic, but humans situated in context, rather than an external and immutable set of standards, would judge.

Perelman held Peter Ramus responsible for creating a divide between rhetoric and logic. Ramus, in vesting philosophy with dialectic (reason and logic) and rhetoric with style and delivery, dealt a critical blow to rhetoric's integrity (*New Rhetoric and the Humanities* 8). Perelman and Olbrechts-Tyteca sought to overcome the Ramistic divide by expanding the range of reason to feature the role of the audience and to include forms of logic beyond deduction and *modes ponens*. Argumentation functions as a response to a rhetorical situation in flux, one that defies a preordained or an apodictic logic. Reflecting this orientation, *The New Rhetoric* is divided into three parts: the framework, starting point, and techniques of argumentation. The first part displays a philosophy of argument, the second describes the psychology of audiences, and the third identifies argumentative schemes. Although the three parts should be read as a blended whole, the authors did recognize that the components of a given argument could be lifted out of its scheme for analysis. In the third part, Perelman and Olbrechts-Tyteca extract arguments from their rhetorical situations to display patterns of reasoning found outside of formal logic.

In part one of the *New Rhetoric,* Perelman and Olbrechts-Tyteca establish a normative framework for the enactment and evaluation of argument. As a response to totalitarianism and the failure of logical positivism and radical skepticism to provide the grounds of reason, Perelman and Olbrechts-Tyteca offered argumentation. Argumentation, they write, offers the human community the means of reasoning about end values, avoiding the conclusion that justice had no basis in reason. They also note that there were times when argumentation was not a sufficient response, and illustrated this claim with a reference to Churchill's decision not to engage in negotiations with Hitler (17). A goal of argumentation is to spur action, but morality should trump the goal of persuasive effect, and argument does not belong everywhere (16).

Two touchstones in the NRP are the audience and the epideictic. Perelman and Olbrechts-Tyteca develop a compelling theory of the rhetorical audience, which Gross and Dearin elucidate in Chapter 3 of their excellent book *Chaïm Perelman* (For an extended review of this book, see Frank, "After the New Rhetoric"). Their vision of rationality shifted the focus from the logical form of apodictic reasoning to the value hierarchies of audiences. Although Perelman and Olbrechts-Tyteca understood the need for coherence and logical relationships among the components of argument, they resisted the confining models of rationality offered by formal logic. They sought to develop a definition of reason, Gross and Dearin write, that resisted the false division of will from understanding, one that embraced the sentient and intellectual capacities of the human being (28).

Johnstone did not find a theory of audience in the NRP, holding that Perelman and Olbrechts-Tyteca were only concerned with categorizing audience techniques ("Rev. *The New Rhetoric: A Treatise on Argumentation*" 225). The pragma-dialecticians blame the NRP's take on audience for reducing judgments of truth to human opinion. In contrast, Gross and Dearin's reading is much more careful and nuanced, giving argument theorists a far better understanding of the NRP's vision of audience than that provided by Johnstone or the pragma-dialecticians.

According to the NRP, all argumentation, including the inner deliberations of the conscience, is designed for an audience. Persuasive effect is not the only objective of the rhetorical encounter as the speaker has an obligation to know when it is wrong or inappropriate to argue, and there are stronger and weaker audiences. Perelman and Olbrechts-Tyteca adopt Henry Stack Sullivan's view that the speaker's vision of an audience is a construction (19). Those who argue have created images of their audiences. Arguments can be effective if the advocate has adequately calibrated the construction of the audience to its reality. There are particular, composite, and universal audiences vying for the attention of the advocate.

The particular audience is one of several interconnected audiences. Although an appeal may be addressed to a particular audience, many who argue often face composite audiences, those made up of individuals holding different and conflicting values. The universal audience, which Perelman reported was a profoundly misunderstood notion in the NRP, offers a normative check on those who present arguments ("The New Rhetoric and the Rhetoricians"). Perelman saw the universal audience as rhetoric's answer to Kant's categorical imperative. The universal audience invites those who argue to use a form of reason that aspires to universality. Gross and Dearin in chapter three of *Chaïm Perelman* provide a cogent explanation of the universal audience and its value in argument theory. They are not alone. The universal audience, which my colleague James Crosswhite in his *Rhetoric of Reason* has developed with care, is a symbolic construction as real as the others fashioned by a speaker. Chapter two of Crosswhite's book provides a sequential guideline for the construction of a universal audience. Chris Tindale in his *Acts of Arguing* also explains how the universal audience can be used in argument with clarity and precision (95–97).

This shift, from the mathematical structures of apodictic logic, to the lived experience of human beings, strikes some as reducing the validity of knowledge claims to audience response. Don Levi raises this concern when he worries that scholars using Perelman may be more concerned with persuasive impact rather than the truth content of an argument. Perelman, having studied formal logic, understood the traditional principles used to assess the correctness of argument. However, he saw that these principles could not lead to sound judgments about values or justice and often did not assist with humans struggling within tragic contexts. Perelman recognized that there are stronger and weaker arguments, with the audience serving as the judge. The NRP does establish normative assumptions, which Crosswhite, Tindale, and others discuss at some length.

First, there is a normative assumption that audiences should have the freedom to judge arguments, opening up the possibility of mistake and misjudgment. Yet, this freedom is ultimately more important than a "truthful" claim that is enforced with violence or the coercion embedded in formal logic. Second, there is an active concern in the NRP for the quality of the audience; some audiences are better able to make judgments. The audience of scientific arguments illustrates this larger point. Alan Gross, in two important books, has outlined the rhetorical components of scientific arguments. In these books, Gross studies science as a form of rhetoric designed to persuade audiences. The scientific community, Gross and his colleagues observe, use the scientific article as a means to communicate knowledge claims to an audience. These claims are judged by an expert audience. As Gross and his colleagues observe, in answering certain questions, the scientific method is superior to others. As Gross and Dearin note, Perelman was not a relativist, and accepted scientific arguments as strong or weak based on the judgments of audiences commanding the necessary expertise.

Perelman's refurbishing and repair of the epideictic, a critically important move in the NRP, highlights a third normative position in the NRP out of which flows a metaphysic, epistemology, and axiology of argument. Epideictic discourse does not merely reinforce values, as Lockwood, in a clear misreading of Perelman and Olbrechts-Tyteca, suggests (75–76). Rather, it assumes some values and facts have gained acceptance and validity through persuasion over time. Values and facts are only as strong as the argumentative proof offered in support. An authentic contact of minds requires some preconditions, including arguers and audiences sharing a symbol system, a desire to engage in communicative exchange, and an attempt by those who argue to address the values of the audience. With the epideictic, those who make arguments to audiences begin with normative assumptions; the scientist, politician, spouse, and artist all start with or develop a common language, value hierarchies and exemplars during argumentation. Arguers may use values and knowledge claims presumed by the audience as touchstones for arguments designed for the immediate exigence and rhetorical situation.

These accepted values and knowledge claim function, in the NRP as a "regressive philosophy," giving the process and products of argumentation a metaphysical status. Perelman, in a landmark article published in 1949, observed:

Regressive philosophy affirms that, at the moment the philosopher begins his deliberation, he does not start from nothing, but from a set of facts, which he does not consider as necessary nor absolute nor definitive but as sufficiently sure to allow him to establish his deliberation. He considers these facts as fragmentary, and he does not believe that the notions that help him to express them are perfectly clear or fully developed. In a way these facts are already associated in his thought; progress in their systematization will allow him to develop the principles of his knowledge and to better understand, describe, and classify the elements of his experience. This experience is never complete; new facts can always provoke a questioning of the notions and principles of the primitive theory, whose revision could lead to a better understanding of the old facts. This revision, this adaptation, will not be done automatically, but will be the work of the thinker who is responsible for his actions and who commits himself by his decisions. (Frank and Bolduc, "Perelman's 'First Philosophies'" 199).

Perelman grounded his faith in a reason linked to experience. Argument helped to determine what could be learned from experience over and through time. The revision and adaptation of knowledge claims functioned as responses to changed circumstances and the influence of time. Indeed, in their 1958 reflection on argumentation, written after the completion of the *Traité*, Perelman and Olbrechts-Tyteca suggest that time is the primary factor distinguishing apodictic logic from argumentative reason:

The contrasts that one can notice between classical demonstration and formal logic on one hand, [and] argumentation on the other, can, it seems, come back to an essential difference: time does not play any role in demonstration; it is, however, essential in argumentation. So much so that one can wonder if it is not the intervention of time that allows [one] to best distinguish argumentation from demonstration. ("De La Temporalité Comme Caractère De L'argumentation" 115)

Argument takes place in time, and serves to test, if necessary, the preconceptions of the audience, or to assume these preconceptions for the purposes of crafting an argumentative response to the exigence.

In turn, this metaphysics was tied to an epistemology of "confused notions." Such notions and concepts defy attempts at ultimate definition, remaining plastic and indeterminate over the long term, but can yield rules of action in the short term. Justice, in Perelman's work, is the critical confused notion, one that Perelman argued could host conflicting and incompatible perspectives. Within the epistemological perspective of the NRP, knowledge claims are as strong as the arguments supporting them. In turn, this vision was grounded in a value pluralism bound together with reason.

Perelman set forth an axiological system in which audiences could hold different values that may conflict. In the realm of rhetoric, value conflicts can be negotiated and mediated through argumentative reason rather than violence or raw power. The capacity for reason, Perelman held, transcends value differences. In preparing for argument, the advocate can assume that audiences adhere to loci. Here, as Warnick (2000) has demonstrated, Perelman and Olbrechts-Tyteca identify five loci, designed to illuminate the touchstones for a contact of minds: quantity, quality, romantic, classical, and the individual. The advocate can move between and among loci in search of adherence. One critical point, often missed in the analysis of the

NRP, is that speakers and audiences are not forced to choose between the classical (stable or more permanent values) and romantic (less stable or impermanent values) loci. Although Perelman was highly critical of the classical tradition, holding that it held to a restrictive view of truth of timeless and immutable values, he did not conclude that the romantic alternative, with its affirmation of novelty, instability, and aporia, was the only remaining option. The advocate could use both the classical and romantic, navigating between the two in search of adherence.

With the loci of argument in place, Perelman and Olbrechts-Tyteca outline the techniques of arguments, viewing them as objects of thought structured by schemes. Argument schemes, which provide a much richer attempt to simulate the argument process than the Toulmin model, invite the critic to view argument as embedded reason supported by a host of hidden tributary springs (187–192). The critic's task is to reveal these springs, and identify how the various components of argumentative reason interact. Perelman and Olbrechts-Tyteca identify a number of argument specimens in the NRP, making it the most important contemporary source of argument description if we use the entries in the *Oxford Encyclopedia of Rhetoric* (2001) as a measure. The contributors turn to Perelman and Olbrechts-Tyteca for many entries, including those on argumentation, arrangement, exemplum, the forensic genre, the conviction-persuasion and demonstration-argumentation distinctions, inference, law and rhetoric, *logos, pathos,* practical reason, irreparable, and rhetoric and religion.

Perelman and Olbrechts-Tyteca's taxonomy of argument is a system—perhaps the first twentieth century codification—of nonformal logic. The authors hoped their system would complement apodictic logic, thereby broadening the domain of reason. However, given the disparaging comments Perelman makes about apodictic reasoning, I can understand why some believe he did not see value in formal logic. His intent was to demonstrate the limitations of formal logic and to broaden the realm of reason to include the judgment of human values. To demonstrate the affinity between formal and non-formal reasoning, Perelman used the traditional vocabulary of logic: identity, transitivity, noncontradiction, etc.

In so doing, Perelman and Olbrechts-Tyteca enacted their theory of argumentation as they used the vocabulary of logic used by their audience. This choice, I believe, is meant to convey to the reader that apodictic and non-formal reasoning, in sharing the same vocabulary, belong in the house of reason. The primary difference between the apodictic and non-formal reasoning expressed through argument is the role played by time and context. Perelman and Olbrechts-Tyteca, in their preview to the third section of the treatise, discuss the nature of the arguments they consider, observing "the meaning and the scope of an isolated argument can rarely be understood without ambiguity: the analysis of one link of an argument out of its context and independently of the situation to which it belongs involves undeniable dangers. These are due not only to the equivocal character of language, but also to the fact that the springs supporting the argumentation are almost never explicitly described" (187). This is a fundamental assumption in their taxonomy of argument as they did not assume one could capture the meaning of lived argument in a univocal language or that argument specimens were purebred. Classical and Aristotelian logic, Perelman and Olbrechts-Tyteca argued, did not account for the role of time, leading them to remodel Aristotle's three laws of thoughts.

Perelman and Olbrechts-Tyteca believe Aristotle based his dialectic in predicative logic, which gave the procedure of his dialectic its form (*The New Rhetoric* 84). This logic, according to Perelman, is based on three laws of thought: identity (A is A), non-contradiction (A cannot be both B and not-B), and the excluded middle (Either A is B or A is not-B). Propositional logic is designed to elicit general and universal truths guided by induction, deduction, and the syllogism (*An Historical Introduction* 58). In the NRP, Perelman and Olbrechts-Tyteca take these laws of identity, non-contradiction, and the excluded middle and reformulate them for the life and functions served by argumentation.

Central to the law of identity is the issue of definition. Perelman and Olbrechts-Tyteca reject the classical divide between "real" and "nominal" definitions, locating instead a third option: definitions supported by reasoned argument. Drawing from the works of Stevenson and Gonseth, Perelman and Olbrechts-Tyteca contend that definitions must be persuasive and open to revision (*The New Rhetoric* 446–447). People can stipulate to certain definitions, Perelman and Olbrechts-Tyteca note, but this agreement is subject to modification. Clear definitions are not a value independent of social context and do not automatically trump attempts to capture denotations that deal with confused notions or essentially contested concepts.

Edward Schiappa, in a recently published book on argument and definitions, makes use of the NRP to display the characteristics of what he calls "definitive discourse" (xi). Schiappa takes a rhetorical perspective on definitions, seeking to explain how those who argue make use of definitions in controversies about abortion, obscenity, and a host of other public policy issues. At several junctures in the book, Schiappa turns to the NRP to underscore the rhetorical nature of definitions (e.g., dominant definitions remain in place until challenged (31); dissociation is used to change definitions (36, 38); the importance of audience in definitions (45); the importance of persuasion in definitional argument (47); choice in definition (49); the role of nouns in definition (115); and metaphors and definition (132)). Schiappa's Perelmanian influenced insights on definitions constitute a critical codification of definition theory and will become an expected citation in argument studies.

The law of non-contradiction, in Perelman and Olbrechts-Tyteca's system of argument, yields to the lived realities of antimony and paradox. In formal logic, contradictions produce incoherence. The problems humans face often feature conflicts between two mutually exclusive values that may both be reasonable in given contexts. Perelman, as Dearin and Gross note, did study the logical antimony before he made his rhetorical turn, and he saw the need for systems of reason that could host conflicting values (3–5). Perelman and Olbrechts-Tyteca in the NRP set forth the notion of incompatibility as non-formal logic's answer to the law of non-contradiction (*The New Rhetoric* 195–210). In the realm of human argument, it is possible, Perelman and Olbrechts-Tyteca suggest, for mutually exclusive values to be placed in a hierarchy, and that a particular value may earn priority because of context and time. Values failing to secure top billing would not be liquidated or denigrated, but would remain viable with the understanding that they might move to the top of an agenda with a change in context and time.

The law of the excluded middle holds that identity cannot be mixed. Perelman and Olbrechts-Tyteca argue that it is possible for separate entities to share something in common, or to coexist within a larger unity. In formal logic, this would be incoherent. With these revisions and amplifications of the rules of logic, Perelman and Olbrechts-Tyteca develop a mode of reasoning that is analogic and paratactic.

In contrast to deductive and hypotactic reasoning, in which a major premise rules the minor premises and conclusion, analogic and paratactic reasoning establishes standards for comparative judgments. Perelman observed:

[S]ince the time of Aristotle, logic has confined its study to deduction and inductive reasoning, as though any argument differing from these was due to the variety of its content and not to its form. As a result, an argument that cannot be reduced to canonical form is regarded as logically valueless. What then about reasoning from analogy? What about the *a fortorio* argument? Must we, in using such arguments, always be able to introduce a fictive unexpressed major premise, so as to make them conform to the syllogism? (*The New Rhetoric and the Humanities* 26)

As the Kneals note in their history of logic, Aristotle's system of logic was dominant through the centuries and blocked the development of analogic thinking. Perelman and Olbrechts-Tyteca explicitly develop analogic thinking: "analogies are important in invention and argumentation fundamentally because they facilitate the development and extension of thought" (*The New Rhetoric* 385). This movement from apodictic-hypotactic reasoning to analogic thinking marked a profound shift in thinking about logic.

Of the many novel contributions made by the NRP to non-formal logic, the notion of "dissociation" is of particular importance. This notion, discussed by Schiappa in a 1985 article in this journal, allows arguers to avoid the binary thinking so prevalent in 20th century argumentation ("Dissociation in the Arguments of Rhetorical Theory"). Dissociative reasoning retains opposing values, refusing to allow the problem of difference to produce solutions that obliterate competing values to achieve conflict resolution. Such reasoning takes into account time and context. Take for example the Israeli-Palestinian conflict. One might assume that one of the two national movements is authentic and has an irrefutable claim to the land. Another assumption might be that both have legitimate, although incompatible claims, calling for dissociation. One product of dissociative thinking in the Israeli-Palestinian conflict would be a vision that the land should be shared, and that sacred spaces, such as Jerusalem, might be rationed through an allocation of timeslots, similar to the approaches used to resolve riparian disputes (For an application of Perelman and Olbrechts-Tyteca's perspective on analogic thinking to the problem of Jerusalem, see Cohen and Frank). Dissociation, according to Perelman and Olbrechts-Tyteca, provides a mode of reasoning that seeks out policies allowing for the co-existence, if not rapprochement, between conflicting values. This expansion of reason to include the possibility of opposites coexisting is a striking advance.

The NRP has been a key source for theoretical insights into argument as a process and a product. However, the work of Perelman and Olbrechts-Tyteca has received criticism from several sources. The most energetic criticism has come from the school of pragma-dialectics in the Netherlands.

ARGUMENTS AGAINST THE NEW RHETORIC PROJECT

The NRP and Perelmanian philosophy have critics. Steven Toulmin believes Perelman did not open "the broader perspectives within which the new rhetoric functions . . ." (Olson, "Literary Theory, Philosophy of Science, and Persuasive Discourse"). Michael F. Bernard-Donals and Richard R. Glejzer write that Perelman and Olbrechts-Tyteca "understand all situations as discursive and therefore rhetorical, thereby failing to note rhetoric's connection with other forms of knowledge, none of which is "objective" in the sense that it is unmediated, but which nevertheless occupy some middle ground between absolute certainty afforded by a metaphysics and the absolute skepticism that some see as the upshot of anti-foundationalism and its rhetorical world" (15). Peter Goodrich argues the NRP is "positively conventional and politically conservative in the extreme in its invocation of the traditional categories of legal reason and of legal interpretation" (111). John Ray suggests the NRP seeks to establish, with the universal audience, standards of judgment that are transcendental, unaffected by experience or a fluid reality.

The most sustained criticism of the NRP's system of argument has come from Frans van Eemeren and his school of pragma-dialectics. This is not the first time I have considered pragma-dialectics and the movement's treatment of Perelman's philosophy. I reviewed van Eemeren and Grootendorst's *Argumentation, Communication, and Fallacies: A Pragma-Dialectical Perspective* for the *Quarterly Journal of Speech*. In this review, I claimed that the authors had been manifestly unfair in their treatment of Perelman and Olbrechts-Tyteca's NRP. I recall recoiling from the book when I read in the introduction that a pragma-dialectical perspective was needed on argumentation because Perelman had a "prejudice against logic" (3–4). I found clear evidence that pragma-dialectics was neo-Ramistic and neo-Platonic, hostile to the rhetorical tradition. In a response to my review, Klinger defended pragma-dialectics:

> It is most certainly not "Neo-Ramistic in attitude and Neo-Platonic in function," nor does it "revive the agenda of Pascal and Descartes," nor is it "globally unfriendly" to the study of rhetoric, as one reviewer has suggested (Frank 252). These are serious charges, and charges that seem generally inconsistent with the spirit of van Eemeren and Grootendorst's program. While they admit that they first approached the study of argumentation from formal logic and Choresklan linguistics, they have expressed a sincere interest in working through the rich rhetorical tradition that has survived in the United States and elsewhere. . . . [T]hese scholars have the desire and intent to build bridges, not to isolate and denigrate. Indeed, their move from formal logic and linguistics to argumentation is an attempt to construct a mediate position between rhetoric and philosophy. (111)

I have sought, in the subsequent writings of the pragma-dialecticians, for this spirit of genuine interest in the rhetorical tradition, looked at the attempts at mediation, and examined the bridges they claim to have built. I still believe van Eemeren et al. have seriously misread Perelman and Olbrechts-Tyteca. Although I will not center on the many flaws in the assumptions of the pragma-dialectical approach, I will respond to their description and critique of Perelman and Olbrechts-Tyteca's system of argument that appears in *Fundamentals of Argumentation Theory*.

Henry Johnstone invited my colleague James Crosswhite to critique the pragma-dialectic take on Perelman for *Philosophy and Rhetoric*. Crosswhite claimed that van Eemeren and Grootendorst misinterpret, misread, and misunderstand Perelman and Olbrechts-Tyteca's NRP. Unfortunately and curiously, the pragma-dialecticians have not responded to Crosswhite's 1995 critique in their many subsequent writings, violating the requirement established in pragma-dialectics that those who argue have an "obligation to defend a standpoint at issue, while the antagonist assumes the obligation to respond critically to the standpoint and the protagonist's defense" (*Fundamentals of Argumentation Theory* 281). Their misreading of Perelman in *Fundamentals of Argumentation Theory* rehearses and repeats the misrepresentations of the NRP in their 1987 *Handbook of Argumentation Theory*. My intent here is to respond to five criticisms of the NRP's system of argument offered by the pragma-dialecticians. This response builds from Crosswhite's earlier effort.

First, the pragma-dialecticians score the NRP for its failure to use a univocal language for argument. "Clear definitions are nowhere to be found" in the NRP (van Eemeren et al., *Fundamentals of Argumentation Theory* 122). As Crosswhite notes, the pragma-dialecticians do not acknowledge nor do they appear to contextualize the motives or the intentions of the Perelman and Olbrechts-Tyteca system of argument ("Is There an Audience for This Argument?" 135). Perelman and Olbrechts-Tyteca's system cultivates an equivocal language for reason and logic, doing so to escape the toxic grip of totalitarian thinking and the misuse of apodictic logic. The NRP is condemned by the pragma-dialecticians for losing its system in elaboration, failing to give "clear insight into the relations between sections" in *The New Rhetoric,* and for failing to provide clear definitions. The payoff of this critique, the pragma-dialecticians declare, is that "any account of the new rhetoric is based on interpretation" (van Eemeren et al., *Fundamentals of Argumentation Theory* 121–122). I am hard pressed to understand how this is a criticism given most argument scholars would agree that any account of anything is an interpretation, although I gather pragma-dialecticians cluster good argumentation theory under the label of clarity and bad argumentation theory under the category of interpretation.

In comparison to the NRP, pragma-dialectics, which is truly a crude form of conflict resolution, seeks to end difference of opinion through argument. Pragma-dialectical argumentation may be suitable when one is planning to construct a building or when one needs, in Michel Foucault's words, a "bureaucratic morality" to "keep our papers in order" (*The Archaeology of Knowledge* 17). Pragma-dialectics is intolerant to interpretation, and most certainly to varied interpretations, and seeks clarity in the face of a reality and experience that is often irreducibly ambiguous, tragic, or in which there are multiple but incompatible truths.

Second, the pragma-dialecticians hold the NRP "offers an extremely relativistic standard of rationality" (*Fundamentals of Argumentation Theory* 120). The pragma-dialecticians believe that if all observers do not agree on the meaning of a particular symbol, then meaning must be relative. There is agreement in the NRP that the norms of reasoning held by arguers and audiences before argument begins are a function of epideictic discourse, a crucial concept van Eemeren et al. fail to include in their account of Perelman and Olbrechts-Tyteca's NRP. These norms are a result of previous argumentation and have withstood the test of critical scrutiny. Unless questioned, they remain in place, serving as the starting points of argument.

Rules of reasoning alone do not guarantee sound and logical decisions. The quality of the argumentation is a function of choices made by the audience and the arguments presented by those who present arguments. There are, in Perelman and Olbrechts-Tyteca's system, audiences of different qualities and standards. An audience might choose to abide by the rules established by the pragma-dialecticians, and move nicely through the various stages of a critical discussion. However, an audience might reject these rules, seeking instead to engage in argumentation for other legitimate purposes. The NRP deliberately leaves open the possibility that those in disagreement might all have truths, some of which must co-exist. Agreement to the rules of critical discussion and the end of an argument in agreement are not sufficient indications of quality. If audiences are the judges of rationality, then the strength of a reason is relative to the quality of the audience. The beauty of Perelman and Olbrechts-Tyteca's pluralistic view of audience is that it starts and ends with a diversity of audiences bound together with a broad sense of reason. No one audience can claim ultimate superiority, nor are the rules of dialogue sacred. The goal, and this is one point of agreement for Perelman and Olbrechts-Tyteca and the pragma-dialecticians, is to improve the habits of reasoning used by arguers and audiences.

Third, the pragma-dialecticians complain that the argument schemes outlined in the NRP are vague. They quibble about Warnick and Kline's 1992 article in this journal indicating the empirical utility of Perelman and Olbrechts-Tyteca's of the argument schemes outlined in *The New Rhetoric,* doing so with the accepted modes of social science. For my purpose, it is important to note that Warnick and Kline found that observers not educated in the nuances of argument could identify the argument schemes in the NRP, and that Perelman and Olbrechts-Tyteca provide "an updated and refined topical system enabling the study of argument patterns" (13). The quibbles of the pragma-dialecticians aside, Warnick and Kline's conclusions remain sound, and the most successful argument textbook in the United States, Edward Inch and Barbara Warnick's *Critical Thinking and Communication: The Use of Reason in Argument,* draws from the NRP in its approach.

A fourth criticism made by the pragma-dialecticians is that Perelman does not "elaborate systematically on how the new rhetoric can be applied to law" (*Fundamentals of Argumentation Theory* 127). This is a failure because Perelman gives "no description of the way in which, and the circumstances in which, the specific kinds of loci constituted by the general legal principles can be effective in convincing an audience" (127). This criticism seems to suggest that Perelman and Olbrechts-Tyteca should have established concrete rules for persuading legal audiences rather than learning from the characteristics of legal reasoning. Their concern was the latter and with the larger philosophical issues concerning justice and jurisprudence; their work might be faulted for not proscribing particular strategies for legal advocates, but that was not their intent.

Yet, legal scholars have drawn from the NRP in addressing legal principles and reasoning. Consider the special issues of *Northern Kentucky Law Review* (1985) and *Law and Philosophy* (1986) devoted to the legal implications of *The New Rhetoric.* A number of legal scholars cite Perelman and the NRP in legal articles devoted to reasoning, justice, and argument. The NRP has served to explain the nature of legal reasoning and to provide the tools necessary for the interrogation of legal claims. I call attention to a recent attempt by Francis J. Mootz III, professor of law at Pennsylvania State University, to build a theory of legal reasoning and argument by yoking the works of Perelman and Hans-Georg Gadamer. In a 63,000-word essay in the *Southern California Interdisciplinary Law Journal,* Mootz values what the pragma-dialecticians find weak in Perelman, the "refusal to collapse his inquiry into just a methodology of rhetorical techniques" (608).

Gadamer's hermeneutics and Perelman's NRP, according to Mootz, allow legal scholars to avoid "apodictic certitude" and "relativistic irrationalism" in favor of "rhetorical knowledge." In grounding legal understanding in rhetorical knowledge and by placing Gadamer in relationship with Perelman, Mootz observes:

> From a hermeneutical perspective, the new rhetoric provides guidance in the face of hermeneutical idealism: by moving from ontology to politics, scholars can foster a critical inquiry oriented toward improving our various rhetorical practices and thereby avoid the conservative implications of replacing the Cartesian model with a model premised on abstract notions of historicity

and finitude. According to this reconfigured approach, the breakdown of the Cartesian paradigm results from the discovery of a better ontological account of communication and understanding rather than an irrational abandonment of objective methodological inquiry. (530)

The system of argument outlined in the NRP adopts a humble stance on questions of truth and justice, remains pluralistic in orientation, and serves as a check on both Enlightenment claims to absolute truth and the radical skeptics denial of any truths. With the help of Perelman, Mootz has embarked on an effort to develop a systematic understanding of legal reason, one that deserves the close attention of argument scholars.

ARGUMENTATION IN THE WAKE OF THE NRP

At this point, we can reconsider Klinger's claim that the pragma-dialecticians "desire and intend to build bridges, not to isolate and denigrate" (111). Those who seek to build bridges between rhetoric and pragma-dialectics would need to be tolerant of multiple perspectives on argument, and embrace the desirability of plurality and the possibility of multiple interpretations that might all be reasonable. Pragma-dialectics explicitly cannot support an ecumenical spirit nor does it sponsor continued dialogue, it seeks an end to disagreement. Pragma-dialecticians speak in one language in search of a unitary truth. At most, the pragma-dialecticians see rhetoric serving the function of "strategic maneuvering" in service to a rule bound dialectic. Rhetoricians may be welcomed in the realm of pragma-dialecticians, but as second-class citizens who offer insight on "rhetorical techniques."

There is a bridge from NRP to pragma-dialectics. If advocates and audiences agree to the use of a univocal language and seek resolution of conflict, which may be justified in certain contexts, the NRP can embrace pragma-dialectics. The adoption of a pragma-dialectical perspective is a choice made by humans in a given context. Humans might make other and different choices that might be reasonable as well. I am joined by other scholars in their criticism of the pragma-dialecticians' misreading of the NRP and concur with Warnick when she notes in her entry in the *Oxford Encyclopedia of Rhetoric* that the "lucid" account of the NRP's "theory of argumentation" in *Fundamentals of Argumentation Theory* is undermined by "unfounded" criticisms and "a misunderstanding of some of Perelman's work" (Conviction 174), Crosswhite when he concludes that van Eemeren's and Grootendorst's interpretation of Perelman is "incredibly crude and backward (138)," and Tinsdale's observation that "A charge that 'anything goes' has no force against Perelman's position, and van Eemeren and Grootendorst's concern that the position promotes undue subjectivism is misplaced (100)."

I am not suggesting the NRP is immaculate, conceived without flaws. Gross and Dearin, who admire Perelman's work, identify his limitations, which they believe include a failure to deal with emotional proof, an underdeveloped process of arguing, and a possible injustice to his collaborator Lucie Olbrechts-Tyteca, for which he is responsible, because her role in the NRP project is not specified or celebrated (3–5). There is an obscurity embedded in some of their ideas that is less than helpful, and English readers may lose the nuances of the original due to what Vickers has called the "undistinguished translation" of the *Traité* (592).

Even with these limitations, scholars of argumentation and rhetoric have and will continue to draw from the many insights in the new NRP. Maneli, who knew Perelman well, in a little-noticed book, declares in its title that the NRP should be the "philosophy and methodology" for this century. This bold title betrays Maneli's more modest aim, which is to cultivate a philosophy of pluralism and tolerance as a response to the violent traumas of the twentieth century. A noted legal scholar and author of two excellent books on legal reasoning, Maneli saw the dialectical perspective developed by Perelman as a philosophy needed to counter the suffering caused by totalitarian movements. Maneli, who escaped from the German concentration camps, and later participated in a negotiation designed to bring the Vietnam War to an end, sought to bring Perelmanian insights to bear on the problems of society. Although he does not address the secondary literature on the NRP, Maneli offers a spiritual interpretation of Perelman's work.

This interpretation is unexpected, as Maneli and Perelman were both atheists. Both faced the ruthlessness of the Nazis, experienced the cruelty of anti-Semitism, and, after the war, sought the reconstruction of a world they believed operated independently of deities and transcendental truths. The Holocaust and the destruction of Europe placed the burden of proof on those who had faith in human reason to redeem it, which Perelman did with the NRP. Maneli and Perelman turned to regressive philosophy, tradition, natural law, and epideictic discourse to avoid metaphysical foundationalism and the problem of infinite regress to ground truths. They did have an abiding faith in humanity, and the capacity of humans to construct humane laws and just societies through argumentation. They did not cede the spiritual to the religious as they had an abiding faith in the power of human reason and its expression through argument. They saw argumentation serving a central role in the humanities and as a humane art as it provided the human community with the means of yoking an expanded sense of reason to liberty.

CONCLUSION

NRP set a course between radical skepticism and certainty by carving out a realm of rhetoric. In this realm, ethical action is a function of the moral power of reasoning, a commitment to irreducible pluralism, and the priority given to the value of dissent. As Perelman and Olbrechts-Tyteca state in the penultimate sentence of the *New Rhetoric*: "The theory of argument will help to [provide] the justification of the possibility of a human community in the sphere of action when this justification cannot be based on a reality or objective truth" (711). This theory of argument should be at the heart of any authentic system of argument or vision of participatory democracy. There is an embedded humility in Perelman and Olbrechts-Tyteca's work as it does not claim transcendent truths. This attitude of humility is complemented by a faith in the ability of humans to make good, if not absolute, decisions. When read in the proper light, the *New Rhetoric* remains a classic, offering deep insight into the meaning and experience of argument.

WORKS REVIEWED

Crosswhite, James. *The Rhetoric of Reason: Writing and the Attractions of Argument*. Madison: University of Wisconsin Press, 1996.

Eemeren, Frans H. van, Rob Grootendorst, and Francisca Snoeck Henkemans. *Fundamentals of Argumentation Theory: A Handbook of Historical Backgrounds and Contemporary Developments*. Mahwah, N.J.: L. Erlbaum, 1996.

Gilbert, Michael A. *Coalescent Argumentation*. Mahwah, N.J.: L. Erlbaum Associates, 1997.

Gross, Alan G., and Ray D. Dearin. *Chaïm Perelman*. Albany: State University of New York Press, 2003.

Maneli, Mieczysaw. *Perelman's New Rhetoric as Philosophy and Methodology for the Next Century*. Boston: Kluwer Academic Publishers, 1994.

Mootz, Frances J. "Rhetorical Knowledge in Legal Practice and Theory." *Southern California Interdisciplinary Law Journal* 6 (1998): 492–611.

Schiappa, Edward. *Defining Reality: Definitions and the Politics of Meaning.* Carbondale: Southern Illinois University Press, 2003.

WORKS CITED

Arendt, Hannah. *Eichmann in Jerusalem: A Report on the Banality of Evil.* Penguin Twentieth-Century Classics. Rev. and enl. ed. New York, N.Y.: Penguin Books, 1994.

Arendt, Hannah. *The Origins of Totalitarianism.* 2d enl. ed. New York: Meridian Books, 1958.

Arnold, Carroll. "Introduction." *The Realm of Rhetoric.* Ed. Chaïm Perelman. South Bend: Notre Dame University Press, 1982.

Brandes, Paul D. "Rev. Traité De L'argumentation; La Nouvelle Rhétorique." *Quarterly Journal of Speech* 45 (1959): 86.

Cohen, Shaul, and David A. Frank. "Jerusalem and the Riparian Simile." *Political Geography* 21 (2002): 745–60.

Conley, Thomas M. *Rhetoric in the European Tradition.* New York: Longman, 1990.

Crosswhite, James. *The Rhetoric of Reason: Writing and the Attractions of Argument.* Rhetoric of the Human Sciences. Madison: University of Wisconsin Press, 1996.

Eemeren, Frans H. van, and Rob Grootendorst. *Argumentation, Communication, and Fallacies: A Pragma-Dialectical Perspective.* Hillsdale, N.J.: L. Erlbaum, 1992.

Eemeren, Frans H. van, Rob Grootendorst, and Francisca Snoeck Henkemans. *Fundamentals of Argumentation Theory: A Handbook of Historical Backgrounds and Contemporary Developments.* Mahwah, N.J.: L. Erlbaum, 1996.

Eemeren, Frans H. van, Rob Grootendorst, and Tjark Kruiger. *Handbook of Argumentation Theory; a Critical Survey of Classical Backgrounds and Modern Studies.* Studies of Argumentation in Pragmatics and Discourse Analysis; 7. Dordrecht, Holland: Foris Publications, 1987.

Foss, Sonja K., Karen A. Foss, and Robert Trapp. *Contemporary Perspectives on Rhetoric.* 3rd ed. Prospect Heights, Ill.: Waveland Press, 2002.

Foucault, Michel. *The Archaeology of Knowledge.* New York: Pantheon Books, 1972.

Frank, David A. "After the New Rhetoric." *Quarterly Journal of Speech* 89 (2003): 253–61.

Frank, David A. "Dialectical Rapprochement in the New Rhetoric." *Argumentation and Advocacy* 33 (1998): 111–37.

Frank, David A. "The New Rhetoric, Judaism, and Post-Enlightenment Thought: The Cultural Origins of Perelmanian Philosophy." *Quarterly Journal of Speech* 83 (1997): 311–331.

Frank, David A. Rev. Frans H. van Eemeren and Rob Grootendorst, *Argumentation, Communication, and Fallacies: A Pragma-Dialectical Perspective* (Lawrence Erlbaum Associates, 1992). In *Quarterly Journal of Speech* 79 (1993): 251–253.

Frank, David A., and Michelle K. Bolduc. "Chaïm Perelman's 'First Philosophies and Regressive Philosophy.'" Commentary and Translation. *Philosophy and Rhetoric* 16 (2003): 177–207.

Frank, David A. and Michelle K. Bolduc. "From *Vita Contemplativa* to *Vita Activa*: Chaïm Perelman and Lucie Olbrechts-Tyteca's Rhetorical Turn." *Advances in the History of Rhetoric.* Forthcoming, 2004.

Gilbert, Michael A. *Coalescent Argumentation.* Mahwah, N.J.: L. Erlbaum Associates, 1997.

Glover, Jonathan. *Humanity: A Moral History of the Twentieth Century.* New Haven, CT: Yale University Press, 2000.

Gross, Alan G. *The Rhetoric of Science.* Cambridge, Mass.: Harvard University Press, 1990.

Gross, Alan G., and Ray D. Dearin. *Chaïm Perelman.* Albany: State University of New York Press, 2002.

Gross, Alan G., Joseph E. Harmon, and Michael Reidy. *Communicating Science: The Scientific Article from the 17th Century to the Present.* Oxford; New York: Oxford University Press, 2002.

Hauser, Gerard A. "Henry W. Johnstone, Jr.: Reviving the Dialogue of Philosophy and Rhetoric." *The Review of Communication* 1 (2001): 1–25.

Inch, Edward S., and Barbara Warnick. *Critical Thinking and Communication: The Use of Reason in Argument.* Boston: Allyn & Bacon, 2002.

Johnstone, Henry W. "New Outlooks on Controversy." *Review of Metaphysics* 12 (1958): 57–67.

Johnstone, Henry W. "A New Theory of Philosophical Argumentation." *Philosophy and Phenomenological Research* 15 (1954): 244–52.

Klinger, Geoffrey D. "Rev. Frans H. Van Eemeren and Rob Grootendorst, *Argumentation, Communication, and Fallacies: A Pragma-Dialectical Perspective.*" *Argumentation and Advocacy* 31 (1994): 111–13.

Lockwood, Richard. *The Reader's Figure: Epideictic Rhetoric in Plato, Aristotle, Bossuet, Racine and Pascal.* Genève, Switzerland: Librairie Droz, 1996.

Maneli, Mieczysaw. *Perelman's New Rhetoric as Philosophy and Methodology for the Next Century.* Library of Rhetorics; V. 1. Dordrecht; Boston: Kluwer Academic Publishers, 1994.

Mootz, Francis J. "Rhetorical Knowledge in Legal Practice and Theory." *Southern California Interdisciplinary Law Journal* 6 (1998): 492–547.

Natanson, Maurice Alexander, and Henry W. Johnstone. *Philosophy, Rhetoric and Argumentation.* University Park: Pennsylvania State University Press, 1965.

Olbrechts-Tyteca, Lucie. "Rencontre Avec La Rhétorique." *Logique et analyse* 3 (1963): 1–15.

Oliner, Samuel P., and Pearl M. Oliner. *The Altruistic Personality: Rescuers of Jews in Nazi Europe.* New York: Free Press, 1988.

Oliver, Robert T. "Philosophy and/or Persuasion." *La Théorie De L'argumentation; Perspectives Et Applications.* Louvain: Nauwelaerts, 1963. 571–80.

Perelman, Chaïm. Letter to Emily M. Schossberger. 29th November 1967. File: Traité de l'Argumentation, Chaïm Perelman Papers, Archives, Université Libre de Bruxelles, Bruxelles, Belgium.

Perelman, Chaïm. "Etude Sur Gottlob Frege (Résumé De La Dissertation De L'auteur)." *Revue de l'Université de Bruxelles* 2 (1939): 224–27.

Perelman, Chaïm. *An Historical Introduction to Philosophical Thinking.* Trans. Kenneth A. Brown. Studies in Philosophy 3. New York: Random House, 1965.

Perelman, Chaïm. *The Idea of Justice and the Problem of Argument.* Trans. Londres, J. Petrie, Routledge & Kegan Paul. New York: Humanities Press, 1963.

Perelman, Chaïm. "The New Rhetoric and the Rhetoricians, Remembrances and Comments." *Quarterly Journal of Speech* 70 (1984): 188–96.

Perelman, Chaïm. *De La Justice.* Bruxelles: Université Libre de Bruxelles, 1945.

Perelman, Chaïm. *The New Rhetoric and the Humanities: Essays on Rhetoric and Its Applications.* Dordrecht, Holland: Boston, 1979.

Perelman, Chaïm, and Lucie Olbrechts-Tyteca. "De La Temporalité Comme Caractère De L'argumentation." *Tempo, Archivio difilosofia* 2 (1958): 115–33.

Perelman, Chaïm, and Lucie Olbrechts-Tyteca. *Traité De L'argumentation: La Nouvelle Rhétorique.* 5e edition, ed. Bruxelles: Editions de l'Université de Bruxelles, 1988.

Perelman, Chaïm, and Lucie Olbrechts-Tyteca. *The New Rhetoric: A Treatise on Argumentation.* Notre Dame: [Ind.] University of Notre Dame Press, 1969.

Schiappa, Edward. *Defining Reality: Definitions and the Politics of Meaning.* Rhetorical Philosophy and Theory. Carbondale: Southern Illinois University Press, 2003.

Schiappa, Edward. "Dissociation in the Arguments of Rhetorical Theory." *Journal of the American Forensics Association* 22 (1985): 72–82.

Sloane, Thomas O., ed. *Encyclopedia of Rhetoric,* Oxford; New York: Oxford University Press, 2001.

Stevenson, Charles L. *Ethics and Language.* New Haven, Connecticut and London: Yale University Press and Oxford University Press, 1947.

Tindale, Christopher W. *Acts of Arguing: A Rhetorical Model of Argument.* Suny Series in Logic and Language. Albany: State University of New York Press, 1999.

Toulmin, Stephen Edelston. *An Examination of the Place of Reason in Ethics.* Cambridge, Eng.: University Press, 1950.

Vickers, Brian. "Philosophy: Rhetoric and Philosophy." *Oxford Encyclopedia of Rhetoric.* Ed. Thomas Sloan. Oxford: Oxford University Press, 2001. 583–92.

Warnick, Barbara. "Conviction." *Oxford Encyclopedia of Rhetoric.* Ed. Thomas Sloan, 2001. 171–75.

Warnick, Barbara. "Lucie Olbrechts-Tyteca's Contribution to the New Rhetoric." *Listening to Their Voices: The Rhetorical Activities of Historical Women.* Ed. Molly Meijer Wertheimer. Columbia, SC: University of South Carolina Press, 1998.

Warnick, Barbara, and Susan Kline. "The New Rhetoric's Argument Schemes: A Rhetorical View of Practical Reasoning." *Argumentation and Advocacy* 29 (1992): 1–15.

Zarefsky, David. "Future Directions in Argumentation Theory and Practice." *Perspectives on Argumentation: Essays in Honor of Wayne Brockriede.* Ed. Janice Schuetz and Robert Trapp. Prospect Heights, Illinois: Waveland Press, 1990. 287–314.

· ·

Persistent Questions
in the Theory of Argument Fields
DAVID ZAREFSKY

At first, the concept of argument fields seemed to be a straightforward matter. In *The Uses of Argument,* Toulmin wrote, "two arguments will be said to belong to the same field when the data and conclusions in each of the two arguments are, respectively, of the same logical type."[1] He proposed that, for any given field, there are accepted standards for judging the worth of arguments. The notion of field dependent standards permitted analysis and criticism according to a criterion which avoided both extremes of universal formal validity and utter relativism.

In the nearly twenty-five years since the appearance of *Uses,* however, the concept "argument fields" has been used in a variety of ways. In *Human Understanding*[2], Toulmin appears to regard fields as "rational enterprises" which he equates with intellectual disciplines. His purpose is different, though: tracing the development and change of concepts rather than judging claims. Other writers have used the term in still other ways. In reviewing the "field" literature, Willard maintained, "It is arguably the case that its diffuse and open-ended nature has been [the field notion's] most attractive feature and that its widespread employment is owed to the fact that it can be made to say virtually anything."[3] There are so many different notions of fields that the result is conceptual confusion rather than whole-some diversity. Faced with so many competing "proto-theories" of fields, the argu-mentation scholar might well wish to eschew the theoretical concept altogether.[4]

But the "field" concept offers considerable promise for empirical and critical studies of argumentation. It may be useful, therefore, to try to dispel confusion without abandoning the concept altogether. Such is the admittedly ambitious purpose of this essay, which extracts from the literature on "fields" a sense of the persistent questions and problems in theory development. The questions are grouped under three headings—the purpose of fields, the nature of fields, and the development of fields.

Often, one's answer to one question, such as the work one wants the "field" notion to do, will affect how one answers other questions, such as whether fields are defined by their subject matter or by their form. It should be possible, therefore, to construct a small number of consistent viewpoints about the "field" concept. At the same time, there are questions which apply regardless of how one defines a field's nature or a scholar's purpose, and these are explored as well.

THE PURPOSE OF FIELDS

(1) For what purpose is the concept of argument fields introduced? Since the prin-ciple of parsimony would call for abandoning an unnecessary construct, we should be certain that the notion of fields is useful. And since identical terms can be used with different meanings, we should be clear about what work the "field" notion is intended to do.

(1a) Does "field" explain how arguments originate? One approach might be to view fields as the places where arguments occur. On this view, since there is argument in the courtroom, we have the field of legal argument. Since scientists argue, we have scientific argument. The logic behind this approach is that disputes develop within a social community. By identifying the shared norms and purposes

of a community, a critic would be sensitized to those matters which are "settled" and those about which there is disagreement. Likewise, the critic could gain a feel for what are the accepted standards for resolving disagreements. In science, for example, a commitment to empiricism reigns; disagreements among scientists are seldom likely to be resolved by appeal to Biblical text or by the toss of a coin.

This approach to the purpose of the "field" concept is both descriptive and sociological, and it is useful if one's research purpose is to investigate the origins of argument within specialized communities. It also may be useful in explaining why an impasse develops when an argument occurs between members of different specialized communities. For example, a dispute about abortion in which one advocate defines the issue as religious and another defines it as a question of personal autonomy is unlikely to proceed very far. The assumptions about what is relevant to the dispute and what already is "settled" will vary between the arguers. This concept of field also may explain disagreements between advocates who define an issue as belonging to a specialized field and those who see it as a more general matter for deliberation by a larger public. In their study of the accident at Three Mile Island, Farrell and Goodnight describe just such a conflict over whether the issue was a matter for science or for public judgment.[5]

In recognizing the uses of this view of "fields," one also should recognize the purposes for which it is *not* suited. Since it is sociological in nature, it characterizes situations or occasions for arguing, not argument products themselves. Situations may influence but do not totally determine the argument products. It does not explain how the claims, data, warrants, and so forth adduced by a theologian will differ from, say, those proffered by an artist. And since it is descriptive, it does not speak to the question of quality either of an argument or of a situation which produced it. Theorists interested in these objectives also have employed the "field" concept, but they appear to have different purposes in mind.

(1b) Does "field" serve to compare and contrast arguments? A second possible purpose for the concept of "fields" is to examine similarities and differences among arguments. Arguments which are alike on the dimensions examined would belong to the same field. This seems to be the approach Toulmin had in mind in *Uses.* On this view, a field would consist of arguments—regardless of the circumstances of their origin—in which the notions of what constituted evidence, what were acceptable grounds for inferring conclusions, and so on, were the same. Law and science might be distinguished, for example, because one relies heavily on reasoning from precedent whereas the other relies primarily on direct observation and reasoning from probabilities. Ethics might differ from either field because of its emphasis on reasoning from an *a priori* nature of the good. Psychoanalysis would be a distinct field from behaviorism on the basis of how each would answer the question of what counts as evidence.

It is important to recognize how this purpose of fields differs from the first. In some cases, the two approaches would lead to different views of the boundaries of a field; in others, to similar views for quite different reasons. Like the first approach, this one is descriptive. But it is a description of argument products rather than of situations in which arguing occurs. It therefore may be a useful conception if one's research purpose is to explore similarities and differences in the arguments which actors produce or to identify recurrent patterns of reasoning by induction from actual arguments rather than by an *a priori* taxonomy.

(1c) Does "field" provide a standard for the validity of arguments? Yet a third view of the purpose of the "field" concept is that it offers a standard for evaluating

arguments. Whereas the first two purposes were descriptive in nature and hence conducive to an empirical research program, this sense of purpose is frankly normative and hence serves the interest of the argument critic.

This point of view represents a midpoint between two unacceptable extremes for answering the question, "What is a good argument?" If goodness, or validity, were treated as a matter of form, then few if any meaningful arguments could achieve the standards of formal validity. Both Toulmin and Perelman have pointed to the difficulties in treating formal logic as the paradigm case of argumentation, noting the inability of this paradigm to accommodate most actual disputes.[6] Recent writing in mathematics calls into question the ability of a formal system fully to account for arguments even in that most formal of realms.[7]

The other extreme position, that an argument is valid if someone thinks it is, seems equally unsatisfactory. It would force the abandonment of any impartial standpoint for assessing the value of arguments, and would lead to the vicious relativism characterized by Wayne Booth: "Charles Manson will be confirmed by the assent of his witches, Hitler by his SS troops, every Christian sect by its hundreds or millions of adherents, and indeed every political and religious program by its ability to present witnesses."[8] If we abandon both the quest for formal validity and a commitment to *any* notion of "reasonableness" which transcends individual occasions, it is hard to see how we could evaluate the soundness of arguments.

Having rejected the absolutism of formal logic and the implications of vicious relativism, one might arrive at the field concept—as Toulmin did—as a middle ground. The fragmentation of knowledge is thus viewable as a temporary setback, held in check by the promise of an impartial standpoint of rationality. Plausibly, the impartial standpoint may turn out to be a procedural principle capable of authorizing evaluations of arguments while doing justice to interfield relativity.

If one uses the field concept to pursue such epistemic/judgmental purposes, identifying fields and their boundaries becomes critically important. Only a clear conception of fields can yield a clear impartial standpoint of rationality since the former is the "ground" from which the latter "figure" emerges. Right now—without the impartial standpoint—the soundness of arguments depends upon their fit with the procedural and substantive ecologies of different fields. This perspective suggests that fields should be defined by their judgment criteria for what counts as "reasonable" or "valid." Whether the mapping of fields which results from such a standard would correspond in any significant way to the maps produced by the other two approaches is an open and largely unexplored question.

It is idle to speculate about whether sociological or argument-centered perspectives, description or evaluation, empirical research or criticism, is the more important task. Certainly we need both. What needs to be recognized is that one's view of fields will depend heavily on the work one wishes the concept to do. Much of the confusion in the extant work on fields may result from using the concept and arguing about its ramifications without making one's research purpose clear.

Whatever the purpose, one must assume that where argument occurs significantly affects its nature, or the concept of "fields" would be superfluous. As Cox puts it in discussing public policy argumentation, we must assume that the concepts of "public" and "policy" *inform* argumentation in a meaningful way.[9] Whether one's goal is description of situations, description of arguments, or critical evaluation, one must posit characteristics which define the nature of a field. There is considerable divergence among writers as to what these characteristics should be.

One approach to this problem may be to employ different labels. In his essay in this issue, Wenzel distinguishes among fields, forums, and contexts of argument.[10] Fields are grounded in the contents of knowledge structures; forums are grounded in the practices of a rational enterprise which attempts to create knowledge structures; and contexts are grounded in the general sociocultural environment. Fields relate to argument products; forums to procedures; and contexts to processes. These distinctions identify different perspectives which can be taken in studying argumentation.

THE NATURE OF ARGUMENT FIELDS

A second persistent question is *(2) For any given argument, what determines the field it is in?* In some respects this question follows naturally from the first—one might be expected to define the characteristics of an argument field consistently with one's goal in invoking the concept of fields. The literature, to be sure, reflects wide variation in how fields are defined. Some of the variation is caused by differing answers to the first question but some is independent. What follows is an attempt to identify the variety of usages.

(2a) Are argument fields determined by the argument's form? If one holds, as Toulmin seemed to in *Uses,* that fields are groups of arguments in which data and conclusions are of the same logical type, it would follow that formal differences would distinguish among fields. Few contemporary writers take this strict position, probably because it assumes a degree of formalism which is not appropriate to practical reasoning.[11] In a recent essay in this journal, Willard makes a cogent case against the equation of fields with logical types.[12]

Toulmin, Rieke, and Janik seem to have adopted a modification of this position. They describe the structure of argument in five different fields—law, science, management, ethics, and the arts.[13] They maintain that what are regarded as acceptable data and warrants vary by field, as do the importance of backing, rebuttals, or qualifiers. But these are not really *formal* differences. Toulmin and his colleagues have first identified fields according to the criterion of subject matter, and *then* have asked how fields differ according to what types of substantive statements count as the various parts of the argument. To see in this procedure a *formal* criterion for the definition of fields is to beg the question.

(2b) Are argument fields determined by subject matter? This approach to defining fields focuses on argument content rather than form. The assumption is that arguments dealing with the same subject are alike in important ways—origins, structural features, validity standards, etc.—and that they differ on those same dimensions from arguments on a different subject.

A particular version of this approach which has received widespread attention is the equation of fields with academic disciplines. Toulmin distinguishes among compact disciplines, diffuse disciplines, would-be disciplines, the undisciplined, and the undisciplinable. Toulmin, Rieke, and Janik identify law, science, management, ethics, and the arts as examples of fields. This same approach is evident in several papers at the Second Alta Conference which attempt to characterize legal argument as a distinct field.[14]

For some purposes this approach may be useful, particularly for understanding the norms and conventions of an academic discipline and how they constrain argumentation. For example, it may help to explain why scientists might dismiss certain data or claims as unscientific while another discipline might embrace the very same data and claims.

But as a way to define fields or to distinguish among them this approach has serious problems. First, where, for example, does psychology leave off and sociology begin? As Gronbeck notes in his recent paper on "socioculture," a concerted effort seems underway to blur disciplinary boundaries.[15] Moreover, different disciplines address common problems (and their members are able to argue meaningfully with one another when they do). And disciplines—psychology or communication studies, for instance—may be so broad that the variance in approach among scholars *within* a discipline is greater than that among scholars *between* cognate disciplines.

There is a more serious difficulty with the equation of fields and academic disciplines. This approach may well recreate the same error which Toulmin finds in formal logic: selection of an inappropriate paradigm for general argumentation. Most instances of argumentation do not occur within the confines of any academic discipline. They involve personal and public matters on which the arguers lack the specialized expertise associated with an academic discipline. Even when arguers concern themselves with, say, the budget and national finance, they often generate arguments uninformed in any meaningful way by the discipline of economics. One could define public and personal arguments as fields in their own right, but doing so would confound our attempt to define fields by the *subject-matter content* of arguments. In short, defining argument fields by reference to subject matter will fail to account for a substantial portion of everyday informal argumentation.[16]

(2c) Are argument fields determined by situational features? Since Bitzer's seminal essay,[17] the concept of "situation" has loomed large in rhetorical theory. A third approach to defining fields is by reference to features in the situation or in the orientation of the arguers to it. Variations on this approach range from Willard's personal-construct assumption that "A is in field X when he thinks he is," to generic exploration as recommended by Fisher, to identify the recurrence of situations of the same basic type.[18]

This approach would seem most useful for researchers investigating arguing as a process, who would be interested in probing the circumstances under which argumentative interactions occur. In viewing argument from a dramatistic perspective, for example, Klumpp is concerned with the enactment of symbolic drama in response to a situation.[19] In adopting a constructivist/interactionist orientation, Willard appears to be concerned with the personal constructs by which people define situations as arguments, and with the sort of behavior for which such a definition of the situation calls. Our literature has seen diverse approaches masquerading under the common label "constructivism." But whether one takes the personal-construct view identified with Willard or the social-construction-of-reality view identified with Kneupper, the common thread is to define fields by reference to aspects of the argumentative situation.[20]

A specific variation on this approach may be worthy of special note. In referring to Freudianism and behaviorism as distinct fields within the subject area of psychology, Willard introduces the possibility that arguers' schools of thought or world-views determine the field in which their arguments reside. Of course, one might regard a world-view as being an integrated set of personal constructs consistently applied. Pepper's work on root metaphors[21] suggests that one's world-view affects argumentative choices in significant ways. This suggestion is borne out by Linder's historical research on the rhetoric of the American Revolution and the anti-war protest movements of the 1960's.[22] In each case she found that arguers who had the same basic conclusions defended them in quite different ways, arguing often from different presuppositions and interpreting data differently.

Defining fields in this manner seems appropriate for one particular type of research objective. It is well-suited to Willard's goal of investigating how people come to decide that they know something.[23] Since this purpose is descriptive and social psychological, it is sensible to define fields according to descriptive features of the social situation. Even such a seemingly broad statement as "A is in field X when he thinks he is" makes sense within the context of Willard's research program. What clouds the matter is either the grafting of this definition onto research purposes for which it is ill-suited, or the criticism of this definition on the grounds that it is unsuited for research purposes for which it never was intended. Here is a good example of how one's answer to the first question—the purpose for invoking the field concept—powerfully influences how one determines what field an argument is in.

(2d) Are argument fields determined by the shared purpose of the arguers? One might regard the arguers' purpose as one dimension of the situation and hence subsume this question under the immediately preceding one. But its implications are sufficiently different to warrant separate treatment.

In a paper for the 1981 Summer Conference on Argumentation, Rowland makes a forceful plea that it is *purpose* which energizes the activity of arguing in the first place.[24] Accordingly, two arguers are in the same field if they share a common purpose, and—probably because of the shared purpose—the arguments they produce will differ in important ways from arguments which derive from a different purpose. Presumably, purpose may be identified either explicitly by the arguers or implicitly in their discourse.

This view has much to recommend it, particularly since purpose (or motive) may well be the root term from which different conceptions of the situation, or different academic disciplines, derive. Rowland's case studies of the law and newspaper criticism do seem to bear out the utility of his approach. Moreover, it is an approach which potentially could serve each of the three objectives mentioned earlier. It could explain how arguments develop, it could explain and predict differences in the structural features of argument, and it could serve as the basis for critical evaluation by prompting the question, "Did the advocate argue appropriately in light of the purpose?"

Still, there are problems in regarding purpose as the defining characteristic of fields. Arguers have multiple purposes. Meaningful discussion does occur among people whose purposes are not only different but incompatible. (Sometimes these exchanges may be productive if either party can step outside his own conception of purpose to imagine the other's. Sometimes they are futile, as in Willard's example in conversation of the dispute between the creationist and the evolutionist over the meaning of the Bible.) Arguers do not always *know* their purposes—much of everyday argument is produced spontaneously, even mindlessly. Even if an arguer knows his purpose, the analyst or critic may not, and hence may be unable confidently to classify the argument according to its field. Finally, for a critic who wishes to avoid the intentional fallacy, the arguer's purpose may not matter. Such a critic would focus on argument as discourse, a product of an interaction which has come to have a life of its own.

(2e) Are argument fields determined by the audience for argument? A final approach to characterizing argument fields is to examine the question of who

constitutes the appropriate audience for the arguments. On this view, fields would be distinguished according to the composition of the appropriate audience to evaluate claims. This approach has its roots in any theory of knowledge which holds that *consensus* is a test for the soundness of claims; the question naturally follows, "consensus among whom?" Perelman and Olbrechts-Tyteca distinguish between the universal audience and particular audiences;[25] presumably the field of argument would be determined by which type of audience was addressed.

More recently, both McKerrow and Goodnight have distinguished among audiences which arguments address. In his paper on "argument communities," McKerrow identifies the social, philosophical, and personal as three distinct "communities" of argument, distinguished by the nature of the audience.[26] To be sure, McKerrow does not offer his view as a *definition* of fields, but he employs the concept of "community" in an analogous way. It is the community who determines what norms are appropriate and what evaluative standards should prevail. In his critique of fields, Rowland identified some of the difficulties of attempting to equate fields with audiences in this manner.[27] Such immense differences may be found among arguments addressed to the same community as to compel the conclusion that the common audience is an incidental rather than essential feature of the argumentation. Moreover, in genuine controversies often multiple audiences are addressed simultaneously. In such a case, it seems impossible to determine which audience's standards of validity or appropriateness should prevail.

Goodnight's view is somewhat different. Since he takes one of the purposes of the "field" concept to be providing grounds for the evaluation of argument, he maintains that to define a field is in effect to define the set of persons competent to evaluate the argument.[28] If we are in the field of science, for example, only scientists ultimately are capable of judging the discourse. The distinction here is between *listener* and *judge*: scientific discourse may be addressed to virtually any audience, but only one audience is presumed competent to assess it. Hence, nonscientific objections to an argument in the field of science can be dismissed precisely on the grounds that they are not scientific. They do not address the special concerns of that audience which is ultimately competent to rule in the matter.

For Goodnight, the fact that arguments are addressed simultaneously to multiple audiences helps rather than hinders his claim. For he explores how, in just such ambiguous situations, one statement of who is competent to judge comes to prevail over another. How is it, for example, that nuclear accidents are seen as falling under the rubric of technological rather than religious authority, or that abortion is a matter for decision by criminal law rather than medicine? There are interests involved in assigning arguments to one field or another, and Goodnight attempts to show how the interplay of interests accounts for the growth and decay of entire realms of argument. Just as Schattschneider called attention to the interests involved in widening or narrowing the scope of a conflict,[29] so Goodnight suggests the strategic interests involved in classifying an argument within one or another field. For him, as for McKerrow, fields designate audiences. If McKerrow focuses more on actual audiences, Goodnight is more concerned with the audiences to whom one attributes standards for evaluation.

(2f) Are inferences from fields to characteristics reversible? There is an additional issue related to the way in which argument fields are defined; it concerns the relationship between a field and its properties. If we have defined and mapped fields correctly, then once we know we are in field X (or witnessing an argument from field X), we would know that the argument would have certain features different

from those of an argument in field Y. But is the converse also true? If, for example, we hear someone make an assertion that sounds "legal," can we infer that the speaker is in the field of law? We used the concept of field to identify the features of an argument within it; can we use the features to identify the field?

In a logical sense, the answer must be no, since the principle, "All As are Bs," does not imply its converse. One could assert that all legal arguments cite precedent cases without knowing that all arguments which cite precedent cases are legal. But in fact we make just this sort of "logically invalid" inference all the time. Perelman and Olbrechts-Tyteca describe the interaction between essence and accident. From repeated observations of an act's accidental features we form an impression of its essential nature, though that nature is not directly knowable. Then, from our impression of its essence we make predictions about the accidental features which might be subsequently displayed.[30] The point is that there is an ongoing interaction between the view one has of a field and one's view of the characteristics displayed by arguments in the field. What prevents the reasoning process from circularity is the cumulation of cases. From an examination of the features of arguments 1, 2, 3, . . , n, all of which are commonly recognized as belonging to field X, we form a notion of the essential nature of X which we then use to predict the features of argument n + 1.

The answer to this question is of special value to the critic. To determine what a speaker's statements mean and hence what their truth conditions are, one must locate the statements in a particular field. (Wenzel employs the terms "context" and "forum" instead of "field" for this sort of usage.)[31] From features of the argument the critic infers the field; from the nature of the field he or she predicts the appropriate validity standards or truth conditions. The question for the critic is whether, in any given argument, the features of one field are more prominent than the features of another. The concept of field, however, provides a principle according to which one can interpret ambiguous claims.

In summary, the extant literature reveals considerable variation in how argument fields are defined. In part, this variation reflects diversity in the work which scholars expect the "field" concept to do. However, variation in definition is at least partly independent of variation in purpose. Some of the approaches to definition either cross-cut various purposes for the concept of "field" or else are compatible with multiple purposes. Moreover, once one has defined a field, the relationship between a field's essential nature and its surface properties is complex and troublesome. One observes the features of arguments universally located within a given field, infers from those features what is the basic nature of the field, and then predicts—based on the assumed nature of the field—the characteristics of other arguments which may be taken to reside in the field. Through this sort of sign reasoning, the field concept enables a critic to determine what ambiguous statements mean and what are the appropriate grounds on which to test them.

THE DEVELOPMENT OF FIELDS

The final question to be considered relates to the growth and decay of argument fields: *(3) How do fields develop?*

The importance of this question can be seen from the consequences of failure to answer it. As with "instincts" in psychology, the temptation is great to "invent" fields as it suits one's purpose to do so. Whenever an argument does not fully fit within existing categories—whether of subject matter, purpose, audience, or whatever—the eager researcher might proclaim the existence of a new argument field. This proliferation of fields, made all the more likely by the amorphous nature of the field concept itself, threatens to rob the idea of its significance. If every argumentative encounter has become its own field, then the concept has been trivialized. It no longer explains the genesis of arguments, except in a tautological way; and it thwarts the possibility of identifying argument structures or evaluation arguments in any way that transcends the details of the particular case. To avoid these pitfalls, we need an account of the growth and demise of fields against which we can check individual claims for the emergence or disappearance of fields. Toulmin offered such an account of how concepts change in *Human Understanding;* what is needed is a similar if less ambitious account of the rise and fall of fields. Several specific aspects of this question are explored here.

(3a) Do arguers create their own field? An affirmative answer to this question seems implied by the several variations of "constructivism." Kneupper, for instance, maintains that fields are formed by actors' creation and transformation of symbols.[32] Willard believes that fields can be understood best as psychological constructs.[33] Both writers appear to share the belief that fields are called into being by arguers in specific situations. What saves this approach from a vicious relativism is the assumption that because arguers validate assumptions intersubjectively there is a finite range of situations and that types of situations recur. Still, this perspective on the evolution of fields is probably more useful in accounting for an argument's genesis than it is for the other possible purposes described above.

(3b) Are fields different from the public? In his essay in this issue, Goodnight poses the possibility that fields, as specialized interests, stand in opposition to the public, a term which refers to a general community interest.[34] On this view, the way a field emerges is by an expert group's successfully defining a topic area or exigence as not the proper concern for the general public. The effect, Goodnight surmises, is to denude the concept of "the public" and to deprive individuals of responsibility for their collective choices. Hence, fields grow at the expense of the public. The motive for their growth is the desire by specialists to assume the power to decide about matters which affect or interest them. This desire can be rationalized with the claim that the public is incompetent. The attempt to see in economic or scientific issues matters which are technical rather than ideological is an illustration of how separate argument fields emerge.

Goodnight's case is cogent, but it depends upon a particular stipulation: the belief that the personal, technical, and public are not only different spheres but wholly different orders of magnitude. On Goodnight's view, fields are subdivisions of the technical sphere. Whether an argument is assigned to one field or another is a matter of little consequence except to the technical experts themselves who are battling for the prerogative to control discussion of the issue. The crucial question is whether a dispute is assigned to the technical sphere *at all* or whether it is reserved for the public domain. If, however, one views public argument as *coequal* with any of the specific specialized fields—as Cox appears to do[35]—the nature of the problem is somewhat different. Advocates for the public would be on an equal footing with advocates for any specific field and hence would not be at the disadvantage Goodnight's essay implies. His account of field origins would be attenuated since the contest to control the discussion would occur between one field and another rather than between *any* field and the more general "public."

(3c) How do time and historical experience influence the demarcation of argument fields? Several scholars have addressed the issue of how fields progress

through time and are affected by experience. For example, Campbell's provocative analysis of historical epochs suggests that they constitute "new model[s] of ultimate explanation," subsuming earlier contexts of argument.[36] And, in his essay in this issue, Goodnight draws upon the relationship among the personal, technical, and public spheres in order to explain how entire realms of argument may come to be lost, no longer representing live options for speakers or audiences.[37] Farrell's forthcoming essay, "Knowledge in Time," also addresses how a society's conception of knowledge is shaped by time.[38] Central to all of these essays is the recognition that an argument field is shaped by the larger sense of chronology. If, for example, there are cycles in the emergence and disappearance of issues of a certain type, or cycles in the optimism or pessimism of a people, or any of the other varieties of historical cycles which have been theorized, these cycles will affect the constellation of argument fields. To cite but one example, in a time of economic expansion social welfare programs are advocated as economic investments, but in tight times the same arguments are assigned to the field of "charity."

Not just the passage of historical time, but experience more generally affects argument fields. Two of the 1981 Summer Conference papers suggest that an audience's notion of validity standards is affected by history. In surmising that fields differ in their assumptions about what is reasonable, I observed that reasonableness is dependent on history: "Audiences are willing to make an inference confidently because the inferential pattern in the past has led to satisfactory results far more often than not."[39] The ways in which experience affects fields should be of particular interest to those whose research purposes are descriptive and sociological. A theory which grounds fields in the experience of social communities needs some account of what in their historical experience leads these communities to spawn significantly different approaches to the nature of argument.

(3d) Other than in their defining characteristics, how do fields differ? If our interest in argument fields is to have value beyond the taxonomic, identifying different fields must somehow make a difference. Having said, for example, that legal argument and scientific argument are discrete fields, we should be able to make sound predictions about how these differences would be manifest. Otherwise little has been gained from the "field" usage. If it were determined, say, that fields were defined by logical types and that they differed only in logical type, we might just as well abandon the "field" construct and say that *arguments* vary by logical type.

Two major answers have been offered to this question. One, represented by Toulmin, Rieke, and Janik, is that fields differ in the component parts of arguments or in their configuration. In *An Introduction to Reasoning,* the authors maintain that the nature and pattern of data, warrants, claims, backing, and so on differ across the range of fields they examine. In like fashion, Klumpp has suggested that fields determine what types of data are even considered relevant to the support of a given claim. And Farrell's recent work involving the concept of "authority" implies the question of whether fields differ according to judgments of what constitutes authority.[40] These and other differences in argument structure should be of special interest to researchers whose goal is to describe argument products as they are affected by fields.

The other major suggestion is that fields differ according to validity standards, or—put more broadly—how they answer the question of what makes an argument reasonable. A reasonable argument is one which most people would accept when they were exercising their critical judgment. This approach to the question assumes that each field has its own "standpoint of rationality" and that these standpoints represent the middle ground between formalism and vicious relativism. Several recent papers suggest that standards of reasonableness may vary from field to field. This possibility is implicit in Gronbeck's suggestion that the correctness of an argument depends on contextual validity standards and that these are determined by a socioculture. It is likewise implied by Fisher's contention that the nature of *reason* varies with genre. It is made explicit in my own hypothesis that fields will differ in the substantive underlying assumptions made about an argument and that these assumptions are a key determinant of an argument's reasonableness.[41] The claim that public policy arguments are deemed reasonable if they appeal to both liberal and conservative presuppositions represents a beginning effort to delineate the ways in which standards for reasonableness are constrained by an argument field. This approach has been of primary interest to scholars seeking to use the field concept as a tool for the critical appraisal of arguments.

For researchers whose goal is to describe argumentative situations, less has been done to explicate the ways in which fields differ, perhaps because there is a strong tendency to regard "field" as synonymous with "situation," assert that fields exist in the minds of the arguers, and then conclude that no two situations are exactly alike. Willard, however, has suggested that fields vary by the audiences for argument. Unlike McKerrow or Goodnight, Willard does not *define* fields by reference to audiences. Nevertheless, he suggests that it may be more productive to view fields as characterizations of audiences than of speakers, because the speaker's affiliation may be difficult to determine and because it is the audience as well as the speaker who bring predispositions and values to the argument.[42] Certainly such a position is consistent with a view of fields as sociological categories, and it is compatible with much of what we know about audience analysis.

CONCLUSION

There is a certain temptation to throw up one's hands in the face of conceptual fuzziness and confusion, abandoning the troublesome concept altogether. But the "field" concept has useful purposes to serve. It is a potential aid to explaining what happens in argumentative encounters, to classifying argument products, and to deriving evaluative standards. To be sure, researchers on argument fields are not yet pursuing a coherent program. By identifying the different jobs that the "field" concept is expected to do and explicating some of the key questions in theory development, we may bring greater coherence to this work.

One value of the field concept is that it has forced argumentation scholars to re-examine their discipline's purposes and methods, and to see the relationship between a purpose or method and the sort of theory it produces. This disciplinary self-consciousness is not only valuable in its own right but essential to the integration of empirical and critical studies on which mature and robust theories of argumentation will depend.

NOTES

[1] Stephen E. Toulmin, *The Uses of Argument* (Cambridge: Cambridge University Press, 1958), p. 14.

[2] Stephen E. Toulmin, *Human Understanding* (Princeton: Princeton University Press, 1972).

[3] Charles Arthur Willard, "Field Theory: A Cartesian Meditation," *Dimensions of Argument: Proceedings of the Second Summer Conference on Argumentation,* eds. George Ziegelmueller

and Jack Rhodes (Annandale, Va.: Speech Communication Association, 1981), p. 21. This anthology hereafter will be cited as *Dimensions*.

4 For example, McKerrow admits to "skepticism regarding the value of 'field theory' as a rationale for the explication of arguments." Ray E. McKerrow, "Field Theory: A Necessary Concept?" paper presented at the Speech Communication Association convention, Anaheim, California, November 1981.

5 See Thomas B. Farrell and G. Thomas Goodnight, "Accidental Rhetoric: Root Metaphors of Three Mile Island," *Communication Monographs,* 48 (December 1981), 271–300.

6 See, for example, Toulmin, *The Uses of Argument*, pp. 146–210; Chaim Perelman and L. Olbrechts-Tyteca, *The New Rhetoric,* trans. John Wilkinson and Purcell Weaver (Notre Dame, Ind.: University of Notre Dame Press, 1969), pp. 1–10.

7 See, for instance, Morris Kline, *Mathematics in Western Culture* (Oxford: Oxford University Press, 1972), pp. 42–43; J. Van Heijenoort, "Gödel's Theorem," *Encyclopedia of Philosophy* (New York: Macmillan, 1967), III, pp. 348–357.

8 Wayne C. Booth, *Modern Dogma and the Rhetoric of Assent* (Notre Dame, Ind.: University of Notre Dame Press, 1974), p. 106.

9 J. Robert Cox, "Investigating Policy Argument as a Field," *Dimensions,* p. 126.

10 Joseph W. Wenzel, "Fields, Forums, and Contexts of Argument," *Journal of the American Forensic Association,* this issue, pp. 204–5.

11 McKerrow does tend in this direction, however, in arguing that fields ought to be regarded as logical types. See Ray E. McKerrow, "On Fields and Rational Enterprises: A Reply to Willard," *Proceedings of the [First] Summer Conference on Argumentation,* eds. Jack Rhodes and Sara Newell (Falls Church, Va.: Speech Communication Association, 1980), esp. p. 403.

12 Charles Arthur Willard, "Argument Fields and Theories of Logical Types," *Journal of the American Forensic Association,* 17 (Winter 1981), 129–145.

13 Stephen Toulmin, Richard Rieke, and Allan Janik, *An Introduction to Reasoning* (New York: Macmillan, 1979).

14 These papers appear in *Dimensions,* pp. 159–278. Also, in the discussion period of the program, "Theoretical Perspectives on Argument Fields," Michael C. McGee argued from the floor that the concepts of "discipline" and "field" were redundant.

15 Bruce E. Gronbeck, "Sociocultural Notions of Argument Fields: A Primer," *Dimensions,* pp. 1–2.

16 For a thorough statement of this problem, see Charles Arthur Willard, "Some Questions about Toulmin's View of Argument Fields," *Proceedings of the [First] Summer Conference,* pp. 348–400.

17 Lloyd F. Bitzer, "The Rhetorical Situation," *Philosophy and Rhetoric,* 1 (1968), 1–14.

18 Charles Arthur Willard, "Cartesian Meditation," p. 34; Walter R. Fisher, "Good Reasons: Fields and Genre," *Dimensions,* pp. 114–125.

19 James F. Klumpp, "A Dramatistic Approach to Fields," *Dimensions,* pp. 44–45.

20 Readers of this journal should be quite familiar with the ongoing dispute between Willard and Kneupper. For their most recent positions, see Charles W. Kneupper, "Argument: A Social Constructivist Perspective," *Journal of the American Forensic Association,* 17 (Spring 1981), 183–189; Charles Arthur Willard, "The Status of the Non-Discursiveness Thesis," *Journal of the American Forensic Association,* 17 (Spring 1981), 190–214.

21 Stephen Pepper, *World Hypotheses* (Berkeley: University of California Press, 1942).

22 See Patricia L. Linder, "World-View and Rhetoric: The Ideological Foundations of American Revolutionary Communication," Thesis Northwestern 1978; "World-View and Rhetorical Choice: The Ideology and Tactics of Selected Antiwar Protest Groups During the Vietnam Era," Diss. Northwestern 1980. For a description of her method, see Linder, "World-View and Rhetoric: A Proposed Methodology for Ideological Definition," paper presented at the Speech Communication Association convention, San Antonio, November 1979.

23 See Charles Arthur Willard, *Argumentation and the Social Grounds of Knowledge* (University, Ala.: University of Alabama Press), in press.

24 Robert C. Rowland, "Argument Fields," *Dimensions,* esp. pp. 61–68.

25 Perelman and Olbrechts-Tyteca, pp. 17–45.

26 Ray E. McKerrow, "Argument Communities: A Quest for Distinctions," *Proceedings of the [First] Summer Conference,* pp. 214–227.

27 Rowland, p. 60.

28 See G. Thomas Goodnight, "The Personal, Technical, and Public Spheres of Argument: A Speculative Inquiry into the Art of Public Deliberation," this issue, pp. 220–23.

[29] E. E. Schattschneider, *The Semisovereign People* (New York: Holt, Rinehart, and Winston, 1960), pp. 16–18.

[30] Perelman and Olbrechts-Tyteca, pp. 293–330.

[31] Wenzel, "Fields, Forums, and Contexts of Argument," this issue.

[32] Charles W. Kneupper, "Argument Fields: Some Social Constructivist Observations," *Dimensions,* pp. 80–87.

[33] Willard writes, "the field notion is most useful to argumentation theorists as a psychological idea, taking account of the idiosyncratic perspectives of situated actors." Charles Arthur Willard, "Some Questions about Toulmin's View," p. 348.

[34] Goodnight, "The Personal, Technical, and Public Spheres," this issue, pp. 219–20.

[35] Cox, "Investigating Policy Argument as a Field," *Dimensions,* pp. 126–142.

[36] John Angus Campbell, "Historical Reason: Field as Consciousness," *Dimensions,* pp. 101–113.

[37] Goodnight, "The Personal, Technical, and Public Spheres," this issue, p. 215.

[38] Thomas B. Farrell, "Knowledge in Time," *Advances in Argumentation Theory and Research,* eds. J. Robert Cox and Charles Arthur Willard (Carbondale: Southern Illinois University Press, 1982), in press.

[39] David Zarefsky, "'Reasonableness' in Public Policy Argument: Fields as Institutions," *Dimensions,* p. 88. For a similar view, though not described in the terms of argument fields, see Dale Hample, "What Is a Good Argument?" *Dimensions,* p. 884.

[40] Toulmin, Rieke, and Janik, *An Introduction to Reasoning,* Part IV; Klumpp, p. 49; Farrell, "Knowledge in Time."

[41] Gronbeck, pp. 1–20, esp. p. 15; Fisher, pp. 114–125; Zarefsky, p. 89.

[42] Willard, "Cartesian Meditation," p. 24.

Chapter 2

Definitions

Few lines of inquiry in argumentation studies reflect the vast interdisciplinary differences like the question of the definition of argument does. The essays in this chapter represent major concerns with defining argument and argumentation that have emerged over the past three decades. They also reflect differences in perspectives among rhetoricians, informal logicians, and philosophers.

The differences arise because discussions of the definition of argument and argumentation are primarily concerned with sharpening and expanding the study within particular disciplinary frameworks. Conceptions of argument function, form, theory, and methodology vary among disciplines and influence their definitions. For some scholars, theory is based on the practice of argumentation; concepts reflect everyday use. For others, argument theory comes first; it prescribes universal constructs of argument as a way to bring practice into conformity with theory. The tension between the two approaches results in a central concern in defining argument and argumentation: are argument studies about describing communicative practices (argument as it exists) or normative constructs (argument as it should be)?

Daniel J. O'Keefe's "Two Concepts of Argument" (1977) is concerned with the confusion that arises from conflating two aspects of argument that are described in rhetorical scholarship. O'Keefe creates a distinction between Argument$_1$ (product) and Argument$_2$ (process). The major contribution of this article is the deliberate focus on argument as a process of interaction (Argument$_2$). Drawing on argumentation scholar Stephen Toulmin's work, O'Keefe redirects argument studies toward seeing and describing as opposed to prescribing. His contribution aims to rescue the concept of argument from abstraction and to define the term as it functions in everyday experience.

Robert C. Rowland's "On Defining Argument" (1987) defines argument in terms of its epistemic function, as an independent means of discovering knowledge. Approaching argument as a human endeavor that people experience with one another, Rowland calls for a definition that explains the form and function of argument, and thereby distinguishes argument from other symbolic acts. As a form, argument is characterized as discourse in which reasons and evidence are presented in support of claims, while the function of argument is to produce knowledge. Rowland claims that, by its nature, argument is a reason-giving activity and is therefore necessarily symbolic. By excluding non-symbolic forms such as music or art from his definition of argument, Rowland positions language at the center of argument.

Christopher W. Tindale, in "A Concept Divided: Ralph Johnson's Definition of Argument" (2002), approaches the definition of argument from an informal logic perspective and gives us a strong sense of how informal logicians have defined argument. Tindale puts forward a conception of argument that builds upon major works in informal logic while addressing theoretical tensions in the current literature. This essay responds to a conception of argument, framed by

Ralph Johnson, another informal logician, that defines argument as an attempt to influence with reasons and support. Tindale lays out the utility of defining argument in this manner and addresses the tensions that arise from definitions of argument that do not fully consider the role audiences play in shaping argument premises. In Tindale's estimation, there is still work to be done to merge the gap between viewing argument as a product or as a process.

The essays in this chapter reflect an evolving understanding of the components of argument. By defining argument in terms of function, the authors establish boundaries and allow for flexibility in defining argumentation. The multiplicity of perspectives illuminates the potential of argumentation as a field of study, in that it shows an interdisciplinary body emerging to further expand the boundaries of argument.

....

Two Concepts of Argument

DANIEL J. O'KEEFE

Students of argument rarely acknowledge that the term "argument" has two importantly different senses. In this essay I attempt to show the importance of distinguishing these senses, taking as a focus for analysis Wayne Brockriede's recent discussions of the concept of argument. I will argue that Brockriede's view suffers from a failure to heed the distinction I emphasize, but that this failure signals important developments in the study of argument.

I

In everyday talk the word "argument" is systematically used to refer to two different phenomena. On the one hand it refers to a kind of utterance or a sort of communicative act. This sense of the term I will call "argument$_1$." It is the sense contained in sentences such as "he made an argument." On the other hand, "argument" sometimes refers to a particular kind of interaction. This sense, "argument$_2$," appears in sentences such as "they had an argument." Crudely put, an argument$_1$ is something one person makes (or gives or presents or utters), while an argument$_2$ is something two or more persons have (or engage in). Arguments$_1$ are thus on a par with promises, commands, apologies, warnings, invitations, orders, and the like. Arguments$_2$ are classifiable with other species of interactions such as bull sessions, heart-to-heart talks, quarrels, discussions, and so forth.

Now I should immediately emphasize that the distinction I am pointing to does not turn on the number of persons involved. We might, for example, find it useful in some situations to speak of one person having an argument$_2$ (with himself); and we might similarly encounter cases where we would want to say that two or more persons had jointly made an argument$_1$. But these cases seem secondary on the paradigmatic senses of "argument$_1$" and "argument$_2$," and so I have in setting out the distinction referred to what seem to be exemplary uses of the two senses of the term.

This distinction is, I think, a plausible and natural one, as evidenced by our everyday ways of speaking. Certainly an argument$_1$ is very different from an argument$_2$. One speaks of arguments$_1$ being refuted, valid, or fallacious, while one does not ordinarily characterize arguments$_2$ in these ways; and one speaks of arguments$_2$

coming to blows, or being pointless or unproductive, while one does not usually characterize arguments₁ in just these ways.[1] There is, in short, an obvious distinction between arguments₁ and arguments₂ embedded in our everyday use of the term "argument." It is this distinction that underlies the curiosity in statements such as "Bob and I had an argument and it was refuted."

I might mention that this distinction is usefully extended to cover related forms, so that (e.g.) a person who is arguing₁ is making an argument₁, and a person who is arguing₂ is in the process of having an argument₂. The distinction here is evidenced in everyday talk by the difference between "arguing₁ *that*" and "arguing₂ *about*," the difference between the sentences "I was arguing₁ that P" and "we were arguing₂ about Q" (or "I was arguing₂ with myself about Q"). Similarly, one might use "arguer₁" to refer to a person in a way that highlights the fact that the person is to be understood as making an argument₁, and "arguer₂" to emphasize that the person is to be understood as engaged in an argument with another person.[2]

The importance of distinguishing arguments₁ and arguments₂ can be displayed by examining Wayne Brockriede's recent analysis of argument.[3] Brockriede offers six general characteristics of argument. These are not, he emphasizes, necessary and sufficient conditions for something's being an argument, but are rather general features to which one can appeal in deciding whether something is (or can usefully be seen as) an argument. My claim is that Brockriede's analysis unfortunately elides arguments₁ and arguments₂, to the detriment of his characterization of argument.

Brockriede's first characteristic is that argument involves "an inferential leap from existing beliefs to the adoption of new beliefs or to the reinforcement of an old one."[4] This first characteristic seems obviously to be a description of arguments₁.

A second characteristic of argument is "a perceived rationale to support that leap."[5] This might initially seem to be an attribute of arguments₁. However, Brockriede's elaboration of this characteristic introduces complications. He writes:

> An arguer must perceive some rationale that establishes that the claim being leaped to is worthy at least of being entertained. The weakest acceptable rationale may justify saying that the claim leaped to deserves entertainment "for the sake of argument." A stronger rationale may justify a person's taking a claim seriously—with the hope that after further thought it may be accepted. A still stronger rationale may convince someone to accept a claim tentatively until a better alternative comes along. If the rationale is too slender to justify a leap, the result is a quibble rather than an argument; but a rationale so strong a conclusion is entailed removes the activity from the realm of the problematic. If the perceived rationale occupies either polar region, it fails to justify the label of argument because the claim either appears ridiculous (not worth arguing about) or too risky to entertain.[6]

Now the locus of perception here is apparently the "persuadee" (i.e., the recipient of the arguments₁ initially advanced by the "persuader"). That is, Brockriede's claim seems to be that the persuadee must see the persuader's claim as "worthy at least of being entertained" before there is (or can be) an "argument." This analysis, it seems to me, confuses not only arguments₁ with argument₂, but also arguments₁ with good (but not too good) arguments₁. I can best explain this as follows.

It is probably true that a persuadee must see at least a scintilla of support (for the leap) before he sees the claim as a serious one—one worth having an argument₂ about. But it does not seem to me that where the persuadee finds this support lacking he cannot recognize that the persuader *has* advanced *some* argument₁, however poor that argument$_1$ may be. That is, a bad argument$_1$ is still an argument$_1$. I might well recognize that someone has advanced an argument$_1$ (has offered putative reasons for a claim) yet also see that argument$_1$ (those reasons) as so unconvincing that I see no need for my advancing counter arguments$_1$ (no need for us to have an argument$_2$). The person made an argument$_1$, but it was a terrible argument$_1$—so terrible that I need not engage him in an argument$_2$. Conversely, if the persuadee finds the rationale so compelling that he, utterly accepts it, he will again likely see no need for having an argument$_2$. But the persuader has still presented an argument$_1$; a convincing argument$_1$ is still an argument$_1$. (I will return to this point shortly in the context of discussing "analytic arguments.") In sum, Brockriede's discussion of this second characteristic not only confuses the conditions that make an argument$_2$ likely to occur with the conditions for an argument$_1$'s having been made, but also unhappily limits the scope of arguments$_1$ in a way that excludes highly successful arguments$_1$ and utterly unsuccessful arguments$_1$.

Brockriede's third characteristic is "a choice between two or more competing claims."[7] He suggests that "people who argue have some choice but not too much. If they have too little choice, if a belief is entailed by formal logic or required by their status as true believers, they need not argue; but if they have too much choice, if they have to deal with choice overload, then argument may not be very productive."[8] The difficulties with this analysis are rather complex. Consider first this claim: "If a belief is entailed by formal logic, then people need not argue." As it stands, this claim is not well put. Any statement can be "entailed by formal logic" given the right kinds of premises. Perhaps Brockriede's intent here can better be expressed as follows: "If a person sees a claim as logically following from premises he accepts, then he need not argue." But this version of the claim will not do either. The fact that I accept the premises which formally entail a given claim does not ensure that others (whom I might wish to persuade) will also accept those premises. If I want those others to accept my claim, then I may well need to argue$_1$ (i.e., make arguments$_1$) for it. Perhaps, then, the point Brockriede wishes to make can be put this way: "If a person sees a claim as logically following from premises that he accepts and that he believes some other person O accepts, then he need not make arguments to O in support of the claim." Now this version might be acceptable if all persons reasoned in a strictly logical fashion, for if this condition were met then the knowledge that O accepts certain premises would give grounds for believing that O accepts claims that are logical consequences of those premises. Under such conditions, there would in fact be no need to make arguments$_1$ (to O) for those logical consequences. As it happens, of course, not all persons always reason in a strictly logical way.

I suspect that theorists of argument have been misled here by examples such as "Socrates is a man, and all men are mortal, so Socrates is mortal." This case presents a conclusion which is on its face acceptable to most persons; one need not construct an argument$_1$ here. But not all conclusions of logically tight arguments$_1$ are so clearly unobjectionable. We are to the point of discussing what are sometimes called "analytic arguments," arguments$_1$ in which the conclusion is logically entailed by the premises. Brockriede, of course, is not alone in suggesting that analytic arguments$_1$ are not really arguments$_1$ at all. My claim, however, is that this exclusion of analytic arguments$_1$ from the realm of argument$_1$ is unwarranted.

Suppose, for example, that I wish to disabuse some philosopher of what Richard Taylor calls "simple materialism," the belief that persons are identical with their bodies. I might attack this belief this way:[9]

(1) If two things are identical, then any predicate meaningfully applicable to one must be meaningfully applicable to the other.

(2) Certain sorts of predicates (e.g., moral assessments and, roughly speaking, intentional characterizations such as "believes that p" and "hopes that q") are meaningfully applicable to persons but not to their bodies.

(3) Therefore, persons are not identical with their bodies.

What are we to make of this? That I haven't really made an argument$_1$ here (by virtue of its analyticity)? But I certainly did something very much like presenting an argument$_1$. That my hearer (if he now abandons his earlier stand) really believed my conclusion all along (it being implicitly contained in premises he accepted)? But in a perfectly straightforward sense he did not initially believe my conclusion. No, I think the most plausible characterization of what I have done is that I have made an argument$_1$—this, even though the argument$_1$ is "analytic." (Notice that nothing turns on my hearer having accepted my argument$_1$. I could properly be said to have made an argument$_1$ even if my hearer had rejected one of my premises as false. Indeed, I could properly be said to have made an argument$_1$ even it my hearer had not thought my claim worthy of being entertained even "for the sake of argument.")

Now to suggest that analytic arguments$_1$ are genuine arguments$_1$ is not to claim that analytic arguments$_1$ occur very often in everyday life, that naive social actors regularly employ logically tight forms of argument$_1$, that the "analytic ideal" is a useful framework for describing or understanding everyday arguments$_1$, or that only analytic arguments$_1$ are arguments$_1$. It is only to claim that analytic arguments are in fact arguments$_1$, that there is no good reason for excluding (as Brockriede does) logically tight arguments$_1$ from the realm of argument$_1$.

So far I have discussed this third characteristic—"a choice between two or more competing claims"—in terms of arguments$_1$. But the same characteristic could be viewed from the perspective of arguments$_2$. Thus, for example, if persons "have too little choice . . . they need not argue"—that is, they need not have an argument$_2$.[10] If you and I are trying to decide what course of action to adopt, and we see only one plausible alternative, it may well be pointless for us to have an argument$_2$. Similarly, if we "have too much choice," if we "have to deal with choice overload, then argument may not be very productive"—that is, it may not be useful for us to have an argument$_2$.[11] Our alternatives are not sufficiently narrowed to permit productive arguments$_2$ to occur. The third characteristic, then, can be read as applying either to arguments$_1$ or to arguments$_2$, and hence it does not distinguish the two senses of "argument."

Brockriede's fourth characteristic is "a regulation of uncertainty." He indicates that "if certainty existed, people need not engage in what I am defining as argument. When uncertainty is high, a need for argument is also high. . . . If people have too little uncertainty to regulate, then they have no problems to solve and argument is not needed."[12] Brockriede notes that usually arguers will attempt to control uncertainty by reducing it, but that on occasion arguers might strategically choose to increase uncertainty.

When one speaks of "arguments" as designed to reduce or increase uncertainty, one seemingly is referring to arguments$_1$. One common purpose in making arguments$_1$ is to regulate the persuadee's uncertainty (especially to reduce his uncertainty about which of two competing claims to honor). Sometimes, however, arguments$_2$ are conducted for the same purpose. Institutionalized arrangements for arguments$_2$, as in the American judicial system, frequently involve purposeful clash where the point of having the argument$_2$ is to present the issues to (and thus regulate the certainty of) a third party; each arguer's arguments$_1$ and counter-arguments$_1$ are primarily directed at the third party (the audience, e.g., judge or jury), rather than at his opponent. Hence Brockriede's fourth characteristic of "argument," while apparently focused on arguments$_1$ can apply equally well to both arguments$_1$ and arguments$_2$. Thus this fourth characteristic does not distinguish the two senses of "argument."

The fifth characteristic is "a willingness to risk confrontation of a claim with peers."[13] This seems an attribute of the arguer rather than of the argument, and apparently focuses on persons who are making arguments$_1$ (i.e., arguers$_1$) but who are not yet engaged in an argument$_2$. Presumably those involved in an argument$_2$ (arguers$_2$) are already engaged in confrontation; for them, that risk has been actualized (though, of course, different risks may now arise).

The sixth characteristic advanced is "a frame of reference shared optimally." The suggestion is that persons "cannot argue with one another very effectively if their presuppositions share too little or are virtually irreconcilable; but argument is pointless if two persons share too much."[14] In characterizing his own essay as an exemplar of "argument," Brockriede makes a telling commentary with respect to this sixth attribute: "I have presumed throughout that our frames of reference overlap at some points but not at too many."[15] Now it might be true that for a person to advance an argument$_1$ he must presume that his frame of reference overlaps at some points with those of his listeners. (Of course, it seems that this is a requirement not merely for a person's advancing an argument$_1$, but for a person's speaking at all.) But this is not the same as saying that for two persons to have an argument$_2$ they must share a frame of reference. The second claim may be true as well, but it is not synonymous with the first.

Further, what I have called the "second claim" here is ambiguous. One is not sure whether Brockriede means to suggest that a shared frame of reference is required ("required" in the loose sense of being a "generic characteristic") for persons to have an argument$_2$, or whether such is required for two persons to have a productive argument$_2$. Now perhaps Brockriede wants to restrict the sense of "argument" (more carefully, "argument$_2$") in a way that includes only productive (worthwhile, good) arguments$_2$, preferring to reserve some other term (say, "squabble") for unproductive arguments$_2$. But this is something left unclear in Brockriede's discussion.

In sum, Brockriede's treatment of "argument" elides two distinct senses of the term. As a consequence, his discussion of the generic characteristics of "argument" is confused. Characteristics one, two, and four appear to focus on arguments$_1$; characteristic six seems to center on arguments$_2$; and the status of characteristics three and five is unclear.

II

I hope it is now clear that a confusion of the two senses of "argument" leads to unhappy consequences. Fruitful work in the study of argument will obviously turn on a recognition of the differences between arguments$_1$ and arguments$_2$. But Brockriede's elision of the two senses of "argument" is important, because it is indicative of shifting concerns in the study of argument.

Broadly put, most contemporary treatments of argument have had two central features: a focus on arguments$_1$ and a prescriptive orientation. Hence the emphasis of textbooks and coursework in argumentation is on teaching one to be a good (effective, ethical, strategic, . . .) arguer$_1$: Here is what a logically sound argument$_1$ is, here are some common fallacies in argument$_1$, these stock issues give you a clue as to what arguments$_1$ you will likely need to make, and so forth.

Brockriede, however, is obviously as concerned with arguments$_2$ as with arguments$_1$ (even while he does not differentiate there clearly). And accompanying this expanded interest is, I think, a descriptive or explanatory concern, rather than a purely normative orientation. That is, Brockriede seems more concerned with understanding and explaining "arguments" (of whatever type) than with offering prescriptions to "arguers" (of whatever type).

This same general shift from prescription to description can be discerned in Stephen Toulmin's *Uses of Argument*. Toulmin notes that logic, as he conceives it, "may have to become less of an *a priori* subject than it has recently been; so blurring the distinction between logic itself and the subjects whose arguments the logician scrutinizes."[16] Toulmin continues:

> Accepting the need to begin by collecting for study the actual forms of argument current in any field, our starting-point will be confessedly empirical. . . . This will seem a matter for apology only if one is completely wedded to the ideal of logic as a purely formal, *a priori* science. But not only will logic have to become more empirical; it will inevitably tend to become more historical. . . . We must study the ways of arguing which have established themselves in any sphere, accepting them as historical facts; knowing that they may be superseded, but only as the result of a revolutionary advance in our methods of thought.[17]

Thus Toulmin suggests that students of argument undertake the task of "seeing and describing the arguments in each field as they are, recognizing how they work; not setting oneself up to explain why, or to demonstrate that they necessarily must work."[18]

Notably, much of the criticism leveled at *Uses of Argument* has focused on prescriptive questions. Thus, for example, Cowan charges that Toulmin "has not shown *how* conformity to the forms and procedures he outlines does provide any support or justification at all. . . . How are we to know whether a proposed backing *really* backs?"[19] This line of criticism is somewhat off the mark, just because Toulmin is much less concerned with justifying the use of the kinds of arguments$_1$ he mentions than he is with simply describing and explicating those arguments$_1$. One might say that for Toulmin, like Wittgenstein, the central task is that of "clarifying those public standards of justification that we all employ in science and in everyday life."[20]

One could, I think, point to many other indications within the study of argumentation of an emerging concern with the description and explication of argument, as opposed to a focus on prescriptive matters: the extensive discussions of the role of formal logic in argumentation,[21] Perelman's work on types of arguments$_1$,[22] Crable's recent textbook *Argumentation as Communication*.[23] But all of these discussions largely focus on arguments$_1$. Arguments$_2$ do not receive very much (explicit) attention. Brockriede's essay, however, makes it clear that a shift from prescription to description will very naturally include an (expanded) interest in arguments$_2$.

Unfortunately Brockriede does not clearly distinguish arguments$_1$ and arguments$_2$. Yet I think it is obvious that a coherent description of everyday "argument" will turn on recognizing that distinction: it is one thing to describe or explain an argument$_1$ that someone makes, and something quite different to describe or explain an argument$_2$ that two persons are having.

But to recognize the distinction between arguments$_1$ and arguments$_2$ is only to have a starting-point for analysis. Very thorny issues immediately arise concerning how one is to delimit arguments$_1$ and arguments$_2$, and how one is to characterize the relation between arguments$_1$ and arguments$_2$. For example: Do we want to say that an argument$_2$ necessarily involves the exchange of arguments$_1$ and counter-arguments$_1$ (so that what we might call "squabbles" or "quarrels," in which—if we define them this way—arguments$_1$ are not exchanged, are not arguments$_2$)? Or are quarrels genuine arguments$_2$, simply different from arguments$_2$ in which arguments$_1$ are exchanged? Again, would we want to say that someone had made an argument$_1$ if no argument$_2$ took place (so that making an argument$_1$ definitionally involves having an argument$_2$)? Or are we willing allow that arguments$_1$ can be made even if no argument$_2$ ensues?

And beyond these initial questions, the distinction points to rather more direct inquiries concerning everyday argumentation: How are arguments$_2$ conducted in everyday life? What strategies are employed in making arguments$_1$? To what (if any) standards do naive social actors hold everyday arguments$_1$? Along what dimensions do arguments$_2$ differ (e.g., institutionalized vs. informal)?

I do not propose to answer these questions here. I am convinced, however, that questions such as these—questions predicated on the recognition of the distinction between arguments$_1$ and arguments$_2$—are central to the understanding of everyday "argument." The emerging shift from prescription to description in the study of argumentation will come to naught so long as theorists of argument do not recognize the two senses of "argument."

NOTES

[1] Now I suppose that, for each characterization I have just mentioned, it could be argued that the description could be extended to apply to both arguments$_1$ and arguments$_2$. This might well be true, but I think that in each case it would be clear that the characterization *was* an extended one, that some shift in the meaning of the characterization had occurred.

[2] These related distinctions are not quite as clear-cut as is the distinction between the two senses of argument. There are several reasons for this. One is that an arguer$_1$ (who is arguing$_1$, who is making arguments$_1$) will often at the same time be an arguer$_2$ (be arguing$_2$, be engaged in an argument$_2$). Another is that some might be inclined to say that a person who seems to be engaged in an argument$_2$ but who is not making arguments$_1$ is actually not engaged in an argument$_2$ at all, but rather is engaged in, say, a quarrel (that is, some might want to restrict the sense of "argument$_2$" so that quarrels and the like are excluded); this restricted sense of "argument$_2$" makes it necessarily true that an arguer$_2$ be an arguer$_1$. But surely one can be an arguer$_1$ without being an arguer$_2$, since one can make arguments$_1$ without becoming engaged in an argument$_2$ (if, for example, one's arguments$_1$ are ignored), and thus one can argue without arguing$_2$. So while these related distinctions are somewhat murky, they still seem to have some merit.

[3] Wayne Brockriede, "Where is Argument?" *Journal of the American Forensic Association,* 11 (1975), 179–82. See also Wayne Brockriede, "Rhetorical Criticism as Argument," *Quarterly Journal of Speech,* 50 (1974), 165–74.

[4] Brockriede, "Where is Argument?" p. 180.

[5] *Ibid.*

[6] *Ibid.,* pp. 180–81.

7 *Ibid.*, p. 181.

8 *Ibid.*

9 Taylor makes something like this argument in his *Metaphysics* (Englewood Cliffs, N.J.: Prentice-Hall, 1963), pp. 8–10.

10 Brockriede, "Where is Argument?" p. 181.

11 *Ibid.*

12 *Ibid.*

13 *Ibid.*

14 *Ibid.*, p. 182.

15 *Ibid.*

16 Stephen Toulmin, *The Uses of Argument* (Cambridge: Cambridge University Press, 1958), p. 257.

17 *Ibid.*

18 *Ibid.*, p. 258.

19 Joseph L. Cowan, "The Uses of Argument—An Apology for Logic," *Mind,* 73 (1964), 31.

20 John Turk Saunders and Donald F. Henze, *The Private-Language Problem* (New York: Random House, 1967), p. 19.

21 See, e.g., Ray L. Anderson and C. David Mortensen, "Logic and Marketplace Argumentation," *Quarterly Journal of Speech,* 53 (1967), 143–51; Glen E. Mills and Hugh G. Petrie, "The Role of Logic in Rhetoric," *Quarterly Journal of Speech,* 54 (1968), 260–67; David W. Shepard, "The Role of Logic," *Quarterly Journal of Speech,* 55 (1969), 310–12; Hugh G. Petrie, "Does Logic Have Any Relevance to Argumentation?" *Journal of the American Forensic Association,* 6 (1969), 55–60; C. David Mortensen and Ray L. Anderson, "The Limits of Logic," *Journal of the American Forensic Association,* 7 (1970), 71–78.

22 C. Perelman and L. Olbrechts-Tyteca, *The New Rhetoric,* trans. John Wilkinson and Purcell Weaver (Notre Dame: University of Notre Dame Press, (1969), esp. Part Three.

23 Richard E. Crable, *Argumentation as Communication: Reasoning with Receivers* (Columbus, Ohio: Charles E. Merrill, 1976).

On Defining Argument

ROBERT C. ROWLAND

Traditionally, argument has been treated as the means by which knowledge claims were justified. Physicists, chemists, historians, philosophers, and the experts in other fields discovered knowledge, while argumentation theorists provided the means of justification. Over the last twenty years this view of the function of argument has been replaced by one treating argument, particularly dialectical argument, as an independent means of discovering as well as of justifying knowledge. For example, Perelman characterizes the New Rhetoric, which is primarily a theory of argumentation, as "the indispensable instrument for philosophy."[1] Rescher argues that "Disputation and debate may be taken as a paradigmatic model for the general process of reasoning in the pursuit of truth."[2] Similarly, Ehninger treats argument as a method of discovering truth,[3] and Hardwig applies the method to moral questions.[4] Wenzel supports a similar perspective: "Argumentation is the methodology above all of rational undertaking."[5] A consensus among argumentation theorists is emerging which identifies argumentation as "the epistemological method."[6]

Some theorists go farther and claim that argument is not only the method through which individuals discover knowledge but is also the means through which a society creates social truths. In this view, social knowledge is created through dialectical interchange between arguers. Farrell writes: "Such argument actualizes social knowledge premises by requiring their conscious application to generalized human interests."[7] Goodnight makes a similar point: "Deliberative rhetoric is a form of argumentation through which citizens test and create social knowledge in order to uncover, assess, and resolve social problems."[8] The view that knowledge is created through argument has even been extended to science. For instance, Weimer argues that rhetoric subsumes both logic and dialectic and that it is through rhetoric that scientific truths are created.[9]

In sum, there is growing agreement that argumentation is more than a means of justifying knowledge claims, but is actually the means through which individuals, citizens, and even scientists discover knowledge. This agreement about the function served by argument would seem to bode well for the study of argumentation. In *Human Understanding*, Toulmin argues that agreement on disciplinary purpose is one of the pre-conditions for consistent progress in a field.[10] Unfortunately, while argumentation theorists are in general agreement about the function of argument, they agree about little else. Some treat argument as a propositional form while others see it as primarily a social process. There is similar disagreement about almost every other question at issue in the study of argument. The remainder of this essay will explore this disagreement and consider an alternative conceptualization of argumentation.

THE PROBLEM

The problem facing argumentation theorists today can be explained quite simply: there is no agreement on the defining characteristics of argument form, the theory which should undergird the study of argument, the proper method of evaluating that study, or even the meaning of the term argument itself. This disagreement is so fundamental that some theorists believe that others are not even studying argumentation. In order to sketch the breadth of the dispute I will focus on three aspects of it: the disagreements about form, theory, and methodology.

For centuries theorists focused on argument as a highly structured form of propositional logic. They treated the syllogism as the model for all argument and tested arguments by applying a set of precisely defined formal rules. Led by Toulmin,[11] contemporary argumentation theorists have moved away from this perspective, because they claim that a strictly formal model cannot explain real-world argument. Real-world argument is less formal, but far more interesting and important than the argument typically found in a syllogism. While most argumentation theorists have rejected a purely formal approach to argument, many still define argument in formal terms as a type of propositional discourse in which premises are combined in support of a claim. Thus, Natanson writes: "An argument consists of at least two propositions, one of them being held to follow from the other."[12] Although Toulmin rejects a definition of argument as a species of formal logic, his description of argument in the Toulmin model focuses on form.[13] Many other theorists also treat argument as a type of propositional discourse. As Rieke and Toulmin note, "the theory of argument taught still tends toward formal rules as the paradigm of all argument."[14]

While many theorists continue to treat argument as a thing, a type of propositional discourse, a growing number of theorists reject this interpretation in favor of a view of argument as a process.[15] In their view, argument is not a thing which people make, but a process which people go through with each other. For example, Willard rejects a definition of argument as a thing in favor of a definition of argument as a type of interaction.[16] He writes: "Formally, argument is a kind of interaction in which two or more people maintain what they construe to be mutually exclusive propositions."[17] In this view there are no formal characteristics which must be present before a certain interchange is labeled as an argument. Rather: "The more holistic view of human nature toward which the communication discipline seems to be moving invites us to regard 'argument' as simply any act of conjoining symbolic structures (propositions or otherwise) to produce new structures."[18] Here, Willard is primarily concerned with the process of argument: "Argument as process ought to be the organizing model [for argumentation theory]."[19] His process view of argument is so broad that virtually any discourse can be treated as argument. This raises difficulties I shall discuss later.

Recently, Hample has argued that argument is best defined not as a product or a process, but as a form of cognition.[20] In its most basic sense, then, argument is a form of reasoning.[21] Thus arguments are not found primarily in discourse or in interaction, but "within the people who are arguing."[22] Hample goes on to claim that the reasoning process includes a "thinking out" step, memory and retrieval, reconstruction, information processing, and creation.[23] In his view, the cognitive process of argument is an essential attribute of argument as both interaction and product and is thus the most basic definition of argument.

There is also widespread disagreement about the proper theoretical model to be applied to the study of argument. Some theorists continue to treat argument as the informal branch of logic. These theorists emphasize the value of logical theory for explaining argument.[24] At the same time, a number of theorists point to other sources for argumentation theory. For example, Willard focuses on the psychological dimensions of argument. He claims that argument "is a psychological phenomenon having no existence apart from the individuals who use it."[25] Willard borrows the man as scientist metaphor from Kelly, who argues that humans define the world in terms of construct systems which they use to gain knowledge and solve problems. Drawing on Kelly, Willard explains argument as the process of social interaction through which people come to understand the world. In his view, people argue when their construct systems interact. Although they share a constructivist approach to argument with Willard, both Kneupper and Burleson come to very different conclusions about the nature and function of argument.[26] Kneupper and Burleson treat argument as both a form of social interaction and a symbolic form possessing certain definable characteristics. They represent a middle ground between a formalist and a psychological approach to argument.

One might suspect that, even if there were disagreement about the defining characteristics of argument and the best theory for explaining it, theorists would agree about general methods of describing, explaining, and evaluating arguments. Surprisingly, there is little agreement even at the level of methodology. This disagreement relates primarily to two issues: the utility of models for describing argument and the legitimacy of evaluation as a goal of argumentation.

Until 1958, the dominant model used to describe argument was the syllogism. Argument theorists often described real-world arguments by first categorizing the premises in the argument and then placing them in syllogistic form. Since 1958 and the publication of *The Uses of Argument,* one main method for describing argument has been the Toulmin model.[27] Although the model is no longer as widely accepted as it once was, it is still used in many basic argumentation textbooks as a method of breaking down and categorizing arguments. Recently, the use of the Toulmin model in particular and of models in general has been challenged. Willard argues that the Toulmin model is too simplistic to be useful.[28] In his view, three models are needed, one each for the hearer, the arguer, and the discourse itself, in order to describe an argument adequately. Willard also claims that the Toulmin model misleads the critic by de-emphasizing the importance of situational and psychological factors in discourse. The model is, he claims, too simple to produce a useful description of real-world argument. Not only does Willard attack the value of the Toulmin model, and by implication any other model for categorizing argument, but he also argues that a critic should not focus mainly on texts in the descriptive process. The problem with texts, according to Willard, is that they contain only part of the data found in real-world argument. They cut the critic off from the social situation in which the argument occurred and from non-discursive communication, which he believes is an essential element in argument. Willard writes: "I think it intuitively obvious that all kinds of communication may be construed along discursive and/or non-discursive lines and that arguments, because they are a kind of communication, reflect the same duality."[29] He goes on to argue that non-linguistic communication plays an important part in argument[30] and is no less rational than strictly propositional discourse.[31]

In addition to the disagreement about the proper methodology for describing argument, there is also disagreement about what to do once that description has been completed. For most traditional argumentation theorists, the next step was obvious; after describing the argument you evaluated it.[32] Thus Toulmin argues: "If I'm talking about arguments, I am concerned with the appraisal of argument, whether or not some arguments are stronger than others, or in better taste than others."[33] This view has been defended in a number of recent essays.[34] Willard has called the evaluative focus of argument studies into question by building a case for a purely descriptive approach to argument criticism. He argues that the standards usually used to evaluate arguments aren't useful. For example, even an argument built on inconsistent assumptions may be true in some situations. His conclusion is that "the form of an argument guarantees neither its truth nor its moral worth."[35] Willard also argues that in principle there can be no ultimately justifiable standards for argument evaluation. The problem is that any proposed standard for evaluating an argument must itself be justified. And in turn that standard must be justified by another standard, and so on. This leads to an infinite regress out of which the critic cannot break.[36] Based on this reasoning, Willard rejects evaluation altogether in favor of description as the goal of the study of argument.[37] In sum, while many critics treat evaluation as an essential element in argument criticism, Willard and others warn that evaluation is inherently unjustifiable.

At this point, the problem facing argumentation theorists should be obvious. There is disagreement about the goal of argument criticism and the proper method of attaining that goal. Nor is there agreement about the theoretical presuppositions upon which the study of argument should be built. Finally, there is no agreement about the defining characteristics of argument itself. Some treat argument as an interpersonal process, while others define it in purely formal terms. It seems that the one point upon which nearly all critics agree is the epistemic function of argument. Yet, this very agreement raises questions. If critics do not agree on the definition or method of analyzing argument how can they agree on its function? Something deserving to be called argument seems to exist and to justify detailed examination philosophically and otherwise. But until some agreement can be reached about what "argument" and "argumentation" are, there can scarcely be scholarly dialogue that is clear.

THE ANSWER

The problem facing theorists studying argumentation is a definitional one. I believe the way in which most theorists have approached defining an "argument" has been self-defeating. The theorists have generally reasoned from what they believed were typical examples of argument to the defining characteristics of "argument." Traditionalists have treated propositional discourse as representative of all argument, which has led other scholars such as Willard to object that this way of defining what argument is ignores the features of ordinary-language social interaction that certainly occur wherever communication can fairly be called "argumentation."[38]

It is not possible to develop an adequate theory of argument by working from allegedly typical examples to theory. This approach will not work because there is no way to identify a typical example drawn from the class "argument" without first knowing what argument is. It does Willard no good to argue that non-discursive argument is more typical than is propositional argument. One has to know what the term "argument" itself means before we can evaluate whether non-discursive or propositional argument is more typical. Argumentation theorists have developed very different definitions of argument because they have treated it as a thing in the same sense that a table is a thing. Argument is a concept which has no existence apart from our definitions of it. Arguments as such do not exist in the real world. They are concepts which come into existence only after we define them.

Here, Richard Robinson's distinction between real and nominal definitions[39] is relevant. According to Robinson, some definitions are about things (the definition of the characteristics of a certain animal) while other definitions are about words or concepts. The definition of argument fits in the second category. The definition of a thing may be evaluated by comparing it to the thing, but the definition of a concept can be evaluated only by considering the function of the concept and asking how well a particular definition serves that function. It is pointless to argue about whether typical arguments are discursive or non-discursive, verbal or non-verbal. The answer to these disputes is inherent in the definition of argument which one chooses.

I have argued that to be useful a definition of argument must be nominal or stipulative. If I am correct, the next task is to discover how such a stipulative definition can be produced. Here it is important to recall the one point upon which nearly all argumentation theorists are agreed, the epistemic function of argument. This agreement on purpose should be treated as a useful clue in defining argument. If the function of argument is to produce knowledge for individuals and society then any definition of the concept should explain that function. The theorist should begin with the assumption that there is some symbolic form out there which serves epistemic and justificatory functions, and reason back to the characteristics which allow a form to serve those functions. Here, the key idea is that form and structure are shaped by function.

There is some support for the view that argumentative form follows function. In a number of recent essays it has been argued that fields of argument are shaped by their social functions.[40] In this view, the force which unifies a given field is the shared problem-solving purpose of a group of arguers. The arguers in the field choose a subject area, argument form, set of evaluative criteria, disciplinary organization, and so on because they believe that those characteristics will best fulfill their purposes. Thus, precise evaluative standards, competitive procedures, and a high degree of formality have developed in law because those characteristics are thought necessary to achieve justice and balance the rights of the individual and society. In science, by contrast, where the purpose is to attain scientific truth, informal procedures and mathematically precise evaluative standards are the norm because they best fulfill that purpose. In both cases form follows function. If the characteristics of various fields of argument can be traced to the shared purposes energizing arguers in the area, it is reasonable to suspect that the general characteristics shared by all argument may also be traced to shared purpose, in this case the general epistemic purpose apparently served by all argument.

In sum, a good definition of argument should explain the form (whether as interaction or product) and function of argument, as well as the link between form and function. In addition to defining what argument is it should define what argument is not. In other words, any definition of argument should distinguish arguments from other symbolic forms. If all communication can be considered argument then the term argument lacks any independent meaning.[41]

It should be possible to begin the process of defining argument by focusing on its epistemic purpose. However, it is not enough to say simply that argument is epistemic. Argument serves two related epistemic functions: justification and discovery. Much argument serves the function of justifying previous conclusions. A teacher justifies conclusions which he or she discovered in studying a subject. A scientist justifies conclusions drawn from an experiment. It might appear that the justificatory and epistemic functions are independent, and it is true that an arguer discovers no new knowledge when he or she justifies a claim. However, justificatory argument can be classified as epistemic when it produces new knowledge in the audience. Here it should be noted that while argument is *an* epistemic method it is not *the* epistemic method. Knowledge may be discovered through other means than argument. Willard has built a compelling case supporting intuition as a means of discovering moral and empirical truths.[42] However, while knowledge may be discovered through intuition or other non-argumentative methods, it is through argument that this knowledge is transmitted. Absent telepathy or some other method of directly sharing my intuitions, I rationally persuade you to accept the knowledge I discovered via intuition, by going through a process of justification. The method of rational justification is what constitutes and distinguishes argument. It may be rational for me to believe my own intuitions simply because I feel them to be true, but it is rational for me to accept someone else's intuitions only if good arguments support them.

In addition to justification, argument is an independent method of discovering knowledge. This discovery process occurs in dialectical argument when an arguer tests his or her claims against competing claims. It is the give and take of the dialectical process which reveals new truths. When I am forced to answer your arguments against my position, I may discover that I am wrong or be forced to modify my beliefs. Alternatively, I may convince you that you are wrong.

To this point, I have claimed that the method of rationally solving problems is argument. Through argument I may justify a previous position or discover the answer to a previously unanswered problem. The next step in securing a functional definition of argument is to identify the characteristics which allow argument to serve this rational function. The answer is obvious: argument solves problems by providing reasons for a particular view and by testing those reasons against competing positions. The epistemic purpose of argument requires arguers to support their positions with reasons and evidence and to test those reasons against competing reasons and evidence. It is the reliance on reason-giving which distinguishes argument from other symbolic forms and makes it rational. At this point, argument can be defined in relatively simple terms. Argument is discourse in which people attempt to solve problems rationally by supporting their claims with reasons and evidence.[43]

It might seem that this view rejects any analysis of argument as a process in favor of an exclusively formal definition of argument. However, a closer look reveals that the proposed definition treats argument as both a form and a process. As a form, argument is that type of discourse in which reasons and evidence are presented in support of claims. An individual uses the formal characteristics of argument in order to justify a claim to an audience. This represents a unilateral application of argument; there is no give and take. In argument as process, an individual tests his or her claims against the claims of other arguers. Alternatively, a single individual may engage in what might be called an internal dialectic, in which he or she tests every claim against counter claims. Argument as process occurs as long as all of the individuals in a dispute support their claims with reasons and evidence. As soon as one party or another refuses to support a position with reason and evidence, or refuses to answer the arguments of the other side, the dispute ceases to be an argument. The process of argument occurs when people produce arguments as product against each other.[44] We cease to argue as soon as we move away from the resources of argument as product.

This explanation of the relationship between argument as product and argument as process is appealing in its simplicity. The characteristic which defines all argument, reason-giving, is also the characteristic which, when applied in a dialectical situation, has the potential to produce new knowledge. Arguments as product and process are really two sides of the same coin. That coin is human rationality, for, as Weimer argues, the defining characteristic of rationality is the ability to respond to counter-arguments and support a claim with a reason.[45] Argument is, then, a unit of discourse. It is also a process. Neither sense is more basic; they are inextricably connected.

The view developed here also clarifies Hample's claim that argument is best defined as a cognitive process. At one level Hample is clearly correct that arguments have no existence outside of the human brain. We would not know of arguments were it not for the brain, and the enthymematic nature of argument means that we interpret arguments through our cognitive structures. However, this same point could be made about any human creation. Language, art, and music all require cognitive interpretation. We would not know of their existence, were it not for our minds. Since humans know the world through their brains, all human constructions are in one sense cognitive. However, in another sense arguments do exist in the world as a form of discourse. The point is that, for argument to serve its epistemic function, a reason or group of reasons must be present. And since argument is a species of communication, that reason or those reasons must be symbolic and thus analyzable apart from a consideration of cognition. Hample is right that the reasons in an argument are interpreted by the human brain, but just as it sometimes makes sense to talk about the notes played by a violinist as opposed to the psychological responses of the audience to those notes, it also may make sense to discuss the reasons and evidence presented in a unit of discourse.

Moreover, the breadth of Hample's definition of argument undercuts its value. If argument is defined to include information processing, retrieval, creative energies, and so forth, then the concept has become so loose that it is not very useful. In addition, when it actually comes to studying argument, Hample admits that the critic must return to texts of some kind.[46] At that point the independent value of his cognitive view of argument is undercut. Argument serves its epistemic function by generating reasoning, but it is the symbolic form of argument that allows it to serve this function. Reasoning and argument are closely related but not identical concepts.

IMPLICATIONS

The functionalist approach to defining argument, which I have sketched, has a number of important implications for argumentation theory. One of the primary benefits of the approach is that it recognizes that argument is an inherently normative concept. We argue in order to solve problems rationally. If we don't argue then we give up on rationality itself. A purely descriptive approach to argument ignores its social function. In a recent essay, Willard cites the opinion of Elliot that "evaluation is a pleasant avocation of critics; and like other human activities it must be earned. No human has a right to evaluate another unless he convincingly can argue that he fully understands that other and he can defend his standards."[47] Willard goes on to defend description as the primary goal of argument study. Here, Willard misunderstands the social function of argument and argument criticism. A literary critic can focus exclusively upon description because the social function of art is to create aesthetic pleasure. Description by itself can enhance that pleasure. Evaluation is not needed. But the social function of argument is different from that of art. Argument is the method by which we evaluate all knowledge. Consequently, argument is inherently normative.

The rational function of argument makes evaluation a necessary component of any adequate theory of argument. When humans attempt to solve problems they don't want just any solution, but the best solution. Thus, it is imperative that we be able to distinguish the relative quality of the arguments which we produce to solve those problems. This analysis leads to the commonsense conclusion that some arguments are better than others and that it is possible to distinguish which ones are better.[48] It is easy to imagine a public debate in which one speaker advocates handgun control based on five or six compelling reasons, while a representative of the National Rifle Association says simply, "Only Commies and queers are against guns." In that situation it would be easy to evaluate the arguments for gun control as superior to the one against it. Although this example is extreme, it is revealing. It suggests that in at least some situations it is possible to evaluate the relative quality of competing arguments. Once it is admitted that evaluation of some type is both feasible and useful, it is only a matter of identifying the most rational standards for evaluation and adapting them to specific circumstances.

A second implication drawn from the functionalist view of argument relates to the proper methodology for analyzing arguments. When viewed functionally, an argument is a claim supported by a reason and evidence. In formal terms, the basic triad of the Toulmin model serves as a good definition of argument. Here,

I do not deny that real world arguments are often complex. Such arguments may be supported by any number of reasons and bits of evidence. Moreover, much of the support for an argument may be implicit. In an enthymeme, an arguer draws upon shared values or social knowledge to support a claim. It also may be difficult for the critic to distinguish between the reason and data presented in support of a claim. However, although it is often difficult to break an argument into its component parts, this in no way denies the utility of models for describing arguments. Models such as the Toulmin model may be difficult to apply, but if the essential form of argument is that of a claim supported by a reason and evidence, they can serve as useful, if flawed, descriptive devices. Here, it is important to understand that the critic of argument should not be concerned with all the persuasive appeals presented in a speech or essay. Nor should the critic be concerned with why an audience is influenced in a particular way or with the motives behind a speaker's actions. The argument critic should be concerned with argument as the rational method of solving problems. He or she is concerned with the reasons and data supporting a conclusion and not with the other aspects of the discourse or situation. In this regard Willard's objections to the Toulmin model point to its limited value as a method of rhetorical criticism, but not necessarily deny its worth as a means of argument criticism. In addition, by focusing only on the descriptive value of the Toulmin model, Willard[49] ignores its most important function, as an evaluative tool. I suggest that the primary value of the Toulmin model is as a means of identifying weaknesses in arguments. By identifying possible rebuttals and by testing the material validity of an argument via a consideration of backing, the critic can evaluate some aspects of the overall worth of the argument.

A rationalistic definition of argument as a problem-solving device also illuminates the methodological dispute about the value of texts as sources of arguments. While a text is an imperfect record of an argument, most of the problems associated with texts lose their importance when it is understood that the argument critic is concerned primarily with the reasons and evidence presented in support of a claim, as opposed to other aspects of the discourse. Although a text may not reflect all of the motives of a speaker, the subtleties in a particular situation, or the non-verbal aspects of a speech, it will contain the reasons and evidence presented in support of a claim. It is those reasons and data which should be of concern to the argument critic.

The functionalist interpretation of argument also suggests a possible means of resolving some of the issues in the discursiveness dispute. Willard may well be correct that much communication is transmitted via non-discursive symbols. He also may be correct about the importance of non-verbal communication. However, the primary function of argument is to resolve problems through reason-giving. And reasons by their very nature are symbolic.[50] In answering this objection Willard points to the crucial role which non-discursive elements play in shaping the reasons behind an action and notes that people often argue for reasons that are explicitly stated in their discourse. He suggests that a definition of argument as a form of propositional discourse ignores the role of such non-discursive reasons in argument.[51] Here, Willard trades on ambiguity in the meaning of the word "reason." In discussing non-discursive argument he in effect defines a reason as the motive behind an action. In this regard, he is clearly correct that non-discursive elements often function as motives or illuminate an arguer's motives. However, Willard proves that non-discursive elements act as reasons only by choosing an improper definition of the term. In argument, a reason functions not as a motive but as a justification, an inference rule supporting a claim. While non-discursive elements may function as motives, they cannot function as rational justification for a claim unless they are translated into a shared symbol system. Reason-giving in the sense of justification is by its very nature symbolic. It is interesting that Willard has yet to cite an example of a non-discursive element that functions as a reason in the sense of justification. Non-discursive forms such as art or music may be perfectly rational and may be important forms of communication, but they cannot function as reasons without being translated into a shared symbol system. The final movement of Beethoven's Ninth Symphony could be used as part of an argument supporting international cooperation, but in such an argument it would not be the notes of the score that were important, but the link between the symphony and the United Nations.

Some might object that by limiting the definition of reason to a rule of inference or justification for a claim I arbitrarily limit the study of argumentation. However, it should be remembered that a good definition of argument both explains the link between form and function and distinguishes between argument and other forms of discourse. By defining reason to include motive as well as justification, Willard produces a definition of argument that is so broad that it is useless. All discourse involves reason-giving, if a reason is defined as a motive. Moreover, such a definition ignores the rational function of argument. Argument serves as epistemic method because in it reasons (in the sense of justifications) are presented in support of claims. Absent reason-giving, discourse cannot solve problems rationally and thus shouldn't be treated as argument. Against this view, Willard argues that since argument is a form of communication, all forms of communication must be present in it.[52] Willard's claim is problematic. The fact that some communication is non-discursive does not mean that all forms of communication (in this case argument) must include non-discursive elements.

Finally, it is important to recognize that the non-discursiveness question is not an empirical issue. I am arguing that by definition argument involves reason-giving and that reason-giving is necessarily symbolic. This view cannot be defeated by citing ordinary-language research showing that much discourse is non-discursive. My position does not deny the non-discursive element in communication, but only notes that non-discursive symbols cannot serve as reasons, absent translation into a shared symbol system, and therefore are not essential to an understanding of argument. The dispute is over the value of a stipulative definition of argument as a form of reason-giving discourse. I suggest that such a limited definition is more useful than the amorphous definitions proposed by Willard and others because it identifies the form and function of argument, explains the linkage between form and function, and distinguishes between argumentative and non-argumentative discourse.

The stipulative definition of argument which I have proposed suggests that the dispute over the importance of language in argument also may be resolved quite easily. Willard is quite correct that argument is not necessarily linguistic. However, argument is by its very nature symbolic, for the process of reason-giving requires a shared symbol system. As a result, most argument is carried on in language. Language is the most universal, precise, and powerful symbol system that humans possess.[53] Robinson explains how language facilitates argument:

> Words are the means to a knowledge of things. Without them an animal's knowledge is confined to his own unanalyzed memories and perceptions of

his own experience. Without them there is little analysis, little generalization, and no transmission of experience from one animal to another. When the cat comes home, he cannot tell you what he has seen. And this is not because he has no leisure, for the busy bees can tell each other that they have found honey; it is because he has no symbols. Without symbols history contracts into a plurality of incommunicable autobiographies, and science into each organism's private rules of thumb.[54]

Argument may be non-discursive or non-verbal, but in such cases it functions as argument only after translation into a discursive symbol system such as language.

The view of argument as a rational problem-solving agent also clarifies a number of other issues in argumentation. For example, Brockriede's list of defining characteristics of argument can be illuminated by considering how function shapes argument. According to Brockriede, six characteristics define argument:

1. An inferential leap from existing beliefs to the adoption of a new belief or to the reinforcement of an old one.
2. A perceived rationale to support that leap.
3. A choice among two or more competing claims.
4. A regulation of uncertainty.
5. A willingness to risk confrontation of a claim with peers.
6. A frame of reference shared optimally.[55]

While characteristics (1) and (2) correspond to the definition of the form of argument which I have presented, the remaining characteristics are not essential to defining argument. Instead, in characteristics (3) through (6) Brockriede identifies those situations in which productive argument is likely to occur. For example, in characteristic (3) Brockriede claims that people do not argue if there is only one option for action. His point is similar to Willard's claim that argument inherently involves disagreement. However, there are situations in which people support claims with reasons and evidence, even though they believe there is only one possible course of action. A group of committed Catholics might continue to build what I have defined as arguments, supporting the existence of God, although they were all in agreement about that issue. It makes sense to characterize such discourse as argument. Despite the absence of disagreement, the committed Catholics are supporting their claims with reasons and evidence. However, while disagreement is not a necessary aspect of argument it is usually the force which motivates people to argue. Similarly, "a regulation of uncertainty" is not a necessary aspect of every argument; it is a goal motivating arguers.

The final two characteristics identified by Brockriede—a willingness to risk confrontation and a shared frame of reference—also are not necessary attributes of argument. People often support their claims with reasons and evidence although they don't share a frame of reference or risk confrontation. When the Soviet and United States ambassadors to the United Nations engage in debate, they support their claims, but there is no risk of self and no shared frame of reference. Thus, characteristics (5) and (6) are not essential to the definition of argument. Rather, they are essential to the successful resolution of argument. Without a shared frame of reference and a willingness to risk the self, there is little chance of rationally resolving a dispute.

CONCLUSION

The functional approach to the study of argumentation is valuable because it provides a clear definition of the scope of argumentation. It recognizes that while all argument is rhetorical, not all rhetoric is argument. One danger associated with some recent work on argument is that the term argument itself becomes so broad that it loses all meaning. If argument is defined to include all disagreement, all comparison of construct systems, and all instances in which an individual believes that he or she is arguing then essentially all communication is argument.

A more useful definitional move is to treat argument as the symbolic form(s) we use to solve problems rationally. This implies that argument is the method of reason. Such a definition sets the limits of argumentation and defines the form of argument in relation to the function of arguing. Moreover, so to define argument recognizes the role of evaluation in the study of argument. Merely to describe an argument or set of arguments leaves their human significance out of consideration. Once the arguments of a speech, essay, or other verbal interaction have been described with accuracy, the next point of critical interest is naturally the arguments' relative quality as efforts to induce closure. The value of examining arguments is undercut if description becomes the only aim of criticism of argumentation. A socially satisfying definition of argument and a useful theory of argumentation must provide at least trained theorists with grounds for distinguishing between weak and strong arguments, as the functional definition does.

Some will perhaps object that the functional definition of argument for which I have contended restricts a student of argumentation to study of propositional discourse. This is true in the sense that my definition identifies reason-giving as a fundamental characteristic of argument, and reason-giving is propositional. On the other hand, an issue that needs clarification in theory of argument, as I have shown, is whether "argumentation" and "rhetoric" are to be considered synonymous. If so, the concept of "argument" becomes unnecessary; the concept of "rhetoric" is sufficient. My contention is that arguments occur *in* rhetoric and need to be recognized, described, and evaluated in light of their unique functional and formal features. Arguments cannot be understood by applying the same kinds of analysis as we would apply if, say, rhythm were our point of interest. Arguments are formally and functionally different from rhythmic patterns, situational constraints, levels of vocabulary, and the like—all features of rhetoric. If argument is taken to be the means by which humans rationally solve problems—or try to, arguments can be identified, described, and evaluated critically as part of the broader enterprise of identifying, describing, and evaluating rhetoric. Across centuries, people have believed there is such a process as trying to arrive at preferred conclusions by rational means, rather than by non-rational means. That process, I have argued, entails distinctive verbal forms appropriate to the function of the process. It is at least useful to give such purposeful forms and function a name. Traditionally and contemporaneously "argument" is philosophically and etymologically the appropriate name.

NOTES

1 Chaim Perelman, *The Realm of Rhetoric,* trans. William Klubach (Notre Dame: University of Notre Dame Press, 1982), 7.
2 Nicholas Rescher, *Dialectics: A Controversy-Oriented Approach to the Theory of Knowledge* (Albany: State University of New York, 1977), 46.

3 Douglas Ehninger, "Argument as Method: Its Nature, Its Limitations and Its Uses," *Speech Monographs* 37 (1970):101–10.

4 John Hardwig, "The Achievement of Moral Rationality," *Philosophy and Rhetoric* 6 (1973):171–85.

5 Joseph W. Wenzel, "In Defense of Criticism," 11. Paper presented at the Speech Communication Association Convention, Louisville, Kentucky, November 1982.

6 Wayne Brockriede, "Argument as Epistemological Method," in *Argumentation as a Way of Knowing,* ed. David A. Thomas (Annandale, Virginia: Speech Communication Association, 1980), 128. Also see Charles Arthur Willard, "Epistemological Functions of Argument Studies: A Constructivist/Interactionist View," in *Argumentation as a Way of Knowing,* 12; Walter R. Fisher, "Rationality and the Logic of Good Reasons," *Philosophy and Rhetoric* 13 (1980): 121; Robert L. Scott, "On Viewing Rhetoric as Epistemic," *Central States Speech Journal* 18 (1967): 13; Thomas B. Farrell, "Rhetorical Argument as Reduplication: The Epistemic Function," in *Argumentation as a Way of Knowing,* 102.

7 Farrell, "Rhetorical Argument as Reduplication," 106. Also see his "Knowledge, Consensus and Rhetorical Theory," *Quarterly Journal of Speech* 62 (1976):1–14.

8 Thomas Goodnight, "The Personal, Technical, and Public Spheres of Argument: A Speculative Inquiry into the Art of Public Deliberation," *Journal of the American Forensic Association* 18 (1982):214.

9 Walter B. Weimer, *Notes on the Methodology of Scientific Research* (Hillsdale, New Jersey: Lawrence Erlbaum Associates, 1979), 78, 84.

10 Stephen E. Toulmin, *Human Understanding: The Collective Use and Evolution of Concepts* (Princeton: Princeton University Press, 1979), 359–60.

11 Toulmin, *The Uses of Argument* (Cambridge: Cambridge University Press, 1958).

12 Maurice Natanson, "The Claims of Immediacy," in *Philosophy, Rhetoric, and Argumentation,* ed. Henry W. Johnstone, Jr. and Maurice Natanson (University Park: The Pennsylvania State University Press, 1965), 11.

13 For a treatment of the Toulmin model emphasizing form see Douglas Ehninger and Wayne Brockriede, "Toulmin on Argument: An Interpretation and Application," *Quarterly Journal of Speech* 46 (1960):44–53.

14 Richard D. Rieke and Stephen E. Toulmin, "Problem Statement and Tentative Agenda," in *Argumentation as a Way of Knowing,* 5.

15 See Daniel J. O'Keefe, "Two Concepts of Argument," *Journal of the American Forensic Association* 13 (1977):121–28.

16 Recently, Willard defined argument as "social comparison processes which undergird knowledge." See his *Argumentation and the Social Grounds of Knowledge* (University, Alabama: University of Alabama Press, 1983), ix and 21; and "A Reformulation of the Concept of Argument: The Constructivist/Interactionist Foundations of a Sociology of Argument," *Journal of the American Forensic Association* 14 (1978):126. Future references will be cited as "A Reformulation."

17 Willard, "A Reformulation," 125. Also see Scott Jacobs and Sally Jackson, "Conversational Argument," in *Advances in Argumentation Theory and Research,* ed. J. Robert Cox and Charles Arthur Willard (Carbondale: Southern Illinois University Press, 1982), 205–37.

18 Willard. "On The Utility of Descriptive Diagrams for the Analysis and Criticism of Argument," *Communication Monographs* 43 (1976):317. Future references will be cited as "On the Utility."

19 Willard, "A Reformulation," 124.

20 Dale Hample, "A Third Perspective on Argument," *Philosophy and Rhetoric* 18 (1985):1.

21 Ibid., 16.

22 Ibid., 3.

23 Ibid.

24 See Glen E. Mills and Hugh G. Petrie, "The Role of Logic in Rhetoric," *Quarterly Journal of Speech* 54 (1968):260–67; Petrie, "Does Logic Have Any Relevance to Argumentation?," *Journal of the American Forensic Association* 6 (1968):55–60. Any number of informal logic texts point to the relevance of logical theory to the study of argument. Even Kahane makes reference to traditional logical theory. See Howard Kahane, *Logic and Contemporary Rhetoric,* 3d ed. (Belmont, California: Wadsworth, 1980).

25 Willard, "On the Utility," 313. Also see his "The Epistemic Functions of Argument: Reasoning and Decision-Making From a Constructivist/Interactionist Point of View, pt. 1," *Journal of the*

American Forensic Association 15 (1979):169–91; "The Epistemic Functions of Argument: Reasoning and Decision-Making From a Constructivist/Interactionist Point of View, pt. 2," *Journal of the American Forensic Association* 15 (1979):211–19; "Propositional Argument is to Argument What Talking About Passion is to Passion," *Journal of the American Forensic Association* 16 (1979):21–27; "The Status of the Non-Discursiveness Thesis," *Journal of the American Forensic Association* 17 (1981);190–214; and "A Note on Burleson's 'Final Comment,'" *Journal of the American Forensic Association* 18 (1982):178–81. Future references to these essays will be cited as "Epistemic, pt. 1 [or] pt. 2," "Propositional," and "SNDT."

26 See for instance Brant R. Burleson, "On the Analysis and Criticism of Arguments: Some Theoretical and Methodological Considerations," *Journal of the American Forensic Association* 15 (1979):137–47 (future references to this work will be cited as "On the Analysis"); Burleson, "The Place of Non-Discursive Symbolism, Formal Characterizations, and Hermeneutic in Argument Analysis and Criticism," *Journal of the American Forensic Association* 16 (1980):222–31; and Burleson, "On Willard's Non-Discursiveness Thesis: A Final Comment," *Journal of the American Forensic Association* 18 (1982):175–78; Charles W. Kneupper, "On Argument and Diagrams," *Journal of the American Forensic Association* 14 (1978); 181–86; Kneupper, "Paradigms and Problems: Alternative Constructivist/ Interactionist Implications for Argumentation," *Journal of the American Forensic Association* 15 (1979):220–27; Kneupper, "Argument: A Social Constructivist Perspective," *Journal of the American Forensic Association* 17 (1981):183–89; Kneupper, "The Status of the Discursiveness Thesis," *Journal of the American Forensic Association* 18 (1982):161–74.

27 Recently a number of theorists have proposed alternative means of describing arguments. See for instance, Michael Scriven, *Reasoning* (New York: McGraw Hill, 1976), 41–44, 79–82.

28 Willard, "On the Utility."

29 Willard, "Argument as Non-Discursive Symbolism," *Journal of the American Forensic Association* 14 (1978):190. Also see his *Argumentation and the Social Grounds of Knowledge,* 50.

30 Willard, "Argument as Non-Discursive Symbolism," 187–93; also see his "SNDT," and *Argumentation and the Social Grounds of Knowledge,* 66.

31 Willard, "Epistemological Functions of Argument Studies," 18; Willard "On the Utility," 315.

32 Traditional argumentation texts include lists of fallacies to facilitate the evaluation of arguments. See for instance Nicholas Rescher, *Introduction to Logic* (New York: St. Martin's Press, 14), 56–92.

33 Stephen E. Toulmin, "Transcript of Closed Discussion," In *Argumentation as a Way of Knowing,* 163.

34 See Robert C. Rowland, "On Argument Evaluation," *Journal of the American Forensic Association* 21 (1985):123–32.

35 Willard, "Argument Fields, Sociologies of Knowledge, and Critical Epistemologies," 9. Paper presented at the Speech Communication Association Convention, Louisville, Kentucky, November 1982.

36 Willard, "Argument Fields," in *Advances in Argumentation Theory and Research,* 27–28. Also see Weimer, 4–6. For a somewhat similar view see Walter R. Fisher, "Toward a Logic of Good Reasons," *Quarterly Journal of Speech* 64 (1978):377.

37 See Willard. "Epistemological Functions of Argument Studies," 9, 11–13, 32.

38 See Willard, "SNDT," 211, 212; Willard, *Argumentation and the Social Grounds of Knowledge,* 31, 36–38.

39 Richard Robinson, *Definition* (Oxford: Oxford University Press, 1954), 16.

40 Robert C. Rowland, "Argument Fields," in *Dimensions of Argument: Proceedings of the Second Summer Conference on Argumentation,* ed. George Ziegelmuller and Jack Rhodes (Annandale, Virginia: Speech Communication Association, 1981), 56–79; Robert C. Rowland, "The Influence of Purpose on Fields of Argument," *Journal of the American Forensic Association* 18 (1982):228–45; Rowland, "Purpose and Field Theory: A Non-Justificationist Approach." Paper presented at the Speech Communication Association Convention, Louisville, Kentucky, November 1982.

41 For a similar position see Kneupper, "Paradigms and Problems," 221; Burleson, "On the Analysis," 138.

42 Willard, "SNDT," 199–200.

43 See Burleson, "On the Analysis," 141–42.

44 This view is similar to that of Brockriede; see Wayne Brockriede, "Characteristics of Argument and Arguing," *Journal of the American Forensic Association* 13 (1977):129.

45 Weimer defines rationality in critical terms. A rational human is ready to support any of his or her positions against criticism. It is the capacity to answer any criticism with reasons which makes humans rational. See Weimer, 40, 47, 48.
46 Hample, 11.
47 Willard, "SNDT," 213.
48 For a more developed version of this argument see Rowland, "On Argument Evaluation."
49 Willard, "On the Utility," 309.
50 Kneupper, "On Argument and Diagrams," 182.
51 Willard, "Epistemic, pt. 2," 211–17.
52 Willard, "SNDT," 190.
53 Kneupper defends a similar position, "The Status of the Discursiveness Thesis," 164–65. Also see Scriven, 2–3; S. Morris Engel, *With Good Reason: An Introduction to Informal Fallacies* (New York: St. Martin's Press, 1976), 2–3; Graeme S. Halford, *The Development of Thought* (Hillsdale, New Jersey: Lawrence Erlbaum Associates, 1982), 4, 35; Gillian Cohen, *The Psychology of Cognition* (London: Academic Press, 1977), 94, 122–23.
54 Robinson, 27–28.
55 See Wayne Brockriede, "Where is Argument?" *Journal of the American Forensic Association* 11 (1975):179–82.

A Concept Divided:
Ralph Johnson's Definition of Argument

CHRISTOPHER W. TINDALE

At the heart of *Manifest Rationality* (2000) (henceforth *MR*) lies a rich and provocative concept of argument:

> An argument is a type of discourse or text—the distillate of the practice of argumentation—in which the arguer seeks to persuade the Other(s) of the truth of a thesis by producing the reasons that support it. In addition to this illative core, an argument possesses a dialectical tier in which the arguer discharges his dialectical obligations (168).

This definition underlies the entire manifest rationality project and, in its author's mind, provides the 'adequate conceptualization of argument' (142) that Informal Logic has lacked. Part of its provocative nature is to be seen in one of the stronger claims associated with it: that 'an argument without a dialectical tier is not an argument' (176). From this it follows that a vast number of the common examples in textbooks are to be excluded from the extension of 'argument' (along with scientific theories, advertisements, and proofs—168), or at least these should be recognized as no more than 'proto-arguments' (170).

But it is my contention that the concept of argument in *MR* is hampered by an internal tension between the product an argument is and the process it captures, and while the project itself suggests a way to resolve this tension, such a resolution is still in the future. My strategy for uncovering this tension will be to look at five distinct ideas that this concept of argument contains.

1. 'AN ARGUMENT IS A TYPE OF DISCOURSE OR TEXT . . .'

In a limiting definition, this is the first limitation. Johnson explicitly values the written over the spoken: 'My theory is focused on argumentative text rather than argumentative speech' (35). This is reiterated later where he distinguishes his approach from that of Habermas and defends the choice by noting that 'written argument is the most stable form of argument and therefore a more suitable candidate as the foundation of the practice' (156). In her Preface to *The Rise of Informal Logic* (1996), Trudy Govier elaborates on this in more detail:

> [Johnson] believes that for the analysis and evaluation of arguments, the written text should be the paradigm, the primary object. A written argument is more fixed and stable than an oral one. It is, notably, a more public object, being available to a greater number of people. Furthermore, greater care has typically gone into constructing a written argument—it is not simply 'off the cuff.' Similarly, responses to written arguments are more thorough and more carefully developed. If one develops a sound theory for written argument, one may go on to determine whether and how that theory may be adapted so as to apply to oral arguments (xii–xiii).

Several things might be observed about Johnson's preference for the written:

(i) At first glance, Johnson seems to have merely marked out his territory, distancing himself from the proposals of other informal logicians and argumentation theorists like Gilbert (1997), Groarke (1996), and Willard (1989). The kisceral, visual, or gestural will not be admitted. This might merely be a consequence of viewing argumentation as rational persuasion rather than, say, as communication (Johnson, 1998, n. 1). But here we are dealing with a definition of argument which purports to stipulate what an argument *is* or should be. To say of written argument, however, that it is the *most* stable form (my emphasis) still acknowledges these other forms, banished now beyond the margins of the definition. But in so doing, it cloaks them in vagueness. Should they count, and to what extent? What is unstable about them? This confusion is compounded by Johnson's acknowledgement that oral argument precedes written argument 'both in sociocultural and personal history'. But this 'oral argument' cannot be argument in the sense of the adopted definition.

(ii) This concern carries over to the remarks on argumentative practice. Written argument is a developed and refined artifact, somewhat artificial. This seems at odds with the calls early in the book for the need to recover 'argument' from its recent mathematization and reinvest it with its natural meanings. But, at the same time, Johnson's ideal of 'practitioners' is philosophers and logicians (166). These are dedicated rather than casual participants in the practice. They set the standard. By contrast the casual practices of everyday arguers and their audiences are secondary.

(iii) Finally, and following on from both the previous two points, we might reflect on Govier's remark that 'If one develops a sound theory for written argument, one may go on to determine whether and how that theory may be adopted so as to apply to oral arguments' (1996, p. xiii). This will give us a top down situation, bringing practice into conformity with theory, rather than the reverse: theory based on the underlying practice. Johnson may reasonably respond that the written argument is part, the central part, of traditional practice. But, still, what he promotes is the practice of specialists and we might wonder whether (a) the practices of everyday casual arguers and audiences *could* be brought into line, and (b) whether something would be lost in doing so.

In commenting on an earlier draft of this paper[1] Johnson reiterated his belief that philosophers produce not just better arguments, but products that 'more truly reflect the nature of argument'. And he draws the analogy between our project of recognizing and appraising arguments and what goes on when we reflect on the paintings of skilled artists or the novels of the better novelists. But this only serves to stress my concern. We might agree that philosophers produce better arguments (generally) and recognize exceptional novels. But when we are interested in the *nature* of the novel, or of argument, surely it is instructive to look at the *range* of things that pass for each without prejudging what is central and what is not? I leave aside the more thorny question of how we decide philosophers produce better arguments without already having a standard (philosophers' arguments) to assist in such judgements.

2. 'THE DISTILLATE OF THE PRACTICE OF ARGUMENTATION . . .'

This distillate, this pure product, that is argument is essentially linked to argumentation and cannot be understood without it (12, 144, 154). Johnson invites us to view argument within the practice of argumentation, 'which includes as components (a) the process of arguing, (b) the agents engaged in the practice (the arguer and the Other), and (c) the argument itself as a product' (154). Indeed, these are dynamic relations, including the distilled product. Yet to speak in these latter terms for (c) is to suggest something that is finished. But to place it alongside (a), the process, suggests something that is yet to be completed. This is the first glimpse of a suggested tension between process and product. As much as Johnson encourages us to see them as interrelated, it is the nature of that interrelation, encompassed by the remainder of the definition, that appears particularly elusive.

3. 'IN WHICH THE ARGUER SEEKS TO PERSUADE THE OTHER(S) OF THE TRUTH OF A THESIS BY PRODUCING THE REASONS THAT SUPPORT IT.'

Here we find the function component of the definition, the best accounts needing to link structure with function. In various forms throughout the book, Johnson offers two components of this purpose. The following quotes capture these:

(a) By the term 'argument,' I understand an intellectual product . . . that seeks to persuade rationally (24).
(b) the fundamental purpose, although admittedly not the only one, is to arrive at the truth about some issue (158).

Note that the definition itself doesn't require that the purpose be fulfilled: 'good' arguments may fail to persuade the Other(s) of the truth of the thesis. Then again, as the first quote would suggest, the tone of discussion throughout the book emphasizes and values *rational* persuasion over any other. This is the feature that will distinguish the better arguments (189).

Hence, the *ad baculum* would not be considered an argument 'because here the reasoning is being used to threaten someone' (145). It isn't a matter of it being a bad move in argument, Johnson suggests; it is simply a non-argument. We might suspect that the person advancing the *ad baculum* is trying to persuade someone of the truth of a thesis (you should/should not do X) by producing reasons (the consequences of doing X or not). Thus, it would meet a strict reading of the definition of argument. But Johnson *means* the definition to be understood within the context of the manifest rationality project, where the argumentation is 'patently and openly rational' to the participants (163). The audience of the *ad baculum* would not consider the threat rational, and so it does not qualify as an argument. Note here how much depends upon the audience.

At several points Johnson discusses the distinctions between rhetoric and logic (here understood as informal logic). Chief among these is the difference in purpose. Rhetoric aims at effectiveness rather than truth and completeness. That is, if there is an objection to the argument of which the arguer is aware, from the point of view of rhetoric he or she has no obligation to deal with it; the argument is effective without it. But from the point of view of logic, the arguer is obligated to deal with it: 'Because even though the audience does not know of the objection, and so the arguer could get by without dealing with it, the argument will be more rational in substance and appearance if it can meet the test of this objection' (270). This requires a much stronger interpretation of Johnson's concept of argument. Because this implies that rational persuasion can be by degrees and the *more rational,* the better the argument. This could seem just a point about evaluation, that better arguments have better reasons or are more complete. But the implication for the definition is more than this: it suggests that rationality is a goal in itself. That, given the dual nature of the purpose I identified in (a) and (b), while (b) is more evident in the definition, (a) is the larger purpose that Johnson promotes. The *ad baculum* fails to be simply a bad argument because its attempts at persuasion are not rational (and we should add) *'to both parties'.* The character of manifest rationality which is not explicit in the definition of argument turns out to completely underlie it.

4. 'IN ADDITION TO THIS ILLATIVE CORE . . .'

An argument has a core, of premises and conclusion, or reasons 'produced to justify a target proposition' (160). This illative core[2] is what most definitions have in common, and hence there might be little that needs to be said about it. For Johnson, it comprises only the first tier of the argument and it is the second, dialectical, tier that is unique to the definition and would seem to warrant more discussion. But the nature of the illative core must be reflected somehow in the criteria used to evaluate it. What is of interest is the addition of a fourth criterion to the standard three that have characterized Johnson's early work. His four criteria, then, are relevance, sufficiency, acceptability and truth (180). The question that should arise for us is why, having been satisfied for so long with the first three, Johnson has seen the need to (re)introduce the fourth as a criterion for argument evaluation? Why is acceptability no longer able to do the job alone?

Truth is important as a criterion of premise adequacy in part because Johnson conceives argumentation as a method for getting at truth. Insofar as people agree with this goal, then the criterion itself may be non-controversial. While the issue of truth as a criterion for premise adequacy requires far greater consideration than can be given to it here, there should be some concern about how this concept is being used in *MR*, about, indeed, *which* concept of truth is at work.

Johnson clearly holds that a premise is true or false in itself (and not in relation to an audience). In his discussion of Hamblin, he imagines two members of an audience, Brilliant and Dull. One finds an argument good because he accepts certain of its premises, and the other finds it bad because he does not. Johnson observes:

> If we take Hamblin's approach, we will say that the argument was a good one
> for Brilliant but not a good one for Dull. We cannot, it seems, ask whether

the argument is a good one in itself, a good one *simpliciter*, or a good one objectively. In other words, acceptance as a criterion leads to the subjectivity and relativity of appraisal of argument (194).

Johnson wants both to ask whether an argument is good in itself and have the answer make sense. He raises the same 'problem' of relativism in defending his position against Robert Pinto (278), and insists later that the fact that people may be justified in accepting a bad argument does not mean it ceases to be a bad argument (339). These points are more contentions than Johnson allows. But more importantly, they *seem* to sit awkwardly within a pragmatic model with its many appeals to context. This, again, hints at a tension in Johnson's core ideas. It is the dialectical tier that will draw more on (and reveal) the context. The illative tier is still in many respects very traditional.

One of the admitted difficulties in using 'truth' as a criterion in argumentation is deciding which theory of truth is at stake. When we turn to *MR* we find it far from clear which theory of truth is to be preferred.

Hamblin's principal objection to the truth requirement—that it presupposes a God's eye view—is seen to apply to some forms of the correspondence theory of truth but overlooks the range of other possibilities: 'Other theories of truth—coherence, idealist, pragmatist, instrumentalist, and, of course, relativist—do not require omniscience, and hence could be adopted by arguers without requiring that they forfeit their posture within the dialogue' (196). Shortly after this, Johnson again seems to shy away from a correspondence theory, since it 'would appear to be open to the sorts of criticisms mentioned by Hamblin,' and to favour a relativistic concept of truth which 'would make for a theory that is largely indistinguishable from theories governed by dialectical criteria' (198). But whether we are to prefer a relativistic concept, and how that is to be worked out, is unclear. In fact, comments made in the last part of the book would seem to rule out a relativistic concept.

In his response to Pinto (1994), Johnson tackles the claim that an argument may have false premises that it would be unreasonable *not* to accept: 'its premises, although false, are beyond reasonable doubt' (280). Johnson believes Pinto's position is too abstract and requires an illustration that would show this possibility. I believe there is the appearance of a confusion here. Pinto (like Hamblin, and Govier elsewhere) seems to be thinking of cases where people quite 'reasonably' accept premises that are false. We can think, for example, of Hume's inhabitants of Sumatra who reject the claim that water freezes in other climates on the reasonable premises that those who state as much must be lying because such an event is contrary to nature. Of course, what I am relying on here is an epistemic standard and Johnson seems to want a stronger truth standard. His reasons for questioning whether Pinto *et al.* can illustrate their case is that he seems to be seeing it as asserting that the argument's premises, though false, are beyond reasonable doubt *yet are known to be false* by those accepting them.

In chapter 11, Johnson offers the clearest statement on how he reads and uses the truth requirement and how it is to differ from acceptability. But in providing this clarification, he seems to fall foul of several of the concerns raised earlier. In a normative theory, he tells us, the truth and acceptability requirements are not incompatible. 'The truth criterion concerns the relationship between the premise and the state of affairs in the world. The acceptability criterion concerns the relationship between the premises and the audience. Hence, it is possible, in principle, for the premises of an argument to satisfy both' (337). This shows that, for Johnson, the two criteria are doing quite different tasks and so each is necessary. It would also allow for the premises to satisfy one criterion but violate the other. 'When there is a tension between the truth requirement and the acceptability requirement, we should tend to resolve the issue in favour or the truth criterion. Why? Because, I will argue, such a resolution fits better with the idea of manifest rationality' (339).

In this regard, he looks at two cases where the assumption is that the arguer *knows* a premise is either false or unacceptable to the audience. In such cases, of course, manifest rationality would mitigate against such a premise. But surely more crucial are instances where the arguer does not know these things?

This emphasis on what the arguer knows supports my interpretation of what Johnson is expecting by way of example from Pinto *et al.* above. Also, when he writes that 'The truth criterion concerns the relationship between the premise and the state of affairs in the world' (337), Johnson aligns himself more closely with a correspondence theory than a relativistic one, and thus, we must believe, is 'open to the sorts of criticisms mentioned by Hamblin' (198).

5. 'AN ARGUMENT POSSESSES A DIALECTICAL TIER IN WHICH THE ARGUER DISCHARGES HIS DIALECTICAL OBLIGATIONS.'

Because of the underlying project of manifest rationality, the illative core cannot be enough. While 'many arguments consist of the first tier only' (in which case it is a misnomer to call them arguments or, at least, complete arguments), the best practitioners 'always take account of the standard objections' (166). It is this taking account that constitutes the dialectical tier. More precisely, it is the addressing of alternative positions and standard objections.

There seems two things to address here: (i) the relationship between the illative and dialectical tiers with respect to the product itself, and (ii) the relationship between the arguer and Other(s) implied by the dialectical tier.

That we should take account of and anticipate objections seems noncontroversial, even if it has not been a feature of the tradition. It is non-controversial in that it is hard to imagine an informal logician denying that this is a valuable practice. But that this feature should be such an essential component of what *an argument is,* such that its absence excludes a discourse or text from being an argument, is controversial. It must be asked whether this dialectical tier is a part of the product or, rather, is something that arises afterwards, as participants reflect on the initial argument or an evaluator begins to work on it.[3] On the whole, insisting that an arguer complete the argument by showing how (s)he intends to handle certain objections must be seen as a very positive development in theory. It forces the acknowledgement that arguing is a complex activity and that many textbook treatments are inadequate. On the other hand, it may have some unexpected consequences. For example, since what separates rhetoric from argumentation is the requirement of manifest rationality (163), then the proposal would seem to project slim prospects for the development of rhetorical argumentation.

One constructive critic of Johnson's dialectical tier is Trudy Govier (1998). She presents ten difficulties with the proposal, several of which bear upon my own remarks. Taking Johnson's proposal on its own merits, she finds (i) that it is 'objectionable to label an argument incomplete because it does not address all objections and consider all alternatives' (7), and (ii) that vagueness remains about how to judge the success of attempts to deal with objections (7).

I believe answers to both of these objections are already contained in the appeal to context that underlies Johnson's model. Johnson himself responds to Govier's concern about not addressing all possible objections by agreeing, but insisting that what is important is that an arguer has dialectical obligations (1998, p. 2). Thus, we might surmise, to be an 'arguer' (and so to produce an argument) the fulfilling of one's dialectical obligations must be part of one's practice. Thus, again, an arguer must address *some* obligations for an argument to be complete. Apparently, Govier and Johnson understand 'complete' in different ways: Govier sees it objectively in terms of covering all possible objections; Johnson views it contextually in terms of the arguer's recognition of obligations.

This helps. But surely we could take things further by observing that the context restricts the possible objections and alternatives to those relevant for the audience in question and so likely to be raised by that audience? That is, insofar as the dialectical relationship between arguer and audience is integral to a specific argument, then the relevant objections should be those internal to that relationship. Possible objections that could be brought against the argument-product dislocated from its dialectical context are not at issue here.

Reading the proposal in these terms also helps us to address the second criticism about the vagueness of judgements. While there are indeed some points of clarification required to help us to understand how the dialectical tier works as a criterion for argument assessment, we can still establish a good sense of how successful an arguer is in discharging her or his dialectical obligations toward the *specific audience*. This will, of course, involve an understanding of that audience and a demonstration of the same.

My main response to this call for a dialectical tier is to support it further because I see it as part of the essential argument, although not exactly on terms that Johnson proposes. There is a profound way in which the anticipation of the Other's objections informs and *forms* the arguer's own utterances and *in this sense* the dialectical 'tier' cannot be divorced from the structure. In fact, understood this way, the line between the two tiers really begins to dissolve, thus addressing the critics' fear about logical or temporal separation of the two tiers.

Johnson accommodates this up to a point. He acknowledges that the arguer is only half the story and that the process is incomplete without the Other, and he gives us a dynamic relationship of back-and-forth responses between the two (157). But this still implies a temporally extended process.[4] To better capture and reflect the activity of arguing some compression is required, and Johnson later suggests just this:

> Genuine dialogue requires not merely the presence of the Other, or speech between the two, but the real possibility that the logos of the Other will influence one's own logos. An exchange is dialectical when, as a result of the intervention of the Other, one's own logos (discourse, reasoning, or thinking) has the potential of being affected in some way.
>
> Specifically, the arguer agrees to let the feedback from the Other affect the product. The arguer consents to take criticism and to take it seriously (161).

I have suggested elsewhere (1999) that the dialectical process at the heart of Mikhail Bakhtin's theory of dialogism is a superior candidate for a model that captures the act of arguing. Writing of the word in living conversation, Bakhtin saw it as 'directly, blatantly, oriented toward future answer-word: it provokes an answer, anticipates it and structures itself in the answer's direction' (1981, p. 280). Here, Bakhtin is involving the dynamic *internal* to discourse. It challenges the notion of the separated, self-reliant thinker/speaker who composes a discourse in isolation and then brings it into a dialogue (or argument) with another. What is described here is what Bakhtin calls the addressivity of speech. In our present terms, an argument is always addressed to someone and that is the most telling part of its structure. The argument is co-authored by the arguer and addressee. This is more than the accommodation of a reply and the anticipation of objections. This is to suggest that a more accurate description of what is involved in arguing sees the anticipated components as influencing the make-up of the structure. The dialectical is not something that takes place after the illative is fixed; it precedes the development of that 'core' (which ceases to be so core since such terminology is no longer warranted if the dialectical infuses it rather than surrounds it).

Johnson, in the passage cited above, moves toward this position in the remarks made about the logos of the Other influencing the arguer. But he draws back from it in the final two sentences where the references to feedback and criticism suggest a more traditional separation of opposing discourses. What works well, though, and is entirely consistent with Johnson's position, is a Bakhtinian collecting of that opposition within the argumentative discourse itself.

6. CONCLUSION

The manifest rationality project does much more than has been indicated here. For example, it offers new suggestions for fallacy theory (178–179) and provides a wealth of ideas for stabilizing and furthering the field of Informal Logic. But at the core of the theory is a concept of argument with its accompanying commitment to a particular understanding of rationality. As I have shown, while there is much to welcome in this development, there are also things to be clarified, developed, and perhaps modified.

The final and crucial question is: does the concept (of argument) hang together? I have noted several things that suggest it is not entirely successful in this. Early on in the discussion of the definition (section 2), we first saw the tension between the process and the product in the practice of argumentation. Does the relationship between the illative and dialectical tiers suggest something that is finished or in process? This is never completely answered. Johnson resists Govier's reading of 'complete', yet at the same time while rhetoric aims at effectiveness, logic aims at truth and completeness. What sense of 'complete' is at work here? Especially since the better arguments, we saw, are the more complete ones. The problem appears to be that, while the dialectical tier captures the dynamic process between those involved, the illative retains much of the fixedness of earlier models. For Johnson, premises are true or false in and of themselves and not in relation to an audience. But his understanding would seem to conflict with the positive reading I gave to the dialectical tier. While this later part of the definition works to close the gap between the illative and the dialectical, and to provide a coherent model of argument, features of the earlier parts of the definition serve to keep the tiers firmly apart.

We can view Johnson's concept of argument, with its insistence on a dialectical tier, as a tremendous advance. But as the new moves forward, questions remain as to how much of the old goes with it and how well the two really fit together.[5]

NOTES

[1] Written comments at Ontario Philosophical Society meeting, October 2000.
[2] The term is taken from Blair (1995).
[3] Trudy Govier suggests as much when she writes that 'an argument is one thing; objections to it, another; responses to those objections yet another' (1998, p. 7).
[4] One of Govier's concerns.
[5] An earlier version of this paper was presented at the October 2000 meeting of the Ontario Philosophical Society at McMaster University. I am grateful to the other panelists and members of the audience for their discussion, and particularly to Ralph Johnson for his written comments.

REFERENCES

Bakhtin, Mikhail: 1981, *The Dialogic Imagination: Four Essays,* Michael Holquist (ed.), Caryl Emerson and Michael Holquist (trans.), University of Texas Press, Austin.
Blair, J. Anthony: 1995, 'Premise Adequacy', in Frans van Eemeren et al. (eds.), *Perspective and Approaches,* Sic Sat, Amsterdam, pp. 191–202.
Gilbert, Michael: 1997, *Coalescent Argumentation,* Lawrence Erlbaum Associates, Mahwah, NJ.
Govier, Trudy: 1998, 'Arguing Forever? Or: Two Tiers of Argument Appraisal', in Hans V. Hansen et al. (eds.), *Argumentation & Rhetoric* (CD Rom), OSSA, St. Catharines, Ontario, 14 pp.
Groarke, Leo A.: 1996, 'Logic, Art and Argument', *Informal Logic* 18, 105–129.
Hamblin, C. L.: 1970, *Fallacies,* Methuen, London.
Johnson, Ralph H.: 2000, *Manifest Rationality: A Pragmatic Theory of Argument,* Lawrence Erlbaum Associates, Mahwah, NJ.
Johnson, Ralph H.: 1998, 'Response to Govier's "Arguing Forever? Or: Two Tiers of Argument Appraisal"', in Hans V. Hansen et al. (eds.), *Argumentation & Rhetoric* (CD Rom), OSSA, St. Catharines, Ontario, 5 pp.
Johnson, Ralph H.: 1996, *The Rise of Informal Logic,* Vale Press, Newport News, Virginia.
Pinto, Robert C.: 1994, 'Logic, Epistemology and Argument Appraisal', in R. H. Johnson and J. A. Blair (eds.), *New Essays in Informal Logic,* Informal Logic, Windsor, Ontario, pp. 116–124.
Tindale, C. W.: 1999, 'Arguing for Bakhtin', in Frans van Eemeren et al. (eds.), *Proceedings of the Fourth International Conference of the International Society for the Study of Argumentation,* Sic Sat, Amsterdam, pp. 786–790.
Willard, Charles A.: 1989, *A Theory of Argumentation,* The University of Alabama Press, Tuscaloosa.

Chapter 3

Structures and Schemes

Structures and schemes are significant dimensions of argumentation theory and analysis. These concepts imply that reasoning by argument is a patterned activity consisting of integral parts. Simply, structures refer to the parts of argumentation; schemes refer to the connection among the parts. To focus on structure is to ask: what are the components of an argument, and how are those components arranged? Schemes are intrinsically tied to an argument's structure. A schema signifies the relationship between an argument's claim and its premises; it justifies the connection of premises to a conclusion. An analysis of schemes focuses on what a given argument relies upon to uphold its conclusion.

The essays in this chapter address the structures and schemes of arguments. Each essay summarizes and expands upon concepts developed in groundbreaking argumentation books by Stephen Toulmin, Chaïm Perelman and Lucie Olbrechts-Tyteca, and Douglas Walton. The essays make distinctions between rhetorical and informal logic approaches to schemes and structures and the approaches used in formal logic. The essays in this chapter also explore the degree to which structures and schemes are bound by context.

Wayne Brockriede and Douglas Ehninger's 1960 essay, "Toulmin on Argument: An Interpretation and Application" introduced Stephen Toulmin, the author of an influential argumentation book *The Uses of Argument,* to United States scholars of rhetoric. Brockriede and Ehninger demonstrate Toulmin's model as an argument structure for evaluating, developing, and criticizing arguments, and argue that the model is superior to formal logic for analyzing human arguments. They also claim that classical argument structures (such as enthymemes and syllogisms) do not adequately describe the full range of arguments that people use. Brockriede and Ehninger use Toulmin's notion of warrant to classify arguments by the type of proofs (logical, ethical, or pathetic) they employ.

In "*The New Rhetoric*'s Argument Schemes: A Rhetorical View of Practical Reasoning" (1992), Barbara Warnick and Susan L. Kline discuss the use of schemes to make inferences in argument. Drawing on Chaïm Perelman and Lucie Olbrechts-Tyteca's book, *The New Rhetoric,* this essay explains the significance of viewing argument schemes—common patterns of inference—as rhetorical constructions. While argumentation scholars know *The New Rhetoric* for advancing a rhetorical perspective of argument in relation to particular and universal audiences, Warnick and Kline contend that these argument schemes also offer a system that helps people classify and track patterns of argument. According to their analysis, the fact that the schemes frequently appear in discourse indicates that they can help us understand arguments.

J. Anthony Blair's essay, "Walton's Argumentation Schemes for Presumptive Reasoning: A Critique and Development" (2001), addresses ideas that Douglas Walton, a contemporary informal logician, presented in his book *Argumentation Schemes for Presumptive Reasoning.* In presumptive reasoning, an inference is made on the basis of a presumption—an assumption that is used to infer a conclusion. (Blair cites the following example: "John's hat is not on the peg. Therefore, John has left the house." The schema that makes this argument work is a presumption that a missing hat is a sign that someone has gone.) Blair synthesizes Walton's ideas, provides a detailed account of schemes, refines the idea of presumptive reasoning, and advocates developing an expansive theory of argumentation that would fully account for schemes.

The three essays in this chapter illustrate the significant attention that argument scholars have paid to structures and schemes. The components of argument and the inferences people make to move from premises to a claim are all important to understanding argumentation. The essays also address and extend primary concepts of argument that are commonly addressed in basic argumentation courses.

··

Toulmin on Argument:
An Interpretation and Application
WAYNE BROCKRIEDE AND DOUGLAS EHNINGER

During the period 1917–1932 several books, a series of articles, and many Letters to the Editor of *QJS* gave serious attention to exploring the nature of argument as it is characteristically employed in rhetorical proofs.[1] Since that time, however, students of public address have shown comparatively little interest in the subject, leaving to philosophers, psychologists, and sociologists the principal contributions which have more recently been made toward an improved understanding of argument.[2]

Among the contributions offered by "outsiders" to our field, one in particular deserves more attention than it has so far received from rhetoricians. We refer to some of the formulations of the English logician Stephen Toulmin in his *The Uses of Argument*, published in 1958.[3]

Toulmin's analysis and terminology are important to the rhetorician for two different but related reasons. First, they provide an appropriate structural model by means of which rhetorical arguments may be laid out for analysis and criticism; and, second, they suggest a system for classifying artistic proofs which employs argument as a central and unifying construct. Let us consider these propositions in order.

1.

As described by Toulmin, an argument is *movement* from accepted *data*, through a *warrant*, to a *claim*.

Data (D) answer the question, "What have you got to go on?" Thus *data* correspond to materials of fact or opinion which in our textbooks are commonly called *evidence*. Data may report historical or contemporary events, take the form of a statistical compilation or of citations from authority, or they may consist of one or more general declarative sentences established by a prior proof of an artistic nature. Without data clearly present or strongly implied, an argument has no informative or substantive component, no factual point of departure.

Claim (C) is the term Toulmin applies to what we normally speak of as a *conclusion*. It is the explicit appeal produced by the argument, and is always of a potentially controversial nature. A claim may stand as the final proposition in an argument, or it may be an intermediate statement which serves as data for a subsequent inference.

Data and claim taken together represent the specific contention advanced by an argument, and therefore constitute what may be regarded as its *main proof line*. The usual order is *data* first, and then *claim*. In this sequence the *claim* contains or implies "therefore." When the order is reversed, the *claim* contains or implies "because."

Warrant (W) is the operational name Toulmin gives to that part of an argument which authorizes the mental "leap" involved in advancing from data to claim. As distinguished from data which answer the question "What have you got to go on," the warrant answers the question "How do you get there." Its function is to *carry* the accepted data to the doubted or disbelieved proposition which constitutes the claim, thereby certifying this claim as true or acceptable.

The relations existing among these three basic components of an argument, Toulmin suggests, may be represented diagrammatically:

Here is an application of the method:

In addition to the three indispensable elements of *data, claim,* and *warrant,* Toulmin recognizes a second triad of components, any or all of which may, but need not necessarily, be present in an argument. These he calls (1) *backing,* (2) *rebuttal,* and (3) *qualifier.*

Backing (B) consists of credentials designed to certify the assumption expressed in the warrant. Such credentials may consist of a single item, or of an entire argument in itself complete with data and claim. Backing must be introduced when readers or listeners are not willing to accept a warrant at its face value.

The rebuttal (R) performs the function of a safety valve or escape hatch, and is, as a rule, appended to the claim statement. It recognizes certain conditions under which the claim will not hold good or will hold good only in a qualified and restricted way. By limiting the area to which the claim may legitimately be applied, the rebuttal anticipates certain objections which might otherwise be advanced against the argument.

The function of the qualifier (Q) is to register the degree of force which the maker believes his claim to possess. The qualification may be expressed by a quantifying term such as "possibly," "probably," "to the five per cent level of confidence," etc., or it may make specific reference to an anticipated refutation. When the author of a claim regards it as incontrovertible no qualifier is appended.

These additional elements may be superimposed on the first diagram:

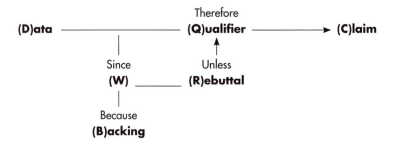

We may illustrate the model as follows:

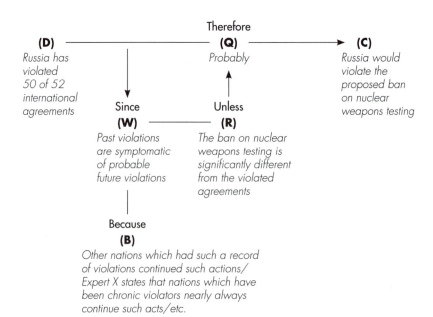

2.

With Toulmin's structural model now set forth, let us inquire into its suitability as a means of describing and testing arguments. Let us compare Toulmin's method with the analysis offered in traditional logic, the logic commonly used as a basic theory of argumentation in current textbooks. We conceive of arguments in the customary fashion as (1) deriving from probable causes and signs, (2) proceeding more often by relational than implicative principles, (3) emphasizing material as well as formal validity, (4) employing premises which are often contestable, and (5) eventuating in claims which are by nature contingent and variable.

The superiority of the Toulmin model in describing and testing arguments may be claimed for seven reasons:

1. Whereas traditional logic is characteristically concerned with *warrant-using* arguments (i.e., arguments in which the validity of the assumption underlying the inference "leap" is uncontested), Toulmin's model specifically provides for *warrant-establishing* arguments (i.e., arguments in which the validity of the assumption underlying the inference must be established—through backing—as part of the proof pattern itself).[4]

2. Whereas traditional logic, based as it is upon the general principle of implication, always treats proof more or less as a matter of classification or compartmentalization, Toulmin's analysis stresses the inferential and relational nature of argument, providing a context within which all factors—both formal and material—bearing upon a disputed claim may be organized into a series of discrete steps.

3. Whereas in traditional logic arguments are specifically designed to produce universal propositions, Toulmin's second triad of backing, rebuttal, and qualifier provide, within the framework of his basic structural model, for the establishment of claims which are no more than probable. The model directs attention to the ways in which each of these additional elements may operate to limit or condition a claim.

4. Whereas traditional logic, with its governing principle of implication, necessarily results in an essentially static conception of argument, Toulmin by emphasizing *movement* from data, through warrant, to claim produces a conception of argument as dynamic. From his structural model we derive a picture of arguments "working" to establish and certify claims, and as a result of his functional terminology we are able to understand the role each part of an argument plays in this process.

5. Whereas the modes based on the traditional analysis—enthymeme, example, and the like—often suppress a step in proof, Toulmin's model lays an argument out in such a way that each step may be examined critically.

6. Whereas in the traditional analysis the division of arguments into premises and conclusions (as in the syllogism, for example) often tends to obscure deficiencies in proof, Toulmin's model assigns each part of an argument a specific geographical or spatial position in relation to the others, thus rendering it more likely that weak points will be detected.

7. Whereas traditional logic is imperfectly equipped to deal with the problem of material validity, Toulmin makes such validity an integral part of his system, indicating clearly the role which factual elements play in producing acceptable claims.

In short, without denying that Toulmin's formulations are open to serious criticism at several points[5]—and allowing for any peculiarities in our interpretations of the character of traditional logic—one conclusion emerges. Toulmin has provided a structural model which promises to be of greater use in laying out rhetorical arguments for dissection and testing than the methods of traditional logic. For although most teachers and writers in the field of argumentation have discussed the syllogism in general terms, they have made no serious attempt to explore the complexities of the moods and figures of the syllogism, nor have they been very successful in applying the terms and principles of traditional logic to the arguments of real controversies. Toulmin's model provides a practical replacement.

3.

Our second proposition is that Toulmin's structural model and the vocabulary he has developed to describe it are suggestive of a system for classifying artistic proofs, using argument (defined as *movement* from data, through warrant, to claim) as a unifying construct.[6]

In extending Toulmin's analysis to develop a simplified classification of arguments, we may begin by restating in Toulmin's terms the traditional difference between *inartistic* and *artistic* proof. Thus, conceiving of an argument as a movement by means of which accepted data are carried through a certifying warrant to a controversial claim, we may say that in some cases the data themselves are conclusive. They approach the claim without aid from a warrant—are tantamount to the claim in the sense that to accept them is automatically to endorse the claim they are designed to support. In such cases the proof may be regarded as *inartistic*. In another class of arguments, however, the situation is quite different. Here the data are not immediately conclusive, so that the role of the warrant in carrying them to the claim becomes of crucial importance. In this sort of argument the proof is directly dependent upon the inventive powers of the arguer and may be regarded as *artistic*.

If, then, the warrant is the crucial element in an artistic proof, and if its function is to carry the data to the claim, we may classify artistic arguments by recognizing the possible routes which the warrant may travel in performing its function.

So far as rhetorical proofs are concerned, as men have for centuries recognized, these routes are three in number: (1) an arguer may carry data to claim by means of an assumption concerning the relationship existing among phenomena in the external world; (2) by means of an assumption concerning the quality of the source from which the data are derived; and (3) by means of an assumption concerning the inner drives, values, or aspirations which impel the behavior of those persons to whom the argument is addressed.

Arguments of the first sort (traditionally called *logical*) may be called *substantive;* those of the second sort (traditionally called *ethical*) may be described as *authoritative;* and those of the third sort (traditionally called *pathetic*) as *motivational*.

Substantive Arguments

The warrant of a substantive argument reflects an assumption concerning the way in which things are related in the world about us. Although other orderings are possible, one commonly recognized, and the one used here, is six-fold. Phenomena may be related as cause to effect (or as effect to cause), as attribute to substance, as some to more, as intrinsically similar, as bearing common relations, or as more to some. Upon the first of these relationships is based what is commonly called argument from *cause;* on the second, argument from *sign;* on the third, argument from *generalization;* on the fourth, argument from *parallel case;* on the fifth, argument from *analogy;* and on the sixth, argument from *classification.*

Cause. In argument from cause the data consist of one or more accepted facts about a person, object, event, or condition. The warrant attributes to these facts a creative or generative power and specifies the nature of the effect they will produce. The claim relates these results to the person, object, event, or condition named in the data. Here is an illustration, from cause to effect:

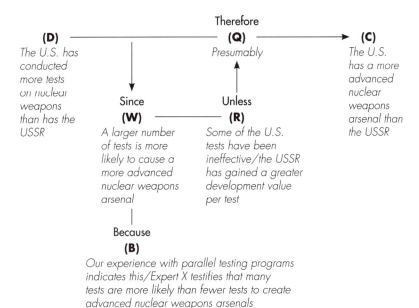

When the reasoning process is reversed and the argument is from effect to cause, the data again consist of one or more facts about a person, object, event, or condition; the warrant asserts that a particular causal force is sufficient to have accounted for these facts; and the claim relates this cause to the person, object, event, or condition named in the data.

Sign. In argument from sign the data consist of clues or symptoms. The warrant interprets the meaning or significance of these symptoms. The claim affirms that some person, object, event, or condition possesses the attributes of which the clues have been declared symptomatic. Our first example concerning Russia's violation of international agreements illustrates the argument from sign.

Generalization. In argument from generalization the data consist of information about a number of persons, objects, events, or conditions, taken as constituting a representative and adequate sample of a given class of phenomena. The warrant assumes that what is true of the items constituting the sample will also be true of additional members of the class not represented in the sample. The claim makes explicit the assumption embodied in the warrant. The form can be diagrammed so:

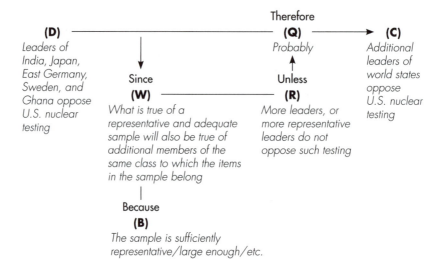

Parallel Case. In argument from parallel case the data consist of one or more statements about a single object, event, or condition. The warrant asserts that the instance reported in the data bears an essential similarity to a second instance in the same category. The claim affirms about the new instance what has already been accepted concerning the first. Here is an illustration:

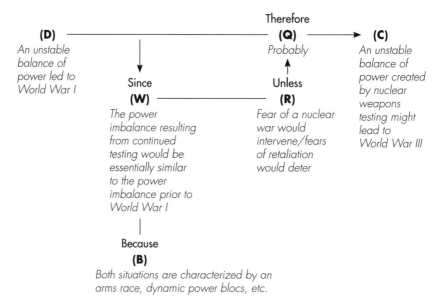

In argument from parallel cases a rebuttal will be required in either of two situations: (1) if another parallel case bears a stronger similarity to the case under consideration; or (2) if in spite of some essential similarities an essential dissimilarity negates or reduces the force of the warrant. The example illustrates the second of these possibilities.

Analogy. In argument from analogy the data report that a relationship of a certain nature exists between two items. The warrant assumes that a similar relationship exists between a second pair of items. The claim makes explicit the relationship assumed in the warrant. Whereas the argument from parallel case assumes a resemblance between two *cases*, the analogy assumes only a similarity of *relationship*. Analogy may be illustrated so:

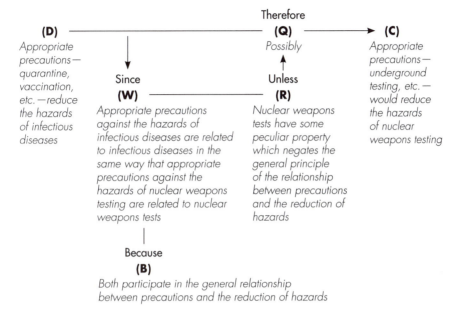

In most cases the analogical relation expressed in an argument from analogy will require a strongly qualifying "possibly."

Classification. In argument from classification the statement of the data is a generalized conclusion about known members of a class of persons, objects, events, or conditions. The warrant assumes that what is true of the items reported in the data will also be true of a hitherto unexamined item which is known (or thought) to fall within the class there described. The claim then transfers the general statement which has been made in the data to the particular item under consideration. As illustrated, the form would appear:

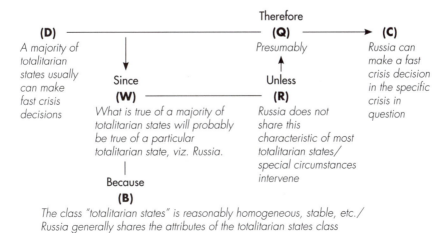

Two kinds of reservations may be applicable in an argument from classification: (1) a class member may not share the particular attribute cited in the data, although it does share enough other attributes to deserve delineation as a member of the class; and (2) special circumstances may prevent a specific class member from sharing at some particular time or place the attributes general to the class.

Authoritative Arguments

In authoritative arguments the data consist of one or more factual reports or statements of opinion. The warrant affirms the reliability of the source from which these are derived. The claim reiterates the statement which appeared in the data, as now certified by the warrant. An illustration follows:

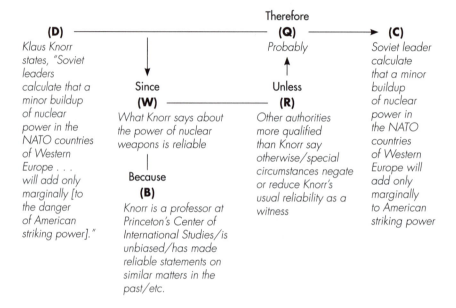

The structure and function of an authoritative argument remains basically the same when the source of the data is the speaker or writer himself. The data is carried to claim status by the same sort of assumption embodied in the warrant. We may infer a claim from what Knorr says about nuclear weapons whether he is himself the speaker, or whether another speaker is quoting what Knorr has said. Thus the *ethos* of a speaker may be studied by means of the Toulmin structure under the heading of authoritative argument.

Motivational Arguments

In motivational arguments the data consist of one or more statements which may have been established as claims in a previous argument or series of arguments. The warrant provides a motive for accepting the claim by associating it with some inner drive, value, desire, emotion, or aspiration, or with a combination of such forces. The claim as so warranted is that the person, object, event, or condition referred to in the data should be accepted as valuable or rejected as worthless, or that the policy there described should or should not be adopted, or the action there named should or should not be performed. Illustrated the form would appear:

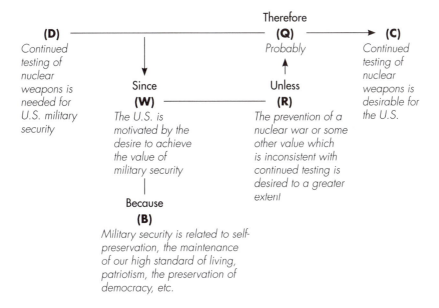

4.

We have exhibited the structural unity of the three modes of artistic proof by showing how they may be reduced to a single invariant pattern using argument as a unifying construct. Let us as a final step explore this unity further by inquiring how artistic proofs, so reduced, may conveniently be correlated with the various types of disputable questions and the claims appropriate to each.

Let us begin by recognizing the four categories into which disputable questions have customarily been classified: (1) Whether something is? (2) What it is? (3) Of what worth it is? (4) What course of action should be pursued? The first of these queries gives rise to a question of *fact*, and is to be answered by what can be called a *designative claim;* the second, to a question of *definition*, to be answered by a *definitive claim;* the third, to a question of *value*, to be answered by an *evaluative claim;* and the fourth, to a question of *policy*, to be answered by an *advocative claim.*

Supposing, then, that an arguer is confronted with a question of fact, calling for a designative claim; or a question of policy, calling for an advocative claim, etc., what types of argument would be available to him as means of substantiating his claim statement? Upon the basis of the formulations developed in earlier sections of this paper, it is possible to supply rather precise answers.

Designative Claims. A designative claim, appropriate to answering a question of fact, will be found supportable by any of the six forms of substantive argument, or by authoritative argument, but not by motivational argument. That is, whether something exists or is so may be determined: (1) by isolating its cause or its effect (argument from cause); (2) by reasoning from the presence of symptoms to the claim that a substance exists or is so (argument from sign); (3) by inferring that because some members of a given class exist or are so, more members of the same class also exist or are so (argument from generalization); (4) by inferring because one item exists or is so, that a closely similar item exists or is so (argument from parallel case); (5) by reasoning that D exists or is so because it stands in the same relation to C that B does to A, when C, B, and A are known to exist or to be so (argument from analogy); and (6) by concluding that an unexamined item known or thought to fall within a given class exists or is so because all known members of the class exist or are so (argument from classification). Moreover, we may argue that something exists or is so because a reputable authority declares this to be the case. Motivational argument, on the other hand, may not be critically employed in designative claims, because values, desires, and feelings are irrelevant where questions of fact are concerned.

Definitive Claims. The possibilities for establishing definitive claims are more limited. Only two of the forms of substantive argument and authoritative argument are applicable. We may support a claim as to what something is: (1) by comparing it with a closely similar phenomenon (argument from parallel case); or (2) by reasoning that because it stands in the same relation to C as B does to A it will be analogous to C, where the nature of C, B, and A are known (argument from analogy). In addition, we may support a definition or interpretation by citing an acceptable authority. Among the substantive arguments, cause, sign, generalization, and classification are inapplicable; and once again motivational argument is irrelevant since emotions, wishes, and values cannot legitimately determine the nature of phenomena.

Evaluative Claims. Evaluative claims may be supported by generalization, parallel case, analogy, and classification, and by authoritative and motivational arguments. By generalization a class of phenomena may be declared valuable or worthless on the ground that a typical and adequate sample of the members of that class is so. By classification, in contrast, we infer from the worth of known members of a class the probable worth of some previously unexamined item known or thought to belong to that class. By parallel case, we infer goodness or badness from the quality of an item closely similar. By analogy, however, we infer value on the basis of a ratio of resemblances rather than a direct parallel. In authoritative argument our qualitative judgment is authorized by a recognized expert. In motivational argument, however, an item is assigned a value in accordance with its usefulness in satisfying human drives, needs, and aspirations. Arguments from cause and sign, on the other hand, are inapplicable.

Advocative Claims. Advocative claims may legitimately be established in only four ways. We may argue that some policy should be adopted or some action undertaken because a closely similar policy or action has brought desirable results in the past (argument from parallel case). We may support a proposed policy or action because it bears the same relation to C that B does to A, where B is known to have brought desirable results (argument from analogy). Or, of course, we may support our claim by testimony (authoritative argument), or by associating it with men's wishes, values, and aspirations (motivational argument).

This analysis concerning the types of arguments applicable to various sorts of claims may be summarized in tabular form:

	Designative	Definitive	Evaluative	Advocative
Substantive				
A. Cause	X			
B. Sign	X			
C. Generalization	X		X	
D. Parallel Case	X	X	X	X
E. Analogy	X	X	X	X
F. Classification	X		X	
Authoritative	X	X	X	X
Motivational			X	X

The world of argument is vast, one seemingly without end. Arguments arise in one realm, are resolved, and appear and reappear in others; and new arguments appear. If one assumes some rationality among men, a system of logical treatment of argument is imperative. The traditional logical system of syllogisms, of enthymemes, of middles distributed and undistributed, may have had its attraction in medieval times. The inadequacies of such a logic, however, have been described by experts; for example, see J. S. Mill on the syllogism and *petitio principii*.[7] The modern search has been for a method which would have some application in the dynamics of contemporary affairs.

Toulmin has supplied us with a contemporary methodology, which in many respects makes the traditional unnecessary. The basic theory has herein been amplified, some extensions have been made, and illustrations of workability have been supplied. All this is not meant to be the end, but rather the beginning of an inquiry into a new, contemporary, dynamic, and usable logic for argument.

NOTES

[1] E.g., such books as James M. O'Neill, Craven Laycock, and Robert L. Scales, *Argumentation and Debate* (New York, 1917); William T. Foster, *Argumentation and Debating* (Boston, 1917); and A. Craig Baird, *Public Discussion and Debate* (Boston, 1928); such articles as Mary Yost, "Argument from the Point of View of Sociology," *QJS*, III (1917), 109–24; Charles H. Woolbert, "The Place of Logic in a System of Persuasion," *QJS*, IV, (1918), 19–39; Gladys Murphy Graham, "Logic and Argumentation," *QJS*, X (1924), 350–363; William E. Utterback, "Aristotle's Contribution to the Psychology of Argument," *QJS*, XI (1925), 218–225; Herbert A. Wichelns, "Analysis and Synthesis in Argumentation," *QJS*, XI (1925), 266–272; and Edward Z. Rowell, "Prolegomena to Argumentation," *QJS*, XVIII (1932), 1–13, 224–248, 381–405, 585–606; such Letters to the Editor as those by Utterback, XI (1925), 175–177; Wichelns, XI (1925), 286–288; Ralph C. Ringwalt, XII (1926), 66–68; and Graham, XII (1925), 196–197.

[2] See, for example, Mortimer Adler, *Dialectic* (New York, 1927); Paul Edwards, *The Logic of Moral Discourse* (Glencoe, Ill., 1955); Carl I. Hovland, Irving L. Janis, and Harold W. Kelley, *Communication and Persuasion* (New Haven, Conn., 1953); Charles Perelman, *Traité de l'argumentation,* 2 vols. (Paris, 1958), and *La nouvelle rhétorique* (Paris, 1952); and John Cohen, "Subjective Probability," *Scientific American,* MCMVII (1957), 128–38.

[3] (Cambridge, Cambridge University Press). See especially the third of the five essays in the book. *Cf.* J. C. Cooley, "On Mr. Toulmin's Revolution in Logic," *The Journal of Philosophy,* LVI (1959), 297–319.

[4] In traditional logic only the epicheirema provides comparable backing for premises.

[5] It may be charged that his structural model is merely "a syllogism lying on its side," that it makes little or no provision to insure the formal validity of claims, etc.

[6] Our suggestion as to the structural unity of artistic proofs is by no means novel. The ancients regularly spoke of *pathetic* and *ethical* enthymemes, and envisioned the *topoi* as applicable beyond the *pistis*. (See in this connection James H. McBurney, "The Place of the Enthymeme in Rhetorical Theory," *SM*, III [1936], 63.) At the same time, however, it must be recognized that especially since the advent of the faculty psychology of the seventeenth and eighteenth centuries, rhetorical thought has been profoundly and persistently influenced by the doctrine of a dichotomy between pathetic and logical appeals. (For significant efforts to combat this doctrine see Charles H. Woolbert, "Conviction and Persuasion: Some Considerations of Theory," *QJS*, III [1917], 249–264; Mary Yost, "Argument from the Point of View of Sociology," *QJS*, III [1917], 109–124: and W. Norwood Brigance, "Can We Redefine the James-Winans Theory of Persuasion?" *QJS*, XXI [1935], 19–26.)

[7] *A System of Logic*, I, Chap. 3, Sec. 2.

···

The New Rhetoric's Argument Schemes: A Rhetorical View of Practical Reasoning

BARBARA WARNICK AND SUSAN L. KLINE

In a lecture delivered in 1957, Chaim Perelman (1958) described the workings of practical reasoning and compared them to the structures of formal logic:

> Why envisage proof always in terms of a single model? . . . [A] final convergence [of a number of indications] can lead to conclusions so sure that only a lunatic would ever think of doubting them. . . .When we have to reconstruct the past [for example] the arguments which we use seem to me very much more like a piece of cloth, the total strength of which will always be vastly superior to that of any single thread which enters into its warp and woof. (pp. 300–301)

In *The New Rhetoric*, Perelman and Olbrechts-Tyteca (1969) developed a description of the various threads making up this cloth; these include the starting points for argument, the conventions governing argument practices, and the mechanisms or schemes for making inferences.[1]

Each of these dimensions of argument is tied in Perelman and Olbrechts-Tyteca's (1969) theory to a conception of what the arguer believes that the audience will accept, since *"it is in terms of an audience that an argumentation develops"* (p. 5; emphasis in original). For instance, the starting points of argument—facts, truths, presumptions, values, hierarchies, and the loci of the preferable—are derived from premises to which the arguer's anticipated audience presumably subscribes. The conventions for conducting arguments also grow out of practices and norms mutually accepted by interlocutors who participate together in a common culture. Likewise, the inferential schemes that move the audience to accept the arguer's claims are generated through commonplaces and structures recognized and accepted by Western society. Over two-thirds of *The New Rhetoric* was devoted to describing these agreed-upon liaisons that make inferences possible, for Perelman and Olbrechts-Tyteca believed that in practical reasoning, inferential moves are made possible rhetorically.

Yet *The New Rhetoric*'s system of argument schemes has not received attention proportionate to its significance. While numerous studies have focused on the concepts of universal audience (Scult, 1976; Ray, 1978; Perelman, 1984; Golden,

1986), presence (Karon, 1976), and the rationality/reasonableness distinction (McKerrow, 1982; Laughlin & Hughes, 1986), attention to the argument schemes themselves has been infrequent, despite the fact that Perelman and Olbrechts-Tyteca (1969) devoted the bulk of their treatise to the rhetorical nature of inference forms. Quasi-logical, analogical, and dissociative scheme types have been individually studied (Dearin, 1982; Measell, 1985; Schiappa, 1985). One critique of the system has appeared (van Eemeren, Grootendorst, & Kruiger, 1984), and various critics have made partial or tentative efforts to apply the schemes to argument practices (Siebold, McPhee, Poole, Tanita, & Canary, 1981; Farrell, 1986). While argument textbooks make general use of the scheme typology to describe argument practices (Katula, 1983; Herrick, 1991), precise study of the individual schemes has been sporadic and indeterminate. Two decades after *The New Rhetoric* was published, Olbrechts-Tyteca (1979) expressed disappointment at the lack of attention given to the study of specific schemes. And in 1986, Thomas Farrell could claim that *The New Rhetoric*'s descriptions of practical reasoning practices "have been the singularly most neglected feature of Perelman's rhetorical theory" (p. 269).

The scheme typology is nonetheless of singular importance because it provides us with a rhetorical account of the operation of argument schemes. Prior to *The New Rhetoric,* our vocabulary for describing inference patterns was limited to formal logical patterns (e.g., categorical, disjunctive, and conditional syllogisms) and the standard classifications of inductive reasoning (analogy, generalization, cause, and sign). Perelman and Olbrechts-Tyteca (1969) generated their schemes through a careful empirical process in which they collected discursive arguments for over ten years, typed them, and added new categories (dissociations, symbolic liaisons, and double hierarchy arguments, among others), thus providing a richer vocabulary for describing reasoning structures. In addition, Perelman and Olbrechts-Tyteca explicitly incorporated a rhetorical theory of argument by shaping audience-accepted commonplaces into the inference structure of schemes.

Our purpose in this essay is twofold: (1) to describe how schemes make use of culturally-accepted commonplaces in their inference structures, and (2) to respond to significant criticism of the schemes by clarifying and elaborating them and indicating their frequency in discourse. Our essay will establish that the schemes recognizably appear in discursive arguments. By showing how rhetors' knowledge of their expected audiences enables them to make use of audience biases, habits of thought, and forms of expression to transfer adherence to the claim, we will indicate the senses in which the schemes are rhetorical.

THE RHETORICAL WORKING OF THE SCHEMES

Because they lie at the very core of Perelman and Olbrechts-Tyteca's theory, argument schemes deserve further systematic study. In Perelman and Olbrechts-Tyteca's (1969) view, a theory of argument must examine the ways in which discursive techniques induce the mind's adherence to theses presented for its assent (p. 4). Such an analysis begins with premises already accepted by the audience; these premises form both the foundation and the starting point of argument. Arguers construct arguments from the coexistential, causal, and symbolic liaisons as well as hierarchies and loci recognized and accepted by particular audiences, or considered to be compelling in relation to a universal audience. While rhetors recognize many kinds of premises, Perelman and Olbrechts-Tyteca divide them into two major types: premises that focus on the real and consist of facts, truths, and presumptions; and premises that focus on the preferable and consist of values, hierarchies, and loci about the preferable (p. 66).

While arguments derive persuasive force from recognized premises, they also derive force from the ways in which rhetors connect opinions to these premises. Perelman and Olbrechts-Tyteca (1969) posit that arguers connect premises to theses by way of inference forms, or *argument schemes,* that pass acceptance from the premises to the conclusion. Schemes create links either through processes of association, in which premises are brought together and unified in particular ways, or through processes of dissociation, in which previously unified premises are disengaged from each other. Thus argument schemes exploit the cultural and cognitive predispositions of the audience as construed by arguers. The schemes themselves are distinct, culturally held beliefs about the ways we form new beliefs from already accepted premises. Hence, argument schemes are themselves loci about arguments in that they are different ways of relating observations to claims that gain force by being recognized and accepted by an audience. It is the recognizability of the forms themselves that gives arguments their persuasive force. The persuasive power of arguments, then, arises from these inference forms, as well as from the recognized liaisons, hierarchies, and loci of the preferable.

It is important to recognize that schemes are able to function persuasively because of the arguer's and the audience's mutual participation in a common culture. Perelman's (1958) opposition to a Cartesian model of proof was emphasized by his rejection of proof that is ahistorical or acultural. Perelman viewed argument as a culturally-constituted activity. (In his view, schemes work rhetorically because their inferences are jointly recognized by a culture common to the arguer and his or her audience.) Thus, Perelman held that the faculty of reason is constituted within us by means of a cultural apprenticeship and because of the rules we are taught and the changes we make in them as a result of their use.

This awareness of both the inference structure of arguments and of their cultural situatedness means that Perelman and Olbrechts-Tyteca's theory combines what Joseph Wenzel (1990) has called a logical approach to the study of argument with a rhetorical one. Arguments are indeed products produced by naive social actors that can, despite the equivocal character of language, be reconstructed and subjected to logical analysis and criticism. For instance, Perelman and Olbrechts-Tyteca (1969) write extensively about the ways arguments containing particular schemes exhibit similarities in syntactic form and semantic content. Yet, because arguments are also efforts to win adherence, these theorists also understand premises and schemes as constituting and being constituted by functional processes of persuasion. Thus, much of *The New Rhetoric* is devoted to the ways symbolic resources can enhance the presence of premises and schemes and motivate persons to agree.

Further, by combining a logical approach with a rhetorical one, Perelman and Olbrechts-Tyteca (1969) suggest that argumentation theorists should examine the conditions under which argument schemes are appropriately applied in relation to particular audiences, and also in relation to a universal audience. In Perelman and Olbrechts-Tyteca's view, the audience is a systematized construction by the speaker. While argument schemes should certainly be studied for their effectiveness in anticipating particular audiences, it is often the universal audience that is invoked when a rhetor makes a judgment about how to use particular argument schemes. Yet since the universal audience varies according to the image formed of it by interlocutors, each culture "has its own conception of the universal audience." So Perelman and Olbrechts-Tyteca suggest that "the study of these variations would be very instructive, as we would learn from it what men, at different times in history, have regarded as *real, true,* and *objectively valid*" (p. 33; emphasis in original).

A CRITIQUE OF THE SCHEMES

Van Eemeren, Grootendorst, and Kruiger (1984) called *The New Rhetoric*'s contribution "remarkable," but launched a critique of Perelman and Olbrechts-Tyteca's schemes. They questioned the power of the argument schemes to describe actual arguments. First, they argued, there is no substantial distinction in the scheme definitions between form and content. If this is true, they observed, arriving at precise and reliable interpretations of the schemes would be very difficult, since "in principle every audience (and hence every interpreter) can discern different argumentation schemata in an argument from those discerned by another audience" (p. 256). As we hope to demonstrate, form and content (as well as context) are indeed fused in *The New Rhetoric*'s scheme system. However, as we will also indicate, this fusion does not prevent the schemes from being recognizable to various interpreters.

Second, van Eemeren and his colleagues (1984) noted that the schemes themselves are couched in ordinary language and in the syntax of common speech. In order to be identified as the exemplar of a particular form, then, an argument often may have to be restated or "reconstructed" to accord with the appropriate form. As the Dutch authors observe, "the form of argumentation must be made to accord with the chosen argument form. . . . For this a certain reduction or specification of meaning is required which must be adapted to the purpose achieved by the argumentation" (p. 230). Quasi-logical arguments, especially, require reduction. As normally stated, they can only be related to their respective subforms (incompatibility, identity, reciprocity, transitivity, etc.) through restatement and reduction. In many cases, interpreters must consider the number of terms in the argument and their relation to each other in order to ascertain what type of quasi-logical argument is involved.

Third, van Eemeren and his colleagues (1984) note the lack of precision and clarity with which Perelman and Olbrechts-Tyteca originally defined and exemplified the schemes (p. 253). Many of *The New Rhetoric*'s examples are esoteric or obscure, and its authors' descriptions of the schemes are quite complicated. In the absence of clear examples and criteria for identifying the various subforms, the Dutch authors wondered whether it was at all possible to differentiate one category from another.

Finally, despite the non-empirical nature of their own critique, van Eemeren and his colleagues (1984) criticized Perelman and Olbrechts-Tyteca for failing to ground their system empirically (p. 256). Even though *The New Rhetoric*'s authors spent over a decade collecting examples of argumentation from discourse in various fields, their efforts were held to be inadequate. Since they presented discourse snippets extracted from various contexts to illustrate the schemes, the Dutch authors wondered whether Perelman and Olbrechts-Tyteca were thereby able to eliminate systematically factors that would be disruptive to the typology.

In part, the present study is intended to respond to this critique. As our treatment of various argument schemes will indicate, it is not possible to separate form and content when examining arguments using Perelman and Olbrechts-Tyteca's system. The form in which an argument is stated is only *one* of the threads constituting its fabric. Extra-formal elements such as notions, loci, hierarchies, function, and argument context are inevitably a part of interpreting and categorizing an argument. Reducing an argument only to its formal features would undermine *The New Rhetoric*'s central purpose which is to reintroduce the culturally recognizable argument features that formal logic has set aside. The speech and syntax in which an argument is stated are also threads making up its meaning. When considered in the context of the argument situation and in relation to the arguer's intention, most variations in interpretation can be resolved.

The treatment of the schemes in *The New Rhetoric* does at times lack clarity. Because of this, we began our study by identifying as precisely as possible the features of each scheme as discussed in *The New Rhetoric, The Realm of Rhetoric,* and other writings by Perelman and by Olbrechts-Tyteca.[2] Consequently, we were able to construct a substantial set of identifiable attributes for each scheme. Precise identification of these attributes enabled us (as members of the culture to which the arguments were addressed) to recognize and categorize individual argument schemes used in each of the five panel discussions that we studied. The texts of the five programs presented a circumscribed universe of discourse for analysis. Since we considered all of the statements that we classified as arguments, and since we actively considered the possibility that some arguments might not fit into *any* category, our examination of the arguments can be said to be inclusive. To clarify how individual scheme types work and to respond in part to van Eemeren and his colleagues' observation that the schemes were originally imprecisely defined and esoterically exemplified, we here provide an account of individual scheme workings and illustrate them with examples.[3]

EXEMPLIFICATION OF INDIVIDUAL SCHEME CATEGORIES

As we have noted, arguers use schemes to connect premises and claims, and this process has both rhetorical and logical dimensions. Such inferential mechanisms as syllogistic inference, cause/effect links, paired hierarchies, and coexistential relations follow logical models tacitly recognized by audiences in Western culture. The role of most schemes is to increase or decrease the presence of certain elements of reality. And, the schemes themselves must have a certain presence for the anticipated audience; they depend upon symbols, beliefs, and values specific to a particular culture. The purpose of this section, then, is to examine and describe the ways in which assumed audience predispositions are resources that establish inferential links in the thirteen scheme categories described by Perelman (1982; see Figure 1). To illustrate scheme workings and their dependence on audience beliefs, examples of the various scheme categories will be provided.

Quasi-Logical Schemes

Quasi-logical arguments are so named because they have the *appearance* of formal logic (and not because they are to be regarded as somehow "less than logical"). In using quasi-logical schemes, arguers draw upon the recognized structures of formal logic to construct nonformal arguments. Transitivity, reciprocity, or disjunction transfers audience allegiance from accepted premises to the arguer's conclusion. The arguments' appeal derives from audience recognition of their logical counterparts and the fact that their syllogistic infrastructure has a certain inherent persuasiveness (Perelman & Olbrechts-Tyteca, 1969, p. 193). Contemporary culture's preference for certainty, simplicity, and parsimony contributes to the effectiveness of quasi-logical arguments. The limited number of terms and the direct connections between them have a compelling air.

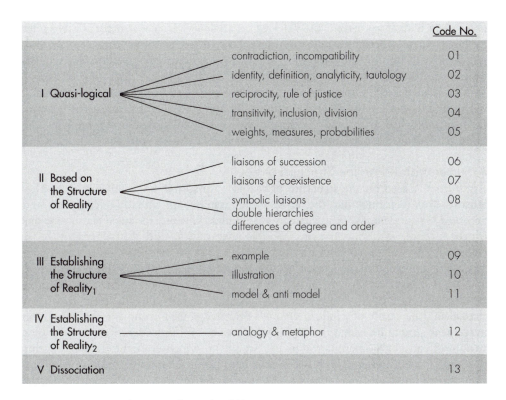

		Code No.
	contradiction, incompatibility	01
	identity, definition, analyticity, tautology	02
I Quasi-logical	reciprocity, rule of justice	03
	transitivity, inclusion, division	04
	weights, measures, probabilities	05
	liaisons of succession	06
II Based on the Structure of Reality	liaisons of coexistence	07
	symbolic liaisons double hierarchies differences of degree and order	08
III Establishing the Structure of Reality$_1$	example	09
	illustration	10
	model & anti model	11
IV Establishing the Structure of Reality$_2$	analogy & metaphor	12
V Dissociation		13

Figure 1   Argument Schemes in *The Realm of Rhetoric*

Transitivity arguments, based as they are on the categorical syllogism, cause audiences to accept theses by way of transference through a middle term. In the *Ethics* series, one panelist in the role of a corporate CEO argued that "we ought to make our case through what's important to this company. There is nothing more important now in our corporate life than the research program. And I want to see us make our case on that." Here, his claim concerning the research program was enabled by transference through the middle term, "what's important."

Quasi-logical simplicity is also manifest in *reciprocity* arguments. Based as they are on a simple conditional relationship between two terms, reciprocity arguments rely upon a perceived symmetry that has a certain inherent appeal. The same CEO might have argued that "sacrificing the research program, the most valuable component of our operation, means that there won't be much of value remaining." The research program's sacrifice is here equated with a profound loss of value in the operation as a whole.

Other quasi-logical relations derive the same sort of persuasiveness from the appeal of formal logical relations. *Contradiction* and *incompatibility* depend upon the commonly-held assumption that asserting "x" and "not x" simultaneously is absurd. *Arguments from the Rule of Justice*—beings in essentially the same category should be treated in the same way—succeed because audiences value precedent. *Arguments by division*, which make a point simply by enumerating the parts or features of something, rely upon a spatialized conception of reality that excludes overlappings, interactions, and fluidity. The concreteness and stipulations of arguments by division also increase the presence of the whole and thus foreground those aspects that the arguer wishes to make salient. For example, in the *Ethics* series, an investment banker argued for the value of his advisory services to a corporate raider by listing them: "First, it's partially our incentive to bring him the idea. Second, we work with him on the strategy and tactics of how to consummate the acquisition. And, if he has to dispose of some pieces, we assist him in these dispositions." *Statistical probabilities,* the last group of quasi-logical arguments, are also supported by a cultural preference for calculative estimates and quantification. In general, then, quasi-logical arguments increase awareness of relationships by reducing the number of terms in an argument and simplifying the connections between them.

Arguments Based on the Structure of Reality

Arguments "based on the structure of reality" are so named because they employ liaisons and relations that the arguer can assume are already recognized and accepted by audiences. This category includes liaisons of succession, liaisons of coexistence, symbolic liaisons, double hierarchies, and differences of order (Perelman, 1982). Arguments of succession include all forms of causal argument wherein phenomena of the same level are connected in an explanatory relationship.

Causal arguments are grounded in culturally held beliefs and presumptions about reality, not the least of which is that events generally must have a cause rather than being the result of random chance. Effective causal argument depends upon agreement among interlocutors about the motives and precedence for action. One variant of causal argument is pragmatic argument, which evaluates acts and events in terms of their consequences and works because of a common audience assumption that the best means is that which requires the smallest sacrifice to obtain the desired end. For example, when asked for a plan behind a proposed acquisition, the aforementioned corporate raider simply responded, "The plan? The plan is that we want to give your stockholders $30 a share and the stock is selling at $20." Perelman and Olbrechts-Tyteca (1969) note that in Western society this utilitarian orientation "enjoys a value . . . inherent in this superiority" (p. 277).

A second subtype based on reality is *coexistential relation.* In arguments of coexistence, one connects terms that belong to unequal levels of reality, such as connecting an unobservable essence to its observable manifestations. The prototype for this inference scheme type is the act/person relation (Perelman, 1951). Act/person relations are reciprocal. Sometimes we classify the person according to his or her acts; at other times, we reason from the act to the person. For example, a journalist in the *Ethics* series argued "If I found out later that the CEO had lied to me, I'd have a very strong feeling about him, his company, and the other information he provided." Act/person and other coexistential ascriptions are driven by the epistemological priority given to what is concrete and empirically accessible. Such preferences are intensified by audiences' spontaneous tendency to classify, exaggerate, and simplify (Perelman & Olbrechts-Tyteca, 1969, p. 304).

Symbolic liaisons and double hierarchies are two other types of argument based on accepted structures of reality. In *symbolic liaisons,* recognized symbols reshape an audience's perceptions. Symbolic liaisons are characterized by a relationship of participation between a symbol and what the symbol evokes. They often function as recognized metonymies (e.g., "level playing field" and "Joe Six-Pack").

Double hierarchy arguments employ accepted value hierarchies to get other hierarchies accepted. As Walker and Sillars (1990) observed, audiences regularly use undisputed hierarchies to weigh or grade values and to resolve conflicts between values. The use of what Perelman and Olbrechts-Tyteca (1969) call the "loci of the preferable" indicates that the existence of certain unquestioned hierarchies is what makes double hierarchy arguments possible. For instance, loci of quantity (greatest good for the greatest number) and of the existent (the concrete is to be preferred to the merely possible) are often used to support choices based on hierarchies (pp. 83–99). Toward the end of the Persian Gulf war, peace advocates argued that "a cease fire now is better than a negotiated settlement later because of the thousands of lives that would be lost on both sides if hostilities continue." This argument used an accepted hierarchy based on a locus of quantity and value (lives saved as opposed to lives lost) to persuade the audience of a second hierarchy (an immediate cease fire is to be valued over an eventual negotiated settlement). On the other hand, opponents of an immediate cease fire maintained that "a decisive victory now followed by a peace conference will lead to a true peace; other alternatives are mere stopgaps." Here another locus of quantity (permanent versus transitory) was used to support a negotiated settlement rather than a temporary cease fire. In both cases, then, established hierarchies have been used to argue for one of the two options.

Arguments Establishing the Structure of Reality

Unlike arguments in the former category that rely upon connections recognized by the audience, arguments establishing the structure of reality seek to call upon existing audience predispositions to create new audience perceptions. Such arguments generally employ a concrete instance, relationship or linguistic form to establish a more abstract or general principle. In *The New Rhetoric,* this category included example, illustration, model and anti-model, analogy, and metaphor.

The *example* seeks to establish a new principle by resort to the particular case. Use of example implies disagreement over a principle while assuming that generalization is possible. To make way for the principle, the example must be factual and striking. *Illustrations* resemble examples in form but their function is different. Instead of establishing a principle, they increase its presence by clarifying it or showing its import. Since the principle is already established, the illustration may be fictive, so long as it engages the imagination, for vivacity is the source of its appeal. When many particular cases are cited, the first ones may serve as examples to establish a principle, while the others act as illustrations. For instance, in the *Ethics* series, an entrepreneur could show the inadequacy of corporate conglomerates by observing that takeovers "created extraordinary contraptions of multi-industry that went from making socks to making electronic engines to making aerospace to whatever you like. These conglomerates didn't work."

Argument from model and anti-model presents a person or group as a model to be imitated or avoided. Attraction for the model (antipathy for the anti-model) is converted into favorable or unfavorable orientation toward the model's behavior. The argument's aim is thus to encourage imitation. Arguments from model can set up a particular model behavior with the aim of inspiring similar behavior by the audience, or, as Perelman and Olbrechts-Tyteca (1969) put it, "incite to an action inspired by" a particular behavior (p. 362). For example, in the *Ethics* series, one CEO said of a community-minded organization:

> We have tried for a long time to get corporations to be more responsible. We have now done it at Peachtree. We're reaching out, supporting the university, supporting cultural activities, and so on. We are the ultimate of what America believes corporate responsibility is all about.

The implied thesis here is that the model corporation is one that is concerned with the well being of its home community and of society. Since most audience members view such an orientation as virtuous, they will be inclined to agree that it should be emulated. In arguments from model, arguers also may invoke the prestige of a person or group to confer added value on their acts.

Analogy and metaphor bring together two structures—a better known structure (the phoros) and one that is lesser known (the theme). *Analogical arguments* succeed to the extent that the arguer can focus audience attention on those features of the theme that s/he considers most important. The arguer must select a phoros that is appropriate because it is familiar within the cultural context of the argument and focuses attention on the features that the arguer wants projected onto the theme. Analogies facilitate the development and extension of thought; they make it possible to give the theme a structure and a conceptual setting. In the *Ethics* series, an entrepreneur reminded his audience that one should not "mix up the difference between doing business and doing good. The bee doesn't make honey because he's doing good; he doesn't have soul searching, 'Am I doing good when I make honey?'" Here the phoros (honey making) focused audience attention on the means/end distinction the arguer wished to feature. Whereas analogies bring together structures from different spheres in a tensive relationship, metaphors consecrate the relation between theme and phoros. The two spheres are no longer separate but are fused. The same entrepreneur coined multiple metaphors in referring to inoperative conglomerates: "you can enshrine them, ossify them, and make them into a monument." Such metaphors are not stylistic but argumentative in that they alter audience perceptions and imply an argumentative thesis—that inefficient and unprofitable conglomerates are like fossils in their rigidity and state of *rigor mortis*.

Dissociations

Whereas analogies bring together two concepts from separate spheres, dissociation modifies a notion's conceptual structure by disengaging incompatible notions that had originally been unified. Dissociation thus begins by assuming "the original unity of elements comprised within a single conception . . ." (Perelman & Olbrechts-Tyteca, 1969, p. 411–412). It then sets a criterion by using the valued term of a hierarchized pair to produce a value reorientation. Dissociation is thus unlike division which allows concepts "to remain as they were . . . , like bricks saved intact from a building that has been pulled down" (p. 413). Dissociating a new concept from an old one remodels the audience's concept of reality and resolves incompatibilities.

Perelman and Olbrechts-Tyteca (1969) reflect that the mere fact that such pairs can be abstracted and have meaning is "the residue of a dominant cultural tradition" (p. 420). The power of dissociation as an argumentative form relies on audience recognition of the appearance/reality pair which Perelman and Olbrechts-Tyteca explain with the prototype of the Term I/Term II distinction. The Term I (appearance) component of the pair, which is actual, obvious, and immediate, is devalued; the Term II concept, a construction that can only be known indirectly, is valued. The appearance/reality pair reflects other, similar pairs composed from pervasive and culturally bound value orderings: verbal/real, means/end, subjective/objective, letter/spirit, opinion/knowledge.

The generality of hierarchized pairs within a society lends a certain stability to dissociations. Dissociations nevertheless represent the presumed hierarchies of an arguer's expected audience. The particular audience appeal of dissociations was dramatized in the discussion of corporate takeovers in the *Ethics* series. The CEO favoring conservative business practices opposed speculative takeovers by arguing:

I don't see a plan that's going to be beneficial to the corporation. It's a one-time hit, where we get a spike in the share price, and we cash out a corporation instead of operating it as a viable entity sometime into the future.

Here the plan "beneficial to the corporation" is a Term II reference and establishes as criteria permanence and inherency. The "one time hit," the quick cash out, is devalued as Term I because its benefits are short term. Thus, the operative pairs here are: means (cash out)/end (corporate benefit); and transitory (quick profit)/permanent (long-term viability). In response to this, the CEO's opponent, a market entrepreneur, made use of an opposing dissociation:

If it's a good plant and it's working efficiently, it will remain and become a better plant because you will have done a remarkable thing, which is marry management and capitalism. If you can't make the plant efficient, either modernize it or close it. You are running a business, not a charity.

The entrepreneur's valuing of capitalist management, efficiency, and opportunism as Term II concepts depend upon his audience's recognition of the locus of quantity and its appropriateness to the business setting.

Close examination of various schemes, then, reveals the senses in which they are inherently dependent upon culturally held beliefs and values. Perelman's theory has been criticized because it is culture bound, but it is difficult to imagine how any theory so dependent upon values and schemes shared by a projected audience could be otherwise. Perelman and Olbrechts-Tyteca's theory of schemes grows out of the habits of thought and intellectual biases of Judeo-Christian Western culture. Recognition of the ways in which the schemes operate rhetorically in a given cultural setting can enable analysts to illuminate the inferential workings of many types of rhetorical discourse.

PATTERNS OF SCHEME USE IN THE *ETHICS* SERIES

To further examine the stability and usefulness of the schemes in *The New Rhetoric*, we applied its categories to arguments used by participants in the *Ethics in America* series. Of the ten programs in the series, we randomly selected and transcribed five dealing with ethical issues in five different areas—business, politics, law, medicine, and journalism. The programs employed a total of 67 different panelists and four different narrators.

To identify the inference schemes used in these discussions, we employed a two-step procedure. First, we identified all the arguments that appeared in the discussions, using a conception of argument articulated by van Eemeren and Grootendorst (1984) and consistent with Perelman and Olbrechts-Tyteca's (1969) theory. For our purposes, an instance of discourse was deemed an argument when it (a) expressed a viewpoint, in (b) an actual or anticipated context of opposition, with (c) a rationale designed to justify or refute that viewpoint. Using these characteristics, we independently identified the arguments in each transcript, then met and resolved through discussion all of our coding differences. Reliability of our coding was determined by calculating a Guetzkow (1950) U on the pre-discussion codings of one transcript; this procedure determined that our identification of arguments was reliable ($U = .04$).

Next, we coded each of the arguments we had identified using the 13-scheme classification provided in Figure 1. To help us in our work we developed detailed coding guidelines identifying the attributes of each scheme category according to descriptions contained in *The New Rhetoric* and *The Realm of Rhetoric*.[4] We applied these guidelines to the transcripts, identifying how many schemes were present in each argument and classifying schemes into major categories and subcategories. For each transcript we identified and classified the argument schemes separately, then met and discussed each of our coding judgments. To help us detect schemes we had missed and to help resolve our coding differences, we employed a third person to code two of the transcripts and join us in our discussions. All of our codings were mutually agreed upon through these discussions.

To estimate the reliability of our codings we first determined whether we identified the same number of argument schemes in each of the arguments we identified. As before, we selected one transcript and computed a Guetzkow U on our prediscussion codings which yielded an acceptable U of .06. We then determined whether our scheme codings were consistent by selecting one of the transcripts and computing Kappas on our prediscussion codings. The resulting Kappas were .78 for major level classifications and .71 for subcategory classifications. These reliability estimates indicate that our coding, while it was not highly consistent, was acceptably consistent and reliable prior to any discussion of our coding judgments.

Our procedures produced a number of observations about scheme use in argumentative discussions. First, we found that the number of arguments and number of schemes used was fairly consistent from discussion to discussion. The distribution of the 622 arguments across discussions was as follows: 111 in the journalism discussion, 118 in the law discussion, 126 in the medicine discussion, 128 in the politics discussion, and 139 in the business discussion ($M = 124$). In these 622 arguments, we identified 1037 argument schemes. These schemes were also relatively consistent across discussions: 216 schemes were detected in the journalism discussion, 221 in law, 213 in medicine, 171 in politics; and 216 in business ($M = 207$). Hence it appears that scheme use is relatively consistent across different topics of discussion and across different groups of people.

A second observation is that while all of the scheme categories were used in the discussion, some categories were used much more than others. The frequency of scheme use by major and minor categories is provided in Table 1. As Table 1 indicates, the great majority of the argument schemes used in the discussions were quasi-logical in nature (37.2%) or based on the structure of reality (41.9%).[5] Only 16% of the schemes established the structure of reality, while dissociation accounted for only 4% of scheme use. Within these major categories, there were substantial differences in the use of particular schemes. Of the quasi-logical schemes (37%) that were used in the discussion, most were definitions (9%), reciprocity (11%), or schemes of transitivity or division (12%). There were very few contradictions and incompatibilities (3%) or quantitative schemes (2%). Of the arguments using schemes based on the structure of reality, most were liaisons of succession or causal schemes (22%) or liaisons of coexistence (12%). Fewer arguments used symbolic liaisons or double hierarchies (8%). Of the 16% of schemes that established the structure of reality, 10% were examples, illustrations, or model/anti-model, while 6% were analogies or metaphors. As we have already mentioned, only 4% of the schemes used in the discussions were dissociations.

We offer two final observations about scheme use in these argumentative discussions. First, we found the frequency of scheme use to be relatively stable across the discussions. For instance, quasi-logical schemes were consistent, ranging from 33% in the business and journalism discussions to 41% in the law discussion. Use of schemes based on the structure of reality was also highly consistent, ranging from

MAJOR CATEGORIES & SUBCATEGORIES	Business	Politics	Law	Medicine	Journalism	TOTAL	(Raw Frequency Totals)
I. Quasi-logical	33.3	38.0	41.8	39.4	33.8	37.2	(386)
01	3.7	3.5	2.3	1.9	2.3	2.7	
02	10.6	8.1	10.0	10.3	4.6	8.8	
03	6.5	12.3	10.0	11.7	13.4	10.7	
04	8.3	12.3	17.7	11.7	12.5	12.5	
05	4.2	1.8	1.8	3.8	0.9	2.5	
II. Based on the Structure of Reality	39.4	43.3	42.3	43.7	40.7	41.9	(434)
06	17.6	21.6	23.1	29.1	19.0	22.2	
07	17.1	13.5	10.0	9.4	10.6	12.0	
08	4.6	8.2	9.1	5.2	11.1	7.6	
III. Establishing the Structure of Reality$_1$	10.6	8.8	8.2	8.5	15.7	10.4	(108)
09	2.8	4.1	5.5	2.8	11.1	5.3	
10	4.6	1.8	2.3	3.8	2.8	3.2	
11	3.2	2.9	0.4	1.9	1.9	2.0	
IV. Establishing the Structure of Reality$_2$							
12	9.3	7.0	2.3	5.6	6.5	6.1	(63)
V. Dissociation							
13	7.4	2.9	5.5	2.8	3.2	4.4	[(46)]
(Raw Frequency Totals)	(216)	(171)	(221)	(213)	(216)		(1037)

Table 1   Scheme Use

39% in the business discussion to 43% in the politics and medicine discussions. Second, we found that many of the arguments were seen to employ more than one argument scheme. A full 22% or 231 arguments were simultaneously coded with two different argument schemes, while 13%, or 135 arguments, employed three or more different argument schemes.

CONCLUSION

Our close study of descriptions of the schemes in *The New Rhetoric* and *The Realm of Rhetoric* enabled us to clarify the attributes of the thirteen schemes so that the three individuals could identify the schemes with an acceptable level of consistency. Identifying the schemes in natural discourse is always difficult because they are culture, context, and audience dependent. Variations in interpretation are inevitable, as Perelman and Olbrechts-Tyteca (1969) themselves realized when they observed that interpretive difficulties "are due not only to the equivocal character of language, but also to the fact that the springs supporting the argumentation are almost never entirely explicitly described" (p. 187). Our own experience, however, indicated that *The New Rhetoric*'s scheme system was no more problematic in this regard than other argument typologies.

An intriguing dimension of Perelman and Olbrechts-Tyteca's system is their introduction of new inference categories. Until recently, our texts and pedagogy have generally neglected double hierarchies, dissociations, and arguments from model and anti-model. Although these schemes were relatively infrequent in our discourse sample (totalling no more than 12% of scheme use), they did play a crucial role in certain parts of the discussions. Dissociations were used to resolve contradictions and incompatibilities, and panelists resorted to double hierarchies to justify values and moral action. Furthermore, the frequency and predominance of quasi-logical schemes indicate their significance. Our study indicates that treatments of informal and inductive logic should not be limited to analogy, generalization, cause, and sign, since a large proportion of ordinary language arguments make use of quasi-logical schemes.

We found the scheme category system to be generally complete, since nearly all the arguments could be categorized into at least one of the scheme types. The only kind of arguments that appeared to be problematic were refutative arguments. Since Perelman and Olbrechts-Tyteca did not study *interactive* arguments, their general neglect of specifically refutational schemes is not surprising. Sometimes refutative patterns emerged (e.g., dissociations used to resolve incompatibilities or challenge analogies). At other times, refutations could not be easily categorized. In our discourse sample, refutations occurred infrequently. Generally, however, the characteristics of refutative arguments merit further study by argumentation theorists.

We found the frequency of scheme use to be relatively stable in the various discussions.[6] The fact that a number of arguments evinced more than one scheme seemed to us to be unproblematic. Perelman and Olbrechts-Tyteca (1969) anticipated multiple scheme use when they observed that "one must not believe that these classes of argumentative schemes are isolated entities. We are often allowed . . . to interpret an argument . . . as belonging to one of the classes of structure as well as to another" (p. 192). Arguments frequently employ multiple schemes simultaneously, and their cogency and appeal may be enhanced as a result.

As our study indicates, Perelman and Olbrechts-Tyteca (1969) offer a heuristic and expanded set of culturally-based scheme categories for the micro level study of inference processes. They have, in fact, provided an updated and refined topical system enabling the study of argument patterns. Sensitized as they were to the arguments' rhetorical dimension, these authors made explicit the hierarchies, metonymies, thought patterns, and habits to which Western audiences subscribe, and they have shown how these are used to make the schemes work. *The New Rhetoric*'s scheme taxonomy should prove to be a resource valuable to argument analysts, rhetorical critics, and other scholars interested in the rhetorical study of argument practices.

NOTES

[1] Perelman and Olbrechts-Tyteca discuss the "schemes," or explicit and implicit linkages in microarguments, in part three of *The New Rhetoric*. In this section they also discuss other techniques of argumentation, such as the interaction and strength of arguments, the amplitude of arguments, and the persuasive effects of various ways of ordering arguments. The emphasis of this essay, however, is on the inferential links, or "schemes," within individual arguments.

2 For our classification of the schemes, we employed the thirteen-scheme breakdown described in *The Realm of Rhetoric* because it was more parsimonious than that in *The New Rhetoric*. However, we consulted the latter work extensively in developing our guidelines for the system as a whole.

3 The examples will be drawn from 622 arguments we found in the *Ethics in America* television series, a set of ten panel discussions first aired by the Public Broadcasting System during the winter of 1989. In this series, prominent journalists, lawyers, judges, doctors, corporate executives, and other public figures discussed the ethics of corporate takeovers, political campaigning, press coverage, medical experimentation, and other practices. In each program, a narrator presented a series of hypothetical situations to a panel of 12 to 17 experts who recommended and defended positions and courses of action. Panelists were expected not to reach agreement but to display and justify their positions in the manner of Kant's categorical imperative. The next section of this essay, which describes the rhetorical operation of the schemes, will draw most of its examples from a single discussion in the *Ethics* series that concerned corporate takeovers.

Because of its unique characteristics, the discourse we study here is not representative of general argumentation. Nonetheless, it does make use of interactive arguments: it uses questions and answers, proposals and refutations; arguments are frequently broken up and interrupted; and claims are often implicit or based on prior speaking turns. Its dissimilarities from general argumentation are largely due to its nature as a *media event*. Based on fabricated hypothetical situations, it is addressed to a media audience as well as to other interactants, evinces the reasoning of skilled experts rather than naive social actors, and is intended to display viewpoints and raise rather than resolve issues. Although this discourse was useful in answering the research questions we posed, we urge caution in applying our findings to analyze interaction in general interpersonal argument.

4 Detailed coding guidelines are available from the authors upon request.

5 The raw frequencies for the occurrence of all schemes in the discourse sample are available from the authors upon request.

6 Our results in their present form are particular to the format and communication situation in which these discussions were held. General statements concerning the patterns and frequency of scheme use can only be made possible by studies of schemes appearing in other communication contexts.

REFERENCES

Dearin, R. D. (1982). Perelman's concept of "quasi-logical" argument: A critical elaboration. In J. R. Cox & C. A. Willard (Eds.), *Advances in argumentation theory and research* (pp. 78–94). Carbondale: Southern Illinois University Press.

Farrell, T. B. (1986). Reason and rhetorical practice: The inventional agenda of Chaim Perelman. In J. L. Golden & J. J. Pilotta (Eds.), *Practical reasoning in human affairs* (pp. 259–86). Dordrecht Holland: D. Reidel.

Golden, J. L. (1986). The universal audience revisited. In J. L. Golden & J. J. Pilotta (Eds.), *Practical reasoning in human affairs* (pp. 287–304). Dordrecht Holland: D. Reidel.

Guetzkow, H. (1950). Unitizing and categorizing problems in coding qualitative data. *Journal of Clinical Psychology, 6*, 47–58.

Herrick, J. A. (1991). *Critical thinking: The analysis of arguments*. Scottsdale AZ: Gorsuch Scarisbrick.

Karon, L. A. (1976). Presence in *The new rhetoric. Philosophy and Rhetoric, 9*, 96–111.

Katula, R. A. (1983). *Communication: Writing and speaking*. Boston: Little, Brown.

Laughlin, S. K., & Hughes, D. T. (1986). The rational and the reasonable: Dialectic or parallel systems? In J. L. Golden & J. S. Pilotta (Eds.), *Practical reasoning in human affairs* (pp. 187–205). Dordrecht Holland: D. Reidel.

McKerrow, R. E. (1982). Rationality and reasonableness in a theory of argument. In J. R. Cox & C. A. Willard (Eds.), *Advances in argumentation theory and research* (pp. 105–22). Carbondale: Southern Illinois University Press.

Measell, J. S. (1985). Perelman on analogy. *Journal of the American Forensic Association, 22*, 65–71.

Olbrechts-Tyteca, L. (1979). Les Couples philosophiques: Une nouvelle approche. *Revue internationale de philosophie, 33*, 81–98.

Perelman, C. (1951). Act and person in argument. *Ethics, 61*, 251–69.

Perelman, C. (1958). Self evidence and proof. *Philosophy, 33*, 289–302.

Perelman, C. (1982). *The realm of rhetoric* (W. Kluback, Trans.). Notre Dame: University of Notre Dame Press.

Perelman, C. (1984). The new rhetoric and the rhetoricians: Remembrances and comments. *Quarterly Journal of Speech, 70*, 188–96.

Perelman, C., & Olbrechts-Tyteca, L. (1969). *The new rhetoric: A treatise on argumentation* (J. Wilkinson & P. Weaver, Trans.). Notre Dame: University of Notre Dame Press.

Ray, J. W. (1978). Perelman's universal audience. *Quarterly Journal of Speech, 64*, 361–75.

Schiappa, E. (1985). Dissociation in the arguments of rhetorical theory. *Journal of the American Forensic Association, 22*, 72–82.

Scult, A. (1976). Perelman's universal audience: One perspective. *Central States Speech Journal, 27*, 176–80.

Seibold, D. R., McPhee, R. D., Poole, M. S., Tanita, N. E. & Canary, D. J. (1981). Argument, group influence, and decision outcomes. In G. Ziegelmueller & J. Rhodes (Eds.). *Dimensions of argument: Proceedings of the Second Summer Conference on Argumentation* (pp. 663–92). Annandale VA: Speech Communication Association.

van Eemeren, F. H., & Grootendorst, R. (1984). *Speech acts in argumentative discussions*. Dordrecht Holland: Foris.

van Eemeren, F. H., Grootendorst, R., & Kruiger, T. (1984). *The study of argumentation*. New York: Irvington.

Walker, G. B., & Sillars, M. O. (1990). Where is argument? Perelman's theory of values. In R. Trapp & J. Schuetz (Eds.). *Perspectives on argumentation: Essays in honor of Wayne Brockriede* (pp. 134–50). Prospect Heights IL: Waveland.

Wenzel, J. W. (1990). Three perspectives on argument: Rhetoric, dialectic, logic. In R. Trapp & J. Schuetz (Eds.) *Perspectives on argumentation: Essays in honor of Wayne Brockriede* (pp. 9–26). Prospect Heights IL: Waveland.

Walton's Argumentation Schemes for Presumptive Reasoning: A Critique and Development

J. ANTHONY BLAIR

1. INTRODUCTION: WALTON'S ACCOUNT

In his book, *Argument Schemes for Presumptive Reasoning* (1996), Douglas Walton offers an account of that kind of reasoning, or argumentation, in which the support that the proffered grounds supply for the claim at issue succeeds (or is intended to succeed) in establishing a presumption in its favour that is at least sufficient to shift the burden of proof to anyone who would deny that claim. Such reasoning, or argumentation, probably constitutes the majority of reasoning and argumentation that we engage in, encompassing much of the thinking and arguing we do involving claims about actions, policies and evaluations, and all of it that proceeds from less than conclusive or firm grounds—reasoning or arguing that is not (or is not intended to be), either deductively decisive or inductively strong. Given the prominence of such reasoning and arguing in our lives, Walton's project is important, and therefore worthy of a critical examination.

In this paper I first sketch Douglas Walton's account of argument schemes for presumptive reasoning. Then I outline some of what I think is missing from the account as presented by Walton. Last, I propose ways of filling in some (not all) of those missing pieces. The sketch of Walton's account will occupy the rest of this introductory section. I should make clear at the outset my general agreement with Walton's project. Although I think his account is incomplete, and I disagree with some details, I believe that the study of presumptive argumentation schemes is important, and that Walton's approach to it is fruitful and suggestive.

In the book under examination, Walton restricts his discussion to the argument schemes to be found in presumptive reasoning. He takes presumptive reasoning to be typified by the pragmatic, 'rough and ready generalizations,' of practical reasoning (reasoning about what to do); it is the 'plausible reasoning' for which Rescher provided a calculus in his *Plausible Reasoning* (1976). A model for presumptive reasoning is default or non-monotonic reasoning discussed in computer science.

Central to Walton's account is his analysis of *presumption*. He presents presumption as related to, but distinct from, *burden of proof*. On his analysis, it is that move in a dialogue which lies between assertion (which incurs the burden of proof) and assumption (which carries no burden whatever). A presumption so conceived has practical value by way of advancing the argumentation, and, in accepting something as a presumption, the interlocutor assumes the burden of rebutting it. Thus a presumption shifts the burden of proof, and this function is at the heart of Walton's analysis. Presumptions come into play in the absence of firm evidence or knowledge, which is why they are typically found in practical reasoning. Presumptive reasoning, in sum, 'is neither deductive nor inductive in nature, but represents a third distinct type . . . , an inherently tentative kind of reasoning subject to defeat by the special circumstances (not defined inductively or statistically) of a particular case' (Walton, 1996, p. 43).

For Walton, argument schemes are structures or 'forms' of argument which are 'normatively binding kinds of reasoning' and are 'best seen as moves, or speech acts' in dialogues (ibid., p. 28). They are normatively binding in the sense that, in accepting premises organized in a 'genuine' scheme 'appropriate' to the type of dialogue in process, one is bound (in some way) to accept the conclusion drawn from them, provided that the 'critical questions' that are 'appropriate to' that scheme are answered satisfactorily (ibid., p. 10).

Walton postulates that the validity of an argument scheme is contextual: a function of the context of dialogue in which it is used in a given case. Remember that the aim of argument in presumptive or plausible reasoning is to shift the burden of proof in a dialogue (not to prove a proposition with a given degree of probability or plausibility). Whether a scheme succeeds in shifting the burden of proof depends on whether the scheme is valid (for the occasion of its use) and on whether the members of a set of 'critical questions' associated with it either have been answered affirmatively earlier in the dialogue or can be later if they are raised. (In making the distinction between choosing a valid scheme and applying it so as to satisfy its associated critical questions satisfactorily, Walton mirrors the distinction between the selection of the scheme and its correct use made by van Eemeren and Grootendorst, 1992, p. 159).

To this distinction between an argument scheme and its associated critical questions there corresponds, in Walton's theoretical structure, a distinction between two (of three) levels of argument criticism. At the 'local' level the scheme itself may be invalid; or the argument may fail to conform to its scheme's requirements; or its premises may lack needed support. The critical questions associated with an argument scheme normally lead to further arguments, when and as their answers are provided and supported, so that the occurrence of a scheme in a dialogue effectively introduces a sequence of exchanges, which Walton labels an 'argumentation theme.' These argumentation themes form the backdrop for the second level of argument criticism: questioning the relevance of an argument at a given point in a dialogical exchange. The idea seems to be that what makes an argument relevant is the appropriateness of its placement in the sequence of questions and answers that constitute the argumentation theme of the dialogue at that point. (The third level of criticism is to question the appropriateness of the dialogue type being used.)

So a presumptive argument scheme is the pattern of a unit of local reasoning that is a move in an argumentative dialogue aiming to provide sufficient grounds to shift the burden of proof with respect to the assertion that is its conclusion.

Walton describes and discusses about thirty such schemes. For each scheme he supplies a description, a formulation, a set of critical questions associated with it, at least one and often several 'cases,' which are actual or invented examples of the scheme in use, and a discussion of the scheme in which he typically draws attention to its salient properties, relates it to other schemes, discusses the fallacies associated with it, comments on its presumptive force, and mentions typical contexts of its use.

An example of one of the argument schemes Walton discusses will illustrate his treatment. Here is the scheme of the 'argument from sign' (Walton, 1996, p. 49):

(1)   A is true in this situation.
       B is generally indicated as true when its sign, A, is true, in this kind of situation.
       Therefore, B is true in this situation.

Walton gives, among others, the following examples of arguments that instantiate the argument from sign scheme (ibid., pp. 47, 49):

(2)   3.1   There are some bear tracks in the snow.
            Therefore, a bear passed this way.
      3.4   Bob is covered with red spots.
            Therefore, Bob has the measles.
      3.5   The barometer just dropped.
            Therefore, we will have a storm.
      3.6   Bob is biting his nails.
            Therefore, Bob is worried about something.

Following Hastings (1962) Walton identifies the following two 'critical questions' as associated with the scheme of the argument from sign (Walton, 1996, p. 48):

(3)   1.   What is the strength of the correlation of the sign with the event signified?
      2.   Are there other events that would more reliably account for the sign?

Although Walton's account is rich in detail, I believe it leaves many theoretical questions and issues unanswered and unaddressed. I will list and discuss these *lacunae* in the next section.

2. WHAT IS MISSING FROM WALTON'S ACCOUNT

A natural first question to ask is, 'Where do argument schemes come from? What is their *provenance*[?]' Are they in the first instance descriptions of patterns to be found in (or, that can be abstracted from) actual argumentation as social events and products? If so, then their normative force requires an explanation, for from the fact that people's arguments happen to exhibit a particular pattern, it does not follow that the conclusions of such arguments are warranted by their premises. True enough, Walton proposes that presumptive schemes result merely in a shift in the burden of proof, and are not intended to make a definitive case for a claim. But in that case the question still remains as to where they get even that presumptive probative force. Alternatively, argument schemes are in the first instance *a priori* prescriptions for cogent or presumptive argumentation—patterns whose instantiations will be cogent or presumptively weighty arguments if they are appropriate for that context and are used appropriately. In the latter case, on what principles are they formed? Where do they get their probative force? As far as I can discern, Walton does not address these questions in this book. In sum, we are left with the following questions.

Q-set 1:   Are the schemes meant to be descriptive or prescriptive? In either case, what gives them normative force?

Other questions concern the *classification* of the schemes. Walton's argument from sign scheme looks like a scheme for causal reasoning: after all, the bear is the presumed cause of the bear tracks. Yet he also includes as a different scheme one he calls 'the argument from cause to effect.' Does 'the argument from sign' amount to 'the argument from effect to cause'? And if so, are these two schemes species of a generic causal argument scheme? Or are they best classified as different types of reasoning? In any case, how is the matter to be decided?

Notice also that Walton has grouped somewhat different types of reasoning together under the label of 'argument from sign.' The paw of a bear is necessary to make a bear track, but worry is not necessary in order to cause nail biting, nor is a storm necessary for the barometer to drop. Also, the connection between worry and nail biting is psychological, whereas that between a brewing storm and a falling barometer is physical. I do not mean to disagree with Walton that these four examples should be grouped as exemplifying one scheme, but it is fair to ask for an explanation of why these somewhat different contents of reasoning end up being classified as exhibiting a single argument scheme. Walton supplies no rationale for his selection of schemes, and the order in which he presents them seems to a large extent arbitrary.

It might be thought that van Eemeren and Grootendorst (1992) have already resolved this matter. They propose 'three main categories of argumentation schemes' (appealing, respectively, to when something is '*symptomatic*' of something else, or something is '*similar*' to something else, or something is '*instrumental*' to something else) (ibid., pp. 96–97). Of each of these 'there are many sub-categories' (ibid., p. 97). But they offer no account of why there are just these three categories, or why these three are the 'main' ones. Moreover, there are types of argument that don't seem to fit any of these three, for example, argument by inductive enumeration. And, van Eemeren and Grootendorst never define these three generic schemes or categories of schemes, but rather explain them by offering synonyms and by providing examples. As a result, while it is therefore difficult for a critic to show that a particular pattern of argumentation does not fit any of their three schemes (for example, that the appeal to authority scheme is not, as they claim, a case of symptomatic argumentation), by the same token it is equally difficult for them to show that it does. It is necessary to appeal to intuitions precisely where intuitions differ.

So we end up with a second set of questions:

Q-set 2:   On what principles are schemes to be classified? How are schemes to be distinguished by type?

Perhaps related to the questions about classifications are questions about the level of generality a scheme should exhibit. It is easy to imagine schemes of different generality for one and the same example of argumentation. For example, if I am fussing about my knee aching, and June says, among other things, 'If your arthritis is bothering you, take some ibuprofen—it's what your doctor prescribed,' which one of the following is the correct, or the better, scheme for her argument?

(4)   D prescribed treatment T for patient P's medical condition C.
       D is an authority with respect to treatments for C-type conditions and about P's condition.
       So, it is presumptively reasonable for P to take T when in C.

(5)   D prescribed action A to solve problem C.
       D is an authority with respect to dealing with C.
       So, it is presumptively reasonable to do A to solve C.

Clearly scheme (4) is less general or abstract than scheme (5), yet both seem exemplified in June's argument. What is the correct, or best, level of abstraction, and why? This issue is discussed in Kienpointner's *Alltagslogik* (1992), but Walton supplies no answers in his book.

Q-set 3:   How general should an argument scheme be? How is the question of the correct level of generality to be properly decided?

Another topic that is not discussed by Walton is the connection between an argument scheme and its 'associated' critical questions. He simply lists a set of critical questions for each scheme, but what motivates these questions? How is it to be decided which are the correct questions, and when a list of critical questions is complete? (The same question can be raised with respect to van Eemeren and Grootendorst's account, which makes a similar use of critical questions, without explanation. See van Eemeren and Grootendorst, 1992, pp. 101–102.)

Q-set 4:   Which are the right kind, and number, of critical questions to ask with respect to any given scheme? How is that to be decided?

I have glossed over the fact that Walton talks sometimes of schemes exhibited in arguments and sometimes of schemes exhibited in reasoning. One wants to know how these are related. So far I have followed Walton's convention of focusing on schemes without distinguishing presumptive reasoning from presumptive argumentation.

Q-set 5:   Are there both argument schemes and reasoning schemes,
or only one, and if so, which one? Or is there no distinction
between arguments and reasoning, or at least between
argument schemes and reasoning schemes?

As I have noted, in the book under consideration Walton devotes his attention
to the argument schemes used in presumptive reasoning or arguing. Are there other
types of schemes as well? Walton seems clearly to concede that possibility:

> We analyze only what we call presumptive argumentation schemes, ...
> Therefore, we do not include, for example, inductive arguments, part-whole
> arguments, or genus-species arguments, presuming that (by and large, at any
> rate) these types of argumentation are not presumptive in nature. (Walton,
> 1996, p. 3)
>   Certainly the problem remains of understanding how many of the most
> common of these [presumptive] argumentation schemes in everyday conversa-
> tion are inherently different from the usual models of deductive and inductive
> reasoning . . . . (ibid., p.3)

If there are other kinds of argumentation schemes besides those for presumptive
reasoning, then it seems that a general theory of argument schemes is needed to
account for them all.

Q-set 6:   How are presumptive argumentation schemes related to those
for inductive or deductive reasoning? What is the correct
general theory of argument schemes?

Finally, I would like to question some of the details of Walton's analyses of
presumption and of argument schemes. In particular I question whether presumptive reasoning is 'inherently tentative,' 'inconclusive' and 'provisional' (ibid., pp. 42,
ix, xi). I also would like at least to mention the possibility of questioning whether a
context of dialogue is essential to the function of argument schemes, or presumptive
or others.

Q-set 7:   Are all the details of Walton's account of argumentation
schemes for presumptive reasoning correct?

To sum up, among the tasks which a more complete theory of argument schemes
than is provided by Walton would have to take on are the following—each task or
set of tasks corresponding to one or more of the above seven question sets.

T1. Explain the descriptive and prescriptive functions of argument schemes
and explain the ground of the normative force of prescriptive schemes.
(Q-set 1)

T2. Identify the types of argument schemes and the principle(s) of
classification for argument schemes. (Q-set 2) Among other things,
determine whether there are inductive and deductive as well as
presumptive argument schemes. If possible, provide a general theory of
argument schemes. (Q-set 6)

T3. Address the question of the correct or appropriate level of generality of
argument schemes. (Q-set 3)

T4. Explain what motivates the critical questions attached to an argument scheme, and how the correct or appropriate number and formulation of these critical questions is to be established. (Q-set 4)

T5. Explain what it is that schemes are appropriately predicated of—arguments, or reasoning, or both. (Q-set 5)

T6. Offer critiques of some of the details of the account. (Q-set 7)

In the next section I will address all of these tasks except T3 and, aside from some comments in passing, T2. Both T2 and T3 have been discussed in detail by Kienpointner (1992), and it would take me beyond the focus on Walton's account to examine that of Kienpointner.

3. FURTHER DEVELOPMENTS

Argumentation and Reasoning

There is by now, thanks particularly to the work of van Eemeren and Grootendorst (1984, 1992), among others, general agreement among argumentation scholars that argumentation is a complex social, speech activity involving more than one party, with practical goals and subject to norms related to those goals. One cannot argue without at least an imaginary audience or interlocutor. Reasoning, on the other hand, whatever its social origins and functions, is a mental activity that can be performed privately. One can reason alone. Argumentation requires that its participants reason, so reasoning is necessary for argumentation; but one can reason without engaging in argumentation, so argumentation is not necessary for reasoning.

One (principal) type of reasoning is inferring—making the judgement that one proposition is implied by another or others (I use 'implied' broadly, to include 'supported.'). When Walton speaks of 'presumptive reasoning,' he is speaking of drawing presumptive inferences, or inferring presumptively. A person can infer without arguing (for example, you think to yourself, 'I need to be alert tomorrow, so I'd better get a good sleep tonight, so I'd better go to bed early.'), but inferring is necessary for arguing, in several respects. In argumentation, inferences are being made constantly by interlocutors in order to ascertain the nature of their activity and to sustain it. (For example, they constantly make inferences to answer such questions as: 'Do we disagree about this claim?' 'Which moves are permitted and appropriate at this point?' 'Which is the best move for me at this turn?') At the heart of the activity of argumentation is the offering of and response to arguments in the more narrow sense of reasons offered in support of or against claims: the illative core of argumentation. Here the interlocutors draw inferences about which propositions are implied by other propositions and about which propositions the other person or the audience will likely deem to be implied by given propositions, and the arguments they offer to one another are in effect invitations to draw inferences (Pinto, 1995, p. 276; Beardsley, 1976, p. 5).

These distinctions may be illustrated by the following schematic description of a dialectical interchange (where, 'a', 'b', 'c', 'd', 'e' and 'f' express variables ranging over what are accepted by an interlocutor as facts or states of affairs; 'p', 'q', 'r', 's' and 't' express variables ranging over propositions; and 'A' and 'B' express variables ranging over interlocutors):

(6)   1. Person *A* judges that proposition *p* implies proposition *q*. (Reasoning, by *A*.)

2. Either *p* does imply *q* or *p* does not imply *q*. (Implication, relationship between propositions.)

3. *A* judges on the basis of facts (*a*, *b* and *c*) that interlocutor *B* accepts *p* and will accept that *p* implies *q*. (Reasoning, by *A*.)

4. *A* invites *B* to accept *q* on the grounds that *p* and that *p* implies *q*. (Argument, offered by *A* to *B*.)

5. *B* accepts *p,* but also accepts *r,* and judges that *p* and *r* imply *not-q*. (Reasoning, by *B*.)

6. *B* invites *A* to accept *not-q* on the ground that *r* and that *p* and *r* imply *not-q*. (Argument, offered by *B* to *A*.)

7. Either *p* and *r* do imply *not-q* or they do not imply *not-q*. (Implication, relationship between sets of propositions.)

8. *A* does not accept *t,* or that *t* implies *not-r,* but believes on the basis of facts (*d*, *e* and *f*) that *B* accepts both. (Reasoning, by *A*.)

9. *A* invites *B* to accept *not-r* on the ground that *t* and that *t* implies *not-r*. (Argument, offered by *A* to *B*.)

10. Either *t* implies *not-r* or *t* does not imply *not-r*. (Implication, relationship between propositions.)

Clearly, reasoning (that is, inferring) is integral to the use of arguments in argumentation (although as 8. and 9. above indicate, one can, in offering an argument, invite one's interlocutor to employ reasoning that one rejects oneself). So what are the schemes to which Walton refers schemes of? Are they schemes of reasoning or of arguments?

I think the answer must be: both, but inference is more basic. Whether or not the arguer draws the inference that he or she invites the interlocutor to draw, he or she recognizes the possibility of drawing that inference. Thus the presentation of an argument presupposes a possible inference, and hence the instantiation of some possible pattern of inference. Thus, an inference scheme is logically prior to its use in any argument. Moreover, if schemes are prescriptive, they function to license inferences, so that is another reason for identifying them with inferences. On the other hand, in uttering an argument that invites the interlocutor to draw an inference, the arguer employs an instance of some pattern of argument, and so might be said to be employing an instance of an argument scheme. There is often no harm in shifting without notice from talk of inferences to talk of arguments, given the central role of inference in argument. However, given the difference between argument and inference, the two should not be conflated.

Walton's Classification of Schemes

Classifications are made with ends in view, and since there can be many compatible purposes for classifications, there are numerous possible compatible classifications. Walton is at pains to distinguish the schemes of presumptive reasoning from those of deductive logic and inductive reasoning. His principle of classification seems to be the strength of commitment to which the reasoner is entitled, given the premises, for each type of inference. When the premises deductively entail the conclusion, one is entitled to absolute confidence in the conclusion, given the premises. In contrast,

Walton thinks, when the premises presumptively support the conclusion, one is entitled to have little confidence in the conclusion, given the premises—just enough confidence to shift the onus of refutation over to anyone who would still deny the conclusion. Walton has little to say about inductive reasoning.

Walton is on the right track, I believe, but he overstates the tentative character of presumptive reasoning. To be sure, some presumptions are supported only very weakly; but others are supported so strongly that it would be no less irrational to lack confidence in their conclusions than it would be to lack confidence in conclusions strongly supported by inductive reasoning. For example, if my doctor prescribes ibuprofen for pain in my arthritic knee, and he knows the condition of my knee, having examined it arthroscopically, and he is an expert on the deterioration of, and the onset of arthritis in, knee joints with damaged cartilage, and there's no reason to distrust his judgement in this case, and his prescription conforms with the standard medical judgement for such cases, and none of the contra indicators against taking ibuprofen apply to me at the moment, then his prescription generates an extremely strong presumption in favour of my taking ibuprofen for arthritic pain in my knee. Again, if Ann has promised to return Bob's book on Monday, and if other things are equal, then unquestionably Ann has an actual (not just a *prima facie*) obligation to return Bob's book on Monday. There is nothing tentative or weak about these inferences.

So I would suggest a slightly different principle than degree of confidence for distinguishing these types of inference. I think the salient difference is whether the conclusion is defeasible in principle, given the premises. In the case of deductive entailments, given the premises, the conclusion is not defeasible, in principle. In the case of inductive and presumptive reasoning, it is. The defeasability criterion has the virtue of drawing the line sharply, while at the same time allowing that presumptive and inductive inferences can be extremely strongly supported, leaving no room for reasonable doubt or tentative commitments. Granted, this criterion fails to distinguish inductive from presumptive reasoning. I do not have a solution for that problem, but perhaps it is not a serious objection that the two cannot be sharply distinguished using this criterion.

The Provenance of Schemes

Kienpointner (1992, p. 241) distinguishes between descriptive and normative schemata, but in doing so he is distinguishing between, respectively, schemes for arguments with descriptive premises and conclusions, and schemes for arguments with descriptive and normative premises and normative conclusions. That is not the distinction I mean to denote by the labels 'descriptive' and 'prescriptive.' Instead, I have in mind the distinction between, on the one hand, a scheme that conveys the pattern of reasoning that someone actually used in a particular instance of reasoning or argument 'on the hoof' (to use the useful expression attributed to John Woods), which entails no endorsement of that reasoning or argument, and, on the other hand, a scheme that portrays a supposedly valid or cogent pattern of inference or argument.

But where do schemes—descriptive or prescriptive—come from? What is their *provenance*? How do Walton and others come up with these schemes, and just these schemes?

In the literature on schemes, many schemes seem to originate from—discussions of schemes in the literature! Thus, Kienpointner (1992) cites many mediaeval and classical sources for the schemes he describes. Walton does not explain the genesis of his list. He cites examples of actual argumentation for some, and provides invented examples for others. The assumption seems to be that the reader will find his invented examples plausible because they illustrate familiar patterns of reasoning or argument. But Walton also appears to cite schemes he takes to be well-known to his readers given their familiarity with the logical literature. Perelman and Olbrechts-Tyteca (1958) find in non-philosophical writing many of the schemes they describe. As noted above, van Eemeren and Grootendorst (1992) propose three generic argumentation schemes that they propose for use both in analyzing argumentative discourse and in assessing the adequacy of the defence of standpoints, which they characterize as 'more or less conventionalized ways of presenting the relation between what is stated in the argument and what is stated in the standpoint' (ibid., p. 96). Later, they refer to 'appropriate selection' of argumentation schemes, and their 'correct application' (ibid., p. 159).

To the extent that these authors provide descriptions of schemes actually selected for use, they are giving empirical reports of patterns found in actual or possible argumentation. To the extent that they are intended to be offering advice for the correct selection of reasoning or argumentation schemes or for the correct application or use of the schemes selected, their prescriptions must satisfy criteria other than simply to have been used. The issue of whether there can be an *a priori* theory of all possible cogent inference or argument schemes is too large to be broached here. It will have to be enough to note for now that any such theory will have to accommodate our logical intuitions about particular cases, from which it follows that unless and until such a comprehensive theory is produced, there is no shame in generating normative schemes from particular arguments or types of arguments in actual use that seem to us to be probatively compelling.

The Source of the Probative Force of Arguments or Reasoning Exhibiting Presumptive Schemes

Describing the schemes that have been used, and determining the cogency of the arguments or reasoning in which they are instantiated, are obviously different tasks. The philosophical interest in schemes relates to the grounds or source of their cogent use. What is the source of the probative force of a 'valid' inference or argument using such a scheme? The short explanation, I take it, lies in the irrationality of accepting the premises but rejecting the conclusion of such an inference or argument in those particular circumstances. Consider the three broad classes of arguments or reasoning that Walton mentions.

In the case of a deductively validity [*sic*], the reasoning or arguing derives its normative force or cogency from the fact that the truth of the premises of such a scheme on that occasion guarantees the truth of the conclusion. Thus, to accept the premises, and yet refuse to accept the conclusion, is irrational by virtue of being strongly inconsistent. In acknowledging that the reasoning or argument using that scheme is deductively valid, one is committed to accepting the conclusion if one grants the premises, so in granting the premises and refusing to accept the conclusion, one contradicts oneself.

Inductively strong reasoning or argument derives its normative force or cogency from the fact that in the use of such a scheme in those particular circumstances, to accept the premises and yet deny the probability of the conclusion, is irrational by virtue of a somewhat different kind of inconsistency. For strong reasoning using inductive schemes, given the evidence the conclusion is more probable than any alternative; and to acknowledge the inductive strength of reasoning using that scheme is to admit as much, yet to deny the conclusion is to hold out for some less probable alternative. There is no self-contradiction here, since it is possible that the conclusion is false, given the evidence, for even the strongest inductive inference.

In the case of presumptively cogent reasoning or argument, it is plausible to understand the probative force of the use of the scheme in question in those circumstances in a similar fashion. The reasoning or argument derives its cogency from the fact that to accept the premises and grant the validity of the inference using that scheme yet deny the plausibility of the conclusion, under the circumstances—without suggesting that any conditions of rebuttal exist—is pragmatically inconsistent. Given a strong presumption, to refuse to accept the conclusion without denying the evidence or finding a rebutting condition implies believing that there is some rebutting condition or circumstance for which there is no evidence. The skeptic in such a case is holding that the less plausible is the more plausible.

In all three cases, the probative force of the reasoning or argument using the scheme derives from one or another type of inconsistency involved, given that pattern of reasoning or argument and the facts of that situation, in accepting the premises, yet refusing to accept the conclusion.

The Motivation and Justification of the 'Critical Questions' of Presumptive Schemes

In this connection, by the way, we can understand what motivates the critical questions that Walton and others (for instance, Hastings, 1963; Schellens, 1987; van Eemeren and Kruiger, 1987; van Eemeren and Grootendorst, 1992) take to be associated with inference or argument schemes capable of use in presumptively cogent argumentation or reasoning, and how those questions play the normative role they do. Given that presumptive reasoning or argument is in principle defeasible, someone who reasons according to such a scheme wants to know how likely it is that the inference will be defeated in the given case. The so-called 'critical questions' are simply information-seeking questions that inquire about the conditions or circumstances that tend to rebut inferences using that scheme. The presumption is strengthened to the extent that the answers to these questions indicate the absence of defeating or overriding conditions. That is why presumptive schemes have critical questions associated with them, and it is the reason that the probative force of any presumptive reasoning or argument is partly a function of the answers to the critical questions associated with the scheme used in that case.

The role of the critical questions also explains why in some cases presumptively-supported claims are so plausible that to doubt them would be completely unwarranted. If answering all the critical questions associated with a scheme reveals that none of the rebutting conditions applies in a given case, then there is simply no reason whatever to deny the conclusion.

The Source of the Probative Force of Reasoning or Arguing Using Particular Schemes

But whence does reasoning or arguing from particular argumentation schemes derive its authority? What, for instance, is the justification of the argument from authority, or the argument from analogy, or the argument from consequences? Why do we accept appeals to expertise, or to similar cases, or to good or bad outcomes, as cogent? The general account of the rationality of presumptive reasoning sketched above does not explain the cogency of the employment of particular schemes, although it indicates what to look for—namely, some source of inconsistency, in that particular instance of reasoning or argument, attached to accepting the grounds but denying the conclusion.

Consider the argument from authority, one form of which is the argument from expert opinion. Why may we rely on the authority of experts? The answers lie in an analysis of authority and expertise. A necessary condition of authority is knowledge. If someone has knowledge in an area, then among other things they know a number of propositions belonging to it. But a proposition cannot be known unless it is true. So there is a connection between the expertise of an authority and the truth of at least some of the propositions for which the expert vouches. Although this account drastically oversimplifies the appeal to authority, I suggest that it is, *au fond,* the connection between authority, knowledge and truth that authorizes inferences from what experts claim to be the case to the plausibility of those claims.

Consider arguments using another scheme, one of the many forms of the argument from analogy: the argument from *a priori* analogy (Govier, 1987). This is an argument for a normative claim based on the similarity of two cases and the treatment already afforded one of them. An example? 'Officer, you should not give me a speeding ticket, because although I was driving faster than the speed limit, you did not give those other drivers speeding tickets, and they were going a lot faster than I was.' Why may we appeal to such analogies? I suggest that the answer lies in the norm of justice or fairness. Fairness requires treating similar cases similarly. To the extent that fairness is a good, similar cases ought to be treated similarly. The argument from *a priori* analogy appeals to the similarity of other cases, presupposing the norm of fairness. (It follows that a complete justification of reasoning or arguments using the scheme for *a priori* analogy would require a justification of fairness.) Unfortunately for the speeding driver, fairness is not the only value, nor always the highest ranking value, which is why the police officer is able validly to rebut this particular argument: 'There is a relevant difference between you and those other speeders,' he will say, 'You are the one I caught.'

In general, I take it that for each scheme we must be able to provide a general account of why reasoning or arguing using schemes of that type is cogent. There must be some particular connection between the premise set and the conclusion in reasoning or arguments instantiating such a scheme that makes it in some way unreasonable in that kind of case and in those circumstances to deny the conclusion while granting the premises, other things being equal.

4. CONCLUSION

It has been the aim of this paper to advance the theoretical discussion of the concept of argument or inference schemes, using the unsystematic approach of trying, first, to identify some unanswered questions that Douglas Walton's account of argument schemes in his book, *Argumentation Schemes for Presumptive Reasoning* (1996) gives rise to, and second, to make some preliminary and tentative suggestions as to how to some of those questions might be answered. In that book, Walton focuses particularly on the schemes of presumptive reasoning and argument, but even within the narrower scope of his treatment, he seems to have left a number of vexing questions unanswered. I have tried to clarify the relation between argument and reasoning, in order to explain how it is possible to shift between talk of schemes for reasoning and argumentation schemes. I proposed a revision to Walton's way of distinguishing deductive from presumptive schemes, in order to account for the fact that reasoning and arguments using presumptive schemes can be strongly compelling. Given that Walton's list of schemes seems to drop from out of the blue, and that he seems to take the cogency of reasoning or arguing according to them for granted, I sought to account for both the origin of schemes and the probative force of their use, both in general and in particular cases. In the process, I proposed a way of explaining the motivation and justification for the critical questions Walton associates with presumptive schemes. Needless to say, a philosophically complete and satisfying theory of argument and inference schemes remains to be written, although I think Walton's book is an important step in that direction.[1]

NOTE

[1] The author is grateful for the corrections and suggestions made by two anonymous referees.

REFERENCES

Beardsley, M. C.: 1976, *Writing With Reason,* Prentice-Hall, Inc., Englewood Cliffs, NJ.
Eemeren, F. H. van and R. Grootendorst: 1984, *Speech Acts in Argumentative Discussions,* Foris, Dordrecht.
Eemeren, F. H. van and R. Grootendorst: 1992, *Argumentation, Communication and Fallacies,* Lawrence Erlbaum Associates, Hillsdale, NJ.
Eemeren, F. H. van and T. Kruiger: 1987, 'Identifying Argument Schemes', in F. H. van Eemeren, R. Grootendorst, J. A. Blair and C. A. Willard (eds.), *Argumentation: Perspectives and Approaches,* Foris, Dordrecht.
Govier, T.: 1987, *Problems in Argument Analysis and Evaluation,* Foris, Dordrecht.
Hastings, A. C.: 1962, *A Reformulation of Modes of Reasoning in Argumentation,* Northwestern University, Evanston, IL, unpublished Ph.D. dissertation.
Kienpointner, M.: 1992, *Alltagslogik, Struktur und Funktion von Argumentationsmustern,* Frommann-Holzboog, Stuttgart-Bad Cannstatt.
Perelman, Ch. and L. Olbrechts-Tyteca: 1958, *La Nouvelle Rhétorique: Traité de l'Argumentation,* Presses Universitaires de France, Paris.
Pinto, R. C.: 1995, 'The Relation of Argument to Inference', in F. H. van Eemeren, R. Grootendorst, J. A. Blair and C. A. Willard (eds.), *Perspectives and Approaches, Proceedings of the Third ISSA Conference on Argumentation,* Vol. I, Sic Sat, Amsterdam.
Rescher, N.: 1976, *Plausible Reasoning,* Van Gorcum, Assen-Amsterdam.
Schellens, P. J.: 1987, 'Types of Argument and the Critical Reader', in F. H. van Eemeren, R. Grootendorst, J. A. Blair and C. A. Willard (eds.), *Argumentation: Analysis and Practices,* Foris, Dordrecht.
Walton, D. N.: 1996, *Argument Schemes for Presumptive Reasoning,* Lawrence Erlbaum Associates, Mahwah, NJ.

PART II

Judging *and* Evaluating Arguments

Chapter 4

Validity

Traditionally, validity has been the concern of formal logic. From this perspective, a valid argument is one in which logically consistent premises necessarily lead to a true conclusion; argument validity is based on formulas rather than on perceptions of soundness. Yet, rhetorical scholars and informal logicians—typically focused on arguments bound by context and adverse to logical formulas—are also concerned with validity. In part, their interest is motivated by charges that an argumentation theory divorced from validity is unable to judge the soundness of an argument in its social or political context.

The essays in this chapter address the issue of what makes an argument sound outside the rules of formal logic. By redefining the definition and standards of validity, the essays provide alternative methods for evaluating the soundness of arguments. They discuss how validity is determined in everyday arguments, the implications of judging rhetorical arguments as valid rather than merely effective, and how fallacies and bias affect the evaluation of arguments in multiple contexts.

Douglas Ehninger's "Validity as Moral Obligation" (1968) contends that most human arguments do not have the logical or empirical certainty to be considered valid. When arguers cannot prove something is absolutely true, Ehninger asks, how is validity supposed to be determined? Ehninger answers this question by defining validity as a psychological, rather than a logical, connection between a case and a claim. A valid argument is one that causes opponents to consciously abandon or refine their position out of psychological necessity. For argumentation to be a valid process and not merely brute persuasion, Ehninger contends, people must engage in argument with goodwill for the adversary. Arguers, he says, have a moral obligation to present relevant cases and abandon unsound positions.

Thomas B. Farrell, in "Validity and Rationality: The Rhetorical Constituents of Argumentative Form" (1977), also explores validity from a rhetorical perspective. Farrell asserts that because validity has not traditionally been associated with rhetoric, it is important to rethink how validity is conceptualized. For instance, how should scholars treat an argument deemed valid by the rules of formal logic but ethically untrustworthy? He proposes exploring characteristics of rhetorical arguments that might provide a basis for reconstructing the idea of validity. The first characteristic is that audiences are a necessary component in the reasoning of an argument. A second characteristic is that some fields of argument (such as legal arguments) have specific ways of moving from evidence to conclusion that are based on probabilities, rather than certainties. A third characteristic is that the foundation for asserted premises is social knowledge—the agreed-upon norms concerning human interests. Taking these characteristics into consideration, Farrell reframes validity to best address the nature of rhetorical arguments.

James Crosswhite's 1989 essay, "Universality in Rhetoric: Perelman's Universal Audience," articulates a conception of validity that is universal, yet applicable to non-formal (rhetorical) arguments that address particular, concrete problems. Crosswhite builds upon Chaïm Perelman's concept of "universal audience" to construct a definition of rhetorical validity in terms of an arguer's conception of reasonable people that transcends the particular audience—that is, a particular group located in a particular place. This essay analyzes Perelman's concept of the universal audience, which rebuts the charge that rhetorical arguments merely pander to an audience. Crosswhite also discusses how arguers construct universal audiences and employ them in their argument use.

Douglas N. Walton's "Bias, Critical Doubt, and Fallacies" (1991) addresses validity from the perspective of informal logic. This essay introduces readers to significant considerations for evaluating arguments, one of which is the fallacy—commonly defined as an invalid argument. Walton has a pragmatic approach to fallacies that evaluates argument based on how it is used in a particular case. He also explores basic, previously unexamined questions about another significant concern for argument evaluation, an arguer's bias, and explores the connection between bias and various logical fallacies. Walton concludes that determining argument bias requires understanding context. He stresses a normative model that recognizes that different types of argument abide by particular rules and procedures.

This chapter reveals a significant friction among argumentation scholars. Evaluating arguments on the grounds of validity is difficult, because the concept originated in a system of formal logic where premises establish a claim to be necessarily true. While these essays define the terms and conditions of validity differently, they share the principle that the study of everyday arguments should not abandon validity standards, partly because significant ethical and moral implications are involved in judging argument.

Validity as Moral Obligation

DOUGLAS EHNINGER

He who maintains that commercial airliners fly from Pittsburgh to Chicago in fifty-five minutes or that water freezes at thirty-two degrees Fahrenheit may establish his claim empirically. He who argues "If p then q; p; therefore q," or affirms the Pythagorean theorem may offer a demonstration that coerces agreement. In many of the disputes that arise among men, however, these methods do not avail. Appeals to printed data are indecisive, experimental procedures are inapplicable, and the premises required for apodeictic proofs may themselves be matters of contention.

Consider the following: Is our Far Eastern policy viable? Should one always obey his impulses? Does reality transcend the limits of sense experience? When confronted with questions of this sort, how do men argue? What method do they use to support their contentions and advance their claims?

As has long been recognized, men resort to a procedure that is *sui generis* to controversy as a mode of decision making, and this is to amass on behalf of the view they espouse a cluster or "bundle" of "independent" inducements to belief or action, no one of which individually or all of which together establish this view conclusively, but which, acting in concert, gradually build up a preponderance of probability in its favor.[1] They cite precedents, report prevailing opinions, raise questions and objections, invoke values, quote authorities, and trace the consequences of admissions. Above all, they point to weaknesses or "evils" in the view they oppose and outline strengths and advantages in the view they maintain.

This procedure, though seen most clearly perhaps in the arguments of the politician as he endeavors to replace the "ins" with the "outs," is equally the method of the lawyer as he poses the claim of "guilt" against the presumption of "innocence," of the school debater as he advocates the acceptance of his "plan," and of the philosopher as he argues before his peers or before an audience of all rational men the superiority of the "system" he advocates.[2] Cut off from the resources of empirical verification on the one hand, and of formal demonstration on the other, each in his role as advocate is obliged to lay out such proofs and persuasives as are available to him in the form of a *causa* or "case"—an organized body of facts, inferences, and appeals designed to remove doubts and hesitations to make his claim appear probable.[3]

If, however, as a more or less miscellaneous collection of *ad hoc* inducements to belief or action, a case consists neither of a formal demonstration nor of a direct appeal to experience, how is its validity to be determined? Under what circumstances are we warranted in accepting the claim it supports, and when should that claim be rejected? Are we to endorse as legitimate any case toward which we are psychologically disposed, or are we to withhold our assent until certain predetermined standards or conditions have clearly been met?[4] It is with these questions that the ensuing discussion is concerned.

UNACCEPTABLE CRITERIA

Let us approach our problem negatively or by a process of elimination, first considering six possible standards or criteria that do not furnish acceptable measures of the validity of a disputant's case.

At the outset we must dismiss the hypothesis that internal consistency or noncontradiction among the various elements of a case constitutes an appropriate test of its validity. For while a case that contradicts itself always is suspect, the mere absence of self-contradiction is not a guaranty of the pertinence or cogency of the arguments presented. Because the inducements of which a case consists are related to its claim psychologically rather than logically—as grounds or motives for believing rather than as proofs by which one is bound—they must appeal beyond noncontradiction to the "state of the world" and the values of the persons addressed.[5] Where assumptions are incorrect or irrelevant and data are outmoded, consistency and formal correctness are at best academic matters. In short, while consistency and non-contradiction may be necessary conditions for the validity of a case, they are by no means sufficient ones.

Secondly, the ability of a case to persuade—to win acceptance of the claim it supports—is equally unsuitable as a criterion of validity. Not only may a case be persuasive for irrelevant reasons, but sometimes it may be persuasive for no reason at all, its success resting on such extrarational factors as the language in which it is couched, the prestige of its proponent, the juncture in affairs at which it is presented, or the ineptness of the opposition. Similarly, a valid case that lacks these advantages may fail. As Charles L. Stevenson remarks, and as one's daily experiences with the blandishments of Madison Avenue confirm, "It is cognitively nonsensical to speak either of 'valid' or of 'invalid' persuasion."[6]

Thirdly, we cannot measure the validity of a case by comparing it with cases that have earlier been judged valid. Because a case *does* rather than *is*—aims at securing agreement rather than at establishing a general truth—it never can be considered apart from the audience to which it is addressed and the environment in which it is embedded. If that environment is identical with a previous one, a claim is accepted without controversy and no case is needed. If the environment is not identical, a case, though it may be word-for-word the same as a preceding one, must be evaluated in its own right. No one pretends that a case that might have been made in 1920 for the dangers of air travel is still valid today.

A fourth possibility that must be discarded is that the validity of a case is to be measured by how well any plan or proposal it entails works out when put into practice. On the one hand, such a proposal may fail because of carelessness or ineptitude on the part of those charged with its administration. On the other, a proposal for which no case can be made at all may work by accident or because of forces and circumstances that lie beyond man's present store of knowledge. Validity and pragmatic success clearly fall into quite different categories and therefore are not to be confused.

Fifthly, the number or kind of facts that can be adduced in support of a case is irrelevant to its validity. In some instances a single crucial fact is sufficient; in others, massive compilations of the most varied data are inadequate. Indeed, a case may be valid even if no facts at all can be entered on its behalf, for it may refer to a completely hypothetical situation or consist of guesswork and suspicions. The presence or absence of facts may, for a variety of reasons, make a case more or less persuasive; it does not, however, render that case either more or less valid.[7]

Finally, neither the prestige of a proponent nor the motives that impel him furnish an acceptable criterion of a case's validity. A man whose reputation is meager or whose motives are base may present a valid case on behalf of his claim. Prestige, like the presence or absence of supporting evidence, relates to persuasiveness rather than to validity. Motives, as such, are irrelevant.

A VALID CASE

If, then, none of the foregoing hypotheses furnishes an acceptable criterion of validity, how are we to measure this property of a case?

Clearly, our standard must meet two conditions: First, it must be broad and flexible enough to cover the myriad of forms that cases assume; and, secondly, it must help to guarantee judgments that are reliable and choices that are wise and productive.[8] In line with these desiderata I propose that as an appropriate test of its validity we ask whether a case, assuming that it is competently presented, forces a fundamental readjustment in the thinking of the person to whom it is addressed— whether, to borrow a phrase from Henry W. Johnstone, Jr., it "strikes home" in such a way that this person either must abandon or revise in a radical fashion the position to which he previously adhered.[9]

As I remarked earlier, no case in support of an arguable claim can hope to survive unscathed the attacks of an earnest and informed critic. But there is a difference between minor alterations and repairs and major revisions or abandonment. The former leave the original position modified in details but unchanged in essentials; the latter call for far-reaching alterations of a thoroughgoing nature. Similarly, there is a difference between adjustments made with a full awareness of why they are required and adjustments made blindly as a result of suggestion or of appeals to emotion or prejudice.

Specifically, therefore, I suggest that in order to be valid a cause must meet three requirements: (1) It must cause an opponent either to abandon his position or to alter it in some fundamental way. (2) It must cause him to do this out of necessity rather than choice. (3) It must make him fully aware of the adjustments he is effecting and of the reasons why these adjustments are required. Even though the argument itself invites rather than coerces agreement, when confronted by a valid case a disputant is therefore no longer a free agent. Instead he is faced by a choice between mutually exclusive alternatives: that, on the one hand, of being a reasonable person and concluding in accordance with the weight of the evidence; or, on the other, of being unreasonable and, ignoring the evidence and inference, concluding as his own desires or prejudices may dictate.

An invalid case, by contrast, poses no such conflict of allegiances, calls for no such crucial choice on the part of a disputant. Following its presentation, one's adherence to his earlier position not only remains unshaken but may actually be strengthened by the failure of the attack to disturb it. For if the definition of a valid case is that it leaves one no choice but to abandon or revise the position it assaults, the defining characteristic of an invalid case is that it can be exposed, explained, or discounted in a way that leaves this original position essentially intact. An invalid case may be shown to be irrelevant to the issue at hand, to be fallaciously argued, or to suffer from a variety of similar maladies. Exposure of one sort or another, however, always is possible. Therefore, an invalid case never forces the position of an opponent to be abandoned or radically revised. Instead, if either of these eventualities occurs, it is to be attributed to obtuseness or ineptitude on the part of the disputant; for it represents an avoidable rather than an unavoidable response to the attack.

The power that a valid case has to force the abandonment or revision of a previously held position makes it an essential element of productive controversy. As a result of the changes and reorderings it necessitates, erroneous assumptions and untenable beliefs are abandoned, and the dispute advances to more tenable ground. An invalid case, by contrast, bears no such fruit. After it has been presented and discounted, the controversy stands exactly where it did before, the challenged position remaining essentially unaltered. Instead of contributing in a constructive fashion to the resolution the disputants seek, an invalid case hampers and delays it.

Finally, it should be pointed out that although, for the sake of convenience, I have delineated validity only in terms of attack, the foregoing analysis applies equally to the second of the major movements in controversy—that of response or defense. For, just as a case that impugns a position may be thought of as valid if it "strikes home" against the position and invalid if it fails to do so, so a case that defends a position may be regarded as valid if it blunts or repels an attack in such a way that the assault either must be abandoned or radically revised.

MORAL OBLIGATION

Earlier we saw that the relation between a case and the claim it supports is a psychological rather than a logical one—that, instead of demonstrating the formal validity of the claim, the case merely presents "reasons" that promote its acceptance. From this it follows that the act of judging—of actively reflecting upon the alternatives offered and of choosing between them—is an indispensable aspect of controversy as a mode of decision making. Instead of supplying answers ready-made, controversy supplies only the grounds on which judgments may be based. Though his decision may not be unrelated to prevailing standards as determined by cultural norms and social practice, in the end each person to whom a case is addressed is obliged to decide for himself whether the evidence and arguments advanced are sufficient to warrant the claim.[10] Not only the juror in the box but also the citizen and voter and even the consumer of goods and services cannot evade this responsibility.

As an important aspect of the judgmental process the decision as to whether a case does or does not "strike home" must likewise be a matter of personal decision or conscience on the part of the person addressed. Because the claims the protagonist advances make statements about the real world—to use technical language, are synthetic rather than analytic—whatever the worth of the evidence and argument amassed in their support, no logical contradiction is involved in continuing to deny them. Because they are evaluative or predictive rather than factual, there is no empirical "club" with which he can be beaten into submission. After a certain point has been reached, it may be impolitic for him to continue to resist if he hopes to retain the respect and good will of his fellows. This, however, is a decision that rests on social rather than logical grounds and therefore is not a measure of validity as such.

Because validity can be guaranteed by neither logical nor empirical means, in the end it always is dependent on the cooperativeness and good will of those persons whom a controversy concerns and in this sense consists of neither more nor less than a moral obligation on their part. When the antagonist in a dispute fully understands the reasons why his present position is untenable, he has the obligation of revising or abandoning it. This in turn places upon the protagonist the corresponding obligation of making his case relevant—of seeing to it that the person addressed abandons his position only for "the right reasons" and with full awareness of why such action is required. The disputant who fails to respond to a relevant argument lies outside the pale of any method for arriving at choices and decisions rationally. The disputant who abandons relevant argument for persuasion by guile or by force resorts to methods for which the very concept of validity is irrelevant. Only when the moral obligation of each party is duly recognized and discharged—only when conscience rather than stubbornness or ambition guides behavior—will an appropriate standard of validity be struck and maintained in the discussion of those problems which men settle by preparing and presenting cases.[11]

NOTES

[1] George Campbell, *The Philosophy of Rhetoric*, ed. Lloyd Bitzer (Carbondale: Southern Illinois University Press, 1963), pp. 45–46.

[2] On the philosopher as "case builder" see especially Friedrich Waisman, "How I See Philosophy," *Logical Positivism*, ed. A. J. Ayer (New York: Free Press, 1959), pp. 345, 372–377; cf. Gilbert Ryle, *Philosophical Arguments* (Oxford: Clarendon Press, 1945), p. 5 and ff.; Mortimer Adler, *Dialectic* (New York: Harcourt, Brace, 1927), p. v; and Karl R. Wallace, "The Substance of Rhetoric: Good Reasons," *The Quarterly Journal of Speech*, XLIX (October, 1963), 239–249.

[3] The notion of a "case" ("cause" or "suit") as an aggregate of data, precedents, and inferences offered to an adjudicating agency on behalf of a claim is developed in Henry Campbell Black, *Black's Law Dictionary*, 4th ed. (St. Paul: West, 1951), s.v. "Case." In those relatively rare instances in which the disputants agree in advance upon a premise in terms of which the claim in contention is to be tested, a case may consist of a single line or thread of proof, moving deductively from that premise to the claim it implies. Cases of this sort, however, actually are exercises in instruction or correction rather than in persuasion; for the purpose is to demonstrate to an antagonist that, contrary to his present assumption, a certain conclusion does or does not follow from the premise he has endorsed. Moreover, because cases of this sort force or compel the conclusion to which they point, response in the form of counter-argument is irrelevant, and rational controversy dies aborning.

[4] For a liberal interpretation of the nature of proofs and hence of the legitimacy of a case, see Ch. Perelman et L. Olbrechts-Tyteca, *Traité de l'Argumentation*, 2 tomes (Paris: Presses Universitaires de France, 1951).

[5] Cf. Richard Whately, *Elements of Rhetoric,* ed. Douglas Ehninger (Carbondale: Southern Illinois University Press, 1963), pp. 5, 35–36.

[6] Charles L. Stevenson, *Ethics and Language* (New Haven: Yale University Press, 1944), p. 152.

[7] At times, of course, a fact may intervene in a controversy in a way that is decisive—in a way that terminates it once and for all by settling the point at issue. This is another situation, however, which is to be attributed to a miscalculation or oversight on the part of the disputants; for had they known of the existence of such an issue-settling fact they would not, except in ignorance of the nature of the decision-making method they were using, have entered upon controversy in the first place.

[8] Stevenson, *Ethics and Language,* p. 154. Stevenson's entire chapter on "Validity," pp. 152–173, is pertinent.

[9] Henry W. Johnstone, Jr., "Self-Refutation and Validity," *The Monist,* XLVIII (October, 1964), 484–485.

[10] On social practice as a criterion of proof see Arnold Levison, "The Concept of Proof," *The Monist,* XLVIII (October, 1964), 547–566. Cf. Douglas Ehninger, "Debate as Method: Limitations and Values," *Speech Teacher,* XV (September, 1966), 181–182.

[11] Cf. Sidney Hook, "The Ethics of Controversy," *Ethics and Persuasion,* ed. Richard L. Johannsen (New York: Random House, 1967), p. 105. "In the last analysis, only self-discipline can prevent the level of public discussion from sinking below the safety line of democratic health."

···

Validity and Rationality:
The Rhetorical Constituents
of Argumentative Form

THOMAS B. FARRELL

The concept of validity has not been an operable part of the rhetorical theorist's vocabulary. And it is not difficult to see why. When the logician characterizes an argument as valid, the attribution is generically a syntactic one, and diverges sharply from the pragmatic compliments paid to arguments by the rhetorical theorist. Historically, validity defined necessary relationships among things, thoughts, or terms, whereas the optimal relationship in rhetorical argument obtained between the assertion of a premise and the belief of an audience. Theorists from George Campbell to Stephen Toulmin have thus considered validity to be a purely formalistic, or "contentless" concept, best represented by law-like, even analytic relationships. By contrast, rhetorical argument at least purported to be substantive, and found its locus in probable relationships of speaker, audience, and position relevant to particular situations of choice and avoidance.

Given these apparent distinctions, it is ironic that so much speculation about the nature of rhetorical argument has recycled concepts and devices from formal logic. Even those innovations of substance (the Toulmin model, and revisitations of the enthymeme, for instance) have themselves been reduced to geometric simplicity and passed along to students in colorful catalogue form.[1] If rhetorical arguments are judged imperfect or inherently "faulty", the fault may lie not with the use of argument, but with the theoretic models guiding conception and judgment. The dilemma is all too clear. If there is an alternative to the analytic prescriptions of formal logic, it has usually been found in the resignation to persuasive sophistry. In what senses, if any, is it possible to speak of a rhetorical argument as *valid*, without contravening the identifiable features of that concept?

This essay *first* reconsiders validity as the "soundness" of a rhetorical argument, thus allowing the concept of validity to partake of distinctly rhetorical features.

Second, several characteristics of rhetorical argument that contribute to this reconsideration are considered here. These include:

i.   The complicity of an audience in argumentative development.
ii. The probable relationship between rhetorical argument and judgment.
iii. The normative force of knowledge presumed and created by rhetorical argument.

While these characteristics can only be sketched here, their cumulative impact would allow a careful judgment of the term, "validity," as extended to an indefinite rhetorical arena.

No one acquainted with theory or practice in argumentation would equate validity (in the formal sense described above) with "soundness," when "soundness" is understood as *rationality.* Arbitrary reconstructions of genus and species are commonly experienced as playful assaults on the phenomenal world. Not so playful, but equally valid (in a formal logic sense) is the following syllogism culled from Hitler's ravings in *Mein Kampf:*

Major premisse: The best men should rule the world.
Minor premisse: The Germans are the best men.
Conclusion: The Germans should rule the world.[2]

It is a characteristic of the autocratic mind to reason "validly" from certain premises which, themselves, seem idiosyncratic and unsubstantiated. Yet an *ad hominem* dismissal of the argument only compounds the sophistry. While the terms in the above argument are perfectly distributed, and the ideology which produced it influenced an entire culture, it should be possible to judge the soundness of the argument according to something other than purely formal or instrumental criteria.

In judging the soundness of the above argument, the theorist would do well to examine *the degree of conscious compliance with argumentative form in accordance with the consensual purposes and interests of a field.* While formal validity demands only that an argument or demonstration necessarily distribute terms on one *consistent* level of analysis (words with other words, thoughts with other thoughts, things with other things, and so forth), rhetorical argument seeks to establish relationships among terms, thoughts, and things through the judgment and action of an audience.[3] As long as the prescriptive force of logic is confined to the interrelationships of one level of analysis, it should not be surprising that descriptive psychological criteria and impressionistic aesthetic criteria are reserved for the actional implications of rhetorical arguments. What is suggested by my alternative conception is that the "rationality" or "soundness" of rhetorical argument is *not* purely internal to the terms of the argument itself. On the contrary, not even the potential soundness of a rhetorical argument may be surmised until an audience has either acted, or has been rendered capable of acting. Henry Johnstone has recently maintained that rationality in philosophical discourse is not sustained through the exchange of formally valid arguments, but rather through the mutual consciousness of a rhetoric, warning each interlocutor against being "taken in."[4] In an analogous sense, a conception of rationality or "soundness" in rhetorical argument would allow a consideration of how Hitler's argument (in this case, through the generation of an "oppositional" form) enabled his audience to be "taken in." Norman Cameron's classic analysis of schizophrenic thought points to the schizophrenic's recurrent incongruity between words and acts.[5] That shadowy juncture, where rationality is determined, is also the locus of rhetoric. The following analysis sketches three considerations that might give substance to a renewed conception of validity as rationality.

I. THE COMPLICITY OF AN AUDIENCE IN ARGUMENTATIVE DEVELOPMENT

In *The Uses of Argument,* Stephen Toulmin has observed, "In logic as in morals, the real problem of rational assessment—telling sound arguments from untrustworthy ones, rather than consistent from inconsistent ones—requires experience, insight and judgment. . . ."[6] Lacking an audience not only narrows arbitrarily the reservoir of experience, insight, and judgment that might structure rational assessment. It also narrows the very perspective of the evaluator—to the reified argument itself, in isolation from the practical grounds of rational assessment. Since it is rhetoric that requires the mediation of an audience to accomplish purpose, attention should be directed to the necessity of audience intervention as a means of furthering the steps of reasoning involved in rhetorical argument. To speak of *necessity* in a rhetorical context may seem rather unusual. Nonetheless, the first constituent of rhetorical validity would reinterpret "formal necessity" as the *necessary* participation of an audience in the elaboration of rhetorical "form."

The concept of *form* has undergone a series of transmutations sufficient to illustrate the sense of "necessity" implied by rhetorical validity. Plato's conception of form was a self-contained realm, removed from worldly experience, where the Good, the True, and the Beautiful merged as ideal realities. Since the truth was regarded as inaccessible through practical choice and action, no person-dependent conception of method or procedure could elevate the status of statements purporting to embody or represent the truth. Aristotle returned the notion of form to the concrete world of experience and action. Yet form was still removed from the human knower, insofar as concrete objects themselves were viewed as partaking inherently of certain identifiable natures. Form was understood to be the identifiable nature of an object; and only through this identifiable nature could any object be known. Not surprisingly, the law-like relationship of knowable objects functioned as an ideal for all of inquiry. While Aristotle acknowledged that the materials and purposes of rhetoric were different from those of the sciences, the formal similarities of rhetorical argument and scientific demonstration are undeniable. The duality of knower and known was not to survive the metaphysical revolutions of the nineteenth century. And in the twentieth century, the pragmatic school has sought a conception of form consistent with the interactive relationship of knower and object. Thus Dewey has regarded form as the ordering of experience sufficient to achieve some sort of fruition.[7] And Kenneth Burke defines form as the arousal and recurrent fulfillment of appetites or expectations in an audience.[8] Both conceptions regard the participation of an audience as a *necessary* condition for the successful completion of form. Given the interdependence of argumentative form and audience complicity, the actual manner in which audience may be employed as a *criterion* of validity is yet open to exploration.

Our point of departure can be given clarification by the traditional argumentative form of the practical syllogism. Here, a worthy object of attainment is acknowledged. And, given some action which enables this worthy object to be attained, there is a practical, "rational" force not fully realized until the action leading to the object is undertaken and completed. Leaving aside, for the moment, the questionable validity of the original formulation,[9] one may yet wonder how this force is to be realistically determined. Without undue trickery, we might translate Hitler's argument into a practical syllogism. Our worthy object to be attained would be to have the best men rule the world. The action, in this case—a complex of actions, which might enable this worthy object to be attained, would be to have the Germans (i.e., the best men) rule the world. And so forth. But here, one must pause. Since our purview of application is the world, and since we are applying grades to segments of the human race in terms of quality, the rationality of such an exercise could not be determined in isolation. Nor does the mediation, however direct, of the German people purify the process. The German people are an audience, but a clearly inappropriate one. And a determination of superior quality might only be made by those who could be expected to sort reasonably among the options. In short, and with a nod to History, Hitler's argument may be regarded as invalid in a rhetorical sense of the term, given its failure to address and include an appropriate audience.

The determination of an appropriate audience is a difficult task, and far beyond the scope of the present undertaking. Nonetheless, we might expect that an appropriate audience be conscious of its "self", i.e. of its common interests, as well as the appropriate *facts* to be considered, i.e. those matters which pertain to these interests. Further, it is the responsibility of the rhetor to generate the material of such a consciousness, or to address an audience which is so empowered, if an argument is to satisfy the first condition for rhetorical validity.

II. THE PROBABLE RELATIONSHIP
BETWEEN ARGUMENT AND JUDGMENT

Having considered one necessary ingredient in a rejuvenated notion of rhetorical validity—an appropriate audience—an important responsibility now rests upon those who are called to complete the indeterminate form of rhetorical argument. The decision and action of an audience, while necessary, is not determinate in its outcome. Rhetorical argument has traditionally centered on matters regarded as probable. There are at least two reasons for this apparently arcane classification. First, the matters usually defined as rhetorical are practical questions: matters of choice and avoidance, in which there are "live" options: one must *choose,* one way or another. A second, and corollary reason for the "probability" found in rhetorical arguments is that the audience itself, as a conglomerate of human agents, retains the responsibility for choice and action. While the audience may be addressed rationally, or cajoled, or manipulated, the speaker is never "entitled" to one particular kind of judgment from an audience. Of course, it is precisely this dimension of probability that has convinced rhetorical theorists to withhold the attribution of validity from rhetorical arguments. Paradoxically enough, a second unique constituent of rhetorical validity turns upon the manner in which probability is defined and resolved through judgment.

Consider, as an example of probability definition, that curious episode in theological history known as Pascal's Wager. Reconstructed liberally by William James, Pascal redefined the question of God's existence (clearly a philosophical or "theoretical" question), as a question of practical judgment and action, i.e. "Should I believe in God?" James described the result of this translation as a set of "forced" options.[10] Quite simply, there is no way of keeping the question of God's existence an *open* question after Pascal's philosophical intervention. The agnostic, for all his protestations, lives as if God did not exist. And one must choose; there is no other way. What Pascal and James have done is translate an abstract and general question (the history of which is marked by formally valid, but practically inconsequential demonstrations) into a practical question (which might now be exposed to James' "rules of rational thinking"). Not all subjects, of course, admit to such translative shifts. Yet the argument that acknowledges the practical consequences of an issue to human conduct must be judged more valid (in the rational, rhetorical sense of that term) than the argument offering a consistent demonstration which is alienated from practical consequence to human knowers.

Validity requires an acknowledgment of probability insofar as probability is the "natural relation" of the human knower to the unfolding of history itself. As Dewey noted early in this century:

> ... the cognitive quest for absolute certainty by purely mental means has been surrendered in behalf of search for a security, having a high degree of probability, by means of preliminary active regulation of conditions. We have considered some of the definite steps by which security has to come to attach to regulation of change rather than absolute certainty to the unchangeable. We have noted how in consequence of this transformation the standard of judgment has been transferred from antecedents to consequents, from inert dependence upon the past to intentional construction of a future.[11]

The resolution of probability must also acknowledge the indeterminance of the knower's historical situation. Indeed, the rhetor can never be expected to exhaust all potential reasons for judgment in a particular situation. Were this to happen, the situation would be neither rhetorically nor historically very realistic. Action would become determinate motion rather than conscious human choice. How does rhetorical argument resolve probability? It establishes conditions for determining whether—*ceteris paribus*—a good reason has been offered for making a particular judgment or decision. The second constituent of rhetorical validity should somehow standardize relational criteria for "good" reasons and audience judgment. Gidon Gottlieb has advocated the field-dependent use of rules as inference-warrants as a ground of rationality within probable situations:

> The concept of a field of argument leads to another concept, to a field dependent model of rational arguments. If the concept of rationality is a function of the boundaries of a field, and if it indicates the applicable concept of validity, it becomes then necessary to elaborate a model procedure for the assessment of the rationality of arguments *in* such field.[12]

Given the diversity of fields in which arguments may be constructed, it would be impossible to stipulate a sufficiently complex meta-model to allow the generation of exhaustive relational criteria. Yet it would not be difficult to question the rhetorical validity of the argument extracted from *Mein Kampf* on probability grounds. First, the argument—as reconstructed earlier—simply neglects to acknowledge the portentous and disputable grounds of probability implied by each of its premises. In treating a culturally-partisan matter as if it were an ahistorical truth, the implications of argument are completely masked, removed from audience judgment. Of course, closer analysis of argumentative development would likely reveal numerous distortions of inference-warrants, even within the somewhat amorphous field of national policy-formation.

III. THE NORMATIVE FORCE OF KNOWLEDGE PRESUMED AND CREATED BY RHETORICAL ARGUMENT

Thus far, constituents of rhetorical validity have been found in the components of rhetorical process and procedures of argumentative development. I now suggest that the actual premises of rhetorical argument may be regarded as valid, based upon their relation to the social knowledge attributed to specific audiences. In an earlier project, social knowledge was defined as "a normative agreement, presumed by communication acts, which generalizes human interests and is applicable to practical questions."[13] Of the many important functions performed by this construct, it is the normative dimension which is most directly relevant to rhetorical validity. All rhetorical statements assume some relation of problems to persons, interests, and actions. Public expression calls such knowledge into operation, as well as committing the rhetor to those interests he would represent. Michael Walzer, in his work, *Obligations,* has suggested that there is a forceful relationship between public expression of the interests of others, and public commitment to those same interests.[14] The normative force of rhetorical validity, then, is to suggest that—given a particular series of reasons, linked by knowledge to human interests—one should do X, at least in the absence of convincing and *forceful* counterarguments. While the interest-dependent knowledge of limited audiences is by no means a sufficient condition for the determination of rhetorical validity, it is surely a necessary condition. And the contravention of such knowledge can render even the most solemn declarations of public policy invalid.

In October 1976 the American President made the following statement during the course of a televised political debate:

> There is no Soviet domination of Eastern Europe and there never will be under the Ford administration. I don't believe the Yugoslavs consider themselves dominated by the Soviet Union. I don't believe the Rumanians consider themselves dominated by the Soviet Union. I don't believe that the Poles consider themselves dominated by the Soviet Union. Each of these countries is independent, autonomous.[15]

As the President was to learn, the only authority on what the Yugoslavs, the Rumanians, and the Poles believe is . . . the Yugoslavs, the Rumanians, the Poles. Over a period of two days, the President was virtually forced, by a limited audience of East European heritage, to alter and eventually abandon his statement. On Oct. 7, came the first revision: "The United States has never conceded, and never will concede, their domination by the Soviet Union." On Oct. 8, came the second revision: "This administration does not concede that there should be Soviet domination of the Eastern European countries." And later the same day: "Perhaps I could have been more precise in what I said concerning Soviet domination of Poland."[16] The proposition set forth by the President may have simply been an extended "slip of the tongue." But what few, including the President, could deny was that this proposition, through the active intervention of an audience whose interests were affected, was shown to be *invalid.*

Thus far, a revised notion of validity has been introduced. And, the constituents of this revised notion have been grounded *first,* in the components of an extended rhetorical process, *second,* in the development of argumentative interrelations, and *third,* in the normative force of knowledge presumed and created by rhetorical argument. However, given the traditional restrictions upon the usage of the term, "validity," it might be asked if the conditions for determining rhetorical validity are not so foreign to traditional usage and application as to undermine all continuity of meaning. Put another way: perhaps we need a term other than validity: I conclude by reconstructing the three sets of conditions for determining validity, hopefully to shed some light upon this final question of usage.

Our first criterion found, in the redefinition of *form,* a revitalized necessity for the participation of an appropriate audience, with a certain concerned consciousness of "facts." The suggestion is that even the formal realization of rhetorical validity must be consensual. A minimum of historical revision reveals the dependence of previous conceptions of validity upon a stable ontological consensus. The problem is that the consensus of any particular epoch may be partisan (at least within the context of "potential" rational alternatives). The German philosopher and social theorist, Jürgen Habermas, has attempted to set certain constraints upon the consensus-formation process so that validity will be grounded in a rational form of life.[17] Among these requirements are (1) an absence of forcible restrictions, i.e. violence; (2) clear differentiation between public and private discourse; (3) the free questioning of all "ideological" assumptions; (4) equal opportunities to initiate and continue dialogue. The stipulations are attractive enough on the face of it, but the matter of their own origin raises uncomfortable questions. As Ray McKerrow thoughtfully observes, all arguers are participating in a social relationship, in which certain standards of acceptable behavior predominate.[18] Alvin Gouldner has pointed to the difficulties of attempting to establish requirements for consensus-formation by self-proclamation.[19] Habermas' criteria must themselves be instituted by a consensual, reason-giving intelligence. In the terminology of McKeon's philosophical semantics, these are "reflexive" principles.

The second criterion for rhetorical validity was found in the definition and resolution of probability through the use of "inference-rules" relating *good reasons* to audiences within specific fields of argument. In this instance, too, the similarity of our criterion to traditional notions of validity is more a problem than a value. While the inference-warrant approach extends to a speaker/discourse/audience relationship, it resembles formal-analytic validity by separating individuated "good reasons" (through the *ceteris paribus* clause) from potential partisan opposition. This isolation of individual "reason-giving" instances may avoid the short-term dangers of strategic, utilitarian morality. But it requires the eventual construction of an elaborate hierarchy of fields and interests—a hierarchy which, of course, can only be established through argument.

It is our third criterion—the social knowledge foundation of asserted premises —which bears least apparent resemblance to traditional conceptions of formal-analytic validity. As noted earlier in this essay, the substantive grounding of individual premises was thought irrelevant to the concerns of valid syllogistic demonstration (where terms were related categorically to other terms). Not until the function of social knowledge is closely examined will any point of correspondence emerge. All rhetorical appeal moves inexorably "beyond" its immediate audience.[20] Principles, purposes, and procedures are endorsed which presumably must apply consistently to others as well. When an assertion expresses or calls for social knowledge it must generalize human interests. Through the accreditation of audiences, interests *become* interdependent. Now as this generality and interdependence of human interests "exists" only as a potential (i.e. it is forever "coming into being"), the generality implied by any rhetor is necessarily abstract. Thus the traditional sense of validity as an "empty" category, established through relationship, is relevant and applicable to rhetorical validity, as conceived here.

This is not to suggest that rhetorical argument should strive for the precision, consistency, and analycity of traditional validity. Nor does the above analysis exclude the usage of another term. Rhetorical argument seeks to render the formulary qualities of validity as concrete as possible. Rather than finding order in the consistent distribution of things, thoughts, or terms in argument, rhetoric looks to an environment in which distribution is equitable and interests are interdependent. The ideals of rhetoric and the Community remain the same: a rational society.

NOTES

1 The reference here is to Speech textbooks which, since they cannot be exhaustively numbered, had best remain nameless.
2 Adolf Hitler, *Mein Kampf* (Boston: Houghton Mifflin, 1943), p. 146.
3 I am indebted to Richard McKeon's Ideas and Methods course, *Aristotle and the Development of Logic,* for the materials of this distinction.
4 Henry Johnstone, "Rationality and Rhetoric in Philosophy," *QJS,* 59 (1973), 381–389.
5 Norman Cameron, "Experimental Analysis of Schizophrenic Thinking," from *Language and Thought in Schizophrenia* (New York: The Norton Library, 1944), p. 58.
6 Stephen Toulmin, *The Uses of Argument* (Cambridge: University Press, 1958), p. 188.
7 John Dewey, *Art as Experience* (New York: Capricorn Books, 1934), p. 147.
8 Kenneth Burke, *Counter-Statement* (Berkeley: U. of California Press, 1968), p. 31.
9 George Henrick van Wright, *Explanation and Understanding* (New York: Cornell U. Press, 1971), p. 118.
10 William James, "The Will to Believe," *Pragmatism and Other Essays* (New York: Washington Square Press, 1963), p. 196.
11 John Dewey, *The Quest for Certainty* (New York: Capricorn, 1968), p. 290.
12 Gidon Gottlieb, *The Logic of Choice* (New York: MacMillan, 1968), p. 29.
13 Thomas B. Farrell, "Knowledge, Consensus, and Rhetorical Theory," *QJS,* 62 (1976) p. 2.
14 Michael Walzer, *Obligations: Essays on Disobedience, War, and Citizenship* (Cambridge: Harvard U. Press, 1970), p. 5.
15 Gerald Ford, cited in *Chicago Tribune,* Oct. 10, 1976, p. 10.
16 *Ibid.,* p. 10.
17 Cf. Jürgen Habermas, *The Legitimation Crisis* (Boston: Beacon Press, 1975), pp. 108–110.
18 Cf. Ray McKerrow, "Rhetorical Validity: An Analysis of Three Perspectives on the Justification of Rhetorical Argument," *JAFA,* 13 (Winter 1977), pp. 133–141.
19 Alvin W. Gouldner, *The Dialectic of Ideology and Technology* (New York: The Seabury Press, 1976), pp. 142–144.
20 *Ibid.,* p. 277.

Universality in Rhetoric: Perelman's Universal Audience

JAMES CROSSWHITE

I. INTRODUCTION

An essential problem for rhetorical theory has been the question of the scope of the validity claims that may be made for non-formal argumentation. Formal argumentation can make universal validity claims because logical systems define validity in terms of logical form. A theory of non-formal argumentation or rhetoric can make no use of such a definition, and consequently rhetorical theory is often believed to have forsaken questions of validity for questions of effectiveness, or is even accused of having conflated the two.

In this paper, I explain, clarify, and develop and apply in new ways Chaim Perelman's concept of a universal audience. I do this to discover what sort of universality there is in rhetoric, and whether rhetorical theory can meet the objection philosophers have made to rhetoric. I claim that, in fact, Perelman has found a way to distinguish valid from effective argumentation. He has done this without succumbing to any of the traditional philosophical dualisms and without limiting validity to formal argumentation. In particular, he has succeeded in developing a criterion of validity which avoids the dilemma of being either universal but empty or concrete but particular. Thus, he has eluded the primary dangers for theories of argumentation, reason, and truth which try to ground themselves in communication. Finally, I claim that there is implicit in his theory an account of rationality which neither disguises nor undervalues the particular ethical interest of reason.

II. AUDIENCE AND ARGUMENTATION

Chaim Perelman's rhetorical theory is founded on the axiom that the purpose of argumentation is to induce or increase people's adherence to theses presented to them for their assent (TNR 4).[1] What immediately follows from this is that argumentation develops in relation to an audience and that audiences are the measures of arguments. There is no measure of an argument, no way of evaluating it, independent of some concept of an audience.

Perelman recognizes that the worth of arguments cannot be immediately surrendered to just anyone who happens to come across a piece of argumentation, so he defines "audience" and distinguishes between kinds of audience in a way that he hopes will overcome the disadvantages of not having a formal or independent standard against which to measure the worth of arguments. Thus, an "audience" is made up not simply of those one explicitly addresses, or those who read one's arguments, but rather, those whom the writer wishes to influence by the argumentation (TNR 19). An audience so defined is always a construction of an author. So conceived, argumentation is not automatically limited by the actual concrete audiences which may take it in.

Further, there are several different kinds of audience an author may construct, and they may be more or less coincident with the actual social group with which an author is faced. The most important of the distinctions Perelman draws between kinds of audience is the distinction between a particular audience and a universal audience.[2] This distinction is made in order to distinguish between argumentation which appeals only to particular groups with particular characteristics in particular places at particular times and argumentation which attempts to transcend such particularity and make its appeals more broadly. By developing an account of the differences between universal audiences and particular ones, Perelman believes he can better distinguish between merely effective and genuinely valid argumentation. One of the advantages of this line of approach is that he can thereby avoid the more vicious dualisms which sometimes afflict theories of argumentation—for example the dualism of reason and emotion which assigns moods and emotions roles to play in persuasion and in effective argumentation, but none in convincing and in genuine argumentation. This approach also avoids similar splits of mind and body, form and content, objective and subjective, intellect and will.

Perelman's strategy is not a perfectly new one. In the introduction to *The New Rhetoric* he refers to the judgment of Socrates that a worthy rhetoric would employ techniques capable of convincing the gods themselves (7).[3] And the most systematic and persistent attempt to develop this kind of theory occurs in modern political thought—in social contract theory. A central concern of modern political theory is to find an audience whose members evaluate one another's arguments in a way that ensures that the most worthy argument will be the most effective one.

In Hobbes, Locke, and Rousseau, human beings are themselves to have the authority for deciding what rules shall order their societies. In order to justify particular forms of government such theorists imagine human beings not as they are, but as they were or would be in a state of nature, and these theorists justify the social contract on the basis of the deliberations individuals would go through in a state of nature and the rules they would adopt in such a state. The advantage of imagining a state of nature is that individuals in such a state have universal human features and follow natural laws. They are not susceptible to appeals made to them as members of particular groups or classes. Thus, the arguments by which they are persuaded have more universal worth than the arguments that persuade actual individuals in actual societies. Of course, such theories seem to have a mythic or literary cast to contemporary political theorists. And they are all bedeviled by a moral valorizing of nature which many people simply will not accept.

A more contemporary effort of this sort is made in John Rawls's *A Theory of Justice,* in which he tries to imagine an audience whose deliberations will result in their adopting genuine principles of justice. However, instead of imagining a state of nature, he imagines a hypothetical situation of equal liberty, what he calls the "original position." In such a position,

> No one knows his place in society, his class position or social status, nor does anyone know his fortune in the distribution of natural assets and abilities, his intelligence, strength and the like. I shall even assume that the parties do not know their conceptions of the good or their special psychological propensities. The principles of justice are chosen behind a veil of ignorance.[4]

Because the reasoning which goes on within the original position is addressed to an audience which has only universal human features and no particular ones, the principles of justice which emerge from such deliberation have a general scope and not merely a particular one.

III. A BASIC PROBLEM WITH THE THEORY

The same general strategy has been recently adopted by Jürgen Habermas, and since his attempt is one of the most contemporary, and is explicitly a part of a theory of communication which has already had a great influence on communication theorists, rhetoricians, and literary theorists, I want to use it as an example of the general problem such attempts face.

Habermas holds to a consensus theory of truth, but he needs a way to distinguish a "rational" consensus from a merely *de facto* one, and thus truth from mere agreement. He comes up with a criterion similar in some respects to Perelman's. The criterion of truth is not mere agreement, but agreement under certain conditions—conditions under which all the particular structural constraints on argumentation are removed and the cooperative search for truth is the only motive in play. There must be no internal or external constraints. Everyone must have an equal opportunity to argue and be heard. Everyone's arguments must be taken equally seriously. No one may attempt to dominate or act merely strategically—either consciously or unconsciously.[5]

Habermas realizes that this is never the concrete situation in which argumentation takes place. It is an ideal, counterfactual, and yet he claims that it is a supposition that we make when we speak of truth claims being rationally grounded in argumentation. Because if we can argue that the outcome of an argument was influenced by other motives, that an audience was acting strategically or neurotically, that some member was threatened by force, and so on, then this would call the truth claim into question—the consensus would not be understood to be a rational one.

However, Habermas has come to realize that there is a serious problem with his concept of an "ideal speech situation." The problem has to do with the emptiness of the motivations of the participants in it, their lack of any other motivation than reaching a consensus on truth. As Habermas writes,

> It is possible that one day an emancipated human race could encounter itself within an expanded space of discursive formation of will and yet be robbed of the light in which it is capable of interpreting its life as something good? The revenge of a culture exploited over millenia for the legitimation of domination would then take this form: right at the moment of overcoming age-old repressions it would harbor no violence, but it would have no content either.[6]

Eventually, Habermas comes to limit the relevance of the "ideal speech situation" to deliberations about social justice, and he is left with the great problem of how rationally to ground claims about all those social goods, actions, and ideals that are *not* simply matters of procedure.

And this is the general problem for theories that attempt to ground conceptions of reasonableness and validity in conceptions of ideal audiences. The argumentation that is persuasive for such abstractly conceived audiences can be conducted only in the most abstract and formal terms. The agreements such audiences are capable of reaching never concern the concrete and substantive kinds of issues such audiences were designed to deal with.

Similar objections have been made to Perelman's concept of a universal audience. They have been made most explicitly and systematically by John Ray, who charges that the concept is "excessively formal and abstract," and that it "loses all validity when it is concerned with particular situations." He claims further that it is supposed to be an "infallible rational standard," "transcendental," and "not determined by empirical experience."[7]

IV. THE OBJECTION OF PHILOSOPHY

In this paper, I want to explain clearly just what the concept of a universal audience is, and what its uses are. Then I want to show the advantages of Perelman's concept of a universal audience and specifically how it avoids the dilemma of being either universal but empty or concrete but particular.

However, one may want to deny that this is a legitimate problem. One could argue that rhetoric is not really concerned with what is universal, but is instead oriented toward particular actions, or judgments about particular actions, in particular situations.[8] It is not concerned with more general kinds of claims. There are two replies to this. First, that is simply not Perelman's concept of rhetoric. For him, rhetoric's domain is all non-formal reasoning, and the texts he analyzes come from all disciplines, all areas of inquiry—from philosophy, history, literature—including fiction and poetry—and the natural and social sciences, as well as law and theology. But one could still say that Perelman had it wrong, that he should have focused solely on practical reason and on judgments about particulars. That is, he should have foregone the talk about a universal audience. But—and this is my second reply—this would have had two undesirable consequences—the first, seriously unfortunate; the second, ruinous. First, it would have left philosophical and theoretical reasoning, and much scientific and social scientific reasoning, in an uncharted territory between logic, on the one side, and practical reasoning, on the other. Second, it would have left rhetoric vulnerable to the charge that it is really only a form of flattery, a pandering to a particular audience with particular interests, desires, and plans.[9] If an unaddressed audience objected that a line of reasoning was foolish or wicked, an author would have no way of being able to acknowledge the force of the complaint *without abandoning the audience which was being addressed*. In Perelman's terms, there would be no difference between an effective argument and a valid one, and rhetoric would once more be vulnerable to the classical philosophical attacks.

Why should one care about the classical philosophical attacks? Why not just let rhetoric be rhetoric, and let philosophy worry itself? Because the fundamental philosophical attack on rhetoric is that rhetoricians—sophists—do not love what is good. They love success with audiences. Thus, they care about being effective with audiences, but they do not care whether their arguments make any deeper claim. The philosopher, on the other hand, says Plato, cares about what is good—that is, cares about whether an audience *should be* persuaded by an argument or not. This is exactly what Perelman cares about and this is why he distinguishes between effective arguments and valid ones on the basis of a distinction between particular and universal audiences. As Socrates says in Plato's *Phaedrus,* "It is noble to aim at a noble goal, whatever the outcome."[10] So much then, for the attempt to deny the importance of the challenge Perelman takes up.

V. HOW TO CONSTRUCT A UNIVERSAL AUDIENCE

Next I want to give an accurate account of what Perelman's universal audience is, first, by looking at the rules he gives us for constructing a universal audience, and, second, by examining the uses to which he puts the concept.

What is interesting about the rules he gives for constructing a universal audience is that they are not systematic and could often yield conflicting results. There are no priority rules about when to follow one rule rather than another, no limiting of particular rules to particular situations or anything of the sort. Instead, Perelman simply offers these rules, sometimes only implicitly, and without ever bringing a consideration of them together at one time and place. Thus, what he really offers is not so much a system of rules for constructing *the* universal audience but a number of techniques for constructing universal *audiences*—techniques which themselves have variable persuasive force as justifications for the universal audience one is constructing. This is because constructing a universal audience is not really much different from inventing arguments to defend one's conception of universality. For in every move toward universality, there lies a technique for achieving universality. This technique itself can be understood as part of an argument for the concept of universality it yields. This is, if one's concept of universality is called into question, then the first line of defense is to show how it follows from what is ordinarily taken to be a universality-producing technique.

All constructions of universal audiences begin with particular audiences. One has a particular audience in mind, and one performs certain imaginative operations on it in order to give it a universal character. One way to do this is to set aside all the particular, local features of the audience and consider only those features of the audience one considers universal. Another similar method is to exclude from the particular audience all those members who are prejudiced, lack imagination or sympathy, or are irrational or incompetent at following argumentation, and to include only those who are relatively unprejudiced and have the proper competence (TNR 33, NRH 14, 48). This rationality and competence qualification is further specified in a number of ways.[11] To be competent, one must be "disposed to hear" the argumentation (RR 17) and must "submit to the data of experience" (TNR 31). One must also have the proper information and training, and in addition one must also have "duly reflected" (TNR 34).

Another way is to add particular audiences together—to be sure that one's argumentation appeals not only to one particular audience, but to many, or even all particular audiences (RR 14). By adding audiences together this way, one could eventually come to the whole of humanity—if such universality were required by the argumentation.[12] Another technique is to imagine one's argumentation addressed not only to the particular audience one faces at the moment, but to similar audiences at other times, in later years, say. Arguments of this sort frequently make appeals to history and ask their audiences to imagine themselves in their historical roles. According to classical philosophers, the most universal of audiences is the "timeless" one, and the more one's arguments have a timeless appeal, the more universal they are usually taken to be (TNR 32).

A way to test and strengthen one's construction of a universal audience is to let other audiences criticize it (TNR 35). For example, if the particular audience one has universalized can corroborate one's judgment about what really are its universal features, then one's concept has greater validity and strength in argumentation than it would otherwise have. For example, pollsters have pretty well established that California voters are racist, that they vote for or against candidates on the basis of race. In constructing a universal audience of California voters, one would reject this characteristic. And my guess is that California voters would see the reason in this—that they would say yes, race is a factor in how we vote, but we recognize that in some important sense it probably shouldn't be, and that political argumentation shouldn't make appeals of this sort.

Once again, these methods are not systematic and can lead to conflicting results. For example, one party may believe that a specialized audience represents the real universal audience for some particular argument. The opponent of the argument may deny this, and claim that the public represents the real universal audience. Thus, one writer may appeal more to the "competence, training and knowledge" criteria, and make them very strong criteria, while another may appeal to the criterion of adding audiences together, or letting "everyone" decide. In such a case, argumentation cannot lead to agreement because each side measures the argumentation differently. Perelman believes that in such a situation we must postpone argumentation until, through dialogue, question and answer, or exploratory discourse we come to a deeper mutual understanding and uncover agreements that can allow us to continue the argumentation (RR 16–17).

VI. THE USES OF UNIVERSAL AUDIENCES

Next, let us consider the uses to which Perelman puts the concept of a universal audience. First, he uses it to distinguish persuading from convincing (TNR 26ff). This is a critical problem in rhetoric, and it is usually taken on by resorting to any of a number of controversial dualisms, especially the dualism of reason/emotion.[13] Second, he uses the concept to distinguish effective from valid argumentation, and thus *de facto* agreement from *de jure* agreement (TNR 463). Third, Perelman appears to use the universal audience to distinguish fact and value. That is, a fact is supposed to be that to which a universal audience assents, while a value is that to which only particular audiences assent (TNR 66). Perelman's aim in making this distinction is to identify which agreements stand fast in argumentation. According to *The New Rhetoric,* argumentation is founded on agreement, and moves from original agreements to new agreements. In any rhetorical situation, certain agreements stand fast, or argumentation is not possible, Thus, there is a rhetorical way to distinguish the domain of the real (what stands fast) from the domain of the preferred, as well as from presumptions and hypotheses about the real (about which one can argue without undermining the rhetorical situation).

However, I argue that although the concept may be used this way for the purposes of understanding the kinds of agreements operating in a rhetorical situation, it doesn't really distinguish fact from value in any philosophical way, even in Perelman's system. For he realizes that values can attain the status of facts—i.e., that ethical life isn't limited to the subjective features of valuing and preferring. As he writes: "An agreement about the conception of reality is linked to a social and historical situation which fundamentally conditions any distinction that one might wish to draw between judgments of reality and value judgments" (TNR 513). And again, "The status of statements evolves: when inserted into a system of beliefs for which universal validity is claimed, values may be treated as facts or truths" (TNR 76). When Perelman refers to "universal values," as he does on occasion, he means values that have attained the status of facts or truths—that is, the adherence of a universal audience. Thus, there seems to be some kind of distinction between facts and values working behind Perelman's recasting of their definitions for his rhetorical theory, a distinction which is in some way still operating within the theory.

Another important use of the concept is to identify the audience for philosophical argumentation, scientific argumentation, and argumentation about morality (TNR 31, 34, PR 293ff). In all these kinds of argumentation, there is an implicit claim that one's arguments ought to be persuasive for more than a particular audience, that the one who is arguing is appealing to universal standards of reason (TNR 34).[14] Perelman also believes that the concept can be used to solve the problems one faces in composite audiences. That is, when an actual audience consists of a number of different particular audiences who ordinarily do not assent to the same arguments, one can construct from them a universal audience, and aim one's arguments at it (TNR 31). Finally, a universal audience may be used as a standard of relevance. Although arguments can be persuasive for particular audiences even if they are one-sided and omit any treatment of opposing arguments, an argument that is convincing, one which gains the assent of a universal audience, must give a proper hearing and proper credit to all sides of an argument, or all relevant arguments (TNR 119).

VII. UNIVERSALITY AND CONCRETENESS

Now that we have a clear notion of what the concept of a universal audience is, how to construct it, and what its uses are, we can better understand the senses in which it is always something more than an abstract and formal concept; in fact, we can see how Perelman has succeeded in avoiding the universal but empty or concrete but particular dilemma.

Consider first the senses in which the universal audience always has some degree of cultural specificity—for it always does. It does not gather in some non-historical sphere, isolated from and immune to human activities and mortal weaknesses. It is rather always a universal of a particular, a concrete generality. It represents a *"sensus communis"* rather than being an abstraction that stands above the agreements reached by actually existing groups.[15] This can be seen clearly in some specific passages from *The New Rhetoric*.

First: "Everyone constitutes the universal audience from what he knows of his fellow men, in such a way as to transcend the few oppositions he is aware of. Each individual, each culture, has thus its own conception of the universal audience" (TNR 33). In other words, any conception of a universal audience has a specific content that comes from the fact that it is constructed by a specific author within the agreements that make argumentation possible within or among specific cultures. Thus, the universal audience is not a pure or transcendental concept. There is always something empirical in it, something which comes from the experience of an author and the traditions of a culture. As Perelman says, "The universal audience is no less than others a concrete audience, which changes with time, along with the speaker's conception of it" (TNR 491). However, this statement must be qualified. For certainly, the universal audience lacks the actual existence of concrete audiences, and is to this extent ideal—after all, as Perelman also writes, the agreement of a universal audience is not a fact, but a unanimity imagined by an author (TNR 31).

Second, what follows from this is: "Each speaker's universal audience can from an external standpoint be regarded as a particular audience" (TNR 30). That is, if we are already outside or if we move outside the rhetorical situation for which an author has constructed a universal audience, we can see the senses in which the construction lacks universality. We can imaginatively take the external point of view by employing the techniques for constructing a universal audience and carrying them farther than the author has. For example, we can imagine an argument's being addressed to a broader group of audiences, imagine its strength in a different historical context, and so on. Of course, if one takes the external point of view, what one is really doing is setting up a new rhetorical situation and appealing to a different universal audience—and not really undermining the concept of a universal audience. For despite this sort of abstract and external criticism, Perelman insists that: "It nonetheless remains true that, *for each speaker at each moment,* there exists an audience transcending all others" (TNR 30, emphasis added). However, this too requires qualification. There exists one universal audience for each speaker in each situation *if there is argumentation going on, if someone is advancing and supporting a claim.* There is another kind of deliberation in which one explores the differences between two conflicting concepts of a universal audience—for example, in the situation of a genuine moral dilemma. This kind of exploratory discourse often takes the form of dialogue, question and answer, in which each interlocutor aims to uncover hitherto neglected agreements. Such "dialogue" can also take place in self-deliberation. The ultimate goal of this dialogue is to uncover agreements significant enough to yield a new, probably more general, universal audience. Only when a universal audience holds sway for both interlocutors can argumentation be resumed.

Third, I mentioned before that one can strengthen one's conception of a universal audience by letting other audiences criticize it. As *The New Rhetoric* says, "Audiences are not independent of one another . . . particular audiences are capable of validating the universal audiences which characterize them. . . . Audiences pass judgment on one another" (TNR 35). This, too, is a way in which the content and specificity of the universal audience is preserved. The universal audience is constructed by performing imaginative operations on a particular audience. It is always the universal of a particular. If the particular audience completely rejects the universal audience constructed from it, it would weaken the argument that the conception of the universal audience is the right one. Thus, the particular audience has a role in validating the universal audience, in keeping it from losing its relation to the particular audience in question. Of course, the particular audience cannot be the only audience that has a role in validating the conception of a universal audience. After all, the construction of a universal audience is itself a judgment on the insufficiencies of the particular audience. Rather, there is always another audience to which an appeal is made in such cases, and I shall come to this shortly.

Before this, however, it should be pointed out that the fact that the universal audience is not a pure concept, that it lacks the necessity and absolute universality to qualify it as "transcendental," does nothing to cast doubt on its universalizing tendency. The techniques for constructing a universal audience are universalizing techniques. Just because they are limited by the traditional conceptions of what is good, appropriate and true, and taken for granted in a specific rhetorical community, does not mean that they do not yield increasing degrees of universality. The imaginative expansion of audiences across cultures and across time and the application of notions like competence and rationality are clear indications of this. Rather, it means that they do not yield a merely formal, abstract concept of an audience, an audience which would assent to nothing but formal proofs, analytical statements, and empty platitudes. Argumentation is rarely an end in itself. The purpose of arguing is usually to achieve some goal, to realize some good that one imagines is best achieved—all things considered—through argumentation. Thus, *the universality of a universal audience is limited by the good that one can achieve by way of participating in argumentation in a particular rhetorical situation*. Agreement may be a part of such a good, but such a good is more often *that for the sake of which the agreement is sought*. I can see only relative merit in the objections that the view from nowhere could raise to this practice, just as I can see little sense in underestimating goods that *can* be achieved by turning loose on such goods a generalizing impulse that eventually overpowers any conception of good whatsoever.

VIII. THE UNDEFINED UNIVERSAL AUDIENCE

A final way to gain some insight into the sense in which the concept of a universal audience is both concrete and universal is to consider a concept which is, as far as I know, almost completely neglected in philosophy and rhetorical theory, and is discussed very little by Perelman himself. This is the concept of an undefined universal audience. The concept has a very specific and very important use. Here is the single passage from *The New Rhetoric* in which it is mentioned:

> It is the undefined universal audience that is invoked to pass judgment on what is the concept of the universal audience appropriate to . . . a concrete audience, to examine . . . the manner in which it was composed, which are the individuals who comprise it, according to the adopted criterion, and whether this criterion is legitimate (TNR 35).

Thus, it cannot be just the concrete audience which passes such judgment, as we have seen. Rather, the undefined universal audience is the audience for our construction of a universal audience. This should not sound strange because, as we have seen, such a construction itself employs argumentative techniques, and implicitly contains a claim that the universal audience we have constructed is the appropriate one. This claim and argument do not hang in empty space; they are offered to an undefined universal audience—one to which we appeal, but one which we cannot make definite.

This can be viewed from a different direction. Once we know that we construct the universal audience within individual and cultural constraints, "as a way" as Perelman says, "to transcend the few oppositions we are aware of" (TNR 33)— once this is known, then don't we know that our concept of the universal audience is always to some degree insufficient? Don't we recognize that there are arguments of some strength which oppose our construction even if we don't know what they are? Don't we know that, in appealing to an undefined universal audience to validate our construction, we have recognized that in some sense the universal audience is not—even for us—the universal audience? Don't we recognize that there is a universal audience beyond the universal audience?

The difficulty one faces in trying to conceive of such an audience is that it is defined as undefined. However, this is partly only an apparent problem. For although the undefined universal audience is unknown, it is never absolutely unknown. Rather, it is a determinate unknown in the sense that the move from a concrete audience to a universal audience establishes a direction and begins to articulate an ideal or a goal. Of course this is always to some degree indeterminate, a matter of interpretation, full of historical ambiguities. And yet the direction established, the pre-conceptual *sense* we have of the undefined universal audience is determinate enough so that we know it when we encounter it, we know it when it does become determinate, when it does come to appearance. For example, there are those occasions when an audience responds in ways we had not anticipated, and in fact goes beyond our argumentation and ideas and interprets them in ways we *could not foresee—but which we nevertheless recognize as legitimate.* How is it that we can recognize such unforeseeable audience responses as legitimate? Because we do have a knowledge of the undefined universal audience—not an explicit conceptual knowledge, but the kind of knowledge which allows us to recognize the legitimacy of its responses once they do come to expression.

This kind of knowledge should not be underestimated. The substitution of a direction, a vector, an ever-better emergent newness for a comprehensively and conceptually grasped universal audience means that this audience is never grasped directly, but only indirectly—often in feelings, inclinations, reservations, hopes, and hunches. I believe it is also at play in our logically underdetermined ability to make practical and aesthetic judgments.[16] But to comport oneself toward this undefined universal audience, even if one does not understand exactly what it is, is a relatively familiar kind of comportment. I take Socrates to be expressing something of this idea when he says that he is more satisfied at losing arguments than winning them, because when he loses an argument—when an interlocutor responds in an unanticipated but legitimate way—then he learns something new; otherwise, he is left in his ignorance. [17]

So the undefined universal audience is both unforeseeable and anticipated—something we both know and don't know. It is at once an unknown ideal and something potentially concrete. It becomes concrete in actual audience responses. Yet once it becomes concrete and definite in this way, it can no longer fulfill the role of the undefined. Instead, it adds further determinations to our concept of a universal audience—it becomes a part of it. It is as if universal audiences come to be out of and through the undefined universal audience, but the undefined universal audience itself forever withdraws into indefiniteness.

IX. CONCLUSIONS

We can draw a number of conclusions from this. First, rhetoric has a philosophical moment that cannot be eliminated except at great cost. This distinguishes rhetoric from any kind of social science and especially from psychology. The idea of a universal audience introduces an instability into rhetoric which makes rhetoric's domain more like history than psychology, except that the instability in rhetoric is a philosophical one, a matter not simply of what is true, but of the *measure* of the truth yielded by argumentation. An advanced psychology may someday be able to measure the effectiveness of arguments—or at least could, in principle—but it could never measure their validity.

This also "solves" or rather places at its proper place—in actual human inter-action and this means within actual historical practices—the problem of avoiding the dilemma between empty universality and concrete particularity. It is a practical historical task to create and preserve societies with the proper balance between universalizing rationality and the goods of particular traditions. Perelman's rhetorical theory is well-adapted to this balance at the theoretical level, but it takes no historical action.

Finally, Perelman has offered a theory of rationality which neither disguises nor undervalues the particular ethical interest of reason. For the universalizing interest of reason is essentially an ethical one, and has a strong orientation toward the future. On this, both Habermas and Perelman are in strong agreement. As Habermas came to say, "I prefer to speak of an anticipation of an ideal speech situation. . . . The anticipation of the ideal speech situation has the significance of a constitutive illusion which is at the same time an appearance of a form of life."[18] Or, as Perelman puts it, an appeal to universal values, which is always an appeal to a universal audience, is indicative of an aspiration for agreement (RR 27). In the end, any appeal to a universal audience signals such an aspiration, and thus announces a willingness to go on seeing one's opponent's side, to go on testing one's reasoning against more and more demanding measures, to make universal agreement one's aim.

And if the universal audience represents an aspiration for agreement, then rationality in the strong sense of valid argumentation is itself such an aspiration. But as Perelman knew at least from the time of *The New Rhetoric,* the good of universal agreement is just one good, and it must be measured and balanced by other conflicting goods, Sometimes the goods about which we disagree are more important to us than our eventually reaching agreement with people who do not share our moral concerns. This is why Habermas's attempt to ground rationality in communication fails—it gives an absolute primacy to truth, and limits its universal audience to rational motivations alone in the sense of motivations to reach a consensus about truth.[19] And this is precisely where Perelman succeeds. He meets the philosophical objection to rhetoric head on without succumbing to an empty rationalism, and thus fulfills philosophy's original aspiration in a philosophically oriented rhetorical theory which includes a rhetoric of philosophy, and provides, so to speak, a way out of rhetoric within rhetoric itself.

NOTES

[1] Page numbers refer to Chaim Perelman and L. Olbrechts-Tyteca, *The New Rhetoric: A Treatise on Argumentation* (TNR), trans. John Wilkinson and Purcell Weaver (Notre Dame, Indiana: University of Notre Dame Press, 1969); Chaim Perelman, *The New Rhetoric and the Humanities* (NRH), trans. William Kluback (Dordrecht, Holland: D. Reidel Publishing Company, 1979); Synthese Library 140: *The Realm of Rhetoric* (RR), trans. William Kluback (Notre Dame, Indiana: University of Notre Dame Press, 1982); "Philosophy and Rhetoric" (PR) in *Advances in Argumentation Theory and Research,* edited by J. Robert Cox and Charles Arthur Willard (Carbondale: Southern Illinois University Press, 1982): 287–97.

[2] There are many references to "universal audience" throughout Perelman's works, most of them duly noted in the indexes. The most important treatment of the concept is section seven of TNR, "The Universal Audience." However, this section has sometimes been misread. In the passage on classical philosophical instantiations of a universal audience, Perelman is presenting a strictly philosophical conception of universality—one which he opposes, and one in response to which he has developed his specifically rhetorical conception of universality. Nevertheless, commentators have sometimes read these lines as presenting Perelman's own views. For Perelman's own clarification of this matter, see "The New Rhetoric and the Rhetoricians: Remembrances and Comments," *Quarterly Journal of Speech* 70 (1984): 189–190.

[3] Perelman is referring to Plato's *Phaedrus* 273E.

[4] John Rawls, *A Theory of Justice* (Cambridge, Massachusetts: Harvard University Press, 1971): 12.

[5] Habermas deploys and defends the idea of an "ideal speech situation" in different ways in a number of different writings. I am indebted here to Thomas McCarthy's helpful discussion in *The Critical Theory of Jürgen Habermas* (Cambridge, Massachusetts: The MIT Press, 1978): esp. 307ff.

[6] *Philosophical-Political Profiles,* trans. Fred Lawrence. (Cambridge, Massachusetts: The MIT Press, 1984): 158. This passage is incorporated into an interesting discussion of the "ideal speech situation" by David Ingram, *Habermas and the Dialectic of Reason,* (New Haven: Yale University Press, 1987): see chapter eleven. Interestingly enough, it also serves as the primary epigraph for David Michael Levin's *The Opening of Vision: Nihilism and the Postmodern Situation* (New York: Routledge, Chapman and Hall, 1988).

[7] Ray compares Perelman to Rousseau and Kant, shows the similarity of the idea of the universal audience to the ideas of the general will and the categorical imperative, and concludes that the idea of a universal audience fails in the same way that the ideas of the general will and the categorical imperative fail. I have chosen not to respond to those particular arguments. Perelman himself addressed Ray's charges very briefly in "The New Rhetoric and the Rhetoricians: Remembrances and Comments." The citations are from John W. Ray, "Perelman's Universal Audience," *Quarterly Journal of Speech* 64 (1978): 361–75. In order, they are from pp. 372, 375, 370, and 372.

[8] Thomas B. Farrell seems to make an objection much like this in "Reason and Rhetorical Practice: The Inventional Agenda of Chaim Perelman" in *Practical Reasoning in Human Affairs,* ed. James L. Golden and Joseph J. Pilotta (Dordrecht, Holland: D. Reidel Publishing Company, 1986) Synthese Library 183: 259–286.

[9] This is, of course, the charge made by Socrates in Plato's *Gorgias* 463A ff.

[10] Plato, *Phaedrus* 274A–B.

[11] Although Perelman attempts to distinguish reasonableness from rationality (NRH 117–123), I do not follow his usage here. By "rationality" and its cognates, I mean no more than "reasonableness" and its.

12 As one would expect, Perelman omits giving us rules for adding audiences together. In this he would encounter some of Rousseau's arithmetical difficulties in adding up the general will—*if,* as some seem to believe, he were recommending a single technique for constructing the universal audience. Of course, I am offering an interpretation of the universal audience which allows for many different, even conflicting, techniques to be employed. For an account of the problems of adding wills (or audiences) together, see John Plamenatz, *Man and Society,* (London: Longman, 1963) 1, 393. This is probably the right place to wonder aloud whether anyone could do for universalizability in rhetoric anything similar to what Marcus G. Singer did for ethical theory in his *Generalization in Ethics* (New York: Alfred A. Knopf, 1961).

13 For an argument against making the persuasion/conviction distinction this way, see James Crosswhite, "Mood in Argumentation: Heidegger and the Exordium," *Philosophy and Rhetoric* 22 (1989): 28–42.

14 On the role of the universal audience in philosophical argumentation and on the relation of philosophy and rhetoric generally, see PR.

15 Although see PR for some problems facing any simple identification of a universal audience's responses with the dictates of common sense.

16 See Davids Ingram's provocative tracing of a nascent Benjaminian concept of aesthetic rationality in Habermas's recent writings (177ff.).

17 This concept suggests a number of more far-reaching applications as well. For example, consider Emerson's rhetoric. Could we interpret his dictum that his writing was meant not to instruct but to "provoke" as a way of recognizing that his true aim was to call into play the undefined universal audience? The audience whose characteristics emerge in newness? If Emerson had understood him better, could Thoreau have functioned in this way for him— someone who took his ideas more seriously than he did? Emerson's remarks on provocation may be found in his "Divinity School Address." His unsuccessful wrestling with Thoreau is most obvious in his 1862 memorial eulogy to Thoreau.

18 Cited by McCarthy in *The Critical Theory of Jürgen Habermas,* 310. Originally from *"Wahrheitstheorien,"* in *Wirklichkeit und Reflexionen: Walter Schultz zum 60 Geburtstag* (Pfullingen: Neske, 1973): 211–265.

19 Habermas has stayed with this formulation, at least through *The Theory of Communication Action.* See Vol. 1, 25, (trans. Thomas McCarthy [Boston: Beacon Press, 1984]).

···

Bias, Critical Doubt, and Fallacies

DOUGLAS N. WALTON

It would appear to be a common, and indeed quite a general presumption in informal logic that bias is a failure in argumentation that students can be taught to identify. This presumption becomes questionable, however, once we realize that there is no general method for determining bias in arguments that is widely accepted in the field of informal logic, or that is known to be itself free of bias. Even more worrisome, it is far from clear that we even understand what bias is, in the sense of being able to offer some clear and coherent definition that would be widely acceptable to those working in argumentation. Moreover, there are certain inherent difficulties in identifying and evaluating bias fairly and correctly, in a given case.

What should be stressed at the outset is that "bias," as used to criticize, is a two-edged sword. "Bias" has a negative, or critical aspect, typically used to condemn, refute or criticize an argument or person as having a deficiency. But "bias" is also often used in a spurious way, to attack a person or argument aggressively when the charge is not really justified. Bias is also subtle in many cases, and it is often simply unclear which party is in the right, the one accused of bias or the accuser. And most importantly, spirited or aggressive advocacy of a particular point of view is not necessarily the same thing as bias (at least bias in the negative sense in which it is an interference with critical argumentation).

As a first step towards developing methods for evaluating arguments for bias, this preliminary study will ask a philosophical question: What is bias? Consequent upon examining various ways of defining bias, one particular definition will be advocated. The view of bias put forward is *pragmatic,* meaning that it relates to how arguments are used in particular cases. The view of bias put forward is also *dialectical,* meaning that it pertains to a context of dialogue in which argumentation is put forward. According to this view, bias is seen as a kind of charge put forward by one party in a dialogue, a charge that can be sustained in some cases, and refuted in other cases. Finally, the view of bias advocated in this essay is *normative,* based on a standard of how participants in dialogue ought ideally to argue if they are to be rational in their reasoning together.

This essay argues that the evidence upon which a charge of bias is best evaluated is the analysis and reconstruction of the argumentation in the given text of discourse found in a particular case. Bias is a property of argumentation as used in a context of dialogue. It is often said that a person can be biased, or that a question can be biased, for example. But, in the sense of this essay, bias is a failure of critical argumentation. In this sense, most important in judging a person biased is how he or she performs in argumentation; most important in judging a question biased is how the question was used in a context of dialogue to perform some purpose associated with argumentation, reasoning, or arriving at a conclusion.

Finally, the essay will show that criticisms of bias are closely associated with certain of the major informal fallacies. The essay will argue that this association is not accidental, and that bias is essentially tied in with certain fallacies, and other wrong uses of argument.

A CASE OF A CRITICISM OF BIAS

An example shows how criticisms of bias work. In this case, two people are part of a panel discussion that has been set up to discuss a controversial problem of public policy. During the discussion, one participant accuses the other of bias.

Case 1:   Bob and Wilma are discussing the problem of acid rain. Wilma argues that reports on the extent of the problem are greatly exaggerated and that the costs of action are prohibitive. Bob points out that Wilma is on the board of directors of a U.S. coal company and that therefore her argument should not be taken at face value. (Walton, *Informal Logic* 149)

Bob's charge of bias is an ad hominem attack, a species of argument directed towards the person. Bob's argument is that Wilma is biased because of her financial involvement with the coal company, and that therefore we should question Wilma's impartiality. The conclusion we should infer, according to Bob's argument, is that Wilma's claim—reports on the extent of the problem of acid rain are exaggerated—is not a credible claim after considering who is making it.

Bob's criticism not only questions Wilma's impartiality, it also makes an attack on her integrity as a sincere participant in the discussion on acid rain who can be trusted to take part in the panel discussion in accord with Gricean maxims of collaborative dialogue. The key thing here is that the dialogue is supposed to be a particular type of critical discussion that openly looks at the arguments on both sides. However, once Wilma's involvement is revealed, questions are raised whether she is covertly engaging in a quite different type of dialogue, perhaps a type of negotiation or bargaining dialogue, in which her goal is to push for special interests. The suspicion is that she may be trying to use the public forum as a platform to push for one side, to support her own special interests at stake.

Another interesting factor in this case is that it would appear that Wilma did not announce her personal affiliation with the coal company at the beginning of the discussion. By revealing it unilaterally, Bob raises the implication that Wilma may have intentionally concealed this fact. This counts heavily in favor of the contention that Wilma has a bias that undermines her credibility as a balanced participant in the critical discussion.

Of course, we normally expect people to have a bias for one side or the other on a controversial issue. In itself, it might not detract from Wilma's credibility that she argues strongly against regulating emissions that are supposed to cause acid rain, even if she does so consistently. Yes, this may show a bias towards one point of view, but that in itself need not damage her credibility as a proponent of this point of view.

However, when we discover she is on the board of directors of a coal company, it is a different story. The problem here is that we naturally begin to question whether she supports this point of view because that is the way she sees the evidence, or whether her personal interest at stake is always causing her to distort the evidence, and "bend" the arguments to the one side.

It follows that in an allegation of bias like the one in case 1, there is an implicature of lack of critical doubt. The suggestion is that the biased party is "bending" arguments toward one side, instead of assessing the arguments in a critically appropriate way by paying attention to the requirements of the argumentation schemes.

Argumentation schemes require that certain kinds of premises need to be supported and certain kinds of critical questions need to be asked when a particular type of argument is put forward in a critical discussion.[1] The suspicion in the case of an arguer who is badly biased is that the accused is not judging the worth of an argument according to the requirements of the argumentation scheme, but always reaching the conclusion, instead, that happens to support the point of view chosen in advance.

This case also reveals that an allegation of bias is a kind of criticism of argumentation that has two sides. The critic comes forward with certain kinds of evidence to support the allegation. The allegation itself can be more or less serious, depending on the circumstances. And finally, the participant accused can raise certain types of defenses against the criticism.

For example, if Wilma had announced her affiliation with the coal company during the opening stage of the panel discussion, she could still be accused of bias. But such a criticism would be much less damaging than the one in case 1, where she had failed to announce this fact and it was brought forward by someone else during the discussion.

The problem of bias in this case was not that Wilma failed to have a neutral (zero) point of view. The problem was that her favoring the one side was judged inappropriate to the context of dialogue that the participants were supposed to be engaged in. They were supposed to be engaged in a public policy discussion where both parties were open to looking at the arguments on both sides. That does not mean that Wilma cannot have a point of view. But when Bob points out that Wilma is affiliated with a coal company, it casts into doubt her fairness in looking at the evidence on both sides. It suggests that Wilma has generally made up her mind in advance how to argue, no matter which way the evidence goes.

Bob's criticism of bias throws a weight of presumption against Wilma's side to refute the charge, if she can. Perhaps she can do it, but given her concealment, the burden is heavy against her. The question of bias arises because of the grounded suspicion of a concealed, unilateral shift in the type of dialogue involved. They are supposed to be engaged in an open critical discussion, but the suspicion is that Wilma is really engaged in a form of concealed bargaining or quarreling dialogue that always pushes for one side only.

The problem is that in the eristic or quarreling type of dialogue, the goal is to attack the other side and win at all costs, disregarding or overriding the evidence and legitimate critical doubt. Quarreling is not necessarily fallacious or logically erroneous in itself as a type of dialogue. But it is a very inefficient way of conducting a critical discussion, and rightly associated with many fallacies and faults of logic when introduced into a critical discussion context of argumentation.

Bargaining or negotiation is also a legitimate type of discourse in its own right. But problems of bias and fallacies arise when there has been an illicit, or even concealed, shift from a critical discussion to a bargaining type of dialogue. The purpose of a critical discussion is to resolve a conflict of opinions by showing your argument is correct, because it is supported by evidence and conforms to rules of reasoned discussion. But in negotiation, such matters of truth and evidence are not the main point. The goal is to make demands and concessions in order to "get the best deal."[2] A move that is quite appropriate in this type of dialogue could be inappropriate, or even highly obstructive, in a critical discussion. The problem in case 1 is the possibility of an illicit shift from one type of dialogue to another.

CONTEXTS OF DIALOGUE

According to the analysis presented here, bias is a general concept that is pragmatic in the sense that, as applied to any real case, it presupposes a context of dialogue. Although the concept of bias has general characteristics that can be expressed in a definition, it will be implemented somewhat differently in different contexts of dialogue.

In *persuasion dialogue,* the goal of each participant is to persuade the other participant that a particular proposition is true, based on premises that this other party is committed to.[3] In the critical discussion (a subspecies of persuasion dialogue) the goal is to resolve a conflict of opinions. In persuasion dialogue, partisan advocacy of one's point of view is normal and necessary.

Van Eemeren and Grootendorst have shown how a critical discussion has four stages: an opening stage, a confrontation stage, an argumentation stage, and a closing stage. At the opening stage, the participants agree to enter into the critical discussion, and not to abandon the discussion until it is properly closed, or until the other party agrees to postpone or end it. The problem of bias was serious in case 1 because of an improper or illicit dialectical shift. Wilma was supposedly engaged in a critical discussion on the issue of acid rain. But covertly, and without either the agreement or knowledge of Bob, she was really engaging in a kind of interest-based negotiation dialogue.

Critical discussion requires a certain openness to concede that one's argument is subject to critical doubt, and can be subject to critical questioning, or even refuted by good evidence put forward by the other side.[4] When one's own advocacy becomes too aggressive, and is closed off from good counterarguments that have arisen in the dialogue, then it can be proper to speak of harmful bias in a critical discussion.

The *inquiry* as a type of dialogue arises from a problem—something is not known to be true or false—rather than from a conflict. The goal of the inquiry is to prove this proposition from premises that are known to be true, or alternatively, to show that it cannot be proved (Walton, *Begging* 43). Although whether scientific argumentation takes the form of an inquiry is widely debated, proponents of the rhetoric of science place scientific reasoning as a form of inquiry. According to Broad and Wade, bias comes into science in two forms: (1) in interpretation of data where the scientist either "fudges" the data intentionally to make results "more acceptable," or unintentional bias where the scientist has some personal preference for the outcome (85), and (2) in the peer review process and referee system which may, for example favor already eminent scientists over young or unknown scientists, in the allocation of credit for findings (99). Recent cases of fabrication of data have raised many questions about fraud and misconduct in science. Bias is an important concept in judging these concerns.

Bias can enter into an inquiry in the collection of data because the inquiry is supposed to be based on premises that can safely be established in order to eliminate the need for later retraction. Bias can also come into an inquiry in deciding what conclusions can be drawn from these premises, according to the methods and standards of a given branch of science.

Another basic type of dialogue is *negotiation dialogue,* where the goal is to divide up a commodity where resources are insufficient. Each side makes concessions and demands. In this type of dialogue, the goal is not to prove anything, or show that your point of view is right, it is to "get the best deal" or bargain for what you want (Donahue, "Development" and "Empirical").

In the *information-seeking type of dialogue,* the goal is to transfer information from one party to the other—one party has access to some information that the other lacks. In this type of dialogue, it is often very important that the information-giving party present the information in a balanced way (Walton, *Begging* 43). One subspecies of information-seeking is expert consultation dialogue. Bias is often very important as a factor in judging argumentation based on appeals to expert opinion.[5] Another subspecies of information-seeking dialogue is news reporting by the media. Bias, in the sense of balanced reporting, is critical. The reporter has to be selective in presenting reports on all sorts of controversial issues. Here we often have a juxtaposition of two types of dialogues, for the reporter may be giving a report to his readers or viewers on the subject of a recent critical discussion. The report would be biased if the reporter engages in promoting one side too heavily, instead of taking a balanced view that does justice to the arguments on both sides.

Eristic dialogue is a type of verbal combat where the goal is to strike out at the other party in order to win at all costs and, if possible, humiliate the other party. The quarrel is a subspecies of eristic dialogue that has the purpose of giving vent to repressed emotions.[6] Bias and other categories of critical evaluation of argumentation mean little in the quarrel. Argumentation in the quarrel is, by its nature, always strongly biased towards one's own side, and against the point of view of the other side. However, the quarrel is important as a model of dialogue in judging cases of bias because bias often occurs where there has been a shift from some other type of dialogue to quarrel. For example, a dialectical shift from a critical discussion to a quarrel is often indicated by the presence of ad hominem argumentation.

A fallacious argument is persuasive, or "seems valid" as an effective trick, because such an argument could be appropriate or non-harmful in the context of a quarrel. It is only a fallacy because it should be evaluated in the original context of dialogue.

Bias, itself, however, is not a fallacy or a fallacious type of argumentation per se. It is rather a type of attitude that often leads to, and is associated with fallacies. Bias is sometimes harmless, and it is only the harmful type of bias that should be subject to criticism, in the same way that fallacies are subject to criticism as serious failures of argumentation.

ARGUMENT AD HOMINEM

The argument ad hominem or "argument against the man" is a kind of attacking or negative type of argument whereby one participant in a dialogue uses information about an opponent's personal characteristics or circumstances to refute the opponent's argument. There are two basic and common ways to carry out this type of attack, both of which have been widely recognized in traditional logic text-books. One way is to attack the person directly, by arguing that the opponent is of bad character, especially bad character for veracity, and cannot therefore be trusted to be a sincere or reliable participant in the dialogue. The other way is to claim that what the opponent has advocated in the argument is a point of view that is inconsistent with the opponent's own personal circumstances. The first kind of argument has traditionally been called the "abusive" ad hominem and the second has been called the "circumstantial" ad hominem.[7]

The name "abusive" is misleading, however, because the first type of ad hominem can sometimes be a reasonable argument. For example, Waller has shown that evaluating the testimony of a witness in legal cross-examinations by raising questions about the person's character, reliability as a witness, past convictions, and so forth, is rightly regarded, within limits, as a legitimate kind of argumentation (108). Also, I have argued through the analysis of many cases that, in election campaigning in political debates, raising questions of a candidate's personal integrity and character are rightly recognized as legitimate (*Arguer's Position*). The abusive ad hominem could be labeled the "personal" or "direct" ad hominem, but the circumstantial type also has a personal element, so possibly the phrase "direct ad hominem argument" is the best term for this species.

In many instances, the circumstantial ad hominem can be used as a non-fallacious type of argumentation to shift a weight of presumption against one side in a dialogue.

> Case 2: Suppose a politician has gone on record as advocating keeping government expenses down by not giving out inflationary salary raises to government officials, but it is later revealed that, once elected, he has given himself a large increase to his already sizable salary. A critic may then use the circumstantial type of ad hominem argument against the politician, saying "You do not practice what you preach!"

In such a case, the argument could be quite reasonable. Only if it is carried to excess in some way, or used in inappropriate circumstances, would it become a fallacy or bad argument.

The direct and the circumstantial types of ad hominem argument are related in some cases. Sometimes the circumstantial argument is used as a kind of lead-in attack which is then extended or more fully developed into a direct ad hominem attack. In such a case, the arguer's personal circumstances are purported to be in conflict with his argument, implying that the arguer is a liar, insincere, hypocritical, or otherwise deficient in character for veracity.

Another variant of ad hominem argument is the *bias* type of attack: one arguer claims that the other is not an impartial or fair-minded participant in an argument on the grounds that he or she is pushing for one side by reason of some special interest in supporting that point of view. Case 1 is an example of this type of ad hominem argument. Consider the following:

Case 3:   Pay no attention to those American Tobacco Institute arguments against restrictions on smoking. You shouldn't take their arguments seriously; after all, those arguments are bought and paid for by the tobacco industry.[8]

In this case, as Waller rightly points out, the ad hominem argument is a fallacy if the conclusion is that the cited arguments against restrictions on smoking have to be absolutely wrong, just because the arguer has special interests. On the other hand, had the argument been put forward in a more qualified way, perhaps merely citing the bias of the American Tobacco Institute without rejecting its argument as being of no possible merit on these grounds, it could have been nonfallacious. As Waller reminded us, if we were to reject any argument presented by a paid advocate as unsound, "a sound argument would be a rare event in the courtroom." The problem is that we often tend to go too far with ad hominem arguments, wrongly concluding that evidence of any bias refutes an argument so decisively that further dialogue may be regarded as closed or pointless.

Another variant is the *poisoning the well* ad hominem argument, an extension of the bias type of ad hominem argument in which an arguer is said to be so dishonest that nothing the arguer might say can ever be trusted as reliable. This even more aggressive ad hominem tends to leave the attacked party no room for further meaningful participation in the dialogue. The suggestion is that the attacked party is so determined to always push a one-sided point of view or special interest that the arguer can never engage in a collaborative critical discussion that meets the Gricean maxims of honesty and sincerity.

As case 3 showed, the ad hominem argument becomes fallacious when its upshot is exaggerated. An allegation of bias may be reasonable enough if taken as a critical questioning of an argument. But if pushed further, and unjustifiably taken as a conclusive refutation of the argument, absolutely and not just relative to the source, it can become a fallacy. Thus the ad hominem fallacy is a species of dialectical failure—a failure of an argument to meet the maxims of successful communication in dialogue. Putting their analysis in the framework of a Lorenzen formal dialogue, Barth and Martens describe the ad hominem fallacy as the following type of incorrect inference: just because the proponent has defended his thesis successfully against an opponent's criticism ex concessis, it does not necessarily follow, nor is it settled, that the proponent's thesis is true. The fallacy is a kind of unjustified logical leap from a weaker to a stronger form of conclusion.

This formalistic analysis, however, leaves plenty of room for examining the given text to judge whether an ad hominem argument is fallacious. There may be quite a number of factors to be taken into account. An illustration is the famous smoking example:

Case 4:   A parent gives a lecture to her son, arguing that smoking is very bad for your health, and that therefore one should not smoke. But the child replies, "What about you? You smoke. So much for your argument against smoking!" (cf. Walton, *Arguer's Position* 67–71)

In a case like this, we have to be very careful to interpret the child's conclusion correctly. If rejecting the parent's argument that smoking is bad for your health per se, then the child could be committing a serious ad hominem fallacy. But if only questioning the sincerity of the parent in following his or her own advice, the child could be raising legitimate grounds for doubt concerning the practical consistency of the parent's commitments. One can easily see from considering this kind of example that each case should be carefully considered on its merits. Sometimes the ad hominem argument should be rejected as a fallacy, while in other cases it is a reasonable kind of argument which can quite legitimately raise critical questions or shift a burden of proof in a dialogue.

It is well to remember, however, that in cases involving witness testimony or appeal to authority, the ad hominem argument can often be a legitimate way of testing the credibility of a contributor to a species of reasoned dialogue like a critical discussion or a legal trial. Used properly and judiciously in such a context, it can be a nonfallacious kind of argumentation that uses a criticism of bias to raise legitimate critical doubts.

Brinton cites knowledge of ethos or character as a positive factor, rightly appealed to in support of argumentation. Such soft support for argument is appropriate where absence of hard knowledge leaves the way open for presumptions to guide a course of action. The rationale for utilizing such a defeasible kind of argumentation follows from Aristotle's remarks in the *Rhetorica* and *Nicomachean Ethics* that the good man's speech is more credible, especially where opinions are divided and certain knowledge that would resolve the issue is not available at the time.

According to Brinton, an ethotic argument is an argument in which ethos (character) is used to transfer credibility, either positively or negatively, from an arguer to argument (248). If ethos is a legitimate factor in argumentation, it follows that ad hominem argument is a legitimate kind of argumentation in some cases.

In such cases, it would be appropriate to have a kind of favorable bias towards a speaker's arguments or opinions if that speaker has a positive ethos. But if the speaker's ethos is legitimate, and appraised correctly by the respondent to it, would it be correct to describe the favorable attitude as bias? This question remains to be settled by an acceptable definition of bias.

We see then that although allegations of bias are associated with traditional fallacies, such arguments can, in some cases, be reasonable criticisms that raise legitimate critical questions in a context of dialogue.

One problem is that such arguments are presumptive in nature, inherently weak kinds of argumentation that shift a burden of proof in a dialogue by raising critical doubts. Because of deductivist and inductivist prejudices in logic, we are not very well equipped to deal with these kinds of argument, and often prejudge them as fallacies because they appear to fall short, or to be suspicious, from a deductivist or inductivist point of view. To begin to come to grips with these fallacies, and with the concept of bias itself, we need to overcome our prejudice against presumptive reasoning.

Just as the ad hominem is often associated with negative bias, the appeal to authority as a type of argumentation is often associated with a positive bias in favor of a speaker.

ARGUMENT AD VERECUNDIAM

Bias also ties in closely with the argument ad verecundiam as a fallacy. The connection is revealed by the following case, concerning a 17-year-old who died after having an illegal abortion. She was from a state where a young woman under eighteen must get her parents' permission before having an abortion. This case became controversial, and was reported on *60 Minutes*, after the young woman's parents claimed that it was the fault of the law that their daughter died from infection because she was forced to get an illegal abortion.

This case drew national attention, and *60 Minutes* interviewed an advocate of the right-to-life movement, who maintained that, in fact, this young woman did not have an abortion, and that therefore "the premise of the campaign against the consent law is false." This right-to-life advocate, called "Mr. Wilke," argued that the autopsy report showed that the young woman had a miscarriage, and did not show that she had an abortion ("Becky's Story" 10). To dispute this argument, Morley Safer, the interviewer, introduced evidence from the physician who performed the autopsy.

Case 5:   *Safer:* [voice-over] But the forensic pathologist who performed the autopsy on Becky, Dr. John Press, says that's just not true.

John Pless, Forensic Pathologist: Becky Bell died as a result of a septic abortion with pneumonia.

Safer: With tainted instruments, presumably?

Pless: Yes.

Safer: That the infection was transmitted up into the main bloodstream?

Pless: That is my belief—that the infection came from the abortion at the time that the fetus was removed—yes.

Wilke: He's wrong and we have any number of letters now from forensic pathologists, from heads of government institutions. Here's one from Dr. Nathanson, who's done a lot of this work in the courts.

Safer: But Dr. Nathanson is an admitted, well known right-to-lifer.

Wilke: I understand.

Safer: Don't you see how his diagnosis might be a little suspect?

Wilke: He's still a physician and what he's saying compares with what the rest of them are saying. There is no evidence in here of an induced abortion.

Safer: You also cite as an expert Dr. John Curry, the former director of the tissue bank at the Bethesda Naval Hospital.

Wilke: His name has been mentioned, yes.

Safer: He told us he's never seen the autopsy, that he's not qualified to make a judgment.

Wilke: I have not talked to Dr. Curry, either. I do have some other letters here, of course.

Safer: But isn't it a bit irresponsible, even brutal of you, to gang up on this girl and her parents, who are both deeply troubled, using questionable medical evidence, playing fast and loose with the facts? Isn't that a bit unfair?

Wilke: If her parents had not gone public and made this a national thing, forcing us to say the things we're saying, I would be the last one to disturb their grief. I feel terrible doing that. (10–11)

Safer made an appeal to expert opinion in consulting Dr. Pless, but it seemed to be a legitimate move, because Pless was the physician who performed the autopsy. And it was the right-to-life group who introduced this medical question into the controversy by maintaining that the young woman did not die of infection produced by an abortion. Up to this point then, there is an argument based on appeal to expert opinion, but it is not a fallacious argument ad verecundiam.

The context of dialogue could be described as follows: The initial controversy posed by the discussion in this case was the issue of the wisdom of the parental consent law. The dialogue is a critical discussion arising from a conflict of opinions concerning the rightness of a particular law. The issue is controversial—the law is on the books in thirty-four states, but not in the rest ("Becky's Story" 7). Medical matters became relevant to this discussion when the one side in the dispute, the right-to-life advocates, made the claim that the young woman in this case did not die from infection due to an abortion. Hence it came about that an expert consultation dialogue was woven into the original critical discussion.

This shift from one type of dialogue to another is not inherently illegitimate, however. In principle, second hand knowledge may be introduced into a critical discussion by consultation with expert sources of opinion. Such practices have been recognized by van Eemeren and Grootendorst under the heading of an inter-subjective testing procedure, a way of bringing expert knowledge into a critical discussion (71); in my own work under the heading of correct appeals to expert opinion in argumentation (*Informal Logic* ch. 7); and in the well-established legal tradition of expert witnesses. According to these methods, expert consultation can improve the quality of argumentation in a critical discussion where a conflict of opinions is at issue.

Where the fallacious ad verecundiam enters case 5, however, is at the point where Wilke responds to the opinion given by Pless. Wilke tried to refute the evidence brought forward in Pless' opinion by citing "any number of letters from forensic pathologists" and "heads of government institutions." In particular, he cited the opinion of one Dr. Nathanson "who's done a lot of work in the courts." One problem with these appeals to expert opinion is that none of the authorities cited can speak on the same footing with Pless, for none of them did the autopsy. This makes Wilke's appeal inherently weak.

Such a weak appeal to expert opinion is open to doubt already, and Safer then punches another hole in the argument by pointing out that Nathanson is "an admitted, well known right-to-lifer." This is a key point in the dialogue. Safer is attacking Wilke's appeal to authority by claiming it is subject to critical doubt on the grounds that Nathanson is a biased source.[9] The suspicion raised is that Nathanson may be just giving his personal opinion as an advocate for one side of the issue at dispute in the critical discussion, instead of impartially giving his expert opinion as a physician.

The problem of bias in case 5, like case 1, arises because of the dialectical shift. It would appear from the evidence that Nathanson is not giving his advice as an *impartial* expert. Instead, there is reason to believe that he is really engaging in advocacy of his own particular moral point of view.

Since Nathanson's opinion—delivered by letter when he has not even personally examined the medical evidence—is weak, as an expert opinion in this case, the allegation of bias is quite a strong and effective rebuttal. The rebuttal is made even stronger by Safer's quite correct and careful use of it as an argument to raise questions by asking whether it makes Nathanson's diagnosis "a little suspect," rather than treating it as an absolute refutation of Nathanson's opinion.

The ad verecundiam fallacy comes in at the next line in the case where Wilke still tried to push forward with his appeal to expert opinion by saying of Nathanson: "He's still a physician, and what he's saying compares with what the rest of them are saying." However, this cited parallel is false. For as Safer pointed out next, another of the physicians cited by Wilke admitted that he had not seen the autopsy. One expert consultation is not necessarily as strong as another. In this case, it is a question of access to, and utilization of, the medical evidence relevant to the case.

The problem is that Wilke did not back off and admit that his appeals to expert opinion are weaker. Nor did he reply to the question of bias, except to reiterate that his expert sources are physicians, and therefore that their opinions are comparable to the opinion of any other physician. By refusing to make concessions or to respond properly to Safer's legitimate critical questions and charges of bias, Wilke took a rigid stance that appears to confirm that he was taking a quarrelsome, dogmatic approach of always pushing for advocacy of his own point of view, instead of adopting a more critical attitude of at least fairly considering both sides of the issue where doubts can be raised.

BIASED QUESTIONS AND POLLS

In some cases, it is neither a person nor an argument that is biased, or the source of bias. In these cases, what seems to be biased is the technique used to collect information. In this sense, the *fallacy of biased statistics* is the kind of error that occurs when a sample chosen as data is not representative of the distribution of the property in a statistical generalization and does not match the distribution in the sample (Walton, *Informal Logic* 207). The problem here is that the kind of technique used to collect data produces a bias in the results. This problem could be called "technical bias," meaning that the bias is in the technique used to collect data, or arrive at a result.

Biased questions also fall into this category. According to the results of a Soviet referendum held March 17, 1991, more than three quarters of those who voted said "yes" to a new union supporting Mr. Gorbachev (European Journal). Although the voting appeared to be like western elections, the referendum question had a different twist.

Case 6:   Do you think that it is necessary to preserve the Union of the
           Soviet Socialist Republics in which the rights and freedom of
           every citizen regardless of ethnic origin will be fully guaranteed?
           (European Journal)

The "yes" vote was for Gorbachev's side, the "no" for Yeltsin's.

This case is a classic case of a *loaded question* of the sort traditionally dealt with by logic textbooks under the heading of fallacies of questioning (see Walton, *Question-Reply*). The problem is that there is a general presumption among the voters in favor of the "rights and freedoms of every citizen regardless of ethnic origin," and hence the question is loaded towards a "yes" vote. This loading would unfairly skew the results toward one side. You can see which side had the power to frame the question.

Votes or polls can also be biased in another way, however. In some cases, a vote can be said to be biased in the sense that the voters are influenced by some interest or consideration, rather than just giving an honest answer to the question.

Case 7:   A Toyota dealer in California sent out a customer satisfaction survey promising a free cleaning of the customer's car provided the ballot was marked in the "correct" way. Attaching a marked sample of "correct" responses to a survey, the letter noted that all "very satisfied" entries means a free "detail" (a good cleaning, inside and out, of the car). ("We Buy" 295)

In this kind of case, it is the question that is said to be biased, as opposed to the argument, or the person advocating the argument. Because the question has been worded in a particular way, it will inevitably appeal to a bias that exists in the population queried, resulting in a misleading or skewed result that unduly favors one side.

Statisticians have developed careful methods for detecting these kinds of bias in polling and other techniques for the collection of statistical data (see Campbell). Hence, in some cases, bias can be measured, at least within the technical requirements imposed by statistical methods. The term "bias" has a special, technical meaning that applies to certain types of cases that occur in statistics. But can this special, technical meaning of "bias" be generalized to cover the variety of different kinds of bias that are encountered in informal logic?

What needs to be recognized in such cases is that question asking is being used as a part of a dialogue. In information seeking dialogue, questions should be *open*— that is, they should not take a side in a critical discussion by, covertly or otherwise, pushing a respondent towards favoring one side of an issue. If the purpose of the question is really to seek information, advocacy of one side is improper. The purpose of a poll is supposedly to seek out the respondents' "real" or honest point of view or opinion. A biased question is biased because it interferes with this primary purpose of its use in information seeking dialogue.

Hence argumentation is involved in biased questions. The respondent is supposed to draw his or her own conclusions, and not be influenced to draw a particular conclusion suggested by the structuring of the question which slants any one possible answer as the "desired" or "favorable" response.

Many of the kinds of cases of alleged bias that need to be dealt with in informal logic are not inductive nor statistical. Instead, these cases involve presumptive reasoning, a kind of reasoning based on normal expectations in a typical case. This kind of reasoning is *defeasible*, or subject to rebuttal as new evidence comes in. Presumptive reasoning is a provisional way of moving forward in argumentation by working on the basis of plausible or practical assumptions, in cases where knowledge, or even good statistical evidence, is either not available, or is insufficient to prove or disprove the proposition in question.

HASTY GENERALIZATION

Another type of fallacy often associated with bias is the *hasty generalization* or *secundum quid* (neglect of qualifications), where an arguer tends to push ahead with some favorite generalization or personal prejudice, ignoring or suppressing good evidence to the contrary. Fearnside and Holther cite many examples of this kind of prejudicial attitude. The following case is cited as an instance of cultural bias.

> Case 8:   Northern travelers often return from the South complaining of the indolence, ignorance, racial attitudes, and general backwardness of certain areas. Typical comments include "They're still trying to live in the antebellum days." "Even their language reflects their backwardness; they drawl their words and drag their feet." "Jim Crow is simply insufferable."

In their comment on this case, Fearnside and Holther note that although some areas of the South could rightly be described as "economically backward," it shows a kind of prejudiced attitude or apriorism (closing one's eyes to contrary evidence) to exclusively emphasize things about the South perceived as unfavorable, backward, or peculiar. The fault they cite is a kind of one-sided point of view that shows bias by always looking at one point of view and ignoring the contrary point of view. The fault is the narrowness of a cultural bias that ignores aspects outside the arguer's personal or cultural experience (119).

Thouless covered this type of problem under the heading of prejudice in reasoning, writing that it is often the strength of our own "hidden emotional inclinations" on a topic that makes it so difficult to seek out right opinions (232). Thouless believes that to contend with bias in a constructive way, we must cultivate an "attitude of detachment of mind" (23). But the problem is a subtle one because merely having emotional inclinations to support a point of view, explicit or not, is not necessarily being biased in a way that interferes with good argumentation. The problem is to judge when such a proclivity becomes a negative bias, a fallacy, a logical failure, an obstacle to good reasoning.

For instance, the speaker in case 8 is showing a kind of bias, or particular point of view. But the discourse in case 8 is not necessarily an argument. It could be, for all we know of the context, just a description of typical comments by some persons describing their experience of travelling in the South. Broadly speaking, their language and description of their experiences express a bias or point of view. But is it a "bias" in the sense we are trying to analyze? The answer is: not necessarily. There is not enough of an argument to decisively reveal a kind of bias that is a critical failure. A person of the sort may or may not be biased, in this sense of "bias." That depends on the reaction to evidence presented by an opponent in subsequent dialogue—evidence that goes against the Northern point of view on the South.

Allport posed the problem succinctly, by beginning with the observation that what he called "over categorization" is one of the most common tricks of thinking: "Given a thimbleful of facts, we rush to make generalizations as large as a tub." For example, a young boy sees a large Norwegian depicted in a saga, and develops the idea that all Norwegians are giants. Nowadays, we often call this "thinking in stereotypes" (9).

However, as Allport put it, "Not every overblown generalization is a prejudice." Some are simply prejudgments or misconstructions. Such judgments, based on insufficient evidence, become prejudices only in cases where they are not reversed when exposed to new knowledge (9).

What Allport is suggesting here is that having an incorrect prejudgment is not necessarily having a bias, in the sense of bias as a critical failure in argumentation. For example, suppose the only Norwegians the little boy has been exposed to are giants in a saga. He is basing his depiction of Norwegians on inadequate evidence, and therefore arriving at an erroneous, distorted or biased point of view. But this is not a critical failure if the saga is the only evidence he has. What matters is how he responds when confronted with the evidence of nongiant Norwegians. If he revises his conclusions, then it is inappropriate to speak of bias, at least as a critical failure of his reasoning.

The problem of bias is to distinguish between biased reasoning and nonbiased presumptive reasoning. Presumptive reasoning goes forward in a dialogue on a provisional basis, in the absence of knowledge that would definitively resolve the question, one way or the other. Presumptions go forward in argumentation in relation to a burden of proof, in order to facilitate a dialogue, or to enable the participants to go ahead with proposals for action to deal with a practical problem, where sufficient knowledge to resolve the issue cannot be collected in time to be of practical value.

Presumptive argumentation is now widely recognized as important in artificial intelligence, where it has been identified with nonmonotonic reasoning. In a deductively valid argument, no matter how many new premises you add, the original inference stays valid. But in nonmonotonic reasoning, an inference that was correct to begin with may become incorrect once new premises are added. The standard example is the following:

Case 9:   Birds fly.
          Tweety is a bird.
          Therefore, Tweety flies. (Reiter 149)

This inference is correct or acceptable, but only as a presumptive or provisional kind of argument that is subject to exceptions. For example, if we find that Tweety is a penguin, the premises still hold, but the conclusion now fails to hold. This particular case is a "default," the exception to the rule.

The major premise in case 9 is best treated not as a universal generalization of the form "All birds fly" (without exception), or even as an inductive or probabilistic generalization of the form "Most, or a certain percentage of, birds fly." Instead, it is a presumptive generalization of the form "The typical bird can be expected to fly under normal conditions."

The presumptive generalization is, by its nature, subject to default in exceptional cases. Presumptive reasoning is based on a tentative kind of inference that goes forward provisionally, subject to correction or defeat, should new, relevant evidence come into the discussion.

Not all presumptive, stereotypical reasoning is fallacious, or biased in the critical sense. Presumptive reasoning commits the fallacy of secundum quid when it is pushed ahead anyway by an arguer, even in the face of new, relevant evidence that defeats it.

Thus in case 9, suppose the proponent is offered good evidence that Tweety is a penguin, but persists in operating on the assumption that Tweety *must* fly, because *all* birds fly, and Tweety is a bird. The proponent is being "logical" in one sense, but he is also exhibiting a prejudice, or bad bias, that is an obstacle to continuing a reasoned discussion. The problem is that the presumption did not default in the dialogue when it should have.

Presumption becomes bad critical bias when there has been a failure in argumentation of openness to new evidence or legitimate critical doubts that have arisen in a dialogue. What matters in case 8 is not the preconception or prejudgment of the individual in question, if he has only seen evidence that supports his own one-sided stereotype of the South. What matters is how he reacts, for example, in a critical discussion where he is presented with evidence supporting the opposed point of view. This will be revealed in a text of discourse, showing his argumentation in the context of that critical discussion, how he responds to appropriate critical questioning, etc. What reveals the bias of the person is the bias shown in his argumentation in a context of dialogue. Now we have identified and defined the kind of bias meant as the target of analysis, we turn to five hypotheses to analyze it.

FIVE HYPOTHESES IN DEFINING BIAS

The first hypothesis defines bias as a failure of neutrality in argumentation. Simply put, this hypothesis defines a biased arguer or argument as one that displays a non-neutral attitude.

The first question with respect to this definition is: What is a neutral attitude in argumentation? Van Eemeren and Grootendorst are of some help here. In a critical discussion, according to their account, there is an externalized dispute about an expressed opinion where one participant expresses doubt about the acceptability of a point of view propounded by the other participant. A neutral attitude is what they call a "zero point of view."

> If we abbreviate the *expressed opinion* in respect of which language users adopt an attitude as O, it is then possible to identify three possible *attitudes to O*: a *positive* point of view, a *negative* point of view and a *zero* point of view. In our example the first language user takes a positive attitude to O, the second a negative and the third a zero attitude. We shall abbreviate the three possible attitudes as follows:
>
> (a) *positive point of view: +/O*
> (b) *negative point of view: -/O*
> (c) *zero point of view: 0/O*
>
> If a language user advances a positive point of view in respect of O, then he is further *positively committed to O* and if he advances a negative point of view he is *negatively committed to O* (unless he revokes his positive or negative point of view). A language user adopting a zero attitude to O is *not committed to O either positively or negatively.* (79)

Externalization is important in this account of the neutral (zero) attitude. Here then, we seem to have a promising framework for defining "bias": "bias" is simply failure to exhibit a neutral (zero) attitude in an argument.

The basic problem with this hypothesis is that it classifies any argument that shows either a positive or negative point of view as biased. This seems far too strong, for it condemns all advocacy arguments of any sort as biased, no matter how well justified, appropriate, and reasonable. Arguments showing a positive or negative point of view can be quite appropriate and useful for contributing to the legitimate goals of a critical discussion. Generally we think of bias as, if not something bad or inappropriate in argumentation, at least something that represents a skewed or illicit type of argumentation that needs to be singled out for special notice. Bias is not just a point of view, but a point of view that has somehow become too dominant and rigid, or has been pressed on another party in argument unfairly or inappropriately.

The problem here is complicated by Blair's distinction between "good bias" and "bad bias." We might try to rescue the first hypothesis by saying that advocacy (having a point of view) does generally show bias, but it is a good bias, rather than a bad bias. And it is only the bad bias that we need to single out for critical censure. But this still leaves us with the problem of distinguishing between good bias and bad bias.

And it still leaves us with a notion of bias that could be perceived as overly broad. For, according to this account, anyone who puts forward any point of view in any argument can always be replied to: "Your argument is biased. Of course, it is a good bias, not a bad bias. But you have shown bias."

A second hypothesis is to define bias as absence of critical doubt. This narrower definition is also more negative. It implies that bias is to be equated with a kind of one-sided argumentation that is not open enough to admit of critical questions and grounds for doubt that are characteristic of impartial or objective argumentation.[10]

The first problem with this hypothesis is the question: How do you define critical doubt? If critical doubt is defined as a neutral attitude in argumentation, then of course we are back to our first hypothesis. On the other hand, if defined after the manner proposed by van Eemeren and Grootendorst, it becomes a complex concept in its own right.

The other problem with this hypothesis is that absence of critical doubt seems to equate more with dogmatism or fanaticism—extreme forms of bias, perhaps. At any rate, absence of critical doubt does not seem to be exactly the same thing as bias, even though it may be related to bias in some way.

A third hypothesis is that bias means that an arguer has something to gain by putting forward a particular argument or point of view. In this sense we speak of a "biased source," meaning someone giving testimony or supporting a particular point of view where it is revealed that this individual is being paid, or has some other personal interest at stake as a reason for supporting that point of view.

This hypothesis is inadequate, by itself, as a definition, however. Someone who has something to gain could, in some instances, put forward a nonbiased argument; conversely, someone who has nothing to gain could put forward a biased argument. Hence this hypothesis is refuted as a general definition of bias. It only gives an identifying sign of bias. It is a criterion, not a definition of bias.

A fourth hypothesis is that bias is a lack of balance in argumentation, favoring one side unduly. A good example to support this view of bias would be the case of a news report on a controversial issue. It is generally a principle of journalism that the report should look at the arguments on both sides, giving a balanced coverage, if the report purports to be a news account.

This hypothesis differs from the first in that bias is not simply defined as non-neutrality, but as a failure of the type and degree of balance required by the dialogue appropriate for the circumstances of the given case. For example, news reporting is a particular type of dialogue or discourse that requires enough balance of perspective so that it is not perceived as one-sided advocacy of a cause, nor even propaganda.

However, in another type of situation, say in an opinion column, a much more one-sided degree of advocacy of a particular point of view might be quite acceptable. Hence this view makes bias relative to a given context of dialogue.

Finally, a fifth hypothesis is that bias is identified with a particular position or distinctive point of view that has been revealed in a discussion. For example, an argument may be said to exhibit a left-liberal bias. Here, what is being identified is not only a non-neutrality, but the existence of a distinct type of position or bias that may be said to be present or recur throughout a whole sequence of argumentation, or even a number of arguments on different occasions or different subjects. Like the third hypothesis, this approach appears to express a characteristic or criterion of bias that is present in some cases, rather than a general definition of bias.

A new definition of bias incorporates some of these hypotheses and excludes some aspects of them.

CRITICAL DOUBT

A leading characteristic of critical doubt as a kind of attitude of a participant in argumentation is restraint. Critical doubt requires a temporary suspension of one's advocacy of one's own point of view. While it is correct and appropriate normally to have a strong stance in favor of one's own point of view, there are circumstances in which this pro attitude must temporarily be restrained or bracketed.

Some might say that critical doubt entails having a neutral attitude—one which is neither pro nor con. But another more complex way to define "critical doubt" is as an attitude that one party in a dispute has toward the attitude of the other party. Van Eemeren and Grootendorst define critical doubt:

> It is important to realize that the doubt expressed by a language user in a dispute does not bear directly on the expressed opinion but on the *point of view or attitude* expressed by another language user *in respect of* the expressed opinion. Perhaps it is also important here to observe once more that expressing doubt, while it may *accompany* the adoption of the opposite attitude, is *not identical* to propounding the opposite point of view. (81)

In a critical discussion, according to van Eemeren and Grootendorst's account, two parties have set out to resolve an externalized conflict of opinions, and each party has a point of view (standpoint). A standpoint has two components: (1) a proposition, representing the thesis (conclusion) a party is arguing for, and (2) an attitude toward this proposition. An attitude can be positive, negative, or neutral (79). "Critical doubt" is an attitude of one party in a dispute towards the attitude of the other party.

This way of defining "critical doubt" is quite a subtle and complex one. It involves an iteration of one attitude to another attitude. This means that if one participant in a critical discussion may be said to have an attitude of critical doubt, it is implied that there is another participant in the discussion who has another attitude, and the first participant has an attitude toward the second participant's attitude.

Such a definition sounds so complicated and subtle that we may be led to try to define critical doubt more simply as a neutral attitude. But there are some questions on whether this simpler type of definition could ever be adequate. Let's say there is a hotly contested dispute between two involved parties, and you are not a supporter or adherent to either of these two points of view, or have anything at stake in the dispute, as far as you know. Then you can easily be neutral with respect to this dispute. But on most issues of ethics or public policy that affect you, you are not going to be neutral. You are going to have bias, one way or the other, whether you are aware of this bias or not. In this type of case, you will have a bias to one side, and in order to have or employ critical doubt, you are going to have to bracket that bias, or work with it. In such a case, critical doubt is not just having a neutral point of view; it is restraining the non-neutral point of view you already have. However, it is still possible for you to have critical doubt with respect to such an argument. How is this possible?

In such a case, critical doubt is possible because you can temporarily suspend your pro attitude or con attitude, and by such an act of suspension of commitment, put yourself in the frame of mind of someone who does not share your own, partisan, point of view. By such an act, to the extent that it is successful, you can discover what the strongest arguments against your own position are. This is a valuable asset in argumentation. To carry out this function of looking at the disputed issue from your opponent's point of view, as well as your own, you have to adopt an attitude of removal from your own partisan viewpoint. Performing such a function does involve a suspension. But it does not necessarily imply that you must have a neutral attitude.

But there is a way in which critical doubt does involve a neutral attitude. In some cases, it can be useful to look at your argumentation from the point of view of a neutral observer, a person who has no strong opinion on the issue of the discussion, one way or the other. In such a case, the neutral observer is best seen as a hypothetical construct, except that neutral observers are easily recognized as a particular type of normal participant: neither strongly pro nor con on the proposition in question, having a lot of general knowledge about familiar things related to the issue of the discussion and with no strong, special, or unusual commitments one way or the other.

The idea of critical doubt developed here is a subtle one, in that it requires an arguer to play two distinct roles at the same time. Sometimes he or she must push ahead with the strongest arguments he or she can find or articulate from his or her own point of view. Other times, she or he must enter into the spirit of the opponent's position to appreciate and anticipate the arguments the opponent is likely to use to defend that position. Needless to say, the abilities required to effectively carry out such functions require flexibility and imagination.

Another skill needed to use critical doubt effectively in a critical discussion is the ability to allow one's opponent to state his or her point of view freely, and, at times even to encourage him or her to expound his or her point of view. To perform this function successfully, a participant in argumentation must resist the natural impulse to press ahead aggressively with the partisan role of arguing forcefully for one's own point of view. The dogmatic or inflexible arguer tends to see the opponent as dogmatic or fanatical.

It is in just this kind of case that the critical discussion tends to focus on personal attack on both sides. The problem in such a case is that the critical discussion deteriorates into a quarrelsome dialogue. This is the type of situation where fallacies tend to be committed, precisely because the quarrel leaves no room for the function of critical doubt necessary for a successful critical discussion. One party tends to presume that the other party is in the wrong, showing no respect for the capability of the other party to recognize a good argument. Such an arguer feels justified in ad hominem argumentation. The opponent is portrayed as a person with no regard for the truth. Each party then tries to browbeat the other with aggressive and dogmatic appeals to expert opinion, and other tactics. These combative tactics, which might in other cases be neither wrong nor inappropriate, are nevertheless so heavy handed, one-sided, and aggressive that they become serious obstacles to the continuation of dialogue. Once both parties give in to participating unrestrainedly in this quarrelling kind of exchange, the reasoned discussion of the issue becomes hopelessly blocked.

Critical discussion is a delicate kind of dialogue to carry on successfully, because it requires a balance between an adversarial partisan dialogue and a collaborative exchange where Gricean maxims of politeness are observed (see Grice). The ability to put these Gricean maxims to use effectively demands flexibility, tolerance, and restraint. One must understand, and engage the real position of one's adversary. One must, from time to time, listen to one's opponent, granting the opponent the freedom to develop a point of view. Even though one is inclined to dislike that point of view, or find it wrong or even biased, one must make an effort not to distort or exaggerate, thus committing the straw man fallacy. But maintaining the right balance in an argument is not an easy skill when one is strongly committed to one's own deeply felt position. Argumentation to support critical discussion, therefore, depends heavily on restraint. And it is through understanding how restraint functions in practice to counteract the impulse to advocacy that we can come to understand critical doubt as a key concept of argumentation.

It seems then that van Eemeren and Grootendorst's more complicated definition of critical doubt may be best. Critical doubt involves appropriate restraint—a participant shows critical doubt by exhibiting an attitude towards the attitude of another participant in a dialogue. This attitude of critical doubt will legitimately have a tactical aspect of attacking the weak points in the other party's arguments, e.g. weak premises or presumptions open to criticism and legitimate doubts, but it must not develop into inappropriately aggressive and underhanded attacks, or even into negative criticism of a partisan sort. So defined, the concept of critical doubt can be very useful in helping us to define the notion of bias.

In the next section, a definition of bias is put forward that profits from the discussion of cases and other considerations that have now enabled us to sketch out a preanalytic target concept of bias.

FIVE CHARACTERISTICS OF BIAS

According to the definition advocated in this paper, bias is said to have five main characteristics, listed below in order of importance. The first three characteristics are essential, they should be applied to all cases of bias. The last two characteristics are accidental, they are typical of many cases of bias, but do not need to be applied to all cases.

1. Bias is a lack of appropriate balance or neutrality in argumentation. The problem here is that an arguer supports one side too strongly and/or too often.
2. Bias is a lack of appropriate critical doubt in argumentation. The problem here is a failure of restraint and/or failure to suspect the natural inclination to push for a point of view one supports.
3. Bias is a lack of balance or critical doubt appropriate for a given type of dialogue that a participant is supposed to be engaged in. It is not merely a

lack of balance, but a lack of sufficient balance for a particular type
of dialogue.

4. Bias is often identified with a particular position supported by an arguer.
5. Bias is often identified with an arguer's having something to gain—a
    personal interest in the outcome of an argument, e.g. a financial interest.

These five characteristics could all be encapsulated in a single, more lengthy definition of bias. But it is useful to list them singly for purposes of applying the definition
to a particular case where an allegation of bias has been made or is appropriate.

The first characteristic expresses the basic idea of bias. The first thing to be
looked to in identifying bias is a lack of balance—a tendency to consistently favor
one side of an expressed conflict of opinions or argument over the other. However,
as Blair noted, not all bias is bad bias. Where evidence of the presence of the second
characteristic comes forth, a criticism of bias becomes more serious and damaging.

The second characteristic implies more than a lack of balance. It implies a critical distortion. This is an even more serious charge, because it definitely implies a
departure from the requirements of reasoned argumentation in a type of dialogue
like a critical discussion. It could perhaps be called, if not "bad bias," a "worse"
kind of bias than that indicated by the first characteristic.

In most cases, there is a shading, or fuzzy borderline between the first and
second characteristics. Generally, the first characteristic is a milder kind of criticism, but typically it shades into the second, by implicature, or expressly leads into
the introduction of the second characteristic.

What is meant by "appropriate" in the statement of the first two characteristics
is made explicit by the third characteristic of bias. Not just any lack of balance or
critical doubt indicates the existence of bias. An advocate of a point of view in a
critical discussion should naturally push ahead to passionately show conviction for
that point of view. That lack of balance is not, in itself, harmful or obstructive bias.
Where lack of balance is inappropriate for the context of dialogue, bias is open to
criticism as blocking Gricean principles or legitimate goals of discussion.

For example, an environmental advocate may consistently and strongly support
one side of the issue of emission restrictions in a public speech at a rally. But given
the purpose and context of the speech, a certain degree of imbalance in the presentation could be quite tolerable and understandable. However, suppose the context
of dialogue is a balanced news report on the controversy. In this case, the same
degree of imbalance could be open to quite serious criticisms of bias.

In judging any particular criticism of bias, or case where such a criticism may be
appropriate, one key factor is to establish the purpose of a dialogue. This factor sets
the normative horizon against which the claim of bias can be evaluated. According
to this approach then, bias is a normative concept which judges the value or appropriateness of argumentation in a context of dialogue against a normative standard
set by the rules, requirements, and maxims for that type of dialogue. This means
that the evidence for or against a charge of bias should come from the given text of
discourse and context of dialogue for that case.

To judge the fourth characteristic, you need to look at the text of discourse to
evaluate how consistently an arguer has taken up a particular position on an issue.
According to Hamblin, an arguer's *commitment store* is a set of propositions that
can be listed, and attributed to a participant in a dialogue in virtue of the various
moves (speech acts) made by that participant in the past sequence of dialogue (264).
A commitment store is a kind of persona of an arguer's beliefs, but is not to be

identified with his actual beliefs. In my earlier work, many cases of determining an arguer's position are studied, especially in relation to ad hominem criticisms where it is alleged that an arguer's position is inconsistent (*Arguer's Position*).

Finally, judging bias is inherently pragmatic because it is often unclear what type of dialogue the participants in argumentation are supposed to be engaged in. The problem in such cases is that there can be a *dialectical shift,* a movement during the sequence of argumentation from one context of dialogue to another.

Criticisms of bias are often especially prominent where there has been a shift from a critical discussion to a negotiation dialogue. Bias is also a problem where there has been a shift from a critical discussion to an eristic dialogue. The problem can be especially acute where the shift is unilateral or where it is a gradual and illicit shift that confuses and undermines the legitimate goals of the initial type of dialogue of the exchange. These shifts are often associated with the existence of problems related to the traditional informal fallacies.

The kinds of argumentation involved in the fallacies are often argumentation schemes based on presumptive reasoning. But presumptive reasoning, to be correctly used in a context of dialogue, requires an openness to the existence or possibility of contrary evidence, should it arise in the course of dialogue. Fallacies are sometimes just errors of reasoning, but in many cases they are types of tricky tactics used to unfairly get the best of an opponent in dialogue. They are associated with a closed, quarrelsome, biased attitude as revealed by performance in argumentation.

SUMMARY

What is bias? How can you tell that it exists in a given case? Bias is showing too strong a partisan support for one side of an argument, in relation to the type of dialogue an arguer is engaged in. It is a kind of attitude which is revealed in an arguer's performance. It can be determined by comparing the given text of an argument to a normative model of the type of dialogue an arguer is supposed to be engaged in. The problem with bias is that it can interfere with having a critical attitude, and with other skills necessary for good argumentation in a dialogue. Bias is not a bad thing or harmful in itself, but it often does have a way of leading to errors and fallacies that block or interfere with legitimate goals of dialogue.

Bias must always be judged relative to a given type of dialogue in which an arguer is supposed to be engaged in argument. For example, an argument is biased in a critical discussion where the partisan or adversarial aspect of it overcomes the tolerance and flexibility needed to sustain functions like empathy and critical doubt, which are necessary for the conflict of opinions to be resolved by the critical discussion. The problem may be that the arguer pushes ahead too strongly in favor of his or her own side, losing the ability to step back and see the argumentation from a critical perspective.

Eristic, partisan dialogue, which always pushes ahead to support one's point of view unquestioningly and to attack the opposing point of view by any means, is a legitimate part of a critical discussion, provided it is restrained and channeled to conform to the rules of critical discussion. Bias comes in when this eristic dialogue gets out of hand, causing an anger to lose the proper restraint and the ability to exercise critical doubt.

Bias is in fact not easy to judge, in many cases. It can be very subtle in some cases, and in many cases, it requires a lot of documentation to prove that it really exists in an argument. Such evidence should come from the text, analyzed by using the appropriate normative model of dialogue.

Bias especially comes into play where an arguer explicitly purports to be giving an impartial account of a disputed issue. In such a case, the account is correctly judged to be biased if it tends too strongly to favor the one side by ignoring or suppressing good argumentation of the opposing side. The perception then, rightly, is that the arguer is concealing a partisan advocacy for the one side over the other, in conflict with a prior commitment to at least look at the arguments in a balanced way.

In contrast, if the account is supposed, at the opening stage, to be a partisan argument which argues only for the point of view of the one side by supporting the case for that side as convincingly as possible, then there should be no perception of a critical bias. Thus, curiously, the very same argument, in the same words, could be biased in the one case, yet unbiased in the other case. It all depends on the context of dialogue. Hence bias is an essentially pragmatic matter.

To accuse someone of being biased is a strong form of criticism, and it is interesting to note that false or unjustified accusations of bias are themselves very powerful and interesting kinds of arguments for the student of argumentation.

NOTES

1 See Hastings; van Eemeren and Kruger for accounts of the various argumentation schemes.
2 See Donahue, "Empirical" and "Development."
3 Fuller accounts of the characteristics of these types of dialogue are given in Walton, *Informal Logic* 3–9; *Question-Reply* ch. 9; and "What is Reasoning?" 412–14.
4 See Jacobs and Jackson.
5 Walton, *Begging* 43. These types of dialogue are systematically described in Walton and Krabbe.
6 Flowers, McGuire, and Birnbaum. See also Walton, *Informal Logic* 3; *Question-Reply* ch. 9; and *Begging* 42. A detailed analysis of the quarrel as a normative model of dialogue is given in Walton and Krabbe.
7 General accounts are to be found in Hamblin; Barth and Martens; Hinman; and Walton, *Arguer's Position*.
8 Waller 108. This case, or a similar one, is discussed in more detail by Blair.
9 Attacking an appeal to expert testimony on the grounds that the expert is a biased source is allowed in legal cross examination as a legitimate kind of argumentation. See Graham. However, it is also a kind of argumentation that can be abused.
10 Blair would appear to disagree with this hypothesis, but sees a connection. He argues that bias is bad when it comes to closed mindedness, or leads to distortion, unfairness, or misinterpretation.

WORKS CITED

Allport, Gordon W. *The Nature of Prejudice*. New York: Doubleday, 1958.
Barth, E. M., and J. L. Martens. "*Argumentum Ad Hominem*: From Chaos to Formal Dialectic." *Logique et Analyse* 77–78 (1977): 76–96.
"Becky's Story." Produced by Richard Bonin. *60 Minutes*. 24 February 1991. CBS News Transcript #24. 7–11.
Blair, J. Anthony. "What is Bias?" *Selected Issues in Logic and Communication*. Ed. Trudy Govier. Belmont CA: Wadsworth, 1988. 93–103.
Brinton, Alan. "Ethotic Argument." *History of Philosophy Quarterly* 3 (1986): 245–58.
Broad, William, and Nicholas Wade. *Betrayers of the Truth: Fraud and Deceit in the Halls of Science*. New York: Simon and Schuster, 1982.
Campbell, Stephen K. *Flaws and Fallacies in Statistical Thinking*. Englewood Cliffs: Prentice-Hall, 1974.
Donahue, William A. "An Empirical Framework for Examining Negotiation Processes and Outcomes." *Communication Monographs* 45 (1978): 247–57.

————. "Development of a Model of Rule Use in Negotiation Interaction." *Communication Monographs* 48 (1981): 106–20.

European Journal. Public Broadcasting Service. 31 March 1991.

Fearnside, W. Ward, and William B. Holther. *Fallacy: The Counterfeit of Argument.* Englewood Cliffs: Prentice-Hall, 1959.

Flowers, Margot, Rod McGuire, and Lawrence Birnbaum. "Adversary Arguments and the Logic of Personal Attacks." *Strategies for Natural Language Processing.* Ed. Wendy G. Lehnert and Martin H. Ringle. Hillsdale NJ: Erlbaum, 1982. 275–94.

Graham, Michael H. "Impeaching the Professional Expert Witness by a Showing of Financial Interest." *Indiana Law Journal* 53 (1977): 35–53.

Grice, H. Paul. "Logic and Conversation." *The Logic of Grammar.* Ed. Donald Davidson and Gilbert Harman. Encino CA: Dickenson, 1975. 64–75.

Hamblin, Charles L. *Fallacies.* 1970; Newport News VA: Vale, 1986.

Hastings, Arthur. *A Reformulation of the Modes of Reasoning in Argumentation.* Diss. Northwestern Univ., 1962.

Hinman, Lawrence M. "The Case for *Ad Hominem* Arguments." *Australasian Journal of Philosophy* 60 (1982): 338–45.

Jacobs, Scott, and Sally Jackson. "Speech Act Structure in Conversation." *Conversational Coherence: Form, Structure and Strategy.* Eds. Robert T. Craig and Karen Tracy. Beverly Hills CA: Sage, 1983. 47–66.

Reiter, Raymond. "Nonmonotonic Reasoning." *Annual Review of Computer Science* 2 (1987): 147–86.

Thouless, Robert H. *Straight and Crooked Thinking.* London: English Univ. Press, 1930.

van Eemeren, Frans H., and Rob Grootendorst. *Speech Acts in Argumentative Discussions.* Dordrecht Holland: Foris, 1984.

van Eemeren, Frans H., and Tjark Kruger. "Identifying Argumentation Schemes." *Argumentation: Perspectives and Approaches.* Ed. Frans H. van Eemeren, Rob Grootendorst, J. Anthony Blair, and Charles A. Willard. Dordrecht Holland: Foris, 1987. 70–81.

Waller, Bruce N. *Critical Thinking: Consider the Verdict.* Englewood Cliffs: Prentice-Hall, 1988.

Walton, Douglas N. *Arguer's Position: A Pragmatic Study of Ad Hominem Attack, Criticism, Refutation, and Fallacy.* Westport CT: Greenwood, 1985.

————. *Begging the Question: Circular Reasoning as a Tactic of Argumentation.* New York: Greenwood, 1991.

————. *Informal Logic.* Cambridge: Cambridge Univ. Press, 1989.

————. *Question-Reply Argumentation.* New York: Greenwood, 1989.

————. "What is Reasoning? What is an Argument?" *Journal of Philosophy* 87 (1990): 399–419.

Walton, Douglas N., and Erik C. W. Krabbe. *Commitment in Dialogue.* In press.

"We Buy Votes." *Consumer Reports* April 1991: 295.

Chapter 5

Normativity

The effort to align theory and practice is a common theme in argument studies. This effort has taken various intellectual forms that have resulted in a steady rethinking of traditional norms and previously accepted concepts. Normativity is a complex term that broadly encompasses socially constructed concepts of what ought (and ought not) to be involved in a good argument. Normativity may also be understood as the process of abstractly evaluating sound argumentation in the absence of context.

Challenges to argument normativity confront objective standards of argument practice and reject concepts of argumentation as comprised of universal features (e.g., reason and structure). Such challenges are built upon the assumption that arguments are developed in specific cultures. For example, a particular culture could use appropriate yet atypical frameworks of reasoning, such as visual argument or feminine rationality, to establish criteria for judgment. However, when theorists emphasize argument normativity, they may not recognize culturally specific practices as argumentation. Cultural critiques of argumentation theory challenge the conventional standards of argument evaluation, practice, and rationality. As the argumentation practices of multiple cultures are integrated into the construction of argument theory, the body of scholarship becomes more nuanced.

The idea of understanding argument exchange via particular cultural practices is relatively new in argumentation studies. The essays in this chapter reflect and critique the major theoretical challenges that multi-culturalist approaches to argumentation studies raise. Collectively, these essays call into question the traditional standards of objective and universal judgment in argumentation theory.

Wouter H. Slob's "How to Distinguish Good and Bad Arguments: Dialogico-Rhetorical Normativity" (2002) addresses normativity by creating a conceptual space between dialectic and rhetoric. Slob shows how normative standards in logic, dialectics, and rhetoric fail to produce conditions where argumentation can be evaluated objectively and consistently. Arguing that pre-determined rules do not accurately assess validity in human discourse, he derives a concept of normativity from the assumption that, in practice, people reach agreement in matters of dispute if they are given enough time and information. He proposes an approach to argumentation, which he terms dialogico-rhetorical, that centers on a normativity that is shaped in discussions rather than consisting of pre-determined rules. According to this approach, participants in a dispute co-create the conditions that determine the norms of their particular argumentative space. Consequently, this approach retains and reformulates normativity as opposed to eliminating the concept all together. With this essay, Slob opens a new framework to evaluate argumentation.

Deborah Orr's 1989 essay, "Just the Facts Ma'am: Informal Logic, Gender and Pedagogy," is a caustic critique of traditional argument studies. The author addresses "common understandings" of rationality as they are reflected in Western educational institutions. Rationality, understood to be the conditions of good sense and sound judgment, is culturally specific and subjective. The premise of this essay is that the style of rationality that most people use is different from the packaged, advocacy-based reasoning—embedded in the Western education system. Drawing on gender research, Orr explores alternative forms of rationality, especially masculine and feminine modes of reasoning. Feminine modes of reasoning could include patterns that are emotive, attend to individuals in their particularity, engage narrative frameworks, and remain open-ended and flexible. She concludes that United States culture favors masculine modes of rationality and challenges other viable styles of rationality, especially feminine modes of reasoning. The essay calls on argumentation scholars to expand their understanding of rationality and consider what humans actually do when they think.

In "Justifying *My* Position in *Your* Terms: Cross-Cultural Argumentation in a Globalized World" (1999), Yameng Liu articulates the conditions of a new historical moment, in which forces of globalization have produced a desire and need to engage argumentatively across international borders. Globalization makes cross-cultural approaches to argumentation practical and necessary, especially when interlocutors may approach argumentation with ideologically incompatible positions. Liu adds a cross-cultural corrective to the traditional scholarship, focusing on the under-recognized necessity of common ground and calling for a focus on cross-cultural arguing as a unique mode of exchange.

In his 1999 article, "Argument Quality and Cultural Difference," Harvey Siegel identifies and rebuts recent philosophical critiques of normativity that he calls "multi-cultural." He explores the theoretical shift from understanding validity as located in the features of an argument to understanding it as located in culturally specific norms. According to Siegel, the multi-cultural perspective assumes arguers are trapped by their own perspectives and criteria for judging arguments. Siegel disagrees: he claims that judgment is not solely determined by cultural specificity. He also suggests that multi-culturalism inevitably prescribes the same theoretical universality that it initially rejects. This essay provides a framework for attempting to reconcile the universal concepts of argument theory with the particular cultures of argumentation.

The essays in this chapter illustrate how theorists have critiqued and defended concepts of normativity in argumentation scholarship. The essays address the grounds from which theorists and critics analyze arguments, and the degree to which culturally specific and socially constructed arguers are bound by context. Collectively, these essays illustrate a major theoretical controversy in argumentation studies, in which the integration of theory and practice evolves into a culturally diverse dialogue.

How to Distinguish Good and Bad Arguments: Dialogico-Rhetorical Normativity
WOUTER H. SLOB

INTRODUCTION

Logic is the study of distinguishing between good and bad reasoning or argumentation, and therefore it is a normative discipline. Determining what are good or bad arguments is not an interesting hobby, but involves the normative evaluation of arguments pertaining to the acceptance or dropping of conclusions. The question is not whether a conclusion is accepted, but whether it *should* be accepted. By formulating sets of rules, logicians try to get a grasp on the norms involved in the process of reasoning or argumentation. But what is it that gives such norms their authority? Where does the *normativity* of logic come from? In an era witnessing the fusion of many norms and values in all kinds of fields and contexts, this question becomes increasingly urgent.

DEDUCTIVISM

The idea that *bad* arguments are logically interesting is rather young. For ages logic was primarily interested in *good* arguments. Bad ones were negatively defined as not-good and, as a distinguishing instrument, logic could be limited to answering the question what accounts for the goodness of arguments. Strictly speaking, a good argument is a *sound* one, involving both the truth of the premises as well as the validity of the inference. Such deductive arguments yield conclusions by necessity: if the premises are true, the conclusion cannot be false. Deductivism might be understood as a truth-preserving method of inference: it warrants that the conclusion never exceeds the information of the premises. But of course, the information of the premises may be defective. 'The conclusion of a deductive argument,' Leo Groarke reminds us, 'is as certain as its premises' (Groarke, 1995, p. 138). Still, from a logical point of view, the status of the premises is hardly interesting. It is the job of the scientist of a relevant discipline to determine the status of the premises. The logician is responsible only for the validity of the inference. In this view, logic does not change the content of the premises and is merely a method of combining information. Here another aspect of deductivism arises: it is not merely a logical technique, but also suggests a specific understanding of normativity. As no information is changed, deductive inference is neutral and objective. Everybody who accepts the premises should accept its conclusions. Deductivism, thus, provides a universal standard of inference. Not merely being a logical tool, it is a theory that serves to understand normativity. It is this aspect of deductivism that raises questions. There is, to my mind, not the least objection to using a deductive method as a logical technique, but as a theory of normativity, providing a neutral and objective standard of evaluation, it fails. Unless indicated otherwise, it is in this latter sense that I shall use the term 'deductivism.'

According to deductivism, an argument can be bad for two reasons: its premises are false, or the inference is invalid. Logic is concerned only with the latter, and, as C. L. Hamblin has shown, it applies a negative understanding of bad arguments: 'a fallacious argument . . . is one that *seems to be valid* but *is not* so' (Hamblin,

1970, p. 12). Hamblin, however, argues that this 'standard treatment' of fallacies is not adequate in accounting for bad arguments. Deductive invalidity is neither a sufficient nor a necessary condition for fallaciousness. Some fallacies are not invalid (e.g. the notorious *begging the question*), and others are invalid but not fallacious (all inductive arguments are, as such, deductively invalid).[1] But if this is so, deductivism fails as normative instrument to distinguish between good and bad arguments and hence fails as a theory of normativity. Many thinkers have followed Hamblin and have expressed doubts on the suitability of deductivism. In a broad gesture of recognition, Ralph Johnson embraces as informal logicians all 'those who reject soundness as being either necessary or sufficient for a good argument' (Johnson, 1995, p. 237). Although informal logicians display many important differences, they share a suspicion towards deductive normativity. Three aspects are to be mentioned.

(1) By aiming at an objective and universal standard, deductivism hopes to yield definite inferences. If the inference is deductively valid, the conclusion follows necessarily. Surely, the definiteness of deductivism is one of its great attractions, but we may see an important shortcoming of this logical ideal: it does not allow for gradations in logical strength. This feature, however, neglects the actual *argumentative performance*. Argumentation is understood as the exchange of arguments both pro and contra, but it is hard to see how deductivism can balance both those 'forces'. 'Deductively,' Trudy Govier complains, 'the category "valid" is of the all-or-nothing kind. If an argument is such that, given its premises, it is absolutely impossible for its conclusion to be false, it is valid. If not, it is invalid. Period: there is nothing in between' (Govier, 1987, p. 3). This disqualifies deductivism as a suitable evaluative instrument for most actual discussions, as discussions typically are about weighing pros and cons. Deductively only support counts, but this means that no account can be given for rebuttals. Although it is obviously possible to argue deductively both for a positive and a negative version of the conclusion, it is not possible to balance them deductively.

(2) Deductive normativity aims at inference by necessity, which cannot be false (if the premises are true) and which therefore cannot be doubted. It requires therefore a monistic understanding of logic: 'there is just one correct system of logic.'[2] The early Wittgenstein echoes a long tradition maintaining that 'we can think nothing unlogical, since if we could, we would have to think unlogically' (*Tractatus*: 3.03). If thinking as such presupposes logic, we are dealing with a universal understanding of human rationality. Deductive normativity requires such a logical monism and hence applies a universal type of rationality. Given the fact that bad arguments exist, however, we must presume that the persons advancing them *do* think 'unlogically'. If monism is to be maintained, we may be facing logical alternatives. Now the problem arises how to decide which logic is the correct system. As logic itself is at stake here, it is clear that we need another normative instrument to decide upon this. This makes the normativity of logic, at least partially, dependent on something else but monistically this is impossible. To substantiate the univocality of deductivism, logicians in the beginning of the 20th century hoped to discover the true foundations of logic, which would form the basis of monistic deductivism. Unfortunately for their project however, the last century witnessed an enormous proliferation of logical systems, not forming a coherent unity.[3] Rather than *yielding* a normative instrument, the proliferation of logical systems *calls* for a way to make a normative choice.

(3) Perhaps the most serious problem for deductive normativity is that it is not at all hard to obtain. Logical validity is easily obtained when the right premises are present. Deductivism allows for a technique to make any argument valid. Generally, it recognizes the so-called *enthymeme* as an argument with a missing premise. In practice, such incomplete arguments are often used and cause no problems because most people will tacitly add the missing premise so that the argument is completed. Deductively, however, an enthymeme is not valid. But clearly, such a verdict is hasty as only the complete argument can be properly evaluated. A deductive analysis, therefore, must add the missing premises. As no valid argument can become invalid by adding premises, completing arguments can deductively only do good. The problem, however, is that *any* argument can be made valid by adding a suitable premise. The associated conditional or the conclusion itself will do.[4] There may be objections regarding the content of the premises, but, as said before, that is of no concern to the deductive logician. This simply means that either an argument is valid, or it can always be made valid. If enthymemes are allowed to be completed, no invalid arguments can exist. Deductive logic, far from providing a suitable normative instrument, has no power to perform its distinguishing task.

If deductivism fails as a theory of normativity, we have lost our universal standard to assess arguments in a neutral and objective way. Are we on our way to relativism?

THE SHIFT TO DIALECTIC

Over the last three decades an increasing number of logicians have dropped deductivism as normative theory in favor of a *dialectical* approach. The term traces back to Aristotle, for whom dialectical arguments differed from demonstrative arguments by applying *acceptable* instead of *true* premises. Dialectical arguments, consequently, do not yield necessity but yield only probability.[5] In its contemporary form, however, dialectical logic is not primarily concerned with the status of the premises, but with the status of logical inference. In contrast to Aristotle modern dialecticians reject monism and acknowledge the plurality of different systems of logic between which *choices* must be made. Modern dialectical logic is about the authorization of a specific logical system in a particular situation. To see how this works, we must see how dialecticians understand the nature of argumentation.

Modern dialecticians understand argumentation as a matter of dialogue. Basically there are two participants involved: the proponent, defending a thesis, and the opponent, resisting the thesis.[6] Whereas deductive monism concentrates on the support of the conclusion only, dialectical logic acknowledges the vital role of opposition in argumentation. Indeed, the opponent generates the discussion. Only when a thesis is disputed, it makes sense to defend it. Supporting an undisputed thesis is at best a waste of time, at worst irrelevant babbling, or an *ignoratio elenchi* in between. Dialectical logic takes disagreement on the status of a thesis as a condition for the possibility of discussions. At least in this sense, the starting positions of the participants are asymmetrical.

There are many different ways to deal with disagreements. We may try to solve the conflict, or stick to investigating where exactly the difference lies. We may want to settle the issue by means of force, or try to tackle the opponent by ridiculing her position. According to dialecticians, different ways of dealing with conflicts yield different types of discussion; and different types of discussions allow for different argumentative moves. What is suitable in a quarrel is not always acceptable in a critical discussion, and vice versa.[7] For every type of discussion, a specific set of argumentative rules can be drawn. When two people want to work on their disagreement, in one way or another, they must first decide what kind of discussion they will engage in and respect the argumentative rules that are in force. Whereas the starting-positions of the participants are asymmetrical, the regulating system of logical rules is not! Obviously, the participants must voluntarily submit to the rules; only on this basis can someone be held committed to the authority of the rules. Dialectical rules are in force if *conventionally* accepted by all participants.[8] Very often the conventional aspect remains implicit: many rules of discussion go without explicitly mentioning them. It would be very tedious to issue a 'dated and signed written declaration' every time an argument is about to begin.[9] Nevertheless, as Douglas Walton says, 'the rules *can* be explicitly stated, and agreed to by the participants, where it is useful and necessary, at the opening stage' (Walton, 1989, p. 10, italics whs). In other words, the participants *would* accept the rules if they were explicitly asked to. Conventional normativity may be called '*would*-normativity'.

Dialectical logic aims at an inter-subjective understanding of normativity, now that objective monism has been shown to be impossible. In our era of conceptual schemes, paradigms, 'language-games', webs of belief, etc. its conventional approach seems to cohere well with the general philosophical climate. The rules of the game determine what is correct and what is incorrect and provide clarity for the participants. But the rules also allow outsiders to evaluate a discussion. Anyone who is aware of the rules of the game is in the position to pass judgement on the argumentative moves that are being made.

Still, dialectical *would*-normativity is not sufficient because, in short, it also allows for *would-not*. In the face of losing a discussion a participant may simply withdraw his commitment, or demand modification, or distinguish exceptions. Indeed, Walton and Krabbe see retraction as 'one of the most fundamental (almost intractable) problems concerning commitment' (Walton and Krabbe, 1995, p. 9). The conventional nature of dialectical normativity leaves us with the fundamental possibility that someone retracts commitment at a decisive stage. Its would-normativity is not what we expect from normativity. It lacks normative force precisely where it is needed most: when somebody does not accept something she *should* accept. To account for such *should*-normativity we must rule out arbitrary or strategic one-sided withdrawals. Dialectically this is only possible if the agreements are controlled in some way.

The problem of retraction is complicated by the fact that conventional normativity often remains implicit. This invites the possibility that 'rules' are kept hidden only to be played out when needed. Any dictator can be 'reasonable' as long as he has the best arguments. But there might also be the 'rule' that in case he is wrong, his adversaries will be silenced. Under these conditions the evaluation of arguments is a feeble business. The dictator will feel confident in applying the additional rule, and may even feel justified in doing so, as everybody implicitly knows that dictators cannot lose discussions. From the interlocutor's perspective the additional 'rule' is mere powerplay and blatantly fallacious. This suggests that the evaluation of argumentative moves cannot simply be trusted in the hands of the participants. Indeed, as Johnson and Blair say: 'many people evaluate arguments by one "standard" only: does it support my view or not? That', they insist, 'is not a logical standard of evaluation but rather a purely idiosyncratic one' (Johnson and Blair, 1983, p. 30). In what way can this idiosyncrasy be overcome?

DIALECTICAL RATIONALITY

The conventional-dialectical answer to this problem is sought in regulating the basic agreement of the participants by means of a modest understanding of rationality. Surely, by dropping monism, no *universal* rationality is feasible any more, but we might still be able to conceive of a *shared* form of rationality. Acknowledging that the starting points of a discussion are asymmetrical for both participants, it is still possible to find substantial moments of agreement. These moments serve as orientation for a modest understanding of rationality. In this fashion Calvin Schrag (1992) develops a notion of *transversal rationality*: although people are irreducibly different, any interaction shows points of agreement that can function as the basis for a local form of rationality. We can also think of Nicholas Rescher's *rationality of ends,* consisting of an anthropological orientation on real interests (Rescher, 1988). The appropriate ends Rescher maintains, 'are not somehow freely *chosen* by us: they are fixed by the (for us) inescapable ontological circumstance that—like it or not—we find ourselves to exist as human beings' (Rescher, 1988, p. 105). Reflecting on the question of normativity, however, we need not delve into the substances of these proposals. What is important for our purposes is the fact that dialectical rationality consists of some form of basic agreement that overcomes the idiosyncratic differences and that provides a suitable form of commensurability. If this succeeds, we have a normative standard for the regulation of discussions. In practice, the common ground will not always be easy to find, and might not even be stable. Indeed, if it were straightforwardly available, it would substantially be indistinguishable from monism. Its function, however, is to provide a normative horizon. Dialectical rationality is a logical *ideal,* deriving its normativity from the idea that ultimately people would come to agreement in matters under dispute if they were given sufficient time and information.[10]

Dialectical rationality performs its task for at least three purposes. First of all there is the question of how conventions are arrived at. Presumably a discussion is required to determine the choice of which logical system is to be in force. But clearly such a meta-discussion needs regulation as well, and a nasty infinite regress impends. Dialectical logicians appeal to a notion of 'logical intuition' or 'natural rules' of normal argumentative behavior. [11] Generally, the idea is that participants of a discussion cooperate because rationally this is in their best interest.[12] This idea is rather troublesome in itself, as the notion of 'best interest' seems to *presume* substantial normativity rather than providing one (at least it must be able to say what is to count as 'best' interest). But even if this problem is surpassed, we should see that cooperation is not simply by definition in the best interest of all participants. No appeal to subversive elements is necessary to make this understandable. Mahatma Ghandi did well not to accept the 'normal argumentative behavior' of colonial Britain to achieve his goals. If his deviation of its argumentative rules defines irrationality, there were good reasons for him to be irrational.

Secondly, dialectical rationality allows controlling the proper conduct of the discussion. If a substantial standard can be arrived at conventionally, it is possible that the observance of its rules is monitored. This is where rationality gets a face. The inter-subjective character of dialectical normativity suggests that 'the control of each discussion is in the hands of the participants themselves' (Hamblin, 1970, p. 283). But we have seen that if idiosyncrasy is to be ruled out, this is not so generously permissible. Indeed, dialectical logicians generally introduce a *third* logical role: that of the rational observer. In an unbiased way, she can determine what type of discussion is going on and apply the corresponding rules. The rational observer embodies the normative conduct of the discussion. As the participants have committed themselves conventionally to the rules, and the rational observer only applies these standards, her verdict is normative for the participants involved. This can only mean that the control of the discussion is in the hands of the partici- pants themselves only in so far as they represent the verdict of the rational observer. Typically, of course, it is the logician or theorist of argumentation who is in the position to perform the task of rational observer.

The third important task for dialectical rationality is to perform evaluation. The rules of any type of discussion determine the 'moving space' of the participants. As long as both can do legitimate moves, the discussion continues, but at some moment it may no longer be possible for one of the participants to make a correct move. In this situation, the interlocutor has won the discussion. Here the role of rationality for our normative problem is cashed out: 'it is not irrational to lose a discussion. . . . But it is—we suggest—irrational not to admit that one has lost' (Barth and Krabbe, 1982, p. 71). Although specific rules determine the distinction between correct and fallacious argumentative moves, it is the notion of rationality that controls the authority of the rules corresponding to a specific type of discus- sion. In this sense rationality is, in Charles Willard's apt phrase, the gold standard of argumentation.

DIALECTICAL NORMATIVITY

If dialectical normativity is to be preferred to monistic normativity, it should at least perform better where monism failed. When we take a closer look at the func- tion of the dialectical understanding of rationality, there appears to be hardly any improvement. Indeed, if this form of rationality is to perform its normative task, dialectical logic turns out to be a monism in disguise and its emphasis on dialogue a cosmetic brush-up. Ironically the objections parallel the objections against monis- tic normativity. Just as in monism the actual argumentative performance is of little importance. Just as in monism it is hard to see how irrationality can arise. And just as in monism it is questionable how the distinguishing instrument is able to perform its task. Let us see what it comes about in more detail:

(1) The dialectical approach emphasizes argumentation and hereby values dialogue. Two perspectives are always taken into account. The proponent supports a thesis, whereas the opponent resists it. Despite the fact that in this way both supporting and rebutting forces in a discussion are present, we may also observe that the dialectical approach hardly leaves room for genuine argumentative exchange. The outcome of any dialectical discussion is a function of the rules and the respective starting points. This means that there is always a 'best solution' to any logical problem, and only a mistake or a limited perspective could spoil it. A perfect observer in ideal circumstances and infinite time could calculate the outcome of any discussion given the points of departure and the rules of inference. This feature erases the actual argumentative performance of the participants. The dialec- tical approach, moreover, seems to limit the choice of logical systems to undecidable

systems only. In decidable systems, after all, the conclusions are predictable and it is hard to see why someone who could foresee the loss of her argumentative strategy would ever want to accept a logical system that leads to her loss.

(2) Rather than a fundamental feature, the dialectical acknowledgement that there are different perspectives is a matter of discomfiture and is the result of the fact that real-life arguers are not perfectly rational. If they were, both perspectives would coincide with the perspective of the rational observer and no conflict would arise in the first place. The question is where and how does irrationality slip in? How can the participants have perspectives that deviate from the rational one? And especially, to what extent? The very fact that both participants engage in a discussion with each other shows that they are prepared to defend their respective positions, or at least that they are not prepared to change them for no reason at all. But to the extent that they are committed to their own position, they surely will consider their own convictions to be rational. And obviously the most stubborn convictions are most strongly considered to meet this general standard so that the interlocutor should also adopt them. What we see is that within a discussion the participants may disagree on what *counts* as rational. It is hard to see how in such circumstances rationality itself can be invoked to perform the task of neutral arbiter,[13] unless of course rationality has a monistic status.

(3) The main problem for a dialectical notion of rationality is that it cannot perform its evaluative task. The perspective of the rational observer is only useful if it transcends the limited perspectives of the discussants. But this means that the rational observer is indeed an observer: an outsider that has no substantial impact on the participants in question. If there is substantial influence, the observer becomes part of the discussion and hereby loses his external position. The perspective of the rational observer cannot be relevant for the discussion unless it becomes a position within the discussion. But if this is the case, it is merely another opposing position and has lost its capacity to perform its determining task in an unbiased way. It becomes a party in the discussion and its perspective is on equal level with the others. Clearly this merely increases the normative problem. When it comes to distinguishing good from bad arguments, we need an instrument that is available within the debating arena. Dialectical rationality offers only an ideal perspective, remaining an external onlooker.

The failure of a dialectical notion of rationality to perform its normative function is shown when we look at the dialectical understanding of fallacies. In the influential pragma-dialectical approach of Frans Van Eemeren and Rob Grootendorst, the notion of fallacies is directly linked to the violation of specific rules for critical discussions: 'the dialectical rules which are violated in case of fallacies are applicable *only in so far as the purpose of the discussion is to resolve a dispute*' (Van Eemeren and Grootendorst, 1987, p. 296, italics whs). This dialectical understanding of rational normativity is conditional: if people engage in a critical discussion they must obey its specific rules. Put in this way, however, any instance of a fallacy may be seen as a negation of the normative conditional: violating the rules negates the consequent, which means that the antecedent is false as well. The occurrence of a fallacy, unless as slip of the tongue or correctable mistake, may be an indication that no critical discussion is going on in the first place. But under those circumstances, as Van Eemeren and Grootendorst argue, it is not possible to apply the standard for a critical discussion and consequently 'there is no point, from a dialectical perspective, in referring to a fallacy'

(Van Eemeren and Grootendorst, 1987, p. 298). Does this not evaporate the entire notion of fallacy? If so, dialectical normativity based on rationality fails to perform its normative task.

There can be little doubt that the dialectical shift in logic has opened up a whole new area of tools and instruments to analyze argumentation. Much better than deductive monism it is equipped to deal with real-life argumentation and in the thirty years of its development it has provided many useful descriptive insights. Yet, its conception of normativity does not solve the problems that encountered deductivism. Its appeal to a modest version of rationality to prevent idiosyncrasy can only work if it transcends the respective perspectives of the participants. But this either mocks the intersubjectivity of the dialectical proposals or becomes irrelevant for its substance. The external rational observer will not do for a suitable notion of normativity, which also means that this cannot be the task of logic. Yet, we need not be sad about this. It may, as Hamblin argued, 'not be the logician's particular job to declare the truth of any statement, *or the validity of any argument*' (Hamblin, 1970, p. 244).

DIALOGICAL RHETORIC

If rationality fails as an instrument to substantiate normativity, it seems that we are left with the idiosyncrasies of the participants. This means that no *shared* standard for evaluation is available, and this may seem to involve a hopeless relativism. I do not think the latter consequence is involved. There is another way of conceiving normativity that can control idiosyncrasy, indeed, a way that makes use of the different perspectives of the participating discussants.

The solution may lie in the point that many traditional logicians will see as the problem to overcome: the argumentative asymmetry in starting positions. Rather than trying to neutralize the differences by postulating a universal or shared form of rationality, we might radicalize the asymmetry and see if there is a blessing in the curse.

As we have seen, dialecticians generally defend the idea that argumentation only makes sense when some thesis is being questioned. There is plenty to be said about this presupposition (for instance: does it allow for gradations? How are logical roles exactly to be conceived of? How should we analyze complicated situations, involving more than one opposition? How do apparent non-discursive situations, such as introspection or scientific inquiry, fit in? How do undefined 'opponents', such as readers of a book, fit in?). But in considering our main question,— proposing a normative alternative for dialectics—, it is not this dialogical aspect that is at issue, but the question of a suitable standard. Regarding this, we can make use of dialogical asymmetry. If it is the opposition that initiates the discussion, then closure of discussion might simply be determined by overcoming the opposition. If the 'why'-question of the opponent is satisfactorily answered, the argument has succeeded. From this perspective, argumentation is fundamentally audience-oriented and 'aims at gaining the adherence of minds' (Perelman and Olbrechts-Tyteca, 1969, p. 14). Chaim Perelman and Lucy Olbrechts-Tyteca use this description to characterize the New Rhetoric. In their minds dialectic and rhetoric are virtually the same, but traditionally philosophy has had a somewhat tense relation with rhetoric. Rhetoric merely aims at *persuading* an audience, whereas philosophy is after a higher goal: truth. Logic serves as its instrument to *prove* its conclusions, rhetoric is at best ornamental and at worst deceptive. The lack of normativity in rhetoric is clearly at stake.

Rhetoric is often associated with the use of beguiling arguments, with opening up the box of illicit tricks and with cheating its audience. Yet applying deceiving strategies is a bad advice for the rhetorician. In rhetorical theory reputation is important and reputation is easily damaged by bad argumentation. Thinking that argumentative bogus can be rhetorically successful, moreover, seems to be quite an underestimation of audiences. In general audiences are not persuaded by arguments they do not consider reasonable. The question, however, is whether we need a larger notion of *rationality* to make sense of argumentative *reasonableness*. My answer is no. The participants themselves determine the reasonableness of the interlocutor's moves and they do so by applying their own standards. Discussants do not need a universal or shared standard of rationality; they need to observe the standards of their respective interlocutor because it is her resistance that launched the discussion in the first place. If we are to convince any interlocutor, we can succeed only if she is given arguments that are convincing to her. Perhaps, we might call this trans-subjective.

Still, there *is* an important normative problem facing rhetoric. The demand to orient oneself to the standards of the audience erodes the position of the speaker herself! If only the standards of the audience were important, the speaker seems to be extradited to the whims of her audience. This surely, would be a very disturbing consequence of audience-orientation. There is a moral objection: it is absurd to demand this orientation if the audience's standards are abject. There is a rhetorical objection in the long run: one disqualifies as a serious partner in discussion when shifting standards according to specific audiences. Most serious, however, is the logical objection that only by observing one's own standards a thesis is worth defending. Much like the dialectical idea that an argument only begins when some thesis is being questioned, we should say that an argument only starts when the speaker is prepared to support it. If only the standards of the audience were decisive, its very resistance would be the end of the discussion. Precisely because the speaker is committed to the thesis, she defends it, but this is only possible if she acknowledges the compelling nature of her own convictions. All this suggests that audience-orientation has limits. But while dialectical logic deploys rationality to set those limits, I propose to leave setting the limits to the participants themselves. The speaker's own standards control her willingness to accommodate the argument to the standards of the audience.[14]

This version of rhetoric pushes the dialogical character of dialectics a little further. The orientation on the interlocutor goes both ways: this rhetoric is dialogical. Not only must the proponent orient her arguments on the opponent, in principle the opponent is as well called to defend his resisting position to the proponent. Dialectical logic granted the opponent the right to ask just any 'why'-question and burdened only the proponent to defend her thesis.[15] Dialogical rhetoric adds that this is only called for if the 'why'-question makes sense. As Aristotle said 'a man should not enter into discussion with everybody or practice dialectics with the first comer' (*Topica*, VIII, 14, 164b). Dialogical rhetoric distributes burden of proof over both participants. Both opponent and proponent must defend their respective positions, if called for. And either can only succeed by convincing the other.

The small clause 'if called for' is an important condition. Just as the proponent is called on to defend her thesis only by instigation of the opponent, so the opponent is only called on to defend his resisting position when the proponent questions it. In many discussions it is not a recommendable strategy that the proponent plays upon this possibility. If one wants to gain the adherence of a mind, positive arguments often work better than the more aggressive tactic of requiring an explanation for not accepting one's own position! Still, doubling the burden of proof allows us to make sense of the idea that not all objections are worth serious attention. It provides moreover a suitable instrument in case of stubbornness: 'why do you still object?'. If only the proponent faced burden of proof, there was no obligation for the opponent to answer this question.

Dialectics hoped to retain normativity in the face of idiosyncratic standards by postulating a commensurating standard of rationality. The rational observer is the virtual third logical role that embodies this idea. Dialogical rhetoric proposes another strategy: not the neutral arbiter, but the players themselves control one another's arguments. The basic idea of dialogical rhetoric is that the two personal or even idiosyncratic standards of proponent and opponent 'span' a normative field that determines the argumentative moving space of a particular discussion. Within this field the participants must convince the interlocutor of the reasonableness of their respective positions, but they will also have to balance their support to the rebutting evidence contributed by the interlocutor. At all times, however, the question is not how to satisfy some external rational observer, but simply how to answer the questions of the specific interlocutor.

Dialogical rhetoric concedes that any discussion begins because an opponent questions a thesis and a proponent is prepared to defend it. They hold a different position from the start and they are argumentatively committed to their respective positions. Clearly the proponent tries to convince the opponent of the reasonableness of the thesis, but dialogical rhetoric maintains that also the opponent tries to convince the proponent of the reasonableness of his opposition. In both cases the arguments advanced are directed to the respective interlocutor. And it is this specific interlocutor that determines whether the other's move is indeed reasonable. Whereas rationality requires that there is a universal or shared standard that is substantially normative for both, dialogical rhetoric allows that both participants apply their own, perhaps idiosyncratic, standard.

Lacking the authority of rationality in no way opens up a normative vacuum. On the contrary. Because of the equally distributed burden of proof, any argumentative move might call for support. Neither of the participants can frivolously dismiss the arguments of the interlocutor, as the dismissal itself can be called for justification. And the reasonableness of this is to the interlocutor to decide. The normative force of dialogical rhetoric lies in the fact that for the establishment of any move both participants are responsible. Obviously the proponent is responsible for the moves she advances. But the opponent also becomes committed when he does not, or no longer, resist the claim.[16] By either advancing or accepting any argumentative move both participants become responsible for both the supporting and the rebutting 'forces'. Together they form a kind of a *vector*, constituting the strength of the argument. The resultant conclusion is binding for both participants, because they are committed to all the constitutive elements. As both discussants may apply different standards, it may very well be the case that the resulting conclusion is accepted for different reasons. But we do not need complete agreement. Dialogical rhetoric is happy with acquiescence.[17]

Some remarks are called for regarding the objections against both monistic deductivism and dialectical rationality. Dialogical rhetoric should do better.

First of all, dialogical rhetoric is genuinely argumentative and concerns only the substantial contributions of the participants themselves. The normative force of any conclusion is the result of the moves that are established during the discussion. This is a matter of accepting argumentative moves advanced by the interlocutor. In contrast to dialectical logic, however, dialogical rhetoric sees the acceptance of moves not as determined by rules, but rather by the question when and to what extent some 'rule' is in force. At stake is a difference in understanding rules and regularities within argumentation. Of course argumentation shows regularities and those regularities can be strategically exploited. From a rhetorical point of view, however, they should be seen as *topoi:* argumentative strategies and not as normative rules. Understanding argumentative regularities as topoi has the advantage that argumentative sliding is easily understandable. Dialectical logic links sets of normative rules to specific types of discussion, but also maintains that discussions can 'slide' into other types.[18] If, however, the type-specific rules are normative, such sliding is simply impossible: deviation from normative rules is by definition illegitimate, unless, of course, exceptions or modifications are allowed during the discussion. But there can be no other reason to do so than if a specific argumentative move compels it. In that case, however, the course of the discussion determines the authority of the rules which turns the idea of rule-regulation upside down. If dialectical rules are understood as rhetorical topoi, this problem vanishes. The regularity forms an integral part of the discussion itself.

Secondly, dialogical rhetoric plays on the disagreement that has got the discussion started in the first place and expands on it. It does not require any form of prior agreement. Consequently, the problem of incommensurability is insubstantial for its understanding of normativity, and there is no need to ponder upon universal or shared rationality. Still, there is no need to defend incommensurability or to emphasize disagreement. In practice argumentative situations are surely much less *différant* than some contemporary philosophers want us to believe. The claim here is merely that commensurability is not required for normativity, but it will not do much harm either. If dialogico-rhetorical normativity works under incommensurable conditions, it also works when the situation involves substantial agreement after all. The only thing that is required is that both participants have an *interest* in the discussion. They do not have to share a set of normative standards, nor do they have to pursue a common goal; they should only consider their interlocutor helpful in some way to achieve their own aims in the discussion. As this 'interest' can have many different shades and forms, it is merely an empty, formal requirement. It is required only to explain the participants' willingness to engage in the discussion and has no substantial normative impact whatsoever.

Thirdly, the control of the discussion is completely in the hands of the participants themselves. The normative force of the conclusion is the result of the standards of both participants and hence fully available. As a kind of a balance between personal, perhaps idiosyncratic standards, many philosophers might object that such a dialogico-rhetorical understanding of normativity involves no standard at all. In a sense this is correct. There is no shared standard operative here that is publicly available and that could also be controlled by an outside observer. Still, when no public standard is required to dispose of a suitable understanding of normativity, this objection loses interest. Whereas dialectical reasonability depends upon a public standard of rationality, dialogico-rhetorical reasonability consists of the acceptance of any move by the interlocutor. The feeble and shifting play of advancing and accepting argumentative moves results in a dynamic and shifting form of normativity. What is lost, however, is that an external rational observer controls the evaluation of a discussion. Dialogical rhetoric takes Hamblin's contentment seriously that the logician 'does not stand above or outside practical argumentation or, necessarily, pass judgment on it' (Hamblin, 1970, p. 244). Being neither a judge nor a court of appeal, however, the logician is certainly a 'trained advocate'. As such, her task is to assist discussants and to train them, perhaps, in logical self-defense. But there is no normative task for her. Yet the importance of normativity is not that an external observer can control it, but that the participants are committed to the conclusions of a discussion. It is my conviction that a dialogico-rhetorical understanding of normativity provides a better account of this than its dialectical counterpart. When all reasonable moves have been made, both participants *must* accept the resultant conclusion, and this surpasses dialectical would-normativity. Obviously this is not to say that any other person is committed to the results of a discussion as well. A bystander, such as an informed logician, may have reasons to question the course of a discussion. But unless she engages in a substantial discussion, such reasons are not relevant to show any mistake that might have been made.

The goodness of arguments is determined by the acceptance of the interlocutor, the badness of arguments by the refusal to do so. This idea has consequences for the notion of fallacy. Without an operative notion of discussion-rules fallacies cannot be seen as violations of rules. Nevertheless the traditional fallacies are to be understood as unadvisable argumentative strategies. Arguments that are usually considered fallacious are bad because they are weak; they can easily be exposed and are not very convincing for the most part. A taxonomy of fallacies is useful to show risky argumentative strategies, and is as such helpful in enhancing argumentative skills. It may improve people's argumentative techniques and may teach them how to respond to fallacious argumentation. But it may also show people how to *use* fallacies. From a dialectical point of view committing a fallacy is disqualifying as such. But this makes it hard to understand why they are all around us. A dialogico-rhetorical understanding makes it possible to explain the phenomenon. Even blatantly fallacious argumentation can have a function: it opens up a possibility to shift the burden of proof to the interlocutor. If she shows non-acceptance by responding to a bad move by saying 'fallacy!', she may be called upon to support her charge. This may put a new item on the agenda, distract attention, and buy time. Acknowledging that fallacies can be used strategically explains their occurrence, whereas merely rejecting them off hand as rule-breaking moves does not. Fallacies should not only be studied for logical self-defense, but also as a means to win a discussion.

CONCLUSION

The dialectical shift of logic improves many aspects of deductive monism, but it does not offer a better understanding of normativity. The problem lies in the fact that dialectics conceives of normativity as something that is determined by a shared form of rationality. Dialecticians acknowledge that participants of a discussion differ in their opinions (indeed, this forms a precondition for the very existence of the discussion), but this leaves them with the problem of idiosyncratic standards. If discussants are allowed to have different perspectives, they might as well have different standards for the discussion. The appeal to a shared form of rationality, that would provide for a suitable form of commensurability runs into similar problems as deductive normativity does. Dialogical rhetoric offers another way to deal with idiosyncrasy. Rather than trying to find a common denominator, it suggests that the idiosyncrasies of the participants 'balance' one another. This results in understanding normativity as a consequence of the argumentative process itself for which commensurability is insubstantial. Perhaps this does not satisfy what was traditionally expected from a normative standard, but it certainly yields 'should'-normativity. As such it offers an understanding of normativity that is applicable in radically pluralized situations.

NOTES

[1] It is possible, however, to reconstruct inductive arguments in a deductive way. This typically applies deductivism as a logical technique without adopting its implied understanding of normativity. Cf. Groarke, 1995.

[2] Cf. Haack, 1978, p. 221. For epistemological reasons I am not entirely happy with the term 'monism,' as it seems to suggest that both thinking and being are structurally the same. This is the problem of (post-aristotelean) epistemology in a nutshell. An alternative for 'monism' may be 'mono-logic,' but this term is easily confused as derived from monologue.

[3] For Barth and Krabbe, 1982 (pp. 3–13, 19–22) this is the main reason to go 'from axiom to dialogue'. For an overview of different logical systems cf. Haack, 1978.

[4] And perhaps even the negation of one of the other premises. Obviously this will make the premises inconsistent. But the problem of inconsistency is its triviality and not its invalidity.

[5] Cf. Van Eemeren, Grootendorst and Snoeck Henkemans, 1996, chapter 2.

[6] The two participants are best understood as logical roles. Actual persons can play these roles, but also groups of people. It is not absurd to think of a 'man talking to himself' as playing both roles. Moreover scientific inquiry can be put in those terms as well. Jaakko Hintikka defended the notion of 'interrogative dialogues' as suitable instrument to analyze communication, but also as 'a model of scientific knowledge seeking'. Cf. Hintikka, 1987, p. 217.

[7] Douglas Walton distinguishes between eight different types of discussion, including eristic discussions: quarrels. Most dialecticians, however, do not recognize the latter as a genuine discussion. Cf. Walton, 1989, pp. 3–11.

[8] It is easily seen that this picture allows for some form of dynamism: during the discussion the process can be suspended to discuss on a higher level the suitability of one or more of the rules. It may be required to modify them. If all participants agree to proceed according to the modified rules, the discussion can be reopened.

[9] Cf. Barth and Krabbe, 1982, pp. 21f, defining a logical convention for a well-defined company.

[10] This feature remains loyal to the idea that rationality performs an epistemological task. If it were *in principle* impossible to arrive unanimously at truth, all epistemological efforts would be hopeless. Dialectical rationality can deal with practical uncertainties in the application of rationality, but ideally unanimity must be secured. Or else the entire notion of rationality evaporates.

[11] Cf., for instance, Barth and Krabbe, 1982, pp. 39, 75.

[12] The emphasis on cooperation leads to a natural preference for a specific type of discussion: the critical or rational discussion. Indeed a distinction is being made between *settling* and *resolving* disputes. Settling concerns forms of dealing with disagreements such as tossing, refereeing, fighting and intimidation. The preference for more civilized forms of discussion is betrayed in sentences such as: 'to really resolve a dispute, the points that are being disputed have to be made the issue of a critical discussion that is aimed at reaching agreement . . .' (Van Eemeren and Grootendorst, 1992, p. 34).

[13] Technically the question of which position reflects the rational standpoint transforms the dialectical understanding of rationality into an epistemological problem. Considering that rationality itself is supposed to be an epistemological notion to arrive at truth, it seems that we doubled a problem rather than solved one.

14 This is a somewhat simplified picture. The starting points of a participant and the aimed at result of the discussion determine the relative 'stake' of the engagement in the discussion. For our present purpose however, abbreviating this as 'standard' will do.

15 If the 'opponent' starts defending a counter-thesis, dialectical logic analyzes this as a different discussion in which the original logical roles are switched. The proponent becomes opponent and vice versa. In this way the burden of proof is always on the proponent only, and hence dialectical logic, like deductive logic, is always supportive. Even when rebuttals have substantial influence, the qualifiers are exclusively supportive. Cf. James B. Freeman, 1991, pp. 111ff.

16 At what stage he does so is not important at this point. In some cases he must be quick to react, because the discussion may pass an irreversible moment after which no return to an earlier stage is possible. In other cases steps may be retraced to an earlier stage. What is allowed is simply to the interlocutor to decide.

17 Despite his rationality of ends consisting of an ideal form of agreement, Nicholas Rescher proposed a suitable understanding of acquiescence. Cf. Rescher, 1993.

18 Cf. for instance Walton and Krabbe, 1995, pp. 100–116.

REFERENCES

Aristotle: 1965, *De Sophisticis Elenchis,* trans. E. S. Forster, Loeb Classical Library, London/Cambridge, Mass.

Aristotle: 1989, *Topica,* trans. E. S. Forster, Loeb Classical Library, London/Cambridge, Mass.

Barth, E. M. and E. C. W. Krabbe: 1982, *From Axiom to Dialogue; A Philosophical Study of Logics and Argumentation,* Walter de Gruyter, Berlin/New York.

Eemeren, Frans H. van and Rob Grootendorst: 1987, 'Fallacies in Pragma-Dialectical Perspective', *Argumentation* 1, 283–301.

Eemeren, Frans H. van and Rob Grootendorst: 1992, *Argumentation, Communication, and Fallacies; a Pragma-Dialectical Perspective,* Lawrence Erlbaum Associates, Hillsdale.

Eemeren, Frans H. van, Rob Grootendorst and Francisca Snoeck Henkemans (eds.): 1996, *Fundamentals of Argumentation Theory; A Handbook of Historical Backgrounds and Contemporary Developments,* Lawrence Erlbaum Associates, Mahwah.

Freeman, James B.: 1991, *Dialectics and the Macrostructure of Arguments; a Theory of Arguments Structure,* Foris, Berlin.

Govier, Trudy: 1987, *Problems in Argument Analysis and Evaluation,* Foris, Dordrecht.

Groarke, Leo: 1995, 'What Pragma-dialectics Can Learn from Deductivism, and What Deductivism Can Learn from Pragma-dialectics', in Frans H. van Eemeren, Rob Grootendorst, J. Anthony Blair and Charles A. Willard (eds.), *Analysis and Evaluation. Proceedings of the Third ISSA Conference on Argumentation,* vol. I, 138–145.

Haack, Susan: 1978, *Philosophy of Logics,* Cambridge University Press, Cambridge.

Hamblin, C. L: 1970, *Fallacies,* Methuen, London.

Hintikka, Jaako: 1987, 'The Fallacy of Fallacies', *Argumentation* 1, 211–238.

Johnson, R. H. and J. A. Blair: 1983, *Logical Self-defense,* McGraw-Hill Ryerson, Toronto etc.

Johnson, Ralph H.: 1995, 'Informal Logic and Pragma-dialectics: Some Differences', in Frans H. van Eemeren, Rob Grootendorst, J. Anthony Blair and Charles A. Willard, *Perspectives and Approaches. Proceedings of the Third ISSA Conference on Argumentation,* Vol. II, 237–245.

Perelman, Ch. and L. Olbrechts-Tyteca: 1969, *The New Rhetoric; A Treatise on Argumentation,* University of Notre Dame Press, Notre Dame/London.

Ray, John: 1978, 'Perelman's Universal Audience', *The Quarterly Journal of Speech* 64, 361–375.

Rescher, Nicholas: 1988, *Rationality; A Philosophical Inquiry into the Nature and the Rationale of Reason,* Clarendon, Oxford.

Rescher, N.: 1993, *Pluralism; against the demand for Consensus,* Clarendon, Oxford.

Schrag, Calvin O.: 1992, *The Resources of Rationality; a Response to the Postmodern Challenge,* Indiana University Press, Bloomington.

Walton, Douglas N.: 1989, *Informal Logic. A Handbook for Critical Argumentation,* Cambridge University Press, Cambridge.

Walton, Douglas: 1996, *Argument Structure; A Pragmatic Theory,* University of Toronto Press, Toronto/London.

Walton, Douglas N. and Erik C. W. Krabbe: 1995, *Commitment in Dialogue; Basic Concepts of Interpersonal Reasoning,* SUNY, Albany.

Just the Facts Ma'am:
Informal Logic, Gender and Pedagogy

DEBORAH ORR

From the time of Aristotle's *Organon* through most of the present century, the study of logic has meant the study of formal logic. Only recently, mainly within the last two or three decades of this century, has this been questioned and challenged by the rapidly growing and influential development of informal logic. Blair and Johnson have identified two major streams which have fed "the informal logic movement".[1] These were the discontent of instructors in introductory logic courses with formal logic as an efficacious tool for teaching reasoning and argumentation and the theoretical insight that formal deductive logic is not commensurate with argumentation in natural language. The meeting of these two streams has proved fruitful: At least two new journals, *Informal Logic* and *Argumentation,* devoted to the study of informal logic, conferences devoted to it, and a large and rapidly growing body of journal articles, monographs and textbooks.[2] The impression I have received over the past decade or so, the time during which I have been following this movement somewhat and using its insights and developments in my own classrooms, has been that informal logic has been received as a breath of fresh air by teachers and students alike, a way of teaching reasoning and argumentation skills that is fresh, exciting and useful. But my own early, and may I say uncritical, enthusiasm for informal logic has abated over the past several years. What first appeared to be a large, if largely unexplored, box of tools for human reasoning now seems a somewhat more limited set of instruments. In this paper I would like to discuss the clues that have led me to believe the toolbox is less than fully equipped and to make some suggestions as to where informal logic might look to enlarge its stock of implements.

There have been three broad types of things which have led to my current discontent with the theory and practice of informal logic. First of all was the nagging but inchoate sense that the sorts of things I was thinking about and the ways in which I thought about them, as an individual, a student and then as a researcher, were, somehow, wrong. For instance, I have long had an interest in ethics but found that there was little if anything in classical statements of theory that bore a relationship to what I did as a moral thinker. Art and literature, I discovered as a student, could illuminate my practice but philosophy and logic largely did not. This sense of being on the wrong track dogged most of my academic career. I dealt with it by learning as quickly and thoroughly as possible the appropriate ways of proceeding in academe—the alternative was failure and personal embarrassment. But the price I paid for this success was the sense that while I was clever to get as good as I did at what was expected of me, on some deep level I was inadequate, that what I was doing did not come 'naturally' to me. The price of success was a continual battle against myself and my deepest inclinations.

In addition to my personal experience as a thinker was my experience as a teacher. During my career I have taught a 'critical skills' course for several years and have also been involved in a fairly wide range of entry level university courses in the humanities and social sciences which have stressed the development of reasoning and writing skills. Among these have been several courses and subgroups within courses comprised entirely of English as a Second Language (ESL) students.

While I have not carried out systematic research, I have developed the same strong impressions which I find are shared by many teaching at this level: Our students lack what we consider to be elementary skills in reading, writing and thinking. They cannot interpret their assignments. They fail to understand the main points or discern the supporting arguments in the material they read. And so forth. While there is a general recognition that ESL students employ different rhetorical styles from Canadian-born English-speaking students, this is largely seen as something to be corrected. My response to all this has been fairly typical: I gripe a lot with my colleagues and try to develop strategies to correct my students' faulty practices, e.g., develop exercises to teach them how to analyze a text or send them off to the Essay Tutoring Centre to learn how to develop and use a thesis statement. In sum, I have seen my students as people with problems which I ought to try to remedy.

Lastly, my research interests in epistemology and women's studies have gradually led me to think that my style of rationality, and in many instances that of my students, is not wrong but rather simply different from the dominant style. However, our differences have not been recognized as such, have not been accorded respect and certainly not been fostered in educational institutions, and more broadly in a culture, dominated by what I have come to see as a too narrow and often inappropriate conception of rationality.

In the rest of this paper I will survey some of the empirical and theoretical support for the contention that this culture's conception of rationality, especially as it is reflected in our educational institutions and the materials and practices we as teachers use, is far too narrow. Particularly I will argue that it is time for the informal logic movement, because of the growing influence it exerts through informal logic texts, introductory logic courses and critical skills courses, to recognize, theoretically ground and incorporate into its texts alternative styles of rationality. My focus will be, in fact, on only one of what I believe is a range of alternative styles. I call this the feminine style, in contrast with the dominant or masculine style because, while it has been empirically linked with women in contemporary North America, it is theoretically grounded in the psychology of femininity as gender. I will not speak to the question of the styles of rationality which a study of such variables as race, class or ethnicity might uncover.[3]

Reasoning has been seen as a masculine activity at least since the time of Aristotle. As Genevieve Lloyd has shown through her incisive historical examination of western philosophy, "Rationality has been conceived as transcendence of the feminine"[4] and the feminine in turn has been defined in opposition to and exclusion of the masculine. The feminine is 'the other' to the masculine 'self' and has been seen as primitive and underdeveloped. Thus she argues that Augustine's conceit that mind has no sex must be abandoned. This culture's conceptions of mind and rationality are overwhelmingly male.

A strong contingent within the feminist movement, at least from Wollstonecraft and Mill onward, has argued that the difference between male and female performance in reasoning lay not in inherent capacity but in socialization. Give women the proper education, they believed, and they would prove themselves fully the intellectual equals of men. Since their time many women have proved that they could use the masculine mode of reasoning as successfully as men. But it was the work of Carol Gilligan[5] which provided some of the earliest and most important empirical evidence for the nature of the difference between men's and women's reasoning as well as a theoretical account of that difference in the psychology of gender.

Stimulated by Kohlberg's research into moral development but skeptical of his generalization of his findings to all of humanity since his initial research was conducted on male subjects only, Gilligan focused in her work on the moral reasoning of girls and women. Her research has uncovered two distinct modes of thinking about moral dilemmas which she calls the ethic of care and the ethic of justice. Although they are not sex-linked, the ethic of care is empirically associated with women and the ethic of justice with men.[6] Each utilizes a different fundamental assumption: "While an ethic of justice proceeds from the premise of equality—that everyone should be treated the same—an ethic of care rests on the premise of nonviolence—that no one should be hurt".[7] But the most striking differences between the two emerge when we examine the style of reasoning each employs. The ethic of justice is consonant with the style reported by Kohlberg,[8] the dominant masculine style, in that it proceeds deductively and at its highest stage of development embraces a universal moral principle such as Kant's categorical imperative or the Golden Rule. It values 'objectivity' and thus will not be influenced by the agent's relationships, concerns for specific others or the particulars of the case. It aims for universal justice. In contrast to the formality and abstraction characteristic of the ethic of justice, the ethic of care employs a style which is 'contextual and narrative'. Relationships, responsibilities and the concrete particulars of the case are definitive of the moral dilemma for this ethic; they can not be filtered out. It seeks solutions which ensure that none are hurt, which "alleviate the 'real and recognizable trouble' of this world",[9] rather than ones which are universalizable.

In Gilligan's analysis, "the logic underlying an ethic of care is a psychological logic of relationships, which contrasts with the formal logic of fairness that informs the justice approach."[10] These logics in turn are formed by the differential experience of gender formation undergone by male and female children in this culture. Female children, because they are raised by women who see them as like themselves, are encouraged to develop a self-identity centering on attachment and relationship while male children are perceived by their mothers as different from themselves and are encouraged to separate and develop a sense of self as isolated and autonomous. In Nancy Chodorow's words, "Girls emerge from this period with a basis for 'empathy' built into their primary definition of self in a way that boys do not."[11] Thus gender theory provides a causal account of two contrasting conceptions of rationality which are instantiated in the ethical styles Gilligan delineates in her work. The two rationalities can be seen as distinct with regard to both 'content', what is thought about, and 'form', how it is thought about.

Similar findings of genderized thought patterns linked to sex have been reported by others including Lyons who has further tested and substantiated Gilligan's findings.[12] Pigott, who views what I call the feminine mode as an impediment to be overcome, reports that not only do entry level university students exhibit this difference but that at a recent meeting which she attended, discussion of topics of concern to women, whether led by academic or nonacademic women, "soon bogged down in 'confessions' from the women in the audience of one personal experience after another".[13] Based on a sample of one thousand writing placement tests, half taken by men and half taken by women, she finds a significant difference in topics chosen and in "male-female thinking patterns".[14] When given the same choices of topics, "The majority of men preferred to write about the politics of the school system; the majority of women preferred to write about themselves and their parents."[15] <u>Men avoid the personal; women prefer it.</u> <u>Male thought patterns</u> were analyzed as <u>deductive, female as inductive</u>, although I would argue that this analysis is a function of Pigott's *a priori* acceptance of those categories of logic and that the examples she reproduces of women's papers could well be read as exhibiting Gilligan's 'narrative' mode rather than falling into the traditional category of induction. Her logical commitments can be deduced from her overall assessment of women students, that they "limit, even thwart, their intellectual development by employing exclusively intuitive analysis. They rely *solely* on personal experience in their thinking, in their focusing on topics, and, most notably, in their writing, scribbling a world of particulars within which the incident is isolated, individual, non-generalizable, and stunted because it does not relate to universal concepts which could give it meaning."[16]

Although he uses the terms 'female mode' and 'male mode'[17] where I have used 'feminine mode' and 'masculine mode' to denote the influence of gender, Thomas Farrell more carefully analyzes and differently categorizes the style of thinking which Pigott has stigmatized as so dysfunctional. Farrell holds that the 'female mode', which he calls the mode of indirection, is distinct from inductive reasoning,

> although in a sense it certainly proceeds inductively. The conventional textbook distinction between inductive and deductive organization, it seems to me, is simply a distinction between two forms of the male mode which proceed by differentiation and antithesis. Both present the product of thought in a carefully controlled way, although the ordering or arrangement of ideas is different. The "indirection" of the female mode, on the other hand, tries to simulate how one might actually reason to a conclusion, and differentiation and antithesis are not especially accentuated. Deductive and inductive organization denote arrangements of discourse that appear to be planned in advance, whereas the "indirection" of the female mode seems to proceed without a readily recognizable plan. The thinking represented in the female mode seems eidetic, methectic, open-ended, and generative, whereas the thinking in the male mode appears framed, contained, more preselected, and packaged. The ideas seem less processed and controlled in the female mode than in the male mode and hence come closer to recreating the process of thinking as it normally occurs in real life . . . The female mode seems at times to obfuscate the boundary between the self of the author and the subject of the discourse, as well as between the self and the audience, whereas the male mode tends to accentuate such boundaries. The emphasis on explicitness (even when understatement is used for ironic effect) in the male mode seems to support a need for closure, whereas the "indirection" and implicitness in the female mode seem to offer an openness that could be useful in reconciling differences.[18]

Farrell also notes that the male mode tends to employ the structural device of beginning with a thesis and ending with a conclusion, thus allowing for more "playfulness" in the development or body of the work because the listener or reader is clear about where the discourse is headed.

His last two sentences in the above quotation indicate that these two styles meet the psychological demands of the gender of their practitioners which I have sketched above. Farrell cites a number of studies, including some work of his own, which show that the indirect mode is to be found in the writing of historical and contemporary women and which go some way to relating the modes employed by men and women to the type of education they had received.[19]

Farrell illuminates the nature of the hegemony of the 'male mode' in western culture when he notes that Peter Ramus, author of influential medieval textbooks on reasoning, censures those who deviate from what he regards as the "'one and only method', that is, reasoning from general principles baldly stated to particulars",[20] i.e., the 'male mode'. Clearly Ramus is teaching a narrow version of what Moulton[21] has called The Adversary Method to the disparagement and exclusion of the feminine mode of reasoning. While Moulton offers many criticisms of the underlying assumptions of The Adversary Method and its claims to historical precedent, a major drawback which she points to which is relevant to my concerns is that it "accepts only the kind of reasoning whose goal is to convince an opponent, and ignores reasoning that might be used in other circumstances: To figure something out for oneself, to discuss something with likeminded thinkers, to convince the indifferent or the uncommitted."[22] Thus its use to the exclusion of other modes fosters not only bad but potentially divisive reasoning. (The adversarial mind-set of informal logic texts today is reflected even in the titles of some of them, e.g., *How to Win an Argument, Logical Self-Defense*.) In contrast Farrell finds that the 'female mode' avoids antagonism, stresses solidarity with its audience and is "generally supportive, conciliatory, and potentially integrative".[23]

It is not my intention in this paper to fully defend the feminine mode but rather to make a contribution to describing and understanding it to the end that it be recognized and taught as a part of what humans do when they reason. I fully subscribe to Wittgenstein's dictum that, if we do not want our conception of logic to be based on superstition and illusion, then we must "look and see", and accept, what people actually do when they think.[24] I will, however, offer a comment on one point and that is the oft expressed fear that modes of thinking which incorporate the affective and relational aspects of the thinker's life, ones that give the subjective dimension an equal place beside, or even primacy over, the objective are bound to be both unreliable and selfserving. As Lloyd and Moulton, among many others, have argued, the masculine mode has been developed with the explicit intent of excluding the emotional and subjective. It will take much argumentation about many interrelated issues to overcome this view and for now I will offer only as an illustrative counter example the methodology of the widely acclaimed geneticist and Nobel Laureate, Barbara McClintock.

McClintock is described by Evelyn Fox Keller as a methodological rebel. Eschewing the 'objective' method of normal science, McClintock employed an epistemological stance and rational style which are closely akin to that of the feminine mode of reasoning I have been discussing. She argued that modern research methods are vitiated by a tendency to impose preconceived answers (the hypothesis or thesis) and to ignore or force fit information which did not cohere with one's preconceptions. Feeding this are assumptions about the world (that its organization can best be understood by dichotomizing divisions, e.g. subject-object, mind-matter, feeling-reason) and the goal of science (to produce unifying laws) which McClintock also rejected. For McClintock the goal of science was to make the differences she saw understandable and this necessitated a kind of respect, even love for and union with her material that ordinary science does not recognize, in fact forbids.

In comparing the 'epistemology of division' of ordinary science with McClintock's 'epistemology of difference', Keller has said, "Division severs connection and imposes distance; the recognition of difference provides a starting point for relatedness. It serves both as a clue to new modes of connectedness in nature, and as an invitation to engagement with nature."25 A methodology of relatedness and connection, of feeling and intuition, enabled McClintock to ask question of nature, to think about it and make discoveries which were all outside the range of ordinary science. But, Keller argues, McClintock's method of empathy with her material, her 'feel for the organism', was not solipsistic: It led to the production of knowledge which is reliable, that can be shared with and reproduced by the scientific community.26

This last claim is supported by McClintock's argument that she was not doing 'feminist' science but claiming science as a fully human endeavour. She believed that she was employing *human* capabilities and she trusted that, contrary to the position taken by centuries of western thinking, the 'subjective' was not unruly and erratic but a reliable and trustworthy source of knowledge. This meant that in her work, while she had been socialized to, and to some degree employed the methodology of, ordinary science, she was able to mitigate that distorted practice with the techniques of her distinctive empathic approach to the world. She believed that as a person and as a scientist she must struggle to transcend gender and Keller reads her work as evidence of her success. In this she is both compatible with the theoretical possibilities of Chodorow's theory of gender which I brought to bear in my discussion above, and in line with a body of evidence which finds that both men and women can and do employ both styles of rationality.

Fundamental to Chodorow's theory is the idea that gender results from the polarization and asymmetrical development of a shared human potential. The psychological process of gender acquisition produces girls who have, as we have seen, "a basis for 'empathy' built into their primary definition of self in a way that boys do not"27 and boys with a psychic structure centered on what Chodorow calls a "pseudo-independence."28 These are the sorts of differences which ground the different styles of rationality uncovered by Gilligan's work. But, to repeat, these difference[s] are not inherent but acquired. Chodorow locates their social roots in the sexed divisions of labour within and among the family, home and workplace in contemporary capitalist society. The clear implication of this is that the transcendence of gender and all that hangs on it, on more than an haphazard and infrequent basis, requires changes in those spheres. But this topic is beyond the scope of my paper.

Besides Keller's discussion of Barbara McClintock's work, Farrell provides other examples of women who successfully use both rational styles. For instance his analysis of Virginia Woolf's *A Room of One's Own* shows Woolf quite consciously using both styles and manipulating them to create a work which combines exposition, fiction and argumentation in a unique and satisfying way.29 But the incorporation of the feminine mode is not unique to highly successful and visible women like McClintock and Woolf as is shown by the in-depth study conducted by Mary Belenky and her colleagues30 of the epistemic styles and development of 135 women drawn from a variety of backgrounds ranging from elite colleges to social agencies. They discovered five distinct epistemic positions which were expressed in the different 'voices' of the women they studied: (1) silence—is the lack of a voice of women who have been abused and abandoned and consequently see external authorities as all powerful; (2) received knowledge and (3) procedural knowl-edge—are the voices of women who try to 'fit in' and accept society's definitions of reason and objectivity; (4) subjective knowledge—is the voice of women who are on a 'quest for self' and in this process reject public definitions of truth and authority for ones which are private and subjectively known; and (5) constructed knowledge—is the most mature voice of women and results from

> an effort to reclaim the self by attempting to integrate knowledge that they felt intuitively was personally important with knowledge they had learned from others. They told of weaving together the strands of rational and emotive thought and of integrating objective and subjective knowing. Rather than extricating the self in the acquisition of knowledge, these women used themselves in rising to a new way of thinking.[31]

An important feature of the thinking of women at this position was that they 'abandoned either/or thinking', the epistemic stance of division, for that of difference.[32] Further, like McClintock, they questioned and recast their paradigms and methodologies alike. Belenky *et al.* report that for their subjects, "Question posing and problem posing become prominent methods of inquiry . . . [they] tend not to rely as readily or as exclusively on hypothetico-deductive inquiry, which posits an answer (the hypothesis) prior to the data collection, as they do on exam-ining basic assumptions and the conditions in which a problem is cast."[33] Thus these women were able to utilize and integrate the techniques of both rational modes to become "passionate knowers", ones for whom "connected knowing is not simply an 'objective' procedure but a way of weaving their passions and intellectual life into some recognizable whole".[34] Clearly, for these women rationality is not partitioned off from the rest of their selves and lives but integrates and serves these.

Finally, Carol Gilligan has found that mature men as well as mature women can and do 'weave together' both modes. Although they might have been initially committed to one ethic or the other, Gilligan found that crises in personal relation-ships or professional life can lead both sexes to critically examine and expand their decision making procedures toward a "convergence"[35] of the two.

> Though both sexes move away from absolutes in this time, the absolutes them-selves differ for each. In women's development, the absolute of care, defined initially as not hurting others, becomes complicated through a recognition of the need for personal integrity. This recognition gives rise to the claim for equality embodied in the concept of rights, which changes the understanding of relationships and transforms the definition of care. For men, the absolutes of truth and fairness, defined by the concepts of equality and reciprocity, are called into question by experiences that demonstrate the existence of differ-ences between other and self. Then the awareness of multiple truths leads to a relativizing of equality in the direction of equity and gives rise to an ethic of generosity and care. For both sexes the existence of two contexts for moral decision makes judgment by definition contextually relative and leads to a new understanding of responsibility and choice.[36]

Gilligan does not find that harmonizing these two voices, these two deeply different styles of rationality, is an easy task for her subjects. One, in grappling with a dilemma in her professional life which challenged the adequacy of her ethic of care by itself, found it necessary to adopt a principle of rights which left her with "two principles of judgment whose integration she cannot yet clearly envision".[37] Nevertheless, Gilligan believes that the dialogue between the two voices can lead to a fuller understanding and transformation of many of the areas of human life and relationship which are so problematic for us today.

Since its inception as a science, logic has conceived of itself as the study of the eternal and universal laws of thought. While they believed that its study might serve as a corrective to faulty practices, thus giving logic a practical role in education, logicians have not seen themselves as recommending one set of procedures from among a collection of valid alternatives but rather as describing the *a priori* 'one right way to think'. Informal logic's recent arrival on the scene has challenged the received belief that formal logic adequately describes how people proceed when they reason in ordinary language. As Blair and Johnson point out, the subject matter of informal logic is "communicative practice" and some of its major theoreticians hold that, "arguments as products of communication in such natural language practices as rational persuasion or rational inquiry are simply not chains of deductive inferences."[38] I believe that in this the informal logic movement has made a genuine and liberating advance but, as the large and growing body of studies of the feminine mode of rationality show, it is time for informal logic to take the next step, to expand its understanding of what rationality and argumentation are when they are understood as human, not masculine, practice. To dismiss the feminine mode of rationality with the stock charge of 'mere psychologism' would be at best question begging, at worst prejudice.

I have drawn on research from a variety of different sources to show first that the feminine mode or style of rationality is, in fact, practiced and can be found quite readily in environments as different as elite colleges and social agencies, in fields as disparate as genetic research and moral practice. While researchers have not used a standardized vocabulary to describe and analyze the feminine mode, to compare it with the masculine or to study the integration of the two, the similarities in their accounts cannot be missed: the very epistemic foundations of the feminine and masculine modes of rationality are different. Within broad areas of thought and inquiry they begin with different assumptions and strive for different goals. In contrast to the masculine mode, the feminine mode does not fit comfortably into the standard categories of induction or deduction. Gilligan has called its form 'narrative', utilizing the 'psychological logic of relationships', and Farrell, 'indirect'. Chodorow and Keller have used the term 'empathic' to mark the blurring of boundaries between thinker and subject of inquiry and Belenky notes the integration of subject and object in her practi[ti]oners of constructive knowledge. Relationship with and concern and respect for the other are central to this method. The affective and relational are integral and can not be suspended, as is attempted in the demand for objectivity of the masculine mode. While the masculine mode proceeds by differentiation and antithesis with the goal of one of a pair of opposites emerging as dominant, the feminine mode preserves differences. The masculine mode has been described as controlled, packaged and having closed boundaries while the feminine is open-ended and more closely simulates actual thought processes. Writing in the masculine mode more frequently begins with a thesis and ends with a conclusion than writing in the feminine and Farrell maintains that the feminine mode places more trust in its audience to draw conclusions. Perhaps we might rephrase this by saying that the feminine mode requires a more active involvement on the part of its audience. Finally, the masculine mode has been characterized as adversarial and potentially divisive while the feminine is conciliatory, integrative and stresses solidarity.

Clearly, these descriptions are preliminary to the fuller study and description of the feminine mode, and its integration with the masculine, as processes of 'rational persuasion and inquiry'. For informal logic this will mean, among other things, a study of the role and use of the 'subjective' in the feminine mode, the study and description of typical patterns of inquiry and persuasion and the identification and study of 'fallacies' typical of this mode. And similar concerns must be brought to bear in a study of the integrated use of the two modes.

Two consequences of the thesis that both the feminine and the masculine modes are rooted in gender need to be stressed. First, it follows that since gender is an acquisition and not sex determined, both modes of rationality are potentially open to both sexes. Second, both theoretical and empirical research support the hypothesis that early influences on an individual's development as well as whether or not she or he receive support and direction in later years influence the individual's access to the various modes of rationality. On the theoretical level Chodorow's work, especially in showing gender acquisition as the polarization of human potential, ground this claim. On an empirical level Gilligan has found that despair and moral nihilism, rather than development toward maturity and the convergence of the moral voices, characterized those women who have felt themselves abandoned and unsupported in their decision making during a time of crisis.[39] And in far greater detail the work of Belenky and her colleagues show how the environment and life experiences of their subjects have helped or hindered their development through the different forms of knowledge.[40] All too frequently these women's experiences in educational institutions have not fostered but suppressed constructed knowing. They have paralleled the experience of the philosopher Sara Ruddick who has written,

> Harvard's training, and the identity it allowed, had become intimately, unconsciously connected with lessons of respectability I had learned as a child . . . Even now, I can surprise myself, wondering whether a question is "really" philosophical, whether I should ask questions I haven't been trained to answer.[41]

The lesson in this for those involved in informal logic, be they developing theory, writing texts or teaching, is that for the full range of human thinking to develop we must collectively recognize the validity of modes of thinking other than the dominant masculine strain and actively foster their development. Among other things this calls for the understanding of thinkers as other than disembodied minds. They are rather persons with useful affective and empathic tools to bring to intellectual life. It is to these tools and their uses and limits which informal logic must now turn its attention.

NOTES

1 Blair, J. Anthony and Ralph H. Johnson, "The Current State of Informal Logic", *Informal Logic,* IX 2&3. Spring & Fall, 1987, pp. 147–152.
2 I have relied on two useful bibliographies: Johnson, Ralph H. and Blair, J. Anthony, "A Bibliography of Recent Work in Informal Logic", prepared for the Symposium on Informal Logic, University of Windsor, June 26, 1978 and "Informal Logic Texts: An Annotated

Bibliography," Prepared by Jean Saindon, York University, July, 1988. The former lists journal articles, monographs and textbooks while the later focuses on texts.

3 Harding, Sandra, "Is Gender a Variable in Conceptions of Rationality: A Survey of Issues", *Beyond Domination,* ed. by Carol C. Gould, Rowman & Allanheld, New Jersey, 1983, pp. 44–62, fn. 5 gives a guide to some of the recent literature on European vs. non-European modes of rationality.

4 Lloyd, Genevieve, *The Man of Reason: "Male" and "Female" in Western Philosophy,* Univ. of Minnesota Press, Minneapolis, 1984, p. 104.

5 Gilligan, Carol, *In a Different Voice,* Harvard Univ. Press, Cambridge, Mass., 1982.

6 *Ibid.,* p. 2.

7 *Ibid.,* p. 174.

8 See especially Kohlberg, Lawrence, "The Development of Children's Orientations Toward a Moral Order: 1. Sequence in the Development of Moral Thought", *Vita Humana,* 6, 1963, 11–33 and Kohlberg, Lawrence, "The Cognitive Developmental Approach to Moral Education", *Phi Delta Kappan,* June 1975, 670–677.

9 Gilligan, *op. cit.,* p. 100.

10 *Ibid.,* p. 173.

11 Chodorow, Nancy, *The Reproduction of Mothering,* Univ. of California Press, Berkeley, 1978, p. 167 quoted in Gilligan, *op. cit.,* p. 8.

12 Lyons, Nona Plessner, "Two Perspectives: On Self, Relationships and Morality", *Harvard Educational Review,* 53, No. 2, May 1983, pp. 125–145.

13 Pigott, Margaret B., "Sexist Roadblocks in Inventing, Focusing, and Writing", *College English,* 40, April 1979, p. 922.

14 *Ibid.,* p. 927.

15 *Ibid.,* p. 923.

16 *Ibid.,* p. 922, emphasis in the original.

17 Farrell, Thomas J., "The Female and Male Modes of Rhetoric", *College English,* 40, April 1979, pp. 909–921. Farrell's position that these modes are rooted in biology (fn. 14) does not affect his description and categorization of them which are my main concerns. Obviously, I reject this thesis.

18 *Ibid.,* pp. 909–910.

19 *Ibid.,* p. 911, especially the studies by Allison Heisch and Patricia A. Sullivan.

20 *Ibid.,* p. 911.

21 Moulton, Janice, "A Paradigm of Philosophy: The Adversary Method" in *Discovering Reality,* ed. by Sandra Harding and Merrill B. Hintikka, D. Reidel Pub. Co., Dordrecht Holland, 1983, pp. 149–164.

22 *Ibid.,* p. 199.

23 Farrell, *op. cit.,* pp. 916–917.

24 Wittgenstein, Ludwig, *Philosophical Investigations,* trans. by G. E. M. Anscombe, Basil Blackwell, Oxford, 1968, see especially section 66.

25 Keller, Evelyn Fox, "A World of Difference", in *Reflections on Gender and Science,* Yale Univ. Press, New Haven, 1985, p. 163.

26 *Ibid.,* p. 166.

27 Chodorow, *op. cit.,* p. 167.

28 *Ibid.,* p. 187.

29 Farrell, *op. cit.,* pp. 913–916.

30 Belenky, Mary Field, Blythe McVicker Clinchy, Nancy Rule Goldberger and Jill Mattuck Tarule, *Women's Ways of Knowing,* Basic Books, Inc., New York, 1986.

31 *Ibid.,* pp. 134–135.

32 *Ibid.,* p. 137.

33 *Ibid.,* p. 139.

34 *Ibid.,* p. 141.

35 Gilligan, *op. cit.,* p. 2.

36 *Ibid.,* p. 166.

37 *Ibid.,* p. 165.

38 Blair and Johnson, "The Current State of Informal Logic" p. 147.

39 Gilligan, *op. cit.,* especially Chap. 4, *passim.*

40 Belenky *et al., op. cit., passim.*

41 Ruddick, Sara, "*A Work of One's Own*" in *Working It Out,* ed. by S. Ruddick & P. Daniels, Pantheon, New York, 1977, p. 137, quoted in Belenky *et al., op. cit.,* p. 96.

Justifying *My* Position in *Your* Terms: Cross-Cultural Argumentation in a Globalized World

YAMENG LIU

Arguing across the boundaries of independent and ideologically or culturally incompatible formations (e.g., West and non-West) is, for many scholars of argumentation, a contradiction in terms. The practice of argumentation presupposes a substantively constituted common ground. And one would have to abandon this disciplinary presupposition in order to believe that controversies can be resolved rationally without there being a shared rhetorical tradition to fall back on as the ultimate guarantee for agreement. Powerful contemporary trends of thought also lend their support to a deep skepticism about the possibility of resolving inter-communal conflicts through an exchange of good reasons.

THE SPECTER OF INCOMMENSURABILITY

Leading philosophers of our time, from W. V. Quine to Richard Rorty, have long expressed their doubt that a rational agreement can ever be reached argumentatively between radically different systems. Quine undercuts such a possibility with his influential doctrine of the 'indeterminacy of translation.' For him, outsiders 'cannot even say what native locutions to count as analogues of terms as we know them, much less equate them with ours term for term' (1960, p. 53). Rorty believes that 'there is no way to step outside the various vocabularies we have employed and find a metavocabulary which somehow takes account of *all possible* vocabularies.' This belief has led him to reject argumentation as the mode of cross-'vocabulary' interactions (1989, pp. xvi, 8). Jean-François Lyotard adds an ethical dimension to the issue of incommensurability with his concept of a *différend*, i.e., 'a case of conflict, between (at least) two parties, that cannot be equitably resolved for lack of a rule of judgment applicable to both arguments.' He maintains that since 'a universal rule of judgment between heterogeneous genres is lacking in general, . . . the rules of the genre of discourse by which one judges are not those of the judged genre or genres of discourse,' and a 'wrong' would necessarily result (1988, p. xi). Even Jürgen Habermas has acknowledged that his earlier formulation of a 'discourse ethics,' based on the principle that 'a norm can be considered objectively right if it would be consented to in free discussion by all concerned as consonant with their interests,' fails to take into proper account 'the power of history over against the transcending claims and interests of reason,' the 'ideas of the "good life"' which 'form an integrated component of the particular culture,' and '*Sittlichkeit*, the concrete customs of a community' (Dews, 1986, pp. 17–18).

Anthropologists' vivid stories of their personal encounters with other cultures give further credence to the skepticism. Clifford Geertz, in an account of a 'debate' he had during his 1971 trip to Indonesia, shows what an impossible task it could be trying to argue with people locked in an acutely different cultural framework. Taking place in a religious school in Sumatra, the 'debate' pitted Geertz against the teacher-director of the institution over the issue of whether American astronauts had indeed landed on the moon. The religious master opened with the declaration that 'no Muslim could believe [the moon-landing],' because the Prophet was 'held to have said that an enormous ocean lies between the earth and the moon and this was the source of [Noah's] flood.' If the Americans had indeed gone to the moon, then (1) they 'would have put a hole in this ocean and a flood like Noah's' would have ensued and would have drowned us all; (2) they would have proved that the Prophet was wrong, which was impossible; (3) what they did was most likely to be a trick played by God who 'had constructed a fake moon off to the side somewhere for them to land on.' Geertz, feeling that he had better not question the 'authority of a *hadith* [a tradition from the Prophet]' there and then, and not quite knowing 'what to do with [the master's] argument,' chose to confine himself to describing what Western science considered the moon to be. To shore up his case, he suggested in conclusion that 'maybe the best thing would be for a Muslim to go along on the trip next time.' This invocation of the 'seeing is believing' presumption did not sound persuasive to people who had accepted the premise that the Almighty God could easily construct a 'fake moon' in the first place. As a result, what promised to be a 'great debate' between two cultures fizzled out, degenerating into a 'clash of narratives' instead, with 'nothing' being 'disturbed' (1995, pp. 82–84).

These perspectives are, to be sure, not without their critics. Donald Davidson famously challenges the notion of 'incommensurability' on the basis of its own 'incoherence.' For if two different 'conceptual schemes' were indeed as radically incommensurable as has been suggested, they would be *mutually unintelligible*. And it would not be possible for us to find other conceptual schemes incompatible to ours on the basis of an intelligent comparison (1973–1974). More recently, Richard J. Bernstein points out that '[incommensurable] languages and traditions are not to be thought of as self-contained windowless monads that share nothing in common. . . . There are always points of overlap and crisscrossing, even if there is not perfect commensuration' (1991, p. 92). Yet there is still no denying the fact that neither a neutral ground nor a commonly acceptable 'metavocabulary' is available when symbolic exchanges take place between independent formations such as the above-mentioned. A culture is definable precisely by the uniqueness of the basic assumptions and beliefs its members subscribe to. If the disputants *insist* on invoking their own first premises, as in the case of Geertz 'debating' the Indonesian religious master, there is no way a mutually agreed-upon decision can be reached on any issue of significance. Large international or inter-cultural formations, moreover, came into being because of an irreconcilable conflict, real or imagined, in vital interests. As a result, within the dominant framework of international relations, the 'complexities of political life are reduced to a calculus of power, justice is reduced to self-interest, appearances are reduced to the reality they conceal, and, ultimately, language is reduced to the world it would represent' (Beer and Hariman, 1996, p. 390).

The apparent intractability of all these epistemological, ethical and geopolitical issues has discouraged argumentation scholars from going beyond an *intra*-cultural context in pursuit of a normative theoretical model applicable to *inter*-cultural debates as well. An incredulity toward the possibility of what the Self and the Other would *both* regard as a rational exchange is deeply embedded in their practices. Perelman and Olbrechts-Tyteca take it for granted that an 'effective community of minds,' constituted of everything from a 'common language,' a shared body of 'norms set by social life,' to a mutual 'wish to enter into conversation,' is a *sine qua non* of argumentation. For an illustration of what an absence of such a community would entail, they refer to Alice's failed attempts to strike a conversation with the denizens of the Wonderland (1969, pp. 14–15). While argumentation theory has undergone significant changes since these comments were first made, the requirement of a unified 'community of minds' remains as much assumed by the discipline as the story of Alice's doomed effort to communicate continues to serve as a cautionary tale for its practitioners. Theorists of 'argument fields' or 'argument spheres,' to be sure, have become increasingly interested in inter-field border crossing since the 1980's. Yet the multiple 'fields' or 'spheres' involved are clearly understood to have come into being within, and to depend for their existence and normal functioning on, the same cultural formation, i.e., the contemporary West (Eemeren and Grootendorst et al., 1996, pp. 204–206).

GLOBALIZATION AND THE NEED FOR CROSS-CULTURAL ARGUMENTATION

Given the apparently unbridgeable gap between a world doomed to incompatibility and argumentation's orientation toward conflict resolution on the basis of shared interests and reasons, the discipline's focus on intra- rather than inter-cultural disputation is not without justification. The basis of the justification, however, has been undercut lately by an emerging new international order and the pressing need such an order has created for different cultural-ideological formations to enter a meaningful dialogue with one another. With the end of Cold War and the unprecedented drive toward globalization, the world as a whole has become so closely interconnected financially, economically, environmentally and communicatively that what happens in one area—not necessarily the center stage of international politics or business—could now have serious effects on other parts (e.g., the worldwide economic and political turmoils triggered by the devaluation of the humble Thai baht), and the notion of a 'generalized interest' across national or continental boundaries begins to make sense. Scholars and public commentators alike have started talking about the need to formulate 'universal ethics' or codify 'planetary legal standards.' In days gone by, writes international relations scholar Stephen Schlesinger, ideological constructs ranging from 'nationalism' to 'historical memories' had such a hold on people that 'the idea of a world of laws' would have seemed 'a laughable proposition.' Today, however, 'the imperatives behind worldwide trade . . . are [so] tightening the bonds among nations' that not only have we been witnessing a steady movement toward 'working together in a lawful fashion around the world,' we have actually started to forge a 'juridical global community,' with treaties governing trade, global warming, land-mines, etc., as its 'building blocks' (1997). Columnist Flora Lewis maintains that 'globalization of economics and technology is no longer a contentious thesis but an irresistible reality with concrete effect on people's lives.' As a result, the idea of 'articulating . . . a global ethic' applicable to 'everybody everywhere' is 'spreading with increasing insistence' (1997). Forward-thinking political scientists are contemplating a 'post-realist world order' (Beer and Hariman, 1996). And communication scholars have come up with a whole spectrum of scholarly arguments 'around the public sphere and its apparent or possible growth into a transnational civil society,' from the suggestion that 'the only possible response to global market forces is . . . a universal public sphere in which common interests can be recognized and acted on' to calls for 'the creation of a global perspective and values in the depths of people's hearts and minds, establishing the idea of a global civil society' (Sreberny-Mohammadi, 1997, pp. 11–12).

Since the global market forces can hardly be expected to 'behave themselves' without being constrained by a commensurate legal-ethical framework, the more economically interconnected the world becomes, the greater the need to foster 'global perspectives and values.' And as there is no way a 'world legal society' or a 'global ethic' can be instituted without there having already been a global rhetorical regime in place to serve as one of its indispensable institutional scaffolds, finding the right mechanisms for arguing across existing cultural or civilizational formations in today's world has also become an imperative of our time. A rhetorical order must be installed to ensure a fair and productive debate over what shape the brave new 'society' would eventually take and how legal cases or ethical issues could be debated and adjudicated cross-culturally. A genuine global community can be constructed only on the basis of a non-coerced global consensus, whose achievement requires *rational* discussions among *all* its would-be members. Give-and-take on the basis of a geopolitical or a geoeconomic calculation of private interests and relative strength, which has been the principal non-violent means of international conflict resolution, can no longer serve as the mechanism upon which the functioning of a 'global civil society' depends.

THE CASE OF THE EAST-WEST DEBATE OVER RIGHTS AND VALUES

While the arrival of such a society is far from imminent, there can be little doubt that the world has been moving in that direction since the end of the Cold War. As a sign of the progress, controversies have erupted between the West and the non-West in recent years over democracy, universal human rights, 'Asian values,' etc. None of these could have become the topic of intense global discussions should the rigid ideological divide of the Cold War era stay intact and an irreconcilable confrontation of radically incompatible systems continue to be presumed as a fact of international life. Under those circumstances, it would have been absurd for a NATO to try to engage the Warsaw Pact in a debate over what form of democracy the latter should adopt, and a dialogue between either block and the Nonaligned Movement over what values were universal would have been equally difficult to imagine. That these are now being taken up as central concerns of the current international discourse testifies to the depth of the on-going global transformation. The way they have been addressed so far, however, draws attention also to how a serious lack of understanding of cross-cultural interactions has hampered the effort to formulate a universally binding set of axiological and ethical standards.

The inadequacy of our thinking about arguing across boundaries is highlighted by three unexpected findings from a close look into the still unfolding East-West contention over values. First, contrary to the assumption that radical differences among incompatible systems constitute the single greatest obstacle to cross-communal argumentation, no incommensurability-caused problems appear to be plaguing the contentious exchange of opinions between the West and the non-West. This is largely due to the fact that the representative 'voices' of the non-Western cultures do not come from people like Geertz's interlocutor in the above-mentioned episode. Rather, they typically come from people such as former Singaporean prime minister Lee Kuan Yew or the current Malaysian prime minister Mahathir Mohamad, who, as Western-educated Third World elite, tend to be conversant in Western rhetoric and capable of understanding, communicating with, and debating champions of Western values. Second, in the absence of a 'meta-vocabulary' in which to phrase and evaluate arguments, whose side's 'terms' should be used in cross-boundary debate is generally taken to be an unsolvable killer issue in cross-cultural argumentation. In reality, this has never become a major point of contention. As their primary strategy, the (often self-proclaimed) spokesmen for the non-Western world prefer to draw from *Western* discursive resources and to frame, formulate, and defend their positions in *Western,* rather than their own native terms. The arguments, presumptions, and modes of reasoning they characteristically deploy are likely to be those authorized or even valorized by *Western* discourses.[1] Third, whereas it seems self-evident that the party whose 'terms' have been adopted as the 'working language' of the argumentative interaction would enjoy a decisive advantage over its opponent, what has happened does not bear out this presumption either. Rather than the non-Western interlocutors being handicapped by the use of Western terms, it is often their Western counterparts that appear to be nonplused when confronted by a cultural/ideological Other who nevertheless talks back in Western terms.

The perplexity shows itself in the stance adopted by many Western interlocutors. Typically, public commentators in the West tend either to ignore the non-Western interlocutors' arguments altogether, or to reject them off-hand as self-serving sophistry in defense of undemocratic institutions and practices at home, not to be dignified with reasoned rebuttals.[2] When they do respond, the counterarguments are often controversial (and hence of questionable validity and limited currency) in contemporary *Western* discourse (e.g., resorting to universalism, apriorism, the notion of 'intrinsic value,' etc. to counter attempts to contextualize human rights culturally).[3] These diverse approaches suggest in common a hesitancy, even a reluctance, to engage the non-Western side's arguments squarely. However this tendency may be interpreted, it indicates that the non-Western interlocutors' acceptance of Western terms does not automatically translate into a Western edge on the debate. On the contrary, it may put the Western interlocutors in a strategically awkward position. Within the framework of Western argumentation, the West as the party that advances a standpoint on the issue of democracy is expected to shoulder the burden of proof and to explain to the satisfaction of the Malaysians, for example, why Malaysia's system is less than democratic and (in response to the predictable objection from the latter) what exactly 'democratic' means, how the meaning is determined, how the meaning ought to be determined (e.g., 'does context matter?'), who has the right to determine the meaning, and so on and so forth. The argumentative weapons and strategies available in the domestic discourse of the West are, moreover, no less effective and damaging when turned against Western positions in international disputes. The current incredulity in the West toward claims of being 'self-evidently,' 'timelessly' or 'universally' valid, and the concurrent Western belief that universal legitimacy can be established only on the basis of a consensus that emerges from a free, unrestricted dialogue involving all the parties concerned, tend to cast doubt on the presumption of 'universal human rights' as a self-evidently valid notion requiring no open and critical discussions for the constant reaffirmation of its legitimacy. And in the Western rhetorical tradition, an agreement to argue with someone carries with it both a tacit acknowledgment that one's own position on the issue is debatable and an implied commitment to changing or withdrawing the position should one fail to defend it conclusively. Offering such an acknowledgment or commitment to interlocutors from an alien culture or community could well turn out to be politically or ideologically unacceptable at home.[4]

All these problems point to an unsettling transformation, at their root, of an East-West debate into a West-West confrontation that a Western-terms-only format of engagement is bound to cause. Turning their attention exclusively to Western means of persuasion, non-Western interlocutors could not but seek to justify their position through its association with perspectives or assumptions privileged in the West. They are almost certain to deploy those eloquent arguments in favor of developing a multicultural society in the U.S., for example, as their first line of defense against aggressive promotion throughout the world of what in effect are contemporary Western values, standards or institutions. In so doing, they force their Western critics to confront a valorized current Western perspective and all the positive values it embodies. Similarly, defenders of non-Western values and institutions would not hesitate to exploit internal differences of the West, availing themselves of the often powerful dissenting voices or counter discourses *within* the West in their bid to ward off criticism from the more 'mainstream' Western perspective. The French and the Canadian, for instance, have long expressed a grave concern over a perceived threat to their distinct cultural identities from the dominant American mass media and cultural industries, and have been using it to justify regulating the inflow and consumption of American cultural and informational products. Radical critics in the West have also directed attention to the commercial motives behind the West's insistence on free movement of information across national boundaries (Roach, 1997; DePalma, 1998). The arguments and evidence presented in these efforts, when enlisted by the developing countries in their debate with the developed world over what global order of information and communication ought to be established, would also create a situation in which some potent Western arguments are confronted with others.[5]

From a Western point of view, therefore, what results from a 'Western terms only' approach could well be a 'domestication' of a purportedly 'cross-cultural' clash of opinions, often at the expense of Western interests. The 'domestication' is by no means difficult to accomplish. Because of the fundamentally heterogeneous and openly contentious character of contemporary Western discourse, whatever is at issue, one can always find arguments and counter-arguments of comparable validity from the West's vast pool of authorized rhetorical resources. Thus for every carefully reasoned Western conclusion that 'current international standards of human rights should and will prevail universally,' there is an equally eloquent explanation by fellow Western commentators as to why the perspective is 'deeply troubling in its ethnocentricity' (on the account, for instance, that it 'fails to heed seriously the critique of those who choose to place less emphasis than does the contemporary West on the atomized autonomous individual,' etc.) (Alford, 1992, p. 75). Scratch the surface of a presumed Western consensus on the meaning of democracy, and one is certain to find 'endless disputes over appropriate meaning and definition' of the term among Western political scientists, who as a whole continue to see democracy as an 'essentially contested concept' (Collier and Levitsky, 1997, p. 433). As a recent illustration of how the concept has remained fiercely 'contested' within the West, Samuel P. Huntington argues that democracy is 'simply a way of constituting, limiting and changing governments' and is in no way a guarantee for 'peace, equality, prosperity, harmony among nations and classes,' that it is hence not 'for everyone,' and that as it 'spreads around the world,' democracy 'is becoming more variegated,' taking on different forms and acquiring different characteristics in different countries (1998).

The non-West, moreover, has much to gain in turning their cross-cultural debates *with* the West into a domestic controversy *of* the West. While a realistic acknowledgment of the asymmetrical relations between the West and the non-West, and of the predominance of Western discourse as well, undoubtedly contributes to their willingness to argue in Western terms, the attitude is more likely to have been prompted by a shrewd calculation than a reluctant resignation.[6] Sophisticated apologists of non-Western values and institutions understand that should they insist on arguing in their own terms, appealing to the existing power structure of international politics as the final arbiter of whatever is at issue would become inevitable. On the other hand, since they have no difficulty accessing Western rhetorical resources, and since Western discourse is itself by no means monolithic, accepting a Western framework within which to articulate and present their own case would enable them to reap huge strategic benefits. It would quietly re-situate them and their perspectives *within* the rhetorical horizon of the West, enabling them to represent the issue in a way understandable and, hopefully, acceptable to a Western audience. A full subscription to Western terms of argumentation would entitle them to the protection of Western rhetorical norms, otherwise applicable only to domestic disputes in the West. By strategically allying themselves with some Western positions and perspectives against others, they would be able to blur the line between Self and Other, or between the protagonist and the antagonist in a cross-communal debate, making it more complicated and difficult for their opponents to maintain their focus on the target of their criticism or to sustain their argumentative offensive. The 'West itself,' as Richard Rorty puts it bluntly in addressing the issue of 'East-West asymmetry' from a historical point of view, in fact

> provides most of the promising tools for undoing what the West has been doing to the non-West. If you were, during the first sixty years of this century, an Arab or an African or an Indian impatient to get out from under the colonialist yoke, what you used were . . . Western guns, Western political and socio-economic categories, Western ideas for social reform, Western means of communication. . . . This was because the devices and categories inherited from your previous traditions just weren't of much use in anti-colonialist struggles (Balslev, 1991, p. 78).

The instrumental intent and design behind their non-Western opponents' willing acceptance of the format of debating cross-cultural issues in Western terms leaves open two basic strategic options for the Western interlocutors. First, refusing to play into the opponents' hand by avoiding any serious argumentative engagement with them. Thus, for example, American public commentators (e.g., William Safire of *The New York Times*) who keep labeling and denouncing Singapore as a 'tin-pot dictatorship' nevertheless decline to accept a challenge from Singaporean officials to a public debate.[7] Mainstream Western media which tends to identify and condemn Mahathir as an authoritarian Third World leader fiercely opposed to all Western values never bothers to respond to his frequent complaints against the West's alleged misrepresentation of his views. And frequently a simple pronouncement that [a] certain position is 'unacceptable' to the West is offered as a self-sufficient response to whatever has been presented in defense of that position. As Mahathir observes bitterly:

> To this and many other questions I asked, I did not get a response. All I received was a public admonition. Although what I said about Europe might be true, came the rebuttal, it was 'unacceptable,' I repeat 'unacceptable.' It was not 'unwise' nor 'injudicious,' but 'unacceptable' that I should have publicly mentioned some of the ills found in Europe. (1995)

The frustration revealed in complaints such as this indicates that the approach of refusing to take the opponent's arguments seriously could be quite effective in thwarting non-Western interlocutors' instrumental employment of Western terms. And if Mahathir was indeed the hardened anti-Western crusader or the recalcitrant detractor of universally valid ideals and values he has been widely perceived to be, it is not unreasonable for Western opinion makers to disqualify him as a legitimate interlocutor. 'By listening to someone' in argumentation, as Perelman and Olbrechts-Tyteca point out, 'we display a willingness to eventually accept his point of view' (17). When one side of a dispute is *sure* that the other side is merely trying, by sophistic or casuistic means, either to call into question those 'core values' which are not subject to reconsideration or to undermine one's fundamental interests, then categorically denouncing, rather than carefully reasoning with, the other party may be the sensible thing to do. The problem with this approach is that in our post–Cold War age, we no longer enjoy the kind of communicative security that a clear-cut dichotomization of the world into two hostile camps only can offer. It is no longer easy to tell with certainty an international foe, with whom one has an irreconcilable conflict of vital interests that warrants a refusal to listen, from a legitimate cross-cultural critic/dissenter who is entitled to a reasoned response to whatever issue he has raised.[8] Unless the West makes no attempt to talk to the non-Western world and to try to *persuade* it to accept Western values and institutions by argumentative means in the first place, there are really no compelling reasons for refusing to give the latter's self-justification a fair hearing and, if it is found specious, a reasoned refutation. The refusal to engage cacophonous dissenting voices, ironically, violates a central component of the very democratic value the West is seeking to promote throughout the world. And worst of all, it would amount to giving up the West's leadership in forging a global civil community or international public sphere.

That these are the kind of costs the West cannot afford to pay has led to the promotion of a second approach in dealing with the problems in question. Advocated and practiced in particular by those who have acquired intimate knowledge of non-Western discourses through intensive personal interactions with them and are hence in a unique position to look at the on-going cross-cultural controversies from both points of view, this approach seeks to justify *Western* positions in *non-Western* terms and thus to meet their opponents' subversive effort with a reversal of the very same course of action. The strategy of 'counter-domestication' takes as its point of departure three assumptions: that 'culture—and with it, definitions of humanity—are hardly static or monolithic within any given society' (Alford, 1992, p. 69), that cross-cultural arguments should be addressed primarily to a cross-cultural, rather than a domestic, audience, and that a non-Western audience can be won over by persuasive means only when the arguments are formulated in terms of the audience's own cultural tradition. Taking advantage of the internal diversity of non-Western cultural traditions, practitioners of this approach endeavor to validate Western positions not by insisting that they embody 'universal' or 'international' standards whose validity is self-evident, but by establishing an association between these positions and certain values and interests with which the targeted non-Western audience has been known to identify. And in order for this approach to work, they also strive to establish their credibility with the targeted audience by, among other means, avoiding ideologically distorted representation and assessment of non-Western arguments and conditions.

The basic principles of this approach were laid down early in the post–Cold War East-West debates by human rights scholars such as William P. Alford. A Harvard specialist in Chinese and East Asian law, Alford cautions that '[appeals] to adopt international standards for their own sake or because their advocates believe that these standards enhance individual freedom as an end in itself are less likely to be successful' in promoting human rights in China than those that 'seek to build on and take account of Chinese circumstances' or those that 'endeavor to portray the instrumental value of human rights in the process of building the state, and thereby securing the collective good [of the Chinese themselves].' This is because the Universal Declaration of Human Rights (UDHR) and the other major international human rights documents, 'after all, were drafted predominantly by Western men having little direct interest in or experience with' the type of social problems 'confronting nations such as China.' Although 'purists might recoil,' Alford insists that 'the more that one can show the relationship between those features of foreign societies that are most desired by the Chinese' and fundamental human rights, 'the more likely it is that one will generate support for such rights' (1992, pp. 74–75).

This perspective has since gained support among Western participants in the global debates[9] and has been more systematically expounded by other scholars with a similar background. Notable among its proponents is Daniel A. Bell, a political philosopher with extensive teaching experiences in Singapore and Hong Kong. Bell's 'strategic considerations' have led him to see that if the 'ultimate aim of human rights diplomacy' is 'to persuade others of the value' of the rights, it is 'more likely that the struggle . . . can be won' only if 'it is fought in ways that build on, rather than challenge, local cultural traditions.' The standard approach adopted by most Western human rights champions, which tends to 'deny the possibility that human rights norms and practices are compatible with Asian traditions,' is for him self-defeating. By assuming that 'human rights is a distinctive invention of the West,' practitioners of that approach 'unwittingly [play] into the hands of nasty forces in East Asia who seek to stigmatize human rights voices as "agents of foreign devils" and defamers of indigenous traditions.' And their insistence that the UDHR be *the* framework and the ultimate authority for discussions on human rights issues is counterproductive for the simple reason that since the document was 'formulated without significant input from East Asia,' 'it is not always clear to East Asians why [the Declaration] should constitute "our" human rights norms,' and it hence 'does not have the normative force and political relevance . . . that emerges from genuine dialogue between interested parties keen on finding a long term solution to a shared political dilemma' (1997, pp. 651–656). There are, on the other hands, compelling reasons for the West to strive to present its case in non-Western terms: building human rights practices 'on traditional [East-Asian] cultural resources is more likely to lead to *long term* commitment to human rights ideas and practices'; paying attention to 'local traditions' may help identify 'the *groups* most likely to bring about desirable social and political change' within East-Asian societies; a heightened 'awareness of cultural traditions' would allow the human rights activists 'to draw on the most compelling [local] *justifications* for human rights practices,' and may 'shed light on the appropriate *attitude* to be employed by human rights activists' regardless of 'the substance or the moral justification for one's arguments'; etc. (1997, pp. 657–660).

The 'traditional cultural resources' and 'local traditions' Bell talks about can be invoked to justify the Western position on human rights because, just like their Western counterparts, they are far from monolithic and homogeneous. As Amartya Sen, a Nobel laureate–cum–human rights activist, points out, 'insofar as we do find arguments championing freedoms in some generic sense in ancient Greek treatises, . . . it is not hard to discover comparable championing of generically described freedoms and tolerance in the writings of many Asian theorists, such as Ashoka, whose inscriptions from the third century B.C. emphasize tolerance and liberty as central values of a good society.' Historically, 'the rhetoric of freedom is abundantly invoked in many of the Asian literatures.' And 'nearer our times, acknowledgment would have to be made to the contributions of national leaders such as Mahatma Gandhi or Dr. Sun Yat-sen' who were 'cogently vocal in defense of the widest forms of democracy and political and civil rights.' It is therefore both necessary and possible, Sen concludes, to stop '[seeing] the conflict over human rights as a battle between Western liberalism on one side and Asian reluctance on the other,' and to recast the debate rather as a battle in which 'the primary parties are Asians of different interests and convictions'—a battle that is 'really about the lives of Asians': 'their beliefs and traditions, their rules and regulations, their achievements and failures, and ultimately their lives and freedoms' (1996).

In calling thus for an 'Asianization' of the controversies over freedom, democracy, etc. in Asia, Sen is of course not urging the Western interlocutors to disengage themselves from the cross-communal ideological/rhetorical 'battle.' Rather, he is merely suggesting that the Western side change its tactics and strive to represent the issues concerned as internal conflicts among 'Asians of different interests and convictions.' For him, as for Bell, Alford, and many others, the 'universal and Western justifications for human rights do not seem particularly promising *from a tactical point of view*,' and '*strategic considerations of political relevance* speak strongly in favor of local justifications for the values and practices that, in the Western world, are normally realized through a human rights regime' (Bell, 1997, pp. 656/660, emphasis added). These candid comments on the instrumental intent of the proposed new course of action help project the second approach as an almost perfect mirror image of the non-Western interlocutors' basic strategy.

JUSTIFICATION IN THE OPPONENT'S TERMS

Juxtapose these two symmetrically reversed approaches, and a peculiar mode of cross-cultural argumentation emerges. Rather than trying in vain to meet in a *neutral* 'battleground' for a *direct* argumentative confrontation before a *common* audience, the two opposing parties in this paradigm would each venture into the other's 'territory' and seek to win the 'battle' by provoking a 'civil war' behind the opponent's line. In other words, the two contending sides would each try to justify its position in the other party's terms, and to turn the inter-communal issue that divides them into an intra-communal conflict between two factions of the opponent's side. The mutual 'infiltration,' appropriation, and persuasion such a mode entails allow cross-cultural interlocutors to bypass the necessary lack of a substantive common ground that would otherwise prevent them from engaging each other. They prevent them from bogging down in a deadlock over whose justificatory system to apply. They, moreover, guarantee that arguments framed in two radically different 'languages' are not just intelligible, but meaningful and persuasive, to their respectively targeted audiences.

The intimate mutuality this special mode of argumentation (henceforth referred to as 'cross-arguing') calls for has a real potential of gradually narrowing down the seemingly unbridgeable cultural gulf between the communities in conflict. When one party invokes and plays up certain aspects of the other party's 'local traditions' in an effort to argue against other aspects of the same 'traditions,' or allies itself with certain 'groups' within the other party's society in order to refute other groups inside the same society, it is, in a way, intervening in the other side's 'domestic affairs.' And their active participation in each other's internal processes is almost certain to contribute to the blurring of the line between Self and Other, inside and outside, internal and external, us and them. Any successful intervention of this kind would also lead to a reconfiguration of the internal forces and interests constitutive of the addressee's domestic cultural formation in response to, or in reaction against, the interests and desires that inform the addresser's arguments, causing the formation to become a little more other-oriented or a little less self-contained each time such a reconfiguration occurs. And the desire to compete and win in such a game will also give both parties much incentive to engage in what Geert-Lueke Lueken calls 'anticipatory practice,' that is, 'a kind of mutual field research' performed by the participants in an 'inter-paradigmatic controversy' to 'understand the alien [system] by participation' or to 'create a new one commonly' (1991, p. 249).[10] In cross-arguing, we have thus a promising mechanism for promoting a rational-critical dialogue between heterogeneous formations and, more importantly, for gradually bringing about a civil society that is truly global in scope.

Serious theoretical and practical difficulties remain to be overcome, however, before the discovery of a magic formula for effecting genuine argumentation across boundaries can be announced. One key issue concerns the jurisdiction of the two different intra-cultural sets of norms involved. When a cross-arguer ventures into a foreign realm of rhetoric in an effort to justify his own side's position in the 'alien' terms, which set should he abide by: that of his own side, which is constitutive of his identity as an arguer, or that associated with the 'alien terms' he is using? If the two sets differ considerably, consistently applying the cross-arguer's domestic norms would amount to exercising a kind of rhetorical extraterritoriality that is bound to antagonize the targeted audience and doom the persuasive efforts, whereas to switch codes according to what terms are being invoked is to risk losing one's identity and appearing inconsistent or even unethical by the standard of one's own community. Closely related to this issue is the problem of how to treat a cross-arguing 'alien' in a community. Must his 'alienness' be bracketed off and he be treated as an in-group member as long as he speaks in 'our' language? Or must he continue to be looked upon as a member of the 'other' community and to be dealt with as such? What importance one side should be allowed to attach to the identity of a cross-arguer in its interpretation of, and response to, the arguments he has advanced? Equally problematic is the distribution of the responsibility to persuade between the two parties. Within an intra-cultural framework, what is a presumptive standpoint and where the burden of justification falls do not usually cause controversies. The prevailing assumptions of a community always offer a sense of the normative in reference to which the presumption and the burden of justification in a case of conflict are determined. In the absence of a single, unified community, and especially with the two sides arguing in each other's terms, it is no longer simple to decide when or under what circumstances one side could claim a presumptive status for a point and expect the other side to explain and justify whatever disagreement it might have with that point. And then there is the problem of what action is expected of the participants as a result of the argument. In intra-cultural argumentation, a 'failed defense' of a standpoint should result in its retraction whereas a 'conclusive defense' should lead to the removal of any doubt about its validity (van Eemeren and Grootendorst et al., 1996, p. 284). Working within the same framework and facing the same audience who are in a position to judge and adjudicate makes it easy to determine the outcome of the debate and to expect a change in attitude or behavior of the losing side accordingly. In cross-arguing, however, the validity of a position usually remains intact domestically even after a failed defense of the position in the alien terms of the 'other' audience. Whether a failed attempt by one side to cross-address the other ought to result in the retraction of the standpoint being advocated is, therefore, very much in doubt.

Difficulties such as these direct our attention to a simple fact about cross-cultural argumentation: before the technique of cross-arguing could allow genuine critical dialogues to take place between incompatible communities, a 'code of conduct' that sets 'the rules of a dialectical procedure' (van Eemeren and Grootendorst et al., 1996, p. 283) would still have to be defined, consented to, and observed by the participants. The importance of a shared set of procedural rules and ethical principles to the goal of a productive and consequential cross-cultural interaction has been widely acknowledged. No one, however, seems to be just as aware that cross-cultural argumentation is amenable only to rules drawn in reference to its peculiar circumstances, mode of interaction and functions, and that whatever shape the code eventually takes, it is bound to differ considerably from any available domestic code of conduct, even though it must necessarily build on the latter also. For such rules to be able to guide the cross-arguers through a complicated process of interaction, their framers would have to confront the kind of special difficulties mentioned above and, more importantly, to address the dilemma underlying these difficulties, caused jointly by the co-presence of two independent justificatory systems, the absence of a final 'court of appeal,' and the imperative to prevent cross-arguing from degenerating into a non-consequential 'doubletalk.'

One possible way out of this predicament may be to focus on what defines cross-arguing as a unique mode of argumentation, namely, the symmetrical mutuality of its operation. This essential feature decides that cross-cultural argumentation, to be at all possible, should always be a 'bi-active' practice, and a clear-cut division of labor between an active persuader (speaker, protagonist, etc.) and a reactive/passive persuadee (audience, antagonist, etc.) that serves so well in structuring intra-cultural argumentation does not apply in its organization. Following this line of thinking, we may want to stipulate, for example, that a standpoint must be retracted only when the party that advances it fails to justify it in the other party's terms *and* the other party succeeds in de-justifying it in the first party's terms. Implicit in this stipulation is the understanding that the first party can claim victory only when it succeeds *both* in justifying the standpoint in the second party's terms *and* in withstanding the second party's deconstructive attack on the standpoint in the first party's own terms, whereas the second party's claim of victory must rest on its success *both* in frustrating the first party's cross-arguing attempt *and* in undermining the validity of the standpoint in the first party's own terms. Such an understanding, and the fact that a cross-cultural controversy is necessarily a mixed dispute involving 'mutual denial of the opposing standpoints' (van Eemeren and Grootendorst, 1992, p. 17), may also lead to the decision that argumentative responsibility should always be evenly split between cross-arguers. Since in cross-arguing, each party 'intrudes' into the other's terministic 'territory' and defends its own against the other's 'counter-intrusion' at the same time, both play the same double role as a protagonist/antagonist and should bear the same burden of justification.

Mutuality as a technical/operational principle, however, may not be transplanted to all aspects of the needed code. How it can apply to the determination of the originative issue or of implied premises, for instance, is far from clear. And for all their symmetrical elegance, whether the above-proposed rules are acceptable still hinges on how they succeed in mediating among the conflicting interests, norms, assumptions and traditions involved.[11] Unpacking the configurations of these incompatible interests and identifying all the conceptual, ethical, ideological and political issues existing among them become therefore the necessary first step toward codifying cross-communal interactions. Many of these issues may require for their solution a larger framework than argumentation studies currently provides. Yet by taking up the challenge to identify, analyze and clarify these issues, to initiate and organize a discussion on their solution among concerned parties, and to offer a solid theoretical basis for an informed consent on a normative code of conduct or model of practice for arguing across communal boundaries, theorists of argumentation will be able to make crucial contributions to the eventual formation of a global civil society, and in the process of doing so, to reinvent their own discipline as well.

NOTES

[1] In none of his speeches addressed to an international audience, for example, has Mahathir appealed to any Islamic doctrine or Asian cultural imperative as the ultimate warrant or backing for his position. Typical of his discourse is rather the approach he adopted in his keynote address to the 1997 IMF–World Bank Hong Kong Convention, where he pleaded for the need to regulate international currency trading. Countering the principle of free market which his opponents have invoked to support their opposition to any regulatory efforts, Mahathir draws an analogy with three milestones in the development of modern capitalist market economy in the U.S.: the anti-trust legislation that outlawed monopolies, the legislation to prevent anyone from 'acquiring controlling interest in companies and then stripping their assets' at the expense of other shareholders, and the legislation that outlawed 'insider trading.' If even the U.S. has in fact always subjected its own market to strict regulations so as to prevent small investors from being victimized by big wheelers and dealers, he asks, why should the *international community* not find a way to prevent similar victimization of small financial entities or players in a globalized market? (1997)

[2] Not much serious journalistic or scholarly attention has been paid to unsavory non-Western speakers such as Mahathir or Lee Kuan Yew. In Western mass media, their views, especially the justification they offer for those views, are either not reported at all, ridiculed as 'foolish remarks' (*L.A. Times*/2 November 1997/High Anxiety Stocks: Asian Markets Are Only an Excuse/By Charles R. Morris), or dismissed casually as 'a ploy to defend authoritarian systems of government and abuses of power against individuals and minorities' (*The International Herald Tribune*/July 30, 1997/ Asian Nations Rally Against U.S. Over Rights/By Michael Richardson).

[3] See the *Journal of Democracy* 8.2 (1997) for a sample of arguments from the Western point of view against what has been presented by Kausikan (1997) et al. as the 'Asian perspective' on democracy.

4 From the normative Western point of view, as human rights activist/scholar Abdullahi Ahmed An-Na'im observes, the validity of the current human rights standards would remain less than universal unless it was re-affirmed 'through cross-cultural dialogue.' The process of cross-culturally legitimating these standards 'must be . . . mutual between cultures.' Those 'of one cultural tradition who wish to induce a change in attitudes within another culture must be open to a corresponding inducement in relation to their own attitudes' and must be prepared to accept 'revisions and/or reformulations of the existing international standards' (1992, p. 5). In reality, few Western interlocutors if any would accept negotiability of the criteria in question as a point of departure for whatever 'dialogue' they wish to enter with their non-Western counterparts.

5 Mahathir again provides a telling illustration here. Responding to Western criticism of the restrictions his government has placed on the international press in his 'Speech given at the Plenary of the 48th Session of the UN General Assembly, Oct. 1, 1993,' the Malaysian leader enlists support for his government's policy from both sophisticated Western cultural criticism of the information industry ('We live in the Information Age. What we see and hear and witness . . . is what the media decide we should see and hear and witness'; 'the people who decide what we should see and hear hold terrible power,' those who 'control the media control our minds, and probably control the world') and enduring Western political commonplaces ('Malaysia believes in press freedom,' which, 'as with other freedoms and rights, must be accompanied by responsibility . . . power without responsibility is the most corrupting influence of all').

6 The strategic calculation is reflected in the following comment from Kevin Y. L. Tan's discussion on 'What Asians Think about the West's Response to the Human Rights Debate':

> Most Asian scholars are very keen on the 'Asian values' debate because it is an opportunity to take on the West in an intellectual exchange where the West does not have a clear and distinct advantage. One noted Japanese academic . . . told me he was tired of the West setting the rules and that it's time to give them 'a taste of their own medicine,' . . . even though he did not agree with the 'Asian viewpoint.' He was also proud of the fact that an Asian like Lee Kuan Yew could stand up to the West and 'give it to them.' [*Human Rights Dialogue* 4 (March 1996), online].

7 Singapore PM Goh Chok Tong had invited William Safire 'to debate with him and to educate Singaporeans on the evils of their government,' but 'Mr. Safire had declined the invitation.' See Chan Heng Chee's 'letter to the editor,' on-line edition, *The New York Times,* Oct. 24, 1996.

8 Those who insist on the clarity of such a distinction are usually the same people who prefer to deal with whatever global issues from a position of strength and are impatient with the notion of international legitimation. The preference often results in an outright rejection of argument as a means of international conflict resolution. Conservative American columnist Charles Krauthammer, for example, openly dismisses the concept of 'international community' as 'vacuous,' 'fictional,' 'an illusion.' 'We have no *international community,*' he maintains, because 'community implies a commonality of interest' whereas '[different] nations have different, often conflicting, interests' and '[what] overlap there is tends to be narrow and temporary.' His conclusion: 'Sooner or later, we will have to dispense with multilateral fictions. . . . We don't care who is with us and who is not. We welcome all. We require none. We are going to act. . . . And if the Chinese or the Russians or the French don't like it, too bad. End of argument' ('What "International community"?'/*Washington Post,* December 26, 1997, A29).

9 The growing popularity of this approach is reflected in Western political and moral leaders' endorsement and practice of its basic tenets. In the addresses made during his June 1998 visit to China, for example, U.S. President Clinton went out of his way to cite Chinese sources in support of his advocacy of human rights and democracy in China. By appealing to authorities from the ancient Chinese classic *The Book of Rites* to Deng Xiaoping, he made the point that what he tried to promote was in line with the best of traditional Chinese thought rather than a mere Western imposition (*Washington Post* June 26, 1998, A23; June 29, 1998, A12). Similarly, in an interview given shortly after she became the U.N. Human Rights High Commissioner, Mary Robinson promised that she would try to bring about an 'open debate about Western and Eastern values.' For her, '[we're] not going to make real progress for women in Afghanistan unless we can do it within their culture' (Crossette, 1997).

[10] Lueken, however, sees in 'anticipatory practice' a means to achieving, as an end in itself, a non-strategic 'mutual understanding' between incommensurate 'systems of orientation.' For him, to participate in the 'anticipatory practice' is to engage in 'an open exchange released from the pressure of reasoning, rules, validity questions' (1991, p. 249), or from everything argumentation, in the proper sense of the term, is about. An instrumentally motivated 'mutual field study' is an anathema to his perspective.

[11] That for the cross-cultural code of conduct to be truly binding, its formulation would have to pay 'maximum attention to the interests at issue' (Perelman and Olbrechts-Tyteca, 1969, p. 60) is vividly demonstrated in the U.S.'s decision to stay out of the first international criminal court, to be set up on the basis of an agreement reached in July 1998 by all but a handful of countries. While admitting that a 'general emphasis [by the U.S.] on the immunity of one's own soldiers would carve out the heart' of such a court, whose 'establishment had been an American goal for decades,' the mainstream American public opinions nevertheless endorsed the Clinton administration's decision as being 'consistent with American interests' ('A Court Without the U.S.'/*Washington Post,* July 21, 1998; Page A18).

REFERENCES

Alford, William P.: 1992, 'Making a Goddess of Democracy from Loose Sands: Thoughts on Human Rights in the People's Republic of China', in Abdullahi A. An-Na'im (ed.), *Human Rights in Cross-Cultural Perspectives: A Quest for Consensus,* University of Pennsylvania Press, Philadelphia, pp. 65–80.

An-Na'im, Abdullahi Ahmed (ed.): 1992, *Human Rights in Cross-Cultural Perspectives: A Quest for Consensus,* University of Pennsylvania Press, Philadelphia.

Balslev, Anindita Niyogi: 1991, *Cultural Otherness: Correspondence with Richard Rorty,* Indian Institute of Advanced Study, Shimla.

Beer, Francis A. and Robert Hariman (eds.): 1996, *Post-Realism: The Rhetorical Turn in International Relations,* Michigan State University Press, East Lansing.

Bell, Daniel A.: 1977, 'The East Asian Challenge to Human Rights: Reflections on an East-West Dialogue', *Human Rights Quarterly* 18(3), 641–667.

Bernstein, Richard J.: 1991, 'Incommensurability and Otherness Revisited', in *Culture and Modernity: East-West Philosophic Perspectives,* University of Hawaii Press, Honolulu, pp. 85–103.

Collier, David and Steven Levitsky: 1997, 'Democracy with Adjectives: Conceptual Innovation in Comparative Research', *World Politics* 49(3), 430–451.

Crossette, Barbara: 1997, 'Mary Robinson: New U.N. Voice Stresses Balance in Approaching Human Rights', *The New York Times,* Internet Edition, October 6, 1997.

Davidson, Donald: 1973–1974, 'On the Very Idea of a Conceptual Scheme', *Proceedings and Addresses of the American Philosophical Association* 47, 5–20.

DePalma, Anthony: 1998, 'U.S. Gets Cold Shoulder at a Culture Conference', *International Herald Tribune* (Internet Edition), Thursday, July 2, 1998.

Dews, Peter: 1986/1992, 'Editor's Introduction', in Jürgen Habermas, *Autonomy and Solidarity,* Verso, London, pp. 1–32.

Eemeren, Frans H. van and Rob Grootendorst et al.: 1996, *Fundamentals of Argumentation Theory,* Lawrence Erlbaum Associates, Mahwah.

Eemeren, Frans H. van and Rob Grootendorst: 1992, *Argumentation, Communication, and Fallacies,* Lawrence Erlbaum Associates, Mahwah.

Geertz, Clifford: 1995, *After the Fact,* Harvard University Press, Cambridge.

Huntington, Samuel P.: 1998, 'Democracy is Nice, But Not for Everyone', *The Pittsburgh Post-Gazette* June 28, 1998, C1.

Kausikan, Bilahari: 1997, 'Government that Works', *Journal of Democracy* 8(2), 24–34.

Lueken, Geert-Lueke: 1990, 'Incommensurability, Rules of Argumentation, and Anticipation', in Frans H. van Eemeren et al. (eds.), *Proceedings of the Second International Conference on Argumentation,* pp. 244–252.

Lyotard, Jean-François: 1988, *The Differend: Phrases in Dispute,* University of Minnesota Press, Minneapolis.

Mahathir, Mohamad: 1997, 'Asian Economies: Challenges and Opportunities' (A Speech Given on September 20, 1997 at the Hong Kong Convention of the World Bank), available on-line at http://www.smpke.jpm.my/pm3.htm. Other speeches of his referred to in this paper are available at the same web site.

Perelman, Ch. and L. Olbrechts-Tyteca: 1969, *The New Rhetoric: A Treatise on Argumentation,* University of Notre Dame Press, Notre Dame.

Quine, W. V.: 1960, *Word and Object,* M.I.T. Press, Cambridge.

Roach, Colleen: 1997, 'The Western World and the NWICO: United They Stand?', in Peter Golding and Phil Harris (eds.), *Beyond Cultural Imperialism: Globalization. Communication, and the New International Order,* Sage Publications, London, pp. 94–116.

Rorty, Richard: 1989, *Contingency, Irony, and Solidarity,* Cambridge University Press, Cambridge.

Schlesinger, Stephen: 1997, 'Moving to One-World Society', *The Los Angeles Times* (Internet Edition) Monday, October 27, 1997.

Sen, Amartya: 1996, 'Thinking about Human Rights and Asian Values', *Human Rights Dialogue* 4, On-line, Carnegie Council on Ethics and International Affairs.

Sreberny-Mohammadi, Annabelle: 1996, 'Introduction', in Sandra Braman and Annabelle Sreberny-Mohammadi (eds.), *Globalization, Communication, and Transnational Civil Society,* Hampton Press, Cresskill, pp. 1–19.

Argument Quality and Cultural Difference[1]

HARVEY SIEGEL

I. ARGUMENT QUALITY AS IMPERSONALLY AND TRANSCULTURALLY CONCEIVED

Central to argumentation theory is the matter of the normative evaluation of argument quality: that is, of argument *normativity.* Argumentation theorists are concerned, among other things, with explaining why some arguments are good, or at least better than others, in the sense that they provide reasons for embracing their conclusions which are such that a fair-minded appraisal of the arguments yields the judgment that those conclusions ought to be accepted—are worthy of acceptance—by all who so appraise them.

Such goodness is an *epistemic* matter. Argument normativity is a variety of epistemic normativity, in that what makes an argument good is that its premises provide reasons for accepting its conclusion. That is, the conclusion ought to be accepted, on the basis of the support provided that conclusion by those premises: the premises justify the conclusion, rendering it worthy of belief.[2]

The feature of this view of argument normativity which is of concern in what follows is its impersonal and transcultural character. The quality of a given argument is impersonal, on this view, in the sense that its normative status is independent of the person(s) evaluating that status.[3] This is not to say that the argument could be evaluated without a person to conduct the evaluation (although some arguments can be successfully evaluated by machine). It is to say, rather, that the quality of the argument is a feature of the argument itself, rather than of the person(s) assessing its quality. Moreover, the quality of an argument is transcultural in the sense that its normative status is independent of the cultural locations and perspectives of its evaluators. It is the character of such impersonal and transcultural evaluation, such that the quality of an argument is as it would appear to a hypothetical 'fair-minded' evaluator—rather than as it actually appears to actual, flesh and blood evaluators, with their own cultural locations and perspectives—that will occupy us in what follows.

2. ARGUMENT QUALITY AS CULTURALLY CONTEXTUALIZED: PRELIMINARY CONSIDERATIONS

This impersonal, transcultural conception of argument normativity makes no reference either to the attributes of the persons appraising the argument and judging its normative force, or to the characteristics of the culture(s) to which such persons belong or the cultural context in which the appraisal occurs. The premises of the argument provide whatever support for its conclusion that they do—from no support whatsoever in the case of a really bad argument, to extremely strong support in the case of a really good argument, with every degree of support in between for arguments of every degree of quality—whoever is conducting the evaluation, in whatever cultural context.

But recent work by a wide range of philosophers, argumentation theorists, and social theorists rejects such an abstract, de-contextualized notion of argument goodness. Instead, these theorists insist upon taking seriously, in the evaluation of arguments, the features and perspectives—and in particular, the cultural locations—of the evaluators. That is, such theorists emphasize the importance of *cultural differences* in argument appraisal. Often locating themselves under the banner of multiculturalism, they argue that the quality of an argument depends upon culturally-specific beliefs, values, and presuppositions. Consequently, they contend, no a-contextual,[4] culture-independent characterization of argumentative goodness can succeed.

A considerable range of writers advocate the view that judgments concerning the goodness or normative force of reasons and arguments (and cultural ideals and values more generally) are inevitably, and perhaps necessarily, culture-specific. Alasdair MacIntyre's celebrated *Whose Justice? Which Rationality?* (1988) announces in its very title the doctrine that rationality—and so the probative force of reasons, and so argument quality—is in some sense relative to cultural/historical tradition, and is in that sense neither impersonal nor transcultural. MacIntyre writes that all rational activity is "inescapably historically and socially context-bound" (1988, p. 4); elsewhere he suggests that one "cannot find . . . any genuinely neutral and independent standard of rational justification" (1989, p. 198)—and so, presumably, any context—or tradition-independent standard of argument quality.[5] Jean-Francois Lyotard is said to champion "the irreducibly local character of all discourse, argumentation, and legitimation" (Baynes, Bohman and McCarthy, 1987, p. 70); he holds, clearly enough, that what counts as knowledge and as justification is itself relative to local, cultural context, and he rejects any sort of transcultural 'metanarrative' that sets out standards of argument quality as 'terroristic.' (Lyotard, 1987) More generally, those thinkers generally classified as 'postmodernists' are typically regarded as holding that "rationality is always relative to time and place," implying that argument quality is similarly relative.[6]

Perhaps the most visible writer in that somewhat vague classification is Richard Rorty, who also rejects the possibility of personally- or culturally-transcendent evaluation of arguments, and of cultures more generally.[7] His favored version of pragmatism famously rejects the search for "an Archimedean point from which to survey culture" (1982, p. 150), in favor of a frank embrace of ethnocentricity or 'solidarity,' according to which there is no non-circular or non-question-begging way to justify our own ideals, values and commitments to those who reject them in favor of their own, equally ethnocentric alternatives: "We pragmatists . . . should say that we must, in practice, privilege our own group, even though there can be no noncircular justification for doing so" (Rorty (1989), p. 44)—including, presumably, our own group's judgments and standards of argument goodness. David Theo Goldberg helpfully summarizes and develops Rorty's view as follows:

> The traditional historical commitment of philosophical liberalism to universal principles of reason and (moral) value presupposes universal ideas like intrinsic humanity, human dignity, and human rights—values, that is, that are thought to mark individuals in virtue of their very humanity. As Rorty insists, there is no transhistorical or supersocial Godly view on which such universal (moral) principles can be grounded or from which they can be derived. Axiological concepts and values are necessarily those of some historically specific community. . . . Thus, any insistence on the universalism of values must be no more than the projected imposition of local values—those especially of some ethnoracial and gendered particularity—universalized. (1994, pp. 17–18)

As Goldberg here suggests, Rorty's ethnocentrism rejects the possibility of 'universal principles of reason' in accordance with which arguments can be impersonally evaluated. While Rorty's denial of the possibility of impersonal, transcultural beliefs, values and ideals is in the first instance directed to moral values and principles rather than to principles of 'reason' or of argument evaluation, it is readily extended there, as Goldberg suggests:

> Axiological relativism is bound to deny neither some basic formal principles of thinking—call them universal, if necessary—nor generalizable value judgments concerning especially pernicious social conditions and practices. So, owning up to formal principles of logical relation implies nothing about the assertive content of thought. . . . Logical formalism enables only that inconsistent and incoherent claims for the most part can be ruled out; it is thoroughly incapable of assertively promoting some coherent or consistent standard over another. (16–17)

So, on the Rorty/Goldberg view, there may be universal 'formal principles' both of 'thinking' and of 'logical relation,' but these will be insufficient to determine the quality of 'the assertive content of thought.' With respect to the quality of thought—and, in particular, the quality of particular arguments—such determinations of argumentative quality cannot be other than the judgments of 'some historically specific community,' which may well differ from the judgments of argumentative quality of other specific communities. How good is a given argument, then? It appears that the Rorty/Goldberg answer to this question can only be: it depends on the cultural identities and commitments of its evaluators, and the cultural circumstances in which the evaluation takes place. But appearances here may be deceiving.

As Rorty and Goldberg both acknowledge, their view suggests a problematic form of epistemological relativism. Rorty explicitly rejects relativism, although it remains unclear whether he is nonetheless committed to it.[8] Goldberg defends 'a more robustly nuanced,' 'multicultural' relativism, as the following two passages indicate:

> If the truth is relative simplistically to the group proclaiming it, then all claims to truth, no matter how much they lack substantiation, are on an equal footing. Pat Lauderdale has noted recently that the critique of "objectivity"

as veiling the imputation of Eurocentric value has buried justifiable concerns about accuracy. A more robust and more robustly nuanced conception of relativism underpinning the multicultural project will enable distinctions to be drawn between more or less accurate truth claims and more or less justifiable values (in contrast to claims to *the* truth or *the* good). (1994, p. 15, emphases in original)

Here Goldberg seems clearly to reject epistemological relativism—at least the 'simplistic' form of it according to which 'the truth is relative simplistically to the group proclaiming it'—in favor of an epistemology that explicitly and legitimately distinguishes 'between more or less accurate truth claims and more or less justifiable values.' There is nothing here that the epistemological 'absolutist' need reject. His version of relativism is spelled out further as follows:

... the relativism upon which a sophisticated form of critical multiculturalism rests is not restricted to value particularism. Multicultural relativism is ready and able to fashion general judgments, that is, revisable inductive generalizations as the specificity of (particular) circumstances and relations warrant. These circumstances and relations will include often, though not necessarily always, racial, class, and gendered articulation. Thus multiculturalists are able to condemn a specific form of racism, say, apartheid, in terms of a general judgment that racist exclusions are unacceptable because they are unwarranted in a specifiable scheme of social value to which we do or should adhere for specifiable (and, perhaps, generalizable) reasons. But there is no transcendental proof or grounds, no universal foundation, for this scheme or any other. (1994, p. 19)

Here again what Goldberg calls 'multicultural relativism' seems not particularly relativistic: it accepts that general judgments, e.g. that 'racist exclusions are unacceptable,' can be warranted within 'a specifiable scheme of social value to which we do *or should* adhere for specifiable (and, perhaps, generalizable) reasons.' (emphasis added) The 'scheme of social value' is one to which we should adhere for specifiable reasons, even if we (or some of us) do not in fact so adhere: we would be wrong not to adhere to it, given the reasons which can be offered for it. This seems not only not relativistic, but the very definition of 'absolutism.' (Siegel, 1987, 1999)

Why, then, given his willingness to distinguish between more or less 'accurate' (15) or warranted claims, does Goldberg consider his view to be a 'relativistic' one? I can only speculate here, but there is considerable textual support for the hypothesis that Goldberg regards his view as relativist because he rejects all claims to "*the* truth" and "*the* good" (15), and to "transcendental proof or grounds," and to "universal foundation[s]," for any particular scheme. (19) That is, it appears that Goldberg is concerned mainly to reject foundationalism, certainty, necessity, and transhistorical and supersocial Godly perspectives from which claims to the truth or the good might be made, and to embrace a thoroughgoing epistemological fallibilism. With all this the non-relativist can happily concur. Whether or not this hypothesis is correct, the important point for present purposes is that Goldberg's 'robustly nuanced multicultural relativism' appears not in the end to hold that argument quality is relative to culture; it holds, rather, that some cultural beliefs, values and practices can be legitimately criticized on the basis of reasons which, while neither necessary nor certain, are nevertheless good ones which we should acknowledge as probatively telling even if we in fact do not. (Only thus are we (on Goldberg's view) within our epistemic rights to condemn racist exclusions as 'unacceptable'—i.e. as wrong—not just for us, who are already convinced of the wrongness of racism, but for everyone, including the racist who does not, but should, accept our scheme of social value on the basis of the reasons which can be offered for it and which itself provides us with reasons adequate to establish the unacceptability of such exclusions.)

If this analysis of Goldberg's view is correct, that view in the end does not, despite initial appearances, support a culturally relative view of argument quality. But I hasten to acknowledge that other passages in Goldberg's discussion do seem to recommend such a view. I consider some of those passages further below.

As is already clear, the thesis that argument goodness depends upon cultural commitments and differences raises problems which also arise in the context of discussions of epistemological relativism; in contemplating the former it will prove necessary to consider the latter as well. In what follows, then, I will discuss difficulties with the view that argument quality depends upon culture which accrue to that view in virtue of its apparent embrace of a problematic epistemological relativism; but I will consider other difficulties as well, which befall it even if it avoids relativistic ones. While I hope in what follows to acknowledge the genuine insights of a multiculturalist approach to argument quality, I will argue that that quality is not rightly understood as dependent upon cultural difference.

3. FOUR DIFFICULTIES WITH A CULTURALLY CONTEXTUAL VIEW OF ARGUMENT QUALITY

3.1. Transcendence

Central to the view that argument quality depends upon culture is the claim, embraced by the view's defenders—and, as we will see, by its critics as well—that there is no possibility of 'transcending,' no escape from, whatever specific historical/cultural[9] location argument evaluators happen to occupy. I consider next a version of the argument that defends that view by appeal to this premise.[10]

One case for a personal, culturally sensitive—rather than an impersonal, a-cultural—conception of argument quality depends upon a rejection of culturally 'transcendent' principles of argument evaluation and criteria of argument quality. According to it, all such principles and criteria, however much they are made to look universal or transcendent, are local; their status varies from locale to locale. As Goldberg puts the point: "As Rorty insists, there is no transhistorical or super-social Godly view on which such universal (moral) principles can be grounded or from which they can be derived . . . any insistence on the universalism of values must be no more than the projected imposition of local values . . . universalized." (18) If the values in question are those relating to argument quality, this claim seems to lead directly to the culturally relative conception of argument quality we are considering.

The point, it must be admitted, is widely acknowledged in contemporary discussion: one can never completely escape one's historical/cultural location, with its associated perspective, framework, or conceptual scheme, and achieve a 'God's eye view' or a 'view from nowhere' (Nagel, 1986); all cognitive activity—including, of course, the evaluation of arguments is inevitably conducted from some ongoing perspective or point of view. A typical expression of the thesis is Quine's:

The philosopher's task differs from the others', then, in detail; but in no such drastic way as those suppose who imagine for the philosopher a vantage point outside the conceptual scheme that he takes in charge. There is no such cosmic exile. He cannot study and revise the fundamental conceptual scheme of science and common sense without having some conceptual scheme, whether the same or another no less in need of philosophical scrutiny, in which to work. (1960, pp. 275–276)

Philosophers generally grant Quine's point: there is no 'cosmic exile' from all conceptual schemes; one cannot cognize except from within the confines of some scheme or other. As Goldberg puts it, there is no 'transhistorical or super-social Godly view' from which human judgments—and in particular, judgments concerning argument quality—can be made. But from the relatively uncontroversial claim that we cannot escape all perspectives and achieve a 'view from nowhere,' it seems a short step to the conclusion that principles of argument evaluation and criteria of argument quality are themselves relative to the cultural frameworks which inevitably limit our judgment; that, since there is no 'perspectiveness' judgment, there is no possibility of achieving a perspective which would allow us to judge the quality of arguments in a culturally transcendent way. That is, the uncontroversial claim that all judgments of argument quality inevitably occur in the context of some cultural location or other might be thought to entail that all such judgments are therefore bound or determined by such inescapable locations—and so that what counts as a good argument is problematically limited by cultural context in such a way, or to such an extent, that a culturally relativistic view of argument quality inevitably results.

However, it does not—or so I will argue. The alleged entailment just mentioned fails; even though we cannot attain a culturally transcendent perspective, in the relevant sense we *can* nevertheless 'transcend' such perspectives in judging argument quality. The key is to distinguish between transcending or escaping *any particular* perspective and transcending *all* such perspectives. Once this distinction is drawn, the 'no transcendence, therefore argument quality is relative to culture' argument collapses.

Consider the question first in general terms, i.e. without regard to the specific case of judgments concerning argument quality, and without restricting ourselves to cultural frameworks or perspectives. Are we limited by our perspectives, such that we cannot achieve any critical perspective on them? Are we really 'trapped' within our perspectives in this way? Common sense and every day experience indicate the contrary. Perhaps the most obvious range of counter-examples involve the cognitive activities of children. Children of a certain age, for example, can count and have a reasonable grasp of whole numbers, but have no understanding of fractions or decimals, i.e., parts of whole numbers. If asked 'is there a number between 1 and 2?,' they will answer in the negative, and will be unable to comprehend any suggestion to the contrary. But, given normal psychological/cognitive development, within a few years such children will answer affirmatively; they will have no problem recognizing that, e.g., 1.5 is a number between 1 and 2, and more generally, that there are non-whole numbers. This seems a perfectly straightforward case of the modi[fi]cation of a framework (or of the abandonment of one framework for another) which belies the claim that we are trapped in, bound by, or limited to our frameworks.[11] (Scientific examples can equally easily be given, e.g., of the recognition of the existence of things too small to see with the naked eye, or of the interanimation of space and time and of the large scale non-Euclidean geometry of the universe.)

Very different sorts of examples can also be given. Consider, for example, the 'male sexist pig' who has no awareness or understanding of women other than as (sex) objects, but who in the course of his experience comes to realize (if only dimly) that he does treat women as objects, that many women want not to be so treated, and that there might well be something objectionable about treating women in that way. Suppose that this benighted male comes eventually to a full(er) awareness of the injustice of his earlier treatment of women; he comes to believe that it is wrong to treat women as objects and, over a considerable period of time and with the help of many women (and perhaps some courses in the Women's Studies Department), he develops a radically different and more respectful view of women and (hallelujah!) treats them accordingly. (Surely many men have had their consciousnesses raised to some extent in this way in recent decades.) Here again it seems that our subject has had his perspective altered and, indeed, improved; that is, he has 'transcended' his old sexist perspective for another.

In these examples not only have perspectives altered; the cognizers considered all regard their later perspectives as improvements, i.e., as better than, superior to, their earlier ones. If asked, these cognizers will be able to offer reasons which purport to justify those judgments of superiority. Those reasons, and the judgment that they are good ones which offer justification for the superiority of those later perspectives, are of course made from the perspective of those later perspectives of frameworks; they are not outside of all frameworks or issued from a perspective-less perspective. Thus is acknowledged the uncontroversial premise of the argument under consideration. But the conclusion is undermined by the several counter-examples offered: epistemic agents always judge from some perspective or other, but there is no reason to think that they are trapped in or bound by their perspectives such that they cannot subject them to critical scrutiny. In this sense, we *can* 'transcend' our perspectives; and this sense is sufficient to defeat the general argument for the relativity of judgment to perspectives which we have been considering. As Popper puts the point:

> I do admit that at any moment we are prisoners caught in the framework of our theories; our expectations; our past experiences; our language. But we are prisoners in a Pickwickian sense: if we try, we can break out of our framework at any time. Admittedly, we shall find ourselves again in a framework, but it will be a better and roomier one; and we can at any moment break out of it again.
>
> The central point is that a critical discussion and a comparison of the various frameworks is always possible. (1970, p. 56)

Here Popper clearly draws the crucial distinction which undermines this path to relativism. While the Quinean point that there is no 'cosmic exile' from all perspectives—that we inevitably judge from some framework or other, and that we cannot judge from a perspectiveness perspective—must be granted, it does not follow that our judgments are necessarily tainted by the fact that they are made from some framework or other, or are 'good' only relative to that framework. On the contrary, we can and regularly do 'transcend' our frameworks from the perspective of other, 'roomier' ones, in which can fit both our earlier one and relevant rivals to it—and in this way fair, non-relative evaluations of both our judgments and the frameworks/perspectives from which they are made are possible.[12]

I have to this point been treating the general question of the degree to which our judgments are determined by, and therefore relative to, our conceptual schemes/frameworks/perspectives. The conclusion to which these musings have led is that, while it is clearly correct that we cannot attain or judge from a 'perspectiveless perspective,' we nevertheless not only can but regularly do attain sufficient critical leverage on our perspectives that we can criticize, evaluate, and improve them—and, consequently, that judgment is not inevitably determined by or trapped within those perspectives. This general point is directly applicable to the special case involving judgments of argument quality.[13] When we evaluate arguments, we inevitably do so from some perspective or other. In particular, we do so from the particular historical/cultural perspective in which we are embedded, with its own particular principles of argument evaluation and criteria of argument quality. Nevertheless, we are not 'trapped' within that perspective; our judgements of argument quality are not wholly determined by it. Indeed, during the long history of the development of principles of argument evaluation within Western/European culture, many such principles have been altered as theorists gained critical perspective on them. Particularly salient examples involve the impact of the development of probability theory on principles of argument evaluation and criteria of argument quality which touch upon probabilistic matters, e.g. principles and criteria relevant to what are now taken to be the gambler's fallacy, the fallacy of hasty generalization, and arguments whose cogency depends upon representative sampling.[14] The moral of the story is clear: while there is a clear sense in which judgments of argument quality are embedded in particular historical/cultural locations, that sense is not such as to challenge the impersonal and transcultural conception of argument normativity with which we began. The argument in question—we cannot transcend our historical/cultural locations, therefore argument quality depends upon the features of and is relative to those locations—founders on the failure to distinguish between 'transcending' all perspectives at once, and in doing so judging from a perspectiveless perspective, and transcending any particular perspective. The former is not possible, but the latter is not only possible but quite common. In particular, judgments of argument quality admit of this latter sort of transcendence. Consequently, this route to a culturally relative conception of argument quality does not succeed.

The argument we have been considering rests upon a failure to distinguish between transcending all perspectives, and transcending any particular one. A related argument suffers from the opposite failing: it draws a sharp, but ultimately untenable, distinction between the locatedness or particularity of principles of argument evaluation and criteria of argument quality, on the one hand, and the possibility of any 'universal' status for such principles and criteria, on the other. It moreover regards these are contraries, and consequently holds that principles and criteria relevant to argumentation, being particular, cannot also be thought to be universal. I turn to this argument next.

3.2. Universality and Particularity
Here, as we have already seen, Goldberg clearly articulates the problematic dichotomy in question: "Axiological concepts and values are necessarily those of some historically specific community. . . . Thus, any insistence on the universalism of values must be no more than the projected imposition of local values . . . universalsized." On this view, all principles and values are local and particular; any claim to universality is nothing more than "the imposition of [the] local values . . . of

some ethnoracial and gendered particularity." (18) The application of this view to principles and criteria concerning argumentation is straightforward: they too are particular, not universal; argument quality is dependent upon the particular location in which evaluation takes place. So a given argument may (for example) beg the question, and be judged to be of poor quality in a locale that takes a dim view of that particular argument form, but be judged to be of high quality in a locale in which that form is regarded with equanimity. To take a real example: any argument of the form which we now call 'the gambler's fallacy' was thought to be a good argument in the environs of the Harvard logicians of the 1870's, but is thought to be a bad argument in the rarefied atmosphere of the Emerson Hall (where the Harvard Philosophy Department is housed) of today.[15]

Let us grant that all principles of argument evaluation and criteria of argument quality are local and particular,[16] in the sense that they are inevitably articulated and endorsed in particular historical/cultural circumstances—just (as granted above) as they are inevitably endorsed from some perspective or other. Does it follow that they are therefore not universal? Two contemporary denizens of Emerson Hall suggest not. Israel Scheffler writes: "I have always supposed that the universal and the particular are compatible, that grounding in a particular historical and cultural matrix is inevitable and could not conceivably be in conflict with universal principles." (Scheffler, 1995, p. 14) Hilary Putnam, in commenting on this passage, agrees:

> When we argue about the universal applicability of principles . . . we are not claiming to stand outside of our own tradition, let alone outside of space and time, as some fear; we are standing within a tradition, and trying simultaneously to learn what in that tradition we are prepared to recommend to other traditions *and* to see what in that tradition may be inferior—inferior either to what other traditions have to offer, or to the best we may be capable of. . . .
>
> . . . [W]e are not forced to choose between scientism and skepticism [or between 'universalism' and 'particularism']. . . .The third possibility is to accept the position we are fated to occupy in any case, the position of beings who cannot have a view of the world that does not reflect our interests and values, but who are, for all that, committed to regarding some views of the world—and, for that matter, some interests and values as better than others. This may mean giving up a certain metaphysical picture of objectivity, but it does not mean giving up the idea that there are what Dewey called "objective resolutions of problematical situations"—objective resolutions to problems which are *situated* in a place, at a time, as opposed to an "absolute" answer to "perspective-independent" questions. And that is objectivity enough. (Putnam, 1990, p. 178, emphases in original)

Putnam is here discussing principles of ethics rather than of argument evaluation, and matters metaphysical as well as epistemological, but the relevance of his remarks to our topic is clear. In regarding argument quality as 'impersonal,' 'transcultural,' or 'universal,' we are not denying that our principles of argument evaluation and criteria of argument quality are local and particular, in the sense that they are *ours:* articulated and endorsed by us, in our particular historical/ cultural context. But acknowledging their particularity does not preclude us from proclaiming their universality: that is, their legitimate applicability to arguments, considered independently of their location.

In holding these principles and criteria to be 'universal' or transcultural, we need not deny their locality/particularity. Goldberg and Rorty are correct in holding that all proclamations of universal principle emanate from particular locales. It does not follow from this, though, that such values have no legitimacy or force beyond the bounds from within which they are proclaimed or embraced. The problematic move is to regard 'particularity' and 'universality' as contraries, such that a principle or criterion's being one precludes it from being the other. Elsewhere (Siegel, 1997, pp. 174–178; Siegel, 1998) I have offered both general arguments against regarding these as contraries, and a range of examples, from mathematics, science, and morality, of claims, theses, principles and criteria which are both particular and universal. I will not repeat these arguments and examples here. I will instead content myself with suggesting that, for the reasons given both here and there, this argumentative path—principles of argument evaluation and criteria of argument quality are particular and local; therefore they cannot be 'universal' or 'transcend' their locales; therefore argument quality is relative to historical/cultural location or context does not succeed.

3.3. 'Transcultural Normative Reach'

I believe that the two problems facing culturally relative conceptions of argument quality just rehearsed are formidable. The main difficulty with conceiving of argument quality in culturally relative terms, however, is that any argument for that conception must presuppose the impersonal, transcultural conception of such quality with which it contrasts. As I will call it, any such argument must presuppose 'transcultural normative reach.'[17] For any such argument will proceed from premises to a conclusion which is said by its proponents to follow from those premises. That it does so, if it does, will not be dependent on the cultural characteristics or commitments of those either advancing or contemplating the argument. The argument is taken by its proponents to provide good reasons for embracing its conclusion, reasons which should be found compelling by any person who fair-mindedly considers it. In this sense the argument's quality—the ability of its premises to justify its conclusion—is what it is, independently of the culture of either the arguer or her audience.

Such transcultural normative reach must be accepted by any advocate of a culturally relative conception of argument quality who thinks that her advocacy is not only non-arbitrary, but *rational*—warranted by the reasons offered in its support. For an advocate who rejects such reach cannot regard herself as advancing reasons which ought to persuade a fair-minded opponent, i.e., an imagined rational and open-minded person interested in determining for herself which conception of argument quality is more worthy of embrace. Neither can she regard her embrace of the culturally relative view as more rational than her opponent's embrace of its rival. But this leaves her in a troubling position: if she can't offer such reasons, why should her opponent, or anyone else, agree with her? If she regards her favored view of argument quality as in any way rationally preferable to its alternatives, she must hold that that view is supported by reasons which have forced beyond the bounds of those who happen to share her own presuppositions and commitments. In short, the rational advocacy of and commitment to the culturally relative view of argument quality presupposes the transcultural character of the normative standing of arguments (and reasons) as such.[18]

It is important to recognize that this 'transcultural normative reach,' which I am claiming must be acknowledged by all parties to the debate concerning argument quality, does not depend upon the presumption that judgments enjoying such reach must be issued from some impossibly neutral perspective. Earlier we saw that Goldberg and Rorty reject the possibility of universal principles or values—

including those concerned with argument quality—on the grounds that any such principles must stem from a 'transhistorical or supersocial Godly' perspective, and there simply is no such perspective available, at least to the likes of us. Goldberg and Rorty are right about the unavailability of such a perspective, and, if such a perspective were to prove necessary for arguments to enjoy transcultural normative reach, they would be right to reject such reach. But it is not. Let us grant that there are no universal or transcultural values in the sense that they are grounded in, or derived from, a perspective outside of history and culture, for there simply is no such 'Godly' perspective available. This is not the sense of 'transcultural' relevant here. All that is required for argumentative principles and criteria to be, in the relevant sense, transcultural, is that it is possible that reasons offered for particular conclusions be such that a fair-minded contemplation of those reasons will result in such conclusions being deemed worthy of acceptance on the basis of that contemplation, independently of the cultural heritage and commitments of those doing the contemplating. And this possibility, we have seen, is presupposed by any argumentative advocate of any conclusion whatsoever and *a fortiori* by the advocate of the culturally relative view of argument quality. Consequently, that advocate, like every other, must accept the viability of what I have been calling 'transcultural normative reach'—and must therefore reject the culturally relative view of argument quality, which is incompatible with it.

A parallel point is powerfully made by Robert Fullinwider:

> Consider the case of Christopher Columbus: did he discover America or invade it? From the perspective of fifteenth century Europe, he discovered it. From the perspective of the Arawak and other indigenous American populations, he invaded it. As descendants of the European immigrants of America most of us take (or took) the perspective of Europe. Why should we give it up or modify it? Because it is inadequate in some way? Saying it is amounts to measuring it against something outside itself, some more comprehensive and better point of view.
>
> However, the strong separatist denies there are any overarching perspectives, just *other* perspectives. Now, no other perspective can claim to supercede our own merely by being *other*. If an Arawak-centered perspective is no better than a Eurocentric perspective or no part of a more comprehensive synthesis, why bother to re-write the books on poor Columbus? The ironic implication of strong perspectivism is that the label "Eurocentric" ceases to be a charge, complaint or criticism; it becomes a mere description. (Fullinwider, 1991, p. 14, emphases in original)

Fullinwider's 'strong perspectivist' may for present purposes be identified with the advocate of a culturally relative view of argument quality; the lesson of the example is the same for both. Since the strong perspectivist denies the possibility of overarching perspectives in terms of which particular, local perspectives can be evaluated, she denies herself the ability to criticize any such particular perspectives. More tellingly for present purposes, in doing so she likewise denies herself the ability to criticize alternatives to her favored 'strong perspectivist' view, and to defend as rationally superior to its alternatives that view itself.

Similarly, by denying the possibility of overarching, transcultural principles of argument evaluation and criteria of argument quality, the advocate of a culturally relative view of argument quality denies herself the ability to criticize particular, culture-bound argument-related principles and criteria; and, in doing so, likewise denies herself the ability to criticize alternatives to her favored culturally relative view, and to defend as rationally superior to its alternative that view itself. But her whole purpose, *qua* advocate of that view, is to establish its superiority. Consequently she must, in order to advocate it, *accept* rather than deny the possibility—and indeed the actuality—of overarching, transcultural principles of argument evaluation and criteria of argument quality. That is, she must accept 'transcultural normative reach,' and, as above, must therefore reject the culturally relative view of argument quality which is incompatible with it.[19]

3.4. Argumentation, Rhetoric, and Power

A final worry, which I can treat only briefly here, concerns a kind of skepticism toward the very idea of argumentative or epistemic normativity. The claim that a given argument is a good one, in that its premises provide justification for its conclusion, is (it may be said) not really a claim about normative status at all, since there is 'in the world' no such thing. Such claims, rather, are simply rhetorical devices, which serve to mask the exercise of power. My persuading you that you ought to believe a conclusion C because it is well supported by its premises P, or that certain standards of probative support (which I endorse) are the standards by which you should judge such support, is simply an exercise of my power over you. That certain principles and criteria of argument quality are seen as legitimate is itself no more than a reflection of the power enjoyed by those able to establish them as such. That some items are thought to be 'good reasons' while others are not is—as van Eemeren, Grootendorst, and Henkemans et al. put it in their helpful review[20] of recent work on argumentation, communication and rhetoric—"systematically to privilege certain kinds of claims over others." (1996, p. 209). As they point out, this claim:

> points to the nexus between argumentation and power. It is power, whether political, social, or intellectual, that permits one to stipulate what sorts of claims "count" in any argumentative situation. Power enables those who hold it to impose a partial perspective as if it were holistic—the definition usually given for the term *hegemony*. The most recent wave of argumentation studies seeks to explore and expose the tendency of power to foreclose discourse, and it seeks emancipation by opening up alternatives. This project focuses on marginalized arguers and arguments, and is given impetus by the widespread concern for matters of race, gender and class.
>
> The intellectual underpinning of argument-as-critique is "postmodernism".... There are many varieties of postmodernism, but the central core seems to be the denial that there are any verities or standards of judgment, and the claim that what passes for such standards really is socially constructed. In its ... location of argument in communities, this perspective is in some measure consistent with the others we have discussed. But it goes on to argue that only *a part* of the relevant community has defined the standards, then hegemonically imposed them on the whole. The goal of critique is thus to shed light on this practice and to promote emancipatory potential by posing alternatives. (1996, p. 209, emphases in original)

As these authors point out, one "implication ... of the postmodern project ... is the denial that there can be any such thing as communal norms or standards for argument." (209)[21]

The claim, and the argument for it, can perhaps be summarized as follows: 'Rational argument' is really just a form of rhetoric. The use of rhetoric is the exercise of power. Judgments of argument quality are likewise rhetorical exercises of power. Thus the impersonal, transcultural view of argument quality defended above can be seen only as an equally rhetorical, power-laden construct; it can be no more than a tool of power wielded to further marginalize those not involved in its construction but expected to judge in accordance with its dictates.

This is a fundamental charge; as such adequate treatment of it requires more attention than I can give it here.[22] But three points in reply seem in order. First, this skepticism concerning the very idea of argument quality (other than as an exercise in power) plagues culture-relative as well as transcultural views of argument quality, since according to it the former as well as the latter are mere rhetorical exercises of power. Consequently, it does not offer a reason for preferring the former to the latter (or vice-versa). Second, it is unclear why this view of argumentation should be itself embraced. If the application of standards of argument quality is *just* a rhetorical exercise, with no genuinely normative epistemic force (which renders the conclusions of some arguments worthy of belief), there seems to be no reason to embrace this rhetorical view of argumentation and judgments of argument quality either. The rational defense of the view requires that some rhetorical efforts are more probatively forceful, and some exercises of rhetorical power more legitimate, than others—and so, that argument quality is not *merely* a matter of rhetoric and power.

Of course, the 'advocate' of the view might simply shrug off the debate concerning the relative merits of her view versus opposing views, regarding all such 'rational' debate as merely rhetorical exercise; she may, in denying any sense of 'rational superiority' other than the rhetorical/power one here being considered, be flatly uninterested in establishing the rational superiority of her view. This stance embodies an admirable consistency, but it comes at a high price: in adopting it, and so rejecting the very possibility of rational advocacy of her view, this 'advocate' seems clearly enough not to be engaging the issue with which this paper is concerned. Indeed, taking this stance would render its defense logically impossible; it would make it impossible either to advocate the view in question as rationally preferable to its alternatives, or to engage the general issue of the relative merits of the rival views of argument quality we have been considering. Consequently, while the stance in question appears at first blush to constitute a possible position to take with respect to that issue, taking it not only renders that position indefensible, it renders the issue itself incapable of being coherently posed—in which case it cannot be seen as an adequate stance to take with respect to that issue.[23]

There is, obviously enough, much more to be said here. Nevertheless, I hope to have said enough to make it clear that view of argumentation as rhetorical, and as fundamentally the exercise of power, has no tendency either to upend a transcultural view of argument quality or to support a culturally-relative view of it.

4. CONCLUSION

I have argued that while there is much merit in the general multiculturalist perspective on argumentation—it rightly warns us against impossible 'perspectiveless' perspectives and 'Godly' perspectives outside of time, space, and culture; and rightly reminds us that argument evaluation is conducted by flesh-and-blood people in specific historical/cultural locations, that it takes place in a context—the multiculturalist argument against impersonal, transcultural conceptions of argumentative quality fails. It fails, first, because its criticism of the possibility of 'transcendence' depends upon a conception of transcendence which, although rightly rejected, is far stronger than that required by a transcultural view of argument quality. It fails, second, because it depends upon a sharp 'universal/particular' dichotomy which is in the end untenable. Most fundamentally, it fails because it itself presupposes just the impersonal sort of argumentative quality it seeks to reject: that of transcultural normative reach. Finally, it gains no support from regarding argumentation as the rhetorical exercise of power.

I conclude that the transcultural conception of argument quality survives at least the multiculturalist challenges to it discussed here.

NOTES

1 I am grateful to the Spencer Foundation, the National Endowment for the Humanities, and the University of Miami for their support. The views expressed are of course solely my own responsibility. This paper was presented at a session sponsored by the Association for Informal Logic and Critical Thinking (AILACT) at the World Congress of Philosophy in Boston, August 1998; I am grateful to Jonathan Adler for the invitation to participate in the session and to those in attendance for their stimulating reactions.

2 For further articulation and defense of this epistemic conception of argumentation, see Feldman, 1994; Lumer, 1991; Wreen, 1997; Biro and Siegel, 1992; and Siegel and Biro, 1997; for criticism see Adler, 1997a and 1997b. For more general consideration of epistemic normativity (in the context of consideration of 'naturalized' epistemology), see Siegel, 1996 and 1996a and references therein.

3 Feldman (1994) appears to disagree, as his treatment relativizes argument goodness to persons: the same argument on Feldman's view can be a good one for you but a bad one for me. But I believe that this apparent relativization to persons is in fact relativization to the evidence that a given argument evaluator has at the time of evaluation. The latter sort of relativization, according to which the quality of an argument depends upon the probative strength of the relevant, available evidence utilized in its premises, is the very hallmark of the epistemic view. Thanks to Richard Feldman for helpful conversation and correspondence on this point.

4 Such theorists can thus also be categorized as 'contextualists,' who hold that standards of argument quality differ from context to context, culture being one such context-type. For references and critical discussion, see Combs, 1995. For insightful discussion of possible cultural bias inherent in critical thinking itself, see Ennis, 1998.

5 Although I must immediately concede that on MacIntyre's view relativism *can* be 'transcended.' For discussion of MacIntyre's view of rationality and relativism, see Siegel, 1999.

6 The quoted passage is taken from Carr (1995, p. 80), which offers a general and plausible characterization of the central themes of postmodernism. For critical discussion see Siegel (1998a).

7 This paragraph borrows from Siegel (1998).

8 For discussion of Rorty and relativism, see Siegel (1999).

9 There is, presumably, equally no ready escape from our gendered, class, and other locations. For ease of exposition I will treat these further dimensions of our locations and identities as understood. I also acknowledge the vexed problem of the constitution and individuation of 'cultures,' which I make no effort to address here.

10 What follows is adapted from Siegel (1999), to which the reader is referred for further discussion.

11 Children typically attain 'a reasonable grasp of whole numbers' by age three or four. Grasp of fractions and decimals usually involves a process which extends over several years and is presumably in part a function of what is taught, when. The classic work in this area is Gelman and Gallistel, 1978; it (including their account of what counts as a 'reasonable grasp' of numbers) is summarized briefly and lucidly in Moshman, Glover and Bruning, 1987, pp. 420–423. Thanks to David Moshman for helpful advice on matters concerning psychological development.

12 For critical discussion of Popper's view, and 'framework relativism' more generally, see Siegel, 1987, ch. 2; for consideration of this issue in the context of arguments for/against naturalized epistemology, see Siegel, 1995, esp. pp. 50–51; for more general discussion of the possibility of 'transcendence,' see Siegel, 1997.

13 It is equally applicable to the special case involving specifically *cultural* context. The example involving a sexist perspective I trust makes this clear.

[14] For discussion of the epistemic status of these and other examples, including a sharp change of judgment concerning the legitimacy of the gambler's fallacy, see Siegel (1992).

[15] For discussion and references, see Siegel, 1992, p. 33.

[16] Of course *persons* are also particular; all people are, in Seyla Benhabib's words, 'embodied and embedded' (1992, p. 6), and have to be understood as such by philosophers if they are to avoid 'the metaphysical illusions of the Enlightenment.' (4) Benhabib strives to reformulate 'the universalist tradition in ethics' (9) in such a way that it respects the 'concrete other' as well as the 'generalized other' (158 ff.); she too rejects the universal/particular dichotomy I am challenging in this section.

[17] This section is adapted from and builds upon the discussion of 'transcultural normative reach' in Siegel (1998).

[18] This parallels the analysis of (and argument against) epistemological relativism offered in Siegel, 1987, ch.1 and rehearsed in Siegel, 1999.

[19] She must, moreover, argue that from the perspective of those transcultural principles and criteria her favored view of argument quality proves to be superior to its rivals. Here she runs into the well-rehearsed incoherence arguments against the relativism implicit in her view, since that view centrally denies the possibility of 'transcultural superiority' which it must nevertheless claim for itself. I will not rehearse again those arguments here. They are laid out in some detail in Siegel, 1987 and 1999.

[20] The review in question appears as chapter 7 of their 1996 [*sic*]. They are here reviewing the literature concerning this point, not endorsing it.

[21] For detailed discussions pro and con, see the several essays collected in Simons and Billig, 1995 and Cherwitz and Hikins, 1995.

[22] I have addressed various aspects of it, though not in the context of argumentation theory, in Siegel, 1997.

[23] This point is developed further in Siegel, 1987 and 1999, and in Siegel, 1997, ch. 5.

REFERENCES

Adler, J.: 1997a, 'Fallacies Not Fallacious: Not!', *Philosophy and Rhetoric* 30, 333–350.

Adler, J.: 1997b, 'Reply by Repetition and Reminder', *Philosophy and Rhetoric* 30, 367–375.

Baynes, K., J. Bohman and T. McCarthy (eds.): 1987, *After Philosophy: End or Transformation?*, Cambridge, MA: The MIT Press.

Benhabib, S.: 1992, *Situating the Self: Gender, Community and Postmodernism in Contemporary Ethics,* New York: Routledge.

Biro, J., and H. Siegel: 1992, 'Normativity, Argumentation, and an Epistemic Theory of Fallacies', in F. H. van Eemeren et al. (eds.), *Argumentation Illuminated: Selected Papers from the 1990 International Conference on Argumentation,* Dordrecht: Foris, pp. 85–103.

Carr, W.: 1995, 'Education and Democracy: Confronting the Postmodernist Challenge', *Journal of Philosophy of Education* 29, 75–91.

Cherwitz, R. A. and J. W. Hikins (eds.): 1995, *The Role of Argument in the Postmodern World and Beyond, Argumentation* 9.

Combs, S. C.: 1995, 'The Evocativeness Standard for Argument Quality', in Eemeren, F. H. van, R. Grootendorst, J. A. Blair, and C. A. Willard (eds.), *Perspectives and Approaches: Proceedings of the Third ISSA Conference on Argumentation,* Vol. 1, Amsterdam: Sic Sat, pp. 439–451.

Eemeren, F. H. van, R. Grootendorst, and F. S. Henkemans et al.: 1996, *Fundamentals of Argumentation Theory: A Handbook of Historical Backgrounds and Contemporary Developments,* Mahwah, NJ: Lawrence Erlbaum Associates.

Ennis, R. H.: 1998, 'Is Critical Thinking Culturally Biased?', *Teaching Philosophy* 21, 15–33.

Feldman, R.: 1994, 'Good Arguments', in F. F. Schmitt (ed.), *Socializing Epistemology: The Social Dimensions of Knowledge,* Lanham, MD: Rowman and Littlefield, pp. 159–188.

Fullinwider, R.: 1991, 'Multicultural Education', *Report from the Institute for Philosophy & Public Policy,* vol. 11, #3, 12–14.

Gelman, R. and Gallistel, C. R.: 1978, *The Child's Understanding of Number,* Harvard University Press, Cambridge, MA.

Goldberg, D. T.: 1994, 'Introduction: Multicultural Conditions', in D. T. Goldberg (ed.), *Multiculturalism: A Critical Reader,* Oxford: Blackwell, pp. 1–41.

Lumer, C.: 1991, 'Structure and Function of Argumentations—An Epistemological Approach to Determining Criteria for the Validity and Adequacy of Argumentations', in F. H. van Eemeren,

R. Grootendorst, J. A. Blair and C. A. Willard (eds.), *Proceedings of the Second International Conference on Argumentation*, vol. 1A, SIC SAT, Amsterdam, pp. 98–107.

Lyotard, J. F.: 1987, 'The Postmodern Condition', reprinted in Baynes, Bohman and McCarthy, pp. 73–94.

MacIntyre, A.: 1988, *Whose Justice? Which Rationality?*, Notre Dame, IN: University of Notre Dame Press.

MacIntyre, A.: 1989, 'Relativism, Power, and Philosophy', reprinted in M. Krausz (ed.), *Relativism: Interpretation and Confrontation*, Notre Dame, IN: University of Notre Dame Press, pp. 182–204. Originally published in 1985, *Proceedings and Addresses of the American Philosophical Association*, pp. 5–22.

Moshman, D., J. A. Glover, and R. H. Bruning: 1987, *Developmental Psychology: A Topical Approach*, Boston, MA: Little, Brown and Company.

Nagel, T.: 1986, *The View From Nowhere*, Oxford: Oxford University Press.

Popper, K. R.: 1970, 'Normal Science and Its Dangers', in I. Lakatos and A. Musgrave (eds.), *Criticism and the Growth of Knowledge*, Cambridge: Cambridge University Press, pp. 51–58.

Putnam, H.: 1990, *Realism with a Human Face*, Cambridge, MA: Harvard University Press.

Quine, W. V.: 1960, *Word and Object*, Cambridge, MA: The MIT Press.

Rorty, R.: 1982, *Consequences of Pragmatism*, Minneapolis: University of Minnesota Press.

Rorty, R.: 1989, 'Solidarity or Objectivity?', in Michael Krausz, ed., *Relativism: Interpretation and Confrontation*, Notre Dame, IN: University of Notre Dame Press, pp. 35–50.

Scheffler, I.: 1995, *Teachers of My Youth: An American Jewish Experience*, Dordrecht: Kluwer.

Siegel, H.: 1987, *Relativism Refuted: A Critique of Contemporary Epistemological Relativism*, Dordrecht: D. Reidel Publishing Company.

Siegel, H.: 1992, 'Justification by Balance', *Philosophy and Phenomenological Research* 52, 27–46.

Siegel, H.: 1995, 'Naturalized Epistemology and "First Philosophy"', *Metaphilosophy* 26, 46–62.

Siegel, H.: 1996, 'Naturalism and the Abandonment of Normativity', in W. O'Donohue and R. Kitchener (eds.), *The Philosophy of Psychology*, London: Sage, pp. 4–18.

Siegel, H.: 1996a, 'Naturalism, Instrumental Rationality, and the Normativity of Epistemology', *Proto Sociology* 8/9, 97–110.

Siegel, H.: 1997, *Rationality Redeemed? Further Dialogues on an Educational Ideal*, New York: Routledge.

Siegel, H.: 1998, 'Multiculturalism and the Possibility of Transcultural Educational and Philosophical Ideals', *The School Field* 9, 5–31.

Siegel, H.: 1998a, 'Knowledge, Truth and Education', in D. Carr (ed.), *Knowledge, Truth and Education*, London, Routledge, pp. 19–36.

Siegel, H.: 1999, 'Relativism', in I. Niiniluoto, M. Sintonin, and J. Wolensky (eds.), *Handbook of Epistemology*, Dordrecht: Kluwer (in press).

Siegel, H., and J. Biro: 1997, 'Epistemic Normativity, Argumentation, and Fallacies', *Argumentation* 11, 277–292.

Simons, H. W., and M. Billig (eds.): 1995, *In Search of a Postmodern Rhetoric of Criticism*, *Argumentation* 9.

Wreen, M.: 1997, 'Absent Thee from Fallacy a While?', *Philosophy and Rhetoric* 30, 351–366.

PART III

Spheres *and* Uses *of* Argument

Chapter 6

Public Sphere and Democracy

A central assumption of argumentation studies is that argument is an essential component of democracy. Yet, Charles Willard reminds us that argumentation is also linked to a "tradition that celebrates discipline and specialism."[1] In other words, argumentation in its study and practice is a highly specialized activity deserving of disciplinary status. Here lies a potential friction between argumentation studies serving inclusive democratic ideals and simultaneously attending to building a discipline with, for example, trained experts establishing the terms, parameters, and standards for using and judging arguments.

Each essay in this chapter speaks to this friction by addressing the possibilities for public argument in democracy. Exploration of public argument within the framework of civic participation has found a home in public sphere theory, which focuses on the argumentative "space" of democratic practice.

G. Thomas Goodnight's 1982 article, "The Personal, Technical, and Public Spheres of Argument: A Speculative Inquiry into the Art of Public Deliberation" frames public argument as critically important to contemporary political and civic activities. Influenced by German philosopher Jürgen Habermas's work on communication and public sphere theory, Goodnight's article focuses on deliberative rhetoric—public argument in which citizens create and test new knowledge in order to overcome civic problems. Goodnight explores the possibilities for public argument and democratic deliberation with his conception of the differences among personal, technical, and public argument spheres. A sphere, according to Goodnight, denotes "the grounds upon which arguments are built and the authorities to which arguers appeal." He describes spheres as channels of social interaction and language use that determine argument practice. An important contribution of this article is its view of contextual spheres as mechanisms to understand argumentation in the service of democracy.

In "The Creation of Publics: Notes on Goodnight's Historical Relativity" (1989), Charles Arthur Willard contends that Goodnight errs in his distinction between public and technical spheres. While Goodnight envisions a public sphere where people who are not specialists engage in rhetorical discourse and a technical sphere where experts engage in specialized discourse, Willard finds rhetorical discourse in both public and technical spheres. He identifies two opposed tendencies in argument studies, which he terms "populism" and "technical competence." Willard argues that Goodnight privileges populism as the goal for argumentation studies at the expense of dismissing the significant role of technical skills in argument competency.

Robert Asen, in "Toward a Normative Conception of Difference in Public Deliberation" (1999), identifies *difference* among people in democratic societies as a core concern of public sphere theory. Asen insists on accounting for difference in the theoretical character of the public sphere, suggesting difference must be "viewed as a resource for—not an impediment to—meaningful dialogue." The essay critiques the lack of democratic inclusiveness in deliberations in terms of who is allowed to participate. Drawing on John Dewey, Jürgen Habermas and Michel Foucault, Asen argues for a model of the public sphere that balances normativity and difference as necessary counterparts. He identifies thin norms (discussion about the conditions of deliberation) as the mechanism to establish common ground.

Erik W. Doxtader's "The Entwinement of Argument and Rhetoric: A Dialectical Reading of Habermas' Theory of Communicative Action" (1991) addresses the balance between normativity (universal standards of what argument should be) and difference. Doxtader employs Jürgen Habermas's work to describe the problem of achieving agreement in a pluralistic society. When people's cultural traditions, backgrounds, and social activities differ, Doxtader argues, they must find common ground in order to achieve agreement and a common process to develop shared reasoning. Doxtader critiques Habermas's theory of communicative action in order to negotiate and make room for the concept of difference within the framework of normativity. Doxtader calls on scholars in both argument and rhetoric to provide a dynamic characterization of the complicated process of building consensus.

In their 1999 essay, "Regulating Disagreement, Constituting Participants: A Critique of Proceduralist Theories of Democracy," Darrin Hicks and Lenore Langsdorf address the relationship between argumentation and democracy. Informed by the three major perspectives on argument (logical, rhetorical, and dialectical) and by Jürgen Habermas's conceptions of the public sphere, the authors identify three distinct models of democratic public deliberation. This essay presents a proceduralist approach, which advocates solving problems through a highly structured critical discussion. This approach views conflict as an inevitable condition of human existence that people need to manage in order to resolve their differences through the democratic process. The authors view deliberative discussions as governed by norms that develop from the rules of discourse and the form of argumentation, but they also caution that focusing solely on procedures ignores other important conditions of deliberation, such as how procedures determine who is involved in the decision-making process and who is left out.

These essays represent an increasingly vibrant and significant aspect of argumentation studies. Scholarly work on argumentation and public sphere theory has been relatively coherent, in part, because most scholars take Jürgen Habermas's work as a point of departure. As these essays reveal, as well, scholars regard argumentation as a vital component of healthy democracy.

NOTES

[1] Charles Arthur Willard, "The Creation of Publics: Notes on Goodnight's Theoretical Relativity," *Argumentation and Advocacy* 26 (Fall 1979): 45–59. Reproduced in this chapter.

The Personal, Technical, and Public Spheres of Argument: A Speculative Inquiry into the Art of Public Deliberation

G. THOMAS GOODNIGHT

Deliberative arguments in the public sphere necessarily pertain to the domain of probable knowledge—that kind of knowledge which, although uncertain, is more reliable than untested opinion or guesswork.[1] Public deliberation is inevitably probable because the future is invariably more and less than expected. The full worth of a policy is always yet to be seen. Argumentation offers a momentary pause in the flow of events, an opportunity to look down the present road as well as paths untaken. As deliberation raises expectations that are feared or hoped for, public argument is a way to share in the construction of the future.

To debate the public good or public policy presupposes that arguers and audiences have a sense of before and after, of that which leads to debate and that which may extend beyond it. To encounter controversy over the course of future events is always to raise the question, where will our deliberations lead? If public argument can yield no more than a probable answer to questions of preferable conduct, it can offer no less than an alternative to decisions based on authority or blind chance.

My purpose here is to consider the status of deliberative rhetoric. My guiding assumptions are that rhetoric is an art, a human enterprise engaging individual choice and common activity, and that deliberative rhetoric is a form of argumentation through which citizens test and create social knowledge in order to uncover, assess, and resolve shared problems.[2] As any art may fall into periods of disuse and decline, so it is possible for the deliberative arts to atrophy. Barring anarchic conditions, though, when one way of fashioning a future is foregone, another takes its place. Distinguishing deliberative argument from the social practices which have replaced it is difficult. Many forms of social persuasion are festooned with the trappings of deliberation, even while they are designed to succeed by means inimical to knowledgeable choice and active participation. The increasing variety of forums, formats, styles, and institutional practices—each claiming to embody the public will or to represent the public voice—demands careful attention. If such practices continue to evolve uncritiqued, deliberative argument may become a lost art.

I hope to elaborate this claim by proving three propositions. First, argumentative endeavors characteristically involve, *inter alia*, the creative resolution and the resolute creation of uncertainty. Second, particular arguments emerge in concert with or in opposition to ongoing activity in the personal, technical, and public spheres. Third, argument practices arising from the personal and technical spheres presently substitute the semblance of deliberative discourse for actual deliberation, thereby diminishing public life. Each claim involves a progressively greater degree of speculation. Hopefully, by attending to the creative enterprises of argument, and by examining the inherent tensions among the variety of alternative groundings, the present status of deliberative rhetoric can be uncovered and critiqued.

UNCERTAINTY AND THE GROUNDING OF DISAGREEMENT

Whatever else characterizes an argument, to be recognizable as such, a statement, a work of art, even an inchoate feeling must partake in the creative resolution and the resolute creation of uncertainty. Some say the argumentative impulse, the quest to advance or dispense with the "incomprehensible, illogical and uncertain," arises from the human capacity for symbolization. Language itself imparts an ought which is forever broken and formed anew.[3] Others maintain that this impulse arises from a primitive feeling of dread, an unquenchable desire for completeness.[4] Of the ultimate source of uncertainty, I am not sure; but, my sentiments are in line with de Gourmont: "All activity has uncertainty for its principle."[5]

To say that all argument arises in uncertainty is not to say that all arguments are immediately controversial. O'Keefe performed a valuable service in directing attention toward ordinary encounters in life where words are exchanged instead of blows, and in pointing out that while these disputes are different from "products" produced in less personal contexts, they are nonetheless significant varieties of argument.[6] But I contend that even self-evident reasoning, the highest form of argument by some standards, while not immediately inviting clash, is argumentative as well. To the medieval world, for example, the stars were luminescenses, intelligences placed in the heavens by God. That they represented the eternal in the world was made self-evident by the fact that they neither disappeared nor varied from their orbits. When a super nova appeared in 1572, as Lewis reports, what had been self-evident became the focus of controversy which ultimately contributed to the collapse of a world view.[7] Not all disconfirmations of the "obviously true" are so dramatic. Nor do all occur in this way. But since arguments involve more than simple sensory perception, being made with some ingenuity, even those propositions which seem to be well instantiated within a cultural perspective persist only against a background of uncertainty.

The recognition that some human endeavors are commonly joined by uncertainty does not lead to any particular theory of argumentation. Indeed, such a recognition is a bit subversive of the traditional task of theorists who, since the breakdown of the Medieval Synthesis, have labored mightily to construct methods, procedures, explanations and even whole philosophies of argument. Scholars, seeking to establish that argument itself is grounded in particular theories of logic, psychology, sociology, or linguistics (or some combination), have sought to discover some underlying capacity of human existence which governs and gives meaning to the process of argument making. The work continues apace. Uncertainty persists. Until such a time when all the creative enterprises are reduced to a single underlying certainty, it may be useful to add to the repertoire of study the investigation of the manifold ways in which individuals and communities attempt to create and reduce the unknown. The study of why uncertainties appear, what they mean, how they are banished only to be reformed, and what practices shape the course of future events is important, for knowledge of argument's varieties may illuminate the values, character, and blindspots of an era, society, or person.

Members of "societies" and "historical cultures" participate in vast, and not altogether coherent superstructures which invite them to channel doubts through prevailing discourse practices. In the democratic tradition, we can categorize these channels as the personal, the technical, and the public spheres. "Sphere" denotes branches of activity—the grounds upon which arguments are built and the authorities to which arguers appeal. Differences among the three spheres are plausibly illustrated if we consider the differences between the standards for arguments among friends versus those for judgments of academic arguments versus those for judging political disputes. Permitting a breadth between personal, professional, and public life is characteristically American. The independence of the spheres is protected by a variety of laws protecting privacy and discouraging government intervention in private affairs.

The standards for deciding which events fit into which spheres are sometimes ambiguous and shifting. Burke's notion of identification, however, lends precision to our thinking about this.[8] One form is invoked when a person tries to show "consubstantiality" with another. Another form is invoked through partisan appeals—partisanship being a characteristic of the public. The third form is invoked through a person's identification with his work in a special occupation— the essential ingredient of technical argument. These alternative modes of identification make the personal, technical, and public groundings of arguments possible.

The term "sphere" is not altogether a felicitous one because of its 18th and 19th century connotations of discrete, unchanging arenas where the virtuous play out life according to prevailing custom. One use of spheres as a grounding for rhetorical argument was to justify discrimination against females. Some anti-suffrage speakers justified discrimination on the basis that God had suited women to rule the home and men the professions. Their arguments were grounded in what appeared to be a natural order.[9] Yet from the changing activities of personal and public life, it should be evident that the spheres of argument are not entirely constant over time, and are subject to revision by argument.

Though it may seem historically inevitable that all groundings of argument change as lifestyles are reconfigured, as methods for discovering knowledge become modified, and as the institutions of governance change. But to reduce the spheres of argument themselves to ephemeral contexts or mere points of view is mistaken because all arguers face a similar problem in dealing with uncertainty.[10] An arguer can accept the sanctioned, widely used bundle of rules, claims, procedures and evidence to wage a dispute. Or, the arguer can inveigh against any or all of these "customs" in order to bring forth a new variety of understanding. In the first case, the common grounds for arguing are accepted, and argument is used to establish knowledge about a previously undetermined phenomenon. In the second, argument is employed as a way of reshaping its own grounds. In classical logic this choice was expressed in the contrast between inductive and deductive logic. In the variety of argument endeavors, this tension is expressed by attempts to expand one sphere of argument at the expense of another.

DISTINCTIONS AMONG THE SPHERES OF ARGUMENT, AND AN EXPLANATION OF HOW THE GROUNDINGS OF ARGUMENT CHANGE

Scholars seek a single explanation of the varieties of argumentative endeavors. Earlier in this century, an attempt was made to ground argument in restricted notions of reasons; variations on the basic forms were imperfections awaiting correction.[11] Contemporary theorists, recognizing that not all arguing is comprised of rigorous adherence to stipulated forms, have turned to psychology and sociology to provide explanatory principles in describing the variety of processes. Cognitive psychologists maintain, roughly speaking, that individuals must make sense of the world through whatever apparatus they can employ; thus, since all argument must be conceived and perceived by individuals, the study of mental processes is preeminent.[12] In contrast, other theorists maintain that humans develop through language into an universe of symbols which shapes and is shaped by intersubjective forms of understanding; hence, since individuals can only be known through social expressions, the study of language is preeminent.[13] Others split the difference by developing theories of interaction among individuals and society.[14] These arguments about arguments are useful in extending our concepts about what any particular disagreement may *mean*. But, if the study of argument *per se* is unhinged from particular epistemological commitments, then the creative tension among alternative groundings of disagreement can be uncovered. From a critic's perspective, argument may be approached as a way of coming to understand the transformations of human activity through the variety of practices employed in making argument.

Studying the current practices of the personal, technical, and public spheres is a useful way to uncover prevailing expressions of the human conditions (the views of the world implicit in particular practices of making argument), and perhaps to discover avenues for criticism. A relatively complete investigation of these practices is the subject of a much longer treatise. However, I would like to present an illustration to demonstrate some of the divergent aspects of practice.

Begin with an example made classic by Willard, strangers arguing in a bar at the airport.[15] This is a relatively private affair. Unless an ethnomethodologist is present, it probably will not be preserved. The statements of the arguers are ephemeral. Since no preparation is required, the subject matter and range of claims are decided by the disputants. Evidence is discovered within memory or adduced by pointing to whatever is at hand. The rules emerge from the strangers' general experience at discussion, fair judgment, strategic guile and so forth. The time limits imposed on the dispute probably have no intrinsic significance to the disagreement. The plane will take off. An interlocuter will leave. Others may join in and continue the discussion. Those formerly involved in the dispute may replay the disagreement, embroidering it in the retelling. But the chance encounter is at an end.

Suppose that the conversation is preserved, however, and that the arguments are abstracted from their original grounding to serve as examples in supporting claims about a theory of argument. Consider Professor Willard's own arguments about the argument. In his transformation of assertions, grimaces, glances, and self-reports from the original dispute into examples which illustrate observations about the nature of argument, the concrete particularity of the original dispute is lost. But what is to be gained is the advance of a special kind of understanding among members of a professional community of which Willard is a part, the community of argumentation scholars. In creating his statement, Willard narrows the range of subject matter to that of the interests of the requisite community. He brings together a considerable degree of expertise with the formal expectations of scholarly argument (footnotes, titles, organization, documentation, and so forth). The technical arguments are judged by referees as worthy of preservation. Once the research is published, the community addressed may join into the dispute. Of course, Willard and his critics may engage in *ad hominem* attacks, vestigial products of the private sphere, but what engages the community—and continues to do so long after the disputants turn to other battles—is the advance of a special kind of knowledge.

Now if the illustration can be extended just one more step, suppose that the disagreement within the technical field grows so vehement that there arises two groups in unalterable opposition: Willard followers and Willard opponents. Then neither informal disagreement nor theoretical contention is sufficient to contain the arguments involved. The dispute becomes a matter of public debate. Both groups may take to the public forums governing the technical community's business, each contesting for leadership and control of scarce resources. If one side or the other is dissatisfied with the verdict, then the boundaries of the special community are in jeopardy, as disgruntled advocates appeal to a more general public. Willard may be taken to court and tried by his peers, or he may attempt to have legislation passed that would outlaw what he and his followers believe to be harmful teachings. Once the public sphere is entered, the private and technical dimensions of the disagreement become relevant only insofar as they are made congruent with the practices of public forums.

If a public forum is appropriately designed as a sphere of argument to handle disagreements transcending private and technical disputes, then the demands for proof and the forms of reasoning will not be as informal or fluid as those expressed in a personal disagreement. Yet, since the public must encompass its sub-sets, the forms of reason would be more common than the specialized demands of a particular professional community. Moreover, whereas the public forum inevitably limits participation to representative spokespersons (unlike a chance discussion), an appropriately designed public forum would provide a tradition of argument such that its speakers would employ common language, values, and reasoning so that the disagreement could be settled to the satisfaction of all concerned. Most characteristically, though, the interests of the public realm—whether represented in an appropriate way or not—extend the stakes of argument beyond private needs and the needs of special communities to the interests of the entire community.

The illustration need not be pursued further. The major point to be made is that the ways of making arguments are various. The notions of private, technical and public spheres are useful in describing the manners in which disagreements can be created and extended in making argument. Some disagreements are created in such a way as to require only the most informal demands for evidence, proof sequences, claim establishment, and language use. These may typify arguments in the personal sphere where the subject matter and consequences of the dispute are up to the participants involved. Other disagreements are created in such a way as to narrow the range of permissible subject matter while requiring more specialized forms of reasoning. These typify the technical sphere where more limited rules of evidence, presentation, and judgment are stipulated in order to identify arguers of the field and facilitate the pursuit of their interests. Transcending the personal and technical spheres is the public, a domain which, while not reducible to the argument practice of any group of social customs or professional communities, nevertheless may be influenced by them. But the public realm is discrete insofar as it provides forums with customs, traditions, and requirements for arguers in the recognition that the consequences of dispute extend beyond the personal and technical spheres.

The preceding illustration is intended to be a starting point in examining the differences among argumentative practices. It is not intended to be the foundation of a taxonomical scheme which approaches the study of argumentation by the classification of statements, situations, and customs within established contexts. In the world of arguers, any particular argumentative artifact *can be taken* to be grounded in anyone of the spheres or a combinatory relationship. But the question confronting those who would create ways of raising uncertainty or settling it (and this includes argumentation theorists and critics as well) is the direction in which the dispute is to be developed.

Some critics of argument attempt to provide the links between one sphere and another. Thus, neo-Aristotelian scholars attempted to explain the relation between private life of orators and their public successes.[16] Others, perhaps musing over the creative possibilities of providing a "perspective by incongruity," rip arguments from generally accepted grounding by idiosyncratically extending the argument by analogy. Hauser and his colleagues, for example, attempted to construe Nixon's Cambodia address as comparable to a potlatch ceremony, a ritual practiced among certain tribes of North American Indians.[17] These informed criticisms *reflect* the ongoing attempts of arguers themselves to reform the grounding of disagreement.

To demonstrate how grounds of argument may be altered, I would like to draw upon several historical examples. In each case, what had been accorded as an appropriate way of arguing for a given sphere was shifted to a new grounding; different kinds of disagreement were created. The first example shows how matters of private dispute can take on a public character. The second demonstrates how matters of public judgment can become subjected to the technical domain. The final illustration involves the cooptation of the technical by the public.

In 19th Century America, the poor were generally considered to be poor because of personal character flaws. As explained by adherents of the Gospel of Wealth, poverty was a sign of God's disfavor. The poor were poor because they were lazy, spendthrift, or simply engaged in pursuits that did not deserve reward. Arguments made to the poor and about the poor were grounded in the private sphere; poverty was essentially an issue between a man and his Maker.[18] Thus harder work, more saving, and greater self-reliance were encouraged so that all could share in a prosperous abundance provided by God. Help was cajoled from the rich only as a gesture of Christian charity. With the advent of the Progressive movement, however, the grounding of arguments about poverty gradually shifted from the private to the public sphere. Converting the doctrines of Darwin and his social proponents to a recognition that the environment shaped people and the environment could be altered, Progressives gradually transformed the issue of poverty to a public concern, one that was a shared rather than an individual responsibility.[19] Even though attempts to return the issue of poverty to the private sphere sometimes arose, the Progressives were successful in placing the issue on the public docket.

The public question of the treatment of the "environment" offers another example of the transformation of argument grounding. Extending from the early part of the 20th century were various public movements to protect the heritage of all Americans from the pursuit of private interests by preserving part of pristine America. The vanishing wilderness was the common concern of artists, preachers, naturalists, indeed any citizens who wished to see nature's works preserved.[20] While these movements were successful in restricting some exploitative practices and protecting some of the wilderness, it was not until the public environmentalist movement of the 1970s that the grounds of appeal became more restricted. Rachel Carson's *Silent Spring*, a work combining lyric style and limited scientific fact, projected a future world where the growing poisonous by-products of industry permeated the cellular structure of all living individuals.[21] So strong was the public concern, that a relatively new technical community blossomed, ecologists. Yet, with the competing demands for energy, a private interest made public in terms of job loss, the ecologists could not take the environmental protection principle to its ultimate extent. Rather, state-of-the art practice becomes a tentative balancing between projections of competing demands of energy and ecology. These complicated equations are the only answer to a public movement that finds itself making opposing demands.[22]

The realm of public argument can give rise to the ascendency of technological fields, but public interest may also circumscribe the practice of technical argument. Certainly one of the most outrageous "perspectives by incongruity" of all times was the forlorn attempt by Nazi partisans to create by act of national will a purely

German science. Less obviously, national governments influence the conduct of argument communities by providing resources for equipment, training, and information transmittal. These inducements made in the "public" interest may influence the selection of subjects, techniques and results that are made by theoretically apolitical communities of inquirers. The degree to which present defense efforts induce scientists away from other possible avenues of research is well known. What the configuration of technical argument communities might be if they were not so subordinated to the limits placed by the public interest is an open question.

In each example, the transformation of grounding is evident. Poverty could be the matter of private disagreement so long as the issue was not grounded in questions of public interest and responsibility. The environment was a public issue; but as the implications of public interest demanded trade-offs that could be made only by technical judgments, ecology was given over largely to the technical sphere. Finally, whereas scientists at least in theory should be able to create communities of inquirers without regard to the demands of the public, public leaders nevertheless provide parameters for scientific argument. Although these examples illustrate how some disputes become transformed, it can be demonstrated that some theories of argument attempt to create an organizing perspective where a single sphere grounds all argument practice.

One example of an attempt to harness the varieties of reason under the aegis of a single sphere is that of Toulmin in *Human Understanding*.[23] In this work, it may be recalled, Toulmin seeks to explain the evolutionary development of fields. In the grand synthesis, the most highly developed forms of reason are mirrored in, but not perfectly reproduced by, developing other disciplines. At the crown sits physics. The court is made up of "compact disciplines;" the hinterlands are ruled by the "diffuse disciplines;" the colonies, by "would be disciplines;" and political and ethical argument are found only in the wilds of the "undisciplinable." The advance of reason is equated with single-mindedness of purpose. Society supports these communities of reasoners, presumably because it benefits from the technological applications of discoveries. Such a hierarchical explanation of the uses of reason, I submit, is a technical view *par excellence*.[24] The rules and procedures of the forums guarantee critique; individual allegiances and commitments make little difference in the long run, and the relationship of the disciplines to the public is guaranteed to be felicitous.

If Toulmin's notion of fields is to be accepted as the governing method by which arguments are to be recognized, constructed and evaluated, then what becomes of the personal and public spheres of argument? One of the contributions of Willard's critique of Toulmin is that he points out the personal dimensions to any argument which cannot be accounted for within a strict technical view.[25] It may be added that it is uncertain whether the personal inclinations, stubbornness, and curiosity of men and women attracted to scientific endeavors influence the ways in which problems come to be known and accepted as resolved as much as the independent methods to which they ascribe. The relation between Toulmin's view of argument and the public sphere is also open to question. Is it the case that a scientist's work is without intrinsic political significance? Opponents of eugenics and proponents of creationism would certainly not agree with the claim that scientific communities are propelled only by a curiosity more intense than lay folk. Is it the case that public reasoning itself can be improved by specialization and compactness? This question will receive more detailed analysis in the latter portion of the essay. For now, though, it is important to note that a theory of argument that would ground reason giving in the technical sphere is in opposition to requirements of personal and public life.

THE STATUS OF DELIBERATIVE ARGUMENT

What sphere of argument seems to be prevalent at this time? This is an important question because changes in the grounds of reason cannot be viewed as unequivocal advances. Susan Langer reminds us that "each new advance is bought with the life of an older certainty."[26] My belief is that the public sphere is being steadily eroded by the elevation of the personal and technical groundings of argument. The decline is not entirely a new phenomenon because it is rooted in the dilemmas of Twentieth Century American life.

Writing in the late 1920s, Charles Beard, a great Progressive historian, saw that America had changed. Whereas his country in the 18th Century was characterized by "congeries of provincial societies," modern technology introduced greater specialization, interdependence, and complexity. These changing conditions challenged the looseknit governmental structure of an earlier era. Psychology did offer new opportunities to serve the common good, especially through public health programs, but it also carried with it new problems. He observed, "Technology brings new perils in its train: falling aircraft, the pollution of streams, and dangerous explosives. It makes possible new forms of law violation: safe blowing, machine-gun banditry, wiretapping, and submarine smuggling."[27] Beyond the capacity of government to deal with new social responsibilities, the historian noted an even more fundamental issue.

Beard believed that the nature of government was being inexorably transformed to "an economic and technical business on a large scale." As "the operations of public administration become increasingly technical in nature," the governors turn increasingly to specialized knowledge provided by "chemistry, physics, and higher mathematics."[28] What startled Beard were the implications of this transformation for democratic self-government. If it is the case that specialization is necessary to make knowledgeable decisions, then what value is the participation of common citizens? Entertaining the notion that the United States might best be ruled by a technically trained elite, he concluded that even though such a group might be better acquainted with a range of facts, "it would be more likely to fall to pieces from violent differences than to attain permanent unity through a reciprocal exchange of decisions." His reason: "[T]ranscending the peculiar questions of each speciality are the interrelations of all the specialties; and the kind of knowledge or intelligence necessary to deal with these interrelations is not guaranteed by proficiency in any one sphere."[29]

Since Beard's time, the bill of particulars has changed. Presently, concerns that trouble the administration of government include unanticipated missile launchings, ozone depletion, and atomic power incidents. New technology makes possible plutonium theft, computer crime, and airplane hijacking. But the essential issue persists. Certainly technical knowledge has burgeoned over the past fifty years, but it is not certain that the general knowledge which Beard thought necessary to govern a Republic has become any more refined.

The reasons for this doubt are many. Even as politicians have come to rely upon pollsters and mass-communication strategists to formulate sophisticated rhetorics, audiences seem to disappear into socially fragmented groups. Denial of the public sphere is accompanied by celebration of personal lifestyle, producing what one critic has called the "me generation,"[30] and another, "the culture of narcissism."[31] As arguments grounded in personal experience (disclosed by averaging opinion) seem to have greatest currency, political speakers present not options but personalities, perpetuating government policy by substituting debate for an aura of false intimacy. Thus is privatism celebrated and the discourse continued.

Meanwhile, issues of significant public consequence, what should present live possibilities for argumentation and public choice, disappear into the government technocracy or private hands. As forms of decisionmaking proliferate, questions of public significance themselves become increasingly difficult to recognize, much less address, because of the intricate rules, procedures, and terminologies of the specialized forums. These complications of argument hardly invite the public to share actively the knowledge necessary for wise and timely decisions. Given the increasing tendency of political rhetoricians to produce strings of "ideographs," untrammeled by warrants or inferences, and given the tendency of government to proceed by relying upon the dictates of instrumental reason, the realm of public knowledge, identified by Dewey and later addressed by Bitzer, may be disappearing.[32]

Of course, what once constituted public argument is not entirely gone. Some of its semblance remains.[33] The mass media continue to present the drama of politics, but some vital elements of a deliberative rhetoric are carefully excised. At this juncture, I would like to reconstruct a series of "news reports," aired on some major networks during the spring and summer of 1981. Actually, the stories were not "news" at all, but projected happenings should the Reagan forces find success in making budget reductions. Each "spot" was presented on a day when the Reagan adherents had made some headway in passing their version of reform.

Typically, a female reporter comes on camera saying that she is in some small town in the hinterlands of the United States. An issue is identified, usually the reduction of funds for domestic policy or the termination of a federal program. Residents are interviewed. Some are led to say that, yes, there is no fraud or corruption, and the money has been well spent by hard working souls. When asked what could be done if the funds were to be terminated, to a person, the interviewees responded with a rueful grin, "I just don't know. There is nowhere else to go." Since my political sentiments are somewhat in line with the implied argument of the narrative, I first mistook the reports for a reinvigorated form of public critique. But, on one evening just after the Reagan administration had won a particularly key vote in the Congressional budget battles, an especially gripping narrative was broadcast.

The media found a woman's prison in Florida, where, in what appeared to be something like a summer cottage, female prisoners were incarcerated but allowed to stay with their newly born offspring. As the camera zooms in, the reporter says that a movement is afoot in the Florida legislature to shut down the program which would permit mother and child to remain together. The scene abruptly shifts to two wizened legislators, speaking in deep southern accents. One says in effect, "We need to save the taxpayer every dime we can." The other rejoins: "These women deserve to be punished." Back to the cottage. The female reporter asks the mother/inmate with babe in arms: "What will you do if they pass the cut?" The woman becomes terrified, and clutching the child, tearfully cries: "I don't know. He is all I have. Don't let them take my baby away."

The story was so startling that I began to wonder what could be done for this person, but upon reflection I found that there was not enough information to even begin acting. Later, as I came to think about the entire series of stories as arguments, I discovered that while the reports superficially appeared to be a form of political propaganda—which although one-sided, invites public participation at least through influencing attitudes—actually, they were a different species altogether. The reports always presented the individual as a victim of social forces. Decisionmaking bodies, apparently bereft of human emotion and lacking common sense, were to make decisions based upon inscrutable principles. Like viewing the winds of a rising hurricane, the signs of power politics were to be seen as a kind of natural disaster, sweeping up the deserving and undeserving alike. The reports were crafted in such a way that no intelligent assessment could be made concerning the issues involved. One had no idea of the reasons for the cuts, the credibility of the sources, the representativeness of the examples, etc. But even beyond these characteristic inadequacies, the stories simply did not invite action. These were reports of human tragedies in the making, and, like witnessing other calamities of fate, the participation invited was that of watching the drama play out.

The paradox of expanding communication technology and the decline of the public sphere is not unique to our own time. Dewey puzzled over the simultaneous appearance of new devices (the telephone, motion picture, and radio) and the disappearance of the public.[34] Another communication revolution is taking place, with the advance of improvements in broadcasting techniques, satellite transmission, and computer processing. Instead of expanding public forums, these devices seem to be geared to producing either refined information or compelling fantasy. That the media could be employed to extend knowledgeable public argument but do not suggests the decline of deliberative practice. Mass communications by and large seem to be committed to technical modes of invention. These artfully capture the drama of public debate even while systematically stripping public argument of consequences beyond the captured attention given to the media itself. And the media's own patterns of argument create a view of life where the trivial and mundane eternally interchange with the tragic and spectacular by the hour. What could be a way of sharing in the creation of a future is supplanted by a perpetual swirl of exciting stimuli. Thus is deliberation replaced by consumption.

While Beard did not project a comfortable solution to the problems of meshing technical and public argument, he did formulate a significant challenge:

> /G/overnment carries into our technological age a cultural heritage from the ancient agricultural order and yet finds its environment and functions revolutionized by science and machinery. It must now command expertness in all fields of technology and at the same time its work calls for a super-competence able to deal with the interrelations of the various departments. It must also reflect 'the hopes and energies, the dreams and consummation, of the human intelligence in its most enormous movements.' Constantly it faces large questions of choice which cannot be solved by the scientific method alone—questions involving intuitive insight, ethical judgment, and valuation as of old. Science and machinery do not displace cultural considerations. They complicate these aspects of life; they set new conditions for social evolution but they do not make an absolute break in history as destiny and opportunity. The problem before us, therefore, is that of combining the noblest philosophy with the most efficient use of all instrumentalities of the modern age—a challenge to human powers on a higher level of creative purpose. Its long contemplation lights up great ranges of sympathies and ideas, giving many deeds that appear commonplace a strange and significant evaluation.[35]

Beard's summary of the dilemmas of The Republic in the Machine Age points to a critical enterprise for argumentation theorists. If the public sphere is to be revitalized, then those practices which replace deliberative rhetoric by substituting alternative modes of invention and restricting subject matter need to be uncovered and critiqued. In pointing out alternatives to present practice, the theorist of argument could contribute significantly to the perfection of public forums and forums of argument. If this task is undertaken, then deliberative argument may no longer be a lost art.

NOTES

1 For a discussion of the relation between knowledge, rhetoric, and the public see Lloyd F. Bitzer, "Rhetoric and Public Knowledge," in *Rhetoric Philosophy, and Literature: An Exploration,* Don M. Burks, ed., (West Lafayette, IN: 1978), 57–58. My own assumptions are that the public argument is a viable mode of arguing to the extent that (1) the future is not seen as completely determined; (2) discourse is viewed as capable of presenting and evaluating alternatives for acting or restraining action; (3) individual judgment and action are relevant to the options at hand; (4) the process adheres to freedom of inquiry and expression, with the longer term goal of establishing a true consensus; and, (5) a community of common interests can be discovered and articulated through discourse. See G. Thomas Goodnight, "The Liberal and the Conservative Presumptions: On Political Philosophy and the Foundations of Public Argument," *Proceedings of the [First] Summer Conference on Argumentation,* Jack Rhodes and Sara Newell, eds. (Annandale, VA: Speech Communication Association, 1980), 308.

2 Thomas B. Farrell, "Knowledge, Consensus and Rhetorical Theory," *The Quarterly Journal of Speech,* 62 (February 1976), 1–14. This essay maintains Farrell's distinctions between social and technical knowledge. Although Carleton's observation that the lines between social and technical knowledge are sometimes ambiguous is correct, the reply is nonresponsive to a basic problematic uncovered by Farrell. The arguer must rely either upon an actual consensus such as that which characterizes a technical field with exact specifications for argument or the arguer must project consensus from his or her own personal experience or estimation of the social milieu. ["What is Rhetorical Knowledge? A Response to Farrell—and More," *Quarterly Journal of Speech,* 64 (October 1968), 313–328.] That some aspects of social knowledge become subjected to technical transformation and that the implications of some fields must be resolved by social knowledge indicates merely that arguers are able to reshape the grounds upon which arguments occur.

3 Charles W. Kneupper, "Paradigms and Problems: Alternative Constructivist/Interactionist Implications for Argumentation Theory," *Journal of the American Forensic Association* 15 (Spring 1979), 223.

4 Charles A. Willard, "On the Utility of Descriptive Diagrams for the Analysis and Criticism of Arguments," *Communication Monographs,* 43 (November 1976), 316; Charles A. Willard, "A Reformulation of the Concept of Argument: The Constructivist/Interactionist Foundations of a Sociology of Argument," *Journal of the American Forensic Association,* 14 (Winter 1978), 126.

5 Remy de Gourmont, *Remy de Gourmont: Selections From All His Works,* Richard Aldington, ed. (New York: Covici-Friede, 1929), 472.

6 Daniel J. O'Keefe, "Two Concepts of Argument," *Journal of the American Forensic Association,* 11 (Winter 1978), 121–128.

7 C. S. Lewis, *The Discarded Image: An Introduction to Medieval and Renaissance Literature* (Cambridge: Cambridge University Press, 1974), 92–198.

8 Kenneth Burke, *The Rhetoric of Motives* (New York: Prentice Hall, 1952), 20–29. Burke establishes three major modes of identification: consubstantiality, "in being identified with B, A is 'substantially one' with a person other than himself"; partisanship, "the ways in which individuals are at odds with one another, or become identified with groups more or less at odds with one another," and "Autonomous" identification [quotation marks Burke's], "the autonomous activity's place in this wider context [a larger unit of action in which a specialized activity takes place], a place where the agent may be unconcerned." Although these modes of identification aid us to understand the groundings of each argument sphere, arguers typically import one kind of argument to serve another's function. Thus, the politician can appeal to

consubstantiality in order to masque partisan interests. A partisan movement can grow by having its participants uncover consubstantial interests, as the consciousness raising techniques of the woman's liberation movement were used to increase awareness of a shared identity. Moreover, disputes over what kinds of activities are autonomous occur as responsibility and authority are contested.

9 Joseph Emerson Brown, "Against the Woman's Suffrage Amendment," *American Forum: Speeches on Historic Issues, 1788–1900,* Ernest J. Wrage and Barnet Baskerville, eds., (Seattle: University of Washington Press, 1960), 333–342.

10 It may be tempting to replace the concept of argument spheres with a more popular term like "social context." Most arguments are social productions. Those that are preserved and seem recurrent enough to be labeled as providing a custom or role may be subjected to sociological mapping. See for example, Bruce E. Gronbeck, "Sociocultural Notions of Argument Fields: A Primer," in *Dimensions of Argument: Proceedings of the Second Summer Conference on Argumentation,* George Ziegelmueller and Jack Rhodes, eds., (Annandale, VA: Speech Communication Association, 1981), 1–21. Such mappings may be useful to arguers, who sometimes must project social expectations in order to frame a useful statement. But to view social characterizations as determinative is but to reify the perspectives of a sociologist who may see argument as independent of any particular arguer. So long as one can speak ironically, cross-up and recross expectations, and transvalue social norms, social context—no matter how delicately construed or thoroughly proscribed—cannot be said to be determinative.

11 William Kneale and Martha Kneale, *The Development of Logic* (Oxford University Press, 1962), 628–651.

12 See for example: Dale Hample, "A Cognitive View of Argument," *Journal of the American Forensic Association,* 16 (Winter 1980), 151–159.

13 Ray E. McKerrow, "Argumentation Communities: A Quest for Distinctions," *Proceedings of the [First] Summer Conference on Argumentation,* 214–228; Brant R. Burleson, "On the Analysis and Criticism of Arguments: Some Theoretical and Methodological Considerations," *Journal of the American Forensic Association,* 15 (Winter 1979), 137–148.

14 For an attempt to bridge the gap see Earl Croasmun and Richard A. Cherwitz, "Beyond Rhetorical Relativism," *The Quarterly Journal of Speech,* 68 (February 1982), 1–16. In the view of these authors, "reality" somehow "impinges" on individuals thereby supplying the prerequisite veridicality to guide the arguer's judgment. While the extramental universe need not be denied as a phenomena which sometimes thwarts the best laid theories of arguers, it is difficult to rid arguers of dialectical maneuvers which not only alter the grounds upon which world views are constructed but also present problems that cannot be resolved in a purely positivistic manner.

15 Charles Arthur Willard, "Some Speculations About Evidence," *Proceedings of the [First] Summer Conference on Argumentation,* 267–268.

16 The changing trends of rhetorical criticism mark the different ways in which the relation between or among spheres of argument can be viewed. Neo-Aristotelian critics often attempted to explain public success by exploring the private training, talents, and inclinations of the orator. Symbolic interactionist criticism often focuses on the public significance of private symbol systems, as movement studies demonstrate how the public sphere is reformed through opposition. Fantasy theme analysis charts the personal responses to public statement through its attempt to uncover social dramas.

17 Richard B. Gregg and Gerard A. Hauser, "Richard Nixon's April 30, 1970 Address on Cambodia: The 'Ceremony' of Confrontation," *Communication Monographs,* 40 (August 1973), 167–181. By taking Nixon's address away from its most obvious grounding, namely the tradition of presidential war rhetoric, the rhetorical critics performed the critical function through poetic extension. In this manner the grounds of argument are extended to the point that the speech itself is made to seem arbitrary. But why compare Nixon's address to a potlatch ceremony? Why not a potato harvest, a pair of cufflinks, or any other random item? Any critic, through analogical extension, can ignore the processes through which the argument is made by a person or institution and supplant his or her private identification. Unless something is made known about the relation between argument and practical grounds, or at least live alternatives, a criticism of an argument may tell us more about the critic than the argument.

18 See for example: *The American Gospel of Success,* Moses Rischin, ed. (Chicago: Quadrangle Books, 1968), 3–91.

[19] Richard Hofstadter, *The Age of Reform: From Bryan to F.D.R.* (New York: Vintage Books, 1955), 174–214.

[20] Roderick Nash, *Wilderness and the American Mind* (New Haven: Yale University Press, 1967), 141–160.

[21] Rachel Carson, *Silent Spring* (Boston: Houghton Mifflin Co., 1962).

[22] Thomas B. Farrell and G. Thomas Goodnight, "Accidental Rhetoric: The Root Metaphors of Three Mile Island," *Communication Monographs,* 48 (December 1981), 271–300.

[23] Stephen Toulmin, *Human Understanding: The Collective Use and Evolution of Concepts* (Princeton, New Jersey: Princeton University Press, 1972), 364–411. There is a variety of views extending and supplementing Toulmin's. See Ray E. McKerrow, "On Fields and Rational Enterprises: A Reply to Willard," *Proceedings of the Summer Conference on Argumentation,* 401–413; Charles Arthur Willard, "Argument Fields and Theories of Logical Types," *Journal of the American Forensic Association,* 17 (Winter 1981), 129–145; see also essays in this issue. Whether fields are differentiated by subject matter, logical type, language use, sociological character, or purpose is a matter of some disagreement. Perhaps one of the major characteristics of a field is the effort to define the boundaries of a specialized community of argument users. Given the tendency of those involved in rational enterprises to see the world through their specialty (Burke's notion of "occupation psychosis"), it would be surprising if a single notion of field could be acceptable.

[24] The rubric of argument fields, in my estimation, is not a satisfactory umbrella for covering the grounding of all arguments. If it is claimed that anytime an arguer takes a perspective there is a field, then one term has been merely substituted for another. Alternatively, to claim that all arguments are grounded in fields, enterprises characterized by some degree of specialization and compactness, contravenes an essential distinction among groundings. Personal argument is created in a durational time dimension, as Willard and Farrell have pointed out. Points at issue can be dropped, appear again years later, be returned to, or entirely forgotten. From an external perspective, the private dispute may seem to be serendipitous, even while the interlocuters pursue the matter in its own time. The establishment of a field more or less objectifies time insofar as common procedures, schedules, measurements and argument/decision/action sequences are set up by common agreement. Herein the personal dimension may seem to be not strictly relevant or even counterproductive, except in special cases. A time of public debate may lead to the enactment of a future which increases or decreases individual and/or field autonomy as an outcome of what are figured to be pressing exigencies. Within a democracy at least, public time is not reducible to the rhythms of any individual (unlike a pure dictatorship) or the objectifications of technicians (unlike a purely positivistic state).

[25] Charles A. Willard, "On the Utility of Descriptive Diagrams for the Analysis and Criticism of Arguments," 308–312.

[26] Susan Langer, *Philosophy in a New Key: A Study in the Symbolism of Reason, Rite, and Art* (Boston: Harvard University Press, 1978), 294.

[27] Charles A. Beard and William Beard, *The American Leviathan: The Republic in the Machine Age* (New York: Macmillan, 1930), 7.

[28] Beard and Beard, 3–19.

[29] Beard and Beard, 10–16.

[30] Richard Sennett, *The Fall of Public Man: On the Social Psychology of Capitalism* (New York: Knopf, 1978), 313–338.

[31] Christopher Lasch, *The Culture of Narcissism: American Life in an Age of Diminishing Expectations* (New York: Norton, 1978), 31–70.

[32] John Dewey, *The Public and Its Problems* (Chicago: The Swallow Press, 1927).

[33] Although all rhetoric uses language, and although all language may be viewed as "incipient action" as it excites attitudes, distinctions should be made between those forms of discourse designed to keep us watching while the symbols continue to dance and those forms which invite the knowledgeable conjoining of motion and action to construct a future. If distinctions are not drawn between the aesthetic and deliberative uses of argument, then the public sphere may be coopted by default, given over to those who control the means of producing elaborate symbolic events. How can untimely, irrelevant and even fatuous "public communication" be critiqued, if all rhetoric is fantasy?

[34] Dewey, *op. cit.*

[35] Beard and Beard, *op. cit.*

....

The Creation of Publics:
Notes on Goodnight's Historical Relativity

CHARLES ARTHUR WILLARD

I want to point to two flaws in G. Thomas Goodnight's theory of the public sphere and to suggest reforms of his position that avoid these defects. The first flaw is an untenable and expendable component of Goodnight's distinction between the technical and public spheres—namely the belief that public discourses are rhetorical and technical discourses are not. The second flaw stems from Goodnight's reliance on an untenable, extraneous, and needlessly vague view of history—the theory of generations.

GOODNIGHT'S POSITION

A sketch of Goodnight's position is the place to start, both to clarify the features of his thinking that are not at issue and to satisfy the reader that my criticisms do not turn on idiosyncratic interpretations.

The nucleus of Goodnight's (1982) thought is a distinction among three spheres of argument: the personal, the technical, and the public. By "sphere," Goodnight means "the grounds upon which arguments are built and the authorities to which arguers appeal" (p. 216). The "grounds" upon which arguments are built are the doubts and uncertainties from which dissensus creates interaction. Thus, grounding, and after it argument, are freed from the control of reason, proof, or any other serial predication characteristic of foundationalist theories. The three spheres are omnibus rubrics with which "disagreements can be created and extended" (p. 220). The resulting concepts differ from similar concepts in field theory, in which "ground" functions in a more foundationalist way. Where field theory plots conventional epistemic structures, Goodnight's triad is a blueprint imposed upon motives for conserving disagreements. Goodnight's "personal sphere" arises in relatively private, etiquette-ruled, and (usually) unpreserved conversation. The "technical sphere" labels discourse guided by the field-specific ideals, norms, and expectations of expert communities. And the "public sphere" arises when disagreements have consequences that transcend the private and technical spheres. Goodnight wants to devise a creative tension among the three spheres that might yield a new basis for criticism.

Goodnight's (1982) organizing concern is that the public sphere "is being steadily eroded by the elevation of the personal and technical groundings of argument" (p. 223). We have lost not only the time and space for public discourse, we have lost the art of deliberation. The elevation of the personal sphere means that people are no longer citizens. They have escaped to privatism: celebrating personal lifestyle over civic responsibility. Here we hear the voices of Tocqueville (1969), Sennett (1978), and Habermas (1974): the deliberative arts have been suffocated by base and degenerate institutionalized communications, including the manipulative languages of public relations and advertising, that masquerade as deliberative discourses. "As arguments grounded in personal experience (disclosed by averaging opinion) seem to have greatest currency, political speakers present not options but personalities, perpetuating government policy by substituting debate for an aura of false intimacy" (Goodnight, 1982, pp. 224–225).

Even worse is the dominance of technical discourses. Where Dewey (1927) views technical discourses with more hope than skepticism, Goodnight, like Habermas, holds that the public sphere is co-opted by technical specialism and the disciplinary control of knowledge. This is a story of necessary evils. A complex world requires specialism and the languages of technique. But instrumental rationality has also brought us to the nadir of human possibility: Auschwitz, environmental disaster, starvation, and—looming over them all—the prospects of a nuclear coda to history. Here, Goodnight (1982) is continuing the thought of the progressive historian Beard:

> Since Beard's time, the bill of particulars has changed . . . . But the essential issue persists. Certainly technical knowledge has burgeoned over the past fifty years, but it is not certain that the general knowledge which Beard thought necessary to govern a Republic has become any more refined. (p. 224)

From Beard's time to our own, the idea of general knowledge has been increasingly subordinated to specialism and technical expertise:

> [I]ssues of significant public consequence, what should present live possibilities for argumentation and public choice, disappear into the government technocracy or private hands. As forms of decision-making proliferate, questions of public significance themselves become increasingly difficult to recognize, much less address, because of the intricate rules, procedures, and terminologies of the specialized forums. These complications of argument hardly invite the public to share actively the knowledge necessary for wise and timely decisions. (p. 225)

In this passage, and many like it, one discerns Weber's (1947) pessimism about the rationalization of society filtered through the sensibilities of a postmodern rhetorical theorist. The result is a populist thesis: the public has been disenfranchised by modes of argument that favor specialism or expertise. Peters (1989) reads Goodnight the same way: a discourse is not genuinely public if it "valorizes modes of reasoning unavailable to the public" (p. 27).

This populism is one reason why Goodnight's work strikes a chord among argumentation theorists. The pedagogical rationale for argumentation and critical thinking is often infused with populism. It is a rhetoric of mass enfranchisement that stresses the importance of mass participation to democracy. The enabling assumptions behind this rhetoric are that governance is fueled by general knowledge and that mass competence in this knowledge is possible.

But this populism is one horn of a dilemma, for traditional teaching in argumentation and critical thinking also celebrates discipline and specialism. The whole point in the textbooks is that deliberative techniques *are* a discipline. And the truth tests championed by current texts are largely theories of expertise. To select but one instance, the chapter on evidence in Warnick and Inch (1989) is largely devoted to principles for quoting sources (pp. 65–89).

This friction between populism and technical competence which infuses our teaching will not be resolved in this essay, but it forms the backdrop for the dispute I want to initiate with Goodnight. One key to reading Goodnight is to appreciate the populism at the center of his thinking. The key to reading my criticisms here is to see that behind them is the belief that the requirements of competence are central to a coherent epistemic. My hunch is that our recognition of the *correctness* of the epistemic demands of specialism and technique will get the better of our populist instincts, thus jeopardizing our beliefs about democratic participation. And, if this hunch is borne out, the question arises: Once we get to the concrete details, do Goodnight's generalizations about the public as a community of nonspecialized interlocutors imply that public deliberation—or what Cox (1981) calls "public policy-making"—is in fact a technical specialty?

Another key to reading Goodnight is to appreciate the importance he attaches to historically grounded criticism. For him, the problem of ordering and perfecting public life is virtually synonymous with the problem of reason; the problem of reason, in turn, is virtually synonymous with criticism. The generations idea is his point of leverage for describing the historical grounding of criticism:

> [S]ociety itself is comprised of successive generations, each in various phases of growth and decay, and among these groups are competing visions of what it means to work out a common destiny. A generation that first encounters its own capacity to act during times of economic prosperity, domestic tranquility, social conformity, and peace comes to view the public sphere differently than one that endures the terrors of depression, civil unrest, social upheaval and war. . . . If reasoned argument is not to remain ungrounded, then it must find a space, effecting a consensus across time. In the struggle to fashion arguments which create continuity among generations yet are authentic to the unique experience of one's contemporaries is found the well-springs of reason in the public sphere. (Goodnight, 1987b, p. 140)

"Criticism" is Goodnight's term for the discourse that trades upon this space.

This brief sketch will have to do, though it is dreadfully sparse. It slights the richness of detail, provocativeness, and literary virtuosity that mark Goodnight's work. Still, the gist of Goodnight's thought is not at issue here. What follows is intended as a friendly amendment.

THE PUBLIC SPHERE IS AT LEAST AS TECHNICAL AS THE TECHNICAL SPHERE IS PUBLIC

The view I want Goodnight to relinquish is the idea that the public sphere is rhetorical while the technical sphere is not. My objections to this distinction are that it is nebulous—it muddies Goodnight's thinking at just the point it should be clearest and that it is untenable—it understates the degree to which public issues are technical and technical issues are rhetorical. And the distinction is doubly dispensable: (1) because most of Goodnight's thought turns on a different basis for distinguishing the public and technical spheres—namely, Dewey's (1927) view that matters become public when their effects transcend private or specialized domains; and (2) because most of Goodnight's insights can be preserved merely by saying that public deliberative discourse differs from technical discourse in important ways: "Rhetoric enters into every kind of discourse, even the most scientific. . . . But the fact that rhetoric is present in all discourse does not mean that all discourse is essentially the same, or that all discourse uses the same kind of rhetoric" (Leff, 1987, p. 31).

Some readers may doubt that Goodnight in fact holds the view I have attributed to him. It is commonplace nowadays to study the rhetorical dimensions of technical discourses. The rhetoric of inquiry (Nelson, Megill, and McCloskey, 1987) and social epistemology (Fuller, 1988) movements join with a burgeoning literature in the sociology of science in an increasing interest in the rhetorical constitution and effects of technical domains. There are disagreements in these ranks, often about the interplay between the social bases of a consensus and norms of rationality. Nonetheless, it is unremarkable in the 1990s to think of technical discourses as rhetorically constituted.

Is Goodnight (1982) swimming against this stream? Listen to his distinction of the three spheres as forms of Burkean identification:

> One form is invoked when a person tries to show "consubstantiality" with another. Another form is invoked through partisan appeals—partisanship being a characteristic of the public. The third form is invoked through a person's identification with his work in a special occupation—the essential ingredient of technical argument (p. 217).

But why does this passage impute partisanship solely to the public sphere? The term "partisan" in ordinary parlance applies equally to Goodnight's description of the defense of theories in technical domains and the defense of claims in interpersonal contexts.

"Partisan" is, I think, being used as a surrogate for "rhetorical." And what we really have is a reiteration of Aristotle's belief that rhetoric and dialectic "are concerned with such things as come, more or less, within the general ken of all men and belong to no definite science" (1354a1–3). One pernicious outcome of this reasoning which Goodnight does not espouse is that rhetoric has no subject matter of its own. Another bad result which he does espouse is an artificial distinction between science and non-sciences. For Aristotle it was simple: science deals with certainties, rhetoric and dialectic with probabilities.

Goodnight (1987b) does not believe in certainty, but he is seeking something that resembles it, for he wants to say that technical discourse differs in kind from public discourse: "public argument concerns matters of common interest that are not susceptible to determination by either personal doubt or technical reason" (p. 133). This implies that technical reason does not require public argument. Certainty is *outre,* so probable versus technical seems to be the operative distinction, perhaps allied with such distinctions as general versus specific, and political versus disciplined. Thus, in speaking of technical reason, Goodnight seems to mean disciplined discourses. The public sphere is thus rhetorical while the technical fields are, well, technical. To be sure I am right in imputing this distinction to Goodnight, consider two more passages:

> [A] theory of argument that would ground reason giving in the technical sphere is in opposition to requirements of personal and public life. (Goodnight, 1982, pp. 223)

> Rhetorical argument addresses those topics that extend beyond individual concerns and reside outside the margins of technical reason. Its forum, the public sphere, is comprised of a community of non-specialized interlocutors who participate in ongoing discussion, debate, and decision-making about common rights and duties, matters of collective preference, contingent choices, and responses to events that could come out this way or that (Goodnight, 1987b, p. 139).

The flaw in this reasoning is that, except for the reference to nonspecialized interlocutors, the last sentence might be found in Heisenberg on quantum mechanics, McCloskey on economics (1987), Rosaldo (1987) or Geertz (1988) on anthropology, Megill and McCloskey (1987) on history, Nelson (1987) on political science, or any number of Popperians on any number of sciences. This is a frustrating flaw, for Goodnight stands to lose more than he gains from a stipulative standoff with the sociology of science. Indeed, the recognition of the rhetorical bases of technical discourses may be just the sort of critical leverage he is seeking. The disciplines are "splendid local adaptations"—to use Gould's (1980) expression—solutions to particular rhetorical problems. Far from being the polar opposite to public discourse, they are local success stories, discourses adapted to specialized publics, and thus potentially valuable sources of public knowledge and precedent. Admittedly, as Goodnight (1987b) says, the technical fields have the bad habit of seeking public hegemony—attempting to "reduce the public to an epiphenomenon" (p. 139). But so do movements, interest groups, organizations, corporations, and even individuals. The important thing is to study the myriad ways domain-specific knowledge is translated into policy influence.

A different way of discriminating the technical from the public spheres—and one that as far as I can see Goodnight can accept—is to say that complexity is the chief problem of the public sphere. I am working on a book in which this claim figures prominently, so I admit a vested interest in the argument. Still, Goodnight's depiction of public issues often turns on the fact that they are too complex for technical settlement. The public decision-maker faces multi-faceted organizations with overlapping jurisdictions, redundancy, multiple objectives, and equifinality. Public issues often draw upon multiple fields, when no single authoritative domain can settle them. So an issue's breadth qualifies it as public property: the public jurisdiction is most clearcut when field jurisdictions are narrowest.

Goodnight's (1982) claim that rhetorical discourse resides outside the margins of technical discourse can also be challenged because it blurs our thinking about how technical authority does, can, and should affect political judgments and about how disciplinary facts may be used in public discourse. He appreciates the need for disciplined expertise, as in the case of the ecology movement which transformed into a technical discourse. He also stresses the degree to which degenerate public discourses can silence or distort expertise (1987a). Still, he underestimates the degree to which public uncertainties turn upon discipline-based questions. Is the bridge sound? Does low level radiation cause cancer? How can ozone depletion be reduced? Should Challenger be launched? Our need for such facts is one reason why we have disciplines; and the degree to which questions of fact intermingle with considerations of collective interest is, to my mind, the core problematic of public discourse.

The intermingling of collective interest and disciplinary property (facts) is not better understood by saying that the former is rhetorical while the latter is not. It is more promising to consider the interconnections among facts and collective values as a rhetorical problem *par excellence*. Why, then, is Goodnight reluctant to take this path? Why insist on the rhetorical versus nonrhetorical instead of focusing on the rhetorical differences between the disciplinary and public discourses?

The answer is that Goodnight's (1987b) contrast between technical and public discourse is based on a baffling view of the epistemic makeup of technical fields. Consider this reasoning:

> To the extent that a field insulates itself—restricting access to its patterns of reasoning by requiring mastery of specialized codes, procedures, knowledge, and language to limit what can count as reasonable argument—it places itself at risk to the more generalized community. Of course such risks may

be worthwhile, as some kind of thought is made possible only through the labor of complex, sustained activity. But as a field departs from what can be translated into the reasoning patterns of adjacent specialized communities, much less made interpretable to common sense, it may lose the possibility of communicating with a wider audience. (p. 138)

This reasoning stumbles at the outset. Insulated fields are not *at risk* to the general community. If authority is indispensable, then insulation is protection, not risk. And why should we suppose that expert disciplines want to maximize their chances of communicating with a wider audience? The recombinate DNA researcher addresses the public only when she must (e.g., the safety hearings of the Cambridge City Council forced advocates of a new research lab onto public turf; their risks became public risks). Otherwise, biologists do biology, physicists do physics, and so on. Fleck (1979), a physician-turned-renegade-epistemologist, predicted a century ago that the outcome of this specialism would be the emergence of a satellite discipline—popular science writing—devoted to translating technical achievements into public language. He predicted that popularization would have rhetorical effects on the technical fields themselves: the catchphrases, analogies, and conceptual short-cuts needed by the popularizers would emanate back into the core of the technical fields. Consider, for instance, why a genetic theory recently imported into anthropology is called the "Eve Hypothesis." So what the first part of Goodnight's claim *should* say is this:

Specialism, discipline, professionalization, and increasing technical sophistication make for arcane knowledge. Insofar as a field is incomprehensible to outsiders, the field's authorities must be trusted or ignored. Decision-makers may resent this forced choice, so they sometimes ignore authorities, e.g., the Challenger disaster. When they do not ignore authorities, however, they often find themselves on the business end of a paternalistic and exploitative relationship.

The second part of Goodnight's (1987b) reasoning—the impenetrability of technical argument—also must be reformed. As it stands, it turns on what is meant by translation and "interpretable to common sense" (p. 138). Nothing good can come from this. First, though translation is a technical problem for analytic philosophers, Goodnight cannot mean it that way. Presumably he would agree with Fuller and Willard (1987) that translation cannot presuppose one unproblematic language of reality to which an alien language must be adjusted. The adjustment process works both ways. Too, does he want to make us neurotically conventional? If we fear departing from well-understood, easily translated conventions, do we not in principle become fearful of conceptual innovation and change? That new ideas within a field may be difficult or impossible to translate into current thinking may be more a political problem than an epistemic one. Nobody, as far as I know, makes intelligibility-by-current-conventions the sole epistemic standard. Part of the problem lies with the notion of "a community of nonspecialized interlocutors" (Goodnight, 1987b, p. 139). Aside from the fact that it is a dubious idealization, it is also misleading, for it implies that the public skills, whatever they are, are not technical skills. Yet members of political publics may also be members of specialized fields who do not check their disciplined cognitive habits at the door to the public arena. Nor should they, for their specialized competencies may be a resource appropriate to public issues. Perhaps we want to say that entry into the public sphere entails adoption of a new persona: one transforms one's professional identity into one's model of citizenship. Such a face shift is a rhetorical accomplishment, but a hard one to understand if technical discourses are thought to be nonrhetorical. Here again the question arises whether Goodnight's view is best seen as a call for the creation of a technical specialty.

Finally, what does Goodnight's (1987b) reference to "common sense" mean? Goodnight argues that any particular field's dominant mode of thought cannot be defended as a hegemonic, universally commensurating order, so he cannot mean that intelligibility to common sense is a standard for deciding what may count as a fact. Thus, following the charity principle, we may presume that Goodnight is not saying that something counts as a fact insofar as it is translatable into a common public vocabulary. A better inference is that, though disciplinary facts may not be translatable to a common public vocabulary, their policy implications are or should be. Of course implications are often as complex and technical as the facts being interpreted. Still, reasoning as we are now, the importance of communication with wider audiences makes sense. We can say that Goodnight should have put the last part of his reasoning this way:

> Public policies depend upon authoritative interpretations of outcomes and risks. But disciplinary authorities often are not competent to assess outcomes and risks, for these involve a broader array of factors than a single discipline controls. The safety of nuclear power, recombinate DNA research, construction methods, etc., involves political, managerial, and administrative facts as well as nuclear, biological, and engineering knowledge. This breadth of public issues is the basis for authorizing the epistemic jurisdiction of public decision-makers, though it does not make public actors less dependent on technical authority.

This amendment, which I think Goodnight might accept, leads to another amendment which he likely will not accept:

> Public policy-making, or deliberative rhetoric, is a complex technical field. The disciplined study of public deliberation may include such questions as: How is technical knowledge translated into testimony or public prose? How do experts reason from their facts to policy inferences? How do technical fields interact, share knowledge and problematize one another's methods? On what bases can rival expert testimony be compared and weighed? How do the narrative structures of entertainment media interfere with the rational evaluation of policy consequences?

By making policy-making a technical discipline, this amendment cuts against the populism and mass enfranchisement rationales, and forces us to debate explicitly whether the idea of mass participation is an empty myth. Goodnight's view of rhetoric is quirky because he fears rationalizing in principle. This plausible fear, however, does not rebut the need to see policy-making as a technical discipline.

These amendments, as far as I can see, do not prevent Goodnight from saying what he most wants to say—namely that public deliberative rhetoric should focus on the creation and maintenance of a discourse space for the public interest. To the catalogue of abuses of the public interest—that it has been commodified, reduced to oversimple cost-benefit equations, and suffocated by sweeping utilitarian claims—Goodnight adds the rhetorical threat that we can no longer easily distinguish between entertainment and real tragedy. The effects of governments seem indistinguishable from fate or natural calamities—hence the disappearance of issues of significant public consequence (Goodnight, 1982, p. 225) and the apparent impossibility of giving voice to the genuinely collective interest in justice, fairness, safety, and innovation.

THOSE WHO REPEAT HISTORY ARE CONDEMNED TO STUDY IT

My second objection is to Goodnight's use of the generations notion to describe the grounding of criticism. To ground reasoned argument, Goodnight (1987b) argues, we need "a space, effecting a consensus across time." In the struggle to create arguments that "create continuity among generations" are "the well-springs of reason in the public sphere" (pp. 140–141).

The meaning of expressions such as "consensus across time" is by no means clear. Indeed consensus across time is a contradiction in terms, for "consensus" implies that parties adjust their positions to achieve a mutually acceptable agreement. But our ancestors are not currently competing for power; they cannot make the move definitive of rhetoric: they cannot strategically adapt and adjust their claims to contexts and audiences. This is one drawback of being dead: one's texts are at the mercy of the hermeneutical exploits of the living. Nonetheless, Goodnight wants to find a space for rhetoric in the struggle to effect a consensus across time. By this he may mean that the ghosts of the past can be pressed into multiple service by the living, put to divergent uses. Since texts are indefinitely construable and our adaptations indefinitely flexible, historical differences may be transcendable. Or he may mean that enduring problematics—in this case the problem of reason—are like Plato's Ideas. That his thinking comes closer to the latter than the former can be shown by a brief sketch of his position.

Goodnight (1987a) is seeking a theory of historically grounded criticism. He hopes to fashion a space for criticism that transcends present concerns and moves argument to a higher level. He concedes much of the thrust of field theory—and sees his work as complementary to it—but he also agrees with Arnold: "A true critic has no contemporaries but is one with the ages" (p. 63). Mark that phrase "one with the ages" for it is often said of dead people.

Imagine theorists of criticism arrayed along a continuum. To the right stands Arnold (1982), to the left Lyotard (1984). In the middle, standing with Weaver (1964), is Goodnight. This is not a logician's continuum; opting for the middle does not rule out, co-opt, or in any way silence, the two extremes. As we listen to Goodnight, we are also to hear—with the full force of their arguments—the voices of Arnold and Lyotard. This is a trio for three voices.

Arnold's critic has an incommensurability problem: an inability to take two perspectives at once. Like Wittgenstein's duck-rabbit image, the past and the present seem mutually exclusive, so Arnold, through Goodnight (1987a), puts the critic in a position of choosing between being timeless and yet having no time, or being timely but transient: "To be timeless is to have no time of one's own, however. So what is gained by a commitment to one's own standards of truth is lost in the capacity to communicate truth to contemporaries. Criticism demands a separation, even alienation, from the times" (p. 63).

Lyotard's critic, conversely, is adrift in an indefinitely expanded present (a predicament Goodnight often attributes to field theorists)—able only to shout imprecations to the future and in continual danger of being co-opted by the system. Science is no help, for it makes only denotative statements: technical reason is too provincial, too focused, limited, and rationalized to address the vast problematic implied by "the problem of reason." An Arnold-like search for eternal truths is no better, for it cannot get around interfield incommensurabilities, the lack of a universal, arbitrating language. The critic is thus an epistemic terrorist, armed with incommensurability arguments and the facts of relativity, striking targets of opportunity in any vulnerable discourse community. Lyotard's critic is as estranged from current conditions as Arnold's, but more like a guerilla than a connoisseur.

In the middle, the Weaver/Goodnight crusader belongs to, but is not wholly of, a culture. Thanks to a temporary alienation, the critic returns to his or her community with a more reflective understanding, ready to wrestle with Lyotard's facts in order to salvage as many of Arnold's ideals as possible. Of course it is easier said than done to ask citizens to acquiesce only to the features of their discourse domains whose epistemic operations are transparent. But Goodnight has a stance in mind: through the struggle to fashion continuities across generations. The theory of generations, then, is Goodnight's (1987b) middle course.

Does the theory of generations create this space? My answer is that it does not. The theory is an ambiguous mix of innocuous truths (our world is filled with people of different ages) joined to claims about common belief that are better explained by such constructs as social movements, audiences, and publics—all cloaked in biology-like or genetics-like language. If the resemblance to biology and genetics is seen as spurious, the theory is seen to be merely a quirky way of vindicating a sweeping prose style.

The theory of generations comes from Spanish philosophy—Goodnight cites Ortega Y Gasset (1958) and Marias (1967)—and from Comte's (1974) proposal that the living are governed by the dead. Ortega and company take the generation notion literally. To Marias it is not a theory but an empirical fact. But this is a rhetorical flourish, for "facts" in Marias' exposition are matters anyone would concede: we are young, middle aged, then old; we are on the scene, then pass from it; fields contain novices, accomplished members (insiders and outsiders), and the elderly. Here the theory is clearest—and innocuous. It would not be innocuous if it predicted a causal relation between one's age and the substantive beliefs one holds. Does it say, in other words, that all people of a certain age hold common beliefs about abortion, welfare, the environment, etc.?

The answer is no. This answer emerges in reply to the oft-made charge that the position collapses to history-as-biology, which Marias (1967) energetically denies. There is a rhythm in humans "because human life has a fairly constant average length and a structure consisting of an invariable sequence of ages. This is not only, or even principally, a question of biological rhythm but rather one of the social functions of successive age groups" (p. 163). This claim would make sense inside a sociology of knowledge, but Marias has nothing of the sort in mind. A generation is

> the life span of a certain kind of world . . . ; [a prevailing] world style includes all who live in the world. The peculiarity of certain groups of individuals only affects partial and for the most part superficial zones. Differences exist between groups of the same generation . . . ; even so, they hardly touch what is deeper and more common to men of a generation: their beliefs— an area of life that lies largely unnoticed and unspoken and perhaps even unknown. (p. 162)

So the generations theory does not predict differences in what communication theorists or sociologists call beliefs: the particular factual claims people agree to.

It relegates such differences to "partial, and for the most part superficial zones." Differences in concrete substantive beliefs are trivial compared to a "deeper and more common" kind of belief that "lies largely unnoticed and unspoken and perhaps even unknown." What sort of belief is this?

The answer may be inferred from Marias' (1967) explanation of why generations may not be the same for people everywhere in the world:

> [D]oes a generation include everyone? . . . evidently not. Generations display a unitary character within the same historical units, which is to say in societies, that are in communication and not merely aware of one another. Europe is a historical unit today, and it has been for some time, because all its parts are effectively in communication. (p. 167)

The last claim—Europe is a historical unit—makes sense only when all the traditional anthropological and epistemic dimensions—differences in language, belief, policy, ideology, and interests—are suspended in favor of a transcendent unity—the historical unit.

One can reread Marias many times and still be uncertain about what he means by "historical unit." It is something like a worldview, but unlike Kuhn's (1972) *"Weltanschauung,"* the historical unit is shared across state, cultural, and field boundaries. The historical unit is also something like old-time structuralism, for it arises from a common situation inherited from the unfolding of social forces and dramatic events.

What is being defended here, I think, is a prose genre: a level of generalization or abstraction at which we speak globally of the postwar generation, the Cold War generation, and more recently the glasnost era. This prose is best suited to epochal claims of the sort one finds in magazines on anniversaries or at the beginnings and ends of decades and centuries. The reader who doubts this point should consult Olson and Goodnight (1989), especially where they describe social change. Here is an instructive sample:

> With the spread of machinery came unprecedented changes in American life. The relative isolation of agrarian and small town life that was the norm until the mid-1870s was rapidly displaced. A society that moved to agricultural rhythms and enjoyed the stability of small, relatively homogeneous communities in which people all knew each other gave way to the forces accompanying industrialism and the technical sphere. (p. 57)

This is a familiar level of generalization which is common, for instance, in history or cultural anthropology. At this level of abstraction, we can see how Marias says that Europe is an historical unit, how it has shared, experienced in common a succession of epochal changes: the end of World War II, the Marshall Plan, the Cold War, the new prosperity, the movement toward federalism, and—in the past six months—the disintegration of the Eastern bloc.

Of course, epochal changes can be described without using the generations idea. Campbell's (1984) work on epochal discourse describes Kuhn-like revolutions in which new worlds arise as old ones are destroyed. Campbell neither assumes, nor needs to assume, that the defenders of old worldviews are always old while the rebels are always young. Indeed, the only published research exemplar of Goodnight's theory that I know of (Olson and Goodnight, 1989) builds a picture of epochal rhetoric in nineteenth century America on Campbell's theory, not the generations theory.

And *Weltanschauung* theory does not need the generations notion except as loose prose technique for saying that fields contain novices and old buffaloes, establishments and outsiders. This usage squares with Kuhn's (1962) Planck Hypothesis—that old ideas give way to new ones not because they are refuted but because their proponents die off (p. 151). But points of view and substantive beliefs also cut across age groups: there can be young mossbacks (which explains how ideas rejected by the mainstream sometimes thrive in peripheral enclaves) or elderly, even venerable rebels (which often explains the prestige of non-mainstream ideas or a community's tolerance of dissent).

So generational identity does not predict the beliefs people hold, their cognitive styles, or their ideologies. If it makes no biological claims, then its generalizations may be made using the generations construct. Thus the theory has no defenses against the claim that a generation is a perspective. A generation, in other words, is a cognitive potentiality that affects the rhetorical possibilities for identification and consubstantiation. If I do not fix on age as a kinship basis, I can see myself in the postwar generation, the Warhol generation, the Vietnam generation, the nuclear generation, the television generation, or the Pepsi generation. The only limit to my flexibility is that I cannot claim membership in an incommensurable group (I am Vietnam generation, but not Vietnamese). These are rhetorical moves—in O'Keefe's (1988) sense—I may make at the invitation of a rhetorical message. Of course once generations are seen this way, there is little left of Marias' theory. The generations no longer stand apart from the concrete beliefs people hold in the indefinitely expanded present.

The degree to which Goodnight's (1987b) position stands or falls with the Ortega/Marias position is unclear. At times, he writes as if he would agree that generations are perspectives. He refers to "a potentiality of public argument" (p. 140) and speaks of generations as a metaphor: "Should the generational perspective be taken not as a literal depiction of argument communities but understood metaphorically as an illustration of the potential stances toward the practices of reason, then the potentialities of argumentative positions in time may be discovered" (p. 137). But in other passages the metaphor hardens. He speaks of the "generational nature of human communication" (Goodnight, 1987a, p. 63) and calls for "an examination of the generational dimensions of reason in history" (Goodnight, 1987b, p. 141). This implies an enduring problematic like genetics, indeed one in which generational identity *does* predict substantive beliefs: society, he says, "is comprised of successive generations, each in various phases of growth and decay, and among these groups are competing visions of what it means to work out a common destiny" (p. 140). And again:

> One might trace the development of a field as its practitioners routinely move through sociological patterns of initiation, ascendancy, maintenance, and decay; but fields, too, may encounter definitive generations that set forth patterns of reason that find influence in defining the basic parameters of argument, the terms in which thought encounters itself, for generations to come. (p. 139)

Here the generations idea does not seem to be a metaphor. The patterns are there to be uncovered.

Ever since McLuhan (1989) compared television to the campfires of primitives, I have harbored the suspicion that some humanists mean tribal unity when they say national unity. Assuming that Goodnight does not want to revive human sacrifice or the other frailties that drew our ancestors to the campfire, assuming that he would not accept revolutionary Iran as a paradigm case of a culture that *has* recovered its historically grounded commonweal, and assuming—I am less sure of this—that he does not hope to revive agrarian simplicity and pastoral virtues, there must lie within us some genetic-like vestige of our ancestors' beliefs: DNA-as-Eternal-Golden-Braid.

The problem is that Goodnight wants to say much more than the generations theory authorizes. Where Marias relegates differences in concrete beliefs to a super-ficial realm, in a manner not unlike Plato's denigration of opinion, Goodnight (though he does not put it this way) appreciates—indeed wants to trade upon—the tension between macro- and micro-prose. It is the same thing as the tension between Arnold and Lyotard. His theory of criticism needs to keep Arnold's voice, and at full throttle. So what Goodnight wants is a rhetorical answer to historical relativity. The things people of different ages have *said* about reason have differed, but the *problem* of reason has endured. In the tensions between the local specifics and the grand problematic, the critic may find useful leverage from maintaining the needed distance from his or her own time while engaging sympathetically with it. In this, a genuine Platonism emerges: the problem of reason is a first form, an Idea. To assume that the differences in what people have said about reason have not transformed the problem of reason is to assume (with Marias) that the particu-lars of people's beliefs are epiphenomena of the Idea. The Idea is unaffected by the particulars.

Whether or not Goodnight would confess to this Platonism, the degree to which he might succeed where Marias stumbles depends on the concrete results of cele-brating the tension between micro- and macro-prose. It is not enough to say that the indefinitely extended present of the field theorist—who attaches central impor-tance to the fine-grained, cluttered epistemic environment—is overarched by the macro-prose of continuities across time. We need to know much more. How do the two relate? And what is to be gained by the critic's stance between them? To these questions, Goodnight's (1987b) answer is more hopeful than concrete: "Because the generational pattern of field 'development' is not synchronous with the flow of historical events, it is necessary to examine how field grounded argument inter-sects with the emergence of generations in the public sphere" (p. 139). Thus one of Goodnight's most oft-used images is "fragmentation across time." The abstract, structuralist-like historical prose lends itself to this focus, and leads Goodnight to charge rhetoric with the task of overarching the fragmentation. The rhetoric of inquiry movement locates rhetoric at the end of philosophy; Goodnight locates it at the end of time.

Goodnight's level of abstraction is an obstacle to getting his point. What are we supposed to do with this? How—concretely—does our stance on the overarching problem of reason give us added insight into (say) Darwinian reasoning, quantum mechanics, or the abortion dispute? How does the continuity of a rhetorical problem affect the discontinuities from age-to-age?

What Goodnight (1987b) finds most irritating in field theorists—perhaps I am the worst offender—is their relegation of our ancestors' ideas to the status of argu-ment fodder. Historical fragmentation is thus made to seem no more than people make it—in much the way that continuities are locally important here but negli-gible there. What the field theorist misses, on this account, is the unfolding of extended controversies. By this Goodnight does not mean that field theorists ignore the historical development of theories. The growth of knowledge, after all, is the pivotal metaphor in field theory. Thus, following Toulmin (1972) and Foucault (1972), we speak of a "genealogy" of problems or the "archaeology of knowledge." Goodnight means, rather, that the study of controversies in the public sphere as continuities and discontinuities is a needed addition to the arsenal of modern criticism.

Most field theorists, I imagine, would say that the differences in concrete beliefs that form the contours of present groups are more important than generations. Goodnight's flaw, it seems to me, is that he provides no basis for disputing this claim. Presumably, the tension between current differences and the struggle to find continuity across time yields a new footing for the dispute. But it is at just this point Goodnight is least clear. What does he want the critic to do? What will the arguments look like?

No field theorist denies historical relativity, though many are in the habit of dismissing it as a curiosity. Life in the present tense has more relativity than it can handle, so epistemic studies tend to immerse themselves—as Goodnight charges—in the particulars of an indefinitely expanded present. Behind this cavalier dismissal is the prejudice that, while historical relativity is relevant to questions of theoretical maintenance and change, it is less relevant to understanding current epistemic differences, Where Goodnight hears the ghosts of the past still arguing, I hold (with Jack Nicholson) that one can only be driven mad listening to ghosts and (with Lord Whitehead) that sciences which hesitate to forget their founders are lost.

Goodnight sometimes writes like Whitman but sounds like Yeats. One detects a yearning for the center that will hold amid current differences. His solution looks foundationalist—as if he is searching for a successor to epistemology capable of repossessing the ground lost in the crisis of modernity. This rhetoric of loss and recovery infuses all of Goodnight's writing. He wants to recover something that has been lost, or become degenerate. His recurring imagery is of dissolution, corruption, and decay. He mourns the lost art of phronesis. He is concerned with our "diminished capacity to act cooperatively in expanding a common good" (Goodnight, 1987c, p. 1). Discourses, he repeatedly says, have been lost—as if they lay somewhere waiting to be recovered. Public discourse is the New Grail—lost somewhere beyond the Dark Wood of techno-talk.

This rhetoric of loss and recovery is a source of unclarity, for words such as "lost" or "diminished" require historical antecedents. To say that something is diminished is to say that it used to be bigger or better. Goodnight disavows nostalgia, but his claims about loss certainly look nostalgic (Biesecker, 1989). This is not a nostalgia for the real attainments of past societies (surely the degree to which any post-Rousseau society actually achieved consensus on a common good other than winning wars is contestable) but for faded visions and dreams. Thus the mood is rather like being nostalgic not for 19th Century London but for the gas-lit dreamscape of a Conan Doyle novel. What I find so unclear in Goodnight's program is the principle, object, quality, procedure—or whatever—he wants to recover.

I doubt that any amendment can capture all of Goodnight's intuitions. Still I wonder if he would accept this substitute:

> We systematize life by giving meaning to events. These meanings are often ones common to our most important social groups—family, friends, disciplines, social movements, organizations, professions, etc. Some people, but not all, feel a need to rationalize their lives, to give them narrative rationality, enduring religious or social meaning, or a position in a social structure.

Hedonists are people who despair of all three options. One organizing principle is our sense of our generation, our *place* in a genealogy, our debts to the dead and obligations to our progeny. This principle is not to everyone's taste. People can complete their lives without taking a position in a generation. Nor is a generational consciousness best for every purpose or time.

Goodnight's concern, remember, is to find a space between Arnold and Lyotard in which Weaver's *savant*-like critic can be estranged from society yet committed to it. My amendment implies that to be timeless or timely is not the critic's only choice. To make sense, the critic presupposes certain facts, assumptions, and values whose epistemic meaning and authority are rooted in the present. If one construes timelessness as freedom from current knowledge, one makes an exaggerated leap, and veers toward Arnold's doctrine.

CONCLUSION

Goodnight (1987a) once said that "no argument is over until complete disagreement is reached" (p. 61). It is apparent, I hope, that Goodnight and I are a long way from complete disagreement. My aim here has been to strengthen his position.

Goodnight's program will be stronger, I think, divorced from the issue of how "rhetoric" is defined. I do not think this is an important matter, and it bogs us down in extraneous issues. More important, and more relevant to Goodnight's hope to establish creative tensions to open new possibilities in criticism, is the fact that while we all believe that there are differences between the rhetorical structures of technical domains and the rhetorical structure of public policy-making, no one, to my knowledge, has concretely described these differences. Thus, acknowledging the rhetorical nature of technical discourses—and the technical nature of public discourses—may give the critic precisely the leverage Goodnight is seeking.

Much of what Goodnight says about history is not at issue. I agree with him that one way to assess the soundness of current beliefs is to know how they were arrived at. And I agree that many public problems persist over time, albeit changed to fit the needs of successive periods. A point of leverage for understanding current predicaments is to consider their similarities and differences with the problems of the past.

The trouble with Goodnight's use of the generations idea is that a convenience idiosyncratic to a prose genre is being mistaken for an enduring problematic. If generations are not biological, and age does not predict substantive beliefs, then generations are awarenesses on a par with audiences, movements, etc., and cognitive options on a par with perspectives or worldviews. We can dispense with generations in favor of these other terms and still agree with Goodnight's main point that there are decisive generations—in societies as well as argument fields. Some epochs are startled by the newness of their problems or befuddled by the irrelevance of their historically derived methods. And just as disciplined theorists struggle to relate innovations to existing theories, so ordinary folk often struggle to find the continuity between current confusions and the good old days.

REFERENCES

Arnold, M. (1982). *Essays in criticism*. (P. J. Keating, Ed.). New York: Penguin.

Biesecker, B. (1989). Recalculating the relation of the public and technical spheres. In Gronbeck (pp. 66–70).

Campbell, J. A. (1984). A rhetorical interpretation of history. *Rhetorica, 2,* 227–266.

Comte, A. (1974). *The positive philosophy*. (H. Martinaeu, Trans.). New York: AMS. (Original work published 1855)

Cox, J. R. (1981). Investigating policy argument as a field. In G. Ziegelmueller & J. Rhodes (Eds.), *Dimensions of argument: Proceedings of the second SCA/AFA conference on argumentation,* (pp. 126–142). Annandale, VA: Speech Communication Association.

Dewey, J. (1927). *The public and its problems*. Chicago: Swallow.

Fleck, L. (1979). *The genesis and development of a scientific fact*. (F. Bradley & T. J. Trenn, Trans.). Chicago: University of Chicago Press.

Foucault, M. (1972). *The archeology of knowledge*. (A. M. S. Smith, Trans.). New York: Pantheon.

Fuller, S. (1988). *Social epistemology*. Bloomington: University of Indiana Press.

Fuller, S., & Willard, C. A. (1987). In defense of relativism: Rescuing incommensurability from the self-accepting fallacy. In F. van Eemeren, R. Grootendorst, J. A. Blair, & C. A. Willard (Eds.), *Argument: Perspective and approaches,* (pp. 313–320). Dordrecht Holland: Foris.

Geertz, C. (1988). *Works and lives: The anthropologist as author*. Stanford: Stanford University Press.

Goodnight, G. T. (1982). The personal, technical, and public spheres of argument: A speculative inquiry into the art of public deliberation. *Journal of the American Forensic Association, 18,* 214–227.

Goodnight, G. T. (1987a). Argumentation, criticism, and rhetoric: A comparison of modern and post-modern stances in humanistic inquiry. In J. W. Wenzel (Ed.), *Argument and critical practices: Proceedings of the fifth SCA/AFA conference on argumentation,* (pp. 61–67). Annandale VA: Speech Communication Association.

Goodnight, G. T. (1987b). Generational argument. In F. H. van Eemeren, R. Grootendorst, J. A. Blair, & C. A. Willard (Eds.), *Argumentation: Across the lines of discipline,* (pp. 129–144). Dordrecht Holland: Foris.

Goodnight, G. T. (1987c). *The language of public policy argument: Toward a rationale for rhetorical and critical studies*. Paper presented at Northwestern University Conference on Argumentation and Public Discourse, Evanston, IL.

Gould, S. J. (1980). *Panda's thumb: More reflections on natural history*. New York: Norton.

Gronbeck, B. E. (Ed.). (1989). *Spheres of argument: Proceedings of the sixth SCA/AFA conference on argumentation*. Annandale, VA: Speech Communication Association.

Habermas, J. (1974). The public sphere: An encyclopedia article. *New German Critique, 7*(3), 49–55.

Kuhn, T. S. (1962). *The structure of scientific revolutions*. Chicago: University of Chicago Press.

Leff, M. (1987). Modern sophistic and the unity of rhetoric. In Nelson, Megill, & McCloskey, (pp. 19–37).

Lyotard, J. P. (1984). *The post-modern condition: Report on knowledge*. Minneapolis: University of Minnesota Press.

Marias, J. (1967). *Generations: A historical method*. University of Alabama Press.

McCloskey, D. N. (1985). *The rhetoric of economics*. Madison: University of Wisconsin Press.

McLuhan, M., & Power, B. R. (1989). *The global village: Transformations in world life and media in the 21st century*. New York: Oxford University Press.

Megill, A., & McCloskey, D. N. (1987). The rhetoric of history. In Nelson, Megill, & McCloskey, (pp. 221–238).

Nelson, J. S. (1987). Stories of science and politics. In Nelson, Megill, & McCloskey, (pp. 198–220).

Nelson, J. S., Megill, A., & McCloskey, D. N. (Eds.). (1987). *The rhetoric of the human sciences: Language and argument in scholarship and public affairs*. Madison: University of Wisconsin Press.

O'Keefe, B. J. (1988). The logic of message design: Individual differences in reasoning about communication. *Communication Monographs, 55,* 80–103.

Olson, K. M. & Goodnight, G. T. (1989). Epochal rhetoric in 19th-century America: On the discursive instantiation of the technical sphere. In Gronbeck, (pp. 57–65).

Ortega Y Gasset. (1958). *Man and crisis*. (M. Adams, Trans.). New York: Norton.

Peters, T. N. (1989). On the natural development of public activity: A critique of Goodnight's theory of argument. In Gronbeck, (pp. 26–37).

Rosaldo, R. (1987). Where objectivity lies: The rhetoric of anthropology. In Nelson, Megill & McCloskey, (pp. 87–110).

Sennett, R. (1978). *The fall of public man: On the social psychology of capitalism*. New York: Knopf.

de Tocqueville, A. (1969). *Democracy in America*. (J. P. Mayer, Ed.; G. Lawrence, Trans.) Garden City NY: Doubleday.

Toulmin, S. E. (1972). *Human understanding*. Princeton: Princeton University Press.

Warnick, B. & Inch, E. S. (1989). *Critical thinking and communication*. New York: Macmillan.

Weaver, R. M. (1964). *Vision of order: The cultural crisis of our time*. Baton Rouge: Louisiana State University Press.

Weber, M. (1947). *Theory of society and economic organization*. (T. Parsons, Ed.; A. M. Henderson & T. Parsons, Trans.). New York: Free Press.

Toward a Normative Conception of Difference in Public Deliberation

ROBERT ASEN

A growing, interdisciplinary literature has developed around the theme of "the end of the public sphere." Pursuing the historical and normative claims suggested by the phrase, scholars have asked whether the public sphere continues to function as an opinion-forming realm and—in any case—whether it ought to be employed as a critical concept for understanding public discourse. Recalling John Dewey's 1927 observation that "optimism about democracy is today under a cloud" (1954, p. 110), contemporary commentators have advanced qualified, sometimes dialectical claims for and against the view of a public in eclipse and a corollary decline in its members' abilities to make judgments about practical, public affairs (e.g., Aronowitz, 1993; Goodnight, 1982; Habermas, 1974, 1962/1989; Rodger, 1985; Schudson, 1995). These and other writers also have considered what principles, if any, ought to structure the public sphere. Some accept the basic premises of a deliberative public sphere, but have called for the inclusion of less familiar, often marginalized voices in conceptual models of public discourse (e.g., Fraser, 1989, 1992a; Benhabib, 1992, 1996; Mansbridge, 1996). Others have held that the public sphere ought to be rearticulated fundamentally, if not supplanted. Various reasons have been offered in support of this position: the public sphere is an integral part of a mass media spectacle that misdirects public attention towards issues of political intrigue while occluding the socioeconomic inequities that affect the everyday lives of citizens (Edelman, 1988); the exclusions that characterize the historical practice of the bourgeois public sphere are constitutive of the concept itself (Griffin, 1996); and the public sphere assumes a self-conscious subject whose speciousness has been demonstrated by developments in poststructuralist theory (Reddy, 1992; Villa, 1992).

The emergence of difference as a key concept in social and political discourse has attached an unusual sense of urgency to these already lively debates. The demands made by new social movements and long-suppressed groups for recognition from social orders—described by Charles Taylor (1995) as the "politics of recognition"—engender an additional set of questions for those who would advance a critical conception of the public sphere. To questions concerning the values and aims of the public sphere, theorists and advocates alike now must append questions that seek to elucidate how diverse participants may be included in public debate as diverse participants rather than (as assumed by the bourgeois public sphere) universal citizens (Zarefsky, 1996; Chesebro, 1996). The issue of democratic inclusiveness is not simply a quantitative matter of the scale of a public sphere or the proportion of members of a political community who may participate in it (Calhoun, 1993, p. 279). The dilemmas entailed in these questions become clear when one considers the history of the bourgeois public sphere told by Habermas. As the "public body expanded beyond the bounds of the bourgeoisie," its new-found heterogeneity produced a fractious rather than an interactive public sphere (1974, p. 54). Habermas recounts this past not to endorse social privilege, but to point to the complexity of the questions identified above. Confronted with the legitimate demands for inclusion by marginalized groups, the bourgeois public sphere could not sustain itself. To be sure, we ignore at our peril the questions that emerge in the interstices of history, norms, and difference.

One way to solve these dilemmas might be to abandon all talk of normative frameworks with respect to the public sphere. In slightly attenuated form, some theorists—most prominently Jean-François Lyotard—have adopted this perspective. This movement away from legitimacy arises partially from an awareness of the ways in which norms subject people to established social orders. Foucault (1980), for instance, writes of the triangle of power/right/truth that operates through discourse and prescribes (among other things) who may speak and what may be addressed. Throughout its history, the bourgeois public sphere has exemplified this tacit form of exclusion. Abstract claims of universal access and open debate in practice have prescribed particular subjects, speaking styles, and topics of discussion. But norms are ineluctable. This is one of the crucial insights of Foucault's theory of the mutual implication of power and knowledge. Norms, like power, both constrain and enable; our awareness of their subjugating capacities ought not preclude attempts to fulfill their emancipatory possibilities. Notions of justice provide subordinated groups with potentially compelling appeals when challenging oppressive orders. It is precisely this kind of appeal that Lyotard employs when he gainsays the terror inflicted on persons threatened with elimination or actually eliminated from language games.

The challenge for theorists, then, is to articulate models of the public sphere that value difference within a common enough framework so that questions of fairness and justice may be broached by participants themselves. For this to be the case, difference must be viewed as a resource for—not an impediment to—meaningful dialogue. As Fraser (1992a) explains, this requires a reversal of a central assumption of the bourgeois public sphere. Rather than bracketing difference as a prior condition of debate, participants ought to seek and thematize it explicitly (p. 120). This dubious assumption—that participants bracket status differentials—also suggests that discursive norms may be conceived thickly or thinly.[1] Thick norms fix core rules or principals, choosing among prospective elements of discussion to prescribe its proper conduct prior to actual dialogue. For instance, a thick norm might restrict topics to matters of common concern. Thin norms identify the necessary conditions of debate that enable participants to make these judgments themselves. A thin norm, for example, might require as a discursive condition that each participant be able to question the topics of discussion. As the title of this essay intimates, difference may be valued within a model of the public sphere that remains committed to deliberation. Moreover, a deliberative public sphere demonstrates a greater commitment to difference than alternative models.

In this essay, I argue that a deliberative model of the public sphere can value difference if one articulates its normative grounds through thin norms and if one recognizes the appearance of deliberation across a multitude of dialectically related publics. Before amplifying these reconfigurations, I identify the constitutive components of the historical/critical bourgeois public sphere and consider three non-deliberative models of the public sphere: tactical, consumptive, and ideological. Though each model gainsays the suppression of difference of the bourgeois public sphere, each one ends up reinscribing it in transfigured form. A deliberative model cannot be retained by default, however. In contradistinction to these alternatives, deliberation has the capacity to engender perspective-taking, which is a form of recognizing difference. Though no model can proscribe all exclusions that may occur in practice, a reformulated public sphere suggests norms that anticipate minimized exclusions of styles, topics, and fora. It also may recover public opinion as both a process and its product.

THE BOURGEOIS PUBLIC SPHERE

The bourgeois public sphere is both a historical and a critical concept. As a historical concept, it describes the emergence of a rational debating public, sustained through political pamphlets and coffeehouses, that flourished in Europe in the seventeenth and eighteenth centuries. Its most notable chronicler has been Jürgen Habermas, whose widely read history has been the subject of considerable debate. An especially significant aspect of this debate is the charge made by some commentators that in failing to explore the contemporaneous functioning of alternative public spheres, Habermas ends up idealizing the bourgeois public sphere (Fraser, 1992a). Historiographers counter that the exclusion of women and laborers played a determinative role in the constitution of the bourgeois public sphere. Alternative histories explicate their exclusion and participation in public life through other means (e.g., Landes, 1988; Ryan, 1990). As a critical concept, the bourgeois public sphere signifies an open forum of debate and an egalitarian community of citizens implicit in the practice of the bourgeoisie and explicit in their legitimation of the public sphere. The contemporary appeal of this critical concept turns on the extent to which theorists believe it may reflect and direct practice. Those who remain committed to deliberation and those who would supplant it begin with the idea of a bourgeois public sphere.

Habermas (1974, p. 49) defines the public sphere as a realm of social life in which public opinion can be formed. The historical bourgeois public sphere consisted of a collection of private persons assembled to form a public. Its political character arose from a world of letters, which enabled the realization of a distinctly bourgeois subjectivity. A political consciousness developed as the bourgeoisie opposed to absolute sovereignty a demand for general and abstract laws and ultimately asserted itself as the only legitimate source for these laws. Yet the bourgeois public sphere retained its autonomy, mediating between civil society and the state. Habermas explains that "in this sense its character was from the beginning both private and polemical at once" (1962/1989, p. 52). Three characteristics describe the operation of the historical/critical bourgeois public sphere: access is guaranteed to all citizens; citizens debate openly; and citizens debate matters of general interest. In the historical bourgeois public sphere, the homogeneous class standing of the bourgeoisie—propertied and educated—engendered a shared vision of the good that prevented the emergence of particular interests that might have threatened the shared interests of the bourgeoisie. Though not directly related to the functioning of the bourgeois public sphere, two additional characteristics elucidate its nature: the bourgeois public sphere presupposes a reasoning public and it is instantiated through discussion.

Acknowledging the historical limitations of the bourgeois public sphere, Habermas argues for the critical value of its defining characteristics. To be sure, significant contradictions plagued this opinion-forming realm. A fiction of a single public structured the bourgeois public sphere. *"The fully developed bourgeois public sphere was based on the fictitious identity of the two roles assumed by the privatized individuals who came together to form a public: the role of property owners and the role of human beings pure and simple* [emphasis in original]" (1962/1989, p. 56). On the basis of this fictitious identity and the supposition that individuals could achieve a propertied standing, actual restrictions to the public sphere could be viewed in accordance with a principle of universal access. Only property owners "had private interests—each his own—which automatically converged into the common interest in the preservation of a civil society as a private sphere" (Habermas, 1962/1989, p. 87). Still, Habermas ascribes to this putative universal human subjectivity positive functions in the context of the political emancipation of civil society from mercantilist and absolute rule. The bourgeoisie debated each other without regard to political or social rank in accordance with uniform rules.

Habermas argues that the bourgeois public sphere marked a crucial transformation of the relationship between power and representation. Feudal lords embodied power; they believed themselves to be consubstantial with a higher order. They represented this power by presenting themselves to a public. If one may speak of a medieval public sphere, then the very presence of the feudal lord created it. The authority of members of the bourgeois debating public, however, arose from a different understanding of representation. Rather than representing power *before* the people, they represented power *for* the people. Against this background, Habermas writes of a kind of refeudalization of the public sphere in contemporary mass society. Since the era of liberal capitalism, the state increasingly has intervened in the conduct of civil society and society increasingly has assumed the functions of public authority, which has enabled "organized private interests" to invade the public sphere and displace rational-critical public debate (1962/1989, p. 179). This interpenetration of public and private realms has engendered feudalistic displays of power. "The public sphere becomes the court *before* which public prestige can be displayed rather than *in* which public critical debate is carried on" (Habermas, 1962/1989, p. 201).

Habermas discerns in the political public sphere of mass society two competing tendencies. Insofar as this sphere represents a collapse of the bourgeois public sphere, it makes way for a staged and manipulative publicity "displayed by organizations over the heads of a mediatized public" (1962/1989, p. 232). And yet, to the degree to which it preserves the positive potential of the bourgeois public sphere, the political public sphere of mass society retains the mandate of a critical publicity that may be set in motion through the very organizations that "mediatize" the public. Habermas envisages a public of organized private people as a replacement for the defunct bourgeois public of private people.

Three explicit and three implicit qualities of the bourgeois public sphere emerge in Habermas' account. The claims of guaranteed access, open debate, and general interest were articulated explicitly by the bourgeoisie to legitimate the public sphere and were fulfilled in varying degrees. The implicit characteristics of rationality, confrontation, and consensus intimate the historical conduct of deliberation within this public realm. As critical/normative principles, these six qualities have been abandoned by some theorists and reformulated by others.

THREE NON-DELIBERATIVE ALTERNATIVES TO THE BOURGEOIS PUBLIC SPHERE

In this section, I consider the tactical, consumptive, and ideological models of the public sphere. Each model asserts that the constitutive qualities of the bourgeois public sphere create tendencies within it that exclude particular voices and homogenize discourse, compelling participants to assume speaking positions located through the practices of dominant groups. All three models turn away from this sphere and from deliberation, believing both to be inherently flawed. From different perspectives, each model purports to highlight difference against the sameness of the bourgeois public sphere. Each model fails to achieve this stated goal, however, ironically reinscribing the pernicious tendencies of the bourgeois public sphere in transfigured form. To illuminate the aims and failings of these three models, in each case I refer to the work of a representative author: Jean-François Lyotard, Michael Warner, and Cindy Griffin.

Lyotard's advancement of a tactical model appears in a work best-known for introducing American readers to a "postmodern condition." For many, the book may be best remembered by Lyotard's contention in the introduction that the postmodern condition is defined as "incredulity toward metanarratives" (1979/1984, p. xxiv). This reduction is unfortunate, for the book raises important questions that cannot be pared down to aphorisms. Lyotard considers the situation of knowledge and the university, but his analysis has implications for sociopolitical spheres generally. Two narratives have legitimated knowledge in its modern form: knowledge as the liberator of humanity and knowledge as the unifier of diverse fields of experience. The rise of technologies and techniques since World War II, the redeployment of capitalism after its retreat under Keynesianism between 1930 and 1960, and (most importantly) the sprouting of seeds of delegitimation within the grand narratives themselves have produced an insuperable credibility gap. This places teachers and students in a potentially disastrous situation, for decision makers have turned to performance-based measures to legitimize their power and evaluate the worth of components within social systems. Invoking a uniform measure of value, decision makers demand that persons contribute to increasing the overall efficiency of the social system or disappear. As modern knowledge is in peril because of the delegitimation of its metanarratives, postmodern knowledge refines one's sensitivity to differences and reinforces one's ability to tolerate the incommensurable.

Because knowledge (and with it sociopolitical orders) can no longer be legitimated on the basis of metanarratives, postmodern knowledge turns to local narratives. In making this move, it relies on a particular method: language games. Lyotard explains that the problem of legitimation is a linguistic one, and "the various categories of utterance can be defined in terms of rules specifying their properties and the uses to which they can be put" (1979/1984, p. 10). Three characteristics describe language games: their rules do not carry their legitimation within themselves, but are objects of an implicit or explicit contract between players; without rules, there is no game; and every utterance should be viewed as a move in the game. Two general principles underlie this method: to speak is to fight and the social bond is composed of linguistic moves (1979/1984, pp. 10–11).

Language games call for an alternative kind of legitimation: paralogy. Viewing consensus as a horizon that can never be reached, Lyotard holds that legitimation must emphasize dissension. This entails a move away from deliberation. Lyotard contends that Habermas' confidence in a dialogue of arguments rests on two dubious assumptions: that it is possible for all speakers to reach agreement on universally valid metaprescriptives and that the goal of dialogue is consensus. The pragmatics of language belies Habermas' belief that the legitimacy of a statement lies in its contribution to the emancipation of humanity. Instead, Lyotard calls for an idea and practice of justice that is not linked to consensus, which entails two steps. The first is a recognition of the heteromorphous nature of language games and a concomitant renunciation of terror: the threatened or actual elimination of a player from a language game. The second step is the adoption of the principle that any "consensus" on definable rules and permissible moves within a language game must be local, "agreed upon by present players and subject to eventual cancellation" (1979/1984, p. 66).

Lyotard's turn from deliberation to language games elides critical reflection. Conceived as a sequence of moves and countermoves, language games preclude the possibility of one player acknowledging and potentially adopting the perspective of the other. Deliberation entails an ability to judge statements (one's own and those of another) critically even as dialogue takes place; it does not exhaust itself at the level of enunciation. Games, however, assume that each player enters each game with an already determined outcome, which is either achieved or not achieved (e.g., a runner either crosses or fails to cross the finish line). The utterances of another player can be engaged only as potential obstacles. Tactical victory replaces social interaction; a focus on the success of the individual player displaces a consideration of dialogue among participants. Moreover, language games assume the status equality of players. Within this model, differences among players cannot be thematized: games disregard considerations of race, class, and gender. Lyotard's notion of tangible justice in a computer age—"give the public free access to the memory and data banks" (1979/1984, p. 67)—suggests that language games require the equality of players as a precondition of their just operation. Yet equality oftentimes must be taken up as a task of social interaction. Finally, Lyotard's renunciation of terror belies a commitment to some (thin) metaprescriptives. That no player should be forcibly removed from language games suggests notions of open access and debate. Lyotard raises significant questions regarding the legitimacy of consensus, but his tactical model suppresses difference.

In his essay "The Mass Public and the Mass Subject," Michael Warner (1993) explicates a cogent version of the consumptive model. Though Warner's account of mass publicity derives from a contemporary development in the public sphere, his essay begins by asserting an element of publicity common to various historical moments. As a precondition of participation, the public sphere requires from individuals a moment of self-abstraction and imaginary reference in which they assume an attitude of indifference to their particularities and refer themselves to an anonymous public as opposed to other individuals. Becoming a public subject requires an individual to mark one's nonidentity with oneself. The specific form taken by this necessary moment, however, has changed through time.

In the historical bourgeois public sphere, the validity of what one said bore a negative relation to one's body. This strategy of abstraction was both a utopian moment and also a major source of obfuscation. The bourgeois public sphere supposed that all particularities have the same status as mere particularity. Each person shared in a putative universal humanity, which was the only proper identity mark among citizens. Yet the ability to assume this universal stance was made available only to particular persons. Warner explains that race, class, and gender differences "already come coded as the difference between the unmarked and the marked, the universalizable and the particular. . . . The bourgeois public sphere has been structured from the outset by a logic of abstraction that provides a privilege for unmarked identities: the male, the white, the middle-class, the normal" (1993, p. 240). Warner labels this contradiction the "minoritizing logic of domination": to call attention to one's marked particularities is to be less than public.

The appeal of contemporary mass subjectivity arises largely from this contradiction between embodiment and negativity. The present-day mass-culture public sphere offers its subject an array of bodily images. These images, moreover, appear in a context in which the discourse of consumption mediates publicity. Warner contends that the pervasiveness of this consumptive discourse makes it "difficult to realize how much we observe public images with the eye of the consumer. Nearly all of our pleasures come to us coded in some degree by the publicity of the mass media" (1993, p. 242). In this milieu, public figures increasingly take on the function of actualizing the otherwise indeterminate image of the people. Warner cites Reagan as an exemplary public figure in this respect. His image blurred boundaries between the political and commodity public. Though much has been made of Reagan's actual popularity (see, e.g., Schudson & King, 1995), Warner suggests that the significance of "Reagan" lay in its function as a relay for a kind of meta-popularity. "Reagan" performed popularity exceptionally well. The mass public sphere tries to minimize the difference between the body longed for and the particular body. Mass publicity promises a reconciliation between embodiment and self-abstraction.

Warner holds that the public sphere is not simply corrupted by its association with consumption. "If anything, consumption sustains a counterpublicity that cuts against the self-contradictions of the bourgeois public sphere" (1993, p. 253). Warner uses the example of graffiti writing to support this position. He explains that graffiti writing takes up the utopian promise of consumer publicity—the promise of a field of choices among infinite goods—and particularly the promise of the brand name. The signatures of graffiti writers claim an imaginary uniqueness promised in commodities but canceled in the public sphere proper. "Whenever mass publicity puts its bodies on display, it reactivates this same promise" (1993, p. 254). Consumptive counterpublicity points to the misdirection of political movements that presuppose the bourgeois public sphere as background and thus take for granted the official strategies of self-abstraction. Warner argues that movements based on identity politics make this mistake. An assertion of the full equality of different identities "would require abandoning the structure of self-abstraction in publicity," which "seems unlikely in the near future" (1993, p. 255).

Though writers as diverse as Paul Ricoeur and Jacques Derrida have argued persuasively that we are never fully self-conscious, the narrower sense of nonidentity explicated by Warner (the imaginary reference of the mass subject) may not be universal—and, even if this were the case, it is likely not uniform. By reducing all public discourse to consumption, Warner elides what may be qualitative differences across publics. This failure to recognize a diversity of publics is one of the significant limitations of the consumptive model. Important questions cannot be answered within this framework: Does discontinuity with oneself persist across various publics? If so, does this discontinuity always follow the same pattern? Does the degree of discontinuity differ across publics? All of these questions assume an answer to a prior, more difficult question: From which self do we abstract? Studies of the discourse of multiple publics suggest that Warner claims too broad a range of application for his consumptive model.

In a study of 5,000 letters sent to Representative Lee Hamilton of Indiana and the House Select Committee on the Iran-Contra investigation, for example, David Thelen (1996) discovers that Americans sometimes resist the allure of media images and insist on dialogue about public affairs as individuals. In the mid-1980s, members of the Reagan administration and the National Security Council were caught selling arms to Iran and, in turn, using the profits to fund Contras seeking to overthrow the Sandinista government of Nicaragua. The media portrayed Lieutenant-Colonel Oliver North, the central figure of the scandal, as a folk hero; commentators termed his putative popularity "Olliemania." Regardless of political affiliation, however, letter writers overwhelmingly rejected North as a hero. Moreover, their letters attempted to establish personal bonds with the representatives and the writers identified themselves most frequently in familial terms (as a father, mother, husband, wife). As this example demonstrates, the consumptive model does not describe all public discourse.

In comparison to the tactical and consumptive models, the ideological model of the public sphere concentrates less on offering an alternative to deliberation and more on revealing some of the pernicious functions of the bourgeois public sphere. Ideology, of course, is a polysemous term (see, e.g., Eagleton, 1991). My designation of an ideological model of the public sphere refers to an understanding of ideology as the representation of the interests of the few as the interests of the many and a view of the public sphere as a social realm for the propagation of such ideology. Cindy Griffin (1996) pursues this line of analysis in an essay on the essentialist roots of the public sphere. She holds that typical theories of the public sphere often reduce it to distinct places, topics, and groups of people. Griffin argues for a conception of the public sphere as an ideology that depends on privilege, subject position, and power. Her specific concern is to explicate the ways in which the origins of the public sphere are rooted in essentialist views of men and women.

Griffin draws heavily on Mary O'Brien's *The Politics of Reproduction* in critiquing this essentialism. According to Griffin, the book demonstrates that male domination over women is grounded in the relationship between anatomy and society. To understand this domination, one must consider ten reproductive moments in the lives of women and men: menstruation, ovulation, copulation, alienation, conception, gestation, labor, birth, appropriation, and nurture. Men involuntarily experience alienation: "the physical experience that occurs when men release the sperm" (1996, p. 25). The separation experienced by men contrasts sharply with the connection women experience as they ovulate, conceive, and carry the fetus through term. Women's reproductive consciousness is a continuous, synthesizing, and mediating consciousness while men's reproductive consciousness is a discontinuous, separated, and isolated one. To compensate for this disparity, men voluntarily engage in appropriation: the attempt to reestablish a connection to the seed. Appropriation entails symbolic rebirth, and the public sphere has functioned as a forum into which men are reborn. Griffin describes O'Brien's argument as a powerful illustration of "how a society can move from anatomy to psychology to symbol: from reproduction to consciousness to the division of social space into separate spheres" (1996, p. 28).

The implications of this reproductive politics for conceptions of the public sphere have been significant, Griffin explains. The primary implication has been the construction of separate realms of public and private and particular discursive forms for each realm. This has lead to a view of persons as separate and divided from each other. This view privileges persuasion as advocates attempt to convince one another of their mutual connection. Appropriation ensues: speakers manipulate other individuals, social spheres, and discourse in an effort to "alleviate alienation from the species and to construct arbitrary systems of connection" (1996, p. 30; see also Foss & Griffin, 1995). Rhetoric thus enacts and perpetuates dichotomies and sustains hierarchies. Recognizing the public sphere as an ideology reveals these and other implications. An ideological view of the public sphere reveals it as a realm where only certain individuals may go to have their voices heard, where an individual's status derives from the experience of certain reproductive moments, and where alienation and mastery rather than connection frame topics.

Given the explicit aims of her essay, Griffin's model produces an unexpected yet glaring contradiction: Griffin advances a biological essentialism to counter the putative essentialism of contemporary conceptions of the public sphere. Her ideological critique raises questions about the public sphere that any deliberative model must take into account, but her biological essentialism occludes social and historical forces that play significant roles in the exclusionary practice of the bourgeois public sphere. This is particularly apparent in her discussion of the ten reproductive moments identified by O'Brien. Among relatively descriptive stages such as ovulation and gestation are historically contested terms like alienation and nurture. In *Keywords,* Raymond Williams begins his entry for "alienation" by noting that it "is one of the most difficult words in the language. . . . It carries specific but disputed meanings in a range of disciplines from social and economic theory to philosophy and psychology" (1985, p. 33). Griffin's use of the term reifies a social product into a natural event. Moreover, her ideological model precludes emancipatory practice. It is surely the case that some people use the public sphere to promote their own interests at the expense of others. But the public sphere cannot be reduced to this ideological function. Within this ideological model, men and women cannot interact across gender divisions and within these divisions—which themselves reproduce the very dichotomies and hierarchies that Griffin criticizes—men and women would have no reason to talk, for their gender would signal already existing agreement.

DIFFERENCE IN DELIBERATION

Neither the tactical, the consumptive, nor the ideological model of the public sphere enables the thematization of difference as a resource. Yet a deliberative model ought not be adopted for this purpose by default. The history of the public sphere suggests that deliberation also has excluded. If difference in deliberation is to be valued, then the bourgeois public sphere must be reconfigured in two significant ways. First, norms that engender questions of justice and fairness need to be conceived thinly so that these questions may be raised by participants themselves.

Second, models of the public sphere need to recognize its instantiation across a multitude of publics.

Deliberation entails a meta-level of critical reflection that promotes perspective-taking, which is a form of recognizing difference. This potentiality arises in the ways that deliberation unsettles and makes available for examination individual desires and suggests their possible transformation through discourse. It asks participants to judge critically their own claims and the claims of others. Seyla Benhabib (1992) argues that deliberative processes generate democratic legitimacy and practical rationality for three reasons, which also illuminate the critically reflective dimension of deliberation. First, deliberative processes impart information. No single person can articulate all perspectives through which social and political issues may be perceived by different persons nor possess all the information relevant to a decision affecting many people. Second, deliberation does not proceed from the methodological fiction of an individual with an ordered set of coherent preferences. Benhabib counters that "it is incoherent to assume that individuals can start a process of public deliberation with a level of conceptual clarity about their choices and preferences that can actually result only from a successful process of deliberation" (1992, p. 71). Third, the very act of articulating a view in public imposes a certain reflexivity on individual preferences and opinions. The publicity of deliberation prompts participants to support their positions with good reasons or risk the dismissal of their views as unsupported assertions. The three alternative models of the public sphere elide critical reflection along these lines, assuming a subject with a fixed set of desires that cannot be modified through dialogue. Language games, for instance, assume that each player enters the contest with an already desired outcome. Like wrong turns in a maze, the statements of other persons are only temporary obstacles that do not alter the quality of the desired outcome. In a similar fashion, the consumptive model portrays the images of others as goods to be purchased by the independently acting consumer. And Griffin's ideological model removes the need for interaction as the outcomes of dialogue across and within sex groups can be known in advance.

Some conceptions of deliberation can block its perspective-taking potential. This prospect is alluded to in the question begged by Benhabib's third justification of deliberation, namely, what counts as a good reason? To the extent to which it answers this question by bracketing status differentials and restricting debate to the common good, which assumes that the common good can be identified prior to dialogue (Fraser, 1992a, pp. 129–30), the bourgeois public sphere forestalls perspective-taking. Its fictitious identity of the citizen and property owner suggests that disjunctures between justification and practice cannot be preempted, but the answers of the bourgeois public sphere are also conceptual exclusions committed through the positing of thick norms. The import of a thin normativism is that conceptual models of the public sphere ought not go beyond elucidating the necessary conditions for valuing difference in deliberation, for theorizing by thick norms posits what ought to emerge through the processes and products of deliberation. Once again, Benhabib's work is instructive. Drawing from discourse ethics, she identifies three conditions that must be met by a valid (i.e., morally binding) agreement reached through public deliberation (1996, p. 70). These conditions are compelling as necessary conditions for the valuing of difference in a deliberative public sphere. First, all participants have the same opportunity to initiate speech acts, to question one another, and to open debate. Second, all participants have the right to question the assigned topics of conversation. Third, all participants have the right to initiate reflexive arguments about the very norms of the deliberative process and their application. These thin norms are not abstractions that constitute objective measures of deliberation. Quite the contrary, deliberative conditions qualitatively inform deliberative substance, adumbrating deliberative processes that may best enable questions of justice and fairness. Moreover, when its potential for perspective-taking is not inhibited conceptually, deliberation implies universal moral respect and egalitarian reciprocity that affirm the integrity of others (Benhabib, 1992, p. 29; see also Cohen, 1997, pp. 77–78; Gutman & Thompson, 1996, pp. 52–94).

Though her discourse ethics enumerates the necessary conditions for valuing difference, Benhabib undermines their thinness to the extent to which she insists that "public reasons take the form of general statements consonant with the rule of law" (1996, p. 83). Against "affective" modes of communication (she offers rhetoric as an example), Benhabib supports a moral ideal of impartiality as a regulative principle governing public deliberation. Habermas' model thickens in this way as well. His recent work presents an intriguing model of the public sphere as a social space of widely diversified and relatively autonomous public spheres that should not restrict access nor topics of deliberation (1992/1996, pp. 308–314, 360–366; 1992, pp. 442–452). But Habermas delimits the public sphere as a context of discovery without decision-making authority distinct from the context of justification of parliamentary bodies. Deliberations in the latter have "less to do with becoming sensitive to new ways of looking at problems than with justifying the selection of a problem and the choice among competing proposals for solving it" (1992/1996, p. 307). This a priori delegation of responsibilities amounts to a topical restriction in circumscribing the deliberation of the public sphere, denying participants modes of political organization they may favor for heightening the receptivity of decision-making processes to difference. Moreover, Habermas' conception of deliberation relies on a consensus too rigidly defined. His assertion that deliberative consensus rests on "identical reasons able to convince the parties *in the same way*" (1992/1996, p. 339) makes rational agreement a near impossibility in situations where participants hold fundamentally different values. Thin norms enable the emergence of what James Bohman has called a "plural public reason," which recognizes that participants may agree with one another for different publicly accessible reasons (1996, p. 83). In this way, rational agreement still is possible in pluralistic societies. Thomas McCarthy explains that participants' "background agreement with the operative political conception of justice may *rationally motivate* them to consent to laws they regard as unwise or unjust in the hope, perhaps, that they will be able to use the same resources eventually to change them" (1992, p. 68).

The necessity of thin norms may be justified intuitively and historically. Though his use of the terms is distinct from my formulation of thin and thick norms, Michael Walzer's association of thinness with recognition marks these two dimensions. Walzer (1994) employs the terms thick and thin to describe the varied accounts that one may give of moral terms. He emphasizes, however, that people live their everyday lives in thick moral language. Our notions of justice, for instance, are embedded in specific contexts that we inevitably invoke in trying to persuade others of our views. "Minimalism, by contrast, is less the product of persuasion than of mutual recognition among protagonists of different fully developed moral cultures" (1994, p. 17). That we recognize in the speech of others, especially people of different backgrounds, our own commitments and beliefs evidences an intuitive resonance to thin norms. They may be discerned as implicated in the perspective of another yet understood through their embedment in our own perspective. Thin norms invoke a mutuality that does not require self-abstraction and assumption of a putatively disinterested stance. This recognition suggests further that thin norms have a history in practice; they may be discovered in deliberative practices that appeal to justice and fairness. In a related manner, Benhabib regards a deliberative model of democracy as explicating the already implicit logic of existing democratic practices (1996, p. 84).

A thin normativism can frustrate perspective-taking if its necessary conditions are circumscribed in a singular conception of the public sphere. It is a fact of contemporary society that the public sphere appears across a variety of publics. A conception of dialectically related publics accounts for social complexity, and welcomes this circumstance as crucial for the valuing of difference. Restricting the public sphere to its frequent and prominent manifestation in the mass media, for example, reduces the concept to particular fora. Moreover, a conception of dialectically related publics reveals that thin norms may not be applied directly to practice; this normative conception does not sketch a single set of procedures.

Embracing a multiplicity of publics reverses an underlying assumption of the bourgeois public sphere: "the institutional confinement of public life to a single, overarching public sphere is a positive and desirable state of affairs, whereas the proliferation of a multiplicity of publics represents a departure from . . . democracy" (Fraser, 1992a, p. 122). Multiple publics expand discursive space in stratified and egalitarian societies. In stratified societies, members of subordinated groups repeatedly have formed "subaltern counterpublics": "parallel discursive arenas where members of subordinated social groups invent and circulate counterdiscourses to formulate oppositional interpretations of their identities, interests, and needs" (Fraser, 1992a, p. 123). Fraser explains that the emancipatory potential of these counterpublics lies in their dual character. They operate both as spaces of withdrawal and regroupment and as training grounds for agitational activities directed toward wider publics. This duality also indicates a publicist orientation: participants in counterpublics view themselves as part of a potentially wider public and aspire to ever widening engagement with others. "Insofar as these arenas are *publics,* they are by definition not enclaves, which is not to deny that they are often involuntarily enclav*ed*" (Fraser, 1992a, p. 124). In egalitarian societies, counterpublics enhance cultural diversity. Fraser holds that cultures act as rhetorical lenses that filter and alter the utterances they frame. Considering this, restricting deliberation to a single sphere would be tantamount to filtering diverse practices and norms through a single, overarching lens (1992a, p. 126). The functioning of counterpublics has been explored in various contexts (e.g., Dawson, 1994; Felski, 1989; Gregory, 1994). For instance, in a study of a women's shelter in Carbondale, Illinois, Maguire and Mohtar recount how the shelter found itself almost immediately serving an explicitly political role. Created as a place for women "to talk about their lives and what it meant to be a women in this culture" (1994, p. 240), the shelter discovered soon after opening that it met an unexpressed need in the community as a place for women who had suffered domestic abuse to seek shelter and make public their experiences.

The bourgeois public sphere has excluded voices and suppressed difference through styles, topics, and fora. A deliberative model that values difference must confront these suppressions and exclusions. Stylistic exclusion refers to the ways in which the bourgeois public sphere tacitly has welcomed, even mandated, particular speaking styles. Iris Young notes that a view of the public sphere as a competitive arena has favored assertive and confrontational speaking styles over tentative, exploratory, or conciliatory ones. She explains that stylistic norms are "powerful silencers or evaluators of speech in many actual speaking situations where culturally differentiated and socially unequal groups live together" (1996, p. 124). Young's reference to social inequality recalls the need for counterpublics and, in situations where persons of unequal status interact, reflexive opportunities to question deliberative processes. No model can proscribe all exclusions that may occur in practice, but a reconfigured deliberative model suggests norms that would minimize the possibility of stylistic exclusion.

Topical exclusions have been aided most significantly by putatively disinterested rules that restrict deliberation to matters of common concern as well as a priori distinctions that deem certain topics "public" and others "private." The mutually implicative relationship of these exclusionary mechanisms often makes introducing topics into larger publics difficult. Social reformers typically must answer the charge that their "issue" is not of general interest. An especially cogent example of an attempt to overcome this exclusion has been the struggle to transform sexual harassment into a public issue. In an analysis of the Senate hearings of charges brought by Anita Hill that Supreme Court Justice Clarence Thomas sexually harassed her when she worked as his subordinate at the Equal Employment Opportunity Commission, Fraser holds that the hearings revealed that relations of power traverse divisions of public/private. They "depended at every point on who had the power to successfully and authoritatively define where the line between the public and the private would be drawn" (1992b, p. 596). In an earlier era, Progressive social reformers fought to publicize poverty. Working against nineteenth century doctrine such as the Gospel of Wealth, which viewed poverty as a sign of God's disfavor, Progressives turned attention away from the supposed faults of the individual to the larger social milieu (Goodnight, 1982). Acknowledging the pluralistic values and conflicting interests of social life, thin norms invite social transformation.

The ways in which fora exclude may not be as explicit as stylistic or topical exclusions, but they are equally significant. Sometimes, stated institutional rules restrict entry to particular fora. At other times, fora afford certain discursive privileges differently to various participants. In her analysis of the Clarence Thomas–Anita Hill hearings, Ashley Armstrong (1995) considers how Senate committee hearings limit witnesses' utterances. Most frequently, however, fora exclude when cultural conventions designate them as appropriate only for certain speakers (see, e.g., Campbell, 1973). As with the bourgeois public sphere, these exclusions belie claims of open access. The letters-to-the-editor section of a newspaper, for instance, purports to select submissions from writers based on their timeliness and cogency. Yet in a study of the letters published in the *New York Times* prior to the US-Iraqi War, Ben Page (1996) reveals that the letters selected came mostly from persons affiliated with prominent social institutions. Moreover, the viewpoints expressed in the letters flanked on the hawkish and dovish sides the paper's "centrist" editorial position on military engagement with Iraq. Page summarizes the implications of his analysis this way: "The indications of constructed deliberation at the *Times*, a highly prestigious publication that purports to conduct a democratic and free-wheeling debate on its editorial and op-ed pages, suggests that such practices may be quite widespread" (1996, p. 37). A model of the public sphere that recognizes a multiplicity of publics confronts these exclusions, recognizing that persons live their lives in a variety of settings. Yet it enables a common enough framework to sustain dialogue among multiple publics. A reconfigured deliberative model retains the bourgeois public sphere's claim of open access while anticipating a reduced likelihood of its betrayal.

CONCLUSION: THE PROCESS OF PUBLIC OPINION

The historical and conceptual exclusions of the bourgeois public sphere have prompted theorists to search for alternative models. I have explored three such models in this essay: tactical, consumptive, and ideological. Each purports to value difference yet each reproduces the homogenizing tendencies of the bourgeois public sphere. An explanation of this performative contradiction may lie in the ways in which each model precludes the potentiality of deliberation to promote perspective-taking—a form of recognizing difference. Deliberation unsettles and makes available for examination individual desires, suggesting their possible transformation through dialogue. In contrast, each alternative model assumes a subject with a fixed set of desires that cannot be modified through dialogue. When individual opinions are hypostatized in this manner, they form a public opinion that appears through the aggregation and comparison of an outside observer. In this way, these alternative models mirror disabling tendencies in the contemporary public sphere.

Explicating the constitutive features of the bourgeois public sphere, Habermas describes public opinion as "the tasks of criticism and control which a public body of citizens . . . practices vis-a-vis the ruling structure organized in the form of a state" (1974, p. 49). Despite its restrictive orientation, this view of public opinion recognizes that it is both a process and its product. This stands in stark contrast to the practices through which mass media and political institutions reify public opinion into a measurable and dissectible product. Diverse viewpoints reduce to fungible units distinguishable only in their accumulation. Harry Boyte notes that "even as public opinion reigns supreme, judgment is precisely what has been lost" (1995, p. 418). For Jean Baudrillard, public opinion has been commodified to a point where "it is no longer necessary that anyone *produce* an opinion, all that is needed is that all *reproduce* public opinion, in the sense that all opinions get caught up in this kind of general equivalent" (1983, p. 126). Calling polls the burlesque spectacle of the political class, Baudrillard contends that its members are the only ones, in the end, who still believe them—though the consequences of this devotion extend across society.

The normative conception developed in this essay assumes a dialectical relation to the contemporary public sphere. It draws from the positive achievements of multiple publics—such as the publicizing of formerly private issues (e.g., sexual harassment)—the need to respect the diverse settings in which people live their lives and to value difference as a resource for deliberation. It draws from the historical experiences of excluded groups and individuals the need for thin norms that anticipate overcoming exclusions of styles, topics, and fora. Thin norms have an intuitive and historical basis, but their location in a deliberative model of the public sphere places these norms in a critical relation to the contemporary public sphere. This essay answers the question of the end of the public sphere by asserting that ends eventually must be determined by participants themselves in the processes and products of deliberation.

NOTES

[1] Michael Walzer (1994) uses the term "thick" and "thin" to refer to the alternative accounts one may offer of the maximal and minimal meanings of moral terms. He locates moral discourse in the former: "Morality is thick from the beginning, culturally integrated, fully resonant, and it reveals itself thinly only on special occasions" (p. 4), in contexts of political and social crisis. Walzer discerns discursive elements—which he describes as "kind[s] of argument[s] (p. xi)"—distinct from the fixed principles or rules (thick norms) and necessary conditions (thin norms) elucidated in this essay. Still, his assertion of the recognizability of thinness, as I shall argue, supports my claim of the necessary quality of thin norms.

REFERENCES

Armstrong, S. A. (1995). Arlen Spector and the construction of adversarial discourse: Selective representations in the Clarence Thomas–Anita Hill hearings. *Argumentation and Advocacy,* 32, 75–89.

Aronowitz, S. (1993). Is a democracy possible? The decline of the public in the American debate. In B. Robbins (Ed.), *The phantom public sphere* (pp. 75–92). Minneapolis: University of Minnesota Press.

Baudrillard, J. (1983). *Simulations* (P. Foss, P. Patton, & P. Beitchman, Trans.). New York: Semiotext(e).

Benhabib, S. (1992). *Situating the self: Gender, community, and postmodernism in contemporary ethics.* New York: Routledge.

Benhabib, S. (1996). Toward a deliberative model of democratic legitimacy. In S. Benhabib (Ed.), *Democracy and difference: Contesting the boundaries of the political* (pp. 67–94). Princeton, NJ: Princeton University Press.

Bohman, J. (1996). *Public deliberation: Pluralism, complexity, and democracy.* Cambridge, MA: Massachusetts Institute of Technology Press.

Boyte, H. C. (1995). Public opinion as public judgment. In T. L. Glasser & C. T. Salmon (Eds.), *Public opinion and the communication of consent* (pp. 417–436). New York: Guilford.

Calhoun, C. (1993). Civil society and the public sphere. *Public Culture, 5,* 267–80.

Campbell, K. K. (1973). The rhetoric of women's liberation: An oxymoron. *Quarterly Journal of Speech, 59,* 74–86.

Chesebro, J. W. (December 1996). Unity in diversity: Multiculturalism, guilt/victimage, and a new scholarly orientation. *Spectra, 32,* 10–14.

Cohen, J. (1997). Deliberation and democratic legitimacy. In J. Bohman & W. Rehg (Eds.), *Deliberative democracy: Essays on reason and politics* (pp. 67–91). Cambridge, MA: Massachusetts Institute of Technology Press.

Dawson, M. C. (1994). A black counterpublic? Economic earthquakes, racial agenda(s), and black politics. *Public Culture, 7,* 195–223.

Dewey, J. (1954). *The public and its problems.* Athens, OH: Swallow. (Original work published 1927)

Eagleton, T. (1991). *Ideology: An introduction.* London: Verso.

Edelman, M. (1988). *Constructing the political spectacle.* Chicago: University of Chicago Press.

Felski, R. (1989). *Beyond feminist aesthetics: Feminist literature and social change.* Cambridge, MA: Harvard University Press.

Foss, S. K., & Griffin, C. L. (1995). Beyond persuasion: A proposal for an invitational rhetoric. *Communication Monographs, 62,* 2–18.

Foucault, M. (1980). Two lectures. In C. Gordon (Ed.), *Power/knowledge: Selected interviews and other writings, 1972–1977* (pp. 78–108). New York: Pantheon.

Fraser, N. (1989). What's critical about critical theory? The case of Habermas and gender. In *Unruly practices: Power, discourse, and gender in contemporary social theory* (pp. 113–143). Minneapolis: University of Minnesota Press.

Fraser, N. (1992a). Rethinking the public sphere: A contribution to the critique of actually existing democracy. In C. Calhoun (Ed.), *Habermas and the public sphere* (pp. 109–142). Cambridge, MA: Massachusetts Institute of Technology Press.

Fraser, N. (1992b). Sex, lies, and the public sphere: Some reflections on the confirmation of Clarence Thomas. *Critical Inquiry, 18,* 595–612.

Goodnight, G. T. (1982). The personal, technical, and public spheres of argument: A speculative inquiry into the art of deliberation. *Journal of the American Forensic Association,* 18, 214–227.

Gregory, S. (1994). Race, identity, and political activism: The shifting contours of the African American public sphere. *Public Culture,* 7, 147–164.

Griffin, C. L. (1996). The essentialist roots of the public sphere: A feminist critique. *Western Journal of Communication,* 60, 21–39.

Gutman, A., & Thompson, D. (1996). *Democracy and disagreement: Why moral conflict cannot be avoided in politics, and what should be done about it.* Cambridge, MA: Belknap.

Habermas, J. (1996). *Between facts and norms: Contributions to a discourse theory of law and democracy* (W. Rehg, Trans.). Cambridge, MA: Massachusetts Institute of Technology Press. (Original work published 1992)

Habermas, J. (1992). Further reflections on the public sphere. In C. Calhoun (Ed.), *Habermas and the public sphere* (pp. 421–461). Cambridge, MA: Massachusetts Institute of Technology Press.

Habermas, J. (1974). The public sphere: An encyclopedia article (1964). *New German Critique,* 1 (3), 49–55.

Habermas, J. (1989). *The structural transformation of the public sphere: An inquiry into a category of bourgeois society* (T. Burger & F. Lawrence, Trans.). Cambridge, MA: Massachusetts Institute of Technology Press. (Original work published 1962).

Landes, J. (1988). *Women and the public sphere in the age of the French Revolution.* Ithaca, NY: Cornell University Press.

Lyotard, J-F. (1984). *The postmodern condition: A report on knowledge* (G. Bennington & B. Massumi, Trans.). Minneapolis: University of Minnesota Press. (Original work published 1979)

Maguire, M., & Mohtar, L. F. (1994). Performance and the celebration of a subaltern counterpublic. *Text and Performance Quarterly,* 14, 238–252.

Mansbridge, J. (1996). Using power/fighting power: The polity. In S. Benhabib (Ed.), *Democracy and difference: Contesting the boundaries of the political.* 46–66. Princeton, NJ: Princeton University Press.

McCarthy, T. (1992). Practical discourse: On the relation of morality to politics. In C. Calhoun (Ed.), *Habermas and the public sphere.* 51–72. Cambridge, MA: Massachusetts Institute of Technology Press.

Page, B. (1996). *Who deliberates? Mass media in modern democracy.* Chicago: University of Chicago Press.

Reddy, W. M. (1992). Postmodernism and the public sphere: Implications for an historical ethnography. *Cultural Anthropology,* 7, 135–168.

Rodger, J. (1985). On the degeneration of the public sphere. *Political Studies,* 33, 203–217.

Ryan, M. P. (1990). *Women in public: Between banners and ballots.* Baltimore: Johns Hopkins University Press.

Schudson, M. (1995). *The power of the news.* Cambridge, MA: Harvard University Press.

Schudson, M., & King, E. (1995). The illusion of Reagan's popularity. In *The power of the news* (pp. 124–141). Cambridge, MA: Harvard University Press.

Taylor, C. (1995). The politics of recognition. In *Philosophical arguments* (pp. 225–256). Cambridge, MA: Harvard University Press.

Thelen, D. (1996). *Becoming citizens in the age of television: How Americans challenged the media and seized political initiative during the Iran-Contra Debate.* Chicago: University of Chicago Press.

Villa, D. R. (1992). Postmodernism and the public sphere. *American Political Science Review,* 86, 712–721.

Walzer, M. (1994). *Thick and thin: Moral argument at home and abroad.* Notre Dame, IN: University of Notre Dame Press.

Warner, M. (1993). The mass public and the mass subject. In B. Robbins (Ed.), *The phantom public sphere* (pp. 234–56). Minneapolis: University of Minnesota Press.

Williams, R. (1985). *Keywords: A vocabulary of culture and society* (Revised ed.). New York: Oxford University Press.

Young, I. M. (1996). Communication and the other: Beyond deliberative democracy. In S. Benhabib (Ed.), *Democracy and difference: Contesting the boundaries of the political* (pp. 120–135). Princeton, NJ: Princeton University Press.

Zarefsky, D. (1996). *The roots of American community.* Boston: Allyn & Bacon.

The Entwinement of Argument and Rhetoric: A Dialectical Reading of Habermas' Theory of Communicative Action

ERIK W. DOXTADER

This essay addresses a common and growing problem in argumentation theory; namely: How do interlocutors address one another in reasonable terms when the expectations for what counts as appropriate, valid, or sound argumentation differ to a substantial degree? This is a problem of concern for a pluralistic society where different cultural traditions, backgrounds, and social activities retain distinctiveness, but social actors still require some modus vivendi for common discussion. It is also a problem for a technologically dependent society whose areas of expertise and labor are increasingly differentiated into fragmented specialties and competing interest groups, but where decision makers also need to find a normatively grounded means of social coordination. Finally, the problem of finding a common process for sharing reasons is an ideological issue to the extent that political groups sunder the shared processes of deliberation in pursuing self-insulated visions of the good life, even while the means of communication reach toward a universal polity. The difficulties and complexities of argumentation in modern society require a sophisticated understanding of the means by which reason is secured through communicative argument.

Contemporary argumentation theory faces a double problematic in explaining the relationship between reason and social action. On the one hand, if argumentation is grounded in a narrow, rule based set of prescriptive standards, theory development may define the reasoning process in such a way as to ignore the social context of argumentation. On the other, if argumentation is equated with any kind of social interaction, then theory relativizes reason into self-defining, fragmented contexts. Such relativism dissolves capacities for constructing common grounds from which distinctions are drawn between valid, good, and sound reasons and their opposites.

Jürgen Habermas' theory of communicative action constitutes an attempt to preserve common bases for reasoning while establishing a role for argumentation in the diverse contexts of social interaction. This essay argues that by excluding rhetorical practice from his theory of intersubjective argumentation, Habermas cannot fully account for the means by which individuals reasonably reach agreements and coordinate actions. The first section of the essay argues that Habermas' theory of argumentation serves to define the relationship between human communication and rational action; that is, the rules inherent to the argumentation process serve as a means by which to reasonably resolve controversy and dispute. While the rules that guide communicative interaction are a central component of Habermas' theory of argumentation, such rules cannot guarantee that argumentation serves the ends of achieving open consensus. As such, the second section of the essay explicates Habermas' attempt to differentiate communicative and strategic action in terms of how human interests inform and sustain consensus building. By linking open communication to specific social contexts, Habermas expands the rational dimensions of argumentation while also ensuring that interlocutors are aware of when open communication is occurring. By examining the tensions in Habermas' attempt to separate strategic and communicative action, the final section of the essay argues that Habermas misunderstands the value of strategic argument in the creation of a consensus based on mutual understanding. Habermas' view of strategic action constricts his ability to fully grasp the relationship of reason and social action coordination. In instances of controversy over the nature of reasoned communication, a recourse to rhetoric is necessary in order to recontextualize situational commonalties, and thus provide new possibilities for achieving consensus.

ARGUMENT AND RATIONALITY

Habermas' theory of argumentation embraces the relation of social development and reason; arguments serve to create a means by which individuals can communicate, establish norms, and enact decisions based on common agreement. By seeking to define the boundaries of social rationalization in terms of argumentation, Habermas' position is important to the extent that it suggests that reasonable action can be defined in terms of a specific rule based process of communicative interchange. In this respect, the primary task of Habermas' theory is to demonstrate how the rules that structure arguments are capable of sustaining a conception of human reason that privileges intersubjective understanding.

Habermas sees argument as a definitive example of how individuals create and enact reasonable forms of action. While this view of argumentation is strongly influenced by Toulmin's position that argumentation can be understood in terms of data, warrant and claim, Habermas believes that the logic of Toulmin's position cannot discern the relative strengths of competing arguments; that is, Toulmin's emphasis on the construction of arguments does not provide a means by which to decide which of two arguments is more reasonable (Habermas, *Theory* 1:35). Instead, Habermas holds that the importance of argumentation for human learning, self-reflection and moral insight suggests that arguments draw their *strength* from explicit appeals to validity standards. Insofar as arguments problematize and question standards of truth, moral-practical correctness, the adequacy of values or sincerity, they provide a certain means by which to test and compare the reasonability of conflicting claims (Habermas, *Theory* 1:23). The ability to recognize these controversial validity claims serves as the means by which interlocutors can openly resolve their differences.

Arguments which test and redeem validity claims can be considered in terms of three different dimensions: a process, a procedure and a production capacity.[1] The processual dimension is important because argument resides in the domain of communicative reasoning where actors engage one another's reasons in an effort to reach an informed consensus. However, while Habermas includes the processual logic of argument in his theory, he believes that considered only as interaction, argument does not provide a means to ground the common rules that undergird consensus building. In other words, if the procedural dimensions of argument are excluded from the theory, there is no way of discerning between claims that are valid and those that are merely popular; hence, no way to distinguish between effective tactics and valid communication. To rectify this problem, Habermas merges the procedural and processual logic of argumentation by showing that universal validity claims presupposed in any communicative utterance structure interactions that lead to mutual understanding. Thus, Habermas maintains that the power of argumentation to circumscribe reasonable practice lays in its ability to reference validity claims raised in the utterances of speakers. By thematizing contested validity claims, argumentation is the primary vehicle by which individuals transform misunderstandings and disputes into constructive consensus (*Theory* 1:18).

> Thus the rationality proper to the communicative practice of everyday life points to the practice of argumentation as a court of appeal that makes it possible to continue communicative action with other means when disagreements can no longer be repaired with everyday routines and yet are not to be settled by the direct or strategic use of force. (*Theory* 1:17)

The communicative office of argumentation, as a means of securing informed and grounded consensus, leads Habermas to a deep suspicion of rhetoric to the extent that rhetorical argument grasps the reasons of others as obstacles to be overcome by deploying strategic means of communication.[2] However, Habermas' theory of argumentation does not fully justify his skepticism of rhetoric to the extent that it does not provide a means by which to discern instances where the rules of argumentative engagement are violated; rules serve as normative guidelines only to the extent that all parties recognize their violation. Thus, the ability to differentiate between open argumentation and the strategic practice of rhetoric depends on whether argumentation can be understood as both a rule governed event and a process that is grounded in social practice.

STRATEGIC AND COMMUNICATIVE ACTION

Habermas is skeptical of strategic argument and rhetoric because such appeals are subservient to instrumental rationality, a form of Enlightenment reasoning which reduces norms of reasoning, values, motives, and competencies to objects of nature, thus reifying human understanding. In this respect, the project of the Frankfurt school has been to expose the defects of Enlightenment reasoning by demonstrating how Western reason is not a neutral means of securing truth. Rather, claims to rationality merely disguise the pursuits of interests. Such a pursuit enshrines means-ends thinking that promises successful intervention into the natural world.[3]

Habermas' social action theory is heavily indebted to this critique of Enlightenment reason. However, he does not share its pessimistic vision to the extent that his theory of argument oriented toward consensus serves as a means by which to regain the normative ground lost to unbridled systems of strategic action (*Philosophical* 106–29). Yet while Habermas seeks to abandon the strictures of negative dialectics, he understands that a theory of argumentation based on universal rules of validity is insufficient to overcome the force of instrumental reason; rules can be exploited and misused. Where the need to follow rules ignores the importance of reflection, the process of reaching understanding risks collapse. Thus, the key issue becomes how Habermas can demonstrate that the potential for open, reflective argumentation emerges from a theory of argumentation that integrates rule based appeals to validity claims and an account of how certain social action contexts resist the effects of instrumentalization.

For Habermas, the ability to overcome the irrationality of Enlightenment instrumentality comes with a consideration of how instrumental and communicative arguments emerge from different forms of human activity; that is, Habermas seeks to isolate modes and contexts of human action which resist purposive rational codification (*Knowledge* 15–19). Habermas believes that it is possible to loosen the grip of purposive rationality by uncovering spheres of individual action which arise in conjunction with, but are separate from, instrumental knowledge (*Knowledge* 47). This expansion of Horkheimer and Adorno's project is significant in that critique is now able to train its eye not just on the external effects of the Enlightenment, but also on the aspects of human action which led to the creation of systems of instrumental reason in the first place; what is, for Habermas, the very site of communicative rationality.

To break the ground for this theory of reflective argument, Habermas returns to Marx's theory of social labor and dialectical materialism. Habermas expands Marx's thinking in order to isolate the differences between the forces and relations of production. Specifically, he argues that Marx's strictly materialist understanding of social relations blinds him to the fact that systems of exchange are sustained only by way of individual and social processes of self-generation; that is, market exchange occurs only in conjunction with forms of practical/communicative action.[4]

In the creation of labor thus comes the first glimpse of humanity as social subjects. Habermas' position is that Marx's materialist dialectic has to be expanded to include both technical and communal interests; the ability to exploit nature is not enough to explain the breadth of human action. What Marx does not account for is the fact that systems of labor and exchange are premised on the ability of individuals to come to an open agreement about how the system should develop and proceed; the exploitive reality of the market is mediated by normative guidelines which are established through a process of social interaction that occurs independent of, yet in conjunction with, forces of exchange (Habermas, *Knowledge* 31–39). By arguing that the creation of meaningful forms of exchange are accompanied by open forms of social interaction, Habermas is thus able to overcome positivism's interpretation of human knowledge by expanding the epistemic potential of human communication.

> . . . [T]he interests constitutive of knowledge are linked to the functions of an ego that adapts itself to its external conditions through learning processes, is initiated into the communication system of a social life-world by means of self-formative processes, and constructs an identity in the conflict between instinctual aims and social constraints. In turn these achievements become part of the productive forces accumulated by a society, the cultural tradition through which a society interprets itself, and the legitimations that a society accepts or criticizes. (*Knowledge* 313)

By reconnecting knowledge and interest through a critique and expansion of the materialist dialectic, Habermas' theory is able to securely ground the theory of intersubjective argument geared toward the achievement of consensus. In order to delineate the exact limits of such communicative practice, Habermas returns to *Dialectic of Enlightenment* and engages its understanding of subjective reason. Habermas agrees with Horkheimer and Adorno that there is in fact, a crisis of reason which occurs insofar as "[t]he rationalization of the lifeworld makes possible a kind of systemic integration that enters into competition with the integrating principle of reaching understanding and, under certain conditions, has a disintegrative effect on the lifeworld" (Habermas, *Theory* 1:342–43). As with Weber, Habermas argues that, when institutionalized, reason has an inherent tendency to instrumentalize social integration and undermine normative development. The result is that meaningful communication and noncoercive forms of socialization are distorted and replaced with preinterpreted symbols that do not admit of either understanding or criticism (Habermas, *Theory* 1:354). Moreover, Habermas argues that the cleavage between instrumental reason and the logic of sociation processes can be understood on a linguistic level: strategic or instrumental speech takes the form of interactions that are based on goal achievement and self-preservation, whereas social integration takes place through speech orientations geared toward reaching intersubjective understanding.[5]

Habermas has two rationales for carefully delineating the boundaries of strategic and communicative action. First, he argues that a fuller understanding of social development signals that a number of interactions depend on an open, cooperative process of understanding. Habermas softens Horkheimer and Adorno's thesis that purposive rationality co-opts meaning, by arguing that many—but not all—important sites of social action have little meaning when placed in an instrumental framework. Using a theory of knowledge constitutive interests, Habermas demonstrates that norms emerge from processes of self-development that cannot be accounted for in an instrumental framework; that is, strategic action undercuts the cooperative, communicative process by which individuals justify and agree to rules of social behavior (*Moral* 66). Consequently, Habermas invokes the distinction between communicative and strategic action in order to account for the dialogic quality of lifeworld interactions and to ensure that ethics are resituated within the boundaries of human knowledge (*Theory* 1:288).

While Habermas is adamant in differentiating instrumental reason and communicative action, he is careful not to make the case that intersubjective understanding and normative development occur in an individual or social context which rejects goal seeking or teleological action. Thus, the second distinction that Habermas makes in his account of strategic and communicative action is that the social pathologies which Horkheimer and Adorno attributed to modernist reason are actually caused by the institutionalization of instrumental rationality. Owing to their need to secure mass loyalty, Habermas argues that institutions use strategic speech in order to ensure that individual and public decisions are made in the name of social stability (*Theory* 2:352). While to some degree inevitable, this form of institutional action potentially distorts the means of communication on which individuals rely to form agreements and coordinate action.[6] Habermas argues that as the institutional mediatization of culture grows, it becomes more and more difficult to understand and criticize the decisions that guide social development. This communicative fragmentation threatens both the individual and the lifeworld to the extent that communication no longer serves the goal of understanding, but rather works to perpetuate the colonization of sociopolitical life (*Theory* 1:355).

In sum, Habermas argues that by understanding argumentation in terms of both its procedures and its social origins, it is possible to establish a theory of communicative action that is resilient in the face of instrumental encroachments. Using both appeals to validity claims and a reflective understanding of the social contexts in which they operate, interlocutors can use arguments as a means of coming to mutual understanding. However, by reading Marx and Horkheimer and Adorno against one another in order to differentiate communicative and instrumental action, Habermas does not address the possibility that in noninstitutionalized contexts, strategic action may, in fact, be necessary to create the conditions for consensus building. Thus, the critical question becomes: How and when does strategy best enter into communicative argument?

THE RHETORICAL DIMENSIONS OF CONSENSUS FORMATION

The viability of Habermas' theory of communicative action is largely contingent on the ability of critique to differentiate instrumental and communicative forms of speech; that is, to establish criteria which explicitly ground the process of openly generating intersubjective consensus. By expanding epistemology to include the human interests that give rise to communication, Habermas is able to provide such criteria through a theory of argumentation that is based on speech acts and the ability of actors to problematize validity claims in discernible social contexts. Once understood in these terms, argumentation becomes a means of mediating action with reason insofar as decisions are based on the intersubjective recognition of the force of the better argument. Habermas recognizes that controversy may undermine attempts to reach consensus based on the force of the better argument. However, his solution to this problem not only serves to reconfigure the boundaries of strategic and communicative action but it also points to an explicit need to include rhetoric within the practice of open argumentation.

In making the case that the goals of social integration, individual development, and action coordination are best secured through intersubjective communication, Habermas isolates two necessary components of consensus formation: the need for participants to share a set of common assumptions that can ground argumentation, and the ability to use these assumptions to rationally discuss a problem, reach agreement and coordinate actions.

> In coming to an understanding with one another about their situation, participants in interaction stand in a cultural tradition that they at once use and renew; in coordinating their actions by way of intersubjectively recognizing criticizable validity claims, they are at once relying on membership in social groups. . . . Under the functional aspect of mutual understanding, communicative action serves to transmit and renew cultural knowledge; under the aspect of coordinating action, it serves social integration and the establishment of solidarity; finally, under the aspect of socialization, communicative action serves the formation of personal identities. The symbolic structures of the lifeworld are reproduced by way of the continuation of valid knowledge, stabilization of group solidarity, and socialization of responsible actors. (*Theory* 2:137)

Habermas' position is problematic on two levels: the theory tacitly makes the assumption that individuals necessarily share background knowledge on which to base argument, and moreover that rational argumentation is always geared to cooperation and action coordination. Goodnight's theory of controversy and oppositional argument problematizes both of these presuppositions (4–9). In addition to the function of reaching agreement, argumentation also creates breaches in accepted patterns of interaction. These breaches, according to Goodnight, can be conceptualized as arguments that question and delegitimize common assumptions about the relationship of reason and argument. Moreover, to the extent that oppositional argument can entail rational, nonrational and irrational components, controversies may serve not to garner agreement among social actors, but rather, to problematize and undermine common frames of reference and communication procedures.[7]

Habermas is not entirely blind to this dilemma and he takes it to mean that his definition of strategic action is too constricting. Specifically, he finds that in situations which lack shared common knowledge on which to base discourse, it is necessary to have a mechanism by which individuals can introduce new terms that can serve as the starting point for communicative action. In essence, what is called for is an expansion of communicative action to allow for the possibility of strategically generating the preconditions of consensual interaction.[8]

> The background of a communicative utterance is thus formed by situation definitions that, as measured against the actual need for mutual understanding, have to overlap to a sufficient extent. *If this commonality cannot be presupposed, the actors have to draw upon means of strategic action, with an orientation toward coming to a mutual understanding,* so as to bring about a common definition of the situation or to negotiate one directly—which occurs in everyday communicative practice primarily in the form of "repair work." (Habermas, *Theory* 2:121; emphasis added)

At face value, the notion of introducing strategic action (perlocutions) into interactions geared toward reaching intersubjective consensus (illocutions) seems to confound Habermas' distinctions between the two forms of behavior. James Bohman suggests that Habermas' inability to strictly distinguish between strategic and communicative action proves that Habermas' theory does not admit to forms of emancipatory-communicative practice necessary for social change (Bohman 186). Working through both Skjei's and Wood's objections to speech act theory, Bohman holds that illocutions and perlocutions overlap such that perlocutions capable of initiating social emancipation fall within the bounds of what Habermas calls communicative action (Bohman 195).

Centering his critique of Habermas on the need to revitalize the mission of the social critic, Bohman ties his theory of "communicative/emancipatory perlocutions" to the rhetorical dimensions of communicative action. Bohman highlights the submerged role for rhetoric in Habermas' position when he writes, "In fact, rhetoric is not at all like ideology or distorted communication, but is the employment of strategic means to achieve communicative effects like changes in beliefs, desires, and attitudes" (202). At base, Bohman is convinced that the need for including this form of rhetoric within the bounds of communicative action stems from a paradox that Habermas is forced into when he draws too strong a distinction between illocutionary and perlocutionary speech (Bohman 200); that is, if a speaker interested in social change cannot employ forms of strategic action, communication with individuals whose language has been subject to systematic distortion becomes impossible to the degree that the interaction becomes one in which the rational force of the better argument has no meaning.

Bohman's sensitivity to the need to investigate the potential for rhetorical practice within Habermas' theory is laudable. Yet his theory falls victim to an overly narrow reading of how Habermas justifies the introduction of strategic speech into communicative action. In particular, Bohman's assertion that perlocutions can be strategic in character, but communicative in intention, is devoid of an analysis of the specific conditions in which rhetorical practice can be introduced into Habermas' theory without distorting its most basic premises. In fact, by not fully appreciating Habermas' claim that "communicative intention" is determined solely by the ability of actors to intersubjectively understand the reasons contained in speech, Bohman's emancipatory rhetoric threatens to unravel Habermas' entire project to the extent that the theory legitimizes speech geared toward social change that is not responsible for its own reasons and justifications (Habermas, *Theory* 1:276–78).

Close scrutiny of Habermas' explanation of how strategic action can generate terms on which to base consensus building underscores the problems with Bohman's theory of communicative perlocutions. By concentrating on the ambiguity of speech act theory, Bohman misunderstands Habermas' central thesis in developing the theory of communicative action; that is, Bohman does not consider that the essential characteristic of communicative speech is not its renunciation of teleological motives, but rather, within an orientation to reaching understanding, individuals are able to intersubjectively recognize and criticize the validity claims that are raised by speech acts (Habermas, *Theory* 1:99). Only through open discussion are speakers able to arrive at a form of mutual understanding that overcomes the concealed power interests that haunt instrumental communication and Bohman's vision of rhetorical practice and criticism.

Admittedly, Habermas is somewhat ambiguous in his justifications for allowing the use of strategic action to create the background agreements necessary for consensus building. However, at base, his position rests on several aspects of his larger critique of the relationship of language and social development. Initially, Habermas' position is premised on the recognition that communicative distortion is not the result of purposive rationality per se, but rather, the institutionalization of instrumental reason into forms of social steering media. Habermas is sensitive to the fact that communicative interaction cannot be conceptualized apart from notions of teleology; intuitively, communication geared toward mutual understanding does not occur solely in contexts that lack goal seeking behavior. Rather, communicative action occurs insofar as participants have the goal of reaching understanding and agreement. Arguing that communicative action is a process by which actors coordinate teleologically structured actions, Habermas maintains that the essential distinction between constructive communication and distorting, purposive rationality is that the latter explicitly dismisses the need to approach interactions in terms which admit to an open and reciprocal examination of the thematized validity claims in speech acts (*Theory* 1:288).

Specifically, by working back through the argument that the interests of labor (instrumental action) and language (orientations geared toward understanding) develop as complementary modes of knowledge, Habermas connects social development to forms of human behavior that submit to an explicit interest in mutual understanding; that is, Habermas holds communicative action to be the means by which individuals orient themselves to the tasks of action coordination, social integration and socialization (*Theory* 2:60). The telos of communicative action is the willingness of actors to openly provide the reasons that undergird their arguments in order to facilitate the process of coming to agreement. Thus, unlike institutionally grounded forms of strategic action, communicative action emphasizes the orientation of speakers to intersubjective understanding and the willingness of interactants to keep their decisions contingent on the outcome of debate and critical reflection.

> These steering media replace language as the mechanism for coordinating action. They set social action loose from integration through value consensus and switch it over to purposive rationality steered by media. Because Weber's action is too narrowly gauged, he is unable to see in money and power the media, which, by substituting for language, make possible the differentiation of subsystems of purposive rational action. It is these media, and not

directly the purposive rational action orientations themselves, that need to be institutionally and motivationally anchored in the lifeworld. (*Theory* 1:342).

At base, Habermas' position is fairly straightforward: communicative action depends on the recognition—now epistemologically grounded—by individuals that the goal of argumentation is to reach understanding. To the extent that all participants share this goal, then the use of strategic action to generate the background conditions for consensus formation is relatively unproblematic; the key is that the strategic action be initiated within the larger context of creating discourse that is open to critical evaluation by all those who have an interest in the outcome of the argument. Thus, Habermas' conception of the nature of strategic action within a communicative setting changes in a subtle way; that is, it is not instrumental per se, but rather, serves to introduce terms which recontextualize and carry the consensus building process forward.

The merger of strategic and communicative action is not a deviation from Habermas' understanding of the original use of language; that is, in the context of communicative action, the creation of a system of social labor requires a means by which to formulate terms (and later meanings) which can serve to undergird the process of consensus building. What is crucial for Habermas in preserving the viability of the theory in the face of its necessary revision is that the coordination and integration functions of communicative action give rise to a conception of consensus which has distinctly normative implications.

Norms are critical components in the consensus building process insofar as they circumscribe acceptable modes of behavior and create the opportunity for equal and full participation. As does Mead, Habermas holds that communicative action and its resultant consensus fulfills the normative dimensions of human open interactions to the extent that individuals use generalized knowledge about each other in order to arrive at common understandings (*Theory* 2:60; *Philosophical* 197). This normative dimension of consensus building serves to insulate communicative action which begins with the strategic action from the pathology of instrumental steering media; the prior consensus needed to instantiate communicative action can stem from strategic action which is grounded normatively and not in the exclusively instrumental function of labor. As such, situations which give rise to an interest in consensus oriented discourse cannot be reduced to questions of instrumentality to the extent that such actions are deemed inappropriate to the normative backdrop of the situation (Habermas, *Knowledge* 91–103).

In sum, Habermas is faced with the problem that actors may not always have the common background by which to begin the process of building consensus. If a consensus cannot be achieved owing to a lack of common background definitions then this usually implicit aspect of communicative practice must be created. Habermas wants to hold that this process can be characterized as the use of strategic action to generate common assumptions in order to initiate consensus formation. At the same time, Habermas argues that the problems usually associated with strategic communication do not unduly taint the openness of the consensus building process because it is strategic action that is situated within an explicit orientation and interest in understanding. In other words, by setting the strategic creation of consensus within the larger normative context of intersubjective understanding, Habermas insulates the interaction from the problems of instrumental distortion (*Moral* 108).

What then is the potential for rhetoric within the context of communicative action? An answer comes with a reconsideration of Goodnight's theory of controversy and its implications for argumentation and consensus. Goodnight's analysis highlights the fact that oppositional argument blocks the creation of consensus by delegitimizing previously unquestioned forms of reason and action (20). Such opposition undermines consensus building on two levels: controversy can deprive speakers of a common basis by which to begin the consensus building process and it can block the agreements that are needed to actually coordinate action. When juxtaposed against the theory of communicative action, Goodnight's position demonstrates that Habermas does not fully account for the ways in which consensus building can be blocked. While Habermas accounts for the need to strategically create the preconditions for consensus building, he is content to make the case that from this common preunderstanding, social actors can coordinate actions and make decisions based on the force of the better argument. However, recalling Habermas' critique of Marx, the power of the theory of communicative action is its ability to not only explain, but also sustain, normative modes of human action. In these terms the theory is obligated to account for the practical dimensions of social action coordination (Habermas, *Theory* 2:137–52).

Habermas' position is that, relative to the problems of actually reaching agreement presented by a theory of oppositional argument, agreements are constructed through recourse to rational argument (*Theory* 1:18). Habermas relies on the idea that the intersubjective recognition of validity claims and the normative interests that arise with a concern for assuring universal participation and recognition of arguments are sufficient for the generation of a rationally ascribed agreement. However, what Goodnight alerts us to is that, in controversial situations, the theoretical power that Habermas ascribes to the "force of the better argument" may beg the question of how actors are to reach agreement and act in relation to that agreement.

The problem facing Habermas is that while he establishes a means by which to secure the initial conditions for consensus building, he does not extend his thinking to account for situations in which actors cannot come to agreement within the context of consensus building itself. For example, in a situation in which individuals share—in principle—the desire to reach a common goal, each may have a radically different means for achieving that goal. The problem becomes that in the ensuing controversy over the most appropriate way of proceeding, each party may introduce arguments that call into question the fundamental reasonability of the other's position. To be clear, the problem here is not one that necessarily involves sheerly instrumental communication or which exists only in the preconsensus building stage—each party can openly express his or her motives, communicate the reasons which back his or her positions and still be unable to arrive at an agreement that is capable of sustaining social action. Rather, the dilemma is that Habermas' notion of the force of the better argument does not have the theoretical teeth to resolve controversies in which each participant delegitimizes the reasons presented by the other. The reason for this problem is that Habermas is committed to an unnecessarily narrow view of rational argument within the larger context of actors working to achieve understanding. What Habermas does not discern is that just as there are *reasons* to strategically generate the background conditions necessary for consensus building, there are also *reasons* as to why forms of strategic action may be necessary to come to a rationally based agreement that can ground social actions.

The productive inclusion of a theory of rhetoric within communicative action comes with the recognition that strategic action's role in consensus building can be extended to explain how forms of oppositional argument are converted into productive forms of agreement and social action. In distinction to Bohman's theory of emancipatory criticism, a dialectical reading of Habermas' introduction of strategic action to generate the potential for consensus indicates how rhetorical practice partially fulfills the action coordination function of the theory of communicative action without distorting its fundamental premises. Rhetoric becomes, in Habermas' terms, a mode of strategic action that is capable of resolving differences that block agreement and which are not reconcilable solely through the force of the better argument.

The rhetorical practice implied by the unrealized dialectic of communicative understanding in Habermas' theory of communicative action can be characterized as the ability of actors to "strategically" substitute appeals geared toward action coordination for those arguments or validity claims which block agreement (*Moral* 67). Rhetoric becomes a mode of reconfiguring action potentials in terms that bracket controversy and which move outside the bounds of the debate in order to provide alternative justifications for action. Like Farrell's conception of social knowledge, rhetoric temporarily attributes a social consensus to interactants in order to offer a basis for action that overcomes the controversial dimensions of the action being debated (Farrell 10). This is not to say that the controversy is necessarily dismissed, but rather, rhetoric informs public practice in such a way that it becomes possible to either return to the dispute in light of the new justifications for action or to recognize that the original dispute no longer precludes action. Thus, in the face of the need to act, rhetoric provides a means by which to overcome the lack of certain agreement in which individuals cannot reconcile their differences.

Although rhetoric is useful in understanding how action coordination can occur in the face of controversy, a consideration of rhetoric in relationship to Habermas' theory must occur reflectively insofar as it is necessary to account for how rhetoric functions with respect to the limit cases of communicative action [*sic*]. Rhetorical theory must not limit its scope to a concern for sheer effectiveness; that is, in the context of communicative interactions, rhetorical practice must acknowledge its own standing and presuppositions through a reflective investigation of its own assumptions and communicative goals. In this regard, by serving as a way of dispelling controversy, rhetoric is an important means by which to understand the relationship between reason and human activity.

Situated within a theory of argumentation geared toward the achievement of understanding, rhetorical theory serves to discern the outer limits of the force of the better argument. Specifically, in situations which do not initially admit to action coordination through argumentation, rhetoric introduces a mode of argument and communication that is capable of both negotiating controversy and creating the possibility for reaching understanding. In Blumenberg's terms, rhetoric serves as a means of initiating the ongoing process of communicative interaction (432–34). Thus, understood within the argumentative and epistemological framework of communicative action, rhetoric is neither an end nor the presentation of the final and definitive word, but rather the beginning of an interaction which privileges intersubjective agreement. If rhetoric is understood as the ability to strategically introduce proposals for action, then it serves as the logical and practical counterpart of argument; rhetoric provides a means by which to engage in argument during instances of controversy and opposition and thus, rhetoric mediates practical action by way of a concern for mutual understanding.[9]

Habermas' attempt to understand the relationship between reason and social development is based on his ability to discern the roots of communicative practice in both the practice of argumentation and an expanded theory of knowledge. This essay has attempted to trace key portions of Habermas' theory of argument in order to demonstrate that social actions which are based on the intersubjective recognition of the force of the better argument require some recourse to rhetoric; that is, a carefully constructed notion of strategic action can serve as means by which to create situational commonality in instances where interlocutors are unable to mutually agree on acceptable standards of reason. Thus, while Habermas' theory demonstrates how argumentation serves the interest of fashioning a vision of the common good, it does not fully realize that controversy can subvert the norms of communication and thus thwart consensus building. In some situations, norms must be recontextualized through rhetorical practice. This recontextualization serves to sustain consensus building by demonstrating that objections can be overcome through the presentation of alternative justifications for action.

In attempting to conceptualize argumentation and rhetoric in terms of how they provide a means of understanding social rationalization, this essay has not sought to develop a specific theory of rhetorical practice; but rather has served what might best be called "the pretheoretical goal" of understanding the necessary ties between forms of communication that are commonly thought to work from largely incompatible ideas of reason. The view, held widely in many philosophical circles, that rhetoric and argumentation are exclusive forms of communicative action is outmoded. To be sure, they have distinct and important differences, but today, the fragmentation of social and cultural decision making requires that critical theorists attempt to fully account for the means by which individuals and public communicate. To this end, if critical theory is to fully realize the connections between action and reason then one of its most important tasks is to investigate how both communicative argument and rhetoric serve the ends of consensus building. Only when these possibilities are fully considered in light of social rationalization will critical theory be able to take up the really interesting problem of how social criticism can account for the ties between human understanding and practical wisdom.

NOTES

[1] Habermas, *Theory* 1:25. This position is developed in much greater detail in Joseph Wenzel's essay on the dialectical, rhetorical and logical nature of argumentation.

[2] For an excellent discussion of rhetoric's reception in critical philosophy see Beiner; Benhabib and Dallmayr.

[3] The effects of the Enlightenment on language are most clearly demonstrated by Horkheimer and Adorno: "Reason is based on an exchange. Specific objectives should only be achieved, as it were on the open market, through the small benefits which power can obtain by playing off one concession against another and following the rules of the game. But cleverness becomes meaningless as soon as power ceases to obey rules and chooses direct appropriation instead. The medium of the traditional bourgeois intelligence—that is, discussion—then breaks down. Individuals can no longer talk to each other and know it: they therefore make the game into a serious and responsible institution which requires the application of all available strength to ensure that there is no proper conversation and at the same time no silence" (209–10).

[4] Habermas is explicit in making the connection between the creation of labor and the need for a mode of communication that can mediate the development of exchange: "The processes of natural history are mediated by the productive activity of individuals and the organization of their interrelations. These relations are subject to norms that decide, with the force of

institutions, how responsibilities and rewards, obligations and charges to the social budget are distributed among members. The medium in which these relations of subjects and groups are normatively regulated is cultural tradition. It forms the linguistic communication structure on the basis of which subjects interpret both nature and themselves in their environment" (*Knowledge* 53).

5 Habermas writes: "A communicatively achieved agreement has a rational basis; it cannot be imposed by either party, whether instrumentally through intervention in the situation directly or strategically through influencing the decisions of opponents" (*Theory* 1:287).

6 For a discussion of communicative distortion see Habermas, "On Systemically."

7 A similar criticism of Habermas' idea of strategic action has been leveled by John Keane: "The supporting consensus that sustains all communicative action has, rather, a profoundly political or public character. Communicative action already and always presupposes the emancipatory, political goal of subjects living together and reaching agreement through reciprocal understanding, shared knowledge, common accord and mutual trust" (159).

8 Habermas writes: "In this phase participants have either to shift the level of metacommunication or to employ means of indirectly achieving understanding. Coming indirectly to an understanding proceeds according to the model of intentionalist semantics. Through perlocutionary effects, the speaker gives the hearer something to understand which he cannot (yet) directly communicate. In this phase, then, the perlocutionary acts have to be embedded in contexts of communicative action. These strategic elements within a use of language oriented to reaching understanding can be distinguished from strategic actions through the fact that the entire sequence of a stretch of talk stands—on the part of all participants—under the presuppositions of communicative action" (*Theory* 1:331).

9 Admitting rhetoric into a communicative action setting does not necessarily mean that the resulting claims lack either reasons or normative standing. Rather, rhetoric works to create modes of action within the larger context of presenting claims that are open to inspection and criticism. The result is that rhetoric functions not simply to encourage social action but to do so against the backdrop of reasons that ground the normative underpinnings of communication.

WORKS CITED

Beiner, Ronald. *Political Judgment*. Chicago: Univ. of Chicago Press, 1983.

Benhabib, Seyla, and Fred Dallmayr, ed. *The Communicative Ethics Controversy*. Cambridge: MIT Press, 1990.

Blumenberg, Hans. "An Anthropological Approach to the Contemporary Significance of Rhetoric." *After Philosophy: End or Transformation?* Ed. Kenneth Baynes. Cambridge: MIT Press, 1987. 429–58.

Bohman, James. "Emancipation and Rhetoric: The Perlocutions and Illocutions of the Social Critic." *Philosophy and Rhetoric* 21 (1988): 185–204.

Farrell, Thomas. "Knowledge, Consensus, and Rhetorical Theory." *Quarterly Journal of Speech* 62 (1976): 1–14.

Goodnight, G. Thomas. "Controversy." *Argument in Controversy: Proceedings of the Seventh SCA/AFA Conference on Argumentation*. Ed. Donn Parson. Annandale VA: Speech Communication Association, 1991. 1–13.

Habermas, Jürgen. *Knowledge and Human Interests*. Trans. Jeremy Shapiro. Boston: Beacon, 1971.

———. *Moral Consciousness and Communicative Action*. Trans. Christian Lenhardt and Shierry Weber Nicholsen. Cambridge: MIT Press, 1990.

———. "On Systemically Distorted Communication." *Inquiry* 13 (1970): 205–18.

———. *The Philosophical Discourse of Modernity: Twelve Lectures*. Trans. Frederick Lawrence. Cambridge: MIT Press, 1987.

———. *The Theory of Communicative Action*. Trans. Thomas McCarthy. 2 vols. Boston: Beacon, 1984, 1987.

Horkheimer, Max, and Theodor Adorno. *Dialectic of Enlightenment*. Trans. John Cumming. New York: Continuum, 1988.

Keane, John. *Public Life and Late Capitalism: Toward A Socialist Theory of Democracy*. Cambridge: Cambridge Univ. Press, 1984.

Wenzel, Joseph. "Jürgen Habermas and the Dialectical Perspective on Argumentation." *Journal of the American Forensic Association* 16 (1979): 83–94.

....

Regulating Disagreement, Constituting Participants: A Critique of Proceduralist Theories of Democracy

DARRIN HICKS AND LENORE LANGSDORF

In his keynote address at the 1995 Ontario Society for the Study of Argumentation conference, Frans van Eemeren contended that '[a]rgumentative discussion is the main tool for managing democratic processes' and therefore, 'argumentation should be valued as the elixir of life of participatory democracy' (1995, p. 145). Because we agree that argumentation is the lifeblood of democratic governance, we believe that it is crucial to explicate the relationship between argumentation and democracy. This relationship is complex, and the lack of a single account of argumentative activity or a unitary conception of democracy makes its analysis difficult.

Joseph Wenzel (1990) identifies three distinct perspectives from which to theorize argumentation:

- a *logical* perspective focuses on relevancy, sufficiency, and acceptability of the arguments made by individuals to justify their convictions;
- a *rhetorical* perspective focuses on the process by which argumentative discourse simultaneously appeals to and creates the communal identities and norms that serve as the bases for persuasion (cf. Greene, 1997); and
- a *dialectical* perspective finds in communicative interaction the resources for developing a set of principled procedures for resolving differences of opinion.

Correlatively, we propose, Jurgen Habermas (1994, 1996a) identifies three normative conceptions of democracy:

- a *liberal* conception understands the role of government as mediating between the conflicting private interests of individuals;
- a *republican* conception understands the purpose of politics as the articulation of a common good embodied in the ethical life of a community; and
- a *procedural* conception claims democratic legitimacy cannot be guaranteed by either the administrative capacities of the state/market or the virtues of ethical communities, but instead is grounded in the very structures of communicative action and the procedures that secure fair and critical discussion.

In this essay we use these three perspectives on argument set out by Wenzel (1990) and the three normative conceptions of democracy formulated by Habermas (1994, 1996a) as a point of departure in order to identify three distinct models of public deliberation:

- a *liberal* model, underwritten by a *logical* argumentation theory, views deliberation as a modus vivendi for mediating the competing claims of special interest groups whose differences can be settled by either the force of universal reason or strategic bargaining;
- a *republican* model, accompanied by a *rhetorical* theory of argument, views deliberation as an opportunity for the citizens of a community to participate in the formulation of a substantive vision of the good life—a vision that is woven into the historical memory of a community and which serves as the foundation of civic virtue (Aune, 1994); and
- a *proceduralist* model presupposes a *dialectical* theory of argumentation and views deliberation as a method for regulating disagreement and resolving

differences of opinion through critical discussion, understood as a method that shifts political power from interest groups and ethical commitments to an institutional framework constituted by a set of rules for managing difference (van Eemeren, 1995).

We focus on proceduralist accounts of democratic deliberation here, because while proceduralist accounts of deliberative democracy have been the focus of a great deal of work in philosophy and political science, their relationship to argumentation theory and pedagogy has been relatively unnoticed.

Proceduralist models of deliberation differ from liberal and republican models in that they claim that the norms of democratic legitimacy do not rely on any descriptive or prescriptive model of the subject. Rather, they promise that legitimate solutions—that is, morally justifiable and rationally produced solutions—to vexing social problems can emerge from critical discussions governed by nothing more than the organic norms arising from the rules of discourse and forms of argumentation. Thus, proceduralist models can claim to avoid reliance upon one or another form of (currently disparaged) subject-centered epistemology and political theory.

We are in sympathy with the aims of proceduralist theories, but believe that this strategy of avoiding discussion of conditions for public deliberation—and specifically, failing to attend to how the participants who are necessary conditions for the sustenance of deliberative democracy are nurtured—threatens their cogency. In effect, the exclusive focus on the procedures regulating public deliberation rests on two presumed dimensions: the value of normatively driven critical debate's product (result), which is deliberative democracy; and the nature of the participants who are crucial conditions for the possibility of deliberation. We focus on the latter dimension here, in order to draw out some implications for argumentation theory and pedagogy that develop from considering who is capable of participating in the deliberative spaces theorized by proceduralist models of public argumentation.

Our critical appreciation and supplement to procedural models of public deliberation develops in three parts. In the first, we set out the contours and assumptions of procedural theories of deliberation. In the second part of the paper we examine a particular presupposition of these theories, namely that they smuggle in *de facto* substantive-ethical commitments embodied in an image of an idealized arguer. In the third part of the paper we propose that procedural theories can be strengthened if we acknowledge that procedures not only govern argumentative activity, but constitute those who engage in argumentation. We conclude by advocating a constitutive proceduralism that can theorize how argumentation theory and pedagogy function as forms of cultural policy and political education.

SECTION ONE: PROCEDURAL THEORIES

Procedural theories work from the presupposition that disagreement is an enduring feature of democratic society and, hence, an interminable element of its political institutions. Seyla Benhabib notes that proceduralist conceptions of democracy proceed on the assumption of value pluralism: 'Disagreement about the highest-goods of human existence and the proper conduct of a morally righteous life are a fundamental feature of our modern value universe since the end of natural law cosmologies in the sixteenth and seventeenth centuries, and the eventual separation between church and state' (1996, p. 73). The sources of disagreement are pervasive and diverse. Gutmann and Thompson (1996) identify four sources of deep moral disagreement: the relative scarcity of material goods, self-interest and limited generosity, the presence of fundamentally incompatible values, and the necessary incompleteness of knowledge and understanding. They propose that each of these sources is an essential feature of the human condition. Thus, even if we could eliminate economic, racial, and gender inequalities, and even if people were better motivated and social resources were less limited, disagreement would remain a 'permanent condition of democratic politics' (Gutmann and Thompson, 1996, p. 9).

Not all forms of disagreement are amenable to democratic life: Gutmann and Thompson (1996, pp. 2–3) distinguish deliberative from non-deliberative forms of disagreement. In deliberative disagreement, citizens who disagree with others still recognize that a position and its advocates are worthy of respect even if they think the position is wrong. Therefore, they will make every effort to listen to their opponents and will accommodate their convictions as much as they can without compromising their own. Non-deliberative disagreement, on the other hand, does not allow room for respect, accommodation, and resolution of conflict through argument. Instead, it settles for defining democracy as a choice between isolation or conquest. It is the challenge of seeing our irreducible differences as resources— and thus, as potential sources of good—as well as obstacles in devising ways of living together in a just and reasonable manner, that warrants the invention of procedural theories of democracy. When people cannot agree on matters of substance, they may not be precluded from agreeing on relatively abstract regulative rules and procedures for governing their critical discussion.

Given that disagreement is defined as both an essential condition of human existence and a potential good, procedural theorists do not advocate avoiding or quarantining disagreement, but rather, managing or regulating it in ways that make it amenable to the democratic resolution of disputes. It is this focus on disagreement that defines the scope and function of procedural theories. Regulation, as defined by Hunt (1993), 'involves the deployment of specific knowledges encapsulated in legal or quasilegal forms of interventions in specific social practices whose resultants have consequences for the distribution of benefits and detriments for the participants in the social practices subject to regulation' (p. 314). For argumentation theory, the focus on regulation takes the form of norms of discursive legitimacy (Habermas, 1996a; Benhabib, 1996; Cohen, 1996; Dryzek, 1990) and codes of conduct for critical discussion that stipulate legitimate argumentative roles and moves (van Eemeren et al., 1993). Although the term regulation carries a negative connotation, because of its association with legal sanctions, we should be careful not to define regulation as a repressive form of power. Regulation can function as a productive form of power that should not be simply equated with control. The procedures that encourage people to speak, to reflect, and to argue are just as much methods of regulation as those that prohibit people from speaking, reflecting, and arguing.

Following Hunt (1993), we can identify four generic aspects of regulation. First is the constitution of an *object* of regulation. There are no natural or ready-made objects of regulation. As Foucault has demonstrated, even taken-for-granted objects of regulation like madness, the economy, and population had to be invented before they could be managed. The recognition of the 'fact of reasonable pluralism' (Rawls, 1993) constitutes disagreement as an object in need of regulation. A second feature of regulation is the designation and creation of regulatory *agents* who collect information, calculate costs, perform evaluations, enforce sanctions, distribute benefits, and accomplish a range of other activities. For procedural theories, it is the arguer who must regulate his or her own conduct. While theorists may design procedures and facilitators may apply them in deliberative situations, the legitimacy of procedures comes from the fact that they are self-imposed and self-enforced. We will address this need for subjects to become self-governing agents in Section Two.

The third generic aspect of regulation is the production of knowledge. As we mentioned earlier, differences can be resources as well as obstacles. When considered as resources, opposing claims instigate alternative possibilities for seeing a situation. When this aspect is exploited, 'argumentation is a means for advancing inquiry by exploring the parameters of oppositions, although it is more typically thought of as a means for bringing inquiry to closure' (Langsdorf, 1995, p. 452). Only after an object has been inscribed as a phenomenon that can be studied, measured, explicated, and criticized—in short, known—can it be regulated. Knowledge must then be translated into the form of regulatory policy and strategy.

This fourth aspect of regulation involves inventing specific *procedures* that serve as norms for managing conduct. These can take the form of prohibitions (e.g., do not advance arguments that are irrelevant to your standpoint), requirements (everyone must be given an opportunity to support his or her claims), and specifications (all participants should have a discussion-minded attitude). The production of regulatory knowledge links the objects of regulation with the formation of regulatory strategies. That is, argumentation theory develops knowledge of the sources, conditions, and consequences of disagreement which in turn makes possible the design of specific techniques for regulating those sources, conditions, and consequences. The regulatory agent, in this case the arguer, functions as both the instigator and the product of regulation. In Section Three we propose that the design of procedural models of argumentation, inasmuch as they constitute the arguer, depends upon and serves as a form of political education, and that implementation of those procedural designs within particular settings such as the classroom operates as a form of cultural policy.

Regulation, Hunt (1993, p. 325) argues, 'needs to be understood as making possible and facilitating certain forms of social relations while discouraging and disadvantaging others.' This is accomplished by articulating the 'form of regulation' (the four generic aspects of objects, agents, knowledge, and procedures) with particular 'modes of regulation' (p. 320). A mode of regulation refers to the ensemble of institutional practices that function to ensure social reproduction. For procedural theories, the mode of regulation consists of rules for managing disagreement space, and so transforming non-deliberative into deliberative disagreement that can lead to effective and democratic resolution of disputes. These rules govern disagreement in public deliberation through four parameters: (1) Identity (who is allowed to deliberate); (2) Locution (how participants should deliberate); (3) Substance (what kind of reasons are allowed); and (4) Forum (where deliberation should be located).

(1) Identity

The principle that all persons have an equal right to participate in deliberation lies at the heart of procedural theories. Yet, two facts of social life make this principle difficult to apply in practice. First, the ideal of universal citizenship is illusory; identity is essentially contestable and diverse. Second, some persons are more likely to be persuasive than others by virtue of being better educated and more eloquent. Conversely some persons are less likely to be listened to despite stating their claims within the dictates of convention and reason. When this 'disregard is systematically associated with the arguments made by those we already know to be systematically disadvantaged, we should at least reevaluate our assumptions about deliberation's democratic potential' (Sanders, 1997, p. 349). Deliberators, if they are to exercise equal rights of participation, must not only possess relative equality of resources and the ability to make arguments cogently. They must also possess relative equality in the capacity to have their claims acknowledged and taken seriously (p. 349).

For example, Wood's (1997) study of deliberation about the clean-up of potentially radioactive debris at the Rocky Flats Nuclear Arsenal (Superior, Colorado) illustrates how, despite an open invitation for all to participate, the implicit devaluing of some persons' voices and concerns—most notably those of Native-Americans, radical environmentalists and homeowners—served to turn public deliberation into a mere ritual designed to legitimate state action. The challenge for procedural theorists is to design a set of procedures that can counter these presumptive logics of exclusion in the background of deliberations. Can we accomplish this without denying some the right to speak? Those excluded from the Rocky Flats deliberations did not think so. They convened their own meetings and barred state officials and state-sponsored scientists from speaking. The meetings were revelatory, in that the concerns heretofore silenced emerged. In other words, knowledge was generated—but at the cost of another exclusionary policy. All too clearly, simply stipulating that all should participate is insufficient. Rather, forming a regulatory strategy that addresses the complex demand for equal and symmetrical participation is a necessary task for any proceduralist theory.

(2) Locution

The range and distribution of locutions that subjects can perform and still be heard as complying with the rules of critical discussion compromise the second mode of regulation. Procedural models begin by positing that all standpoints should be expressed, or at least translated into, the idiom or argumentation. Pragma-dialectical theories further stipulate the range of legitimate speech-acts that participants can perform at each stage of argumentation (van Eemeren et al., 1993). Iris Marion Young's (1996) critique of procedural conceptions of democracy focuses on this locutionary parameter. Governance that narrows the conception of deliberation to critical argumentation, she argues, assumes a culturally biased style of public discussion, for that form valorizes a disembodied, dispassionate, formal, and abstract style of speaking that excludes and devalues the styles of some individuals and groups. Young's insight into how the ways we speak are constitutive of social power provides a much needed corrective to procedural models that assume culturally neutral and universal forms of argumentation.

This assumption is refuted in Reed's (1990) ethnographic account of the implementation of Robert's Rules of Order in the Portuguese Assembly. This purportedly neutral change created a division of elected officials into those who effectively used the procedures of Robert's Rules and those who systematically refused to speak within the confines of parliamentary procedure as governed by those rules. One result of this division was the delegitimization of the assembly's ability to represent all of the citizens. The narrowing of speech into a constraining and foreign form served, in large part, to nullify the promise of democratization.

Young (1996) advocates broadening procedural theories to include a plurality of speaking styles including greeting, rhetoric, and storytelling as techniques for managing disagreement. In contrast, Benhabib (1996) strongly objects to Young's proposal to incorporate informal, relational modes of speaking into the 'public language of institutions and legislatures,' on the grounds that greetings, rhetoric, and stories are too embodied and situated to appeal to all participants (p. 83). Our sympathies lie with Young, yet we recognize that she fails to consider how increasing styles of speech appropriate to public deliberation entails increasing the reach of the regulatory apparatus. The regulation of how persons should speak is a central aspect of procedural models, yet it is one that often remains under-theorized by those who endorse discursive plurality.

(3) Substance

The requirement that persons should phrase their needs, desires, and ideals in the form of argumentative claims enables procedural theories to regulate the substance of the reasons given in support of those claims. Proceduralists do not advocate explicitly censoring ideas from public discussion. However, reasons which claim that some ideas are worth less than others and that the interests of one group should be given priority over those of others are not suitable for public delibera-tion. Although pluralism appears value neutral it embodies an inclusive stance towards diversity, which requires the 'exclusion or transformation of certain value preferences' (Rosenfeld, 1994, p. 1180). Proceduralism depends upon accepting pluralism as a substantive good: 'The process of articulating good reasons in public,' Benhabib (1996) notices, 'forces the individual to think of what would count as a good reason for all others involved. . . . Reasoning from the standpoint of all involved . . . forces one to adopt a standpoint that Hannah Arendt, following Kant, had called the "enlarged mentality"' (pp. 71–72). Would the land ethic of the radical environmentalists present at the Rocky Flats deliberations count as 'good reason for all others involved'? Benhabib's use of the word 'force' is no accident, given Hunt's (1993) reminder that regulation makes possible and facilitates 'certain forms of social relations while discouraging and disadvantaging others' (p. 325). Moreover, her claim underscores the transformative potential of procedures. We will argue, in Section Three, that procedures constitute the critically reflective agent as one imbued with an 'enlarged mentality.'

(4) Forum

It is not sufficient for procedural theories to call for the maximum number of people to be involved in deliberation and to specify the forms and types of claims and reason suitable for deliberation without taking into account where in society these procedures are to occur. Deliberation can break out at three different levels: in personal relationships between friends, families, and coworkers (the micro level), in groups such as neighborhood associations, social movements, trade unions, and religious groups that constitute the institutions of civil society (the meso level), and in state and international political organizations (the macro level) (Blaug, 1996, p. 56). The communicative demands of each level are significantly different; hence, regulatory strategies will have to adapt to the specifics of each forum. Procedural theorists have specified models for each of these contexts: Pragma-dialectical models focus on face-to-face interaction, Habermasian models focus on the network of dialectically related publics constituting civil society, and the 'new constitutional-ists' (Solum and Elkin, 1996) focus on large scale political institutions.

The demands of any particular deliberative situation raise unforeseen problems and opportunities for regulating disagreement. All procedural theories define the function of argument as disagreement-management and, therefore, devise procedural schemes for regulating the sources, conditions, and consequences of disagreement. Where they differ is in their invention of particular regulatory strategies and their selection of which of these four dimensions of regulation (identity, locution, substance, and forum) is to manage disagreement and foster deliberation. Regardless of whether a particular theory focuses on locution (e.g., pragma-dialectical theory) or substance (e.g., Rawlsian inspired models such as those sketched by Cohen, 1996), it is important to note that intervention in one of the four dimensions will have effects across the others. For instance, Young's (1996) critique of locution-based regulations points to how favoring a certain style of speech results in excluding certain identities from equally participating in public discussion.

Procedural theories must negotiate the ever-present need to balance effective resolution of disputes with the preservation of difference. On the one hand, procedural theories are resolution-centered; they do not aim to describe practices that merely settle conflicts, but to invent 'methodic procedures that enable discussants to really resolve disputes on the merits' (van Eemeren et al., 1993, p. 22). On the other hand, close attention to the application of regulatory strategies reveals exclusionary practices embedded in some procedural designs. Advocates of procedural solutions to ongoing democratic problems who see differences as potential resources, and so value pluralism, take the danger of exclusion as primary. The problem, Sanders (1997) argues, 'is how more of the people who routinely speak less—who, through various mechanisms or accidents of birth and fortune, are least expressive in and most alienated from American [sic] politics—might take part and be heard and how those who typically dominate might be made to attend to the views of others' (p. 352).

Contra Sanders (1997), we do not think that the failure of procedural models of deliberation to accommodate all forms of difference entails their outright rejection. Rather, we believe that the introduction of a principle of reflexivity can equip procedural models to address the dynamics of inclusion and exclusion (Hicks, 1995; Benhabib, 1996). That is, if we design procedures that are mutable and dynamic and that build in space for constant challenge and revision, they will not threaten heterogeneous argumentation (Broda-Bahm, 1995, p. 314). The question of how much to trade off between efficiency and fairness then would be open to discussion, review, and debate. In other words, regulation that builds in a self-correcting capacity does not continue despite its failures. It continues precisely because of and inasmuch as it fails. Thus, incompleteness and failure are resources that provide the impetus to regulate (Hunt and Wickham, 1994, p. 80). The persistence of difference is not a threat to procedural theories; rather, it is the engine that drives them.

Although introduction of a principle of reflexivity can help procedural theories manage the constant tension between efficiency and fairness, it is insufficient in itself. Democracy is not simply a matter of discursive design, or of just following rules. Every procedure must be applied in the fluid context of everyday practices of embodied, situated social agents who may be selfish, shortsighted, passionate, committed, and display all of the other characteristics involved in making us human. The problem, then, is how historically effective individuals who do not possess the 'pure legal understanding' delineated by Cornelius Castoriadis (1997) could ever carry out the rigorous demands of procedural theories. The solution emerges in the observation that every act of regulation should be understood as not only externally stipulating legitimate action but also as constituting the very subjectivity of the agents who are both the targets and instruments of regulation.

The crucial aspect of that constitutive process is inculcation of a discussion-minded attitude.

No procedural design will work if the parties do not have a discussion-minded attitude. Persons engaged in argumentation must be willing and able to 'express their opinions, listen to the opinions of others, and to change their own opinions when these fail to survive critical examination' (van Eemeren et al., 1993). Van Eemeren et al. (1993) describe the motivations, competencies, and intentions constituting this discussion-minded attitude as second-order conditions of critical discussion. Second-order conditions are the presuppositions of rational arguers who

> appeal to reasoning and evidence acceptable to themselves and to the other party, adjusting to their interlocutor's frame of reference and establishing a common ground or identification of interests from which they might reason together or otherwise transcend their divisions. They would be expected to conduct themselves in ways that maintain a mutual openness to criticism and to the demand for justification (p. 142).

If interlocutors fail to satisfy these conditions they can be held accountable for not doing so and sanctioned for failing to 'live up to standards of rational conduct' (p. 143).

We are particularly interested in the model arguer specified by these second-order conditions. What are the moral and intellectual comportments attributed to these persons? How do individuals acquire the capacities and dispositions required if they are to be considered rational discussants? To begin focusing our reflection on that question, in the next section we review a particular objection to the conception of the arguer set out in procedural theories of argument; namely, that this conception of the arguer is underwritten by unacknowledged substantive-ethical commitments. We then, in Section Three, propose a way that this objection can be answered by invoking a particular reading of the second-order conditions presupposed in critical discussion—namely that procedures constitute the substantive identity of the arguer.

SECTION TWO: A PRESUPPOSITION OF PROCEDURAL THEORIES

Cornelius Castoriadis (1997, p. 10) claims that procedural theories must smuggle in two *de facto* substantial beliefs if they are to avoid incoherence: (1) The existing social and political institutions of society are compatible with the functioning of democratic procedures; and (2) The citizens of this society are willing and able to apply these procedures in a manner that is compatible with their spirit, and they can defend and revise those procedures if required. He doubts that our political institutions are capable of supporting these demands of procedural models of democratic deliberation without a substantial overhaul. The second presupposition (critically reflective agents capable of implementing these procedures) rests on an extensive political education; an active 'democratic paideia,' which inculcates the habits of critical reflection and a democratic ethos into all citizens. Absent a radically democratic political culture and well-educated citizenry, a 'deliberative democracy' could easily become a 'formalist' simulation of democracy. Hence, an adequate proceduralist account of democratic deliberation must attend to the material conditions of its existence—including and especially, the formation of arguers imbued with a democratic ethos.

The promise of deliberation, Richard Bernstein (1996) argues, does not merely point to formal rules of communication but to the ethos of debate, discussion, and persuasion:

> democratic debate, ideally, requires a willingness to listen to and evaluate the opinions of one's opponents, respecting the views of minorities, advancing arguments in good faith to support one's convictions, and having the courage to change one's mind when confronted with new evidence or better arguments. There is an ethos involved in the practice of democratic debate (p. 1131).

Bernstein goes on to argue that deliberation involves substantial ethical commitments:

> We might even say that the practice of debate in a democratic polity requires the democratic transformation and appropriation of classic virtues: practical wisdom, justice, courage, and moderation. Democratic versions of these virtues are required for engaging in democratic debate (p. 1131).

If Bernstein's claim that procedural theories depend upon substantial ethical commitments and virtues is correct, what, if anything, distinguishes a procedural from a rhetorical perspective on deliberation? The moral status of procedures could not be derived independently of the substantive values that constitute the identities of those engaging in argumentation. This dependence of procedure upon substance undercuts any attempt to maintain a functional dichotomy between procedure and substance. Hence, there is no hope of finding a set of normative principles for evaluating argumentative practice that does not rest upon prior commitment to a conception of the good. A theory of argument would have to limit its scope to the community whose values it took into account as the foundation for its normative principles. Such a theory, as Richard Rorty (1989) has observed, would have to content itself with being frankly ethnocentric.

Proceduralists respond to this charge in two ways. The first response is to acknowledge that it is impossible to maintain a strict dichotomy between procedure and substance. No procedural model is entirely self-referential, but depends upon the presence of 'a liberal political culture and a population accustomed to freedom' (Habermas, 1996, p. 1481). Pragma-dialectical theories, for instance, posit the necessity of a set of 'higher-order' conditions which set out the psychological makeup of the arguer and the ideal socio-political conditions necessary for conducting critical discussion (van Eemeren et al., 1993). These 'higher-order' conditions serve as both empirical preconditions for the theory's application, and ideals that participants refer to in resolving meta-procedural disputes. While this acknowledgement of the interdependence between theory and substance is welcome, we concur with Maier (1995) that this strategy of simply stipulating the presence of higher-order conditions is far less satisfactory than an argument explaining how these higher-order conditions come into being.

A second strategy, employed by Habermas (1996) in response to Bernstein's claim, shifts the burden of normative expectations from the virtues of social actors to the forms of communication embedded in the procedures regulating deliberation. 'To sharpen his thesis into an objection,' Habermas argues,

> Bernstein must ultimately place the burden of democratically legitimating law entirely on the political virtues of united citizens. By contrast, in explaining

the democratic process, discourse theory employs a structuralist argument that relieves citizens of the Rousseauian expectation of virtue—the orientation to the common good only needs to be exacted in small increments insofar as practical reason withdraws from the hearts and heads of collective or individual actors into the procedures of communication of political opinion—and will-formation. In other words, practical reason shifts from the individual level of ethical motivations and insights to the social level of gathering and processing information (pp. 1481–1482).

Hence, democratic proceduralism remains distinct from (rhetorical) republicanism because democratic legitimacy is not founded in the rhetorical self-fashioning of ethical communities, but in the ethical substance built into the procedures themselves.

We find ourselves persuaded by aspects of both Bernstein's and Habermas's positions here. Bernstein's claim that formal rules are certainly necessary but in and of themselves insufficient for the practice of democratic deliberation, and that deliberation requires critically reflective social actors engaged in the pursuit of the common good, concurs with our experience. On the other hand, Habermas's insistence that the interaction order is *sui generis,* and therefore, contains its own political and ethical substance, comports with our theoretical commitments. What we want to understand from this exchange is how practical reason withdraws from the 'hearts and heads of individual actors into the procedure of communication' only to continually return and transform those individual agents into critically-reflective, tolerant, and deliberative citizens.

We want to propose that procedural accounts do not have to assume that arguers already posses the ability and desire to conduct themselves in a rational manner, if they are combined with a constitutive communication theory. They could then contend that the interests and capacities that define the self are not wholly determined prior to participating in deliberation. Rather, the very experience of participating in critical discussion produces individuals with more critical-rational and democratic dispositions; individuals who are more tolerant, better able to examine their preferences, more willing to take the claims of others seriously, and more prepared to submit their judgments to the test of critical scrutiny. Hence, the application of procedures that regulate disagreement would themselves be a form of 'democratic paideia.'

SECTION THREE: HOW PROCEDURES CONSTITUTE PERSONS

We want to now look more closely at how procedural rules constitute and thus govern those who engage in argumentation, while appearing merely to regulate argumentative activity. More broadly stated, we want to argue that communicative interaction plays a major role in constituting the persons who participate in argumentation, rather than merely serving already-formed persons as an instrument for the publication of their thinking. Thus particular ways of regulating locution in argumentation (as one form of communicative interaction) will institute and maintain—which is to say, produce—two different sorts of products.

The first and more evident product is arguments of particular kinds. For example, a deductive procedure that begins from an accepted axiom, such as a building code's specification for the acceptable limits of rise in a staircase, is useful in constructing an argument for approving a particular staircase as conforming to that code. Likewise, this procedure can begin from the U.S. Constitution's declaration that 'all men are created equal and endowed with certain inalienable rights' and proceed by applying that general principle to particular 'men' who identify with specific ethnic, gender, or racial categories. We take these examples as evidence for the unproblematic nature of the claim that particular procedures produce particular kinds of arguments.

We are especially interested in a second and relatively ignored (even, denied) product, namely, those human beings who argue—and we expect that identifying this product is not unproblematic. There are rather profound reasons for our tendency to ignore and even deny that argumentation procedures produce persons (the agents who argue) as well as propositions (which in combination are the claims and conclusion of an argument). Although we cannot discuss those reasons at length here, we do need to mention them briefly, since they may be used to support opposition to the connections between procedural theories of argumentation and the nurturing of participants of deliberative democracy that we explore here.

Both ontological and epistemological reasons, rooted in influential philosophical traditions, are relevant to denying the productive activity that we see operating in regulating deliberation. These traditions hold that epistemic activity is a matter of sensory experience or rational structures, and that our attention thus should be directed toward accurate reception of what is experientially accessible for our research, or toward correct use of the ideas or forms held to be characteristic of human reason. For both ways of thinking (which promulgate varieties of empiricism or rationalism) epistemic activity is directed away from the subjects who conduct it and toward objects understood as independent of those subjects (i.e., the researchers). Even when the domain of research is psychology or sociology, traditional social science decrees that the human beings who are the object of study must not be assimilated to those who are conducting research. In contrast, our focus here on the constitutive function of communicative activity, including argumentation, derives from affiliation with contemporary human-scientific arguments for the rejection of that decree as grounded in an untenable 'subject-object dualism.' Rejecting that traditional dualism is instrumental for our recognition of communication as constitutive, rather than merely constative (descriptive or representational), and so we want to give some brief indication of the support for that rejection.

One way of arguing against social science's presupposition of subject-object dualism is by analogy from contemporary theorizing in physics: Insofar as we accept arguments for the impossibility of observing on the (sub) microscopic level without contributing thereby to the display under observation, we come to see that observing on the macroscopic level appropriate to the human sciences (including communication studies) cannot maintain its independence from the objects under study. The result of this line of thinking is a refocusing on experience as composed of aspects usually labeled 'the object,' 'the subject,' and 'the context' of research. Another way of arguing against subject-object dualism as a presupposition of social science is by extension of the recognition, perhaps most explicitly developed in anthropology, that subjects nurtured in different cultures typically perceive their own environments, including elements that are also present in other cultural environments, differently.

A variation on this latter support develops along lines of thinking that are more political, in contrast to social or physical. For this line of thinking, within which we locate our own work, discerning the genesis and operation of the interests and ideas which contribute to producing 'culture' is of primary importance. In other words, this last research strategy refrains from assuming that whatever researchers find is 'natural,' in contrast to 'humanly produced.' Instead, it orients us toward seeking out the conditions for the production of any and all aspects or components of what's found. In effect, this line of thinking leads us to expand our concept of an 'object' of research to include three dimensions: *conditions* (why this, now), *process* (how this transpires), and product (what results). The 'denaturalization' of these components means that 'digging' for even-more basic levels of production is an intrinsically open-ended task.

We need now to tie this identification of grounds for different ways of understanding the proper 'object' of research to our claim that argumentation procedures constitute persons as well as propositions, and that argumentation theory needs to investigate how procedural rules contribute to the constitution of the agents who use them. This recognition of procedural argumentation's tacit functioning leads us to proposing that any model of argumentation serves as cultural policy and informs political education. Before doing so, however, two potential difficulties in understanding our concept of 'conditions' need discussion. The first is contributed by philosophical tradition and the second is due to the intricacy of argumentation as an 'object' of research.

We would argue that there is a particular philosophical tradition embedded in our everyday ways of thinking about knowing and typically advocated in our teaching as essential to theorizing. This tradition understands 'conditions' as the 'necessary and sufficient' conditions sought by epistemology and holding for all knowers regardless of the particulars of their situations. For example, a supply of ink is a necessary condition for an ink-jet printer's functioning, and that general principle can be applied in producing an argument (probably, in enthymatic form) for why a particular printer just churned out a blank piece of paper. Granted, identifying sufficient conditions is a far more complex matter—even in regard to printers, and certainly in regard to far more complex objects such as deliberative democracy. Yet the traditional assumption, regardless of the nature of the object, is that there are necessary and sufficient conditions for that object to be as it is, for anyone.

Argumentation, for this tradition, is a neutral process culminating (whenever possible) in claims that take the form 'P is x' or, 'S knows that P is x.' Such claims are presumed justifiable for any 'S' who engages in the epistemic activity of knowing 'P.' This conception is abetted by including in 'knowing' background expectations without which 'S' might be said to look at 'P'; might describe, manipulate, or even enjoy 'P'; but would not be acknowledged as knowing 'P.' When we reject this conception of argumentation and its object, in favor of a human-scientific model oriented toward experience conceived as an intricate interaction of 'subjective' and 'objective' features, we need also to respecify the notion of 'conditions.' Rather than pertaining to any 'object in itself'—that is, objects existing as they are, independently of epistemic processes—conditions now pertain to the interactions which are the (respecified) object of research. Thus localized rather than universal conditions are of interest, and theorizing means discerning the particular conditions and components that constitute a particular object, including a particular occasion of epistemic activity organized in argumentative form.

As something of a by-product of this respecification, argumentation ceases to be merely an externalization of epistemic activity and instead appears as an aspect of the interaction that produces the (respecified) object. (More generally, communication ceases to be merely transmission of thinking.) The second potential difficulty that we mentioned as arising from 'denaturalizing' argumentation's components relates to this shift from externalization to interaction. Argumentation is an especially intricate 'object,' for the *process* (argumentation) that produces the *product* (argument that 'P is x') is regulated by the very procedures which are *conditions* for constituting the participants (arguers) as the persons they are, in this interaction. This is not to say that these procedures are all that is involved in the constitution of these persons, or that how these persons are in a particular instance of epistemic-argumentive activity is all they are, in other activities of their lives. However, it does mean that any claim by procedural theorists to the effect that the procedures they advocate are neutral in regard to the sort of persons (agents) who use those procedures, cannot be sustained.

There is an implication of this thesis that especially concerns us when we carry this acknowledgment of argumentation's double constitution into our work as teachers of argumentation theory and practice: any theory of argumentation, and perhaps especially this procedural theory, is a force for cultural policy and political education. We want to advocate the importance of recognizing that what we do in educating for argumentation competence is nothing less than constitute—which is to say, provide, nurture, and discipline for—the reflexive, self-correcting agents who are able to create and sustain deliberative democracy. Two theorists provide the basis for this line of thinking.

The first instigation is the work of Henry Giroux, who has translated (so to speak) Paulo Freire's critical pedagogy into the North American context in which we teach. Giroux understands pedagogy as 'a form of cultural production implicated in the construction and organization of knowledge, desire, social practices, and values that takes place in a variety of cultural sites' (1994, p. 155). Cultural policies necessary for deliberative democracy, then, are produced in the course of educating for competence in the procedures in which deliberative democracy is practiced. These cultural policies, we propose, take a formative role in constituting democratic citizens who embody the second order conditions identified by van Eemeren et al. that we discussed earlier.

Our recognition of the pedagogical implications of a constitutive proceduralism also is instigated by Michel Foucault's thesis that discourse is woven on what he calls a truth-axis and a power-axis. Any communicative event, he argues, can be analyzed to reveal an intricate interdependence of what is known and how power is operative. When we regulate deliberation, then, we understand ourselves as engaging in the use of power in the service of truth. As participants, we find ourselves situated at a highly unstable intersection of centripetal (order and unity) and centrifugal (turmoil and diversity) forces. On a larger scale, these are the needs of effective resolution and preserving differences that must be kept in balance, if deliberative democracy is to be sustained.

Regulation is vital, then, to keeping this volatile combination from disintegrating into verbal quarrel or physical violence; which is to say, in keeping argumentation from deteriorating into fighting. There seem to be only two ways that regulation can be made effective: rules can be imposed, either hegemonically (implicitly) or autocratically (explicitly); or, rules can be chosen by participants. Insofar as the latter course is taken, these participants constitute themselves, through their choices, as agents who employ strategies for furthering their interactions. They are also forming themselves, by virtue of this practice, as beings who can choose.

If we choose the latter mode of regulation as preferable, we are accepting deliberation as a cultural policy. Our teaching of argumentation is then a teaching of values, habits, and strategies that we see as vital to civilization, although they may not be prevalent in a particular social location. However, they may well be identifiable in participants' background practices. Ethnographic evidence suggests that this is the case: members of all social groups recognize values, habits, and strategies that accomplish deliberation, although they may not employ them for various reasons in any given situation. A likely site for foregrounding those background practices, and advocating them in thematic form as advantageous, is the classroom—and in particular, in communication classes devoted to rhetoric and argumentation.

A paradox threatens this advocacy of cultural policy in the classroom. We seem to be saying, in effect: if you want to engage in deliberation as a cultural policy that sustains democracy, do just as I say in regard to adopting certain strategies, habits, and values. Yet the basic value of this cultural policy does not lie in doing just what anyone says—that is, accepting hegemonic or autocratic authority—but rather, in engaging deliberative habits in the service of choice. How can a paradoxical reimposition of such authority be avoided when we promote deliberation as a cultural policy? Our response is a roundabout one that requires consideration of several implications of what we have said thus far. We want to discuss those implications under two general topics: values are constituents of content, agents, and procedures—and thus, of the contexts they form and are formed by; and, procedures are neither 'objective' nor 'relativistic.'

There is a tradition within social science that valorizes 'value-free' research. Explicit formulations of that tradition have become increasingly rare—perhaps because they present performative contradictions, and perhaps also because they run afoul of work in the philosophy of science during the past several decades. Yet we find evidence within academic practice of a yearning for research that focuses on content to the exclusion of value questions. One example would be teaching argumentation as the effective use of means toward prespecified ends, since avoiding deliberating about those ends (goals) is avoiding argument over their comparative value. Another example would be the use of terms such as 'the student,' 'the respondent,' and 'the researcher' in ways that imply a standardized entity in contrast to other, variable entities—which are usually the characteristics or qualities of interest (i.e., value) to the perpetrator of a research project. These purportedly standardized components are presented as simply present to the researcher's gaze, rather than as formed by inclusion (of what the researcher sees as vital or essential) and exclusion (of what the researcher sees as trivial or irrelevant).

We want to argue that examining such practices for their efficacy in establishing habits, rather than assuming them as neutral preliminaries, reveals that they promote avoidance of the value dimension despite its omnipresence in the content and contexts as well as procedures and conditions of deliberation. The issue is not whether to include value, but whether to accept hegemonically-imposed values—and so avoid engaging the power-axis under cover of purporting to adhere solely to the truth-axis. Recognizing that there is no knowledge without power (understood not merely as 'control' over 'data' and methods but as stipulation of what shall 'count' as deliberation) enables us to investigate what we know (content) as developing interactively with how we move towards knowledge (procedure) within limitations that are often less than evident (context). We can then seek out, and make choices about, what would otherwise remain as unexamined presuppositions of deliberation.

Recognizing the constitutive presence of values requires us to reject claims of neutrality achieved through stripping away values embedded in social positions indicated by categories such as race, class, gender, religion, age, and ethnicity. The result of that effort would be a neutral participant; what Michael Sandel calls an 'unencumbered' self, 'free to construct principles of justice unconstrained by an order of value antecedently given' (Sandel, 1984, p. 87). This thoroughly unrealistic concept has a long history, traceable to John Locke's notion of human thinking as a 'blank slate' on which experience 'writes.' We are then to erase those effects thoroughly enough to leave no trace—without damaging the medium, which can then support new, and somehow more pure, inscriptions. We may recognize this line of thinking as an immoral demand, implying (in terms of modern technology) thought-control, brainwashing, or surgical alteration of the brain. Less evidently, although even more relevantly to our present focus on communication as constitutive, we need to recognize that the being resulting from these efforts wouldn't know enough or care enough to engage in deliberation about anything.

Yet the constant balancing of preserving differences (of values, beliefs, ways of acting) and effective resolution (of disputed policies) required for deliberative democracy relies upon our ability to temporarily suspend adherence to the particular beliefs, values, and attitudes that form each of us. This does not mean rejecting, denying, ignoring, or effacing that constitutive process. It does, however, mean recognizing one's fallibility as well as the strength of whichever values (etc.) are securely embedded in any way of life, and so being willing to scrutinize what one usually simply assumes and affirms. Typically, the unanticipated clamor of other possibilities instigates this process. We do have local practices for enlarging rather than erasing the slate (so to speak), although ethnographic research would be required before affirming the generality, much less universality, of those practices. They are exemplified in Locke's own understanding of political order as a matter of people placing their sovereignty in revocable trust when choosing a sovereign. A smaller-scale contemporary example is the practice of elected officials placing their assets under a 'blind trust' management while they're in office.

Phenomenology contributes a useful image here: a suspended adherence would be one that we choose to 'bracket'; to leave out of account for the moment, by analogy with solving equations in piecemeal fashion. A related model is available in George Herbert Mead's conceptualization of the self as both a 'me' of sedimented experience and an 'I' of present innovation. These analogies are not without their dangers, since adherences, assumptions, and alliances—as well as habits, customs, and memories—cannot be as neatly delineated as the components of arithmetical and logical equations. Yet we also have real political exemplars, such as Locke's political theory and everyday solutions to conflict-of-interest, to remind us that an imperfect process still provides a useful model. That's especially so if a watchdog or whistle-blower function can be incorporated. Broadly-intersubjective validation performs that function—albeit, imperfectly. Indeed, the need to improve the reliability of this procedure is a highly practical value of educating for argumentation competence, which develops abilities to recognize and articulate elements in a situation that make it other than it purports to be.

Even this brief consideration of how values can be both constitutive and sufficiently suspended to allow for the consideration of alternatives has involved us in proposing models for that procedure. This move takes us to the second topic implied by our understanding of procedures as constitutive of the agents who use them, the contexts of that use, and the content to which they're applied. Procedures, we hold, are neither 'objective' nor 'relativistic'; not wholly independent of, but also not merely endemic to, the situations of their use. We come to this characterization by understanding procedures as the engine (so to speak) of that perspective on argumentation called 'dialectic procedure,' in contrast to 'rhetorical process' and 'logical product,' by Joseph Wenzel (1990).

A logical perspective understands argumentation as objective in the sense of independent of, yet universally applicable to, all contexts, content, and conditions. This character is achieved by formalization; that is, by abstracting from the particularity of any situation in order to effect its reduction to a complex of connectors and entities. This claim of objectivity is plausible because there are practices in everyday life—and not only in our own local lifeworld—that are objective in this sense. Arithmetic provides ready examples, since we record and manipulate quantities without regard for the peculiarities of what is recorded and manipulated. We can reckon the age, count the occurrences, or record the diminished presence of the fossils just as we do that of futons and fairy tales.

A rhetorical perspective understands argumentation as relativistic in the sense of being attuned to the interests and needs of particular audiences (conditions) seeking to make wise decisions in their situations (contexts and content). There is no claim that strategies that make the best possible case for a position in one situation can be (so to speak) lifted from that situation and applied identically in another. What counts as 'good reasons' in one situation may be tangential or even irrelevant in another, and so no independent status for that 'goodness' can be claimed. Although Plato used the comparison in a derogatory way, we can appropriate his remarks about rhetoric and cookery with a more appreciative attitude toward the methods of everyday life: good cooks don't simply follow recipes, but they do browse in the cookbook for inspiration and consult it occasionally for guidance.

The procedures which drive a dialectical perspective are neither field-dependent (Toulmin, 1958) nor universally applicable. They are assembled and assessed by argumentation theorists and advocated as ways to regulate deliberations when we educate for argumentation competence. Unlike rhetorical processes, they are not attuned to a theoretically unified audience, but to the actual plurivocal audiences which characterize deliberative democracies. Unlike logical products, they are not applicable to all situations. But they do have a high degree of transferability across the type of situations that are composed when multiple identities and interests are brought into deliberation under the exigencies of balancing a democracy's need to effectively resolve disputes, while preserving differences among participants.

When we bring this orientation to argumentation into the classroom and use it to advocate deliberation as a cultural policy, we are also engaged in political education. The latter accomplishment is more difficult to articulate because we typically associate political education with transmitting information (content) about the relative merits of systems of government (products). In the academic context within which we work, those tasks are the purview of political science departments. When we engage in political education, as argumentation theorists within communication departments, we rely upon (but do not repeat) that information about systems in order to teach—typically, through performative modeling—procedures for deliberation. Rather than accepting hegemonically or autocratically imposed procedures, we draw upon—bring into the foreground and thematize—more or less developed capacities for choosing that our students bring to the classroom. These are communicative (rather than psychological) habits and dispositions that establish a basis for participation as agents in a political context.

Emphasizing argumentation competence does not mean minimizing citizens' need for information about the issues that confront us. It does mean stressing the equal importance of competence in deliberating about both the value of procedures used in a deliberative democracy and the value of positions advocated by the means of those procedures. Rather than adopt procedural theorists' tendency to assume a certain model of human being as equipped with particular reasoning skills, we have argued here that education for argumentation competence constitutes human beings as agents who can choose to engage in deliberation and continue to make the diverse choices intrinsic to being an agent. As such, they can propose and evaluate strategies for regulating deliberative activity in the service of furthering democratic ideals.

REFERENCES

Aune, J. A.: 1994, *Rhetoric and Marxism,* Westview, Boulder CO.

Benhabib, S.: 1996, 'Toward a Deliberative Model of Democratic Legitimacy', in S. Benhabib (ed.), *Democracy and Difference: Contesting the Boundaries of the Political,* Princeton University Press, Princeton, pp. 67–94.

Bernstein, R. J.: 1996, 'The Revival of the Democratic Ethos', *Cardozo Law Review* 17, 1127–1145.

Blaug, R.: 1996, 'New Theories of Discursive Democracy: A User's Guide', *Philosophy and Social Criticism* 22, 49–80.

Broda-Bahm, K. T.: 1995, 'Meta-procedure: The Bases for Challenging Operative Norms of Argument', in S. Jackson (ed.), *Argument and Values: Proceedings of the Ninth AFA/SCA Conference on Argumentation,* Speech Communication Association, Annandale VA, pp. 314–320.

Castoriadis, C.: 1997, 'Democracy as Procedure and Democracy as Regime', *Constellations* 4, 1–18.

Cohen, J.: 1996, 'Procedure and Substance in Deliberative Democracy', in S. Benhabib (ed.), *Democracy and Difference: Contesting the Boundaries of the Political,* Princeton University Press, Princeton, pp. 95–119.

Dryzek, J.: 1990, *Discursive Democracy,* Cambridge University Press, Cambridge.

Eemeren, F. H. van: 1995, 'A World of Difference: The Rich State of Argumentation Theory', *Informal Logic* 17, 144–158.

Eemeren, F. H. van, R. Grootendorst, S. Jackson and S. Jacobs: 1993, *Reconstucting Argumentative Discourse,* Alabama University Press, Tuscaloosa.

Giroux, H.: 1994, *Disturbing Pleasures: Learning Popular Culture,* Routledge, New York.

Greene, R. W.: 1997, *Tropes travel: The rhetorical perspective on argumentation and the question of effectivity.* Paper presented at the Tenth NCA/AFA Conference on Argumentation (Alta, Utah).

Gutmann, A. and D. Thompson: 1996, *Democracy and Disagreement,* Harvard University Press, Cambridge MA.

Habermas, J.: 1994, 'Three Normative Models of Democracy', *Constellations* 1, 1–10.

Habermas, J.: 1996a, *Between Facts and Norms: Contributions to a Discourse Theory of Law and Democracy* (W. Rehg, Trans.), MIT Press, Boston.

Habermas, J.: 1996b, 'Reply', *Cardozo Law Review* 17, 1477–1573.

Hicks, D.: 1995, 'Disagreement and Democratic Pluralism', in S. Jackson (ed.), *Argument and Values: Proceedings of the Ninth AFA/ SCA Conference on Argumentation,* Speech Communication Association, Annandale VA, pp. 302–307.

Hunt, A.: 1993, *Explorations in Law and Society: Towards a Constitutive Theory of Law,* Routledge, New York.

Hunt, A. and G. Wickham: 1994, *Foucault and Law: Towards a Sociology of Law as Governance,* Pluto, London.

Langsdorf, L.: 1995, 'Argument as Inquiry in a Postmodern Context', in F. H. van Eemeren, R. Grootendorst, J. A. Blair and C. A. Willard (eds.), *Perspectives and Approaches,* Foris, Dordrecht, pp. 452–463.

Maier, R.: 1995, 'Argumentation and Identity', in F. H. van Eemeren, R. Grootendorst, J. A. Blair and C. A. Willard (eds.), *Perspectives and Approaches,* Foris, Dordrecht, pp. 260–270.

Rawls, J.: 1993, *Political Liberalism,* Columbia University Press, New York.

Reed, R. R.: 1990, 'Are Robert's Rules of Order Counterrevolutionary? Rhetoric and the Reconstruction of Portuguese Politics', *Anthropological Quarterly* 63, 134–144.

Rorty, R.: 1988, *Contingency, Irony, Solidarity,* Cambridge University Press, Cambridge.

Rosenfeld, M.: 1994, 'Law as Discourse: Bridging the Gap between Democracy and Rights', *Harvard Law Review* 108, 1146–1189.

Sandel, M.: 1984, 'The Procedural Republic and the Unencumbered Self', *Political Theory* 12, 81–96.

Sanders, L.: 1997, 'Against Deliberation', *Political Theory* 25, 347–376.

Soltan, K. E. and S. Elkin: 1996, *The Constitution of Good Societies,* Pennsylvania State University Press, University Park.

Toulmin, S. E.: 1958, *The Uses of Argument,* Cambridge University Press, Cambridge.

Wenzel, J.: 1990, 'Three Perspectives on Argument', in R. Trapp and J. Schuetz (eds.), *Perspectives on Argumentation: Essays in Honor of Wayne Brockriede,* Waveland, Prospect Heights IL, pp. 9–26.

Wood, R. V.: 1997, *Voice as a Preemptive Force in Environmental Decision Making,* Unpublished manuscript.

Young, I. M.: 1996. 'Communication and the Other: Beyond Deliberative Democracy', in S. Benhabib (ed.), *Democracy and Difference: Contesting the Boundaries of the Political,* Princeton University Press, Princeton, pp. 120–136.

Chapter 7

Places and Uses

The essays in this chapter investigate the practice of argument in various contexts. They are concerned with where we find arguments and how they are used in public discourse. Several of the essays work to expand the scope of argumentation. For instance, two pieces focus on visual arguments in postcards and in paintings; another views the use of the human body in argument. Other essays provide examples of argument in practice, including the Palestinian Declaration of Independence and the legal case *Texas v. Johnson*. Collectively, the essays in this chapter explore how arguments, located in diverse places, function in public deliberation.

In "Social Argumentation and the Aporias of State Formation: The Palestinian Declaration of Independence" (1993), Ronald Walter Greene explores the major focus on context in contemporary argumentation scholarship. He asserts that argumentation studies are undergoing a "social turn" marked by increased awareness of the contextual dynamics, including identity and difference, that influence and constrain arguments. The essay explains social argumentation theory in terms of three constructs: social formation, subjectivity, and agency. Greene uses these constructs to read the Palestinian Declaration of Independence as a social argument precipitated by multiple contexts. Greene's critical approach belongs to a growing and influential body of argumentation scholarship.

In "Toward a Theory of Visual Argument" (1996), the opening essay in the journal *Argumentation and Advocacy*'s visual argumentation series, David S. Birdsell and Leo Groarke introduce scholars to the emerging study of visual argument. Photographs, paintings, and moving images, they explain, are often used as a form of argument that is distinct from traditional conceptions of argumentation. The authors dispute traditional definitions of argument that focus exclusively on verbal arguments and dismiss the possibility of other forms. They argue that visual and verbal expressions can both advance arguments, just as both can be ambiguous and indeterminate. Birdsell and Groarke urge further study of visual argumentation, including identifying visual elements and tracking changes in visual perspectives over time.

In "The Male Madonna and the Feminine Uncle Sam: Visual Argument, Icons, and Ideographs in 1909 Anti–Woman Suffrage Postcards" (2005), Catherine H. Palczewski explores the intersection between icons (which represent identifiable characteristics of people) and ideographs (idealistic symbols that guide and warrant behaviors and beliefs). Building upon earlier scholarship that questioned whether visuals were fit for argumentative analysis, Palczewski demonstrates how anti–woman's suffrage postcards functioned as visual arguments. More important, she contends that these images present arguments that were absent in the verbal discourse about the suffrage movement; and, therefore, that visuals do argumentative work that is not necessarily addressed with language.

Kevin Michael DeLuca, in "Unruly Arguments: The Body Rhetoric of Earth First!, Act Up, and Queer Nation" (1999), further expands the boundaries of argumentation scholarship by exploring the use of the human body as argument. This essay recognizes visual displays of human bodies as image events that can open up argumentative possibilities not possible in traditional, rational modes of argument. Focusing on the bodily image events orchestrated by several social movement organizations, the author demonstrates that bodies form public arguments in ways that go beyond the capacity of words. The essay encourages scholars to consider argumentative forms that operate outside words and reason.

David Fleming's 1998 essay, "The Space of Argumentation: Urban Design, Civic Discourse, and the Dream of the Good City," extends the reach of argumentation studies in another direction by turning to the design arts. The author questions whether the deterioration of public spaces (such as town squares) is intrinsically connected to the health of public discourse and civic engagement. Argumentation scholars and designers, Fleming contends, share a common civic interest; they should collaborate to create places that foster deliberations. Ultimately, Fleming works to reconnect classical concepts of "logos" (reason) and "polis" (self-governed community) by moving across an expansive scholarly terrain that includes demonstrating how design practices and discourse theories might be used together to guide the building of good communities.

In "The Search for Grounds in Legal Argumentation: A Rhetorical Analysis of *Texas v. Johnson*" (2001), S. J. Balter uses a case study to explore how various audiences shape arguments advanced in legal opinions. The legal realm attracts significant attention from argumentation scholars. Balter contends that the construction of legal arguments, commonly accepted as rhetorical arguments, is highly constrained by the multiple audiences that will scrutinize them. Using the interpretive strategies of communication theorist Stanley Fish and legal philosopher Richard Dworkin, Balter conducts a detailed reading of the United States Supreme Court case *Texas v. Johnson* to illustrate that legal decisions are grounded in the construction of an audience. Balter's essay also offers an example of how case studies can be employed for argument analyses.

These essays expand the reach of argumentation studies. They point to emerging areas of concern in contemporary argumentation scholarship. Focusing on visuals, displays of the human body, and the design arts draws argumentation scholars into vibrant interdisciplinary areas of study. Through detailed analysis of political and legal texts, the essays offer students and scholars various methods to analyze arguments and expand argumentation studies.

··

Social Argumentation
and the Aporias of State Formation:
The Palestinian Declaration of Independence

RONALD WALTER GREENE

Argumentation theory is in the grips of a social turn. Arguments as objects of study are being dispersed within the social categories of fields, spheres and communities.[1] This dispersion of the object of study contributes to an increasing awareness of the contextual dynamics which influence and constrain argumentative practices.[2] However, to position argumentation theory within the category of the social by claiming that arguments exist in context only begs the question of what is meant by the social. The social is a complex space of multiple contexts.

Burke writes that the principal effect of rhetoric is its ability to construct identifications at the same time as it creates division.[3] My argument is that the dialectic of identity and difference is at the heart of social argumentation. By the dialectic of identity and difference, I mean to suggest the process in which the subjectivity of social actors is constituted by argumentative practices. The theoretical benefit of a social turn in argumentation studies is dependent on the ability to understand how identity and difference are deployed, articulated and produced for the purposes of creating, maintaining and/or transforming a social formation.

This paper will analyze the Palestinian Declaration of Independence as a social argument. My analysis will focus on how the Declaration negotiates the contradictions inherent within the dialectic of identity and difference in an effort to create a democratic state formation in the context of colonial domination. My argument will be subdivided into two parts; the first will explicate the theoretical contours of social argumentation, and the second will consist of a close reading of the Palestinian Declaration of Independence. In so doing, this project explicates a theoretical apparatus sensitive to the demands of a critical rhetoric concerned with creating the conditions of possibility for a radical democracy.[4]

SOCIAL ARGUMENTATION

A social theory of argumentation must begin with a theory of the social. The social should not be thought of as simply the context in which argumentative practices take place. This contextual theory of the social transforms the social into historical background, a multiplicity of independent contexts, and/or conceives of the social as prefiguring argumentative practices. By social argumentation, I mean to suggest a process in which the social sets limits and exerts pressures on argumentative practices in ways that are often contradictory and contested. In this way, we can begin to understand how context is not simply prior to argumentative practices but often the result of argumentative practices. To flesh out this theory of the social I will discuss the importance of a social formation, subjectivity and agency.

Social Formation

A social formation consists of a complex structure of practices which produce heterogeneous social relations among human beings.[5] The complex structure of practices refers to the economic, political and cultural modes of production in any given society. The structure of practices are considered complex for two reasons. First, no single practice can be said to determine another. While all practices do interact with one another, each practice maintains a relative autonomy. Therefore, it is not possible to posit a one-to-one correspondence between practices. The notion of relative autonomy reminds us that the effects of different practices are not synonymous with the intentions of social actors, nor is one mode of production considered primary and the other modes of production derivative. Instead, the effects of different practices often circulate within multiple contexts with contradictory effects.

A social formation is considered complex for a second reason: namely that the interaction of the different practices determines relationships of domination and resistance. As Stuart Hall argues, "a social formation is a 'structure in dominance.' It has certain distinct tendencies; it has a certain configuration; it has a definite structuration."[6] Social argumentation directs our attention to how the different practices of a social formation are sutured together constructing relationships of domination. Social argumentation as a critical rhetoric is less an interpretive project then a geographical project concerned with mapping the effects of argumentative practices in the production of a social formation.

However, while a social formation is a structure in dominance it is not without contradictions. A social formation is an active space of conflict and contestation; it is an unstable "structure in dominance" that must reproduce itself through time by producing new articulations among practices.[7] According to Althusser, "As Marx said, every child knows that a social formation which did not reproduce the conditions of production at the same time as it produced would not last a year."[8] To understand how a social formation is reproduced demands an investigation of the concept of subjectivity.

Subjectivity

A tremendous amount of time and energy has gone into the explication of the concept of subjectivity.[9] By subjectivity, I mean the position from which one experiences the world. In contrast to a humanist project that views this position as a site of originality by which the subject comes to understand itself and the world, I want to follow a more critical stance that understands this position as an effect of the modes of production (economic, political, and cultural) in any given social formation. Subjects are not autonomous producers of the social, but rather, the effects of the different practices within a social formation. A critical turn in the understanding of subjectivity agrees with Marx, that subjects make history but not under the conditions of their own making. Critical rhetoric argues that our object of study should not be public address but the addressing of publics. Similarly, subjectivity is the result of being addressed (or what Althusser calls interpellated) by the practices of a social formation. Social arguments are practices which address individuals as subjects in the creation, maintenance and/or transformation of a social formation.

Subjectivity is not monolithic but represents a multiplicity of identities. A woman, a lawyer, a racist, a mother, and a democrat can all be the same person. The practices of a social formation create a dispersed subject. By dispersed subject, I mean to suggest all the different positions from which one experiences the world. These different positions can be understood as one's identity. The dispersed subject is interpellated into a number of identities which are often contradictory. Social arguments create a unity in difference among these different identities. Of course, one way in which social arguments address a subject is by privileging one identity over another. If a social argument reduces subjectivity to one identity, then social arguments can be said to be ideological. When social argumentation fails to recognize the multiplicity of subject positions by which subjects live their lives it risks failing to understand the complexity of a social formation.

Subjectivity represents the ways in which subjects are positioned in a social formation. Since a social formation is a structure in dominance it is important to understand how particular identities are articulated and disarticulated for the purposes of maintaining, creating, and/or transforming relationships of power. To recognize the multiplicity of positions from which a subject can experience the world is to recognize how subjectivity is located within a complex and contradictory web of power relationships. For example, a woman lawyer may be oppressed due to her subordinate position in a patriarchal social practice, but she may also be the oppressor in a capitalist social practice. It is in and through the concept of subjectivity that social formations are reproduced.

A social formation as a structure in dominance reproduces itself through the production, deployment, and articulation of subjectivities who consent to the prevailing norms (norms that can change over time and across practices), which serve to legitimize asymmetrical relationships of power among (social) individuals in different practices. If violence is to be avoided in maintaining a social formation, a chain of equivalences must be constructed that privilege certain practices and their subsequent subject-effects with a normative force. For example, the equation, capitalism = freedom functions to privilege the social relations produced by capitalism while glossing over the antagonism and contradictions within and between capital and labor. The strength and stability of a social formation is a result of how tightly social practices are stitched to a normative force to which subjects can grant their consent.[10]

It is important to keep in mind that while subjectivity is the result of social practices, subjectivity is not a passive category. One's status as a subject is lived, experienced, contested, deployed, reproduced and disarticulated everyday in a number of different social practices. The struggle manifested in contradictory interpellations highlights the importance of agency in understanding a social formation.

Agency

The paradox of a critical turn in our understanding of subjectivity is that if subjectivity is the effect of social practices, then how are subjects capable of resisting the dominant power relationships which define a social formation as a structure in dominance? The answer to this paradox resides in our description of subjectivity as a contested and contradictory position from which people experience the world. To suggest that subjectivity is an effect of different practices in a social formation is not to suggest that human beings are dupes incapable of interrogating the taken-for-granted presuppositions of different social relationships. By agency, I mean to suggest that very process by which subjects negotiate the contradictory interpellations of social practices.

Agency is an affective investment in one's status as a subject. When a subject makes an affective investment in a particular identity from which to experience the world, he/she does so for the purpose of defending and/or contesting that particular subject-position. The point of understanding a social formation as an articulation of different subjectivities and practices is that there is no necessary correspondence between a particular subjectivity and a political project. One's identity as a woman can support either progressive or reactionary social practices concerning the status of women in a social formation. Agency serves as a useful critical concept when it refers to the actions which subjects take in negotiating the multiple and contradictory subjectivities they occupy in a social formation. However, agency need not implicate a voluntaristic metaphysics. As Giddens remarks, "the dialectic of control is built into the very nature of agency, or more correctly put, the relations of autonomy and dependence which agents reproduce in the context of definite practices."[11] Agency is an analytical concept that recognizes the active and contested space of a social formation.

Agency as an affective investment in one's status as a subject can be experienced in and through a number of discursive and non-discursive practices. A gay man makes an affective investment in his status as a gay subject every time he has sex with another man. He also makes an affective investment in his status as a subject when he produces arguments against anti-sodomy laws. Social arguments can be understood as a practice which is the result of an affective investment in a particular subjectivity. Giddens describes the relationship between reason-giving and agency this way: "the reflexive monitoring of behavior operates against the background of the rationalization of action—by which I mean the capabilities of human agents to 'explain' why they act as they do by giving reasons for their conduct."[12] This conception of the relationship between agency and social argumentation should not limit the study of social arguments qua arguments to the production of valid and invalid truth claims. Instead, the relationship between social arguments and agency should be concerned with how agency is determined by the subject-positions addressed by argumentative practices so that subjects can act in the creation, maintenance and/or transformation of a social formation. Agency is the effect of an affective investment in one's status as a subject, and social arguments are one site in which agency is expressed.

Social Argumentation

As the above analysis has suggested, arguments saturate a social formation. By a social argument, I mean a complex practice which articulates different practices and subject-positions together for the purpose of creating a unity in difference. A social argument is both an effect of different economic, political and cultural practices as well as a social practice which has effects in the articulation of a unity in difference. This unity in difference reveals an affective investment in one's status as a subject capable of acting to create, maintain and/or transform a social formation. The dialectic of identity and difference must be constantly negotiated by social arguments to reproduce a social formation and the legitimacy of particular social relationships. A critique of social arguments as a critical rhetoric must be concerned with the effects of these different articulations for the possibility of creating a radically democratic social formation.

PALESTINIAN DECLARATION OF INDEPENDENCE

The kernel of the Arab-Israeli conflict is embodied in the struggle for Palestinian self-determination. The establishment of the Israeli state and the subsequent first Arab-Israeli War culminated in the diaspora of the Palestinian people from their native land. At the end of the June 1967 War, Israel occupied all the land partitioned by the United Nations as the site for a two-state solution in U.N. resolution 181 as well as the Sinai Peninsula and the Golan Heights. The 1967 war established Israeli military supremacy in the region. The Israeli victory shattered the legitimacy of the different Arab states, particularly Egypt and Syria, as the dominant agents of Palestinian self-determination. The occupation of the West Bank and the Gaza Strip re-positioned Palestinians as colonial subjects under Israeli domination who must take the lead in establishing the conditions for the possibility of Palestinian self-determination. In the aftermath of twenty years of Palestinian nation-building and the increasing exploitation of the Palestinian population in the "occupied territories" the Intifada commenced in December of 1987.[13]

In an effort to capitalize on the momentum of the Intifada, the Palestine National Council held its 19th meeting in Algeria in the Fall of 1988. At this historic meeting, the Palestinian National Council (PNC) produced two crucial documents in an effort to establish a new rhetorical context in the struggle for self-determination. In a "political resolution" and a declaration of statehood, the PNC accepted U.N. resolution 181, which calls for the partition of the pre-1947 land into two states. The PNC also accepted U.N. resolutions 242 and 338 as the basis of an international peace conference, renounced terrorism, and advanced direct negotiations with Israel as the basis for resolving the Palestinian-Israeli conflict.[14]

The effects of the 19th meeting of the Palestine National Council continue to have a material impact on the conditions for the possibility of establishing the State of Palestine. In particular, the PNC declaration of statehood serves as an important document for investigating the aporias associated with establishing a democratic state in the context of colonial domination. The primary aporia of state formation facing the Palestinians is the need to establish and maintain a revolutionary collective identity strong enough to end colonial occupation, while at the same time creating the internal space for a "politics of difference" in the new nation-state.

The Palestinian Declaration of Independence is a political argument in the on-going struggle for Palestinian self-determination. As a political argument it functions as a democratic antagonism. Chantal Mouffe draws a distinction between a democratic antagonism and democratic struggles: "Democratic antagonism refers to resistance to subordination and inequality: democratic struggle is directed toward a wide democratization of social life."[15] The point Mouffe wants to make is that democratic antagonisms are polysemic and can be articulated to either reactionary or progressive social practices. In reading this document as a social argument, I am concerned with how a "unity in difference" is reproduced and deployed as a democratic antagonism at the same time that it enables and constrains the production of a democratic social formation.

A Unity in Difference: The Palestinian Arab People
The Palestinian Declaration of Independence begins, "In the name of God, the compassionate, the Merciful. Palestine, the land of the three monotheistic faiths, is where the Palestinian Arab people was born, on which it grew, developed and excelled" (p. 213).[16] The document represents the Palestinian Arab people as an organic unity capable of birth, growth, development and excellence. Notice that this organic unity exists within a space of religious difference. A collective subject—the Palestinian Arab people—is produced in and through an affective investment in being Palestinian as it unproblematically attempts to contain religious difference.

The people as an organic unity functions as a universal anchor to construct arguments in support of Palestinian self-determination. It is in light of the existence of a Palestinian people that social practices are to be judged as either contributing to or preventing self-determination. By deploying organic imagery, the Palestinian people embody stability in change. The people have an essential nature that can be traced over time which serves as a warrant for creating, maintaining, and/or transforming social practices.[17]

The rhetorical effect of the Declaration is to reproduce and deploy a collective subjectivity based on national identity. The Declaration proclaims, "The Palestinian people was never separated from or diminished in its integral bonds with Palestine. Thus, the Palestinian Arab people ensured for itself an everlasting union between itself, its land, and its history" (p. 213). In the next paragraph, the Declaration evokes the tragedies of the past in an effort to transcend differences in the name of political independence: "Resolute throughout that history, the Palestinian people forged its national identity, rising even to unimagined levels in the defense of invasion, the design of others and the appeal special to Palestine's ancient and luminous place on that eminence where power and civilization are joined. . . . All this intervened thereby to deprive the people of its political independence" (p. 213. Ellipses in the original translation). A collective subjectivity grounded in a national identity and political independence makes it possible to link the different histories of "the old Hashimite-supported and the newer pro-PLO leadership, between the PLO and local organizations, communists and religious fundamentalists, rightists and leftists, moderates and radicals"[18] as well as the differences between politically active women and religious fundamentalists. Political independence functions as a normative force which articulates different social practices together for the purpose of creating the State of Palestine.

At this point it is necessary to step back and investigate how a national identity can surface as the anchor for a unity in difference. At the same time, we should be able to understand how the Declaration represents a democratic antagonism. The contradictions within a social formation are never simple. As argued above, it is a mistake to define one contradiction as the principal contradiction of a social formation. A social formation determines and is determined by a vast accumulation of contradictions. However, the accumulated contradictions of a social formation can be fused together in a moment of revolutionary rupture.[19] It is in and through the reproduction and deployment of a national identity that the Declaration enacts an agent capable of self-determination. As a revolutionary rupture, the Declaration is able to identify a unity of oppression which can focus attention on the particular conditions and circumstances which reproduce the social formation as a structure in dominance.

Political independence has the normative force to create revolutionary agency in the name of a unity of oppression. The Declaration circulates as both an effect and a cause of attempts to create a unified Palestinian subject. The Declaration privileges the struggle for political independence as a primary site from which Palestinian subjects should experience the world. However, the contradictions in the social formation go beyond the colonizer/colonized binary represented by the Declaration. The force of political independence to create a unity among different struggles can be seen in the discourses of different social groups.

For example, an alliance of classes is possible based on national identity. According to a statement by the Palestinian Workers Youth Movement, "Let us all, workers and employers, work together to realize the aim of our Palestinian people: the liberation of the land."[20] A chain of equivalences is made possible between workers and employers based on the normative force of political independence and a collective subjectivity—the Palestinian people. Not only can an alliance of classes be articulated, but a unity in oppression between the subject-identities of Palestinian and worker can be fused together. According to a statement by the Workers Unity Bloc, ". . . the effects of the Israeli economic crisis . . . were reflected in the Occupied territories, leading to an intensive exploitation and oppression of the working class, particularly those working in Israeli enterprises. So the working class suffered the most from occupation policy. Hence it badly needs and fights for the end of occupation: it started to use its important role and influence amongst the ranks of the Palestinian people in the battle of liberation and national independence."[21] The struggle for political independence can also be described as a necessary condition for the rights of workers. According to a statement by the Progressive Workers Bloc, "Our main work is union work, but we believe that workers cannot get their rights as long as there is no independent Palestinian state."[22] The normative force of political independence can also negotiate the contradictions among gender within the working class. The Federation of Palestinian Women's Action Committees remarks, "The working woman is part of the Palestinian working class, and therefore she should struggle from the same position as her male colleagues against class discrimination and national oppression. Therefore, the unionist program of the working women coincides with the aims of the general program of the unionist movement and the working class, i.e. to remove the occupation and achieve the aims of our people: the right of return, the right of self determination, and the right to establish our national independent state on Palestinian soil."[23] In this example, the subjectivity of working class women and men is coupled in and through the people and the normative force of political independence.

In constructing a chain of equivalences among the different instances of oppression a unity in difference can be stabilized in and through "the people." Political independence is a normative force as well as the essential characteristic which defines the Palestinian people. According to the Declaration, "In generation after generation, the Palestinian Arab people gave of itself unsparingly in the valiant battle for liberation and homeland. For what has been the unbroken chain of our people's rebellions but the heroic embodiment of our will for national independence? And so the people were sustained in the struggle to stay and prevail" (pp. 213–214). A contradiction within a social formation must go through the people if it is to gain the status of a general contradiction capable of stitching together the vast accumulation of contradictions in a social formation as a revolutionary rupture. In the case of a number of working class men and women, the contradictions of class and gender can be articulated to the lack of political independence.

The Declaration reproduces a democratic antagonism within the social formation revolving around the lack of political independence. Mouffe argues that "an antagonism can emerge when a collective subject . . . that has been constructed in a specific way, to certain existing discourses, finds its subjectivity negated by other discourses or practices."[24] The Declaration positions the Palestinian Arab people within an international regime which has excluded the Palestinians: "when in the course of modern times a new order of values was declared with norms and values fair for all, it was the Palestinian Arab people that had been excluded from the destiny of all other peoples by a hostile array of local and foreign powers" (p. 214). A subjectivity-in-subordination is shown to be in contradiction to the stated norms of the international community opening up the possibility for the subordination of the Palestinian people to be challenged. The Declaration functions as a democratic antagonism by deploying an essential characteristic of the Palestinian people—the struggle for political independence—whose subordination reveals a contradiction in a global social formation. However, since a democratic antagonism must go through the people, it remains polysemic. It does not necessarily lead to a vast democratization of social life. Nationalism as the site of a democratic antagonism risks reproducing a reactionary social formation.

State Formation and the Politics of Difference

The Palestinian Declaration of Independence textually represents a revolutionary rupture in a social formation. Namely, the document establishes the State of Palestine. According to the Declaration, "The Palestine National Council, in the name of God, and in the name of the Palestinian Arab people, hereby proclaims the establishment of the State of Palestine on our Palestinian territory with its capital Jerusalem" (p. 215). The Declaration offers a break from an ongoing social formation which denies Palestinian Statehood, at the same time as it reproduces a Palestinian nation-state in and through the will of the people. The Declaration is able to construct a position in which the agency of the Palestinian people can be enacted through the establishment of a nation-state. By proclaiming the State of Palestine, the Declaration has the rhetorical effect of creating a unity such that "the people will appear, in everyone's eyes, 'as a people', that is, as the basis and origin of political power."[25] Hence, the question arises, what is the relationship between the reproduction of the Palestinian people in and through the formation of a State, and what are the possibilities for creating a democratic social formation?

A State represents a peculiar type of articulation. According to Hall, "the State remains one of the crucial sites in a modern capitalist social formation where political practices of different kinds are condensed" (his emphasis).[26] The State functions as a social space in which contradictory practices and social identities can be articulated for the purpose of "transmitting and transforming" relations of power. Analogous to a condensation symbol, the State represents a number of different practices and meanings such that the State remains a polysemous social construct.[27] However, to perform this condensation the State must allow "that site of intersection between different practices to be transformed into a systematic practice of regulation, of rule and norm, or normalization, within society."[28] Hall draws our attention to the way in which the state is a complex unity which must articulate different social practices and subjectivities for the purpose of governing.

A State determines and is determined by the reproduction of a unity in difference for the purpose of constituting a new social formation. In the Palestinian Declaration of Independence, Statehood becomes a necessary spatial site for the achievement of political independence. The struggle for a national identity becomes synonymous with the fight for space. According to the Declaration, "By stages, the occupation of Palestine and parts of other Arab territories by Israeli forces, the willed dispossession and expulsion from their ancestral homes of the majority of Palestine's civilian inhabitants was achieved by organized terror; those Palestinians who remained, as a vestige subjugated on its homeland, were persecuted and forced to endure the destruction of their national life" (p. 214). In defense of a national identity, Statehood allows for a "reterritorialization" of the land.[29] Consequently, the Declaration pledges "that our struggle shall be continued until the occupation ends, and the foundation of our sovereignty and independence shall be fortified accordingly" (p. 216). It is my argument at this point of the paper that the Palestinians risk reproducing a social formation as a structure in dominance in and through this act of reterritorialization in the name of national identity and the State of Palestine.

One's subjectivity is the result of being addressed by a number of different social practices. In maintaining a new social formation as a nation, the practices of the State of Palestine are likely to privilege a national identity over other identities such as gender, class or religion. According to Balibar "a social formation only reproduces itself as a nation to the extent that, through a network of apparatuses and daily practices, the individual is instituted as *homo national* is from cradle to grave, at the same time as he or she is instituted as *homo economicus, politicus, religiosus.* . . ."[30] Balibar's argument is that the differences among social individuals are not suppressed so much as they are relativized and subordinated to the individual's status as a citizen. The Declaration proclaims, "The State of Palestine is the state of Palestinians wherever they may be. The state is for them to enjoy in it their collective national and cultural identity, theirs to pursue in it a complete equality of rights. In it will be safeguarded their political and religious convictions and their human dignity by means of a parliamentary democratic system of governance, itself based on freedom of expression and the freedom to form parties" (p. 215). In this section of the Declaration, the Palestinian National Council moves from an account of the legitimacy of the Palestinian struggle to a vision about how the State will be organized. The Declaration implies that in and through an affective investment in their status as a citizen Palestinians can actualize other desires concerned with the production of a democratic social formation.

The Declaration's organic imagery of a people whose essential characteristic is the achievement of political independence risks the reproduction of a structure in dominance in and through the practices of the State of Palestine based on this same organic unity. In other words, the construction of a resistant presence in and through a national identity relativizes oppression within the social formation as a nation. Notwithstanding the formal procedures of a democratic state formation, unresolved contradictions within the social formation which have been strategically articulated to the national question are likely to remain not only unresolved but blocked in and through the "nationalization of society."[31] The Declaration represents not only a literal reterritorialization of the land, but the reterritorialization of individual Palestinians as citizen-subjects reproducing the State of Palestine and displacing the unresolved contradictions of a Palestinian social formation.

The democratization of social life cannot proceed without producing an active gender equality beyond the procedural guarantees of a democratic state. In the case of Palestine, the role of women has been increasingly problematized by the demands of the intifada and the fight for an independent state. The active role of women in the fight against occupation has contributed to a growing backlash against the fight for women's equality. The most significant sign of this backlash has been the success of the Islamic Resistance Movement (HAMAS) to force women to wear the traditional head-scarf (*hijab*) in public. Professor Hanan Ashrawi, an activist in both the women's and nationalist movements and currently the official spokesperson for the Palestinian delegation to the Middle East peace talks, highlights the growing contradiction between Islamic fundamentalism and the women's movement: "I think the emergence of the fundamentalist movement is most immediately and directly felt by women—because women are the most direct targets. The most visible aspect of this victimization is the *hijab*. To me, that sums up the way you view a women: as a sex object, as shameful, so you cover her up: as a commodity, the possession of the man; as a secondary member of society—she is supposed to stay at home to support the master."[32] The Declaration's only reference to women states: "we pledge special tribute to the brave Palestinian women, guardian of sustenance and life, keeper of our people's perennial flame" (p. 216). This statement from the Declaration does not offer much support against a conservative backlash directed toward women. The statement reduces women to their bodies, in particular their breasts and wombs. According to Hiltermann, "The only roles assigned to women in the new state are to protect, preserve, and procreate."[33] The subordination of gender equality to political independence contributes to the ongoing oppression of women in the name of political independence.

The Declaration's positioning of women within the traditional practices of domesticity reinforces a particularly insidious form of reterritorialization; the reterritorialization of the woman's womb to demographically reproduce the State of Palestine. Ashrawi remarks, "the demographic argument is . . . a convenient excuse to keep women as hatcheries."[34] A growing number of women activists in the national movement are becoming aware of the tensions between the national issue and the role of women. According to one representative of the Union of Palestinian Working Women's Committees, "We haven't had a feminist agenda. We have been preoccupied with political concerns, and as a result we often become alienated in our society . . . Recently, we have come to realize that this approach doesn't work. We realize that if we don't raise issues now, we won't be able to push them later on, and we'll be abused by the national movement."[35] Women are becoming increasingly sensitized to the need to prevent a dis-articulation of the struggles of women and labor (often, of course, the same people) from the national issue. According to Amal Wahden, an activist in the Worker's Unity Bloc and a founder of the Federation of Palestinian Women's Action Committees, "The struggle for our rights as workers and as women should start now or we'll end up with another bourgeois state and another kind of regime that will oppress women and the working class. It all has to go side by side."[36] The insight of these two arguments is found in their recognition that the construction of a democratic social formation cannot be reduced to the resolution of one contradiction—the fight for political independence. To the extent that a Palestinian social formation is produced in and through the fight for political independence, this social formation as nation reproduces itself as a structure in dominance.

The struggle for Palestinian self-determination demands more than the construction of a Palestinian State. The struggle for political independence has served to create a unity in difference among a vast accumulation of different contradictions and sites of democratic struggle. The arguments of Ashrawi and Wahden highlight the difficulty and importance of maintaining a political stance which does not relativize oppression. Efforts to dis-articulate the struggles of women and labor from the struggle for political independence only exacerbate a reactionary tendency of state formations to reterritorialize the lives of social individuals as citizens blocking social practices which are necessary for a vast democratization of a social formation.

CONCLUSION

Franz Fanon writes that, "colonialism is not satisfied merely with holding a people in its grip and emptying the native's brain of all form and content. By a kind of perverted logic, it turns to the past of the people, and distorts, disfigures and destroys it."[37] The Palestinian Declaration of Independence constructs an argument against colonial amnesia by constructing a narrative of political struggle and commitment to a homeland. It reproduces a Palestinian subjectivity capable of revolutionary agency in a time of brutal oppression. In so doing, the document creates an oppositional space from which Palestinians can organize for the purpose of transforming a structure in dominance. In light of Fanon's argument, the rhetorical achievements of the Declaration should not be easily dismissed.

However, nationalism represents a particularly dangerous contradiction in which to create a revolutionary rupture. The logic of statehood is one that relativizes and subordinates oppression in the name of political independence. This critique of the logic of statehood has demonstrated how the subjectivity of Palestinians-as-Palestinians can block the transformation of social practices which keep Palestinians-as-women in a subordinate subject position. In the case of Palestine, this paper has illustrated how political independence contributes to the reterritorialization of women's bodies for the purpose of demographically reproducing the State of Palestine.

The Palestinian Declaration of Independence represents a social argument in the production and articulation of a unity in difference. This paper has contributed to a theoretical understanding of how arguments circulate in a social formation for the purpose of maintaining, creating and/or transforming relationships of domination. While this essay has pointed to the aporias of constructing a revolutionary rupture around the contradictions of colonialism, we should be reminded that the Palestinians of the occupied territories continue to live under the constant threat of deportation, martial law, and soldiers with real bullets. The challenge for the Palestinians is to articulate the struggle for political independence to a vast democratization of their new social formation.

NOTES

[1] The notion of argument fields has received a tremendous amount of attention in argumentation theory. For a representative sample of how the concept of fields has contributed to argumentation theory, see Charles Willard, "Argument Fields" in *Advances in Argumentation Theory and Research,* Robert J. Cox and Charles Arthur Willard, eds., (Carbondale: Southern Illinois University Press, 1982), 24–77. For a discussion of argument spheres, see G. Thomas Goodnight, "The Personal, Technical, and Public Spheres of Argument: A Speculative Inquiry into the Art of Public Deliberation," *Journal of the American Forensic Association,* 18 (1982), 214–227 as well as his "Toward a Social Theory of Argumentation," *Argumentation and Advocacy,* 26 (1989), 60–70. For a discussion of argument communities, see Raymie McKerrow, "Argument Communities," in *Perspectives on Argumentation: Essays in Honor of Wayne Brockriede,* Robert Trapp and Janice Schuetz, eds., (Prospect Heights, IL: Waveland Press, 1990), 27–40. Hereinafter cited as *Perspectives on Argumentation.*

[2] The relationship between social argumentation and contextualism is best expressed by James F. Klumpp, "Taking Social Argument Seriously" in *Perspectives on Argumentation,* 110–120.

[3] *A Rhetoric of Motives* (Berkeley: University of California Press, 1969), 19–46.

[4] I consider my project to be consistent with what McKerrow calls a "critical rhetoric." However, I believe that the practice of critical rhetoric does not have to abandon a close reading of defining texts within a social formation. Critical practice is not dependent on embodying a "post-textual" stance. On the contrary, what is often at stake in relationships of power is who has the "right" to produce and read particular texts. Whether our critical practice chooses to focus on one text or a number of "textual fragments," the point of a progressive critical practice is to investigate the possibilities for constructing radical democratic social practices. Raymie McKerrow, "Critical Rhetoric: Theory and Praxis," *Communication Monographs,* 56 (1989), 91–111. Hereinafter cited as "Critical Rhetoric." For an example of a critical practice which combines close reading with a Foucauldian conception of power, see Edward Said, *Orientalism* (New York: Vintage Books, 1979).

[5] My understanding of a social formation comes primarily from the work of Louis Althusser. I keep some of Althusser, primarily the notion of relative autonomy and his concept of a social formation as a structure in dominance, while resisting the theoretical baggage associated with his concept of ideology as a mode of production. My purpose in this section is to explore what makes arguments social, and not simply to import another continental theorist into argumentation theory. For those interested in the work of Althusser, see *For Marx,* Trans., Ben Brewster (New York: Random House, 1970). Hereinafter cited as *For Marx, Lenin and Philosophy and Other Essays,* Trans., Ben Brewster (New York: Monthly Review, 1971). Hereinafter cited as *Lenin and Philosophy,* and Louis Althusser and Etienne Balibar, *Reading Capital,* Trans., Ben Brewster (London: New Left Books, 1970). For an example of how Althusser's conception of ideology would work in rhetorical studies, see Maurice Charland, "Constitutive Rhetoric: The Case of the Peuple Quebecois," *Quarterly Journal of Speech,* 73 (1987), 133–150. Hereinafter cited as "Constitutive Rhetoric."

6 Stuart Hall, "Signification, Representation, Ideology: Althusser and the Post-Structuralist Debates," *Critical Studies in Mass Communication,* 2 (1985), 93. Hereinafter cited as "Althusser and the Post-Structuralist Debates."

7 I am using the term articulation in a very specific sense. Stuart Hall defines articulation as "a connection or link which is not necessarily given in all cases, as a law or a fact of life, but which requires particular conditions of existence to appear at all, which has to be positively sustained by specific processes, which is not 'eternal' but has constantly to be renewed, which can under certain circumstances disappear or be overthrown, leading to the old linkages being dissolved and new connections—rearticulations—being forged. It is also important that an articulation between different practices does not mean that they become identical or that the one is dissolved into the other. Each retains its distinct determinations and conditions of existence. However, once an articulation is made, the two practices can function together, not as 'immediate unity' . . . but as 'distinctions within a unity.'" "Althusser and the Post-Structuralist Debates," 113–114.

8 "Ideology and Ideological State Apparatuses (Notes Toward an Investigation)" in *Lenin and Philosophy,* 127.

9 For a discussion of the debates concerning the term subjectivity, see Paul Smith, *Discerning the Subject* (Minneapolis, University of Minnesota Press, 1988).

10 The process of social formation reproduction I have just described has its roots in Gramsci's notion of hegemony. I am particularly indebted to Chantal Mouffe's explication of the concept. Chantal Mouffe, "Hegemony and New Political Subjects: Towards a New Concept of Democracy," Trans., Stanley Grey, in *Marxism and the Interpretation of Culture,* Cary Nelson and Lawrence Grossberg, eds., (Urbana, University of Illinois Press, 1988), 89–101. Hereinafter cited as "Hegemony and New Political Subjects."

11 *Central Problems in Social Theory* (Berkeley: University of California Press, 1979), 149. Herein after cited as *Central Problems.*

12 *Central Problems,* 57.

13 For a more detailed description of the relationship between Palestine and the Arab-Israeli conflict, see Lisa Hajjr, Mouin Rabbani and Joel Beinin, "Palestine and the Arab-Israeli Conflict for Beginners," in *Intifada: the Palestinian Uprising Against Israeli Occupation,* Zachary Lockman and Joel Beinin, eds., (Boston: South End Press, 1989), 101–111. Palestinian mobilization in the occupied territories is described by Joost R. Hiltermann, *Behind the Intifada: Labor and Women's Movements in the Occupied Territories* (Princeton: Princeton University Press, 1991), 3–16. Hereinafter cited as *Behind the Intifada.* For a discussion of Palestinian nation-building, see Dov Shinar, *Palestinian Voices: Communication and Nation Building in the West Bank* (Boulder: Lynne Reinner Publishers, 1987). Hereinafter cited as *Palestinian Voices.*

14 For a discussion of the 19th meeting of the Palestine National Council, see Edward Said, "Palestine Agenda," *The Nation,* (December 12, 1988), 637–638.

15 "Hegemony and New Political Subjects," 96.

16 The Palestinian Declaration of Independence was drafted by the Palestine National Council. This paper uses the English translation of the Declaration which was published in *The Journal of Palestine Studies,* 18 (1989), 213–216. All references to the Declaration come from this translation and hereafter are indicated parenthetically within the text of the paper.

17 It is the organic imagery of a people which constitutes what Charland refers to as an "ideological trick" of constitutive rhetoric since "it presents that which is most rhetorical, the existence of a people, or of a subject, as extrarhetorical." In other words, the organic imagery functions to position the people as if it was a unity waiting for its story to be told as opposed to a "unity in difference" that must always be reproduced through discursive practices. "Constitutive Rhetoric," 137. I am also indebted to Chaim Perelman and L. Olbrechts-Tyteca for their discussion of the relationship between an organic sociology, and the relation between argumentation and the stability and change of a person. See, *The New Rhetoric: A Treatise on Argumentation.* Trans. John Wilkinson and Purcell Weaver (Notre Dame: University of Notre Dame Press, 1969), 293–331.

18 *Palestinian Voices,* 13.

19 This part of my essay is informed by my reading of Louis Althusser, "Contradiction and Overdetermination" in *For Marx,* 89–116. Hereinafter cited as "Contradiction and Overdetermination."

20 *Behind the Intifada,* 77.

21 *Behind the Intifada,* 76.

22 *Behind the Intifada,* 76.

23 *Behind the Intifada,* 162.

24 "Hegemony and New Political Subjects," 94.

25 Etienne Balibar, "The Nation Form" in Etieene Balibar and Immanuel Wallerstien, *Race, Nation, Class* (London: Verso, 1991), 93–94. Hereinafter cited as "The Nation Form."

26 "Althusser and the Post-Structuralist Debates," 93.

27 For a discussion of condensation symbols in rhetorical studies, see David Zarefsky and Victoria J. Gallagher, "From 'Conflict' to 'Constitutional Questions': Transformations in Early American Public Discourse," *Quarterly Journal of Speech,* 76 (1990), 247–261.

28 "Althusser and the Post-Structuralist Debates," 93. Hall believes that the state is missing in much of Foucault's analysis of the social because Foucault fails to understand difference within a complex unity. That is to say, Foucault is forced into a "post-structuralist" stance of defending difference as the mirror opposite of unity (identity). The theoretical importance of the concept of articulation is that it allows us to think about unity (identity) and difference at the same time.

29 My understanding of the process of deterritorialization and reterritorialization is informed by the work of Felix Guattari. According to Guattari, "capitalism has always combined two fundamental practices: first the destruction of social territories, collective identities, and traditional value systems (that is what I call deterritorialization); then the recomposition, often by the most artificial methods imaginable, of personological categories, patterns of power and models of submission, which are, if not formally similar to those that have been destroyed, at least homoetical from the point of view of their function. This last practice is what I call reterritorialization." My argument in this section is that the State represents a form of reterritorialization. See Felix Guattari, "The PostModern Dead End," *Flash Art,* 125 (1986), 40.

30 "The Nation Form," 93.

31 Etienne Balibar, "The Nation Form," 90–92.

32 "The Feminist Behind the Spokeswomen—A Candid Talk with Hanan Ashrawi," *Ms.* (March/April 1992), 15. Hereinafter cited as "A Candid Talk."

33 *Behind the Intifada,* 202.

34 "A Candid Talk," 16.

35 *Behind the Intifada,* 203.

36 *Behind the Intifada,* 165.

37 *The Wretched of the Earth* (New York: Grove Press, 1965), 210.

Toward a Theory of Visual Argument

DAVID S. BIRDSELL AND LEO GROARKE

These special, two issues are motivated by the conviction that argumentation theorists do not pay enough attention to the visual components of argument and persuasion. A better understanding of these components is especially important if we want to understand the role of advertising, film, television, video, multi-media, and the World Wide Web in our lives. A decision to take the visual seriously has important implications for every strand of argumentation theory, for they all emphasize a verbal paradigm which sees arguments as collections of words. Most scholars who study argumentation theory are, therefore, preoccupied with methods of analyzing arguments which emphasize verbal elements and show little or no recognition of other possibilities, or even the relationship between words and other symbolic forms. Students of argumentation emerge without the tools needed for proficiency in assessing visual modes of reasoning and persuasion. We hope that these essays will help spur the development of a more adequate theory of argument which makes room for the visual.

Though we are committed to the development of a theory of visual argument, we have chosen to begin with an article in which David Fleming details his skepticism.

Visual images ("pictures") cannot, he claims, be arguments. We have begun with his paper because we want to recognize that many theorists explicitly or implicitly reject this possibility (Fleming has provided a useful bibliography), and because an answer to their objections must be the basis of a convincing account of visual argument. The rest of our issue therefore answers these objections. J. Anthony Blair attempts to meet them in a defense of the possibility and the nature of visual arguments. Cameron Shelley and Gretchen Barbatsis (appearing in the fall issue) examine cases which illuminate different kinds of visual argument, and propose conceptual distinctions necessary for dealing with different kinds of visual materials. The review essay by Lenore Langsdorf discusses an important book on images and persuasion and reflects more generally on the questions raised by contemporary attempts to understand visual persuasion.

In the present introduction we would like to add some comments on those concerns that strike us as most important when one considers the development of a theory of visual argument. The first issue which must be addressed is a prevalent prejudice that visual images are in some intrinsic way arbitrary, vague and ambiguous. This presumption encourages the view that visual images are less precise than words, and especially the written word. We think that this prejudice is a dogma that has outlived its usefulness, and that the first step toward a theory of visual argument must be a better appreciation of both the possibility of visual meaning and the limits of verbal meaning.

Visual images can, of course, be vague and ambiguous. But this alone does not distinguish them from words and sentences, which can also be vague and ambiguous. The inherent indeterminacy of language is one of the principal problems that confront us when we try to understand natural language argument. This is why historians endlessly debate the interpretation of historical documents, law courts struggle continuously with the implications of written and spoken claims, and personal animosities revolve around who said what and what was meant. The point that visual images are frequently vague and indeterminate cannot, in view of the demonstrable indeterminacy of verbal expressions, show that images are intrinsically less precise than spoken or written words (especially as we often clarify the latter with visual cues—as we may make the tone and meaning of a statement clear with a smile or a wink).

We can best illustrate the possibility of verbal meaning with some simple examples. We will begin with the following anti-smoking poster, which was produced by the U.S. Department of Health, Education and Welfare (now the U.S. Department of Health and Human Services). We must begin by noting that this poster is an amalgam of the verbal and the visual (see Figure 1). The important point is that this does not make its visual components redundant or superfluous. Without the visual elements we could not understand the poster, for the verbal message it contains— "don't you get hooked!"—is vague and ambiguous. It does not explicitly refer to smoking or cigarettes and could as easily refer to drugs, alcohol, or anything else which is potentially addictive. We know it is a message about smoking only because it depicts a fish which is "hooked" to a cigarette. The message of the poster is straightforward. It can plausibly be rendered as "You should be wary of cigarettes because you could get hooked and—like a fish on a lure—endanger your health." This is a quaint argument by analogy. It does not match the sophistication of the visuals which crowd our television sets—and increasingly, our computer screens— but it is an argument in the standard sense: it provides a reason for a conclusion.

Figure 1   Anti-Smoking Poster, U.S. Department of Health, Education and Welfare (1976).

This and countless similar examples make it difficult to sustain the kind of skepticism of those who maintain that the visual is radically indeterminate and cannot, therefore, sustain an argument. Consider Fleming's claim that a picture itself "makes no claim which can be contested, doubted, or otherwise improved upon by others. If I oppose the 'position' you articulate in a picture, you can simply deny that your picture ever articulated that, or any other, position." As common as such views are in academic discussions of the visual, they make little sense in the context of examples like the present one. Here the argument that you should be wary of cigarettes because they can hook you and endanger your health is forwarded by means of visual images, even though it is just the sort of claim that can be contested, doubted and improved upon. We too easily forget that there was a time when debates raged about the addictive qualities and the health effects of cigarettes. If someone viewing our sample poster did not "read" it as an attack on smoking (or arbitrarily denied that it "ever articulated that, or any other position"), then we are forced to the conclusion that they have radically misunderstood the visual image—to a point where we might reasonably wonder about their ability to comprehend the visual (much as we would wonder about someone's ability to understand English if they did not understand the corresponding verbal argument to be an attack on smoking).

Consider a second case which also illustrates the point that visual meaning can be in some cases neither arbitrary nor indeterminate. The following drawing is based on a 1926 editorial cartoon by S. K. Suvanto. The original cartoon was published in *The Daily Worker,* a socialist newspaper published in Chicago from 1924–1958 (see Figure 2). Though we are far removed from the context which produced this cartoon, we still readily understand it, even if we ignore its title (the words in the title add nothing which is not obvious in the image itself). In the background we see the flag of the former Soviet Union—a hammer and sickle—and the silhouette of a Russian worker. The sky suggests dawn. The lattice of new buildings suggests the new industrial communist society. In the foreground we see a painter with an easel. His exaggerated obesity, his suit and his bald head are standard symbols of the capitalist. He is painting the scene in the background but what he paints bears scant resemblance to the "actual" image we see. In his canvas, the hammer and sickle in the flag—symbols of work—become a skull and cross bones. The hammer in the worker's hand becomes a bloody dagger which the worker—who has become a ruthless soldier—is plunging into a victim he grasps with his other hand.

Once again, meaning in our example is straightforward. We can discern a whole set of visual claims: Soviet communism is hard at work building a new industrial society; commentators who portray the Soviets as bent on violence and repression distort the facts; they themselves are greedy and self-interested capitalists. Taken together, these claims lead to the obvious conclusion that we should not listen to those who attack the new Soviet experiment.

Figure 2 "The Model and the Painting," (After K. A. Suvanto).

Such examples leave little room for the presumption that visual meaning is necessarily arbitrary or indeterminate. The claims Suvanto makes in his cartoon are, moreover, just the sorts of claims which are open to debate, confirmation and argument. Someone who does not see his cartoon as an answer to criticisms of Soviet communism has radically misunderstood the point. Of course, one might debate specific points of interpretation (whether there is, for example, some significance in the fact that the *left* hand of the soldier in the painter's painting clutches his victim's throat) and one might fail to understand the visual vocabulary (a teenager might, for example, not understand the references to the Soviet Union or to capitalism). But these issues of interpretation are comparable to the issues that arise in the attempt to interpret verbal claims—the remarks of a political speaker, for example—and cannot be used to show that visual claims are radically indeterminate.

What we have said about these two examples applies equally well to more sophisticated visual images. In the articles in this double issue, Blair shows how a Benetton ad can reasonably be deciphered, Barbatsis illustrates how a television camera can convey an argument and Shelley shows how drawings taken from articles on paleontology forward two different kinds of visual arguments. Fleming is right to point out that argumentation theory lacks a well developed account of the distinction between visual premises and conclusions, but this is because we have not taken seriously the possibility of visual meaning, not because visual images are—as so many commentators presume—necessarily indeterminate.

It does not follow that verbal and visual meanings are equivalent or identical. There are good reasons for questioning whether they have a similar capacity to convey relatively precise meanings. We merely observe that both can be ambiguous or cogent and that both can convey claims and arguments. The meaning of a visual claim or argument obviously depends on a complex set of relationships between a particular image/text and a given set of interpreters. The recognition that visual meaning is not necessarily arbitrary is the crucial first step that we must take in our development of a theory of visual argument.

The importance of context is the second issue that we feel must be addressed in developing such a theory. We do not expect words (at least not all words) to have solid, unassailable meanings of their own. Instead, we look to companion sentences and paragraphs to ascertain contextual meanings which may or may not be corroborated by dictionary definitions. The word "well," standing alone, could refer to my health, my skepticism, or the municipal water supply. If you read the sentence "I am well, thank you," then the context makes it clear that the first meaning is intended. Context plays a similar role when you hear someone ask me how I feel, in which case the single word "well" would be a terse but perfectly intelligible reply.

There is of course more to the process of assessing meaning and its context than examining words on a page or puzzling through sounds we hear. "Context" can involve a wide range of cultural assumptions, situational cues, time-sensitive information, and/or knowledge of a specific interlocutor. The immediate verbal context of a sentence is only one source of information interpreters use in determining the meaning of a string of words. Imagine that you overhear the following exchange:

Jonathan: Do you think the faculty will get a raise this year?

Maryann: Oh, sure. Now that we have a growing deficit, enormous new demands on our operating budget, flat revenues, and a government hostile to public education, I expect 15%!

In such circumstances, it is hard to imagine Jonathan concluding that Maryann actually means that a 15% raise is in the offing, or, more naively still, that Maryann has made a poor argument. Assuming minimal communicative competency on Maryann's part, tone of voice alone will indicate her sarcasm. Assuming that there has never been a raise as significant as 15%, the contextually initiated will recognize that Maryann's response should not be taken at face value. The words alone do not convey these meanings, which are instead conveyed by the contextual cues.

Considered against the background of this familiar feature of verbal communication, there is no reason to assume that a visual image must conduct its contributions to argument in perfect isolation. Yet this assumption undergirds David Fleming's examination of visual argument and drives a good deal of the thinking that presupposes significant, inherent, and universal differences separating the verbal and the visual. We would never banish the consideration of contextual evidence when we consider verbal arguments, especially if we wish to understand their real-world efficacy. It would make no sense to take single words as units of argumentation unless they were clearly understandable as truncated references to more complete propositions. Why then would we assume that photographs should be examined in isolation from one another, or from verbal statements with which they are juxtaposed?

At least three kinds of context are important in the evaluation of visual arguments: immediate visual context, immediate verbal context, and visual culture. The significance of immediate visual context is most obvious in film, for it incorporates a progression of images which allows us to recognize a single frame as part of an overarching argument. Depending on the sequence of frames of which it is a part, an image of a man holding a knife may represent someone preparing to cook, a knife salesman or, more insidiously, evidence that someone is prepared to commit a murder. Sequences of images also play a role in other contexts. Instructional diagrams often use a progression of images to show viewers how to perform simple tasks. Cameron Shelley (in part two of this issue) shows that such diagrams can forward arguments.

Immediate visual contexts, however, encompass more than sequences of images. In judging such contexts we must often pay attention to visual cues beyond a single message source. Elements of the ambient visual environment can be equally influential in providing contextual cues to the interpretation of visual materials.

Immediate verbal context also provides a basis for the interpretation of visual images. A number of commentators (see Fleming in this issue) treat captions and other direct verbal references acting in concert with images as special cases, as indeed they are. It does not follow that the role of the image in a verbal-visual equation is unimportant, or secondary. Words can establish a context of meaning into which images can enter with a high degree of specificity while achieving a meaning different from the words alone. We see this in our first example, in which the words tell us that we are dealing with something which is addictive and harmful, while the visual image establishes that the topic is smoking.

Fleming explains another verbal-visual relationship in his remarks about visual evidence. But Fleming's formulation is limited by his emphasis on immediate verbal contexts which incorporate explicit claim/image interactions. The drawing based on the Suvanto cartoon invokes a much richer relationship between a larger and more general verbal context (communist narratives of the hostility of capital to the achievements of labor) and a specific visual rendition of the assertion that capitalists lie about communism. The implicit verbal backdrop that allows us to derive arguments from images is clearly different from the immediate context created by the placement of a caption beside an image.

When we incorporate conventionalized, situation-specific meanings within the process of interpreting visual arguments, we effectively extend the traditional verbal enthymeme. Suvanto's capitalist, for example, is a conventionalized image, easily recognizable as a type that could be invoked in a narrative description as readily as a visual depiction, particularly in the pages of *The Daily Worker*. But the imagistic recall is likely to be different from the verbal; we still need to be attentive to the way that a given image calls attention to the type. In this case, the drawing emphasizes physical characteristics, implicitly arguing against romantic images of capitalism—the beauty, glamor and power of Hollywood, for example—by emphasizing "undesirable" physical traits like corpulence, baldness and age. In other images, the dyslogies of depiction extend to demonizing qualities, such as the appearance of fangs and claws. In part two of this double issue, Shelley shows how subtle physical characteristics portrayed in a visual image can convey arguments about human evolution.

A third kind of context is supplied by visual culture, which differs from the first two categories principally in its indirect influence on the production of visual meaning. Many scholars have argued that visual culture changes significantly over time, and that developments in art, technology, philosophy, and science promote different ways of seeing over time. These scholars are for the most part careful to distinguish between the notions of "change" and "progress." They argue not that painting, or sculpture, or any other form of art has necessarily improved over time, but quite precisely that it differs, reflecting different values, conditions of production, and habits of interpretation. Cultural conventions of vision in this sense include what it means to see, or to represent seeing, as well as changes in the meaning of particular elements of visual vocabulary.

This is not the place for a comprehensive discussion of such complex ideas, but the basic concept can be illustrated readily by changes in television styles over the past thirty years. In the 1960's, television shots were considerably longer than those we find in the jumpy, quick edits typified by music videos in the 1990's. This change reflects something more than the difference between the evening news and MTV. Shot length has been reduced in almost all commercial television, and the number of shots per minute has surged. Much as cubism tried to present multiple perspectives unfolding over time and/or space on a single, two-dimensional frame, the quick-cut video editing style of the 1990's prefers several quick perspectives on a subject over the single, probing, shot that holds an image for minutes at a time. The result is a combination of visuals that decenters a unitary perspectivalism. No one camera is all-knowing and the subject is deliberately distorted with the use of negative effects or other filters that "reveal" different elements of the subject-as-source for videographic play.

Visual culture provides the broad master narratives of design which are the background for more specific visual (or for that matter, verbal) texts which perpetuate or challenge those narratives. Martin Jay's work identifies "scopic regimes" peculiar to historical periods. Students of argumentation have accepted since Aristotle the influence of acculturation in the production of verbal enthymemes. We are now arguing that the same allowances must be made for visual commonplaces as well, allowing potential visual arguments to draw on the same range of resources that we afford potential verbal arguments.

The changes in visual meaning made plain in studies of visual culture suggest a third issue which must be the basis of a satisfactory theory of visual argument. It concerns the meaning of "resemblance." In his article, David Fleming restricts his analysis to images that are created in an effort to resemble what they represent. We do not dispute the existence of a category of imagery that purports to represent reality, but we want both to problematize the notion and note that argumentation plays a key role in determining resemblance and representation (which constitute another way in which visuals are linked to argument). At issue here is a complex set of relationships having to do with representation and resemblance per se. The topic is too large to address thoroughly in this introduction, but three of its elements bear mention: the disjunction between resemblance and representation, the consequent conventionalization of representation, and the susceptibility of resemblance to visual and verbal challenge.

While most observers would say that a well-executed "realistic" portrait *resembles* the sitter, it may or may not adequately *represent* the sitter. If I sit for a portrait wearing a gorilla suit, a realistic painting, even a photograph, will resemble me (sitting in front of the artist, in a gorilla suit). But does it represent me? A caricaturist's line drawing (consider the famous profile of Alfred Hitchcock that became the lead-in to his television series) that cannot be said to resemble anyone in any detailed way may serve as a good representation of a sitter. Such examples show that while representation is a more ambiguous concept than resemblance, resemblance is itself fraught with judgment. What, exactly, should a successful visual image of a sitter "resemble?" Should it be the sitter's present attitude, the sitter's most common expression, a characteristic gesture?

These difficult questions posed by resemblance and representation have encouraged a wide reliance on conventionalized representations that are easily used in arguments. Heraldry is a conventionalized representation of a family. King Francis I of France was represented by the salamander, though he could hardly be said to have resembled one. In the sixteenth century, the Visconti family was visually represented by a serpent eating a child. While there is no "photographic" resemblance one might say that this demonstration of raw power represents (or metaphorically "resembles") the family's own. Likewise, the President of the United States is represented by his seal, which does not "resemble" him. In fact, because the seal's eagle motif is highly abstracted, appearing in a posture that no "real" eagle could attain in life, it is debatable whether the symbol even resembles a real eagle.

The shifting standards applied to resemblances make them subject to challenge on two argumentative levels. First, they may not in fact resemble (anyone who has argued with a photographer over the quality of a graduation or a wedding picture will have no trouble coming up with cases), and second, they may not represent. The kinds of arguments this implies can be conducted either visually or verbally. In this double issue they are reflected in Barbatsis' analysis of visual images in advertisements aired during the 1988 presidential campaign. One of the principal visual techniques she identifies is the deconstruction of an apparent resemblance in favor of an allegedly more accurate representation in political advertising. The point is not that the preferred alternative is or is not "genuinely" more accurate, but that through the application of visual techniques rather than verbal narrative, the question of resemblance has entered directly into the argument.

So far, we have suggested three prerequisites for a satisfactory account of visual argument: we must accept the possibility of visual meaning, we must make more of an effort to consider images in context, and we must recognize the argumentative aspects of representation and resemblance. We want to finish by more tentatively noting another issue raised by the attempt to formulate a theory of visual argument. Blair raises the issue in his article when he offers an account of visual argument which places significant limits on the visuals we can classify as arguments. In part, these limits are imposed by his distinction between argument and persuasion, suggesting that many of the visuals one might consider arguments are instances of persuasion *rather* than argument. Intuitively, there is something to his suggestion that such visual presentations are attempts to convince in a way that purposely circumvents argumentation and the reflection it implies. Considered from this point of view, the attempt to convince a dieter to eat a piece of cake by holding it under his or her nose is not, it seems, an argument.

Or is it? Why not take the holding of the cake in front of the dieter's nose to be a particularly forceful way of expressing the argument that "Eating this cake would be wonderful, therefore you should forget your diet and eat it"? So construed this is an argument. One might compare the ancient story that Diogenes the Cynic is said to have responded to Zeno's famous arguments against motion by walking a few steps and declaring "I refute Zeno thus." Surely this *is* an argument. But it is also an attempt to circumvent the reasoning and the reflection that accompanies Zeno's paradoxes.

Forbes I. Hill (1983) locates, in Aristotle's *Rhetoric,* support for the notion that visual appeals to desire influence our actions. As Hill puts it, "Aristotle's view of the pathe [feelings] is extremely intellectualized. To come into a state of feeling an auditor must make a complex judgment about himself in relation to external events. If he is incapable of making this judgment, he will not come into the state of feeling" (p. 47). Such a view collapses the distinction between "psychological and logical proof" by making appeals to feelings appeals to certain kinds of judgments. From this point of view, we "argue a person into a state of feeling."

At the very least it must be said that this way of extending the theory of visual argument has some intriguing consequences that are worth exploring. Most importantly, it allows for a significant expansion of the theory of argument. Without this expansion, argumentation theory has no way of dealing with a great many visual ploys that play a significant role in our argumentative lives—even though they can frequently be assessed from the point of view of argumentative criteria. Aristotle's notions of logos, ethos, and pathos can, for example, frequently be used to shed light on such circumstances, even when we have something that falls short of what we would normally count as a fully fledged argument. It is in view of this that the standard distinction between argument and persuasion needs to be reconsidered in the realm of visual argument.

Any account of visual argumentation must identify how we can a) identify the internal elements of a visual image, b) understand the contexts in which images are interpreted, c) establish the consistency of an interpretation of the visual, and d) chart changes in visual perspectives over time. These issues have been explored at length—albeit without a full appreciation of their relevance to argumentation studies—in the fields of art history, cognitive psychology, media studies, semiotics, and visual culture. The rich diversity of perspectives discussed in Langsdorf's review in this issue provides a good starting point for fruitful explorations of the literature this implies, but students of argument interested in the visual should obviously go beyond the single collection she discusses if they wish to engage the burgeoning scholarship in visual theory.

In the highly selective annotated bibliography that follows, we have chosen a few titles that speak very clearly to concerns that parallel the sort of broad understanding any argumentation scholar would want to bring to the examination of a verbal enthymeme. It is a literature to which we may reasonably expect to contribute ourselves. Missing from much of the analysis of visual imagery is the careful consideration of argumentation evidenced in the close readings of cases provided by Blair, Shelley, and Barbatsis. Though arriving at different conclusions about the project of visual argumentation, David Fleming exhibits much the same kind of concern by insisting that we actually find elements of something recognizable as argument before proceeding to an "argumentative" analysis of a picture, a condition that we feel the other three authors to have amply demonstrated in their essays.

Our contributions to understandings of the visual will come from our ability to flesh out theories of visual argumentation as rich and as rigorous as those we have developed for verbal argumentation. In the process of developing a theory of visual argument, we will have to emphasize the frequent lucidity of visual meaning, the importance of visual context, the argumentative complexities raised by the notions of representation and resemblance, and the questions visual persuasion poses for the standard distinction between argument and persuasion. Coupled with respect for existing interdisciplinary literature on the visual, such an emphasis promises a much better account of verbal and visual argument which can better understand the complexities of both visual images and ordinary argument as they are so often intertwined in our increasingly visual media.

SELECTED ANNOTATED BIBLIOGRAPHY

Brennan, T. and Jay, M. (Eds.). (1996). *Vision in context: Historical and contemporary perspectives on sight.* New York: Routledge. A highly eclectic collection of essays on vision from scholars in a wide range of disciplines. Argumentation scholars will find particularly useful the first five essays on the changed and changing roles vision at different points in history [*sic*]. Later essays address issues relating to vision and gender, vision and subjectivity, and visual studies and interpretation.

Bryson, N., Holly, M. and Moxey, K. (1991). *Visual theory: Painting and interpretation.* New York: Harper Collins. The articles in this collection range from elements of semiology to situated seeing. Every article is followed by at least one commentary, making this volume a particularly rich exploration of the issues raised. Argumentation scholars will want to pay close attention to the authors' treatment of arguments about visual materials and visual theory.

Foster, H. (1988). *Vision and visuality.* Seattle: Bay Press. This collection, sponsored by the Dia Art Foundation, is a brief (135 pp.) introduction to several important themes in the study of visual culture. Particularly valuable are Martin Jay's essay "Scopic Regimes of Modernity," and Norman Bryson's discussion of interpretive subjectivity in "The Gaze in the Expanded Field."

Gombrich, E. H. (1989). *Art and illusion: A study in the psychology of pictorial representation.* Princeton: Princeton UP. This classic work, originally published in 1960, sets out to explore the relationships among culture, perception, and forms of artistic production. Written before the development of most visual theories based on postmodernism or electronic media, *Art and Illusion* is a useful starting point for those who find the latter perspectives uncongenial.

Horace, B., Blakemore, C. and Weston-Smith, M. (Eds.). (1990). *Images and understanding.* Cambridge: Cambridge UP. This collection of essays, based on the Rank Prize Funds' International Symposium in October 1986, emphasizes cognitive approaches to visual understanding in the context of commentary from art historians and theorists.

Jay, M. (1993). *Downcast eyes: The denigration of vision in 20th century French thought.* Berkeley: U of California P. Here Jay explores vision as a cultural product, and particularly as the product of intellectual/artistic culture. The analyses of Bataille's and Lacan's contributions to perspectives on vision are invaluable.

Jenks, C. (Ed). (1995). *Visual culture.* London: Routledge. This volume contains essays on visual culture from a British cultural studies perspective. Readers interested in visual issues in electronic media will find this study particularly useful.

Melville, S. and Readings, B. (Eds.). (1995). *Vision and textuality*. Durham: Duke UP. This volume collects essays oriented around questions of disciplinarity in visual studies. Argumentation scholars hoping to understand academic institutionalization of vision will find several essays useful. Helpful as well is a repeated emphasis on verbal/visual issues.

Mitchell, W. J. T. (1986). *Iconology: Image, text, ideology*. Chicago: U of Chicago P. This is an enormously influential study of the shifting fortunes of visually and verbally based systems of meaning in western culture. Mitchell provides a lucid explanation of the stakes in preferring the visual to the verbal and vice versa. His is also the best single-volume exploration of the broad sweep of intellectual history on these issues.

Panofsky, E. (1995). *Meaning in the visual arts*. Garden City: Doubleday Anchor. This is in part Panofsky's most accessible text on the nature of pre-iconographic, iconographic, and iconological analysis. These distinctions are very helpful for anyone attempting to "read" an image.

Sherman, C. R. (1995). *Imaging Aristotle: Verbal and visual representation in fourteenth century France*. Berkeley: U of California P. This richly illustrated volume examines the use of manuscript illumination in the first French translations of Aristotle. Sherman shows how the illuminations themselves conveyed important arguments about state power generally and Charles V in particular. The fact that the analysis focuses on the works of Aristotle makes this book uniquely accessible to argumentation scholars.

SOURCE CITED

Hill, F. I. (1983). The Rhetoric of Aristotle. In J. J. Murphy (Ed.), *A Synoptic History of Classical Rhetoric* (pp. 19–76). Davis: Hermagoras Press.

···

The Male Madonna and the Feminine Uncle Sam: Visual Argument, Icons, and Ideographs in 1909 Anti–Woman Suffrage Postcards

CATHERINE H. PALCZEWSKI

Although we now think of postcards as mass-produced slips of paper (festively decorated with generic images or off-color jokes) to be sent to family and friends from vacation destinations, the social import of postcards during their "Golden Age" (1893–1918)[1] rivals the power of the Internet in contemporary times. The postcard industry was technologically and artistically prepared to play a part in the 1908 presidential election,[2] with postcards reaching the height of their popularity during that campaign.[3] Although it would be impossible to quantify their direct effect on the election, postcards "offer a vivid chronicle of American political values and tastes."[4]

Postcards, and their chronicling of American political values, were not confined to electoral politics. Postcard historian Frank W. Staff remarks, "The detail and unusual items of domestic and social history which [postcards] show are of inestimable value to the historian"[5] and, I would add, to those who study the rhetoric of historical movements. In her comprehensive study of British women's suffrage[6] campaign imagery, Lisa Tickner cites John Fraser's research on the postcard, suggesting "that the pictorial postcard was 'possibly the great vehicle for messages of the new urban proletariat between 1900 and 1914' (it was cheap to buy and to post, simple to use, and quick to arrive in an age of frequent postal deliveries)."[7] In Britain, middle-class collectors formed and joined postcard clubs, subscribed to postcard journals, and attended shows where they would place their collections in competition for medals and awards.[8] During postcards' heyday in the United States, "no 'drawing room table' was complete without one of the special albums in which picture postcards could be preserved"[9] and "one's social standing could be determined by the style and quality of the picture postcards in the album."[10] Thus, it is no surprise that postcards both supporting and opposing woman suffrage in the U.S. were common during the movement's legislative doldrums from 1890–1915 and its developing organizational and philosophical renaissance from 1896 to 1910.[11] Accordingly, a fascinating intersection occurred between advocacy for and against woman suffrage, images of women (and men), and postcards.

Woman suffrage advocates recognized the utility of the postcard as a propaganda device. In the United States, the majority of the postcards supporting woman suffrage contained real-photo images of the suffrage parades,[12] verbal messages identifying the states that had approved suffrage, or quotations in support of extending the vote to women.[13] However, the most visually evocative images in the United States, as in Great Britain, came not from postcards officially commissioned by woman suffrage groups, but from ones produced by commercial postcard publishers.[14] Simply by tapping into prevailing ideology, postcard producers assisted anti-suffrage forces "almost incidentally" by creating "a public imagery of the female form" that used suffragists as "topical or humorous types."[15]

The intersection of postcards, images of women and men, and the U.S. woman suffrage battle is best represented by a twelve-card set of full-color lithographic cartoon postcards lampooning, satirizing, and opposing woman suffrage produced in 1909 by the Dunston-Weiler Lithograph Company of New York.[16] Although many companies produced series of woman suffrage related postcards,[17] the Dunston-Weiler set is noteworthy for its graphic appeal. Two postcards show fashionably dressed white women, one declaring that her love for the vote was more than her love for her husband (Suffragette Series No. 12) and the other a cigarette-smoking *Queen of the Poll* (Suffragette Series No. 9). Two other images depict white women fraudulently electioneering, either by bribing older women with money (Suffragette Series No. 2) or men with kisses (Suffragette Series No. 4). Gender-bending images are provided by a white high-heeled *Suffragette Coppette* in a police uniform (Suffragette Series No. 5), a white *Pantalette Suffragette* in overalls (Suffragette Series No. 3), and a white beardless *Uncle Sam, Suffragee* wearing a skirt (Suffragette Series No. 6). The remaining five images show white men at home, caring for infants and toddlers, while women left the home to vote, were away at suffrage rallies, or simply absent. In particular, the *Suffragette Madonna* (Suffragette Series No. 1) shows a white man with a halo behind his head bottle-feeding a small child.[18] This last image's deployment of a Catholic icon also makes clear that not only are the citizens depicted in the other images presumed white, but they also are presumed Protestant.

Accessing images of women and men, images that speak to the many intersecting and countervailing pressures at the turn of the century, warrants a turn to the images depicted in popular culture forms such as postcards. Michael Calvin McGee encourages scholars to look to "popular" history, such as "novels, films, plays, even songs" when tracking the vertical structures of ideographs,[19] ideographs being the "vocabulary of concepts that function as guides, warrants, reasons, or excuses for behavior and belief."[20] Although McGee believed "the political language which manifests ideology seems characterized by slogans,"[21] Janis L. Edwards and Carol K. Winkler persuasively argue that scholars should attend not only to verbal slogans, but also to visual ones.[22]

No. 1   No. 2

Edwards and Winkler distinguish the *"representative form"*[23] of the visual ideograph from the icon, citing Lester Olson's definition of icons as "a type of image that is palpable in manifest form and denotative in function."[24] Icons operate referentially, in this case denoting specific people (the Madonna and Uncle Sam) with identifiable characteristics. Particularly with the Madonna icon, the referential element is central; in many ways, the Madonna icon came not only to depict the person Virgin Mary, but was believed to be, at least in the pious conception, "a transparent avenue to and from the divine."[25] Extending work on the visual ideograph and its relation to icons, Dana L. Cloud has explored how visual ideographs, as more than recurring iconic images, can index and make concrete verbal ideographs.[26] This essay advances another way to read the interaction between visual icons and verbal ideographs, particularly as they relate to our understandings of sex/gender.

The images in these anti-suffrage postcards offer an interesting location in which to explore how the (necessarily visual) icons of the Madonna and Uncle Sam, as well as non-iconic images of women, were deployed to reiterate the disciplinary norms of the verbal ideographs of <woman> and <man>. This project embraces E. Michele Ramsey's call for a positionalist critical perspective when studying representations of women, a perspective that enables scholars to understand better the broader social context to which historical women rhetors reacted.[27]

No. 3   No. 4

While it initially may seem strange to present <woman> and <man> as ideographs, as McGee notes, "many ideographs . . . have a non-ideographic usage."[28] Pointing to my department head, and saying "John is the brunette man" is a non-ideographic usage; however, telling my department head to "be a man" is, insofar as I use the word as an agency of social control, imbuing the word with an intrinsic force.[29] Thus, the images in the postcards present one location in which to assess the "public vocabulary" defining <woman> *as well as* the public vocabulary defining <man>.[30]

This essay contributes to a happily expanding body of communication studies literature on woman suffrage in general,[31] and on images of <woman> emerging from the suffrage era in particular.[32] This essay adds to the insights of these studies by focusing on the images found in *anti*-suffrage items, and by attending to the way in which <man>, as well as <woman>, was ideographically deployed through images and icons.

In addition to exposing the intersection of icons and ideographs, the postcards analyzed here are fascinating both for how they reflect, and for how they depart from, verbal arguments concerning woman suffrage prevalent during this time period. Accordingly, this essay moves through the following arguments. First, I recognize that the postcards offer visual forms of the arguments against suffrage that highlight the coarsening effect the vote would have on women; the postcards

No. 5   No. 6

offer visual indexes to measure the departure from the verbal ideograph of <woman> caused by suffrage. The postcards show women forsaking their motherly duties and acting masculine by smoking, wearing masculine clothing, and engaging in the debauchery of the polls.

Second, I explore how the postcards present an argument that was absent in the verbal discourse surrounding suffrage: just as women would become de-feminized by the public activity of voting so, too, would men become feminized by the private activity of caring for infants, an activity forced on them by women's public activities. To detail the feminization of man argument, I specifically analyze *Uncle Sam, Suffragee* and the *Suffragette Madonna* postcards. In particular, the *Suffragette Madonna* postcard negotiated the anti-Catholic bias that was present in both suffrage and anti-suffrage arguments. In many ways, this postcard encapsulated the complex arguments concerning gender, sexuality, religion, nationality, and citizenship that circulated throughout the suffrage controversy.

REFLECTING THE VERBAL ARGUMENTS:
WOMAN SUFFRAGE TAINTS AND DE-FEMINIZES WOMAN

During the Victorian era (1837–1901), clearly defined roles for men and women emerged, roles that persisted into the Edwardian era (1901–circa 1918). Women

No. 7   No. 8

were to be the "angel in the house," while men were to face the vagaries of the public world of politics and commerce. Of course, these separate spheres were not impermeable. Woman suffrage advocates challenged the notion that women and the vote were unfit for each other, whether it be that women were unfit to vote, or that the vote would make women unfit to be women. These challenges to the prevailing conception of womanhood did not go unanswered.

At the turn of the century, the "cult of domesticity," and its attendant images of man and woman, was a prevalent theme in "Victorian literature, art, and social commentary."[33] Women who violated the separation of spheres became the "Fallen Woman,"[34] modified in the case of suffrage to also include the "nagging wife" or the "embittered spinster."[35] Particularly in relation to suffrage, "the assumption that the 'public' woman was an unsexed harridan ran deep in contemporary thought."[36] Thus, women were disciplined to remain in the private sphere or risk losing their femininity. However, even those opposed to woman suffrage did not eschew the public realm as a locus of action for women.

The complexity and development of anti-suffrage (antis)[37] arguments should not be ignored or underestimated. As Manuela Thurner argues, "a case can be made for studying the losing side of a protracted historical struggle, such as the contest over woman suffrage" because "a fuller picture of the period's cultural and political climate emerges when both, or more, sides of the debate are taken into

No. 9   No. 10

consideration."[38] Thus, even though woman suffrage may have been won, anti-suffrage postcards offer valuable insights into how sex and citizenship were negotiated through visual argument. But, to recognize the distinctiveness of anti-suffrage images, like those contained in the Dunston-Weiler series, an understanding of the antis' verbal arguments is necessary.

Many male political leaders condemned the idea of a woman voting on the grounds that women were not biologically suited to such an endeavor, and male-run liquor interests played a significant role in combating suffrage. However, men were not the only opponents. Well-organized groups of women, known as remonstrants, also opposed suffrage, claiming as their motto "Home, Heaven, and Mother."[39] Remonstrants believed woman suffrage was a misguided and unnecessary reform.[40] For them, women of good character would be better able to influence public policy by means other than the vote; concomitantly, granting to all women the right to vote might enable those women with less than savory character to overwhelm their more upstanding sisters, as implied by the *Suffragette Vote-Getting* and *Queen of the Poll*.[41]

Typical verbal arguments against suffrage, made by men and used extensively in remonstrant literature, emphasized the effect of the vote on women. Daniel Webster (lawyer, congressperson, and statesperson) decried, "The rough contests of the political world are not suited to the dignity and the delicacy of your sex."

No. 11   No. 12

Cardinal James Gibbons (Catholic archbishop and the youngest prelate at the First Vatican Council) worried, "If woman enters politics, she will be sure to carry away on her some of the mud and dirt of political contact." Dr. S. Weir Mitchell (celebrated clinician and neurologist) exhorted, "woman accepts the irrevocable decree which made her woman and not man. Something in between she cannot be." And antis noted that not only would women be coarsened, but that suffrage would be "an appeal to the coarser strength of men."[42] Those opposed to suffrage were worried *more* about how women would be tainted and de-feminized, than about whether men would be feminized.

In many ways, one can read the visual arguments in pro- and anti-woman suffrage literature as responding to each other. E. Michele Ramsey argues that *The Woman Citizen*'s World War I era cartoons reconfigured citizenship's relationship to sex and gender by presenting woman as a "competent citizen" and redefining the meaning of "loyal citizen."[43] Functioning as a response to this argument, the Dunston-Weiler postcard series depicted the verbal anti-woman suffrage arguments that highlighted women's unsuitability for citizenship duties. Two themes in particular reinforce the verbal arguments opposing woman suffrage and supporting masculine conceptions of citizenship: (1) women lacked the physical power necessary to enforce their vote, and (2) the public realm was unsuited to proper women.

Suffragette Coppette

The *Suffragette Coppette* (No. 5) postcard reflected the antis' verbal arguments concerning women's inability to enforce the effect of their votes. Aileen S. Kraditor, in her germinal history of the movement, outlines the argument linking physical power to voting rights:

> If women were to vote, the thesis continued, half the electorate would be incapable of enforcing its mandate and vicious elements would be encouraged to resort to violence. A vote was not simply the registering of an opinion; it was a demand and consequently would be meaningless unless exercised only by the muscular portion of the community.[44]

The New York Association Opposed to Woman Suffrage, in a circa 1910 statement presented to both houses of the U.S. Congress, noted: "To extend the suffrage to women would be to introduce into the electorate a vast non-combatant party, incapable of enforcing its own rule."[45] Goldwin Smith (British-born historian and journalist), in his commentary on the question of woman suffrage, explained: "Political power has hitherto been exercised by the male sex . . . because man alone could uphold government and enforce the law."[46] In other words, physical power was needed in order for a vote to carry any force.

The *Suffragette Coppette* postcard,[47] one of six that focused on women in public, presented the idea of a woman being a law enforcement officer as laughable. Armed with a rolling pin instead of a truncheon, and accompanied by a demure puppy instead of a vicious police dog, her high-heeled stance makes clear her lack of power. In fact, the subtitle of the postcard makes clear where the real threat of force lies: "Beware of the dog."

Public Woman

The remainder of the postcards depicting women in public reflected the antis' verbal arguments concerning the coarsening effect the vote would have on women and their fear that improper women would populate the polls. Jane Jerome Camhi analyzes how the antis visualized "womanhood of consisting of set types," consisting of "the better class, the indifferent, and the degenerate."[48] Of particular worry to antis were the prostitutes, whom they feared would overwhelm their more upstanding sisters at the polls because "the best of women would shun political life and the most unprincipled would have the field to themselves."[49] Such worries were reflected in the smoking *Queen of the Poll* (No. 9), the bribery of *Electioneering* (No. 2), and the aggressive kissing of *Suffragette Vote-Getting, the Easiest Way* (No. 4).

Interestingly, and in contrast to the oft-seen renderings of suffragists as masculine, the Dunston-Weiler postcards depict women acting in public as still feminine in appearance, wearing attractive dresses and having beautiful faces. However, it would be a mistake to read these postcards as unqualifiedly liberatory. Instead, these images represent a moment in which "sex is both produced and destabilized in the course of this reiteration,"[50] where sex norms are both maintained and challenged. In these images, a public woman may not be a masculine woman, but that did not make her a good woman.

As Judith Butler notes, as sex is reiterated "gaps and fissures"[51] emerge and present opportune moments for resistance. Yet it would be incorrect to read the postcard images of women as subversively progressive because they contradicted the representations of suffragists as unsexed harridans.[52] These images are not an example of the widening of a fissure in our understanding of woman as citizen just because, in these images, woman maintained her femininity even as she voted. Why?

The type of femininity the voting woman was allowed to maintain is one that is sexualized. The connection between sexuality and publicity is not accidental. At this time, a prostitute was considered a "public woman"; thus, being a public woman meant one was a publicly accessible woman.[53] As Lisa Maria Hogeland points out in her discussion of public sex scandals and Victoria Woodhull, "'public women' are sexual(ized) women."[54] Thus, even as the postcards presented a public woman as still a feminine woman, she was not a good woman. Instead of using the loss of femininity as a disciplinary mechanism, the postcards instead deployed the loss of virtue. Either only bad women would vote, or if a woman voted she would be presumed bad.

Evidence of how the voting (public) woman was presented as the sexualized (public) woman is contained in the repeated theme of the exposed ankle, appearing in Suffragette Series Nos. 2, 3, 4, and 12. The repeatedly exposed ankle is not accidental. My argument here is not that actual 1909 women never exposed their ankles. Rather, my argument is that the exposed ankle functions as code, indicating that the woman who voted was to be read as a bad woman.

The sexual significance of the ankle was one that began long before the turn of the nineteenth into the twentieth century. For example, "The provocative effect of the exposed ankle or leg was a source of both moral outrage and ribald jests throughout the [eighteenth] century."[55] Although the story of Victorian piano legs prudishly being skirted in order to avoid exciting the erotic sentiments may be apocryphal,[56] one can still argue that the ankle was coded sexually. In 1850s United States, one of the primary objections to the dress reform represented by the Bloomer outfit was that it exposed the ankle, thus lending the outfit an erotic quality.[57] For a middle-class woman, showing an ankle was shocking, even up until 1909.[58] A cursory review of the *Sears Catalogue*, "the arbiter of fashion to small-town America,"[59] makes clear that women's dresses skirted to the floor were the norm in 1909, with barely a toe peeking out from underneath. Not until 1912 would ankles appear consistently as an acceptable fashion statement. Thus, the repeatedly exposed ankle (and even the, gasp!, calf in No. 4) appearing in these postcards is noteworthy.

Even as these postcards allowed women to maintain their attractiveness as they ventured into the public, the postcard images were not really progressive nor did they rearticulate an understanding of <woman>. Instead of women being disciplined by the loss of their looks, they were disciplined with the loss of their purity. The publicity of the voting woman was the publicity of a "public woman." In fact, the only images in which the woman's ankles were not exposed were still coded as sexual. *Queen of the Poll* (Suffragette Series No. 9) stands with a lit cigarette, and the woman in *Election Day* (Suffragette Series No. 7) sports a low cut bodice as she bids farewell to her husband.

Half of the postcards in the Dunston-Weiler series reflected the verbal arguments concerning the effect of suffrage on women and <woman>. Should women venture into the public world of electoral politics, they risked losing their purity and good standing as women or, conversely, only those who had already lost their good standing would venture to the polls. However, the de-feminization/sexualization of women is not the only argument the postcards depict. In fact, the remaining images advance an argument that was not present in the verbal discourse, an argument appealing to the ideograph of <man> via the icons of Uncle Sam and the Madonna.

DEPARTING FROM THE VERBAL ARGUMENTS: WOMAN SUFFRAGE FEMINIZES MAN

E. Michele Ramsey and Cheryl Jorgensen-Earp both provide examples of how diffuse images of women found in the expansive cultural contexts of the dominant discourse structure the ideograph of <woman>.[60] Katherine Meyer, John Seidler, Timothy Curry, and Adrian Aveni, in their analysis of images of women in Fourth of July cartoons, demonstrate how cartoons are one of the expansive cultural mediums which structure the meaning of <woman>, even when that is not the intentional purpose of the cartoon.[61] Supplementing these scholars' work, this essay explores one location in which the dominant discourse and cultural images gave structure to the concept of <man> as well as <woman>, in part by presenting what is not manly and by presenting men in locations typically populated by women. The corollary to the woman unsexed (or oversexed) by the masculine vote was the man unsexed by the voting woman.

Popular culture images of men in the home appear to be the only traces of a potentially inarticulable fear of the emasculated man, a man made suitable for the private world of childrearing. Most often at this time, dominant cultural images showed men as incompetent in the nursery, the location perhaps most identified with "women's work."[62] Quite simply, by virtue of being a man, men were incapable of pursuits in the domestic realm. A number of British and U.S. postcards show men trying to do laundry, as the cat gets into the milk and the children sit squawking.[63] Consistent with this theme as presented in mass media and other postcard images, every time a man appears in the Dunston-Weiler series (which is in six of the twelve images), they are shown feminized. However, the specter of the feminized man was absent in the verbal discourse opposing suffrage.

The Dunston-Weiler series also presents a variation on the home-bound man theme, with its images of men competently caring for infants, as in the *Suffragette Madonna* (No. 1) and Suffragette Series Nos. 8 and 11. Yet even the competent male caregiver appealed to anti-suffrage sentiments, for then the image was of "the poor, tired husband home from his day's labor only to find that he must mind the baby or do the dishes so that his wife may prepare a speech or attend a public meeting."[64] He was the martyr to the suffrage cause.

As woman suffrage advocates attempted to stretch the meaning of <woman> to incorporate the public act of voting into their role as citizens, those opposed (or indifferent) to woman suffrage formulated images depicting the effect of women's vote on men. This demonstrates that the conflict over gender roles is always simultaneously about femininity and masculinity. In the dominant discursive structure, one cannot expand the meaning of <woman> without necessarily shrinking the understanding of <man>. Writing twenty years after the appearance of the Dunston-Weiler postcards, Virginia Woolf plays out why a gain by women is always simultaneously read as a loss on the part of men:

> Women have served all these centuries as looking-glasses possessing the magic and delicious power of reflecting the figure of man at twice its natural size. . . . That is why Napoleon and Mussolini both insist so emphatically upon the inferiority of women, for if they were not inferior, they would cease

to enlarge. That serves to explain in part the necessity that women so often are to men. . . . How is he to go on giving judgement, civilising natives, making laws, writing books, dressing up and speechifying at banquets, unless he can see himself at breakfast and at dinner at least twice the size he really is?[65]

More recently, Judith Butler has spoken to the theme of how the masculine/feminine binary constitutes what it means to be man or a woman.[66] Gender and sex are something we do, not something we are[67] and thus "'persons' only become intelligible through becoming gendered in conformity with recognizable standards of gender intelligibility."[68] The unintelligibility of a male Madonna and a feminine Uncle Sam speak to this move, as do the images of male caregivers.

The series contains five images of men in the home (Suffragette Series Nos. 1, 7, 8, 10, and 11), all of them caring for children. Perhaps best reflecting the idea that a zero-sum tradeoff exists between men and women's rights, *I Want to Vote But My Wife Won't Let Me* (No. 11) pictures a man washing clothes while also watching over an infant and cat. In this image, a woman's exercise of voting rights has stripped a man of those rights. However, the most interesting male caregiver image is represented by the *Suffragette Madonna,* which completes the transformation of a man (bottle-feeding an infant) into the mother of all mothers. Not only are fathers feminized in the Dunston-Weiler series, but so too are uncles, in the form of Uncle Sam. The remainder of this essay focuses on these two postcard images, primarily because of the way they represent intersections of icons and ideographs. I discuss the intersections of religion, gender, and the vote presented by the *Suffragette Madonna* later, but for now turn to a discussion of *Uncle Sam, Suffragee.*

Uncle Sam, Suffragee

The name Uncle Sam was first used to criticize the United States during the War of 1812,[69] and the first images of Uncle Sam appeared in 1832.[70] Although Brother Jonathan was the more popular image leading up to the Civil War, by the war's end, Uncle Sam became the dominant image, being used both as a positive icon and as a way to challenge the government. Uncle Sam was not depicted with facial hair until 1856, and the facial hair persisted most likely because the figure of Abraham Lincoln so influenced the depictions that after the Civil War, the bewhiskered Uncle Sam was the universally used and recognized likeness.[71] In fact, Uncle Sam would become known in slang as "Mr. Whiskers."[72] In the 1870s, Thomas Nast's cartoons solidified Uncle Sam's characteristics. As a result of Nast's illustrations, the adult Uncle Sam was always depicted with a beard, as he is in the most widely distributed and recognizable image: the 1917 James Montgomery Flagg recruiting poster "I Want You for the U.S. Army." In a collection of Uncle Sam images, all show him with a beard when he is not depicted as a child, except for the image of *Uncle Sam, Suffragee.*[73] In his comprehensive history of Uncle Sam, Alton Ketchum notes that one of the "last appearances of a beardless Uncle Sam" was in 1865.[74] As this postcard series demonstrates, however, Mr. Ketchum was off by 44 years.

Although not possessing the religious power of the Madonna icon, Uncle Sam still functions more like an icon than an ideograph. Although the form of Uncle Sam has changed across time, what he denotes has remained relatively constant.[75] According to the government official responsible for asking Herbert Noxon, at the behest of the State Department, to create the official version of Uncle Sam in 1950, "He is the United States. . . . He is our composite American personality—the symbolic projection of what our country means to us and to other nations."[76]

Uncle Sam denotes the United States. Although typically shown as "benign, friendly, yet firm,"[77] manipulating the image enables one to play with the image of the United States. Thus, a cross-dressing Uncle Sam (or United States) warrants analysis. *Uncle Sam, Suffragee* depicts Uncle Sam clean-shaven, in star-spangled skirt, with hand on hip, and jaunty bonnet atop his head, giving a whole new meaning to "I want you."

The feminization of Uncle Sam is achieved through the change in clothes, the stripping of his secondary sex characteristic of facial hair, minimizing his height, and making him the object of the act of suffrage—the suffragee. Instead of wearing his traditional trousers, top hat, and tails, Uncle Sam is shown in a long skirt, red and white striped duster coat, heels, and oversized bonnet. Whereas many other postcards depicted women in masculine dress (as in *Pantalette Suffragette* and *Suffragette Coppette*), this one turned the tables, putting Uncle Sam in drag. The transformation is completed with the clean-shaven face. In this moment, Uncle Sam was stripped of his masculinity and lost a characteristic that had come to be part of his identity as the representative of the United States. Coupled with his posture, with hands on hip, his stature completes the transformation of the larger than life representative of U.S. power to a figure who is acted upon and passive.

Thomas H. Bivins, in his analysis of the changing shape of Uncle Sam across the decades, posits that part of his heroic nature is embodied in his stature. With the average man standing six and a half heads tall, comic characters are made to appear heroic by having smaller heads and larger bodies, so that they are eight or more heads tall. When Nast finally stabilized the image of Uncle Sam, he was "tall and Lincolnesque, about 7½ heads, and would probably fall somewhere between thin (ectomorphic) and muscular (mesomorphic)."[78] This image persisted well into the 1900s, where his mesomorphic body depicted him as "paternal, protective and the epitome of strength."[79] In contrast, the *Suffragee* image shows him not as muscular, but as curvy with a suspicious bulge at his chest. He also stands only about six heads tall, including his high heels but excluding his patriotic bonnet.

Finally, as "suffragee," Uncle Sam as representative of the United States is on the receiving end of suffrage, not as a right but as something wielded against him. He is the one to whom suffrage is done, and the result of having suffrage done to him is the loss of his masculine power. But Uncle Sam is not the only one feminized by the vote.

The Suffragette Madonna

While the series as a whole negotiated the conflict between de-feminized women and feminized men, the *Suffragette Madonna* postcard in particular also negotiated the anti-Catholic bias that was present in both pro- and anti-woman suffrage arguments. In many ways, this postcard encapsulated the complex arguments concerning gender, sexuality, religion, nationality, and citizenship that circulated throughout the suffrage controversy. The image operated on multiple levels: it appealed to the anti-woman suffrage Catholic population by highlighting how the vote would violate the religious admonition that woman's place was in the home, it appealed to anti-Catholic sentiments fed by the fear that Catholics as a voting block would overtake Protestants, and it deployed the stereotype of Catholicism as effeminate to intensify the feminizing effect of the vote.

Anti-Catholicism was neither new to the time period, nor unique to either suffragists or remonstrants, as both responded to the influx of immigrants from a nativist perspective. During the early decades of the nineteenth century, immigration from Europe to the United States fueled the rapid growth in the Catholic Church until Catholicism represented the country's largest religious denomination by mid century.[80] For the Irish and Germans who had arrived during this first wave of immigration, a unique period of Catholic religious vitality and political and economic stability occurred from 1870 to 1896. During the second half of the nineteenth century, however, new waves of Italian and Polish immigrants, with their "alternative expressions of Catholicism," arrived, presenting a challenge to this stability.[81] This second wave of growth in Catholicism, with its "massive waves of Catholic immigration to industrial and mining centers of the Northeast and Great Lakes states,"[82] combined with "a pre-existing distrust of Catholicism to precipitate an anti-Catholic, nativist reaction."[83] In these regions, most Protestants "banded together in the Republican party as a means for preserving the quasi-official . . . Protestant quality of American life."[84] These reactions made clear the way in which conceptions of American-ness, and citizenship, were bound up with issues of ethnicity and religion.

Given the depth of anti-Catholicism, it was unavoidable that both anti- and pro-woman suffrage groups would appeal to the bias. Anti-immigrant prejudice was evident within the suffrage movement, whose members bemoaned the fact that well-educated native women did not have the vote while expanded suffrage enabled illiterate immigrant men to overwhelm the polls. In order to limit the power of ethnic, often Catholic, political machines, suffragists argued that women should be given the vote. Such arguments were persuasive enough that in the 1890s the American Protective Association endorsed woman suffrage as a way of combating the rising political power of Irish Catholics.[85]

Immigrant communities were well aware of the implications of the suffragists' arguments. Immigrant organizations feared how the native-born population would use woman suffrage against them and, thus, stubbornly opposed any change in voting laws. Not only did immigrants fear the political effect of women's voting, but they also feared its social effect. Immigrant men saw suffragists as "dangerous radicals who sought to destroy the harmony of their traditional family unit by introducing the issue of 'women's' rights into the household. . . . [M]ale immigrants refused to see the 'Votes for Women' campaign as anything less than the destruction of their solitary refuge amid a life of turbulence and danger: the home."[86] These political and social fears explain why, even though the Catholic Church never took an official position, it functionally was the most unified national religious body to oppose woman suffrage.[87]

Remonstrants appealed to this anti-woman suffrage bias of recent Catholic immigrants, even as they also appealed to their Protestant audiences, by highlighting the threat of illiterate immigrant women overwhelming the polls. Even though antis made cursory appeals to the Catholic anti-woman suffrage vote, with the Massachusetts remonstrants publishing a brochure in Polish prior to a 1915 referendum campaign, generally "antis treated the immigrant community and the Catholic Church with disdain"[88] for the "root of anti-immigrant bigotry among remonstrants was anti-Catholic."[89] Thomas Jablonsky vividly explains antis' fear of how woman suffrage would supplement the immigrant vote:

> Of special concern was the alleged nightmarish march of a female Catholic army descending upon the polls under orders of their priests and bishops. "Cathedrals and ignorance" awaited the future of America. Alarmed by the rise of urban political machines, which, in turn, were fueled by the votes

of Irish, Polish, and Italian men, antis feared that the country would suffer greater harm at the hands of "Bridget," "Natasha," or "Maria."[90]

Into this anti-Catholic and highly sex-segregated society, the image of the *Suffragette Madonna* was introduced.

The *Suffragette Madonna* postcard advances the idea that when woman gains (masculine) political power, man becomes feminized, relegated to caring for infants, a duty typically delegated to women and to the domestic sphere. No longer the public citizen, the man becomes the private caregiver, a martyr to the suffrage cause. With its play on the Madonna image, this postcard also reflected a bias against Catholics (even as it appealed to Catholic males' fear that the vote would undermine the sanctity of the home) as it hinted that an expanded franchise might benefit the growing Catholic immigrant community to the detriment of Protestant groups.

It would be impossible to understand the significance of the Madonna image without understanding the concept of "visual piety."[91] For many, the act of looking upon a religious image is deeply spiritual; Catholics in medieval times believed that simply "looking upon relics afforded forgiveness of sin."[92] This led Middle Age European art and architecture to focus on the presentation of the relic and the host, converting the sacred into a visual experience, much as the icon had done in the East. Because the most powerful Catholic female role model is the Virgin Mary,[93] appropriation of the icon is fraught; it is likely to be extremely distasteful, if not outright sacrilegious, to Catholics unless the image, itself, were attempting to stabilize the meaning behind the icon.

However, if the Madonna icon functions so powerfully for Catholics, what enabled it to resonate at all with Protestants? During the nineteenth century, many homes would have displayed Murillo's *Immaculate Conception,* such that the Catholic Madonna and Child "were reinterpreted to be any mother and her child. The Mary was emblematic of all mothers and not merely the mother of Jesus."[94]

During the Victorian era, the standard up to which women had to live was the "angel in the house," with the "preeminent Angel in the House" being the Virgin Mary.[95] The angel ideology was premised on the notion that women's domestic duties were essentially a spiritual calling. In fact, the postcard's use of a child highlights the effeminate nature of care-giving, since the child was of an age where it most likely still required breast-feeding, substituted in this case by the bottle held by the man. The man is not left caring for a young adult, or even a toddler, but an infant—that creature most dependent on parental care. This image employs the representative form of the Madonna icons that show Mother Mary and infant Jesus, but it also highlights the hyper-feminized role of caregiving for infants.

The image appealed to the universally shared belief that woman's place was in the home, particularly with small children. But, even as the image spoke to Catholic men's fears of the loss of their (idealized) home, it also tapped into Protestant men's biases against Catholic immigrants. Although the "angel in the house" ideal transcended religious denominations, Protestants distrusted what they perceived to be Catholics' penchant for idol-worship, most typified by the new immigrant love of mass-produced Mary images.[96] Because the Madonna icon is identified with the Catholic love of religious images, the postcard was a subtle reminder that the type of woman voting would be a Catholic woman, with her Catholic husband caring for their (precipitously expanding number of) children while she was at the polls.[97]

Even as the image of a male caregiver appealed to Protestant and Catholic men's fear of emasculation (caused by the loss of their monopoly on the vote), and as the postcard appealed to Protestants' fear of an ever-burgeoning Catholic vote, it also played on Protestant men's fear of the emasculating effect of Catholicism. Religion scholars have recently focused on how gender and religion intersect, and it is now commonly accepted that "there were distinctive patterns of men's spiritual experience."[98] In contrast to the effeminacy of Catholicism (as perceived by non-Catholics given Catholic priests' celibacy and clothing), Protestants touted the ideal of "muscular Christianity."[99] In other words, not only were men in general emasculated by the vote, but when Catholics overwhelmed the polls and imposed their religion on everyone, Protestant men in particular would be emasculated by Catholicism.

The *Suffragette Madonna* potentially appealed to both Catholic men and to those with an anti-Catholic bias. For Catholic men, the image represented their greatest fear: loss of the sanctity of their home life, which for many was the only stable location in their tumultuous immigrant world. Given that Catholics tended to see women's calling in the home as even more scripturally determined than their non-Catholic counterparts, the appeal made clear that supporting woman suffrage would constitute sacrilege. For Protestants who feared the influx of Catholic immigrants, the image appealed to their fear that Catholic women would overwhelm the polls. However, even as the image spoke in a split voice to the two groups, it also appealed to both on the same level. The image tapped into men's fear, regardless of religion, that the vote would feminize them.

A POSTCARD POSTSCRIPT

For anyone interested in the study of sex/gender, <man> and <woman> should be a central focus of study. As Judith Butler consistently reminds us, "[s]exual difference, however, is never simply a function of material differences which are not in some way both marked and formed by discursive practices."[100] Construction of what it means to be a man or a woman is "a temporal process which operates through the reiteration of norms."[101] As this study and the existing literature examining the function of images in the suffrage controversy make clear, discursive and *non*discursive practices produced by suffragists, anti-suffragists, and institutions of popular culture mark and form understandings of sexual difference.

As Ramsey notes in her call to study the images of woman appearing in "non-traditional texts"[102] norms are reiterated even when not produced by any entity officially allied with a movement. Supplementing Ramsey's call to study non-traditional texts such as advertisements, this study establishes the need to look beyond news media outlets when studying political and suffrage images, at least when examining controversies that occurred during the golden age of postcards. Interestingly, most rhetorical studies of political cartoons analyze ones that appeared in newspapers and magazines.[103] Although critical studies of postcards do exist,[104] none examine the intersection of political cartoons and postcards, even though postcards were cheap, easily accessible, and did not present the demands of literacy that newspapers did.[105]

Postcards were circulated more widely than magazines, were not dependent on literacy, and did not allow audience self-selection (one could not control what postcards one would receive). Studying the images of political controversies from the turn of the century, but ignoring the role of postcards, would be equivalent to studying a contemporary political campaign and ignoring the use of televised commercials and the Internet. Postcards were ubiquitous, cheap, easily accessible, and clearly participated in the suffrage controversy in a way that developed and extended the argument beyond what can be found in the verbal arguments contained in broadsides and print media. The postcards analyzed here represent one location of reiteration of what it means to be a <man> and to be a <woman>.

However, as critical race scholars note, identity is intersectional. One is never *only* a woman or *only* a man. We also are composed of races, genders, sexualities, classes, religions, ethnicities, etc. One cannot study sex/gender distinct from other identity ingredients, for no scholarly alchemic process exists by which to extract a description of sex pure of race, gender, sexuality, class, religion, ethnicity, etc.[106] How we do woman is informed by how we do race, how we do man is informed by how we do gender, and how we do citizenship is informed by how we do religion. Accordingly, I foregrounded the whiteness of the bodies depicted in the postcards when I described them earlier. I intentionally made clear that the images of <man> and <woman> are images of *white* men and *white* women.

In fact, it may be that the very ideograph of <woman> is raced white in the United States. For example, Barbara Welter, in her extremely influential book *Dimity Convictions*, notes how womanhood was defined as pure, pious, domestic, and submissive.[107] Yet, as Chandra Talpede Mohanty makes clear, such an idealized conception of womanhood was confined to white women of the middle and upper classes.[108] Women of color and poor women could never attain the ideal because of their race and class. This, of course, does not mean that the ideograph held no power over them; it was still able to discipline them, to declare each of them a bad <woman> as Sojourner Truth's query of "Aren't I a woman?" made clear. Ultimately, all the postcards in this series, and the *Uncle Sam, Suffragee* image in particular, offer a way to assess the means by which the nation and citizenship are presumed masculine and white.

Even as the postcards do not trouble the normativity of whiteness, the *Suffragette Madonna* postcard's deployment of religion allows recognition of the way in which nationality, ethnicity, religion, and citizenship are intertwined. Whiteness was not nearly as undifferentiated a race category at the turn of the century as it is now. Distinctions were made between native citizens and recent immigrants. Between immigrants, distinctions were made between Western and Eastern European, between Irish and German, Polish and Italian, etc. Thus, the Madonna image offers one way to explore the visualization of the ideograph of white <woman> and white <man> as informed by different strands of Christianity, particularly those strands embraced by immigrants.

In addition to exploring how white <woman> and white <man> was indexed through visual depictions, this essay also demonstrates how visual arguments function as part of a larger public controversy, in this case the controversy over woman suffrage which also necessarily implicated the controversies over sex, gender, citizenship, and religion. Studies of visual rhetoric populate our journals. However, when it comes to recognizing visuals' role in the rhetorical sub-species of argument, some continue to insist that visuals cannot argue,[109] despite a growing body of literature that recognizes visuals can function as argument, both in its propositional and in its process form.[110] This essay should resolve that dispute insofar as it demonstrates that a complete, and significant, argument in the suffrage controversy (that suffrage would feminize men) cannot be discerned and traced without recognizing the possibility of visual argument. Recognizing the role of visual argument, in this case represented by the postcard images although certainly contained in other visual forms, enables critics to read the clash of argument across symbolic forms. Argumentative engagement, thus, is not confined to discursive clash, but can be manifested by occupation of alternate cultural forms. The "answers" to woman suffrage arguments are to be found not only in the discursive creations of organized opposition, but also in the visual products of diffuse popular culture forms.[111]

Accordingly, this study also takes exception to one of the basic assumptions found in the study of political cartoons: that visual arguments merely reflect or intensify existing discursive arguments. Michael A. DeSousa and Martin J. Medhurst "believe the real significance of the political cartoon lies *not* in its character as propositional argument or as persuasion but in its ability to tap the collective consciousness of readers in a manner similar to religious rituals, civic ceremonies, and communal observances."[112] Although I agree with their assessment that cartoons tap into collective consciousness, I disagree that cartoons lack a significant propositional character. The postcards analyzed here demonstrate that political cartoons' propositional function is of real significance insofar as they present an argument in visual form that was absent in discursive form. As the icons of Uncle Sam and the Madonna evoke the ideographs of <man> and <woman>, the postcards make visible the argument that men will be feminized, sacrificing their masculinity and full citizenship to woman's sullied citizenship of equal suffrage.

As Robert Hariman and John Louis Lucaites' work on iconic photographs[113] makes clear, images can embody notions of civic and public identity as they form public culture. They believe the images they studied "become iconic because they coordinate a number of different patterns of identification."[114] This study provides an explanation not of how publicity is formed via the emergence of icons, but of how preexisting icons are deployed to contain emerging expansive definitions of citizenship. Once we accept the "constitutive function of public discourse,"[115] not only must we search for places where publicity is reconstituted and expanded, where a gap and fissure is exploited, but also those locations where it is reiterated through the re-inscription of binary sex/gender norms that are tied to race, religion, and class.

The postcard images studied here offer compelling visual arguments about the effect of the vote on white men's and white women's citizenship. Recognizing this is important, given that even contemporary studies of anti-suffrage arguments focus on how the vote would affect women, not men. Jean H. Baker's introduction to *Votes for Women: The Struggle for Suffrage Revisited* does note that men feared the vote because "political equality with women cut into their households, endangering domestic arrangements"; however, her description of the explanations offered as to why the arrangements existed was that "women were ill-suited to participate in public life because of their domesticity . . ."[116] The fact that men might be ill-suited to tend the home because of their publicity is not noted. Thomas Jablonsky, in his study of the antis, also focuses on the effect on women as represented in the antis' arguments: "The world of women . . . was blending too quickly with the world of men."[117] The point was not that the world of men was blending too quickly into the world of women. Although contemporary scholars note, and advocates from the period decried, the erosion of the distinction between who populated the public and private (home) spheres, almost all mention the detrimental effect women crossing spheres would have on the public and women's ability to care for the home, while none mention the possible effect women's crossing spheres would have on men's location in the spheres.

What might account for this theme appearing in postcards when it is absent in the verbal discourse? Cartoons are a particularly apt way in which to explore some of the enthymematic arguments present in anti-suffrage discourse. If it is true that "[c]artoons often seem to project unconscious desires and fears,"[118] then it seems plausible that while no suffrage opponent (especially a male one) would want to speak of man's (his) possible emasculation, such a fear could be explored in cartoon images where a clothes-washing man is not allowed to vote. Cartoons enabled deep-seated culturally grounded beliefs to be expressed visually, re-entrenching cultural ideals, even while those beliefs were verbally proclaimed to be biologically determined and, thus, not in need of reinforcement.

The recognition of the distinctiveness of the visual arguments against suffrage carries implications for the theory of visual ideographs and where we should search for them. Two forms of visual ideographs have been identified thus far. Edwards and Winkler argue that visual ideographs are representative forms in which depictive rhetoric functions ideographically.[119] Cloud has identified the way in which visual ideographs can "index verbal ideographic slogans, making abstractions . . . concrete."[120] This study presents a third version of the play between icons and ideographs: iconic images can be used to maintain the social control power of verbal ideographs, in this case the ideographs of <man> and <woman>. Instead of the Madonna carrying multiple connotations across multiple images (something Edwards and Winkler note is typical of a visual ideograph), or the Madonna meaning shifting depending on context (as Cloud notes), I believe the Madonna's connotation remains stable here and across her images in other postcards. The referential fixity of the iconic image assists in the proof of the unintelligibility of the feminine man. In fact, instead of multiple connotations appearing across multiple images, multiple connotations resonate within this one postcard depending on whether one is Catholic or not.

Although the Madonna image, as well as Uncle Sam, were appropriated and recontextualized, what Edwards and Winkler identify as the "central features of the transformation of visual images into representative forms,"[121] I do not believe this means the Madonna and Uncle Sam function as *representative forms* of the Madonna and Uncle Sam. Instead, the representative form was <man> and <woman>, of which Uncle Sam and the Madonna are examples. *Uncle Sam, Suffragee* and the *Suffragette Madonna* are not parodies, the form Edwards and Winkler argue often is used in visual ideographs. Instead, they are cautionary tales. They warn that the very meaning of core religious and secular icons would be altered should woman suffrage come to pass. These two postcards depict anti-icons and thus do not function as representative forms. They are referential forms, as icons always are. They are appeals to fix and stabilize the iconic form of Uncle Sam and the Madonna in the face of social pressures of destabilization. Taken together, the visual arguments of the Dunston-Weiler postcard series fix and stabilize the ideographs of <woman> and of <man>.

NOTES

[1] Susan Brown Nicholson, *The Encyclopedia of Antique Postcards* (Radnor, PA: Wallaca-Homestead Book Co., 1994), 196.
[2] Valerie Monahan, *An American Postcard Collector's Guide* (Poole: Blandford Press, 1981), 84.
[3] Roger A. Fischer, *Tippecanoe and Trinkets Too: The Material Culture of American Presidential Campaigns, 1828–1984* (Urbana: University of Illinois Press, 1988), 148.
[4] George Miller, forward to *Political Postcards 1900–1980, A Price Guide*, by Bernard L. Greenhouse (Syracuse: Postcard Press, 1984).
[5] Frank Staff, *The Picture Postcard and Its Origins* (London: Lutterworth Press, 1966), 8.

6 British suffragists referred to "women's suffrage" while U.S. suffragists spoke of "woman suffrage." Accordingly, when referring to British suffrage activities, I use the phrase "women's suffrage" and when referring to U.S. suffrage activities, I use the phrase "woman suffrage."

7 Lisa Tickner, *The Spectacle of Women: Imagery of the Suffrage Campaign 1907–1914* (Chicago: University of Chicago Press, 1988), 50.

8 Tickner, 50–1.

9 James Laver, foreword to *The Picture Postcard and Its Origins* by Frank Staff, 7.

10 Staff, 64.

11 Eleanor Flexner, *Century of Struggle: The Woman's Rights Movement in the United States* (New York: Atheneum, 1973), 248: and Sara Hunter Graham, "The Suffrage Renaissance: A New Image for a New Century, 1896–1910," in *One Woman, One Vote: Rediscovering the Woman Suffrage Movement,* ed. Marjorie Spruill Wheeler (Troutdale, OR: NewSage Press, 1995), 159.

12 The visual power of the suffrage parade is best explained in Linda J. Lumsden, "Beauty and the Beasts: Significance of Press Coverage of the 1913 National Suffrage Parade," *Journalism and Mass Communication Quarterly* 77, no. 3 (Autumn 2000): 593–611. She argues: "The parade marked a milestone in the incorporation of American women into Society. Part of that incorporation involved the portrayal of women in media" (602).

13 This summary of postcard types comes from the author's personal collection, a review of postcards available on-line, examination of collections put up for auction, and consultations with suffrage postcard collectors. The differences between pro- and anti-suffrage postcards are not limited to their style and content. Their uses also differed: "Though most cards were heavily anti-suffrage, some were pro-suffrage. When the pro-suffrage cards are found today, they usually have not been postally used. Perhaps the social climate was such that these cards were hand exchanged or merely kept by the purchaser" (Nicholson, 196).

14 Tickner, 51–2.

15 Tickner, 162.

16 Although I have not yet found exact production numbers for the series, it does appear to be the most widely circulated set of suffrage images in the United States. At least, if survival rates are any indication, it was the most widely produced since postcards from this series are the most commonly available to contemporary postcard collectors,

17 The National American Woman Suffrage Association produced a series of motto and state postcards. I & M Ottenheimer of Baltimore, MD, and the Leet Bros. of Washington, DC, produced a number of real-photo images from suffrage parades. "Just by Way of a Change" was a series produced in Saxony but mailed in the United States. Walter Wellman produced the cartoonish "The Suffragette" series.

18 This is not the only instance of the *Suffragette Madonna*. In 1910, another postcard by that name was circulated, showing a man with halo feeding a girl doll a bottle (available at http://winningthevote.org/anti4-big.html). The Nash postcard company also circulated a similar image.

19 Michael C. McGee, "The 'Ideograph': A Link Between Rhetoric and Ideology," *Quarterly Journal of Speech* 66, no. 1 (February 1980): 11.

20 McGee, 6.

21 McGee, 5.

22 Janis L. Edwards and Carol K. Winkler, "Representative Form and the Visual Ideograph: The Iwo Jima Image in Editorial Cartoons," *Quarterly Journal of Speech* 83, no. 3 (August 1997): 289–310.

23 Edwards and Winkler, 289–90.

24 Lester C. Olson, "Benjamin Franklin's Representations of the British Colonies in America: A Study in Rhetorical Iconology," *Quarterly Journal of Speech* 73, no. l (February 1987): 38, note 1.

25 David Morgan, *Visual Piety: A History and Theory of Popular Religious Images* (Berkeley: University of California Press, 1998), 124.

26 Dana L. Cloud, "'To Veil the Threat of Terror': Afghan Women and the <Clash of Civilizations> in the Imagery of the U.S. War on Terrorism," *Quarterly Journal of Speech* 90, no. 3 (August 2004): 285–306.

27 E. Michele Ramsey, "Addressing Issues of Context in Historical Women's Public Address," *Women's Studies in Communication* 27, no. 3 (Fall 2004): 352–76. Ramsey uses "woman" to refer to "discursively constructed representations" and "women" to denote the literal human

beings (see Ramsey, 373, fn 3). Following other studies of ideographs, I use < > to designate when I am using the ideographic form of a word.

28 McGee, 15.

29 McGee, 6.

30 Ramsey, "Addressing," 353. See also Celeste Michelle Condit, *Decoding Abortion Rhetoric* (Urbana-Champaign: University of Illinois Press, 1994); Celeste Michelle Condit and John Louis Lucaites, *Crafting Equality* (Chicago: University of Chicago Press, 1993).

31 For examples of scholarship analyzing advocacy of woman suffrage, see Karlyn Kohrs Campbell, *Man Cannot Speak for Her* (New York: Praeger, 1989): Bonnie J. Dow, "Historical Narratives, Rhetorical Narratives, and Woman Suffrage Scholarship," *Rhetoric and Public Affairs* 2, no. 2 (Summer 1999): 321–40; Bonnie J. Dow, "The 'Womanhood' Rationale in the Woman Suffrage Rhetoric of Frances E. Willard," *Southern Communication Journal* 56, no. 4 (Summer 1991): 298–307; Susan Schultz Huxman, "Perfecting the Rhetorical Vision of Woman's Rights: Elizabeth Cady Stanton, Anna Howard Shaw, and Carrie Chapman Catt," *Women's Studies in Communication* 23, no. 3 (Fall 2000): 307–36; Sara Hayden, "Negotiating Femininity and Power in the Early Twentieth Century West: Domestic Ideology and Feminine Style in Jeannette Rankin's Suffrage Rhetoric," *Communication Studies* 50, no. 2 (Summer 1999): 83–102; Donna M. Kowal, "One Cause, Two Paths: Militant vs. Adjustive Strategies in the British and American Women's Suffrage Movements," *Communication Quarterly* 48, no. 3 (Summer 2000): 240–55; Wil A. Linkugel, "The Woman Suffrage Argument of Anna Howard Shaw," *Quarterly Journal of Speech* 49 (April 1963): 165–74; and Amy R. Slagell, "The Rhetorical Structure of Frances E. Willard's Campaign for Woman Suffrage, 1876–1896," *Rhetoric and Public Affairs* 4, no. 1 (Spring 2001): 1–23. For scholarship analyzing opposition to woman suffrage, see Elizabeth V. Burt, "The Ideology, Rhetoric, and Organizational Structure of a Countermovement Publication: 'The Remonstrance', 1890–1920," *Journalism and Mass Communication Quarterly* 75, no. 1 (Spring 1998): 69–83; Martha Hagan, "The Antisuffragists' Rhetorical Dilemma: Reconciling the Private and Public Spheres," *Communication Reports* 5, no. 2 (Summer 1992): 73–81; and Kristy Maddux, "When Patriots Protest: The Anti-Suffrage Discursive Transformation of 1917," *Rhetoric and Public Affairs* 7, no. 3 (Fall 2004): 283–310.

32 For scholarship analyzing images of woman and women's rights, see Jennifer L. Borda, "The Woman Suffrage Parades of 1910–1913: Possibilities and Limitations of an Early Feminist Rhetorical Strategy," *Western Journal of Communication* 66, no. 1 (Winter 2002): 25–52; Katherine Meyer, John Seidler, Timothy Curry, and Adrian Aveni, "Women in July Fourth Cartoons: A 100-Year Look," *Journal of Communication* 30, no. 1 (Winter 1980); and E. Michele Ramsey, "Inventing Citizens During World War I: Suffrage Cartoons in *The Woman Citizen*," *Western Journal of Communication* 64, no. 2 (Spring 2000): 113–47; and Ramsey, "Addressing." For other disciplines' studies of images, see Brian Harrison, *Separate Spheres: The Opposition to Women's Suffrage in Britain* (London: Croon Helm, 1978); Ian McDonald, *Vindication! A Postcard History of the Women's Movement* (London: Bellew Publishing, 1989); Alice Sheppard, *Cartooning for Suffrage* (Albuquerque, NM: University of New Mexico Press, 1994); and Tickner.

33 Cheryl Jorgensen-Earp, "The Lady, the Whore, and the Spinster: The Rhetorical Use of Victorian Images of Women," *Western Journal of Speech Communication* 54, no. 1 (1990): 83.

34 Jorgensen-Earp, 84.

35 Tickner, 164.

36 Tickner, 151.

37 The label "antis" generally refers to any person opposed to suffrage. Remonstrants, however, were exclusively women opposed to woman suffrage.

38 Manuela Thurner, "'Better Citizens Without the Ballot': American Anti-suffrage Women and their Rationale During the Progressive Era," *Journal of Women's History* 5, no. 1 (Spring 1993): 33.

39 Thomas Jablonsky, "Female Opposition: The Anti-suffrage Campaign," in *Votes for Women: The Struggle for Suffrage Revisited*, ed. Jean H. Baker (New York: Oxford University Press, 2002), 123.

40 Maddux, 287.

41 Jane Jerome Camhi, *Women Against Women: American Anti-suffragism, 1880–1920* (Brooklyn, NY: Carlson Publishing, 1994); J. Howard, "Our Own Worst Enemies:

Women Opposed to Woman Suffrage," *Journal of Sociology and Social Welfare* 9 (1982): 463–74; Billie Barnes Jensen, "'In the Weird and Wooly West': Anti-suffrage Women, Gender Issues, and Woman Suffrage in the West," *Journal of the West* 32 (1993): 41–51; Mrs. A. T. Leatherbee, *Why Should any Woman be an Anti-Suffragist?*, pamphlet issued by the Massachusetts Association Opposed to the Further Extension of Suffrage to Women, Room 615, Kensington Building, Boston, MA, n.d.; and Susan E. Marshall, *Splintered Sisterhood: Gender and Class in the Campaign Against Woman Suffrage* (Madison, WI: The University of Wisconsin Press, 1997).

[42] *Opinions of Eminent Persons Against Woman Suffrage,* pamphlet issued by the Massachusetts Association Opposed to the Further Extension of Suffrage to Women, Room 615, Kensington Building, Boston, MA, October 1912.

[43] Ramsey, "Inventing," 118, 140.

[44] Aileen Kraditor, *The Ideas of the Woman Suffrage Movement, 1890–1920* (New York: W. W. Norton, 1965), 28.

[45] Quoted in Mrs. B. Hazard, "New York State Association Opposed to Woman Suffrage," *The Chautauquan* (June 1910): 88.

[46] *Opinions of Eminent Persons,* 6.

[47] A similar postcard appeared in 1912. Produced by the C. Wolf company of New York, it is a black and white drawing of an attractive woman in a dress patterned after a police uniform. The caption of the postcard (sarcastically) reads, "Safely the males may walk on the street while such cops are patrolling the beat."

[48] Camhi, 53.

[49] Camhi, 55.

[50] Judith Butler, *Bodies That Matter: On the Discursive Limits of "Sex"* (New York: Routledge, 1993), 10.

[51] Butler, *Bodies,* 10.

[52] For a discussion of the dialectical function of "conflicting representations of woman," see Ramsey, "Addressing," 361.

[53] Glenna Matthews, *The Rise of Public Woman: Woman's Power and Woman's Place in the United States, 1630–1970* (New York: Oxford University Press, 1992), 3. Matthews opens her book with the story of the 1895 arrest of Lizzie Schauer, a young working class woman arrested when she asked for directions from two men. Because she was out at night, and unescorted, she was assumed to be a "public woman" or prostitute.

[54] Lisa Maria Hogeland, "Feminism, Sex Scandals, and Historical Lessons," *Critical Studies in Mass Communication* 16 (March 1999): 98.

[55] Kimberly Chrisman, "Unhoop the Fair Sex: The Campaign Against the Hoop Petticoat in Eighteenth-Century England," *Eighteenth-Century Studies* 30, no. 1 (1996): 18.

[56] Matthew Sweet, *Inventing the Victorians* (New York: St. Martin's Press, 2001).

[57] Shelly Foote, "Challenging Gender Symbols," in *Men and Women: Dressing the Part,* ed. Claudia Brush Kidwell and Valerie Steele (Washington: Smithsonian Institution Press, 1989), 148; see also Carol Mattingly, *Appropriate[ing] Dress: Women's Rhetorical Style in Nineteenth Century America* (Carbondale: SIU Press, 2002).

[58] Sarah A. Gordon, "'Any Desired Length': Negotiating Gender through Sports Clothing, 1870–1925," in *Beauty and Business: Commerce, Gender, and Culture in Modern America,* ed. Philip Scranton (New York: Routledge, 2001), 27.

[59] JoAnne Olian, ed., *Everyday Fashions 1909–1920: As Pictured in Sears Catalogues* (New York: Dover Publications, 1995), i.

[60] Jorgensen-Earp, 93; and Ramsey, "Addressing," 353.

[61] Meyer, Seidler, Curry, and Aveni, 21.

[62] Jorgensen-Earp, 88.

[63] A plethora of postcards, other than those in the Dunston-Weiler set, employed the image of the home-bound and/or care-giving male. However, unlike the Dunston-Weiler set, the vast majority of these other images depicted men as incompetent caregivers. A circa 1910 American Colorgravure postcard (Series 138, Subject 2773) shows a man wheeling a baby buggy with a squalling infant inside, two circa 1910 Bamforth and Co. Publishers postcards (Nos. 1240 and 1048) show a man cleaning house (while caring for crying infants) proclaiming "my wife's joined the suffrage movement, (I've suffered ever since!)", a circa 1911 postcard (698/24) shows the "results of the Suffrage victory" to be a man taking care of a crying infant while the woman leaves, and a 1910 C. Hobson postcard also shows a man caring for children (and

a hissing cat) as his wife leaves. English postcards also carried a similar sentiment (see B. B. London series A17).

64 Jorgensen-Earp, 89.

65 Virginia Woolf, *A Room of One's Own* (New York: Harvest /HBJ, 1929, 1957), 35–36.

66 Judith Butler, *Gender Trouble: Feminism and the Subversion of Identity* (New York: Routledge, 1990).

67 John M. Sloop, *Disciplining Gender: Rhetorics of Sex Identity in Contemporary U.S. Culture* (Amherst: University of Massachusetts Press, 2004), 6.

68 Butler, *Gender*, 16.

69 Maymie R. Krythe, *What So Proudly We Hail* (New York: Harper and Row Publishers, 1968), 49.

70 Alton Ketchum, *Uncle Sam: The Man and the Legend* (New York: Hill and Wang, 1959), 61.

71 Ketchum, 74, 80.

72 Ketchum, 79.

73 Gerald E. Czulewicz, Sr., *The Foremost Guide to Uncle Sam Collectibles* (Paducah, KY: Collector's Books, 1995), 35.

74 Ketchum, 86.

75 Thomas H. Bivins, "The Body Politic: The Changing Shape of Uncle Sam," *Journalism Quarterly* 64, no. 1 (Spring 1987): 13–20.

76 Ketchum, 9.

77 Ketchum, vii.

78 Bivins, 15.

79 Bivins, 15.

80 Harvey Hill, "American Catholicism?: John England and 'The Republic in Danger,'" *Catholic Historical Review* 89, no. 2 (April 2003): 240.

81 Colleen McDannell, *Material Christianity: Religion and Popular Culture in America* (New Haven: Yale University Press, 1995), 133.

82 A. James Reichley, "Faith in Politics," *Journal of Policy History* 13, no. 1 (2001): 158, 240.

83 Harvey Hill, 240.

84 Reichley, 158.

85 Thomas J. Jablonsky, *The Home, Heaven, and Mother Party: Female Anti-suffragists in the United States, 1868–1920* (Brooklyn, NY: Carlson Publishing, 1994), 66–7.

86 Jablonsky, *The Home*, 66.

87 Jablonsky, *The Home*, 67.

88 Jablonsky, *The Home*, 69.

89 Jablonsky, *The Home*, 45.

90 Jablonsky, *The Home*, 45.

91 David Morgan, *Visual Piety: A History and Theory of Popular Religious Images* (Berkeley: University of California Press, 1998).

92 Morgan, 60.

93 Eleanor Heartney, "Thinking Through the Body: Women Artists and the Catholic Imagination," *Hypatia* 18, no. 4 (2003): 3–22.

94 McDannell, 61.

95 Christine L. Krueger, review of *Women of Faith in Victorian Culture* and *Women's Theology in Nineteenth-Century Britain*, *Victorian Studies* 43, no. 1 (2000): 179.

96 Protestants questioned the significance of Mary: "Mariology—the veneration of the Virgin Mary—is one of the points of doctrine that most clearly separates Protestants and Catholics. While Protestants tend to downplay Mary's role, seeing her simply as an exemplary woman, for Catholics she performs multiple functions. She is the embodiment of perfect motherhood . . ." (Heartney, 5). The differences over the role of Mary were not simply ones of degree. In fact, within Victorian England, the Virgin Mary was an extremely controversial figure, "a powerful presence who embodied what many Victorians considered to be the errors of the Roman Catholic Church. These included pagan idolatry, superstition and willful ignorance of the Bible, all of which were summed up in a single word: Mariolotry" (Carole Maire Engelhardt, "Victorian Masculinity and the Virgin Mary," in *Masculinity and Spirituality in Victorian Culture,* ed. Andrew Bradstock, Susan Gill, Anne Hogan, and Sue Morgan [New York: St. Martin's Press, 2000], 44).

97 The history of the icon within Catholicism also resonates with some of the anti-suffrage arguments concerning illiteracy overtaking the polls. The visual itself was not without

controversy within Catholicism. Ultimately, iconoclasts supported the utility of images in "decorative arts and devotional devices to stimulate piety" because the "uneducated, women, and children were particularly responsive to sacred images" and "illiterate Christians needed them to understand and express their faith" (McDannell, 9). Protestant reformers in the sixteenth century, however, tended to limit the use of images only to instruction, and prohibited their presence in the church, lest worshipers confuse sign and referent, as "[a]rt and objects tempted a weak humanity that fell too easily into idolatry" (McDannell, 10).

[98] Andrew Bradstock, Sean Gill, Anne Hogan, and Sue Morgan, eds., *Masculinity and Spirituality in Victorian Culture* (New York: St. Martin's Press, 2000), 2.

[99] For discussions of muscular Christianity, see Donald E. Hall, ed., *Muscular Christianity: Embodying the Victorian Age* (Cambridge: Cambridge University Press, 1994); Tony Ladd and James A. Mathisen, *Muscular Christianity: Evangelical Protestants and the Development of American Sport* (Grand Rapids, MI: Baker Books, 1999); and Clifford Putney, *Muscular Christianity: Manhood and Sports in Protestant America, 1880–1920* (Cambridge: Harvard University Press, 2003).

[100] Butler, *Bodies*, 1.

[101] Butler, *Bodies*, 10.

[102] Ramsey, "Addressing," 353.

[103] For example, Michael A. DeSousa, "Symbolic Action and Pretended Insight: The Ayatollah Khomeini in U.S. Editorial Cartoons," in *Rhetorical Dimensions in Media: A Critical Casebook*, ed. M. J. Medhurst and T. W. Benson (Dubuque, IA: Kendall/Hunt, 1984, revised printing), 204–30; Michael A. DeSousa and Martin J. Medhurst, "The Editorial Cartoon as Visual Rhetoric: Rethinking Boss Tweed," *Journal of Visual Verbal Languaging* 2 (Fall 1982): 43–52; Michael A. DeSousa and Martin J. Medhurst, "Political Cartoons and American Culture: Significant Symbols of Campaign 1980," *Studies in Visual Communication* 8, no. 1 (1982): 84–97; Janis L. Edwards, *Political Cartoons in the 1988 Presidential Campaign: Image, Metaphor, and Narrative* (New York: Garland Publishing, 1997); Janis L. Edwards and H. R. Chen, "The First Lady/First Wife in Editorial Cartoons: Rhetorical Visions Through Gendered Lens," *Women's Studies in Communication* 23, no. 3 (Fall 2000): 367–91; Alette Hill, "The Carter Campaign in Retrospect: Decoding* the Cartoons," *Semiotica* 23, nos. 3 and 4 (1978): 307–32; Martin J. Medhurst and Michael A. DeSousa, "Political Cartoons as Rhetorical Form: A Taxonomy of Graphic Discourse," *Communication Monographs* 48, no. 3 (September 1981): 197–236; Matthew C. Morrison, "The Role of the Political Cartoonist in Image Making," *Central States Speech Journal* (Winter 1969): 252–60; John F. Sena, "A Picture is Worth a Thousand Votes: Geraldine Ferraro and the Editorial Cartoonists," *Journal of American Culture* 8 (1985): 2–12; and James D. Steakley, "Iconography of a Scandal: Political Cartoons and the Eulenberg Affair," *Studies in Visual Communication* 9 (1983): 20–51.

[104] Lisa Z. Sigel, "Filth in the Wrong People's Hands: Postcards and the Expansion of Pornography in Britain and the Atlantic World, 1880–1914," *Journal of Social History* 33, no. 4 (2000): 859–85, available from Project Muse; and Yoke-Sum Wong, "Beyond (and Below) Incommensurability: The Aesthetics of the Postcard," *Common Knowledge* 8, no. 2 (2002): 333–56.

[105] Sigel, 860.

[106] Kimberlé Crenshaw, "Demarginalizing the Intersection of Race and Sex: A Black Feminist Critique of Antidiscrimination Doctrine, Feminist Theory and Antiracist Politics," *University of Chicago Legal Forum* (1989): 139–67; and Adrien Katherine Wing, ed., *Critical Race Feminism: A Reader* (New York: New York University Press, 1997).

[107] Barbara Welter, *Dimity Convictions: The American Woman in the Nineteenth Century* (Athens; OH: Ohio University Press, 1976).

[108] Chandra Talpede Mohanty, *Feminism Without Borders* (Durham: Duke University Press, 2003), 55.

[109] David Fleming, "Can Pictures be Arguments?" *Argumentation and Advocacy* 33, no. 1 (Summer 1996): 11–22.

[110] David S. Birdsell and Leo Groarke, eds., "Toward a Theory of Visual Argument," Special Issues on Visual Argument, *Argumentation and Advocacy* 33, nos. 1–2 (Summer and Fall 1996): 1–10; Randall A. Lake and Barbara A. Pickering, "Argumentation, the Visual, and the Possibility of Refutation: An Exploration," *Argumentation* 12 (February 1998): 79–93; and Catherine H. Palczewski, "Keynote Address: Argument in an Off Key," in *Communicative*

Reason and Communication Communities, ed. G. Thomas Goodnight et al. (Washington, DC: NCA, 2002), 1–23.

111 The insights of this paragraph owe much to conversations with G. Thomas Goodnight and his work with Kathryn M. Olson on the function of nondiscursive oppositional argument in controversy. See Kathryn M. Olson and G. Thomas Goodnight, "Entanglements of Consumption, Cruelty, Privacy, and Fashion: The Social Controversy over Fur," *Quarterly Journal of Speech* 80, no. 3 (August 1994): 249–76.

112 DeSousa and Medhurst, "Political Cartoons," 84. Emphasis mine.

113 Robert Hariman and John Louis Lucaites, "Dissent and Emotional Management in a Liberal Democratic Society: The Kent State Iconic Photograph," *Rhetoric Society Quarterly* 31, no. 3 (Summer 2001): 5–31; "Performing Civic Identity: The Iconic Photograph of the Flag Raising on Iwo Jima," *Quarterly Journal of Speech* 88, no. 4 (November 2002): 363–92; and "Public Identity and Collective Memory in U.S. Iconic Photography: The Image of 'Accidental Napalm,'" *Critical Studies in Media Communication* 20, no. 1 (March 2003): 35–66.

114 Hariman and Lucaites, "Dissent," 8.

115 Hariman and Lucaites, "Performing," 364.

116 Jean H. Baker, ed., *Votes for Women: The Struggle for Suffrage Revisited* (New York: Oxford University Press, 2002), 6.

117 Jablonsky, "Female Opposition," 129.

118 Alette Hill, 308.

119 Edwards and Winkler, 290.

120 Cloud, 287.

121 Edwards and Winkler, 305.

....

Unruly Arguments: The Body Rhetoric of Earth First!, Act Up, and Queer Nation

KEVIN MICHAEL DELUCA

To save old growth forest, an Earth First! activist sits on a platform suspended 780 feet up in a redwood. Protester and platform are dwarfed by the ancient giant. Deep in the woods, a blue-capped, smiling, bearded head pokes up out of a logging road. The rest of the person is buried in the road. This attempt to stop logging by blockading the road extends the meaning of the term passive resistance.

To protest governmental and corporate policy with regards to AIDS research, ACT UP (AIDS Coalition to Unleash Power) activists chain their bodies to the White House gates and conduct kiss-ins in public spaces. ACT UP occupies St. Patrick's Cathedral and interrupts Mass with a "die-in." Police carry out the bodies of 734 "dead" demonstrators. Together, healthy bodies, emaciated bodies, and wheelchair-bound bodies stop traffic on Wall Street. Queer Nation activists "sit-in" Cracker Barrel restaurants to protest employment policies that discriminate against them for failing to practice "normal" values. They invade straight bars and shopping malls to kiss and otherwise display gay sexual identity.

These contemporary activist groups, whether termed new social movements or postmodern social movements, are particularly notable for three reasons. They reject traditional organizational structures while forming radically democratic disorganizations. They neglect conventional legislative and material goals while practicing the powers of naming, worldview framing, and identity-making. Finally, and most significantly for this essay, they slight formal modes of public argument while performing unorthodox political tactics that highlight bodies as resources for argumentation and advocacy.

In terms of their stance towards organizational form, Earth First! is exemplary. It is an anti-hierarchical disorganization with no official leaders, no national head-quarters, no membership lists, no dues, no board of directors, and no tax-exempt status (Setterberg, 1995, p. 70; Kane, 1987, p. 100). This was a conscious decision, as Earth First! co-founder Dave Foreman explains: "We felt that if we took on the organization of the industrial state, we would soon accept their anthropocentric paradigm, much as Audubon and the Sierra Club already had" (1994, p. 21). ACT UP and other groups are similarly radically democratic and decentralized. AIDS activist and writer David Feinberg's description of meetings is revealing: "ACT UP has no leaders. Meetings are run according to Roberta's Rules of Order and are democratic to the point of near anarchy. The facilitator's role is to try to allow as full a discussion as possible without letting things slide into complete chaos, and to lower the level of vituperative and personal aggrievement to an acceptable level" (1994, p. 10; for descriptions of Queer Nation's designed disorga-nization, see Cunningham, 1992, Berlant and Freeman, 1993).

Typical of these groups, ACT UP's aims are neither limited to nor centered on the conventional goals of electoral, legislative, legal, and material gains. As Sean Strub, founder and editor of the AIDS magazine POZ explains,

> Someone 25 years old, gay or straight, with AIDS or not, has a different view of their doctor than they would have 10 years ago. There's a reason ACT UP never incorporated, never sought to build a staff. The idea was not to build an institution with a budget and a bureaucracy. The objective was to change people's relationship to the epidemic and the health care system in general, to make us all players. To analyze its impact, don't look at how many people show up at ACT UP's meetings. Look at how many people took ACT UP's values into their lives (quoted in Schoofs, 1997, pp. 42, 44).

These groups, then, are eschewing conventional goals in favor of contesting social norms, deconstructing the established naming of the world, and suggesting the possibilities of alternative worlds.

In performing these goals, Earth First!, ACT UP, and Queer Nation are practicing a form of argumentation that is an important manifestation of what has become known as constitutive rhetoric: the mobilization of signs, images, and discourses for the articulation of identities, ideologies, consciousnesses, communities, publics, and cultures.[1] For all of these groups, formal public address and argumentation are not primary practices, as denoted by the absence of the eloquent orator of Earth First! or ACT UP.[2] Instead, these activist groups practice an alternative image poli-tics, performing image events designed for mass media dissemination. Often, image events revolve around images of bodies—vulnerable bodies, dangerous bodies, taboo bodies, ludicrous bodies, transfigured bodies. These political bodies consti-tute a nascent body rhetoric that deploys bodies as a pivotal resource for the crucial practice of public argumentation.[3]

In considering the use of bodies by these groups as argument, it is important to consider such usage as in part an adaptation to the unique possibilities and constraints of television, the *de facto* national public forum of the United States at the close of the 20th Century. Unable to buy time like corporations and main-stream political parties do, groups such as Earth First!, ACT UP, and Queer Nation "buy" air time through using their bodies to create compelling images that attract media attention. Even when they have the media's eye, however, these groups' options remain severely restricted. First, the protocols of sound bite journalism that dominate commercial news suggest that most issues will receive only precious seconds and that a few minutes are an eternity. Hardly the time to practice the methods of the Lincoln-Douglas debates. Second, since these groups do not own their time, they know neither if they will be allowed to speak nor for how long. In addition, as radical groups questioning societal orthodoxies, they can expect news organizations to frame them negatively as disrupters of the social order (Gitlin, 1980; Parenti, 1993). These groups are in hostile territory with little control. What they do have some control over, however, is the presentation of their bodies in the image events that attract media attention. Their bodies, then, become not merely flags to attract attention for the argument but the site and substance of the argument itself.

The aim of this essay is to explore the power and possibilities of bodies in public argumentation. After briefly chronicling the relative neglect of the body in criticism of social movement protests, I will perform close readings of the bodies in the performances of Earth First!, ACT UP, and Queer Nation. The purpose of this analysis is not to valorize these groups or to privilege body rhetoric, but, rather, to suggest that we must account for their bodies in order to understand the force of these groups' protests, for Earth First!, ACT UP, and Queer Nation have challenged and changed the meanings of the world not through good reasons but through vulnerable bodies, not through rational arguments but through bodies at risk.

THE ARGUMENTATIVE FORCE OF UNRULY BODIES

Although there is beginning to be some attention to the argumentative and rhetorical potential of images,[4] bodies remain virtually invisible. Even when the tumultuous street politics of the 1960s and the early 1970s forced rhetorical critics to look beyond the boundaries of conventional politics and formal argumentation and consider the implications of extra-linguistic confrontational activities, the scope was limited and bodies escaped sustained attention.[5] As Brant Short points out, "Although critics acknowledged the rhetorical aspects of confrontation, protest, and agitation, these studies suggest that theoretical accounts of seemingly *nonrational* discourse remained linked to traditional notions of logic, rationality, and artistic proofs" (1991, p. 173). Contrary to this perspective, I propose that Earth First!, ACT UP, and Queer Nation's tactics are arguments in their own right and that their bodies are central to the force of their arguments.

To suggest that bodies and images of bodies argue is controversial and defies the traditional delimitation of argumentation as linguistic. Even those sympathetic to the argumentative force of body images hesitate. Celeste Condit's discussion (1990, pp. 79–95) of fetus images is illustrative of the hesitation yet demonstrative of the argumentative force of bodies. In a discussion of the role of images of fetuses in the public debate over abortion, Condit offers a nuanced account of the force of images in public argument. Although Condit starts by granting that images can replace narratives and offer a form of grounding, she asserts the primacy of words, contending that the power of images is dependent on their translation into verbal meanings (1990, p. 81). As Condit shouts, "Without verbal commentary, pictures DO NOT ARGUE propositions" (1990, p. 85; see also pp. 81, 86, 87, 88, 90). Despite such protestations, Condit's own argument remains conflicted. First, Condit admits that images can provide general substance for a ground (1990, pp. 81, 85, 91). In Condit's reading of the fetus images of the pro-Life movement, she asserts that "the pro-Life pictures bring us a weighty set of grounds and that those grounds substantiate the claim that fetuses are important and valuable and ought to be protected" (1990, p. 91). Second, Condit seems to be subtly stretching the bounds of public argument and tacitly suggesting that these fetus images *do* argue. For instance, Condit argues that images offer "a different kind of under-standing" (1990, p. 81) and, in referring to images, Condit writes "like any other form of argument" (1990, p. 81). Most explicitly, Condit later declares, "I believe that the pictures argue forcefully for the substance and value of the fetus" (1990, p. 91). Finally, belying her earlier assertions privileging verbal commentary, Condit does not argue that the pro-Life argument was more persuasive than the pro-Choice argument due to superior verbal commentary. Rather, it was a battle of images. As Condit herself concludes, "The persuasive force of the image of the fetus, towering over the meager pro-Choice images, would powerfully influence the popular consciousness, eventually establishing elements of the pro-Life vocabulary deeply within popular culture and within the lives of polarized subcultures" (1990, p. 94). Significantly, then, not only were images, not words, decisive, but body images, those of fetuses, trumped other images, like those of a hanger.

I side with those who accept that the non-linguistic can argue.[6] Indeed, in an age of mixed media dominated by a televisual discourse composed of visual, aural, and verbal codes, to cling to an anachronistic definition of argumentation risks rendering it irrelevant. That said, I am not suggesting that a naked, pre-discursive body constitutes an argument. There are no *a priori* bodies. Bodies are enmeshed in a turbulent stream of multiple and conflictual discourses that shape what they mean in particular contexts. I am contesting, however, that bodies are in any simple way determined or limited by verbal frames. To think of bodies as crucial elements of arguments in a televisual public forum, then, requires imagining forms of argu-ment that exceed the protocols of deliberative reasoning.

Bodies in Nature

Since their founding in 1980, Earth First!, a radical, no-compromise environ-mental group, has deployed an array of tactics as they attempt to change the way people think about and act toward nature. In their efforts to put onto the public agenda issues such as the clearcutting of old growth forests, overgrazing by cattle on public lands, depredations by oil and mineral companies on public lands, loss of biodiversity, and the general ravaging of wilderness, Earth First! activists have resorted to sitting in trees, blockading roads with their bodies, chaining themselves to logging equipment, and dressing in animal costumes at public hearings. As this brief listing of Earth First! image events makes clear, their tactics are dependent on their bodies. Although these direct actions sometimes succeed and often fail in their immediate goals, their effectiveness as image events can be partially measured by the emergence of clearcutting, old growth forests, spotted owls, cattle grazing, and the 1872 mining law as hot-button political issues. Earth First!, like Greenpeace before them, understands that the significance of direct actions is in their function as image events in the larger arena of public discourse. Although designed to flag media attention and generate publicity, image events are more than just a means of getting on television. They are crystallized argumentative shards, mind bombs, that shred the existing screens of perception and work to expand "the universe of think-able thoughts" (Manes, 1990, p. 77).

The image events of Earth First! interrogate the fundamental beliefs of industrialism while contesting the actions such beliefs warrant. For analysis, let us look at a protester sitting on a platform 100 feet up in a giant Douglas fir and a protester buried up to his neck in a logging road.[7] What is striking about both of these images is the utter vulnerability of the protesters as they intervene on behalf of nature. Quite clearly, the Earth First!ers, human beings, are putting at risk their bodies, their lives for wilderness, for trees.[8] This is an almost incomprehensible act in a modern, humanist, secular culture. In Western culture nature has been displaced in numerous narratives, including Christian, Enlightenment, scientific, capitalistic, socialistic, and industrial, that place human reason and humans at the center. Humans risking their lives for animals shakes the *a priori* anthropocentric assumption of these narratives, breaks the Great Chain of Being, and disobeys the command in *Genesis* to: "Be fruitful and multiply, and replenish the earth, and subdue it: and have dominion over the fish of the sea, and over the fowl of the air, and over every living thing that moveth upon the earth" (*The Holy Bible: King James Version,* 1974, Genesis 1:28, p. 9). In refuting human-centered worldviews, the protesters' bodies give presence (Perelman, 1982) to the proposition that humans are not apart from the natural world but a part of it. They disclose the possibility of an ecocentric world.

While lowering the position of humans in the hierarchy, by risking their bodies for trees the Earth First!ers simultaneously challenge the understanding of animals and nature as mere machines or matter in motion, a storehouse of resources for humans to exploit. These notions are the products of a centuries-long process that Berman felicitously calls "the disenchantment of nature" (1982). In short, by placing themselves at risk, Earth First!ers challenge the anthropocentrism of Western culture and proffer the humble thought that other animals have a right to live and have intrinsic value, not merely economic value.

Perhaps in identification with the forms of nature that they are attempting to save, trees and ecosystems, both protesters have rendered their bodies relatively immobile. The Earth First! activist on the 8-by-4 platform 100 feet up the tree is helpless if the loggers decide to cut the tree despite the protester's presence (this has happened). The Earth First!er buried up to his neck in the road is utterly helpless. He is exposed not only to the potential anger of loggers or law enforcement officers, but to the torturous immobility of not being able to use his hands, whether to swat away a mosquito or scratch an itch. In performing these image events, the activists translate their humanist bodies into ecocentric bodies. Perched high in the Douglas fir, the protester sees the world from the tree's point of view and "becomes" the tree. Rendered relatively immobile, his movements are limited to the swaying of the tree. The protester, like the tree, depends on nourishment to come to him. Finally, their fates are entwined as the protester depends on the tree for support and shelter while the tree depends on the protester's presence to forestall the chainsaw. This mutual dependence is particularly clear in the case of Julia "Butterfly" Hill, who has lived in a 1,000 year-old redwood, Luna, since December 10th, 1997. She has told of how the tree sheltered her during the worst El Nino storms in California's history. Her presence, meanwhile, has stopped Pacific Lumber from killing Luna. Butterfly's bodily presence is a direct response to Pacific Lumber's practice of clearcutting old growth forests. Her body *is* a NO. Indeed, it is the only "no" that Pacific Lumber respects. Often logging illegally (they were cited for over 200 violations of California's logging laws in the past two years), Pacific Lumber cut the trees surrounding Butterfly and Luna. In the road blockade, the protester buried in the earth becomes the earth. He adopts a ground level view of the world. People and equipment tower over him. He is immobile and must be spoon fed. But his vantage point allows him to speak for the earth: "Defending what's left of the wilderness, defending what's left of the world." In clinging to treetops and embedding themselves in the earth, the Earth First! protesters both literally perform and symbolically enact humanity's connection to nature. In dislodging the blinders of a human-centered worldview, the protesters bring into being an ecocentric perspective. In identifying with the tree and the earth, the protesters invite viewers to also identify with the natural world.

As the protester buried in the road speaks, the camera zooms in on him. Technology brings his face and the face of the tree-sitter into my world. Their faces confront me, compel my attention. "A face turned to us is an appeal made to us, a demand put on us . . . there lies the force of an imperative that touches us, caught sight of wherever we see a face turned to us" (Lingis, 1994, p. 167). The weary face of the tree-sitter and the bespectacled, bearded, smiling face popping out of the road testify to their thoughtfulness, resolution mixed with resignation, and humanity. In my encounter with these faces, "I find all that I am put into question by the exactions and exigencies of the other. In the face of another, the question of truth is out on each proposition of which my discourse is made, the question of justice put on each move and gesture of my exposed life" (Lingis, 1994, p. 173). The imperative of these faces call to us and call us to account. They call us to account for proposing an anthropocentric worldview that reduces the rest of the world to a storehouse of resources. They call us to account for industrial practices that destroy a natural world so intimately connected to their bodies, our bodies.

Being buried in the road is significant. In blocking a road, the protester is disrupting literally and symbolically a major artery of industrialism. Indeed, the restructuring of the economy, foreign policy, housing, and social practices around the needs of automotive transportation suggest that our society in the late 20th Century could be termed a "car culture." Although the blocked road is a dirt road, it is key to industrialism in that it is a road for resource extraction. In blocking this road, then, the protester confronts the productive and symbolic capital of the culture and violates social norms:

From an early age, all children are inculcated with a necessary respect: pedestrians should

> always *give way* to automobiles. Such rules are mostly concerned with letting road users "go about their (and capitalism's) business," and are intended to coerce those who might obstruct their "rights of way" or infringe on their liberty. . . . For these reasons, if no other, the advent of recent road protests marks a radical challenge to the instrumental, one-dimensional, and codified ethos of the modern road (Smith, 1997, p. 349).

This body in this road interrupts the industrialization and homogenization of time and space and calls us to slow down and consider this place. By forcing the industrial juggernaut to pause, if only for a moment, this body gives us pause. Such pause opens a space for refuting the oft-repeated assertion of industrialism that progress is inevitable. In pausing, we stop the clock for a moment. In the moment, we can take the time to notice this particular place.

In short, these images of bodies at risk are encapsulated arguments challenging the anthropocentric position granting humans dominion over all living creatures and implicitly advocating ecocentrism as an alternative. By arguing against reducing trees and ecosystems (old growth forests) to economic resources and instead proposing that they have intrinsic value and inalienable rights, Earth First! contests the linking of economic progress with nature as a storehouse of resources, thus deconstructing the discourse of industrialism that warrants the use of technology to exploit nature in the name of progress.

The bodies of Earth First!, then, question the possibility of property and the definition of the land as a resource and, instead, suggest that biodiversity has value in itself and, following Leopold's land ethic, "[a] thing is right when it tends to preserve the integrity, stability, and beauty of the biotic community. It is wrong when it tends otherwise" (1949/1968, pp. 224–25). Progress, then, is not the increasing production of goods through the technological exploitation of nature as a storehouse of resources, but, rather, the recognition of the intrinsic value and fundamental importance of ecosystems and the need for humans to live within limits as a part of larger ecosystems. By implacing their bodies in a region through burying themselves in the ground, perching in trees, hugging trees, and living in these areas until forcibly removed, Earth First!ers constitute an ecocentric community. Through the care of a neighbor, a tree becomes *this* tree, a mountain *this* mountain. The formation of an ecocentric community argues for the possibility of an alternative to the dominant industrial consumer culture.

The inhabiting of trees and regions by Earth First! activists is important. As brief glimpses of camp sites suggest, Earth First!ers often live in the places they are trying to protect. They dwell in the woods. Trees sitters live with the trees. As mentioned, Julia "Butterfly" Hill has lived at 180 feet in one redwood for over a year now. Through inhabiting the tree, she feels, "I have become one with this tree and with nature in a way I would never have thought possible" (quoted in Hornblower, 1998). In dwelling in the woods, the activists compel us to dwell on our relation to nature, to meditate on our fundamental relation as dwelling on the earth. I am using the word dwelling in the sense suggested by Heidegger: "The way in which you are and I am, the manner in which we humans *are* on the earth is *baun,* dwelling. To be a human being means to be on the earth as a mortal. It means to dwell" (1993, p. 349). By placing their bodies in the woods, the Earth First! activists bring the wilderness to us and bring us to the wilderness. They make present a natural world too often obscured by the overlaid technosphere that envelops the majority of Americans as they go about their daily routines. In dwelling in the woods they strip away the technological veneer, they reveal nature, and encourage us to confront our fundamental relation to the world as that of dwelling on earth.[9]

The body rhetoric of Earth First!, besides being a sustained critique of the articulation of nature and progress in the discourse of industrialism, also interrogates the accepted universalization of humanity as "rational man," the Cartesian subject. In the image events discussed, we witness people acting passionately ('irrationally') on behalf of nature and place, commitments that owe as much to love and emotional connections as they do to instrumental reason. Indeed, often these image events are refuting the results of a scientific rationality that uses the methods of cost-benefit analysis and risk assessment to sanction environmental destruction and extinctions in exchange for profits. Earth First! is questioning the very possibility of "science" (a neutral universal practice based on reason) as it condemns the science of the US Forestry Service that recommends clearcutting and other practices that most clearly benefit the timber, oil, and mining industries. In putting their bodies on the line in solidarity with trees and ecosystems, the Earth First! activists enact an embodied and embedded defense of nature that belies anthropocentrism's abstraction of "man" from the natural world and contests science's contextless universalization of nature. Finally, in the acts of their bodies, the activists transgress a notion of subjectivity anchored in reason and proffer their bodies as the founding texts for an embodied subjectivity that radically expands the bounds of human identity. Importantly, in using their bodies to perform their arguments, Earth First!ers are enacting a mode of argument that supports the substance of their argument. That is, they are practicing a mode of argument that is less focused on an abstract, universalized reason and more attune to the feelings that accompany lived experiences.

The most explicit proposition and refutation dynamic revolves around the network news' consistently negative framing of Earth First!. The framing states two explicit propositions: 1) Earth First! is violent; 2) Earth First!ers are terrorists. These claims are presented by the reporters or Earth First! critics through direct charges or through descriptive language of Earth First! activities. ABC News titles the first in-depth national network news story on Earth First! "War in the Woods" (August 10, 1987). Peter Jennings' introduction begins, "Now, the war in the woods" and ends by claiming that Earth First! "is so angry . . . it has been particularly extreme fighting back." Later in the story, reporter Ken Kashiwahara claims Earth First! has turned the forests into "a battlefield for guerrilla warfare." Kashiwahara interviews a US Forest Service official who warns against going "to war over it . . . Ultimately somebody could be murdered in this whole event." Then-head of the National Wildlife Federation Jay Hair chillingly pronounces judgment and punishment: "I reject out of hand their being environmentalists. They're terrorists, they're outlaws. They should be treated as such." Kashiwahara's final description labels Earth First! "terrorists or freedom fighters." Though the terms carry different valences, both ensconce Earth First! in the terminology of war.

Other network news stories echo the terminology. Earth First!ers are "outlaws" or "zealots" (NBC News, July 5, 1990). ABC's Sam Donaldson opens a report, "On the American Agenda tonight, what some people are calling civil disobedience, what others are calling a form of terrorism" (ABC News, August 19, 1993). The report goes on to describe a "battle over logging" and "running battles." Reporter Barry Serafin asserts that tourists "have been scared away by guerrilla war being waged by this country's most radical environmental group."

The verbal framing in these stories of Earth First! activists as violent terrorists is refuted by two sets of body images. The bodies of Earth First! immobilized in a tree or in the earth, chained to logging equipment, holding hands and sitting in front of a bulldozer, bloodied from attack by loggers, peacefully submitting to arrest, are not violent but vulnerable. They embody the counter-proposition: Earth First! practices non-violent civil disobedience.

Many of the images of Earth First!'s opponents in action suggest that the violent framing has been misplaced. Law enforcement officials roughly arrest protesters. Loggers violently confront Earth First!ers. A logger in a pickup trucks speeds toward men, women, and children sitting in rocking chairs blocking a road. A log truck inexorably pushes an Earth First! activist trying to block a road. A leading citizen of a small town sits astride his horse and threatens to rope an Earth First! demonstrator. He tells the sheriff, "I guarantee you're gonna have to arrest me to keep me from dragging that sucker down the street" (ABC News, 1993).

The loggers who beat an Earth First!er follow their bloodied victim to camp. Though Earth First! members significantly outnumber the four loggers, all they do is talk with them. Overall, the bodies of the Earth First! activists and their opponents belie the verbal framing and attest to the non-violence of Earth First!.

Acting Up

Although ACT UP was founded in 1987 with the express purpose of improving care for AIDS patients by violating the veneer of civility that was shrouding the deaths of thousands, it is not too much to claim, as the headline on one article proclaims, that the members of ACT UP are "THE AIDS SHOCK TROOPERS WHO CHANGED THE WORLD" (Schoofs, 1997, p. 42). Besides speeding drug approval, challenging drug prices, and obtaining numerous changes in health care and policy, ACT UP has forced the United States to confront its homophobia on state, institutional, civil, and private levels. It also has given rise to many other gay and lesbian activist organizations, including Queer Nation. Thanks to these groups, mainstream politicians must acknowledge and deal with gay and lesbian issues, the idea of same-sex couples as parents and marriage partners is now imaginable and possible, and homosexuals are becoming a presence in popular culture.

Central to the success of ACT UP and Queer Nation has been an in-your-face body rhetoric. The body is front and center in their arguments for it is the body that is at stake—its meanings, its possibilities, its care, and its freedoms. In their protest actions, the activists use their bodies to rewrite the homosexual body as already constructed by dominant mainstream discourses—diseased, contagious, deviant, invisible. In order to explicate these body arguments, let us take a closer look at some of the actions mentioned in the opening of this essay.

The force of the body makes it a sublime and contested site in cultures, subject to feverish and multiple modes of disciplining and constructing (Foucault, 1977, 1978; Lingis, 1994). In our culture at this time, homosexual bodies are a particularly hot site for they serve as the necessary foil for heterosexuality and yet are evidence of the failure of discursive disciplining and the excess of bodies. Additionally, they are marked not due to physical features but sexual practices, which provokes erotophobia, "the terrifying, irrational reaction to the erotic which makes individuals and society vulnerable to psychological and social control in cultures where pleasure is strictly categorized and regulated" (Patton, 1985, p. 103). More specifically, homosexuality represents an especially potent boundary transgression that violates the hegemonic discourse of heterosexuality and threatens the social order. As Judith Butler explains, "Since anal and oral sex among men clearly establishes certain kinds of bodily permeabilities unsanctioned by the hegemonic order, male homosexuality would, within such a hegemonic point of view, constitute a site of danger and pollution, prior to and regardless of the cultural presence of AIDS" (1990, p. 132). Taking advantage of their liminal status, ACT UP and Queer Nation activists deploy their dangerous bodies in their tactics.

At a basic level, the presence of their openly homosexual bodies is stunning in a culture where gay bodies do not exist or, if they must, their proper place is still the closet. In many regions of the country, to refuse to be proper, to pass as straight, is to risk being bashed. The penalty for exposing one's gay body ranges from verbal abuse to physical beatings to death (with the horrific murder of Matthew Shepherd serving as a ghastly reminder). Thus, by their very presence at a protest the activists are enacting a defiant rhetoric of resistance.

This resistance is intensified in the context of a social field permeated by medical and homophobic discourses that constitute gay bodies as diseased plague carriers bearing the mark of God's disfavor. Germphobia constructs AIDS as a modern plague that calls for quarantine (Patton, 1985, pp. 51–66). The New Right and Christian fundamentalists read AIDS as a message from God and a warrant for oppressive social policies. As Patton observes, "AIDS is a particularly potent symbol for the hard-line radical right because it is evidence of sin, God's disfavor, and an ultimate solution: it is both a sign and a punishment embodied in one of the groups targeted for political decimation long before AIDS" (1985, pp. 86–87). Medical fears and religious prejudice merge in the comments of a doctor in the *Southern Medical Journal*: "Might it be that our society's approval of homosexuality is an error and that the unsubtle words of wisdom of the Bible are frightfully correct? Indeed, from an empirical medical perspective alone, current scientific observation seems to require the conclusion that homosexuality is a pathologic condition" (quoted in Patton, 1985, p. 87). In such a hostile context, the presence of gay bodies, sick, emaciated, and healthy, constitute an eloquent and courageous response to discrimination and hate. It is a refusal to be quarantined, isolated, marginalized, silenced. In making their bodies visible, present, exposed, the ACT UP activists call on society to care.

The same-sex kiss-in ups the ante. The romantic kiss, the portal to heterosexuality, marriage, children and the family values that function as the ideological bedrock of patriarchy is subverted, made "bi." The same-sex kiss instantiates the claimed identity of homosexuality and provokes erotophobia. As a performance of gay or lesbian sexuality it violates two taboos—the taboo on homosexuality and the backup taboo on visibility. The same-sex kiss-in, whether at a public protest, straight bar, or shopping mall, turns the normalized terrain of heterosexuality into an alien landscape. It embodies the Queer Nation slogan, "We're here. We're queer. Get used to it."

The kiss-ins of ACT UP were a specific response to the intensification of homophobic discourses as the AIDS crisis developed. As activist Douglas Crimp explains, a kiss-in was "a public demonstration of gay and lesbian sexuality in the face of homophobia" (1990, p. 50). A poster for an April 29, 1988, kiss-in, created by Gran Fury, "a band of individuals united in anger and dedicated to exploiting the power of art to end the AIDS crisis" (quoted in Crimp, 1990, p. 16), shows two male sailors french kissing. One sailor has his arms around his partner's waist. The other sailor's arms are around his partner's neck. In other words, it is a classic kiss, made famous in celluloid dreams and here transformed into a transgressive political act, charged freedom rhetoric. Part of the charge comes from the bodies of the sailors in uniform, since the armed forces represent the first and last purified bastion of masculinity. At the time, the military was an institution dedicated to weeding out homosexuality in its ranks. Even the Clinton Administration's "Don't Ask, Don't Tell" policy is simply an official version of The Closet. The poster of the sailors kissing is a symbolic coming out that refutes the twin assertions of nonexistence or at least invisibility. More than just a refutation, it also asserts the presence of gays and lesbians in the military. The artists know the argumentative force of the body, for the poster's caption simply says, "READ MY LIPS." Although ACT UP distributed a flier explaining "why we kiss," the force of a kiss-in rests with the body, not the linguistic rationale, which cannot compel attention and is not disseminated through mass media broadcasting.

The Catholic Church is another institution that does not accept the practice of homosexuality. Besides condemning homosexuality and not allowing gays to be priests (of course, the patriarchal Church does not allow straight or lesbian women to be priests), the Church also opposes AIDS education and safe sex. For ACT UP in New York City, the Church's positions and John Cardinal O'Connor's active lobbying against the availability of condoms in public schools "promotes violence against gays" (quoted in Bullert, 1997, p. 125). On December 10, 1989, ACT UP responded to these positions with a "die-in" during Mass in St. Patrick's Cathedral. The "die-in" is designed to violate the veil of sanctity that shrouds the Church and O'Connor. It makes present the fatal consequences of the positions of an institution that purports to preach love, compassion, and understanding. In presenting themselves as symbolic victims and potential actual victims of Church policies, the ACT UP activists practically embody the consequences of Church policies tied to dusty dogma and abstract principles. In interrupting the Mass, the bodies in the "die-in" refuse to be sacrificed on the altar of Church doctrine. In using their gay and lesbian bodies to intervene in a public policy debate over AIDS prevention, ACT UP injects an emotional urgency into the debate. The presence of their individual bodies personalizes the debate and gives faces to the statistics. As one protester shouts, "You're murdering us! Stop killing us! We're not going to take it anymore! Stop it!" (Quoted in Bullert, 1997, p. 126).

Queer Nation, founded at a New York City ACT UP meeting in 1990, deploys the body arguments and other tactics of AIDS activists in the service of the more general aims of challenging heterosexism and queering public spaces. Co-founder Michael Signorile describes the group's tactics: "Utilizing ACT UP's in-your-face tactics to take on gay bashers and increase visibility, Queer Nation spawned chapters across the country. Its members invaded bars and restaurants to hold kiss-ins. Dressed in the most fabulous gay regalia, Queer Nation went into suburban shopping malls" (1993, p. 88). In reterritorializing the terrain of the straight bar or shopping mall through kiss-ins and "fashion shows," Queer Nation activists transgress heterosexist spaces, make them uncomfortable for taken-for-granted heterosexuality, transform these spaces into alien landscapes. This is only a first step. As Berlant and Freeman suggest, "Queer Nights Out" are acts of sexual desegregation that hope to broadcast the ordinariness of the queer body and the banality of same-sex kissing (1993, p. 207). Queering public spaces is a deconstructive rhetoric that does not reverse the heterosexual/homosexual hierarchy, but instead hopes to displace it and create public spaces that are safe for visible manifestations of multiple sexualities: "*Visibility* is critical if a safe public existence is to be forged . . . secure spaces of safe embodiment for capital and sexual expenditures . . . safe spaces, secured for bodies by capital and everyday life practices. . . . 'Being queer is not about a right to privacy: it is about the freedom to be public'" (Berlant and Freeman, 1993, p. 201)—the freedom to be visible, to exist.

Reterritorializing the mall is especially significant in an America where the mall has become the public space for the display of the normative ideals of its consumer culture. It is the contemporary version of Main Street. Teenagers hang out there and conduct the dating rituals of heterosexual adolescence. Families shop for the goods of the American Dream. Seniors power walk into their Golden Years. Into this mythic space Queer Nation activists assert their public place.

The body rhetoric of the kiss-ins also work to "normalize" homosexuality through denaturalizing the conventions of heterosexuality. In consciously imitating and thus parodying the ritual practices of heterosexuality in a bar or mall, the activists reveal in the possibility of imitation the constructedness and contingency of the practices of heterosexuality. As Butler suggests, "As imitations which effectively displace the meaning of the original . . . parodic proliferation deprives hegemonic culture and its critics of the claim to naturalized or essentialist gender identities" (1990, p. 138). In using their bodies as billboards to disrupt the straight spaces of these places, Queer Nation activists recreate these spaces as sites for multiple significations of sexuality.

CONCLUSION

The aim of this essay is fairly limited. This essay is not meant to offer a theory of the body and, indeed, is implicitly incoherent with respect to a theory of the body, for the body is a site of incoherence. Still, the discussions of bodies in this essay does suggest that the body is *both* socially constructed and excessive. That is, bodies simultaneously are constructed in discourses and exceed those discourses. This essay is not an argument about or for postmodern politics or new social movements, though others have made those arguments about ACT UP, Earth First!, and other contemporary social protest groups.[10] Still, if postmodern or new social movements are understood as being concerned with discursive issues relating to identity, social norms, ideologies, power, and worldviews; forming grass roots groups practicing radical participatory democracy; and performing unorthodox rhetorical tactics; the interpretation of the groups in this essay is consonant with such a characterization of postmodern politics. Finally, this essay is not an argument about image politics, though since the focus is on bodies that often appear to people as images of bodies through mass media dissemination, the argument of this essay is supportive of what Mitchell (1994) terms "the pictorial turn" and provides further evidence of the need for a visual rhetoric.

This essay is an argument for the necessity of considering the body when attempting to understand the effects of many forms of public argument, especially social protest rhetoric in a televisual public forum. In close readings of the unruly acts of Earth First!, ACT UP, and Queer Nation, it is evident that both the meaning and force of their arguments is dependent on the deployment of their bodies. I would suggest that these groups are not atypical. Bodies are central to the activism of environmental justice groups, Operation Rescue, and other groups. In attempting to understand the dynamics of social change and the role of rhetoric in constituting identities, ideologies, communities, and cultures, critics must analyze bodies as a rich source of argumentative force. Such a task requires a reconsideration of argumentation so as to take account of public arguments that exceed the bonds of reason and words. Through its readings of body arguments, this essay makes a contribution to such a task.

NOTES

[1] Greene (1998) provides a compelling history of the development of constitutive rhetoric.

[2] Dave Foreman and Larry Kramer are important speakers, but their speeches are mostly for internal group consumption and are unheard in the larger public sphere. These groups' primary public rhetoric is the body rhetoric of their image events.

[3] In this essay I conflate bodies and images of bodies. My analysis largely focuses on images of bodies represented on televisual news. To get into issues of representation would take me

far afield from the thrust of this essay. In addition, an argument could be made that images of bodies on television news are perceived transparently, that is as real bodies, in a way that bodies in Hollywood films, for example, are not.

[4] See Olson (1987), Jamieson (1988, 1994), Condit (1990), Gronbeck (1992, 1993, 1995), Birdsell and Groarke (1996), Lucaites (1997), and Lake and Pickering (1998).

[5] For examples, see Haiman (1967), McEdwards (1968), Scott and Smith (1969), Bowers and Ochs (1971), and Simons (1972).

[6] See Jamieson (1988, 1994), Gronbeck (1992, 1993, 1995), Birdsell and Groarke (1996), and Lake and Pickering (1998).

[7] These image events appeared on ABC World News' report "War in the Woods" (August 10, 1987) and are typical of the images of Earth First! bodies on the news. For an extended discussion of grassroots environmental groups and the media, see DeLuca (1999).

[8] For accounts of violent incidents against environmental activists, see Foreman (1991, pp. 124–127), Helvarg (1994), and Rowell (1996). On September 17, 1998, an irate logger felled a redwood with Earth First! protesters in the area. The falling tree killed Earth First!er David Chain. For a compelling account of the confrontation, see Goodell (1999).

[9] For more on the importance of piercing the technological veil, plus a consideration of the paradoxical role of technology in making possible the environmental movement and a new understanding of nature, see DeLuca (1996).

[10] See Aronowitz (1996), Cohen (1985), Crimp (1990), Offe (1985), Patton (1985, 1990), and Touraine (1985).

WORKS CITED

ABC News (1987, August 10). War in the Woods. New York: ABC.

ABC News (1993, August 19). American Agenda. New York: ABC. [ref]

Aronowitz, S. (1996). *The death and rebirth of American radicalism*. New York: Routledge.

Berlant, L. and E. Freeman. (1993). Queer nationality. In M. Warner (Ed.). *Fear of a queer planet: Queer politics and social theory*, pp. 193–229. Minneapolis: University of Minnesota.

Berman, M. (1984). *The reenchantment of the world*. Toronto, Canada: Bantam Books.

Birdsell, D. S. and L. Groarke (1996). Toward a theory of visual argument. *Argumentation and Advocacy*, 33, 1:10.

Bowers, J. W., and Ochs, D. J. (1971). *The rhetoric of agitation and control*. Prospect Heights, Illinois: Waveland Press.

Bullert, B. J. (1997) *Public television: Politics & the battle over documentary film*. New Brunswick: Rutgers University Press.

Butler, J. (1990). *Gender trouble: Feminism and the subversion of identity*. New York: Routledge.

Cohen, J. L. (1985). Strategy or identity: New theoretical paradigms and contemporary social movements. *Social Research*, 52, 663–716.

Condit, C. M. (1990). *Decoding abortion rhetoric: Communicating social change*. Urbana: University of Illinois.

Crimp, D. (1990). *AIDS demo graphics*. Seattle: Bay Press.

Cunningham, M. (1992, May). If you're queer and you're not angry in 1992, you're not paying attention; if you're straight it may be hard to figure out what all the shouting's about. *Mother Jones*, 17:3, pp. 60–68.

DeLuca, K. (1996). Constituting nature anew through judgment: The possibilities of media. In S. Muir and T. Veenendall (Eds.) *Earthtalk: Communication and empowerment for environmental action*. Westport, CT: Praeger.

——— (1999). *Image politics: The new rhetoric of environmental activism*. New York: Guilford Publications.

Feinberg, D. B. (1994). *Queer and loathing: Rants and raves of a raging AIDS clone*. New York: Penguin Books USA Inc.

Foreman, D. (1991). *Confessions of an eco-warrior*. New York: Harmony Books.

Foucault, M. (1977). *Discipline and punish: The birth of the prison*. New York: Vintage Books.

Foucault, M. (1978). *The history of sexuality: Volume I: An introduction*. New York: Random House.

Gillin, T. (1980). *The whole world is watching*. Berkeley: University of California Press.

Goodell, J. (1999, January 21). Death in the redwoods. *Rolling Stone*, 60–69, 86.

Greene, R. W. (1998, Summer). The aesthetic turn and the rhetorical perspective on argumentation. *Argumentation and Advocacy, 35,* 19–29.

Gronbeck, B. (1992, August) Negative narrative in 1998 Presidential campaign ads. *The Quarterly Journal of Speech, 78,* 333–346.

——— (1993). The spoken and the seen: Phonocentric and ocularcentric dimensions of rhetorical discourse. In J. F. Reynolds (Ed.), *Rhetorical memory and delivery: Classical concepts for contemporary composition and communication* (pp. 139–155). Hillsdale, NJ: Lawrence Erlbaum Associates.

——— (1995). Rhetoric, ethics, and telespectacles in the post-everything age. In R. H. Brown (Ed.), *Postmodern representations: Truth, power, and mimesis in the human sciences and public culture* (216–238) United States: University of Illinois Press.

Haiman, F. S. (1967). The rhetoric of the streets. *Quarterly Journal of Speech, 53,* 99–114.

Heidegger, M. (1993). Building dwelling thinking. In D. Krell (Ed.: *Martin Heidegger: Basic writings.* San Francisco: Harper San Francisco.

Helvarg, D. (1994). *The war against the Greens: The Wise-use movement, the new right and anti-environmental violence.* San Francisco, CA: Sierra Club Books.

Hornblower, M. (1998, May 11). Five months at 180 ft.: An ecowarrior who calls herself Butterfly has set a tree-squatting record. *Time, 151:18.*

Jamieson, K. H. (1988). *Eloquence in an electronic age.* New York: Oxford University Press.

——— (1994, September 28). Political ads, the press, and lessons in psychology. *The Chronicle of Higher Education.* (A56)

Kane, J. (1987, February). Mother nature's army. *Esquire,* 98–106.

Lake, R. A. and B. A. Pickering (1998). Argumentation, the visual, and the possibility of refutation: An exploration. *Argumentation 12,* 79–83

Leopold, A. (1949/1968). *A Sand county almanac.* Oxford: Oxford University Press.

Lingis, A. (1994). *Foreign bodies.* New York: Routledge.

Lucaites, J. L. (1997). Visualizing "The People": Individualism vs. collectivism in *Let Us Now Praise Famous Men. The Quarterly Journal of Speech, 83,* 269–28

Manes, C. (1990). *Green rage, radical environmentalism and the unmaking of civilization.* Boston, MA: Little, Brown & Co.

McEdwards, M. G. (1968). Agitative rhetoric: Its nature and effect. *Western Speech, 32,* 36–43.

Mitchell, W. (1994). *Picture Theory.* Chicago: University of Chicago Press.

NBC News (1990, July 5). Assignment Earth: Earth First! New York: NBC.

Offe, C. (1985, Winter). New social movements: Challenging the boundaries of institutional politics. *Social Research, 52,* 817–868.

Olson, L. (1987). Benjamin Franklin's pictorial representations of the British Colonies in America: A study in rhetorical iconology. *Quarterly Journal of Speech, 73,* 18–42.

Parenti, M. (1993). *Inventing Reality.* New York: St. Martin's.

Patton, C. (1985). *Sex and germs: The politics of AIDS.* Boston: South End Press.

Patton, C. (1990). *Inventing AIDS.* New York: Routledge

Perelman, C. (1982). *The realm of rhetoric.* Notre Dame: University of Notre Dame.

Rowell, A. (1996). *Green backlash: Global subversion of the environment movement.* New York: Routledge.

Schoofs, M. (1997, March 25). ACT UP: 10 years and counting—The AIDS shock troopers who changed the world. *Village Voice, 42: 12,* pp. 42, 44–47.

Scott, R. and Smith, D. (1969). The rhetoric of confrontation. *Quarterly Journal of Speech 58,* 1–8.

Setterberg, F. (1987, May/June). The wild bunch: Earth First! Shakes up the environmental movement. *Utne Reader,* 68–76.

Short, B. (1991). Earth First! and the rhetoric of moral confrontation. *Communication Studies, 42,* 172–88.

Signorile, M. (1993). *Queer in America: Sex, the media, and the closets of power.* New York: Random House.

Simons, H. W. (1972). Persuasion in social conflicts: A critique of prevailing conceptions and a framework for future research. *Speech Monographs, 39,* 227–47.

Smith, M. (1997, Winter). Against the enclosure of the ethical commons: Radical environmentalism as an "ethics of place." *Environmental Ethics, 18,* 339–353).

Touraine, A. (1985, Winter). An introduction to the study of social movements. *Social Research, 52,* 749–787.

....

The Space of Argumentation: Urban Design, Civic Discourse, and the Dream of the Good City

DAVID FLEMING

INTRODUCTION

The profession or discipline of urban design presents the argumentation scholar with two distinct intellectual projects. In one, the object of inquiry is the role of reason-giving, value-laden, socially-situated discourse in the planning of urban space. This project participates in the so-called 'rhetorical turn' of contemporary social analysis, in which a discursive or argumentative component is located in endeavors previously thought to be matters of artistic expression or technical reason.[1] Such inquiry can be useful, both by alerting experts to the 'rhetoric' of their work and by illustrating how arguments in specialized fields are both different from and similar to those in the public realm. As critics have begun to note, however, such work often amounts to little more than a 'dimensionalization' of the special field: it shows how a particular practice can be redescribed in the terms of rhetoric, but it is unclear what theoretical or practical gains actually accrue from such a hermeneutic exercise (see, e.g., Gaonkar, 1990, 1997).

The second project, by contrast, couples argument and design in a more necessary relationship. From this perspective, urban design is seen not simply to *involve* argument but to be, at bottom, *about* argument. The focus of such inquiry is on the ways buildings and cities themselves enable and constrain argument, how the 'built world' influences the production and reception of social discourse. In this kind of inquiry, the planning and design of urban space is literally the 'housing' of rhetoric. It is this kind of project I attempt here. I will argue that, just as different theories of argumentation embody different attitudes towards public space, different theories of public space embody different attitudes towards argumentation. I begin by laying out historical connections between argumentation theory and the idea of civic virtue. I then analyze discourse norms implicit in three theories of urban design. Finally, I propose a 'civic' vocabulary of potential interest to both urban designers and argumentation theorists.

I.

Historically, the art of rhetoric (where much of the early development of argumentation theory can be located) and the self-governing city are closely linked; in some places and during certain periods, to think about one was essentially to think about the other. Rhetoric, in such contexts, served as the primary instrument of civic life; and the city served as the primary scene of rhetoric. The connection is apparent in a story Cicero tells at the beginning of *De Inventione*. Long ago, Cicero writes, men were dispersed, wandering at large in the fields and forests, and relying chiefly on physical strength to survive. It was through one man's reason and eloquence ('*rationem atque orationem*') that they were induced to assemble together, where they transformed themselves into a 'kind and gentle folk' (I.ii.2). And eloquence continued to play a role in city life even after this foundational act:

> [A]fter cities had been established how could it have been brought to pass that
> men should learn to keep faith and observe justice and become accustomed

to obey others voluntarily and believe not only that they must work for the common good but even sacrifice life itself, unless men had been able by eloquence to persuade their fellows of the truth of what they had discovered by reason? (I.ii.3)

In Cicero's story, rhetoric accounts for the origins of the city; the city, in turn, provides a function and context for rhetoric. Just as virtue cannot be voiceless if it is to be effective, speech cannot be politically unanchored if it is to be useful—for Cicero, rhetoric is worthy precisely because it subordinated to 'civil' affairs (I.v.6). Similar myths describing a mutual relationship between rhetoric and the city are common in the classical era. Carolyn Miller (1993) has compared various Greek versions of the myth, showing how Plato and Aristotle tried to weaken the logos/polis bond first articulated by Protagoras and later re-affirmed by Isocrates and Cicero. 'Protagoras' teaching', Miller writes, 'makes rhetoric and politics inseparable dimensions of each other: the democratic city requires rhetoric for its self-constituting operation, and rhetoric must take place within and concern the affairs of the city' (p. 223).

There may be some truth to the mythical connection between rhetoric and the city. The rise of the agora, or central gathering place, in ancient Greek cities during the first half of the First Millennium, B.C.E., is contemporaneous with the rise of both democracy and rhetoric. R. E. Wycherley (1969) has traced the gradual separation of the agora and acropolis and the privileging of the former during that period. Where the acropolis was situated on high ground and served primarily military and religious functions, the agora was situated on flat ground and served primarily commercial, political, and social functions. Where the acropolis was fundamentally aristocratic or monarchical in nature, the agora was democratic. As Wycherley argues, '[T]he gradual emergence of a large body of free and equal citizens, all taking a full and active part in political and social life, guided the architectural growth of the city' (p. 7), which now required a central, open, and well-drained space for citizens to gather and conduct business. Discussions of the Greek 'discovery of politics' too often ignore this spatial dimension of early experiments with democracy (see, e.g., Meier, 1990). One sign of the agora's importance in the social, political, cultural, and economic life of Greek cities during this period is the number and virulence of complaints about it. Aristophanes, Plato, and Aristotle all denounced the wrangling that occurred in the agora; and the Persian King Cyrus is supposed to have remarked:

I never yet feared the kind of men who have a place set apart in the middle of the city in which they get together and tell one another lies under oath (Herodotus, *History*, I.153; qtd. in Wycherley, p. 55).

The specific connection between the agora and rhetoric is made by Jean-Pierre Vernant (1982), who argues that writing (re-introduced into Greece in the 9th C., B.C.E.) made social and political decisions more widely accessible and allowed for the transference of political sovereignty from the monarch to the agora, where problems of general interest could be debated and resolved. And, according to Vernant, once you have the agora, you have the polis, because the polis implies first of all the preeminence of speech (specifically, the antithetical demonstrations of public oratory) over all other instruments of power. What emerges, then, is a reciprocal relationship between politics and logos:

The art of politics became essentially the management of language; and logos from the beginning took on an awareness of itself, of its rules and its effectiveness, through its political function (p. 50).

Eugene Garver (1994) has made a similar point about Aristotle's rhetorical theory; it is, he claims, 'embedded in the particular circumstances of the polis', a context which was 'natural' for Aristotle but 'unnatural' for us (p. 55). Because we no longer live in the kind of community Aristotle lived in, we have transformed rhetoric into a portable *techne,* usable in all sorts of *non-*political contexts. For Aristotle, rhetoric was a restricted, civic art rather than a universal, professional one. It was the art of the citizen; and a citizen was, more than anything else, someone unwilling to delegate the practice of rhetoric (p. 48). (On the connection between eloquence and civic virtue in the Athens of the 5th and 4th C., B.C.E., see also De Romilly, 1992; Murray, 1990; Schiappa, 1991; and Yunis, 1996.)

The Italian Renaissance offered another sphere for this reciprocal relationship to be played out, especially in the independent republics of the northern communes. Petrarch, for example, was aware of the virtues of the contemplative life but was also strongly attracted to rhetoric. He knew instinctively that to be a rhetor was to be committed to the practical affairs of one's city; and to be active in one's city was to be, almost by definition, a rhetor. 'It is a peculiar characteristic of orators,' he wrote, 'that they take pleasure in large cities and in the press of the crowd, in proportion to the greatness of their own talents. They curse solitude, and hate and oppose silence where decisions are to be made' (qtd. in Seigel, 1968, p. 43). According to J. G. A. Pocock (1975), Petrarch was just the beginning of what would soon become a revival of 'the ancient ideal of *homo politicus* (the *zoon politikon* of Aristotle), who affirms his being and his virtue by the medium of political action, whose closest kinsman is *homo rhetor* and whose antithesis is the *homo credens* of Christian faith' (p. 550). Pocock writes that the 'civic humanists' of the 15th C., especially those associated with the Florentine republic, sought to raise rhetoric to the level of philosophy, to legitimize the world of 'face-to-face political decisions' where '[t]he rhetorician and the citizen [are] alike committed to viewing human life in terms of participation in particular actions and decisions, in particular political relationships between particular men' (pp. 59–60). Later, Vico would also attempt to revive the Ciceronian equation of rhetoric and civic virtue. According to Michael Mooney (1985), Vico held that none of nature's gifts was more critical for the orator than a *civil* education:

> simply growing up as part of a city's life, coming to know its streets and its buildings, learning its language and its lore, its history and its ways, and in time being trained in its schools, especially in the company of one's peers. There is nothing, he concluded, that can instruct one better in that *sensus communis,* which is the norm of all prudence and eloquence (p. 84).

Cartesian analysis, Vico thought, made students incapable of managing civic affairs; what they needed was the fullness and pliability of rhetoric.

Why does this coupling of discourse and the city seem so strange to modern sensibilities? Is it because the nation has become the central site for political argument in our time? Because modern transportation and communication technologies appear to have made shared space irrelevant for social interaction? Because the public realm has become increasingly private? Because our urban centers have experienced such deterioration and decay? According to Hannah Arendt (1958), the history of the West since the disappearance of the city-state is the story of the gradual abasement of the *vita activa*: 'a way of life in which speech and only speech made sense and where the central concern of all citizens was to talk with each other' (p. 27). Thomas Bender (1984) has depicted a crucial moment in this story, the time at the end of the 19th C. when the close connection between civic and scholarly culture in American higher education was broken. In the 18th C., Bender writes, learned associations typically included lay intellectuals as well as professional ones; but by the 1880s, academic scholarship had oriented itself towards national rather than civic associations. The result, Bender argues, was that the emergent professionals severed intellectual life from place, leaving Americans with an impoverished public culture. Michael Halloran (1982) tells a similar tale about the rise and fall of rhetoric in American colleges. In the late 18th C., he argues, rhetoric was the central subject in the post-secondary curriculum. Consequently, the role of the English language in the world of practical affairs was emphasized; oral communication (especially forensic disputation and political declamation) was privileged; and the ability to speak to diverse audiences, including local dignitaries, was a prominent goal. One hundred years later, rhetoric had been demoted to a minor place in higher education, diminished by the concept of *belles lettres,* the specialization of the curriculum, and the changing role of education itself, which came to be seen not as the preparation of leaders for the community but the means by which individuals could advance in society.

The time may be ripe for a re-coupling of *logos* and the *polis.* The rhetoric revival of the past half century has reminded us that language is very much a communal affair, its study requiring an appreciation for local knowledge, situated practice, and cultural values. In argumentation theory, for example, the traditional interest in formal validity has been supplanted (or, at least, enriched) by a growing interest in informal analysis and evaluation, where logical considerations are embedded in ethical and political norms, where theories of good reason are informed by theories of good character and good community. In Douglas Walton's (1989) model of 'persuasion dialogue,' for example, the arguer is seen to be under a double obligation: to prove his or her theses from the concessions of his or her interlocutor and to cooperate with that interlocutor's attempts to do the same (pp. 3–9). Frans van Eemeren and Rob Grootendorst (1992) have proposed a 'Ten Commandments' of critical discussion with similar rules. And Jasper Neel's (1988) notion of 'strong discourse' also effects a union of good reason and good community. 'Strong discourse,' Neel claims, is discourse which has been tested in public life; it is strong both by finding adherents and by generating and tolerating competitor discourses (p. 208). For Sandra Stotsky (1991), meanwhile, a good writer is above all else someone who meets certain *moral* responsibilities, who considers other writers as intelligent as him- or herself, who gathers all relevant information on a topic, who uses facts accurately, who assumes an open-minded reader, etc. Finally, Stephen Toulmin's (1992) recent model of rationality explicitly connects logical, ethical, and political norms. Here, reasonableness is a matter of several kinds of 'respect', of which respecting the demands of 'basic intelligibility' (i.e., formal validity) is only one component. Rationality also entails respect for the 'natural grain of the world,' respect for the 'projects of others' (as both individuals and collectives), respect for the special nature of the case at hand, and respect for the standpoints of one's hearers or readers. The very word 'respect' here is reminiscent of Protagoras' myth of the city, where physical attributes and technical skills are distributed differentially, but where mutual respect and justice are shared by all; without them, Protagoras says, the city cannot even survive, much less flourish (Plato, *Protagoras,* 320D–328D).

My question is this: do such theories of argumentation—which make reasoning a matter of formal validity *and* sensitivity to others—presuppose a particular organization of physical space? That is, does good argument require contexts in which arguers are daily confronted with *other* arguers holding *different* views but united by *common* problems? Does argument benefit when arguers have easy access to central and safe public places devoted to informal and formal social contact, when interlocutors believe that they share in the governance of a shared world? Finally, when rhetoricians, argumentation theorists, and political philosophers talk about public discourse, shouldn't they be talking with architects and urban designers as well? After all, scholars and professionals in all these fields share an interest in the 'public sphere'—that metaphorical or literal *realm* of public discourse that many believe to be in a state of decline. Among rhetoricians, argumentation theorists, and political philosophers, the decline of the public sphere is manifest in the contemporary impoverishment of moral discourse (Bellah et al., 1985, 1991; Booth, 1974; MacIntyre, 1981), the failure of civil disagreement (Elshtain, 1995; Glendon, 1991), and the victory of information over argumentation (Habermas, 1970, 1989; Lasch, 1990). But architects and designers are also concerned about the decline of the public sphere. The urban landscape of North America, they claim, is in trouble: our cities (with their suburban sprawl and shopping malls) don't seem like 'real' cities at all: they're centerless, socially fragmented, and restlessly commercial; they're ugly, depressing, and scary; they lack livability and community. In the words of 'edge city' residents asked to describe their town, they are places without soul (Garreau, 1991, p. 8; see also Kay, 1997; Kowinski, 1985; Kunstler, 1993; Rybcyznski, 1995; and Sorkin, 1992).

Is it possible that these two critiques are related? Is the rhetorician's complaint about the deterioration of public discourse also a complaint about the decline of public *space*? And is the designer's complaint about the deterioration of public space also a complaint about the decline of public *discourse*? What follows is an attempt to answer these questions through a reading of three theories of urban design.

II.

Jane Jacobs was an 'urbanologist' who served during the 1950s as associate editor of *Architectural Forum.* Her landmark 1961 book, *The Death and Life of Great American Cities,* has a design appeal not found in other sociological analyses of the city. The book is an attack on orthodox urban planning of the 1950s, particularly the influence of such luminaries as Ebenezer Howard, Lewis Mumford, Sir Patrick Geddes, Clarence Stein, Raymond Unwin, and Le Corbusier. According to Jacobs, city planning in her time privileged central control by experts and relied on the inappropriate model of the English country town. These theories evinced a hostility for large cities, a preference for low-density settlements, a preoccupation with private housing, and an obsession for simplicity, order, and self-sufficiency. Against all of this, Jacobs' model city is the old mixed-use, crowded streets of her own Greenwich Village.

For Jacobs, cities are by definition full of strangers. In this, she resembles Richard Sennett (1977), who would later make the presence of strangers in cities the key social fact behind the 18th C. rise of the public sphere. It is the absence of intimacy in public life that, for Jacobs, Sennett, Arendt, and others, creates the very possibility for 'civilized' social behavior. Because she treats cities as places full of strangers, Jacobs emphasizes those places where strangers are most likely meet: streets and sidewalks.2 Good streets and sidewalks, for Jacobs, are diverse and lively places which generate three social benefits.

First, a city of good streets and sidewalks is safe. Peace is kept by the people themselves; there is a clear demarcation between public and private space (the streets and sidewalks being public); people watch the public spaces ('their eyes are on them,' in Jacobs' terms); and the sidewalks are in constant use. The streets of the safe city are store-, bar-, and restaurant-filled and therefore lively at all hours. 'Under the seeming disorder of the old city,' Jacobs writes, 'is a marvelous order for maintaining the safety of the streets and the freedom of the city. It is a complex order. Its essence is intricacy of sidewalk use, bringing with it a constant succession of eyes' (p. 50).

Second, the city of good streets and sidewalks is one that generates contact. But note that this contact is neither the intimate contact of the home nor the formal contact of the assembly or courtroom. It is the casual contact of strangers and acquaintances. 'Cities are full of people,' Jacobs writes, 'with whom, from your viewpoint, or mine, or any other individual's, a certain degree of contact is useful or enjoyable; but you do not want them in your hair. And they do not want you in theirs either' (p. 56). Such casual contact, over time, among people on non-intimate but civilized terms, gradually builds up 'a feeling for the public identity of people, a web of public respect and trust, and a resource in time of personal or neighborhood need' (p. 56). Jacobs' description of this contact leaves no doubt that it is primarily discursive in nature: getting and giving advice, comparing dogs, admonishing children, admiring babies, complaining about landlords. The trust generated by such contact is illustrated by the old New York City custom of leaving one's keys in a neighborhood store for a guest or visitor. To be able to do this, Jacobs says, you must have someone whom you trust but who will not question your private habits (p. 60). In this way, a good street achieves a balance between an intimate society, where everything is shared, and a fragmented society where nothing is. It is also a place of great tolerance: in such a place, Jacobs writes, possible 'to be on excellent sidewalk terms with people who are very different from oneself' (p. 62).

The third benefit of good city streets and sidewalks, Jacobs argues, is the assimilation of children. Diverse city streets, because they are rich in interest, variety, and material for the imagination, are good places for children, who are fascinated by them. Sidewalks provide children with an 'unspecialized outdoor home base from which to play, to hang around in, and to help form their notions of the world' (p. 81). And, because the incidental play of children on sidewalks is supervised by ordinary, untrained adults, in the course of carrying on their other pursuits, children learn from playing there that people without ties of kinship, close friendship, or formal responsibility will take a modicum of public responsibility for them (p. 82).

Besides the street, Jacobs' other units of social geography are the city district and the city as a whole. The neighborhood, much beloved by urban planners, is meaningless here; it is too large to possess the competence of a good street, too small to have the political power of a district, and never self-sufficient in a big city, where people can move around in a large area for services, friends, and goods.

How can we produce such cities? First, the street must serve more than one primary function; it must contain a mix of uses, and not be limited to exclusively residential or commercial activity. Second, it must have small blocks and thus provide frequent opportunities for turning corners. Third, it must mingle buildings that vary in age and thus allow for varied economic yields. And fourth, it must have a sufficiently dense concentration of people. Such a city, Jacobs argues, will be a place where very different people can live together on civilized terms.

From a rhetorical point of view, Jacobs' city is more than anything else a *talkative* city. It is a place of casual conversations among diverse, non-intimate but mutually dependent strangers and acquaintances. Her design principles can be seen, then, as creating and protecting space for informal talk. Interestingly, the Greek *polis* has been described as just such a place: Arendt calls the city-state the 'most talkative of all bodies politic' (p. 26). But unlike Jacobs' city, the Athens of the 5th and 4th C., B.C.E., also had vital spaces for *formal* public discourse: the assembly, the law court, the theater, etc. Jacobs has nothing to say about these kinds of spaces. She does attempt at one point to draw a direct connection between informal and formal contact (see p. 56); but this is not emphasized and never clearly explained.

Like Jacobs, Christopher Alexander and his colleagues at the University of California at Berkeley, authors of *A Pattern Language: Towns, Buildings, Construction*, set about to formulate principles for building and maintaining the good city. But if Jacobs' key virtues were aliveness and diversity and her enemy the dullness of 1950s urban renewal, Alexander's virtues are wholeness and health and his enemy the societal insanity of the 1960s and 70s (much of the funding for this 1977 book came from the National Institutes of Mental Health). The book is comprised of 253 'patterns,' each pattern consisting of a problem that occurs in the human environment and a design guideline for solving the problem. It is the relationship among the patterns, however, that is the central message of the book: when you build a thing, Alexander writes, you 'must also repair the world around it and within it' (p. xiii). The patterns proceed from the largest (#1 is work toward independent, self-governing regions in the world, each with a population between 2–10 million) to the smallest (#242 is build a bench outside your front door, so people can watch the street). In between are patterns such as #190: vary ceiling heights throughout the building and #71: in every neighborhood provide still water for swimming. Many of the patterns evince a profound concern for good communication; for example, #159 is locate each room so that natural light comes from more than one direction. The reason?

> Rooms lit on two sides create less glare around people and objects; [this] allows us to read in detail the minute expressions that flash across people's faces, the motion of their hands . . . [L]ight on two sides allows people to understand each other (p. 748).

Alexander has much to say about the relationship of geography to self-government. For example, the book prescribes an intricate layering of political communities. First, there is the region of 8 million (#1). Such a region, Alexander writes, has natural boundaries and its own economy; it is autonomous, self-governing, and has a seat in world government. Beyond this size, people are too remote from the political process; smaller than this, the region has no voice in global affairs. Alexander writes of this pattern:

> We believe the independent region can become the modern polis—the new commune that human entity which provides the sphere of culture, language, laws, services, economic exchange, variety, which the old walled city or the polis provided for its members (p. 13).

Second, there is the city of 500,000 (#10). Alexander argues that only with concentrations of 300,000 people or more, can you have a centralized business district with 'magic,' that variety of life that only great concentrations of people have. He's more interested, however, in the next layer of political space: the community of 7,000 (#12). Here the pattern language seems to support Plato's contention that the perfect community has a population of 5,040 (factorial 7); it also seems to accord with the old rule that in a polis everyone should be able to gather in one place and hear an unamplified speaker; and it is about the size of the old direct democracies of New England. On this score, Alexander quotes Paul Goodman, whose rule of thumb for self-government is that no citizen should be more than two friends away from the highest member of a local unit; Alexander computes this to roughly 5,500 people, assuming 12 good friends per person. In spatial terms, the optimum size for Alexander's self-governing community is 75 acres, an area that can be traversed by walking in about 10 minutes; at a density of 60 persons per acre, this would amount to about 4,500 people. All of this, of course, sounds suspiciously like the 'neighborhood' of modern planning lore, which is often defined as the population surrounding a single elementary school and typically comes in at about 7,000 residents. Whatever the rationale, Alexander argues that in a city subdivided into communities of 5–10,000 people, there is the possibility of a direct connection between the man or woman on the street and his or her local officials and representatives. Each such community should have the power to initiate, decide, and execute its own affairs (police, schools, welfare, streets, etc.). And Alexander recommends that local political forums be situated in highly visible and accessible places, so that each community has a political 'center of gravity,' a place where each resident feels at home, and where he or she can talk directly to the person in charge.

Next comes the neighborhood of 500 (#14). People need an identifiable spatial unit, Alexander argues. Because most people limit their 'home base' to just a few blocks, roughly 300 yards across, and because human groups cannot coordinate themselves to reach basic agreements if they are too large, Alexander recommends neighborhood groupings of approximately 500. The fifth layer of political geography is the house cluster of 50 (#37). People tend to confine their local visiting, Alexander claims, to their immediate neighbors, so he recommends arranging houses to form identifiable groups of 8–12 households around common land and paths. 'With one representative from each family, this is the number of people that can sit round a common meeting table' and make wise decisions (p. 200). Finally, there is the self-governing work or office group of about 10 (#80): decentralized, autonomous, face-to-face, self-regulating, and personal.

In laying out this political geography, Alexander says very little about how self-government would actually work at the level of speech acts. He does, however, include several patterns explicitly devoted to political discourse. So, for example, #44 says that visible and accessible town halls need to be placed in each community of 7,000. Such places would include common territory where people can debate policy and where they are encouraged to linger and gather. This territory, Alexander continues, should contain both a public forum, with sound system, benches, walls for notices, etc., and a 'necklace' of community projects, including free office space, meeting rooms, office equipment, etc.

Also of rhetorical interest here are patterns that attempt to limit the intrusion of the automobile into human space (e.g., #11). The problem with cars, Alexander argues, is that they spread people out and keep them apart.

It is quite possible that the collective cohesion people need to form a viable society just cannot develop when the vehicles which people use force them to be 10 times farther apart they have to be. It may be that cars cause the break-down of society simply because of their geometry (p. 66).

In another pattern, Alexander argues that no more than 9 percent of any 10-acre area should be devoted to parking (#22).

> People realize that the physical environment is the medium for their social intercourse . . . when the density of cars passes a certain limit, the environment is no longer theirs . . . social communion is no longer permitted or encouraged (p. 122).

The book also recommends that each community have a promenade, a place where people can go to see and be seen, to rub shoulders, and confirm their community (#31). And there is a pattern (#21) recommending that residential buildings be limited to four stories in the belief that people who live in high rises are isolated from ground-level, casual society.

Alexander's project is more ambitious than Jacobs'; the casual contact of the street, with which Jacobs is exclusively concerned, is here integrated into a vision that also prescribes an intimate geography and formal, public spaces as well. And this, in fact, may be its weakness for our purposes; because he describes the good human landscape with an almost religious comprehensiveness, Alexander may not provide the vocabulary we are after if our primary concern is separating out public discourse as a bounded problem.

If Jacobs' city is lively and diverse; and Alexander's town, whole and healthy; the kind of space associated with 'the New Urbanism' is explicitly intended to evoke 'community.' According to Peter Katz's 1994 book *The New Urbanism: Toward an Architecture of Community*, this recent approach to architecture and planning is self-consciously bent on repairing our fragmented social landscape.

Unlike Kevin Lynch's (1981) *Good City Form*, which is skeptical of a direct, primary relationship between settlement form and the quality of social life, proponents of the New Urbanism claim emphatically that bad urban design creates weak communities, and good urban design creates strong ones. Peter Katz (1994), for example, writes that suburban sprawl—a big enemy here, along with the automobile, modern architecture, and free-wheeling capitalism—has 'fragmented our society—separating us from friends and relatives and breaking down the bonds of community that had served our nation so well in earlier times' (p. ix). Similarly, Peter Calthorpe (1994) argues that the 40-year growth of suburbs and edge cities in North America has left us with a 'profound sense of frustration and placelessness' (p. xii). Our urban and regional geography, he writes, 'seem to have an empty feeling, reinforcing our mobile state and the instability of our families' (p. xii). For Elizabeth Moule and Stefanos Polyzoides (1994), the traditional American model of city-making, in which a grid was cut for *both* public and private use, has been abandoned. Architecture is now about self-expression; transportation needs dominate planning; and the private realm is privileged over that which is common, the 'shared space' which brings people together to relate to one another (p. xxi).

The New Urbanism, Katz writes, returns to a 'cherished American icon': the compact, close-knit community (p. ix). Perhaps the most explicit statement of the New Urbanism has been developed by Andres Duany and Elizabeth Plater-Zyberk (1994). Their focus is on what they call Traditional Neighborhood Development (TND), which contains five principles. First, a neighborhood should have a center and an edge. This contributes, they argue, to the 'social identity of the community' (p. xvii). The center is always public space (a square, green, or important intersection), and it is the locus of the neighborhood's public buildings (post office, city hall, daycare center, churches, shops, etc.). The edge is typically recreational open space or thoroughfare. Second, the optimal size of the neighborhood is a quarter-mile from center to edge, equivalent to a 5-minute walk at an easy pace. This makes the neighborhood accessible without cars. Third, according to Duany and Plater-Zyberk, the neighborhood should have a balanced mix or fine grain of activities: dwellings, shops, workplaces, schools, churches, and recreations all interspersed with one another. This is especially important for residents, like the very young and very old, who are unable to drive. The mix should also contain a range of housing types, from above-shop apartments to single family houses. Fourth, the neighborhood should structure building sites and traffic on a fine network of interconnecting streets. This shortens pedestrian routes, diffuses traffic, and slows cars down. And, because the streets are designed for both pedestrians and automobiles, casual meetings that 'form the bonds of community' (p. xix) are encouraged. Fifth, priority is given to public space and to the appropriate location of civic buildings (government offices, churches, schools, etc.). This, proponents of TND argue, fosters community identity and civic pride. To Duany and Plater-Zyberk's five principles, Calthorpe (1994) adds the tenet that the New Urbanism should be applied throughout the region, at any density, and also to the region as a whole (p. xi).

Seaside, Florida, is Duany and Plater-Zyberk's most famous design. Built in the early 1980s on 60 acres of seaside land, it is a self-contained community with a projected population of 2,000, including 350 houses and another 300 dwellings in apartments and hotel rooms. According to Katz (1994), the overriding goal in the conception of the town was that of 'fostering a strong sense of community' (p. 3) and reversing the trend toward alienation in suburban life. Seaside does this, he claims, by, first of all, asserting the primacy of public over private space. Located first in the plan were the public places: the school, town hall, market, post office, shops, etc.; attention was also given to the streets, the walks, and the beach, all of which are clearly *common* property. The houses are close together, each of a unique design, with consistent setbacks, required front porches, no garages, etc. And everything is within a 5-minute walk. To Vincent Scully (1994), Seaside has succeeded 'more fully than any other work of architecture in our time has done, in creating an image of community, a symbol of human culture's place in nature's vastness' (p. 226). Scully is savvy enough to know, however, that the real force behind Seaside is its draconian building code:

> Architecture is fundamentally a matter not of individual buildings but of the shaping of community, and that is done by the law (p. 229).

The law makes us free, Scully writes, by binding us together so we can live without fear.

Unfortunately, Seaside may be a bit *too* precious; 'community' here turns out to be what people think community should *look* like and not necessarily a place of communal *activity*. In addition, there's the problem of strangers, which Jacobs, Sennett, and others had posited as the social fact around which all urban thinking should revolve. There are no strangers in Seaside; and here we run up against another problem with 'community.' As Maurizio D'Entreves (1994) has claimed about Hannah Arendt's project, politics is not about integrating individuals around a single or transcendent good, it is about active engagement and deliberation, which proceed best—given the unavoidable condition of human plurality—not in an environment of intimacy and warmth but in one of impartiality and trust.[3]

III.

Good reasoned discourse, most argumentation theorists now believe, is more than just a matter of logical form and valid inference; it is also a matter of ethical and political considerations and the cooperative inquiry, dispute resolution, and good deliberation that they facilitate. If such discourse requires not just respect for basic intelligibility but also respect for the projects of others, then, as arguers, we would seem to benefit from having frequent formal and informal contact with many others, especially those who hold views different from our own, who demand reasons from us when we advance our arguments, and from whom we demand reasons when they advance their arguments, but who nonetheless share with us the responsibilities of managing a common world, who are, in a sense, our 'civic friends,' although we may not be intimately connected to them, and we may differ in almost every way from them. I don't know what the common world that promotes such discourse would look like in all its material configurations; but I believe that argumentation theorists and urban designer have much to teach one another as they pursue that world. One of the things that the preceding analysis has revealed, I believe, is a set of underlying issues or problems shared by argumentation theorists and urban designers, a joint vocabulary for talking about, and building, good community. That vocabulary contains at least six key terms: size, density, heterogeneity, publicity, security, and identity. The first three—size, density, and heterogeneity—are perhaps implicit in the idea of the city itself. They are all contained in Louis Wirth's (1938) definition:

> For sociological purposes a city may be defined as a relatively large, dense, and permanent settlement of socially heterogeneous individuals (p. 8).

Unfortunately, a community can have size, density, and heterogeneity and still not have good public discourse. So we also need, I believe, three other terms: publicity, security, and identity.

First, there is settlement *size*. Although there is a long tradition of philosophical speculation about the ideal size (i.e., population) of towns, neighborhoods, and communities, what may end up being most important—and here I am following Alexander (1977)—is an intricate *layering* of political communities, so that individuals have a range of opportunities for both voice and affectivity. The good thing about large communities is that they offer so many possible political groupings, a large community being divisible in so many different ways. Unfortunately, the center of political gravity seems always to drift to the largest sphere, and a problem for public discourse now is the dearth of *local* opportunities for learning about, articulating, and testing political positions. Still, larger communities seem to present the arguer with a greater range of opportunities for observing, learning, and practicing argument.

Second, there is settlement *density*. Although crowding in cities is one reason people often prefer to live in suburbs and small towns, it may be density alone which generates the chance encounters needed for a dynamic public sphere. Density implies a plurality of people sharing a well-defined common world; and this may be a necessary condition for the kinds of good dialogue and strong discourse described above. Because if good discourse is that which is made rational *for others* and that which is tested *in public* against competitor discourses, then a dense settlement will likely have greater potential than a sparsely-populated one for bringing interlocutors into both informal and formal contact.[4]

Third, there is settlement *heterogeneity*. In a city, heterogeneity can refer to either a diverse mix of inhabitants (by age, race, class, culture, ideology, etc.) or a diverse mix of city forms and functions (what Jacobs celebrates as the 'mixed-use' neighborhood, where places of residence, recreation, and business commingle). The first kind of heterogeneity would seem to force arguers to more effectively and responsibly consider diverse points of view when advancing their own positions; the second would seem to promote communities where the public and private spheres are closer to one another, where the different parts of citizens' lives are more effectively integrated, where government, for example, is a more visible part of the human landscape rather than a separate domain somewhere downtown or in Washington. From a rhetorical point of view, a fine grain of use would seem to make public discourse less opaque.

Fourth, there is settlement *publicity*. The issue here is what proportion of a community should be open, accessible, shared, common, and criticizable; or, to put it somewhat differently, how much 'action' should be *social* action, where citizens are *responsible* to one another rather than simply pursuing private projects. Bellah et al. (1991) define publicity as 'that which is expressed in speech or writing in public' (p. 159). Similar notions can be found in Habermas (1989); Gutman and Thompson (1996), where the 'principle of publicity' states that '[t]he reasons that officials and citizens give to justify political actions, and the information necessary to assess those reasons, should be public' (p. 95); and Crick (1992), where 'the unique character of political activity lies in its publicity' (p. 20). Clearly, good public discourse requires territory where all residents have the right to appear, to see and be seen, to hear and be heard. A participant in the 1990 *Harper's* Forum 'Whatever Became of the Public Square' argued that the common space of New York City's subway system may be one reason there is less racial tension there than in Los Angeles: 'Although the public interaction is inchoate—rolling our eyes together at fools or irate passengers, perhaps an occasional courtesy—at least the people *see* one another' ('Whatever Became,' p. 51). As Jacobs, Sennett, Arendt, and others argue, a strong public life requires common space that is somewhere in between intimacy and isolation, between familial warmth, on the one hand, and absolute segregation on the other. There must be places, like streets and sidewalks, where we can appear to one another as strangers and acquaintances; but there must also be places, like libraries and political parties, where we can learn and build factions, and places like town halls and courthouses, where we can debate differences and resolve conflicts.

Fifth, there is settlement *security*. The issue here is how 'human' we want our landscape to be, how protective we are of our smallness and fragility. As a matter of security, in other words, we might want to limit the intrusion of cars in our social space; to ensure that there is density but not too much; that there is mixed use but not chaos; that there is publicity and contact but also privacy and protection.

Finally, there is settlement *identity*. To what extent should we be committed to creating and maintaining cities and communities that we collectively identify with, that we feel we belong to, whose history we know, that have a soul, that are outward manifestations of shared values. From a discursive point of view, the design of cities could contribute to the tendency of rhetors to think more often in the first person plural.

A settlement that scored high on all of these dimensions—a place with large numbers of different people in frequent contact, a place where people identify with one another even as they reveal their differences, a place with safe public spaces for gathering and decision-making—may provide a better context for the development and flourishing of argument than a place that scored low on these factors—a place that was sparsely populated, homogeneous in citizenry or function, and predominantly devoted to private pursuits. The former kind of community is what Michael Sorkin (1992) calls a place of 'authentic urbanity'—a city based on physical proximity, free movement, and a desire for collectivity (p. xv), and which he sees as an ally in the effort to reclaim democracy. The latter, meanwhile, evokes the contemporary North American suburb, a place that would seem to be an unpropitious context for learning and practicing good public discourse. But my primary objective here has not been to bash suburbs or lament the passing of the polis, but rather to help develop an interdisciplinary language for describing, building, and maintaining 'good community' whatever its size and shape. More than anything else, the analysis contained here suggests, I believe, that the design of the built world is always, implicitly or explicitly, the design of the discursive world; and that the promotion of good discourse may well require certain kinds of spatial arrangements. In this regard, rhetoric and urban planning cannot and should not be neutral towards one another; as if we could talk about discourse without talking about the common world that brings us together and separates us, or talk about buildings and towns as if they were not part of our social landscape as well.

NOTES

1 For general introductions to what is variously called 'the rhetoric of inquiry,' 'the rhetoric of science,' or 'the rhetoric of the disciplines and professions,' see Nelson, Megill and McCloskey (1987) and Simons (1989, 1990). For work specifically on the rhetoric of design, see Ackerman and Oates (1996), Cuff (1985, 1989, 1991), Dunlap (1992), Fischer and Forester (1993), Fleming (1996, 1997), Forester (1989), Margolin (1989), Medway (1996), and Schon (1983).

2 Whyte (1988) also gives primary place in urban studies to the street; for him, it is 'the river of life of the city' (p. 7).

3 In the interests of space, I have omitted a fourth theory of urban design of potential interest to rhetoricians and argumentation theorists, that described in Kevin Lynch's 1981 book *Good City Form*. Lynch's book is primarily concerned with the adaptation of form to individual behavior; because of this, and because it is presented at such an abstract level, it is somewhat different from the other three books discussed in this paper. Lynch proposes a set of five performance dimensions for gauging such adaptation: vitality, sense, fit, access, and control. Two additional dimensions are meta-criteria, always appended to the others: efficiency and justice. *Vitality* is the degree to which settlement form supports and protects human biological requirements and capabilities, like sustenance and safety. These are values very widely held, Lynch argues. *Sense* is the degree to which a settlement can be mentally perceived, differentiated, and structured. The first component of a 'sensible' settlement is identity, the extent to which a person can recognize a place as unique. The second component of sense is structure, the extent to which one knows where one is and how other places are connected to it. Such orientation enhances access, enlarges opportunity, and reduces confusion. Other components of sense are congruence, the match between spatial and non-spatial structures; transparency, the degree to which one can perceive how the settlement works; legibility, the degree to which residents can communicate via symbolic features; and, finally, significance, the degree to which the settlement form as a whole communicates certain values, processes, history, the nature of the universe, etc. *Fit* is the degree to which settlement form matches the actions people engage in or want to engage in. But 'action' here is mostly labor and work-oriented; and, in fact, the first example concerns factory labor and the extent to which physical form impedes or enables behavior. The key criterion for fit is adaptability, the ability of a place to be adapted to future functions. *Access* is the ability to reach other persons (e.g., family, friends, etc.), activities (residence, work, recreation), material resources (food, water, etc.), places (shelter, open space, landscapes), and information. Key criteria for measuring this dimension include equity, diversity of accessible resources, and control over access. Finally,

control is the degree to which use and access to settlement form are controlled by its users. Lynch distinguishes among many different kinds of control: right of presence, right of use and action, right of appropriation, right of modification, and right of disposition. The dimensions of good control are congruence, the extent to which the actual or potential users of a space control it; responsibility, the extent to which those who control a place have the commitment, power, and information to do it well; and certainty, the degree to which people understand the control system.

[4] See Gordon and Richardson (1997) and Ewing (1997) for a recent exchange on the benefits and ills of 'sprawl.'

REFERENCES

Ackerman, J. and S. Oates: 1996, 'Image, Text, and Power in Architectural Design and Workplace Writing', in A. H. Duin and C. J. Hansen (eds.), *Nonacademic Writing: Social Theory and Technology*, Lawrence Erlbaum, Hillsdale, NJ.

Alexander, C., S. Ishikawa and M. Silverstein (with M. Jacobson, I. Fiksdahl-King and S. Angel): 1977, *A Pattern Language: Towns, Buildings, Construction*, Oxford UP, New York.

Arendt, H.: 1958, *The Human Condition*, University of Chicago Press, Chicago.

Bellah, R. N., R. Madsen, W. M. Sullivan, A. Swidler and S. M. Tipton: 1985, *Habits of the Heart: Individualism and Commitment in American Life*, Harper & Row, New York.

Bellah, R. N., R. Madsen, W. M. Sullivan, A. Swidler and S. M. Tipton: 1991, *The Good Society*, Alfred A. Knopf, New York.

Bender, T.: 1984, 'The Erosion of Public Cultures: Cities, Discourses, and Professional Disciplines', in T. L. Haskell (ed.), *The Authority of Experts: Studies in History and Theory*, Indiana UP, Bloomington, pp. 84–106.

Booth, W. C.: 1974, *Modern Dogma and the Rhetoric of Assent*, University of Chicago Press, Chicago.

Calthorpe, P.: 1994, 'The Region', in P. Katz (ed.), *The New Urbanism: Toward an Architecture of Community*, McGraw-Hill, New York, pp. xi–xvi.

Cicero: 1968, *De inventione*, Trans. H. M. Hubbell, Harvard UP, Cambridge, MA.

Crick, B.: 1962/1992, *In Defense of Politics*, 4th ed., University of Chicago Press, Chicago.

Cuff, D.: 1985, 'Collaboration and the Ideal of Individualism in Architecture', in P. Heyer and S. Grabow (eds.), *Architecture and the Future: Proceedings of the 72nd Annual Meeting of the Association of Collegiate Schools of Architecture*, 1984, ACSA, Washington, DC, pp. 188–195.

Cuff, D.: 1989, 'Mirrors of Power: Reflective Professionals in the Neighborhood', in J. Wolch and M. Dear (eds.), *The Power of Geography: How Territory Shapes Social Life*, Unwin Hyman, Boston, pp. 331–350.

Cuff, D.: 1991, *Architecture: The Story of Practice*, MIT Press, Cambridge, MA.

D'Entrèves, M. P.: 1994, *The Political Philosophy of Hannah Arendt*, Routledge, London.

De Romilly, J.: 1992, *The Great Sophists in Periclean Athens*, Trans. J. Lloyd, Clarendon Press, Oxford.

Duany, A. and E. Plater-Zyberk: 1994, 'The Neighborhood, the District, and the Corridor', in P. Katz (ed.), *The New Urbanism: Toward an Architecture of Community*, McGraw-Hill, New York, pp. xvii–xx.

Dunlap, L: 1992, 'Advocacy and Neutrality: A Contradiction in the Discourse of Urban Planners', in A. Herrington and C. Moran (eds.), *Writing, Teaching, and Learning in the Disciplines*, Modern Language Association, New York, pp. 213–230.

Elshtain, J. B.: 1995, *Democracy on Trial*, Basic Books, New York.

Ewing, R.: 1997, 'Is Los Angeles–Style Sprawl Desirable?', *Journal of the American Planning Association* 63(1), 107–126.

Fischer[,] F. and J. Forester (eds.): 1993, *The Argumentative Turn in Policy Analysis and Planning*, Duke UP, Durham, NC.

Fleming, D.: 1996, 'Professional-Client Discourse in Design: Variation in Accounts of Social Roles and Material Artifacts by Designers and Their Clients', *Text* 16(2), 133–160.

Fleming, D.: 1997, 'Learning to Link Artifact and Value: The Arguments of Student Designers', *Language and Learning Across the Disciplines* 2(1), 58–84.

Forester, J.: 1989, *Planning in the Face of Power*, University of California Press, Berkeley.

Gaonkar, D. P.: 1990, 'Rhetoric and Its Double: Reflections on the Rhetorical Turn in the Human Sciences', in H. W. Simons (eds.), *The Rhetorical Turn: Invention and Persuasion in the Conduct of Inquiry,* University of Chicago Press, Chicago.

Gaonkar, D. P.: 1997, 'The Idea of Rhetoric in the Rhetoric of Science', in A. G. Gross and W. M. Keith (eds.), *Rhetorical Hermeneutics: Invention and Interpretation in the Age of Science,* State University of New York Press, Albany, pp. 25–85.

Garreau, J.: 1991, *Edge City: Life on the New Frontier,* Doubleday, New York.

Garver, E.: 1994, *Aristotle's* Rhetoric: *An Art of Character,* University of Chicago Press, Chicago.

Glendon, M. A.: 1991, *Rights Talk: The Impoverishment of Political Discourse,* The Free Press, New York.

Gordon, P. and H. W. Richardson: 1997, 'Are Compact Cities a Desirable Planning Goal?', *Journal of the American Planning Association* 63(1), 95–106.

Gutman, A. and D. Thompson: 1996, *Democracy and Disagreement,* Belknap Press (Harvard UP), Cambridge, MA.

Habermas, J.: 1970, *Toward a Rational Society: Student Protest, Science, and Politics,* Trans. J. J. Shapro, Beacon Press, Boston.

Habermas, J.: 1962/1989: *The Structural Transformation of the Public Sphere: An Inquiry into a Category of Bourgeois Society,* Trans. T. Burger with F. Lawrence, MIT Press, Cambridge, MA.

Halloran, S. M.: 1982, 'Rhetoric in the American College Curriculum: The Decline of Public Discourse', *Pre/Text* 3(3), 245–269.

Jacobs, J.: 1961, *The Death and Life of Great American Cities,* Random House, New York.

Katz, P.: 1994, *The New Urbanism: Toward an Architecture of Community,* McGraw-Hill, New York.

Kay, J. H.: 1997, *Asphalt Nation: How the Automobile Took Over America, and How We Can Take it Back,* Crown, New York.

Kostoff, S.: 1991, *The City Shaped: Urban Patterns and Meanings through History,* Bullfinch Press (Little Brown), Boston.

Kowinski, W. S.: 1985, *The Malling of America: An Inside Look at the Great Consumer Paradise,* William Morrow, New York.

Kunstler, J. H.: 1993, *The Geography of Nowhere: The Rise and Decline of America's Man-Made Landscape,* Simon & Schuster, New York.

Lasch, C.: Spring, 1990, 'Journalism, Publicity, and the Lost Art of Argument', *Gannett Center Journal,* n.p.

Lynch, K.: 1981, *Good City Form,* MIT Press, Cambridge, MA.

MacIntyre, A.: 1981, *After Virtue, A Study in Moral Theory,* Notre Dame, UP, Notre Dame, IN.

Margolin, V. (ed.): 1989, *Design Discourse: History, Theory, Criticism,* University of Chicago Press, Chicago.

Medway, P.: 1996, 'Virtual and Material Buildings: Construction and Constructivism in Architecture and Writing', *Written Communication* 13(4), 473–514.

Meier, C.: 1980/1990, *The Greek Discovery of Politics,* Trans. D. McLintock, Harvard UP, Cambridge, MA.

Miller, C. R.: 1993, 'The *Polis* as Rhetorical Community', *Rhetorica* 11(3), 211–240.

Mooney, M.: 1985, *Vico in the Tradition of Rhetoric,* Princeton UP, Princeton.

Moule, E. and S. Polyzoides: 1994, 'The Street, The Block, and the Building', in P. Katz (ed.), *The New Urbanism: Toward an Architecture of Community,* McGraw-Hill, New York, pp. xxi–xxiv.

Murray, O.: 1990, 'Cities of Reason', in O. Murray and S. Price (eds.), *The Greek City from Homer to Alexander,* Clarendon Press, Oxford, pp. 1–25.

Neel, J.: 1988, *Plato, Derrida, and Writing,* Southern Illinois UP, Carbondale.

Nelson, J. S., A. Megill and D. N. McCloskey (eds.): 1987, *The Rhetoric of the Human Sciences: Language and Argument in Scholarship and Public Affairs,* University of Wisconsin Press, Madison.

Plato: 1956, *Protagoras and Meno,* Trans. W. K. C. Guthrie, Penguin, London.

Pocock, J. G. A.: 1975, *The Machiavellian Moment: Florentine Political Thought and the Atlantic Republican Tradition,* Princeton UP, Princeton.

Rybczynski, W.: 1995, *City Life: Urban Expectations in a New World,* Scribner, New York.

Schiappa, E.: 1991, *Protagoras and Logos: A Study in Greek Philosophy and Rhetoric,* University of South Carolina Press, Columbia, SC.

Schön, D. A.: 1983, *The Reflective Practitioner: How Professionals Think in Action,* Basic Books, New York.

Scully, V.: 1994, 'The Architecture of Community', in P. Katz (ed.), *The New Urbanism: Toward an Architecture of Community,* McGraw-Hill, New York, pp. 221–230.

Seigel, J. E.: 1968, *Rhetoric and Philosophy in Renaissance Humanism: The Union of Eloquence and Wisdom,* Petrarch to Valla, Princeton UP, Princeton.

Sennett, R.: 1977, *The Fall of Public Man,* Alfred A. Knopf, New York.

Simons, H. W. (ed.): 1989, *Rhetoric in the Human Sciences,* Sage, London.

Simons, H. W. (ed.): 1990, *The Rhetorical Turn: Invention and Persuasion in the Conduct of Inquiry,* University of Chicago Press, Chicago.

Sorkin, M. (ed.): 1992, *Variations on a Theme Park: The New American City and the End of Public Space,* Holt, New York.

Stotsky, S.: 1991, *Connecting Civic Education and Language Education: The Contemporary Challenge,* Teachers College Press, New York.

Toulmin, S.: 1992, 'Logic, Rhetoric & Reason: Redressing the Balance', in F. H. van Eemeren, R. Grootendorst, J. A. Blair and C. A. Willard (eds.), *Argumentation Illuminated,* SICSAT, Amsterdam, pp. 3–11.

van Eemeren, F. H. and R. Grootendorst: 1992, *Argumentation, Communication, and Fallacies: A Pragma-Dialectical Perspective,* Lawrence Erlbaum, Hillsdale, NJ.

Vernant, J.-P.: 1962/1982, *The Origins of Greek Thought,* Cornell UP, Ithaca, NY.

Walton, D. N.: 1989, *Informal Logic: A Handbook for Critical Argumentation,* Cambridge UP, Cambridge.

'Whatever Became of the Public Square?': 1990, Forum with J. Hitt, R. L. Fleming, E. Plater-Zyberk, R. Sennett, J. Wines, and E. Zimmerman, *Harper's* (July), pp. 49–60.

Whyte, W. H.: 1988, *City: Rediscovering the Center,* Doubleday, New York.

Wycherley, R. E.: 1947/1969, *How the Greeks Built Cities,* 2nd ed. Garden City, Doubleday, NY.

Wirth, L: 1938, 'Urbanism as a Way of Life', *The American Journal of Sociology* 44(1), 1–24.

Yunis, H.: 1996, *Taming Democracy: Models of Political Rhetoric in Classical Athens,* Cornell UP, Ithaca, NY.

··

The Search for Grounds in Legal Argumentation: A Rhetorical Analysis of *Texas v. Johnson*

S. J. BALTER

Legal opinions are essentially rhetorical documents; they pronounce a decision then justify that decision through a series of arguments aimed at particular audiences. Although law has often been identified as an archetype of practical argument, legal arguments must adhere to a stricter level of scrutiny then many other types of argument because courts must not only reach a decision in a particular case, but also justify the authority of the legal system. Jurgen Habermas in his work *Between Facts and Norms,* an exhaustive analysis of the legal system, notes,

> In order to fulfill the socially integrative function of the legal order and the legitimacy claim of law, court rulings must satisfy simultaneously the conditions of *consistent decision making* and *rational acceptability* (1994, p. 198) (emphasis in origin).

Thus, courts are ever mindful of the particular constraints under which they must operate.

Court decisions, particularly those written by members of the Supreme Court, are scrutinized by a variety of audiences including the other members of the Court, lower courts, members of the legal community at large, the media and the public (Golden and Makau, 1982). These audiences constrain the possible means of persuasion that may be incorporated into a judicial opinion. These constraints serve to limit the types of arguments that may be made in a case, the types of evidence that may be used to support the argument, and the very form that the argument may take (Ferguson, 1990; White, 1990). Although it will come as no surprise to argumentation and legal scholars that Supreme Court justices create their arguments under serve constraints, much can be learned by isolating the strategies that justices use to negotiate these constraints. These strategies, especially in highly disputed cases, provide argumentation scholars the opportunity to uncover the grounds that judges use to maintain and create the law.

Legal argumentation covers a wide variety of issues. Each issue contains a different set of questions that must be addressed by the Court when writing a decision. Free speech cases provide a limited set of non-legal concepts that the judge may integrate into the decision. These concepts, which are of particular interest to argumentation and rhetorical scholars, include the speaker, the speech, and the audience for the speech. The interpretation of these materials in the case is one way by which a justice may create an argument that works within the constraints imposed by the legal community while simultaneously creating new argument.

In this article, I will examine the way in which the majority and dissenting opinions in the Supreme Court case of *Texas v. Johnson* use the concept of 'audience' to ground their different decisions. It is useful to pause here to clarify the concept of audience as used by the Court. There are four types of audiences that may be invoked in any free speech case, two of which shape the opinion and two of which exist in the opinion. The first two audiences, the reading audience and the empirical audience, exist outside of the opinion and function to control the types of arguments that may be made in the opinion. The third and fourth audiences, the constructed actual audience and the event's attributed audience, only exist within the opinion. They are rhetorically constructed by the justice; neither is an exact representation of the empirical audience but they are based on the empirical audience and on broader conceptions of the public.

The first of these audiences is one that exists outside of the case. This audience, which I refer to as the reading audience, consists of any possible individual who the justice writing an opinion believes may read the decision. This audience transcends any individual decision; it exists prior to the case, the justices write the opinion with this audience in mind, and it exists after the opinion is written. This audience serves as a check on the argumentation used in the opinion; it is the Court's universal audience (Christie, 1986).

The second audience that shapes the opinion is the audience that was present for the speech event being considered by the Court. In *Texas v. Johnson,* the event that precipitated the case was the burning of an American flag. Thus, the audience present for this event were those who witnessed the flag being burned. This audience does not appear in the decision, indeed it is only present at the moment of the event, but is the foundation for the arguments that the justices will make about the audience in the opinion. This audience is an empirical audience, it could have only been observed at the moment of the event, it can never be fully represented in the decision.

There are two types of audiences that appear in the opinion: the constructed actual audience and the event's attributed audience. The constructed actual audience refers to individuals who were present at the event; it would describe the actions and reactions of particular individuals as they witnessed the flag burning. The event's attributed audience does not make mention of a particular individual, but instead refers to the public as an abstract entity that is imbued with the judge's vision of how an audience should or would react. The constructed actual audience is based on the real while the event's attributed audience is based on an ideal. Or, to use Habermas' distinctions, when judges create a constructed actual audience they are relying on claims of truth; when they use the event's attributed audience they are relying on normative claims (1984).

Texas v. Johnson provides a strong case study for a number of reasons. First, the issue being decided in the case, whether flag burning should be protected as expression under the First Amendment, is highly controversial. Although the Court had heard many flag desecration cases prior to this one, this case marked the first time that the Court dealt directly with the issue of flag burning (Hundley, 1997). Immediately after the Court announced its opinion, both President George W. Bush and the Congress initiated efforts to pass a constitutional amendment to ban flag burning (Pollitt, 1992). This opinion continues to have repercussions in the American political sphere. Second, this issue invokes many accepted American values and the Court is forced to construct hierarchies to justify its opinion, thus scholars can view the positioning of value arguments by the Court. Third, Brennan's majority and Rehnquist's dissenting opinions offer vastly different audiences that serve to frame the use of precedent invoked in the case. This case provides an excellent illustration of how constructions of audience in the opinion serve as the grounds for legal argument. Finally, because the case involves issues at the core of democracy, the right to protest and the right to preserve symbols of nationhood, it allows scholars insight into the Court's construction of its own place in the American political sphere.

1. NEGOTIATING JUDICIAL CONSTRAINTS

The Supreme Court of the United States is under pressure in any given case to not only come to a decision in the case being decided, but to also uphold its legitimacy as the final arbiter of American law. Thus, each opinion is constrained in three ways; by the facts of the particular case, by the prior law that the reading audience believes must be read in relation to the current fact situation, and by the reading audience's expectations that the Court will behave in a fashion that upholds its own legitimacy. The first of these constraints, as I will illustrate in the case of *Texas v. Johnson*, provides judges the most freedom in the construction of an argument. The second and third constraints are not formally codified; they exist in authors' conceptions of the expectations of their reading audience. The reading audience judges the correctness of a justice's interpretation of the law, and the author of the opinion internalizes this judgment. James Boyd White has argued that every opinion issued by the Supreme Court serves two purposes, it pronounces a decision and it validates the Court's reasoning in that decision (1988). Owen Fiss claims that these constraints 'constitute the institution in which judges find themselves and through which they act' (1988, p. 233). Both of these theories, while not explicitly defining the particular constraints that Supreme Court Justices find themselves negotiating, underscore the importance of understanding the argument strategies employed by the Court.

Stare decisis is the most pressing constraint on a Supreme Court Justice. The Justice is under a great deal of pressure to uphold the law as it has been previously decided. Golden and Makau note, 'Use of stare decisis gives the court's readers greater confidence in the Justice's impartiality' (Golden and Makau, 1982, p. 160).

The tapestry of the law forms the backdrop for the finding of any particular case. The author of an opinion must weave his or her finding into the cloth in such a way as not to radically disrupt the patterns that the audience has come to expect for the type of case being decided. These patterns consist of the materials that a justice may use to justify the opinion including the constitution, state law, and prior court cases. Stare decisis may account for what Paul Campos claims is the 'hyper-trophied . . . species of bureaucratized document' that has come to characterize the modern Court decision (1993, p. 855).

Stanley Fish contributes the notion of the 'interpretive community' to an understanding of legal argument. The interpretive community is reminiscent of Perelman and Olbrechts-Tyteca's theory of audience. Perelman and Olbrechts-Tyteca argue that the primary criteria for whether an argument is reasonable are the universal audience. This audience is bounded by the culture; a culture shared by both the speaker and the audience (1969, p. 33). Fish's interpretive communities distinguish these boundaries; he defines the cultural expectations under which both the Supreme Court and its audience operate.

Fish's theory of interpretive communities provides valuable insight into the norms of the legal community. The interpretive community of the law legitimizes a way of thinking about the law that is inculcated into its practitioners at each level of participation from law school through judgeship. Central to this socialization is the judicial opinion, it is studied by law students, read by lawyers, and written in respect to other opinions by judges. The judge must begin the discourse with a particular case; past cases are read in relation to the present circumstances. The community expects that the present case will be understood in relation to the past, but the present case also molds the past. Yet these constraints also free the opinion writer to manipulate the texts on which the opinion is based, as long as this manipulation is justified within the bounds of the community's expectations. Fish writes,

> Interpreters are constrained by their tacit awareness of what is possible and not possible to do, what is and is not a reasonable thing to say, what will and will not be heard as evidence in a given enterprise; and it is within these same constraints that they see and bring others to see the shape of the documents to whose interpretation they are committed (1989, p. 98).

Stanley Fish explains that the materials that the judge uses to justify an opinion are constrained, but he does not explain precisely the expectations the reading audience has for using these materials as grounds for an argument. Ronald Dworkin's theory of interpretation is an attempt to determine how materials are used to support a legal argument. His position complements Fish's interpretive communities; Dworkin is interested in what counts as good evidence in a judicial opinion given the expectations of the community. Fish and Dworkin are not often read as complementary writers; Fish is decidedly anti-foundationalist while Dworkin is committed to the notion that law has integrity. However, taken together, their theories of judicial constraint provide a picture of how judges create and support arguments within the expectations of their reading audience.

Dworkin views judicial opinion writing as argumentation. His primary goal is to discover the grounds of legal argument that serve as valid starting points for the legal community. His work exemplifies the constraints placed by the audience on Supreme Court opinions; his search for correct interpretation of the law is an explanation of what first principles are accepted by the legal community.

Dworkin is in search of these theoretical disagreements, or what he calls 'law's grounds.' Like Stanley Fish, Dworkin notes that the community determines the grounds for legal argument:

> Legal practice, unlike many other social phenomena, is argumentative. Every actor in the practice understands that what it permits or requires depends on certain propositions that are given sense only by and within the practice; the practice consists in large part in deploying and arguing about these propositions. People who have law make and debate claims about what law permits or forbids that would be impossible . . . without law and a good part of what their law reveals about them cannot be discovered except by noticing how they ground and defend these claims (1986, p. 13).

For Dworkin, interpretation should be constructive. He defines this as, 'a matter of imposing purpose on an object or practice in order to make of it the best possible example of the form or genre to which it belongs' (1986, p. 53). Following Gadamer's theory, Dworkin notes that the object under question is constrained by the history of a practice. An interpreter of social practices, of which law is a subset, engages in creative interpretation. Creative interpretations using a constructive approach is 'a matter of interaction between purpose and object' (1986, p. 52). The purpose, or context, of the interpretation sets the standards by which an object is to be judged. Dworkin does not believe that context provides an Archemdian point, but allows for a judgment to be made about an interpretation.

There are three stages, or steps, to interpretation in Dworkin's theory. The first is called the 'preinterpretive' stage. During this time, 'the rules and standards taken to provide the tentative content of the practice are identified' (1986, pp. 65–66). According to Dworkin, there is a strong need for consensus at this stage in order to preserve harmony amongst the interpretive community. This is when the raw materials of interpretation are decided upon. A judge must determine what counts as evidence to the audience in terms of the particular decision being rendered.

The second stage is called the 'interpretative stage.' During this period the interpreter, 'settles on some general justification for the main elements of the practice identified at the preinterpretive stage' (1986, p. 66). Here the interpreter finds a value judgment that shows the practice of law at its best. For Dworkin, this act of justification is solitary, but is performed against the knowledge of the values of the community. This step parallels Perelman and Olbrechts-Tyteca's vision of the persuader who creates a message alone but is always mindful of the standards of the universal audience.

The justification process involves two types of issues: does the justification 'fit' the practice that is being interpreted, and what types of substantive issues would show the practice in the best light? The justification for both of these issues includes an argument as to why the decision is worth pursuing; what values does it uphold for the community? The second stage allows judges to escape the constraints of the legal community, if only for a moment. It is in this stage that a judge frames the opinion and establishes the value hierarchy to which the legal materials gathered in the pre-interpretive stage will be applied. Here judges may mold the facts to support the value hierarchy being advanced by their opinions.

Finally, there is a 'postinterpretive' or 'reforming' stage. During this stage interpreters adjust their conception of what is 'really require(d) so as better to serve the justification he accepts at the interpretive stage' (1986, p. 66). Dworkin notes that, in the real world, interpretive judgments do not progress cleanly through each of these stages, but instead they are more a matter of, 'seeing at once the dimensions of their practice, a purpose or aim in that practice, and the post-interpretive consequence of that purpose' (1986, p. 67).

Dworkin's most valuable contribution to understanding judicial argument is his explanation of why conflicts of interpretation occur. He identifies core beliefs that can be used by an interpreter to explain where interpretations differ,

> at the first level, agreement collects around discrete ideas that are uncontroversially employed in all interpretations; at the second the controversy latent in this abstraction is identified and taken up. Exposing this structure may help to sharpen argument and will in any case improve the community's understanding of its intellectual environment (1986, p. 71).

At the abstract level, there is no controversy, it is only when values are applied to concrete issues that interpretations differ. This echoes Perelman and Olbrechts-Tyteca's claim that it is only the creation of hierarchies, necessitated by particular concerns that will bring values into conflict (1969, p. 80).

Value arguments play a pivotal role in the justification of legal argument. However, these value arguments need connection to particular situations. The particularization of a value construct is done through the creation of a paradigm. Dworkin argues that the paradigms play a more important role in legal argumentation than abstract value propositions,

> The role the paradigms play in reasoning and argument will be even more crucial than any abstract agreement over a concept. For the paradigms will be treated as concrete examples any plausible interpretation must fit, and argument against an interpretation will take the form, whenever this is possible, of showing that it fails to include or account for a paradigm case (1986, p. 72).

Conceptions are values; universal and timeless, but they cannot be brought into the opinion without a connection to the events that precipitated the controversy being decided. Paradigms are specific to a particular set of events, they are the application of values.

Dworkin draws the most criticism from his claim that law has integrity. While this statement may not seem problematic on its face, Dworkin uses the notion of integrity to ground what he considers to be a valid interpretation,

> Law as integrity asks judges to assume, so far as this is possible, that the law is structured by a coherent set of principles about justice and fairness and procedural due process, and it asks them to enforce these in the fresh cases that come before them, so that each person's situation is fair and just according to the same standards (1986, p. 239).

Integrity in law accounts in some measure for the constraints placed on the judge. There is an expectation that judges will justify their opinion by relating it to other cases; i.e. use precedent. If the finding of the case is different than other cases like it, the judge must distinguish the present case from those that came before it.

Habermas embraces Dworkin's project in his proposal for a reconstructive approach to law and legal argument in his work *Between Facts and Norms*. As with many of Habermas's works, this book covers a wide range of issues dealing with the law, but as David Rasmussen observes, Habermas's primary goal is to discover what makes law valid (1996). Habermas argues that law claims validity, in part, through the process of legal argumentation. Law must negotiate the tensions between facts and norms; that is, it must be both applicable to a specific case and speak to a possible future cases. Habermas explains:

> We can think of the hermeneutical process of norm application as weaving together a description of the circumstances and a concretization of general norms. What finally decides the issue is the meaning equivalence between the description of facts making up part of the interpretation of the situation and the description of the facts that sets out the descriptive component of the norm, that is, its application conditions (1994, p. 218).

Thus, in order for a justice to create a legitimate argument about an interpretation of the law, that justice must use as grounds those elements of the case that clarify the norm being constructed by the Court.

Fish, Dworkin, and Habermas contribute two important concepts to a theory of legal argumentation. First, argumentation takes place against the expectations of a community. This community functions to provide the material for interpretation, as well as constrain how that interpretation is judged. Second, there is a sense of the political inherent in the community. Institutions are created by human beings and they reflect the concerns of humanity. Law is a social system that must serve not only its own interests, but also those of the lifeworld of which it is a part. Justices create arguments that reaffirm the value of law, the principle of integrity.

Often, cases that invoke first amendment precedent are conflicts between the government and an individual. Jurists are asked to interpret the Constitution or to decide if a state or federal statute conflicts with their interpretation of first amendment protections. These cases invoke classic questions of hermeneutic theory—how do justices read precedent in relation to the complexities of speech rights in the present?

Dworkin notes,

> Contemporary lawyers and judges must try to find a political justification of the First Amendment that fits most past constitutional practice, including past decisions of the Supreme Court, and also provides a compelling reason why we should grant freedom of speech such a special and privileged place among our liberties (1996, p. 199).

The Supreme Court, when faced with a free speech case, must balance the needs of the community with its decision in a particular case.

The legal community expects that certain materials, most notably similar cases, will be used to justify the decision a judge is making [in a] particular case. Yet these cases alone cannot establish a conclusion in a particular case. Drucilla Cornell points out, 'no line of precedent can fully determine a particular outcome in a particular case because the rule itself is always in the process of reinterpretation as it is applied. It is interpretation that gives us the rule, not the other way around' (1992, p. 157).

Non-legal concepts allow judges a moment of freedom in argumentation. During the first stage of the decision making process, a judge must determine the relevant facts. Although the issue bounds these determinations, this step allows a judge to determine the raw materials of a case. These facts are not nearly as constrained as the precedent used in the decision. In the case I have chosen to illustrate this point,

Texas v. Johnson, each opinion creates visions of the constructed actual audience and the event's attributed audience that were present at the burning of the flag to shape its application of precedent.

2. *TEXAS v. JOHNSON*

During the 1984 Republican National Convention in Dallas, Gregory Lee Johnson participated in a march to protest the policies of the Reagan administration and the activities of some Dallas based corporations. At the end of the march, in front of the Dallas City Hall, Johnson was handed a flag that he burned while other protesters chanted 'America, the red, white and blue, we spit on you' (*Texas v. Johnson,* 1989, p. 399). Johnson was the only one of the protesters to be arrested for the demonstration. He was charged with desecration of a venerated object in violation of the Texas Penal Code.

In a 5-4 decision, the Supreme Court held that the Texas statute infringed on Johnson's speech rights. Four opinions appear in this case: a majority opinion authored by William Brennan, a very brief concurring opinion written by Anthony Kennedy, a long and passionate dissent authored by William Rehnquist, and a short dissent authored by John Paul Stevens. While all four opinions provide insight into the Court's battle over this divisive issue, for the purpose of this article I will concentrate only on Brennan's majority and Rehnquist's dissent. These two opinions provide the clearest articulations of the constitutional issues being decided in this case.

The majority opinion, written by Justice Brennan, divided the issues in the case into two: (1) was Johnson's burning of the flag expressive conduct, and (2) if his conduct was expressive, was the State's regulation of it related to the suppression of his message? Brennan created a quasi-logical frame for his argument; if the State intended to regulate viewpoints, then the Court must apply strict scrutiny to the Texas law. If the State did not intend to ban a particular message, then the Court would apply a more lenient standard in order to judge the constitutionality of the statute. Kent Greenwalt notes that this argument is of major importance in the decision because had the Court applied the more lenient standard to the Texas statute, Johnson's conviction would have been upheld (1990).

Brennan examined Texas's two justifications for its statute (1) that it prevented breaches of the peace, and (2) that it preserved the flag as a symbol of national unity. The majority opinion argued that the first justification was not supported given the facts in the case. Although some members of the actual audience reported that they were seriously offended by Johnson's message, no actual disturbance occurred. Brennan then argued that Texas's second justification was, in fact, a viewpoint regulation because the statute was only intended to punish those who burned the flag in protest. These two major themes are the basis of the majority decision and constructions of audience are integral to both arguments.

The constructed actual audience is used by the majority opinion in order to dismiss Texas's claim that it was trying to prevent a breach of the peace. Brennan begins by recounting the scene that culminated with Johnson's burning of the flag, highlighting only the aftermath of the demonstration, 'After the demonstrators dispersed, a witness to the flag burning collected the flag's remains and buried them in his backyard' (p. 399). Brennan continues his interpretation of the constructed actual audience by noting that, 'No one was physically injured or threatened with injury, though several witnesses testified that they had been seriously offended by the flag burning' (p. 399). This interpretation of the audience establishes two of the premises that Brennan will base his argument upon. First, because there was no threat to the actual audience, Johnson's speech rights should be paramount. Second, the interpretation of a message as offensive was not sufficient justification for abridging speech rights because no breach of the peace was likely from Johnson's action. These constructed audiences are presented before Brennan actually makes the argument that there was no likelihood of a breach of the peace, thus setting the stage for his conclusion.

When Brennan does finally approach the question of whether flag burning was likely to lead to a breach of the peace, he privileges the use of the constructed actual audience. Brennen first restates Texas's version of the event's attributed audience, 'The State's position, therefore, amounts to a claim that an audience that takes serious offense at particular expression is necessarily likely to disturb the peace and that the expression may be prohibited on this basis' (p. 408). He rejects the use of an event's attributed audience for determining the likelihood of breach of the peace, 'we have not permitted the government to assume that every expression of a provocative idea will incite a riot, but have instead required careful consideration of the actual circumstances surrounding such expression . . .' (p. 409). This dovetails nicely with his own constructions of audience to argue that Texas did not have a legitimate interest in preventing a breach of the peace in this particular case. In essence, Brennan is arguing that there can be no normative statement that warns of breach of the peace; this law can only be enforced after a disruption actually occurs.

Brennan then uses the lower court's constructed actual audience to reinforce his argument, 'the flag burning in this particular case did not threaten such a reaction. "Serious offense occurred," the court admitted, "but there was no breach of peace nor does the record reflect that the situation was potentially explosive"' (p. 401). His argument stays consistent by developing the constructed actual audience as support for the argument that no breach of the peace was likely as a result of Johnson's burning of the flag. Thus Brennan is able to simultaneously create a justification for protecting Johnson's message while maintaining a consistent application of precedent that he supports with reference to the *Brandenburg* decision.

Brennan does, however, offer an event's attributed audience to argue that restrictions on flag burning could not be justified by classifying Johnson's action as fighting words. 'No reasonable onlooker would have regarded Johnson's generalized expression of dissatisfaction with the policies of the Federal Government as a direct personal insult or an invitation to exchange fisticuffs' (p. 409). This event's attributed audience does not hold the flag as a personal symbol, but is able to distinguish a critique of the government from their own emotional response concerning the importance of the flag. Also note that Brennan creates a norm of the 'reasonable listener' that privileges critical thinking and the ability to make distinctions about messages in the heat of an emotionally charged protest (Lewis, 1994).

Brennan primarily uses the event's attributed audience to argue that Texas's second stated interest, to protect the flag as a national symbol, is a violation of the first amendment because it is a restriction of a particular point of view. He presents his version of Texas's event's attributed audience in order to show that the Texas law would stifle expression critical of the flag,

> The State apparently is concerned that such conduct will lead people to believe
> either that the flag does not stand for nationhood and national unity, but

instead reflects other, less positive concepts, or that the concepts reflected in the flag do not exist, that is, that we do not enjoy unity as a Nation (p. 410).

The majority opinion ends with Brennan's event's attributed audience, one that is expressly contrasted with Texas's version of this audience,

> We can imagine no more appropriate response to burning a flag than waving one's own, no better way to counter a flag burner's message than by saluting the flag that burns, no surer means of preserving the dignity even of the flag that burned then by—as one witness here did—according its remains a respectful burial. We do not consecrate the flag by punishing its desecration; for in doing so we dilute the freedom this cherished emblem represents (p. 420).

Brennan thus presents an audience who uses expression to counteract the message of flag burning rather than taking serious offense and resorting to violence. This is an attributed audience that would justify the constitutional protections afforded by and protected by the Court; it is an audience that needs freedom to pursue the democratic values of protest and counter-protest.

The majority opinion's constructed and attributed audiences provide powerful justifications for protecting speech. When the reading audience is presented these visions of audience, they are persuaded that Johnson's speech should not be abridged by the State. Texas's reasons for restricting flag burning are premised on protecting (1) the safety of the people and (2) the sanctity of the symbol of the American flag. Brennan's construction of a public that can dissociate themselves from the emotionally stirring visual image of the flag burning and recognize the values inherent in allowing this type of expression are neither likely to riot nor likely to disrespect the values that the flag represents.

Rehnquist authored a powerful dissenting opinion, on which Byron White and Sandra Day O'Connor join. He focused much of his long dissent on the unique role the flag plays in ensuring American unity and nationhood (Dry, 1990). Rehnquist devotes nearly one half of his opinion to a history of the United States that places the flag at the center of its nationhood. Throughout this part of the dissent, the flag is equated with America's war efforts and Rehnquist repeatedly quotes the sentiments of soldiers about the importance of the flag to their efforts. Readers of this dissent are immediately situated in the emotional realm; Rehnquist does not begin to argue the points of law until he finishes this exhaustive tribute to the flag. It is only after the value of the flag has been established that Rehnquist refutes the primary contentions of the majority opinion. He argues that flag burning is not expression; it is likely to cause a breach of the peace, and the state has a legitimate interest in protecting the integrity of the symbol. Rehnquist uses conceptions of the collective as evidence for each of his arguments.

Rehnquist begins his support of Texas's justification for its statute by equating flag burning with fighting words, 'his (Johnson's) act, like Chaplinsky's provocative words, conveyed nothing that could not have been conveyed and was not conveyed just as forcefully in a dozen different ways' (p. 431). After this analogy is made, he uses an event's attributed audience to justify the restriction of flag burning, 'The highest source of several States have upheld state statutes prohibiting the public burning of the flag on the grounds that it is so inherently inflammatory that it may cause a breach of public order' (p. 431). Interestingly, Rehnquist does not take up Brennan's challenge to provide specific instances where flag burning has provoked violence; instead he offers an interpretation of a collective that is overcome by the emotional drama of watching a flag burn.

Rehnquist's second main argument is that the state has a legitimate interest in protecting the flag. Rehnquist argues that the reaction of the collective is the most important factor in determining whether to protect flag burning, 'The concept of "desecration" does not turn on the substance of the message the actor intends to convey, but rather on whether those who view the act will take serious offense' (p. 438). This claim is supported by his drawn out history of the emotional attachment that the event's attributed audience would have to the flag. Rehnquist imbues this audience with a 'uniquely deep awe and respect for our flag' (p. 434).

Early in his opinion, Rehnquist notes the importance of the flag to the nation, 'Millions and millions of Americans regard it with an almost mystical reverence regardless of what sort of social, political, or philosophical beliefs they may have' (p. 429). The attributed audience created by Rehnquist is enamored with the power of the symbol. Such a collective would be so overcome by their emotional response that they would not recognize the value of the dissent it was witnessing.

Thus, Rehnquist comes to the conclusion, 'sanctioning the public desecration of the flag will tarnish its value—both for those who cherish the ideas for which it waves and for those who desire to don the robes of martyrdom by burning it' (p. 437). This event's attributed audience is typical of the strategy Rehnquist employs to counter Brennan's majority opinion; he uses his attributed audiences to support his value hierarchy that would place the protection of the symbol of the flag over the expression of dissent.

Brennan and Rehnquist both ground their legal arguments in constructions of audiences. Brennan's visions of audience were more persuasive to a slight majority of the justices; his constructions provide the foundation for protecting individual rights. Although Rehnquist's dissent does not enjoy the support of Brennan's majority, his visions of the audience may provide grounds for future Courts. The two opinions, read against each other, provide very different visions of audience; the majority envisions a public that is able to understand and appreciate dissent even when faced with the shocking vision of a burning venerated object, the dissent envisions a public so invested in the flag that it cannot get past its offense to engage in reasoned communication. In fact, Rehnquist argues emphatically that flag burning is no more than an 'inarticulate grunt', unworthy of constitutional protection (p. 432).

3. IMPLICATIONS AND CONCLUSION

Texas v. Johnson illustrates the power that constructions of the event's attributed audience and constructed actual audience have in defining the law. These characterizations serve not only to ground the decisions of the Court, but also to illustrate the types of arguments that the Court makes about the public that it serves. As Habermas notes:

> Here we find just that intersection of institutional procedure and an argumentation process whose internal structure eludes legal institutionalization. This intersection of two quite different 'procedures'—legal and argumentative—shows that the universe of law can open itself from the inside, as it were, to argumentation processes through which pragmatic, ethical, and moral reasons find their way into the language of law without either inhibiting the argumentation game or rupturing the legal code (1994, p. 178).

The analysis of audience in this case exemplifies Habermas's conception of these two procedures; Brennan and Rehnquist both invoke constructions of audience in order to negotiate the requirements of the legal procedure while creating moral and factual representations of audience to ground their visions of law.

The Supreme Court primarily functions as an epidictic speaker. It establishes value hierarchies as a precursor to action. In free speech cases, the Court must balance the needs of speakers with the interests of the collective. Implicit in this balancing is the creation of a value hierarchy; when the Court rules that one interest is more important than another it is declaring a specific ordering of values. Some of the values called upon in free speech cases—the promotion of a marketplace of ideas, the protection of individual self expression, and the promotion of democratic self government—are what Ronald Dworkin labels as concepts (1986, pp. 70–71). Concepts are universalized values that serve as starting points in legal argument. The audience accepts these values in the abstract; the role of the author of an opinion is to connect these values to the extant case. This is what Dworkin labels the creation of a paradigm.

Paradigms are exceptionally persuasive arguments, but they are not static. Each time a judge encounters a new case he or she has the opportunity to create a new paradigm. Dworkin writes, 'Paradigms anchor interpretations, but no paradigm is secure from challenge by a new interpretation that accounts for other paradigms better and leaves that one isolated as a mistake' (1986, p. 72). In order for a justice to create these new interpretations he or she must explain how the case being decided is distinguished from prior case law. Interpretations of the audience allow judges to make these types of arguments. *Texas v. Johnson* illustrates the power the constructed audience has in forming these paradigms. Brennan was able to successfully argue that the audience values expression over the symbolism of the flag. Rehnquist reverses this hierarchy in the hope that it may some day become a new paradigm. Joseph Raz's theory of the analogical arguments illustrates the role that audience may play in the determination of these contested values. He notes:

> The fact that whichever rule the court adopts is analogical to some existing rule is still relevant in showing that the court is not introducing a new pragmatic conflict, but is supporting one side in existing dispute, so to speak (1979, p. 205).

Rehnquist is thus able to position his construction of audience as a way for a future Court to adopt his paradigm.

Constructions of the audience serve not only to ground legal argument, but to define the public itself. While First Amendment cases present easily identifiable statements about audience, the Court defines publics in many different constitutional conflicts. It would be useful to examine other areas of law in order to uncover the Court's conceptions of publics in different spheres. Habermas believes that the Court is likely to construct norms about the public that reify its position as the arbiter and protector of the Constitution (1994). In other words, the Court is likely to define the public as a body that is able to function in a democratic society; one that is imbued with the abilities that make it a rational decision maker. First Amendment judicial opinions are a natural body of law on which to start the project of determining how we the people are constituted by the Court, but the search for the definitions of public should not end with this set of decisions.

REFERENCES

Campos, P. F.: 1993, 'Advocacy and Scholarship', *California Law Review* 81, 817–861.

Christine, G.: 1986, 'The Universal Audience and Predictive Theories of Law', *Law and Philosophy* 5, 343–350.

Cornell, D.: 1992, 'From the Lighthouse: The Promise of Redemption and the Possibility of Legal Interpretation', in G. Leyh (ed.), *Legal Hermeneutics: History, Theory and Practice,* University of California Press, Berkeley, 147–172.

Dry, M.: 1990, 'Flag Burning and the Constitution', in G. Casper, D. Hutchinson and D. Strauss (eds.), *Supreme Court Review,* University of Chicago, Chicago, 69–104.

Dworkin, R.: 1985, *A Matter of Principle,* Harvard University Press, Cambridge.

Dworkin, R.: 1986, *Law's Empire,* Belknap, Cambridge.

Dworkin, R.: 1996, *Freedom's Law: The Moral Reading of the American Constitution,* Harvard University Press, Cambridge.

Ferguson, R. A.: 1990, 'The Judicial Opinion as Literary Genre', *Yale Journal of Law and the Humanities* 2, 201–219.

Fish, S.: 1989, *Doing What Come Naturally: Change, Rhetoric and the Practice of Theory in Literary and Legal Studies,* Duke University Press, Durham.

Fish, S.: 1994, *There's No Such Thing as Free Speech, and It's a Good Thing, Too,* Oxford University Press, New York.

Fiss, O. M.: 1989, 'Objectivity and Interpretation', in S. Levinson and S. Mailloux (eds.), *Interpreting Law and Literature: A Hermeneutic Reader,* Northwestern University Press, Evanston, 229–249.

Gadamer, H. G.: 1989, *Truth and Method,* J. Weinsheimer and D. Marshall (trans), Continuum, New York.

Golden, J. L. and J. M. Makau: 1982, 'Perspectives on Judicial Reasoning', in R. E. McKerrow (ed.), *Exploration in Rhetoric: Studies in Honor of Douglas Ehninger,* Scott Foresman, Glenview, 157–178.

Greenwalt, K.: 1990, 'O'er the Land of the Free: Flag Burning as Speech', *UCLA Law Review* 37, 925–947.

Habermas, J.: 1984, *The Theory of Communicative Action, Volume 1: Reason and the Rationalization of Society,* T. McCarthy (trans), MIT Press, Cambridge.

Habermas, J.: 1994, *Between Facts and Norms,* W. Rehg (trans), Beacon Press, Boston.

Hundley, H.: 1997, 'The Signification of the American Flag: A Semiotic Analysis of *Texas v. Johnson*', *Free Speech Yearbook* 35, 45–55.

Lewis, W.: 1994, 'Of Innocence, Exclusion, and the Burning of Flags: The Romantic Realism of the Law', *Southern Communication Journal* 60, 4–21.

Makau, J. M.: 1984, 'The Supreme Court and Reasonableness', *Quarterly Journal of Speech* 70, 259–278.

Perelman, C. and L. Olbrechts-Tyteca: 1969, *The New Rhetoric: A Treatise on Argumentation,* J. Wilkinson and P. Weaver (trans), University of Notre Dame Press, Notre Dame.

Perelman, C.: 1963, *The Idea of Justice and the Problem of Argument,* Routledge, London.

Pollitt, D. H.: 1992, 'Reflection on the Bicentennial of the Bill of Rights: The Flag Burning Controversy: A Chronology', *North Carolina Law Review* 70, 553–614.

Rasmussen, D.: 1996, 'How is Valid Law Possible: A Review of Between Facts and Norms by Jurgen Habermas', in M. Deflem (ed.), *Habermas, Modernity and Law,* Sage Publications, London, 21–44.

Raz, J.: 1979, *The Authority of Law: Essays on Law and Morality,* Clarendon Press, Oxford.

Texas v. Johnson: 1989, 491 US 397. US Supreme Court.

Tushnet, M.: 1991, 'Critical Legal Studies: A Political History', *Yale Law Journal* 100, 1515–1541.

Unger, R. M.: 1990, *The Critical Legal Studies Movement,* Harvard University Press, Cambridge.

White, J. B.: 1988, 'Judicial Criticism', in S. Levinson and S. Mailloux (eds.), *Interpreting Law and Literature: A Hermeneutic Reader,* Northwestern University Press, Evanston, 393–410.

White, J. B. 1990, *Justice as Translation,* University of Chicago Press, Chicago.

Selected Bibliography

This selected bibliography includes scholarly articles published in peer-reviewed academic journals and represents argumentation scholarship that complements the essays in this book. Numerous books and conference proceedings are found in the citations of the articles included in this book and listed below. Argumentation conferences that generate proceedings most connected to the topics represented in this text are the International Conference on Argumentation (ISSA), the NCA/AFA Alta Summer Conference on Argumentation, and the Ontario Society for the Study of Argumentation (OSSA).

BODY AS ARGUMENT

Darwin, Thomas. "Intelligent Cells and the Body as Conversation: The Democratic Rhetoric of Mindbody Medicine." *Argumentation and Advocacy* 36 (Fall 1999): 35–49.

Harold, Christine L. "Tracking Heroin Chic: The Abject Body Reconfigures the Rational Argument." *Argumentation and Advocacy* 36 (Fall 1999): 65–76.

Hauser, Gerard. "Incongruous Bodies: Arguments for Personal Sufficiency and Public Insufficiency." *Argumentation and Advocacy* 36 (Summer 1999): 1–8.

Torrens, Kathleen M. "Fashion as Argument: Nineteenth Century Dress Reform." *Argumentation and Advocacy* 36 (Fall 1999): 77–87.

CLASSICAL CONCEPTS

Benjamin, James. "Eristic, Dialectic and Rhetoric." *Communication Quarterly* 31 (Winter 1983): 21–26.

Braet, A. C. "The Oldest Typology of Argumentation Schemes." *Argumentation* 18 (2004): 127–148.

Braet, A. C. "The Common Topic in Aristotle's Rhetoric: Precursor of the Argumentation Scheme." *Argumentation* 19 (2005): 65–83.

Dieter, Otto A. L. "Stasis." *Speech Monographs* 17 (1950): 345–369.

Hill, Hamner H., and Michael Kagan. "Aristotelian Dialectic." *Informal Logic* 17 (Winter 1995): 25–42.

Rubinelli, Sara. "The Ancient Argumentative Game: τόποι and Loci in Action." *Argumentation* 20 (2006): 253–272.

Timmerman, David M. "Ancient Greek Origins of Argumentation Theory: Plato's Transformation of Dialegesthai to Dialectic." *Argumentation and Advocacy* 29 (Winter 1993): 116–123.

CRITICAL DISCUSSION

Henkemans, A. F. Snoeck. "Complex Argumentation in a Critical Discussion." *Argumentation* 17 (2003): 405–419.

Richardson, John, and Albert Atkin. "'You're Being Unreasonable': Prior and Passing Theories of Critical Discussion." *Argumentation* 20 (2006): 149–166.

van Eemeren, Frans H. and Rob Grootendorst. "A Pragma-Dialectical Procedure for a Critical Discussion." *Argumentation* 17 (2003): 365–386.

CULTURE AND DIFFERENCE

Bench-Capon, T. J. M. "Agreeing to Differ: Modeling Persuasive Dialogue Between Parties with Different Values." *Informal Logic* 22 (Fall 2002): 231–245.

Combs, Steven C. "Challenging Greco-Roman Argumentation Trajectories: Argument Norms and Cultural Traditions." *Argumentation and Advocacy* 41 (Fall 2004): 55–57.

Combs, Steven C. "The Useless/Usefulness of Argumentation: The Dao of Disputation." *Argumentation and Advocacy* 41 (Fall 2004): 58–70.

Frank, David. "Arguing With God, Talmudic Discourse, and the Jewish Countermodel: Implications for the Study of Argumentation." *Argumentation and Advocacy* 41 (Fall 2005): 71–86.

Littlefield, Robert S., and Jane A. Ball. "Factionalism as Argumentation: A Case Study of the Indigenous Communication Practices of Jemez Pueblo." *Argumentation and Advocacy* 41 (Fall 2004): 87–101.

Rocci, Andrea. "Pragmatic Inference and Argumentation in Intercultural Communication." *Intercultural Pragmatics* 3 (2006): 409–422.

Tzu-Hsiang, Yu, and Wen Wei-Chun. "Monologic and Dialogic Styles of Argumentation: A Bahktinian Analysis of Academic Debates between Mainland China and Taiwan." *Argumentation* 18 (2004): 369–379.

Zulick, Margaret D. "Pursuing Controversy: Kristeva's Split World Subject, Bahktin's Many-Tongued World." *Argumentation and Advocacy* 28 (Fall 1991): 91–102.

DEFINITIONS

Blair, J. Anthony. "Arguments and Its Uses." *Informal Logic* 24 (Summer 2004): 137–151.

Brockriede, Wayne. "Arguers as Lovers." *Philosophy and Rhetoric* 5 (1972): 1–11.

Brockriede, Wayne. "Characteristics of Arguments and Arguing." *Journal of the American Forensic Association* 13 (1977): 129–132.

Ehninger, Douglas. "Argument as Method: Its Nature, Its Limitations and Its Uses." *Speech Monographs* 38 (1970): 101–110.

Frogel, S. "Philosophical Argumentation: Logic and Rhetoric." *Argumentation* 18 (2004): 171–188.

Hample, Dale. "A Third Perspective on Argument." *Philosophy and Rhetoric* 18 (1985): 1–22.

Hample, Dale. "Argument: Public and Private, Social and Cognitive." *Journal of the American Forensics Association* 25 (1988): 13–19.

Trapp, Robert. "A Special Report on Argumentation: Introduction." *Western Journal of Speech Communication* 45 (Spring 1981): 111–117.

van Eemeren, Frans H. "A World of Difference: The Rich State of Argumentation Theory." *Informal Logic* 17 (Spring 1995): 144–158.

van Eemeren, Frans H. "A Glance behind the Scenes: The State of the Art in the Study of Argumentation." *Studies in Communication Sciences* 3 (Winter 2003) 1–23.

Weigand, Edda. "Argumentation: The Mixed Game." *Argumentation* 20 (2006): 59–87.

Wenzel, Joseph W. "Toward a Rationale for Value-Centered Argument." *Journal of the American Forensic Association* 13 (1977): 150–158.

DIALECTICS

Finocchiaro, Maurice A. "Dialectics, Evaluation, and Argument." *Informal Logic* 23 (Winter 2003): 19–49.

Krabbe, Erick C. W. "Formal Systems of Dialogue Rules." *Synthese* 63 (1985): 295–328.

Rescher, N. "The Role of Rhetoric in Rational Argumentation." *Argumentation* 12 (1998): 315–323.

DIALOGUE AND CONVERSATION

Blair, J. Anthony. "The Limits of the Dialogue Model of Argument." *Argumentation* 12 (1998): 325–339.

Jackson, Sally, and Scott Jacobs. "Structure of Conversational Argument: Pragmatic Bases for the Enthymeme." *Quarterly Journal of Speech* 66 (1980): 251–265.

Jacobs, Scott, and Sally Jackson. "Argument as a Natural Category: The Routine Grounds for Arguing in Natural Conversation." *Western Journal of Speech Communication* 45 (1981): 118–132.

Jacobs, Scott, and Sally Jackson. "Strategy and Structure in Conversational Influence Attempts." *Communication Monographs* 50 (1983): 285–304.

Kleiner, Brian. "The Modern Racist Ideology and its Reproduction in 'Pseudoargument.'" *Discourse in Society* 9 (1998): 187–215.

Norman, A. P. "The Normative Structure of Adjudicative Dialogue." *Argumentation* 15 (2001): 489–498.

EMOTION

Ben-Ze'ev, Aaron. "Emotions and Argumentation." *Informal Logic* 17 (Spring 1995): 189–200.

Crosswhite, James. "Mood in Argumentation: Heidegger and the Exordium." *Philosophy and Rhetoric* 22 (1989): 28–42.

Gilbert, Michael A. "Emotional Messages." *Argumentation* 15 (2001): 239–249.

Gilbert, Michael. "Emotion, Argumentation and Informal Logic." *Informal Logic* 24 (Fall 2004): 245–264.

Kauffman, Charles. "Poetic as Argument." *Quarterly Journal of Speech* 67 (1981): 407–415.

Manolescu, Beth Innocenti. "A Normative Pragmatic Perspective on Appealing to Emotions in Argumentation." *Argumentation* 20 (2006): 327–343.

Wreen, Michael. "A Feeling Disputation (Douglas J. Walton on Argumentation)." *Dialogue: Canadian Philosophical Review* 36 (Fall 1997): 787–812.

Zulick, Margaret D. "The Normative, the Proper, and the Sublime: The Notes on the Use of Figure and Emotion in Prophetic Argument." *Argumentation* 12 (1998): 481–492.

ENTHYMEME

Bitzer, Lloyd. "Aristotle's Enthymeme Revisited." *Quarterly Journal of Speech* 45 (1959): 399–408.

Braet, Antoine. "The Enthymeme in Aristotle's Rhetoric: From Argumentation Theory to Logic." *Informal Logic* 19 (Summer/Autumn 1999): 101–117.

Goulding, Daniel J. "Aristotle's Concept of the Enthymeme." *Journal of the American Forensic Association* 2 (1965): 104–108.

Hitchcock, David. "Does the Traditional Treatment of Enthymemes Rest on a Mistake?" *Argumentation* 12 (1998): 15–37.

Jacquette, Dale. "Charity and the Reiteration Problem for Enthymemes." *Informal Logic* 18 (Winter 1996): 1–15.

Mudd, Charles. "The Enthymeme and Logical Validity." *Quarterly Journal of Speech* 45 (1959): 409–414.

Walton, Douglas. "Enthymemes, Common Knowledge, and Plausible Inference." *Philosophy and Rhetoric* 34 (2001): 93–112.

Walton, Douglas, and Fabrizio Macagno. "Common Knowledge in Argumentation." *Studies in Communication Sciences* 6 (Summer 2006): 3–26.

EPISTEMOLOGY

Cherwitz, Richard. "Rhetoric as 'A Way of Knowing': An Attenuation of the Epistemological Claims of the 'New Rhetoric.'" *Southern Speech Communication Journal* 42 (Spring 1977): 207–219.

Cherwitz, Richard, and Thomas Darwin. "On The Continuing Utility of Argument in a Postmodern World." *Argumentation* 9 (1995): 181–202.

Cherwitz, Richard, and James Hikins. "The Role of Argument in the Postmodern World and Beyond." *Argumentation* 9 (1995): 119–122.

Crable, Richard E. "Knowledge-as-Status: On Argument and Epistemology." *Communication Monographs* 49 (1982): 249–262.

Goldman, Alvin. "An Epistemological Approach to Argumentation." *Informal Logic* 23 (Winter 2003): 51–63.

Willard, Charles A. "The Epistemic Functions of Argument: Reasoning and Decision-Making from a Constructivist/Interactionist Point of View." *Journal of the American Forensic Association* 15 (1979): 169–191.

FALLACIES

Burke, Michael B. "Denying the Antecedent: A Common Fallacy?" *Informal Logic* 16 (Winter 1994): 23–30.

Chichi, Graciela Marta. "The Greek Roots of the Ad Hominem-Argument." *Argumentation* 16 (2002): 333–349.

Clark, Lynn E. "Liars and Ghosts in the House of Congress: Frank's Ad Hominem Arguments in the Case against Doma." *Argumentation and Advocacy* 26 (Spring 2000): 196–210.

Cummings, Louise. "Argument as Cognition: A Putnamian Criticism of Dale Hample's Cognitive Conception of Argument." *Argumentation* 18 (2004): 331–348.

Cummings, Louise. "Rejecting the Urge to Theorise in Fallacy Inquiry." *Argumentation* 18 (2004): 61–94.

Hintikka, J. "The Fallacy of Fallacies." *Argumentation* 1 (1987): 211–238.

Metcalf, R. "Rethinking the Ad Hominem: A Case Study of Chomsky." *Argumentation* 19 (2005): 29–52.

Siegel, Harvey, and John Biro. "Epistemic Normativity, Argumentation, and Fallacies." *Argumentation* 11 (1997): 277–292.

Talisse, Robert, and Scott Aikin. "Two Forms of the Straw Man." *Argumentation* 20 (2006): 345–352.

Tindale, Christopher W. "Fallacies in Transition: An Assessment of the Pragma-Dialectical Perspective." *Informal Logic* 18 (Winter 1996): 17–33.

Tindale, Christopher W. "Fallacies, Blunders, and the Dialogue Shifts: Walton's Contribution to the Fallacy Debate." *Argumentation* 11 (1997): 341–354.

van Eemeren, Frans H., Bert Meuffels and Mariel Verburg. "The (Un)reasonableness of Ad Hominem Fallacies." *Journal of Language and Social Psychology* 19 (December 2000): 416–436.

Walton, D. "Argumentation Schemes and Historical Origins of the Circumstantial Ad Hominem Argument." *Argumentation* 18 (2004): 359–368.

Walton, Douglas. "Classification of Fallacies of Relevance." *Informal Logic* 24 (Winter 2004): 71–103.

Walton, Douglas. "Begging the Question in Arguments Based on Testimony." *Argumentation* 19 (2005): 85–113.

Walton, Douglas. "Poisoning the Well." *Argumentation* 20 (2006): 273–307.

Woods, John. "Is the Theoretical Unity of the Fallacies Possible?" *Informal Logic* 16 (Spring 1994): 77–85.

FEMINISM

Bruner, M. Lane. "Producing Identities: Gender Problematization and Feminist Argumentation." *Argumentation and Advocacy* 32 (Spring 1996): 185–198.

Crenshaw, Carrie. "The Normality of Man and Female Otherness: (Re)Producing Patriarchal Lines of Argument in the Law and the News." *Argumentation and Advocacy* 32 (Spring 1996): 170–184.

Fulkerson, Richard. "Transcending Our Conception of Argument in Light of Feminist Critique." *Argumentation and Advocacy* 32 (Spring 1996): 170–184.

Gilbert, Michael A. "Feminism, Argumentation and Coalescence." *Informal Logic* 16 (Spring 1994): 95–113.

Griffin, Cindy. "A Web of Reasons: Mary Wollstonecraft's *A Vindication of the Rights of Women* and the Re-Weaving of Form." *Communication Studies* 47 (Winter 1996): 272–287.

Miller, Kathleen. "A Feminist Defense of the Critical Logical Model." *Informal Logic* 17 (Fall 1995): 337–346.

Orr, Deborah. "On Logic and Moral Voice." *Informal Logic* 17 (Fall 1995): 347–363.

Palczewski, Catherine Helen. "Special Issue: Argumentation and Feminisms." *Argumentation and Advocacy* 32 (Spring 1996): 161–169.

Pickering, Barbara A. "Women's Voices as Evidence: Personal Testimony is Pro-Choice Films." *Argumentation and Advocacy* 40 (Summer 2003): 1–22.

FIELDS OF ARGUMENT

Dunbar, Nancy R. "Laetrile: A Case Study of a Public Controversy." *Journal of the American Forensic Association* 22 (1986): 196–211.

Prosise, Theodore O., Greg R. Miller, and Jordan P. Mills "Argument Fields as Arenas of Discursive Struggle: Argument Fields and Pierre Bourdieu's Theory of Social Practice." *Argumentation and Advocacy* 32 (Winter 1996): 111–128.

Roland, Robert. "The Influence of Purpose on Fields of Argument." *Journal of the American Forensic Association* 18 (1982): 228–245.

Wenzel, Joseph W. "On Fields of Argument as Propositional Systems." *Journal of the American Forensic Association* 18 (1982): 204–213.

Zarefsky, David. "Persistent Questions in the Theory of Argument Fields." *Journal of the American Forensic Association* 18 (1982): 191–204.

HABERMAS, JÜRGEN

Cooke, M. "Argumentation and Transformation." *Argumentation* 16 (2002): 79–108

Cramer, P. A. "The Public Metonym." *Informal Logic* 23 (2003): 183–199.

Farrell, Thomas B. "Habermas on Argumentation Theory: Some Emerging Topics." *Journal of the American Forensic Association* 16 (1979): 77–82.

Feteris, Eveline. "The Rationality of Legal Discourse in Habermas's Discourse Theory." *Informal Logic* 23 (2003): 139–159.

Fusfield, W. "Communication without Constellation? Habermas's Argumentative Turn in (and away from) Critical Theory." *Communication Theory* 7 (1997): 301–320.

Goodnight, G. Thomas. "Predicaments of Communication, Arguments and Power." *Informal Logic* 23 (Summer 2003): 119–137.

Rehg, W. "Habermas, Argumentation Theory and Science Studies." *Informal Logic* 23 (Summer 2003): 161–182.

INFORMAL LOGIC AND PHILOSOPHY

Fisher, Alec. "Informal Logic and Its Implications for Philosophy." *Informal Logic* 20 (Summer 2000): 109–115.

Freeman, James B. "The Place of Informal Logic in Philosophy." *Informal Logic* 20 (Summer 2000): 117–128.

Hitchcock, David. "The Significance of Informal Logic for Philosophy." *Informal Logic* 20 (Summer 2000): 129–138.

Johnson, Ralph H. "The Relation between Formal and Informal Logic." *Argumentation* 13 (1999): 265–274.

Woods, John. "How Philosophical is Informal Logic?" *Informal Logic* 20 (Summer 2000): 139–167.

LEGAL

Bertea, Stefano. "Certainty, Reasonableness and Argumentation in Law." *Argumentation* 18 (2004): 465–478.

Bruschke, Jon. "A Critical Analysis of Objectivity in the Legal Sphere." *Argumentation and Advocacy* 30 (Spring 1994): 220–236.

Bruschke, Jon. "Deconstructive Arguments in the Legal Sphere: An Analysis of the Fischl/Massey Debate about Critical Legal Studies." *Argumentation and Advocacy* 32 (Summer 1995): 16–29.

Feteris, Eveline. "The Rational Reconstruction of Argumentation Referring to Consequences and Purposes in the Application of Legal Rules: A Pragma-Dialectical Perspective." *Argumentation* 19 (2005): 459–470.

Feteris, Eveline. "The Rational Reconstruction of Complex Forms of Legal Argumentation: Approaches from Artificial Intelligence and Law and Pragma-Dialectics." *Argumentation* 19 (2005): 393–400.

Feteris, Eveline T. "A Survey of 25 Years of Legal Argumentation." *Argumentation* 11 (1997): 355–376.

Hannken-Illjes, Kati. "In the Field—The Development of Reasons in Criminal Proceedings." *Argumentation* 20 (2006): 309–325.

Hasian, Marouf, Jr. "In Search of 'Ivan the Terrible': John Demjanjuk and the Judicial Use of Ironic Argumentation." *Argumentation and Advocacy* 39 (Spring 2003): 231–253.

Hasian, Marouf, Jr., and Trevor Parry-Giles. "'A Stranger to Its Laws': Freedom, Civil Rights, and the Legal Ambiguity of *Romer vs. Evans* (1996)." *Argumentation and Advocacy* 34 (Summer 1997): 27–43.

Hohman, Hanns. "Logic and Rhetoric in Legal Argumentation: Some Medieval Perspectives." *Argumentation* 12 (1998): 39–55.

Kloosterhuis, Harm. "Reconstructing Complex Analogy Argumentation in Judicial Decisions: A Pragma-Dialectical Perspective." *Argumentation* 19 (2005): 471–483.

Mathewson, Gwen C. "Outdoing Lewis Carroll: Judicial Rhetoric and Acceptable Fictions." *Argumentation* 12 (1998): 233–244.

Plug, H. "Reconstructing and Evaluating Genetic Arguments in Judicial Decisions." *Argumentation* 19 (2005): 447–458.

Scofield, R. G. "The Economic, Political, Strategic, and Rhetorical Uses of Simple Constructive Dilemma in Legal Argument." *Argumentation* 20 (2006): 1–14.

MEDIA AND TECHNOLOGY

Barker, Simon. "The End of Argument: Knowledge and the Internet." *Philosophy and Rhetoric* 33 (2000): 154–181.

Slade, Christina. "Reasons to Buy: The Logic of Advertisements." *Argumentation* 16 (2002): 157–178.

Walker, Gregg B., and Melinda A. Bender. "Is It More than Rock and Roll?: Considering Music Video as Argument." *Argumentation and Advocacy* 31 (Fall 1994): 64–79.

Warnick, Barbara. "Analogues to Argument: New Media and Literacy in a Posthuman Era (Review Essay)." *Argumentation and Advocacy* 38 (Spring 2002): 262–271.

Weger, Harry, Jr., and Mark Aakhus. "Arguing in Internet Chat Rooms: Argumentative Adaptations to Chat Room Design and Some Consequences for Public Deliberation at a Distance." *Argumentation and Advocacy* 40 (Summer 2003): 23–38.

NARRATIVE

Fisher, Walter R. "Narration as Human Communication Paradigm: The Case of Public Moral Argument." *Communication Monographs* 51 (1984): 1–22.

Fisher, Walter R. "The Narrative Paradigm and the Assessment of Historical Texts." *Argumentation and Advocacy* 25 (Fall 1988): 49–53.

Hollihan, Thomas A., Kevin T. Baaske and Patricia Riley. "Debaters as Storytellers: The Narrative Perspective in Academic Debate." *Argumentation and Advocacy* 23 (Spring 1987): 184–193.

Hollihan, Thomas A. "Narrative Studies of Argument." *Argumentation and Advocacy* 25 (Fall 1988): 47–48.

Jasinski, James. "(Re)constituting Community through Narrative Argument: *Eros* and *Philia* in *The Big Chill*." *Quarterly Journal of Speech* 79 (1993): 467–486.

McGee, Michael Calvin, and John S. Nelson. "Narrative Reason in Public Argument." *Journal of Communication* 35 (1985): 139–155.

Verene, Donald P. "Philosophy, Argument, and Narration." *Philosophy and Rhetoric* 22 (1989): 141–144.

PEDAGOGY

Carillo, M. Jesus Cala, and Manuel L. De La Mata Benítez. "Educational Background, Modes of Discourse and Argumentation: Comparing Women and Men." *Argumentation* 18 (2004): 403–426.

Cros, Anna. "Teaching by Convincing: Strategies of Argumentation in Lectures." *Argumentation* 15 (2001): 191–206.

Gehrke, Pat, J. "Teaching Argumentation Existentially: Argumentation Pedagogy and Theories of Rhetoric Epistemic." *Argumentation and Advocacy* 35 (Fall 1998) 76–86.

Goodwin, Jean. "What Does Arguing Look Like?" *Informal Logic* 25 (Winter 2005) 79–93.

Goodwin, Jean. "Theoretical Pieties, Johnstone's Impiety, and Ordinary Views of Argumentation." *Philosophy and Rhetoric* 40 (2007): 36–50.

Mallin, Erwin, and Carrin Vasby Anderson. "Inviting Constructive Argument." *Argumentation and Advocacy* 36 (Winter 2000): 120–133.

Mendelson, Michael. "Quintilian and the Pedagogy of Argument." *Argumentation* 15 (2001): 277–293.

Ruhl, Marco. "Emergent versus Dogmatic Arguing: Starting Points for a Theory of the Argumentative Process." *Argumentation* 15 (2001): 151–171.

Siegel, Harvey. "Why Should Educators Care about Argumentation?" *Informal Logic* 17 (Spring 1995): 159–176.

Winkler, Carol K., and David M. Cheshier. "Revisioning Argumentation Education for the New Century: Millennial Challenges." *Argumentation and Advocacy* 36 (Winter 2004): 101–105.

PERELMAN, CHAÏM

Abbott, Don. "The Jurisprudential Analogy: Argumentation and *The New Rhetoric.*" *Central States Speech Journal* 25 (1974): 50–55.

Arnold, Carroll. "Perelman's New Rhetoric." *Quarterly Journal of Speech* 56 (1970): 87–92.

Corgan, Verna C., "Perelman's Universal Audience as Critical Tool." *Journal of American Forensics Association* 23 (1987): 147–157.

Frank, David A. "The New Rhetoric, Judaism, and Post-Enlightenment Thought: The Cultural Origins of Perelmanian Philosophy." *Quarterly Journal of Speech* 83 (August 1997): 311–332.

Frank, David A. "Dialectical Rapprochement in the New Rhetoric." *Argumentation and Advocacy* 33 (Winter 1998): 111–137.

Frank, David A. "After the New Rhetoric." *Quarterly Journal of Speech* 89 (2003): 253–261.

Gross, Alan. "A Theory of the Rhetorical Audience: Reflections on Chaim Perelman." *Quarterly Journal of Speech* 85 (1999): 203–211.

Perelman, Chaïm. "The New Rhetoric and the Rhetoricians: Remembrances and Comments." *Quarterly Journal of Speech* 70 (1984): 188–196.

Schiappa, Edward. "Dissociation in the Arguments of Rhetorical Theory." *Journal of the American Forensics Association* 22 (1985): 72–82.

Scult, Allen. "Perelman's Universal Audience: One Perspective." *Central States Speech Journal* 27 (1976): 176–180.

POSTMODERN / POSTSTRUCTURALIST

Aden, Roger C. "The Enthymeme as Postmodern Argument Form: Condensed, Meditated Argument Then and Now." *Argumentation and Advocacy* 31(Fall 1994): 54–63.

Chase, Kenneth R. "The Challenge of Avant-Garde Argument." *Argumentation and Advocacy* 29 (Summer 1992): 16–31.

Greene, Ronald W. "The Aesthetic Turn and the Rhetorical Perspective on Argumentation." *Argumentation and Advocacy* 35 (Summer 1998): 19–29.

Hatcher, Donald L. "Critical Thinking, Postmodernism, and Rational Evaluation." *Informal Logic* 16 (Fall 1994): 197–208.

Keith, William. "Argument Practices." *Argumentation* 9 (1995): 163–179.

Langsdorf, Lenore. "Argument as Inquiry in a Postmodern Context." *Argumentation* 11 (1997): 315–327.

PUBLIC SPHERE AND DEMOCRACY

Asen, Robert. "Pluralism, Disagreement, and the Status of Argument in the Public Sphere." *Informal Logic* 25 (Summer 2005): 117–137.

Batt, Shawn. "Keeping Company in Controversy: Education Reform, Spheres of Argument, and Ethical Criticism." *Argumentation and Advocacy* 40 (Fall 2003): 85–104.

Blair, J. Anthony. "Norms and Functions in Public Sphere Argumentation." *Informal Logic* 25 (Summer 2005): 138–150.

Cooke, Maeve. "Argumentation and Transformation." *Argumentation* 16 (2002): 79–108.

Doxtader, Erik W. "Learning Public Deliberation through the Critique of Institutional Argument." *Argumentation and Advocacy* 31 (Spring 1995): 185–203.

Farrell, Thomas B. "Sizing Things Up: Colloquial Reflection as Practical Wisdom." *Argumentation* 12 (1998): 1–14.

Goodnight, G. Thomas. "Toward a Social Theory of Argumentation." *Argumentation and Advocacy* 26 (Fall 1989): 60–70.

Goodwin, Jean. "The Public Sphere and the Norms of Transactional Argument." *Informal Logic* 25 (Summer 2005): 151–165.

Jorgensen, Charlotte. "Public Debate—An Act of Hostility?" *Argumentation* 12 (1998): 431–443.

Mitchell, Gordon R. "Public Argument Action Research and the Learning Curve of New Social Movements." *Argumentation and Advocacy* 40 (Spring 2004): 209–225.

Ray, Angela G. "The Permeable Public: Rituals of Citizenship in Antebellum Men's Debating Clubs." *Argumentation and Advocacy* 41 (Summer 2004): 1–16.

Rehg, William. "Assessing the Cogency of Arguments: Three Kinds of Merits." *Informal Logic* 25 (Summer 2005): 95–115.

Zompetti, J. P. "The Role of Advocacy in Civil Society." *Argumentation* 20 (2006): 167–183.

Zulick, Margaret. "Generative Rhetoric and Public Argument: A Classical Approach." *Argumentation and Advocacy* 33 (Winter 1997): 109–120.

RATIONALITY AND REASON

Bruschke, Jon. "Toward Reviving Rationality in Argument: Adding Pieces to Johnson's Puzzle." *Argumentation and Advocacy* 40 (Winter 2004): 155–172.

Campolo, Chris, and Dale Turner. "Reasoning Together: Temptations, Dangers, and Cautions." *Argumentation* 16 (2002): 3–19.

Finocchiaro, Maurice A. "Two Empirical Approaches to the Study of Reasoning." *Informal Logic* 16 (Winter 1994): 1–21.

Harpine, William. "Is Modernism Really Modern? Uncovering a Fallacy in Postmodernism." *Argumentation* 18 (2004): 349–358.

Healy, Paul. "Rationality, Judgment, and Argument Assessment." *Informal Logic* 16 (Winter 1994): 31–38.

Johnstone, Henry. "Rationality and Rhetoric in Philosophy." *Quarterly Journal of Speech* 59 (1973): 381–89.

Ohler, Amy, "A Dialectical Tier within Reason." *Informal Logic* 23 (Winter 2003): 65–75.

Rowland, Robert. "In Defense of Rational Argument: A Pragmatic Justification of Argumentation Theory and Response to the Postmodern Critique." *Philosophy and Rhetoric* 28 (1995): 350–364.

SCHEMES AND STRUCTURES

Allen, Mike, and Nancy Burrell. "Evaluating the Believability of Sequential Arguments." *Argumentation and Advocacy* 28 (Winter 1992): 135–144.

Braet, Antoine C. "The Oldest Typology of Argumentation Schemes." *Argumentation* 18 (2004): 127–148.

Henkemans, A. Francisca Snoeck. "State-of-the-Art: The Structure of Argumentation." *Argumentation* 14 (2000): 447–473.

Juthe, A. "Argument by Analogy." *Argumentation* 19 (2005): 1–27.

Katzav, J., and C. A. Reed. "On Argumentation Schemes and the Natural Classification of Arguments." *Argumentation* 18 (2004): 239–259.

Liu, Yameng. "Argument in a Nutshell: Condensation as a Transfiguring Mechanism in Argumentative Discourse." *Argumentation* 18 (2004): 43–59.

Warnick, Barbara. "Rehabilitating AI: Argument Loci and the Case for Artificial Intelligence." *Argumentation* 18 (2004): 149–170.

SCIENCE

Ceccarelli, Leah M. "Let Us (Not) Theorize the Space of Contention." *Argumentation and Advocacy* 42 (Summer 2005): 30–33.

Cummings, Louise. "Analogical Reasoning as a Tool of Epidemiological Investigation." *Argumentation* 18 (2004): 427–444.

Czubaroff, Jeanine. "The Public Dimension of Scientific Controversies." *Argumentation* 11 (1997): 51–74.

Depew, David. "The New Philosophy of Science and its Lessons." *Argumentation* 15 (2001): 9–20.

Gorham, Geoffrey. "Does Scientific Realism Beg the Question?" *Informal Logic* 18 (1996): 225–233.

Gross, Alan G. "Scientific and Technical Controversy: Three Frameworks for Analysis." *Argumentation and Advocacy* 42 (Summer 2005): 43–47.

Keränen, Lisa. "Mapping Misconduct: Demarcating Legitimate Science from 'Fraud' in the B-06 Lumpectomy Controversy." *Argumentation and Advocacy* 42 (Fall 2005): 94–113.

Lyne, John. "Science Controversy, Common Sense, and the Third Culture." *Argumentation and Advocacy* 42 (Summer 2005): 38–42.

Miller, Carolyn R. "Risk, Controversy, and Rhetoric: Response to Goodnight." *Argumentation and Advocacy* 42 (Summer 2004): 34–37.

Solomon, Miriam. "It Isn't the Thought that Counts." *Argumentation* 15 (2001): 67–75.

TOULMIN, STEPHEN

Bermejo-Luque, Lilian. "Toulmin's Model of Argument and the Question of Relativism." *Informal Logic* 24 (Summer 2004): 169–181.

Freeman, James B. "Systematizing Toulmin's Warrants: An Epistemic Approach." *Argumentation* 19 (2005): 331–346.

Hitchcock, David. "Good Reasoning on the Toulmin Model." *Argumentation* 19 (2005): 373–391.

Hitchcock, David, and Bart Verheij. "The Toulmin Model Today: Introduction to the Special Issue on Contemporary Work using Stephen Edelston Toulmin's Layout of Arguments." *Argumentation* 19 (2005): 255–258.

Loui, Ronald P. "A Citation-Based Reflection on Toulmin and Argument." *Argumentation* 19 (2005): 259–266.

Reed, Chris and Glenn Rowe. "Translating Toulmin Diagrams: Theory Neutrality in Argument Representation." *Argumentation* 19 (2005): 267–286.

Toulmin, Stephen. "Reasoning in Theory and Practice." *Informal Logic* 24 (Summer 2004): 111–114.

Verheij, Bart. "Evaluating Arguments Based on Toulmin's Scheme." *Argumentation* 19 (2005): 347–371.

Voss, James F. "Toulmin's Model and the Solving of Ill-Structured Problems." *Argumentation* 19 (2005): 321–329.

VALIDITY

Ennis, Robert H. "Argument Appraisal Strategy: A Comprehensive Approach." *Informal Logic* 21 (Spring 2001): 97–140.

Ennis, Robert H. "Applying Soundness Standards to Qualified Reasoning." *Informal Logic* 24 (Winter 2004): 23–39.

Inbar, Michael. "Argumentation as Role-Justified Claims: Elements of a Conceptual Framework for the Critical Analysis of Argument." *Argumentation* 13 (1999): 27–42.

McKerrow, Ray. "Rhetorical Validity: An Analysis of Three Perspectives on the Justification of Rhetorical Argument." *Journal of the American Forensic Association* 13 (1977): 133–141.

Van Den Hoven, Paul. "The Dilemma of Normativity: How to Interpret a Rational Reconstruction?" *Argumentation* 11 (1997): 411–417.

VISUAL ARGUMENT

Blair, J. Anthony. "The Possibility and Actuality of Visual Arguments." *Argumentation and Advocacy* 33 (Summer 1996): 23–39.

Cameron, Shelley. "Aspects of Visual Argument: A Study of the March of Progress." *Informal Logic* 21 (Spring 2001): 85–96.

Finnegan, Cara A. "The Naturalistic Enthymeme and Visual Argument: Photographic Representation in the Skull Controversy." *Argumentation and Advocacy* 37 (Winter 2001): 133–149.

Fleming, David. "Can Pictures Be Arguments?" *Argumentation and Advocacy* 33 (Summer 1996): 11–22.

Groarke, Leo. "Logic, Art and Argument." *Informal Logic* 18 (Summer 1996): 105–129.

Jensen, Robin. "The Eating Disordered Lifestyle: Imagetexts and the Performance of Similitude." *Argumentation and Advocacy* 42 (Summer 2005): 1–18.

Lake, Randall, and Barbara Pickering. "Argumentation, the Visual, and the Possibility of Refutation: An Exploration." *Argumentation* 12 (1998): 79–93.

LaWare, Margaret R. "Encountering Visions of Aztlan: Arguments for Ethnic Pride, Community Activism and Cultural Revitalization in Chicano Murals." *Argumentation and Advocacy* 34 (Winter 1998): 140–153.

Shelley, Cameron. "Rhetorical and Demonstrative Modes of Visual Argument: Looking at Images of Human Evolution." *Argumentation and Advocacy* 33 (Fall 1996): 53–68.

Index

About the Editors

Angela J. Aguayo
is Assistant Professor of
Communication Studies at Eastern
Illinois University, where she teaches
courses in Persuasion and Public
Culture, Argumentation, Rhetorics
of Resistance, and Documentary
Production. She earned her B.A.
and M.A. from California State
University, Long Beach, and her
Ph.D. at University of Texas, Austin.
She has published book chapters
and essays focused on documentary
video discourse as a site of social
contestation, protest, and social
change. Dr. Aguayo also produces
documentary video shorts, which she
has screened at several film festivals,
including the New York Underground
Film Festival and the Cinematexas
International Film Festival.

Timothy R. Steffensmeier
is Assistant Professor of Speech
Communication at Kansas State
University, where he teaches courses
in Communication and Democracy,
Rhetorical Criticism, and Classical
Rhetoric. He earned his B.A. from
Hastings College and his M.A. at
Wake Forest University. He earned his
Ph.D. at University of Texas, Austin,
where he also received the Texas Exes
Teaching Award. Dr. Steffensmeier
serves as a research associate with
the Institute for Civic Discourse
and Democracy, an interdisciplinary
institute focusing on research, teaching,
and extension efforts that facilitate
civic discourse. He has published
book chapters and essays focused on
deliberative democracy, argumentation,
and visual rhetoric. These interests
inform his scholarship concerning
sustainable community development.